Community
POLICING

PARTNERSHIPS FOR PROBLEM SOLVING

EIGHTH EDITION

Linda S. Miller

Former Executive Director of the Upper
Midwest Community Policing Institute
Sergeant (Retired), Bloomington,
Minnesota, Police Department

Kären Matison Hess, Ph.D.

Normandale Community College,
Bloomington, Minnesota

Christine Hess Orthmann, M.S.

Orthmann Writing & Research, Inc.

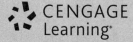
CENGAGE
Learning·

Australia • Brazil • Mexico • Singapore • United Kingdom • United States

Community Policing: Partnerships for Problem Solving, 8th Edition
Linda S. Miller, Kären Matison Hess, Christine Hess Orthmann

Sr. Product Director: Marta Lee-Perriad
Product Manager: Carolyn Henderson-Meier
Content Developer: Cathy Castle, Lumina Datamatics, Inc.
Product Assistant: Diane Chrysler
IP Analyst: Jennifer Bowes
IP Project Manager: Carly Belcher
Art and Cover Direction, Production Management, and Composition: Lumina Datamatics, Inc.
Cover and Internal Images: © thejimcox/ Fotolia

For product information and technology assistance, contact us at **Cengage Learning Customer & Sales Support, 1-800-354-9706.**

For permission to use material from this text or product, submit all requests online at **www.cengage.com/permissions**. Further permissions questions can be e-mailed to **permissionrequest@cengage.com.**

Library of Congress Control Number: 2017932176

Student Edition:
ISBN: 978-1-305-96081-7

Loose-leaf Edition:
ISBN: 978-1-305-96092-3

Cengage Learning
20 Channel Center Street
Boston, MA 02210
USA

Cengage Learning is a leading provider of customized learning solutions with employees residing in nearly 40 different countries and sales in more than 125 countries around the world. Find your local representative at **www.cengage.com**.

Cengage Learning products are represented in Canada by Nelson Education, Ltd.

To learn more about Cengage Learning Solutions, visit **www.cengage.com**.

Purchase any of our products at your local college store or at our preferred online store **www.cengagebrain.com**.

Printed in the United States of America
Print Number: 01   Print Year: 2017

BRIEF CONTENTS

CONTENTS

3   Understanding and Involving the Community   64

4   Problem Solving: Proactive Policing   93

5   Implementing Community Policing   124

Section II: Building Relationships and Trust   149

6   Communicating with a Diverse Population   150

7 Building Partnerships: A Cornerstone of Community Policing 185

8 Forming Partnerships with the Media 214

Section III: Community Policing in the Field: Collaborative Efforts   **237**

9 Early Experiments in Crime Prevention and the Evolution of Community Policing Strategies   239

10 Safe Neighborhoods and Communities: From Traffic Problems to Crime   264

11 Community Policing and Drugs   299

13 The Challenge of Gangs: Controlling Their Destructive Force   368

14 Understanding and Preventing Violence   396

16 The Future of Community Policing   466

A democratic society has to be the most difficult environment within which to police. Police in many countries operate for the benefit of the government. Police in the United States operate for the benefit of the people policed. Because of that environment, we are compelled to pursue ways to advance our policing approach, involve people who are part of our environment, and enhance our effectiveness. Our policing methodology is changed or molded by trial and error, the daring of some policing leaders, the research and writing of academics, and the response of our communities to the way we do business.

For more than 40 years, we have tried a variety of approaches to doing our job better. Some have remained. Many have been abandoned, thought to be failures. They may, however, have been building blocks for our current policing practices and for what is yet to come. For instance, the community relations and crime prevention programs of the 1960s and the experiments with team policing in the 1970s are quite visible in the business of community policing. So should be the knowledge gained from research such as that conducted in the 1970s and 1980s associated with random patrol, directed patrol, foot patrol, one-officer/two-officer cars, and the effectiveness (or lack thereof) of rapid response to all calls for service. If we look at our past, we should not be surprised at the development of and support for community policing as the desired policing philosophy in our country today. It merely responds to the customers' needs and their demand for our policing agencies to be more effective. And therein lies the most important outcome of community policing— effectiveness. Yes, we have responded to millions of calls for service, made millions of arrests, and added thousands to our policing ranks. If we're honest about it, however, we may be hard-pressed to see the imprint of our efforts in our communities. Community policing, involving problem solving, community engagement, and organizational transformation, can contribute significantly to the satisfaction of the community policed and to those policing.

This text provides insight into the meaning of community policing and presents many dimensions necessary to consider when developing a community policing strategy. Its content should help readers to understand the practical side of community policing, recognize the necessary community considerations, and develop methods applicable to their unique environments.

Donald J. Burnett
General Partner
Law Enforcement Assistance Network

PREFACE

Welcome to *Community Policing: Partnerships for Problem Solving*, Eighth Edition. The complex responsibilities of departments embracing the community policing philosophy are challenging. Changes in technology and society continually present new challenges to police officers, requiring them to be knowledgeable in a wide variety of areas.

Community policing offers one avenue for making neighborhoods safer. Community policing is not a program or a series of programs. It is a philosophy, a belief that by working together the police and the community can accomplish what neither can accomplish alone. The synergy that results from community policing can be powerful. It is like the power of a finely tuned athletic team, with each member contributing to the total effort. Occasionally heroes may emerge, but victory depends on a team effort.

Community policing differs from earlier efforts such as team policing, community relations, crime prevention programs, or neighborhood watch programs. Community policing involves a rethinking of the role of the police and a restructuring of the police organization. Its two core concepts are community–police collaboration and partnerships and a problem-solving approach to policing. These dual themes are present throughout the text.

ORGANIZATION OF THE TEXT

Section I of this text discusses the evolution of community policing and the changes in our communities and our law enforcement agencies that have occurred over time. The section then examines the problem-solving approach to policing and how community policing might be implemented.

Section II emphasizes the development of the interpersonal skills needed to build good relationships with all those the police have sworn "to serve and protect." This includes those who are culturally, racially, or socioeconomically different from the mainstream; those who are physically or mentally disabled; and those who are elderly. It also includes youths (both as victims and as offenders), gangs and gang members, and victims of crime. In addition, building partnerships and interacting effectively with members of the media are vital to the success of community policing.

Section III describes community policing in the field. It begins with a look at early experiments in crime prevention and the evolution of community policing strategies. The remainder of the section is entirely new material dealing with community problems ranging from traffic to crime to the fear of crime. It then takes a close look at the drug problem, bringing youths into community policing, addressing the gang problem, and understanding and preventing violence, including domestic violence, workplace violence, and terrorism. The final chapter explains what researchers have found and explores what the future might hold for community policing.

NEW TO THIS EDITION

The Eighth Edition has been thoroughly revised with hundreds of new citations and a plentiful amount of new terms, figures, tables, and photographs. Chapter-specific additions made to the Eighth Edition include:

- Chapter 1: The Evolution of Community Policing
  - Included all 9 of Peel's principles (had only 6 in previous edition)
  - Introduced the President's Task Force on 21st Century Policing and noted that findings from the final report would be presented throughout the text as applied to topic of community policing
  - General updating to include discussion of the growing challenge of police authority, increasing loss of trust in police, demands to prosecute officers involved in shooting, and so on.
- Chapter 2: Inside Police Agencies: Understanding Mission and Culture
  - Added key terms: *deadly force, excessive force, force, less-lethal force, procedural justice, reasonable force*
  - Updated statistics throughout
  - Mentioned the FBI's training program *Law Enforcement and Society: Lessons of the Holocaust*
  - Updated data regarding diversity (racial, gender) in police departments
  - Included content from the President's Task Force on 21st Century Policing regarding officer training and education (Pillar 5)
  - Added the President's Task Force call for police to move from a warrior to a guardian mindset
  - Updated the discussion on the impact of negative police contacts
  - Added a new discussion on the abuse of discretion and the Justice Department's investigation into events that occurred in Ferguson, Missouri
  - Updated data regarding face-to-face contact between the public and the police
  - Expanded the discussion of use of force, per reviewer feedback, including definitions of reasonable force, excessive force, and deadly force as well as the two landmark cases of *Graham v. Connor* (1989) and *Tennessee v. Garner* (1985).
  - Noted how police agencies are trending away from use of force continuums.
  - Added a new section on re-engineering training on police use of force
  - Added a section about most recent high-profile police shooting deaths, per reviewer feedback, and how they have contributed to erosion of public trust in the police
  - Added a new "Technology in Community Policing" box—body cameras

- Chapter 3: Understanding and Involving the Community
  - Added key term: *charge bargaining*
  - Deleted terms: *bowling alone, ghetto*
  - Moved a term to another chapter: *restorative justice*
  - Removed the section on Bowling Alone, per reviewer feedback
  - Added to the Broken Windows discussion: studies that question the effectiveness of focusing police resources on minor crime and order maintenance
  - Added content regarding theories of crime and criminality, per reviewer feedback
  - Moved section on Restorative Justice to Chapter 7, per reviewer suggestion
  - Updated population and demographic discussions based on census data
  - Expanded the discussion on civilian review, including President's Task Force (Pillar 2: Policy & Oversight)
  - Added to the discussions on citizen patrol
- Chapter 4: Problem Solving: Proactive Policing
  - Added key term: *entrapment*
  - Slightly reorganized to place lists (elements and steps of POP) together and reduce redundancy
  - Added a Critical Thinking (What Would You Do?) exercise
  - Added a paragraph under "ethical decision" explaining entrapment
  - Added a new "Technology in Community Policing" box—*Enhancing Community Policing through GPS Tracking Technology* (addresses concerns about revictimization and builds public trust and police legitimacy)
  - Added a new figure to illustrate hot spots map
  - Included two new examples of POP programs in action (from POP Center web site)
- Chapter 5: Implementing Community Policing
  - Updated the section on hiring for diversity, recent statistics on minority officers
  - Included a new strategic plan for Columbia, SC Police Dept (replaced Portland's—was outdated)
- Chapter 6: Communicating with a Diverse Population
  - Added key term: *implicit bias*
  - Added a Critical Thinking Exercise
  - General updates in illegal immigration
  - Added a discussion of implicit bias and new office training
  - Added a discussion of FBI director Comey's comments (2015 Georgetown University speech) regarding law enforcement and race
  - Added to the discussion of religious diversity with new poll figures regarding American attitudes toward Muslims and Islam
  - Expanded on homelessness data
  - Updated suicide statistics
  - Included mention of the President's Task Force Recommendation for CITs

- Chapter 7: Building Partnerships: A Cornerstone of Community Policing
  - Added key terms: *community justice, criminogenic needs, dynamic risk factors, static risk factors*
  - Added a new Ideas in Practice: Building Partnerships and Trust
  - Streamlined the discussion on call management, focusing only on text that spoke directly to partnership formation, to address reviewer criticism that content was misplaced
  - Expanded the discussion on key collaborators and emphasized the trend toward community justice, explaining how community policing fits within that paradigm
  - Moved the section on Restorative Justice (including key term) from Chapter 3 to this chapter (within Community Justice section) per reviewer suggestion
  - Expanded the discussion of community courts to include Red Hook Community Court in Brooklyn, NY, per reviewer suggestion
  - Expanded the discussion on community corrections per reviewed feedback, including the importance of offender assessment in selecting appropriate sanctions and the C.A.R.E. model
- Chapter 8: Forming Partnerships with the Media
  - New key term: *CSI effect*
  - Added material on how media coverage alters our perception of crime
  - Expanded the discussion of copycat killings, including guidelines to take following mass killings to de-incentivize further violence
  - Moved McGruff National Media Campaign discussion from Chapter 9 to this chapter
  - Moved Crime Stoppers section from Chapter 9 to this chapter
  - Added a new Ideas in Practice: Improving Media Relations (Prince George's County, Maryland, Police Department (PGPD) hosts a media breakfast twice yearly)
  - Added a new Ideas in Practice: Media Campaigns about Community Standards for Tolerance (partnership between NCPC and Anti-Defamation League)
- Chapter 9: Early Experiments in Crime Prevention and the Evolution of Community Policing Strategies
  - New key term: *dark side of crime*
  - New Technology in Community Policing: Nextdoor social network app for neighborhood crime prevention
  - Brief mention of warrior versus guardian mindset and the influence on community policing implementation
- Chapter 10: Safe Neighborhoods and Communities: From Traffic Problems to Crime
  - Updated statistics throughout
  - New Technology in Community Policing—Waze App Makes Neighborhood Traffic Worse
  - New section on Police Pursuits, the danger of them to communities, and a Technology Box (StarChase)

- Added a critical thinking exercise (hypothetical situation) for students to solve a neighborhood traffic problem per reviewer request
- Added mention of two new cases (*Torrey Dale Grady v. North Carolina*, 2015; *United States v. Jones*, 2012) to caution about Fourth Amendment search issues associated with using GPS to track suspects
- Moved sections on acquaintance rape and human trafficking to Chapter 14
- Included a critical thinking exercise using the Center for Problem Oriented Policing's interactive module (MOOC: Policing Street Prostitution) to allow students to apply their problem-solving (SARA) skills to a realistic, research-based scenario, per specific reviewer request

- Chapter 11: Community Policing and Drugs
  - Updated statistics throughout
  - Added new terms: *doctor shopping, drug diversion*
  - Added a brief section on Controlled Prescription Drugs (CPDs) as a rising drug threat
  - Added a discussion about rising heroin epidemic, providing Naloxone (Narcan) to police
  - Made Drugged Driving its own section
  - Deleted section on raves

- Chapter 12: Bringing Youths into Community Policing
  - Reorganized chapter to improve flow
  - New key term: *polyvictimization*
  - Added content pertaining to the recommendations of the President's Task Force on 21st Century Policing
  - Included a discussion of the TAPS program to build relationships between youth and police
  - New Ideas in Practice: NYPD Summer Youth Police Academy, per reviewer suggestion
  - Added a paragraph on youth courts, per reviewer suggestion
  - Updated statistics and data regarding Indicators of School Crime and Safety

- Chapter 13: The Challenge of Gangs: Controlling Their Destructive Force
  - New terms: *outlaw motorcycle gang* (*OMG*), *prison gang*
  - Updated statistics throughout
  - Added a new section on the role of public health in preventing gang membership
  - New *Ideas in Practice*: mentoring gang members

- Chapter 14: Understanding and Preventing Violence
  - Added key terms: *Ferguson effect, violent crime*
  - Updated statistics throughout
  - Added the DoJ NotAlone initiative to the discussion of acquaintance rape of college students
  - Moved the section on Human Trafficking from Chapter 10 to here
  - Updated the CeaseFire Ideas in Practice
  - Added a new section on bystander intervention (sexual violence)

- Chapter 15: Understanding and Preventing Terrorism
  - Added terms: *fusion center, Islamic State of Iraq and the Levant (ISIL)*
  - Updated statistics throughout
  - Added a discussion of homegrown violent extremism (HVE) and "lone wolf" attacks
  - Added information about fusion centers and joint terrorism task forces (JTTFs)
  - Included new information on public-private police partnerships (from ASIS International)
  - Mentioned that media coverage displays a bias in reporting on Western countries to a much larger extent than those that happen in the Middle East
- Chapter 16: The Future of Community Policing
  - New term: *predictive policing*
  - Added a new section on Predictive Policing (PredPol)
  - Added new technologies and how they will impact policing
  - Added new content to recruiting and training future police officers

HOW TO USE THIS TEXT

This text is a carefully structured learning experience. The more actively you participate in it, the greater your learning will be. You will learn and remember more if you first familiarize yourself with the total scope of the subject. Read and think about the Contents, which provides an outline of the many facets of community policing. Then follow these steps for *triple-strength learning* as you study each chapter.

1. Read the learning objectives at the beginning of the chapter. Assess your current knowledge of the subject of each objective. Examine any preconceptions you may hold. Look at the key terms and watch for them when they are used.

2. Read the chapter, underlining, highlighting, or taking notes—whatever is your preferred study method.

   a. Pay special attention to all highlighted information.

   LOx
   The key concepts of the text are highlighted in this way.

   b. Pay special attention to the terms in bold print. The key terms of the chapter appear this way the first time they are defined.

3. When you have finished reading the chapter, read the summary—your third exposure to the chapter's key information. Then return to the beginning of the chapter and quiz yourself. Can you answer the learning objectives? Can you define the key terms?

4. Read the Discussion Questions and be prepared to contribute to a class discussion of the ideas presented in the chapter.

By following these steps, you will learn more information, understand it more fully, and remember it longer.

A Note: The material selected to highlight using the triple-strength learning instructional design includes only the chapter's key concepts. Although this information is certainly important in that it provides a structural foundation for understanding the topics discussed, do not simply glance over the Learning Objective highlighted boxes and summaries and expect to master the chapter. You are also responsible for reading and understanding the material that surrounds these basics—the "meat" around the bones, so to speak.

INSTRUCTOR SUPPLEMENTS

MindTap® for Community Policing in Criminal Justice The most applied learning experience available, MindTap is dedicated to preparing students to make the kinds of reasoned decisions they will have to as criminal justice professionals faced with real-world challenges. Available for virtually every Criminal Justice course, MindTap offers customizable content, course analytics, an e-reader, and more—all within your current learning management system. With its rich array of assets—interactive visual summaries, decision-making scenarios, and quizzes—MindTap is perfectly suited to today's students of criminal justice, engaging them, guiding them toward mastery of basic concepts, and advancing their critical thinking abilities.

Online Instructor's Manual with Lesson Plans The manual includes learning objectives, key terms, a detailed chapter outline, a chapter summary, lesson plans, discussion topics, student activities, "What If" scenarios, media tools, and sample syllabi. The learning objectives are correlated with the discussion topics, student activities, and media tools.

Downloadable Word Test Bank The enhanced test bank includes a variety of questions per chapter—a combination of multiple-choice, true–false, completion, essay, and critical thinking formats, with a full answer key. The test bank is coded to the learning objectives that appear in the main text, and identifies where in the text (by section) the answer appears. Finally, each question in the test bank has been carefully reviewed by experienced criminal justice instructors for quality, accuracy, and content coverage so instructors can be sure they are working with an assessment and grading resource of the highest caliber.

Cengage Learning Testing Powered by Cognero, the accompanying assessment tool is a flexible, online system that allows you to:

- Import, edit, and manipulate test bank content from the text's test bank or elsewhere, including your own favorite test questions;
- Create ideal assessments with your choice of fifteen question types (including true/false, multiple-choice, opinion scale/Likert, and essay)

- Create multiple test versions in an instant, using drop-down menus and familiar, intuitive tools that take you through content creation and management with ease;
- Deliver tests from your LMS, your classroom, or wherever you want—plus, import and export content into other systems as needed.

Online PowerPoint Lectures Helping you make your lectures more engaging while effectively reaching your visually oriented students, these handy Microsoft PowerPoint® slides outline the chapters of the main text in a classroom-ready presentation. The PowerPoint slides reflect the content and organization of the new edition of the text and feature some additional examples and real-world cases for application and discussion.

ABOUT THE AUTHORS

This text is based on the practical experience of Linda S. Miller, who has spent 26 years in law enforcement; the expertise of Kären Matison Hess, who developed instructional programs for 30 years; and Christine Hess Orthmann, who has been deeply involved with this text since its inception. The text has been reviewed by numerous experts in the various areas of community policing as well.

Linda S. Miller is the former executive director of the Upper Midwest Community Policing Institute (UMCPI) as well as a former sergeant with the Bloomington (Minnesota) Police Department. She was with the department for 22 years, serving as a patrol supervisor, a crime prevention officer, a patrol officer, and a police dispatcher. She also worked as the training coordinator for the Minnesota Coalition against Sexual Assault.

Ms. Miller is a member of the International Police Association, the International Association of Women Police, and the Public Safety Writers Association. In 1990 she was a member of the People-to-People's Women in Law Enforcement delegation to the Soviet Union.

Kären Matison Hess, Ph.D. (1939–2010), was the author who first developed this text with Miller and carried it through five very successful revisions. Dr. Hess held a Ph.D. in English and in instructional design from the University of Minnesota, was an instructor at Normandale Community College (Bloomington, Minnesota), and crafted a line of enduring, practical textbooks in the fields of law enforcement and criminal justice. Other Cengage texts Dr. Hess coauthored include *Criminal Investigation* (10th edition), *Introduction to Law Enforcement and Criminal Justice* (9th edition), *Introduction to Private Security* (5th edition), *Juvenile Justice* (5th edition), *Management and Supervision in Law Enforcement* (4th edition), *Police Operations* (5th edition), and *Careers in Criminal Justice: From Internship to Promotion* (6th edition).

Dr. Hess was a member of the Academy of Criminal Justice Sciences (ACJS), the American Association of University Women (AAUW), the American Society for Industrial Security (ASIS), the International Association of Chiefs of Police (IACP), the International Law Enforcement Educators and Trainers Association (ILEETA), the Justice Research and Statistics Association (JRSA), the Police Executive Research Forum (PERF), and the Textbook and Academic Author's Association (TAA). In 2006 Dr. Hess was honored by the University of Minnesota College of Education and Human Development at the school's 100-year anniversary as one of 100 alumni who have made a significant contribution to education and human development. Her tireless dedication to authorship and the education of criminal justice students will forever be an inspiration to us.

Christine Hess Orthmann, M.S., has been writing and researching in various aspects of criminal justice for more than 25 years. She is a coauthor of numerous Cengage books, including *Constitutional Law and the Criminal Justice System* (7th edition), *Criminal Investigation* (11th edition), *Introduction to Law Enforcement and Criminal Justice* (12th edition), *Juvenile Justice* (6th edition), *Management and Supervision in Law Enforcement* (7th edition), and *Police Operations: Theory and Practice* (6th edition), as well as a major contributor to *Introduction to Private Security* (5th edition), and *Careers in Criminal Justice and Related Fields: From Internship to Promotion* (6th edition).

Ms. Orthmann is a member of the Academy of Criminal Justice Sciences (ACJS), the American Society of Criminology (ASC), the Text and Academic Authors Association (TAA), and the National Criminal Justice Honor Society (Alpha Phi Sigma), and is a former reserve officer with the Rosemount (Minnesota) Police Department. Orthmann has a Master of Science Degree in criminal justice from the University of Cincinnati.

Tetra Images/Getty Images

The community and the police depend on each other. The common police motto—"To serve and protect"—suggests a target population of individuals who require service and protection. Most police departments stress the importance of community relations, and many have taken community relations beyond image enhancement and crime prevention programs and have started involving the community itself in policing.

This section begins with a discussion of the evolution of police–community relations. Since people first came together in groups, they have had some responsibility for ensuring that those within the group did as was expected. The U.S. method of "preserving the peace," modeled after that used in England, has evolved through several stages. The relationship between the community and its police has been severely strained at times, and attempts to improve it have taken several forms. Recently, emphasis on improved public

1

relations and crime prevention has expanded to a more encompassing philosophy of community policing, including problem-solving policing in many jurisdictions (Chapter 1).

Next, an in-depth look at the police is presented (Chapter 2). Who are the people behind the badges? How have they changed over the years? How might they change in the future? How does the public generally view the police? What aspects of the police role contribute to this view?

The focus in Chapter 3 is on the people and agencies involved in community–police relations. Who are the members of a community?

AP Images/DAN LOH

How do communities differ? How have they changed over the years? What future changes might be anticipated? What aspects of a community must be understood by those working within it? What is expected of community members? What do community members expect?

This is followed by an examination of problem-solving policing, a key component of the community policing philosophy (Chapter 4). The section concludes with a discussion on implementing community policing guidelines and cautions (Chapter 5).

The Evolution of Community Policing

Learning Objectives

LO1 Define community policing.

LO2 Explain what Sir Robert Peel's principles emphasize.

LO3 Summarize the three eras of policing.

LO4 Identify and describe the four essential dimensions of community policing.

Key Terms

community policing
community relations
frankpledge system
hue and cry
human relations
paradigm
paradigm shift
patronage system
political era
proactive
professional model
progressive era
public relations
reactive
reform era
spoils system
thin blue line
tithing
tithing system

On June 13, 2016, in Toulminville, AL, a suburb of Mobile, AL, a 19-year-old African American male, Michael Moore was fatally shot by a 4-year veteran of the Mobile Police Department, Harold Hurst, a White officer. This shooting has sparked much debate and provocation in this suburb among law enforcement members, elected officials, civil leaders, and many outraged community members. By reading accounts provided by the Mobile Police Department, one can determine Officer Hurst was on his way to roll call on June 13, 2016, when he chose to engage the vehicle in which Michael Moore was a passenger. Prior to being pulled over, the vehicle had made a left turn into oncoming traffic, almost causing an accident in front of the officer.

Hurst conducted a traffic stop on the vehicle, the license plate of which turned out to be stolen. When the officer inquired as to the identities of the driver and passengers, Michael Moore gave a false identity, whereby Hurst requested Moore to vacate the vehicle for further inquiry.

After Moore stepped out of the vehicle, Hurst saw a handgun in Moore's waistband and phone in Moore's hand. Hurst ordered Moore to keep his hands up and away from the gun. In what can neither be supported by video nor collaborated by witnesses, actions by Moore led the officer to shoot him. Once on the ground, Moore was again shot by Hurst, who feared the suspect was reaching for the weapon in his waistband. After the second shot was fired, Moore was handcuffed until responding officers arrived, which was standard operating procedure for the police department. Once responding officer arrived on scene, many of whom were wearing body cameras issued by the local government, the prominent footage showed a severely injured suspect who was handcuffed and awaiting medical attention. Moore later died at a local hospital.

Although there were many contentious issues that sparked debate in this incident, the most glaring of all was the lack of video footage from Hurst's body-worn camera or cruiser. In this age of accountability and community policing, these videos often serve as a historian, detailing the events that transpire between the officer and the civilian. The lack of video footage in this encounter, in which Hurst was engaged with a civilian in a contact that resulted in an officer-involved shooting, was detrimental to the corroboration of the officer's account of the incident. Certainly, there was social outrage over the incident.

The FBI offered $10,000 to anyone who could bring forward a video of Hurst and Moore interacting prior to the shooting. To date, no video has been submitted.

Understandably, there was much political outrage and protest by community members following this event. Although still under investigation, the incident has sparked peaceful vigils and activism. Other consequences of this incident include a lack of desire by community members to become police officers, a shortage of applicants applying for local law enforcement positions, and the abrupt departure of many from their policing careers.

In the following chapter, students will review the embryonic beginnings of community policing, the evolving nature of law enforcement, and the progressive problem solving that has surfaced today due to the importance of serving and protecting every community member, regardless of age, sexual orientation, socioeconomic level, gender, religion, or race.

INTRODUCTION

Community policing is often regarded as one of the most significant trends in the history of American policing. However, community policing did not just magically appear as a panacea for society's ills. Its roots can be traced back several centuries to policing in another country, and its evolution in the United States has spanned many decades. Many scholars and practitioners suggest that community policing continues to evolve, now serving as a stepping stone to new innovations and further emerging trends in American law enforcement. Indeed, as society's needs change, so do the methods it uses to "keep the peace."

Community policing is not an isolated phenomenon. Efforts to involve the community are occurring throughout the entire criminal justice system as many criminal justice professionals explore and research the concept of *community justice* and the contention that all citizens have the right and the responsibility to participate in the justice system. Community justice is both a strategy and a philosophy.

WHAT IS COMMUNITY POLICING?

Community policing is a challenging concept to define, and no single definition can satisfy all of those who study it or practice it. The following definitions illustrate the various ways community policing has been described:

- Community policing is an organization-wide philosophy and management approach that promotes (1) community, government, and police partnerships; (2) proactive problem solving to prevent crime; and (3) community engagement to address the causes of crime, fear of crime, and other community issues (Upper Midwest Community Policing Institute, n.d.).

- "It is a philosophy and not a specific tactic; a proactive, decentralized approach, designed to reduce crime, disorder, and fear of crime, by involving the same officer in the same community for a long-term basis" (Trojanowicz & Bucqueroux, 1990, p.154).

- "Four general principles define community policing: community engagement, problem solving, organizational transformation, and crime prevention by citizens and police working together" (Skogan, 2004, p.160).

- "In its simplest form, community policing is about building relationships and solving problems" (Melekian, 2011, p.14).

Ford (2007, p. 321) presents another way to view community policing: "Community policing is an organizational strategy that emerged in the 1980s and '90s for dramatically improving the delivery of police services.... The strategy requires greater emphasis on knowledge management, teamwork, and partnerships with the community in order for the police agency to become more proactive and adaptable in dealing with crime as well as becoming more focused on enhancing the quality of life for the community." As Kelling (1994) asserts: "Whether one calls community policing a philosophy, a strategy, a model, or a paradigm, it is a complex set of ideas that simply cannot be put into a simple one-sentence definition."

Although no one has been able to define community policing in a way that satisfies everyone, most will agree that it includes two vital components: a proactive, problem-solving approach to crime and disorder and partnerships involving both the police and the community in solving the problems. These are also the two core components identified by the Community Policing Consortium, comprised of the International Association of Chiefs of Police (IACP), the National Organization of Black Law Enforcement Executives (NOBLE), the Police Executive Research Forum (PERF), the National Sheriffs' Association (NSA), and the Police Foundation.

Without solving the problems they encounter, the police are doomed to handle the same problems and suspects again and again. Without community partnerships, the chances that the police can successfully solve problems also are slim. A community without input and ownership in the solutions will unintentionally or even intentionally undermine police efforts. A look at the history of policing helps in understanding how community policing has evolved.

LO1

"**Community policing** is a philosophy that promotes organization strategies that support the systematic use of partnerships and problem-solving techniques to proactively address the immediate conditions that give rise to public safety issues, such as crime, social disorder, and fear of crime" (Office of Community Oriented Policing Services, 2014, p. 1).

community policing
A philosophy that promotes organization strategies that support the systematic use of partnerships and problem-solving techniques to proactively address the immediate conditions that give rise to public safety issues, such as crime, social disorder, and fear of crime.

A BRIEF HISTORY OF POLICING

Throughout history societies have established rules to govern the conduct of individuals and have devised punishments for those who break the rules. The earliest record of an ancient society's rules for controlling human behavior dates back to approximately 2300 BCE, when Sumerian rulers codified their concept of offenses against society. Since then such rules have been modified and adapted. In Europe, as the mighty Roman Empire disintegrated during the Dark Ages, an Anglo-Saxon presence rose up in its place. Germanic invaders swept into the old Roman territory of Britain and intermarried with those they conquered. They also brought their own laws and customs to their new territory. The Anglo-Saxons grouped their farms around small, self-governing villages that policed themselves. This informal arrangement became more structured under King Alfred the Great (849–899), who required every male to enroll for police purposes in a group of 10 families, known as a **tithing**. The **tithing system** established the principle of collective responsibility for maintaining local law and order.

tithing
A group of 10 families.

tithing system
The Anglo-Saxon principle establishing the principle of collective responsibility for maintaining local law and order.

The tithing system worked well until 1066, when William the Conqueror, a Norman, invaded and conquered England. William, concerned about national security, replaced the tithing system of "home rule" with 55 military districts called shires,[1] each headed by a Norman officer called a reeve, hence the title shire-reeve (the origin of the word *sheriff*). William also established the **frank-pledge system** that required all free men to swear loyalty to the king's law and to take responsibility for maintaining the local peace.

frankpledge system
The Norman system requiring all free men to swear loyalty to the king's law and to take responsibility for maintaining the local peace.

By the 17th century, law enforcement duties were divided into two separate units, a day watch and a night watch. The day watch consisted of constables who served as jailers and fulfilled other government duties. Citizens worked on the night watch. Each citizen was expected to take a turn watching for fires, bad weather, and disorderly individuals. Some towns also expected the night watchman to call out the time. If a watchman or any other citizen saw a crime in progress, he was expected to give the **hue and cry** summoning all citizens within earshot to join in pursuing and capturing the wrongdoer. Preserving the peace was the duty of all citizens.

hue and cry
The summoning of all citizens within earshot to join in pursuing and capturing a wrongdoer.

By the end of the 18th century, most people with sufficient means paid others to stand their assigned watch for them, marking the beginning of a paid police force and, in effect, the original neighborhood watch.

The system of day and night watchmen was very ineffective. Because wealthy citizens could avoid the watch duty by hiring someone to take their place, those they hired were hesitant to invoke their authority against the well-to-do. According to Richardson (1970, p.10), by the mid-1700s New York City's night watch was "a parcel of idle, drinking, vigilant snorers, who never quelled any nocturnal tumult in their lives … but would, perhaps, be as ready to join in a burglary as any thief in Christendom."

London, suffering from the impact of the Industrial Revolution, was experiencing massive unemployment and poverty. It had become a disorderly city with enormous, crime-ridden slums and a significant juvenile delinquency problem. Some citizens had even begun to carry weapons for self-protection. In an attempt to address the problems, Parliament convened five parliamentary commissions of inquiry between 1780 and 1820. When Sir Robert Peel was

---

[1] A shire is equivalent to a U.S. county.

appointed as home secretary, he proposed that London appoint civilians, paid by the community, to serve as police officers. The Metropolitan Police Act was passed in 1829 and modern policing began.

THE BEGINNINGS OF "MODERN" POLICE FORCES

"Modern" policing began with the formation of the London Metropolitan Police, founded by Sir Robert Peel in 1829. Peel set forth the following nine principles on which the police force was to be based:

- The basic mission for which police exist is to prevent crime and disorder.
- The ability of the police to perform their duties is dependent upon public approval of police existence, actions, behavior, and the ability of the police to secure and maintain public respect.
- The police must secure the willing cooperation of the public in voluntary observance of the law to be able to secure and maintain public respect.
- The degree of cooperation of the public that can be secured diminishes, proportionately, to the necessity for the use of physical force.
- The police seek and preserve public favor, not by catering to public opinion, but by constantly demonstrating absolutely impartial service to the law, in complete independence of policy, and without regard to the justice or injustice of the substance of individual laws; by ready offering of individual service and friendship to all members of society without regard to their race or social standing.
- The police should use physical force to the extent necessary to secure observance of the law or to restore order only when the exercise of persuasion, advice, and warning is found to be insufficient.
- The police at all times should maintain a relationship with the public that gives reality to the historic tradition that the police are the public and the public are the police; the police are the only members of the public who are paid to give full-time attention to duties which are incumbent on every citizen in the intent of the community welfare.
- The police should always direct their actions toward their functions and never appear to usurp the powers of the judiciary by avenging individuals or the state.
- The test of police efficiency is the absence of crime and disorder, not the visible evidence of police action in dealing with them.

Peel envisioned a close police–citizen relationship that helped the police maintain order in London. As originally envisioned by the architects of London's Metropolitan Police, a police officer's job was primarily crime prevention and social maintenance, not crime detection. Police were to serve as local marshals who actively maintained order by interacting with the neighborhoods they served.

Those who came to America in 1620 and their descendants, through the American Revolution, rejected the British Crown's rule that permitted British soldiers to take over homes and to have complete authority over the

L02

Peel's principles emphasized the interdependency of the police and the public as well as the prevention of crime and disorder and sought to give reality to the historic tradition that *the police are the public and the public are the police.*

colonists. Our founders wanted to ensure that no such power would exist in the newly created nation. As former Chief Justice of the U.S. Supreme Court Warren E. Burger (1991, p. 26) stated: "The Founders, conscious of the risks of abuse of power, created a system of liberty with order and placed the Bill of Rights as a harness on government to protect people from misuse of the powers." Nonetheless, the system of policing and maintaining order in the northern part of the United States was modeled on the police system developed in England.

Early Policing in the United States

At the time the Metropolitan Police Force was established in London, the United States was still operating under a day-and-night watch system similar to the one that had been used in England. In the 1830s, several large cities established separate paid day watches. In 1833, Philadelphia became the first city to pay both the day and night watches. Boston followed in 1838 with a six-officer police force.

In 1844, New York City took the first step toward organizing a big-city police department similar to those that exist today across the country when it consolidated its day and night watches under the control of a police chief. The police department was modeled on the London Metropolitan Police and Peel's principles. Other cities followed the example set by New York. By 1857, Boston, Chicago, New Orleans, Newark, Cincinnati, Philadelphia, and Baltimore had consolidated police departments modeled on London's Metropolitan Police. The new police chiefs of these departments faced the beginning of tremendous personnel problems and disarray among their officers:

> What those first chiefs of police found in their newly consolidated forces was a motley, undisciplined crew composed, as one commentator on the era described it, principally of "the shiftless, the incompetent, and the ignorant." Tales abounded of police officers in the 1850s who assaulted their superior officers, who released prisoners from the custody of other officers, who were found sleeping or drunk on duty, or who could be bribed for almost anything. (Garmire, 1989, p. 17)

Despite these problems, and because there were also many honest, dedicated police officers, the citizens considered the police a source of assistance. Early police officers' duties included more community assistance and service than often imagined. Even at the beginning of the 20th century, law enforcement was one of the only government-sanctioned services to help citizens around the clock. Welfare, parole, probation, and unemployment offices did not exist. Police in New York, for example, distributed coal to the poor, monitored the well-being of vulnerable citizens, served as probation and parole officers, and helped establish playgrounds.

It was more than a decade after the formation of the first police forces in the United States that attempts were made to require police officers to wear uniforms. Police officers' well-known resistance to change was apparent even then. The rank-and-file reaction against uniforms was immediate. Police officers claimed that uniforms were "un-American" and "a badge of degradation and servitude." In Philadelphia, police officers even objected to wearing badges on their coats. It was a bitter 4-year struggle before they were finally persuaded to wear a complete uniform.

In 1856, New York City required its officers to be uniformed, but each local ward[2] could determine the style of dress. As a result, in some sections of the city, police officers wore straw hats, whereas in others they wore felt hats. In some wards, summer uniforms were white "duck" suits; in other wards, they were multicolored outfits.

Policing in the Southern States

Policing in the South had different origins—the slave patrols found in the Southern colonies and states. By 1700, most Southern colonies, concerned about the dangers the oppressed slaves could create, had established a code of laws to regulate slaves. These codes prohibited slaves from having weapons, gathering in groups, leaving the plantation without a pass, or resisting punishment.

Predictably, many slaves resisted their bondage. According to Foner (1975), the resistance usually consisted of running away, criminal acts, and conspiracies or revolts. Compounding the problem was the fact that slaves outnumbered the colonists in some Southern states. For example, in 1720, South Carolina's population was 30 percent White and 70 percent Black (Simmons, 1976). The White colonists' fear of the slaves as a dangerous threat led to the development of special officers with general enforcement powers as a transition to modern police (Reichel, 1999). Thus, a strong argument exists that these slave patrols were the first truly American police system (Williams & Murphy, 1990; Dulaney, 1996). In fact, by 1750, every Southern colony had a slave patrol that formally required all White men to serve as patrollers (Dulaney, 1996). In actuality, however, the patrollers were generally poor White men.

In most colonies and states, patrols could enter any plantation and break into slaves' dwellings; punish slaves found outside their plantation; and search, beat, and even kill any slaves found to be violating the slave code. Even after the Civil War and abolition of slavery, "free men of color" were hired as police officers only to enforce Jim Crow laws that supported segregation and to keep the nation's Black population in line (Potter, 2013). Until the civil rights movements swept through the country in the 1960s, Black police officers had no arrest power over White citizens.

The evolution of law enforcement in both the North and South is often divided into three distinct eras.

THE THREE ERAS OF POLICING

Three major paradigm shifts have occurred in the evolution of policing in the United States. A **paradigm** is a model or a way of viewing a specific aspect of life such as politics, medicine, education, and even the criminal justice system. A **paradigm shift** is simply a new way of thinking about a specific subject. Kelling and Moore (1991) describe these paradigm shifts as specific "eras" of policing in the United States.

paradigm
A model or a way of viewing a specific aspect of life such as politics, medicine, education, and the criminal justice system.

paradigm shift
A new way of thinking about a specific subject.

---

[2] A ward is an administrative division of a city or town.

The Political Era (1840 to 1930) *1*

political era
Extended into the first quarter of the 20th century and witnessed the formation of police departments.

The **political era** extended into the first quarter of the 20th century and witnessed the formation of police departments. During this era, police were closely tied to politics. This was dissimilar to the situation in England, where the police were centralized under the king, and the police chief had the authority to fire officers. In the United States, the police were decentralized under the authority of the municipality in which they worked. The chief had no authority to fire officers; therefore, the police were often undisciplined. "The image of 'Keystone Cops'—police as clumsy bunglers—was widespread and often descriptive of realities in U.S. policing" (Kelling & Moore, 1991, p.9). Police officers usually lived in their community and were members of the majority group. Because foot patrol was the most common policing strategy used, officers became close to the public.

During this era, chiefs of police were politically appointed and had a vested interest in keeping those who appointed them in power. Politicians rewarded those who voted for them with jobs or special privileges. This was referred to as the **patronage system**, or the **spoils system** from the adage "To the victor go the spoils."

patronage system
Politicians rewarded those who voted for them with jobs or special privileges; prevalent during the political era. Also called the *spoils* system.

spoils system
Politicians rewarded those who voted for them with jobs or special privileges; prevalent during the political era. Also called the *patronage system.*

In 1929, President Herbert Hoover appointed the National Commission on Law Observance and Enforcement to study the criminal justice system. Hoover named George W. Wickersham, former U.S. attorney general, as its chairman. When the report was published in 1931, it became one of the "most important events in the history of American Policing" (Walker, 1997, p.154). The Wickersham Commission focused two reports on the police. Report 11, *Lawlessness in Law Enforcement*, described the problem of police brutality, concluding that "the third degree—the inflicting of pain, physical or mental, to extract confessions or statements—is extensively practiced." Specific tactics included protracted questioning, threats and intimidation, physical brutality, illegal detention, and refusal to allow access of counsel to suspects (National Commission on Law Observance and Enforcement, 1931, p.4). Report 14, *The Police*, examined police administration and called for expert leadership, centralized administrative control, and higher standards for personnel—in effect, for police professionalism. The inefficiency and corruption of the police led to the second era of policing, the reform era.

The Reform Era (1930 to 1980) *2*

reform era
Emphasized preventive automobile patrol and rapid response to calls for service. Also called the *progressive era.*

The **reform era** is often referred to as the **progressive era**. August Vollmer and O.W. Wilson are usually attributed with spearheading the reform movement that called for a drastic change in the organization and function of police departments.

progressive era
Emphasized preventive automobile patrol and rapid response to calls for service. Also called the *reform era.*

August Vollmer is often credited as the father of American policing. He was elected to be the Berkeley city marshal in 1904, a position that was changed to chief of police in 1909 and which Vollmer held until 1932. During his tenure at Berkeley, Vollmer created a police force that became a model for the country. His innovations included radios in patrol cars, a fingerprint and handwriting classification system, a workable system for filing and using modus operandi (MO) files, motorcycles and bicycles on patrol, and a police school at his department. Vollmer believed police should be trained professionals who were also social workers with a deeper responsibility to the community than simply fighting crime. Vollmer's book, *The Police and Modern Society* (1936), is still a classic in law enforcement. Vollmer also helped create the first college police program at the University of California at Berkeley.

O.W. Wilson, a protégé of Vollmer, continued the move toward professionalizing the police. One of Wilson's greatest strengths was his firm belief in honest law enforcement. Although very aware that the police had little control over the root causes of crime, Wilson advocated the concept of preventive patrol. Wilson's most noted works are *Police Administration* (1950) and *Police Planning* (1952).

One basic change during this era was to disassociate policing from politics, which was accomplished in a variety of ways. In Los Angeles, for example, the chief of police position became a civil-service job that required applicants to pass a civil-service test. In Milwaukee, the chief of police was appointed for life by a citizen commission. With the disassociation of policing from politics came a change in emphasis in the police role as citizens began to equate policing with fighting crime. The police considered social-service-type functions less desirable and avoided them when possible.

The relationship between the police and the public also changed during the reform era, with police leaders commanding their officers to maintain "proper" professional neutrality and emotional distance with citizens and politicians in order to achieve impartial law enforcement (Kelling & Moore, 1991). The public viewed the police as professionals who remained detached from the citizens they served.

During this era, the concept of the **thin blue line** developed, a phrase referring to the line that separates law-abiding, peaceful citizens from the murderous, plundering criminals who prey upon them. The thin blue line describes the dangerous threats to communities, with police standing between good and evil. The phrase also suggests a distance between the police and the public they serve. It evokes both police heroism and isolation.

thin blue line
The distancing of the police from the public they serve.

Adding to the distancing of police from the public during the reform era was the replacement of foot patrols with motorized patrols. O.W. Wilson's preventive patrol by squad car, coupled with an emphasis on rapid response to calls for service, became the dual focus of policing during this era. The police image became one of professional crime fighters roaring through city streets in high-powered squad cars, lights flashing and sirens wailing. Consequently, policing during the reform era is often referred to as the **professional model**, which emphasized crime control by preventive automobile patrol coupled with rapid response to calls.

professional model
Emphasized crime control by preventive automobile patrol coupled with rapid response to calls. The predominant policing model used during the reform era (1970s and 1980s).

The problems the first police administrators faced did not change much, but under the professional model, their answers did. Many police methods were challenged during the 1960s, when social change exploded in the United States as the result of several significant events occurring almost simultaneously.

The Civil Rights Movement began in the late 1950s as a grassroots effort to change the blatantly unequal social, political, and economic systems in the United States. Confrontations between African Americans and the police, the ranks of which were comprised almost exclusively of White males, increased during this time. Representing the status quo and defending it, the manner in which the police handled protest marches and civil disobedience often aggravated these situations.

sound familiar

Punctuated by the assassinations of President Kennedy, Malcolm X, Martin Luther King, Jr., Medgar Evers, and Robert Kennedy, the events of the decade were, for the first time in history, documented in detail and seen by millions of U.S. citizens on television. The antiwar movement, based on college campuses, was also televised. When demonstrators at the 1968 Democratic convention in Chicago were beaten by the Chicago police, the demonstrators chanted: "The whole world is watching." Viewing what was later termed a police riot, the public was shocked.

Plagued by lack of training and confronted by a confusing array of social movements and an emerging drug culture, the police became the "enemy." Officers heard themselves referred to as "pigs" by everyone from students to well-known entertainers. Law enforcement represented the status quo, the establishment, and everything that stood in the way of peace, equality, and justice. Police in the 1960s were at war with the society they served. Never had the relationship between the law enforcement community and the people it served been so strained.

The 1960s changed the face of the United States, and law enforcement was no exception. In addition to the questionable way police handled race riots and antiwar demonstrations during this decade, several big-city police departments were facing corruption charges. Studies in the 1970s on corruption and criminal behavior among police agencies brought great pressure to bear on the entire criminal justice system. Media coverage of law enforcement practices educated the public, who ultimately demanded change in police methods, attitudes, and image. The Bureau of Justice Assistance (1994, 6–7) describes the social and professional "awakening" that occurred during the 1960s and 1970s:

> Antiwar protesters, civil rights activists, and other groups began to demonstrate in order to be heard. Overburdened and poorly prepared police came to symbolize what these groups sought to change in their government and society. Focusing attention on police policies and practices became an effective way to draw attention to the need for wider change. Police became the targets of hostility, which ultimately led police leaders to concerned reflection and analysis. ...

> A number of organizations within the policing field also became committed to improving policing methods in the 1970s. Among those on the forefront of this movement for constructive change were the Police Foundation, the Police Executive Research Forum, the National Organization of Black Law Enforcement Executives, the Urban Sheriffs' Group of the National Sheriffs' Association, and the International Association of Chiefs of Police. These organizations conducted much of the basic research that led police to reevaluate traditional policing methods.

Commissions Established to Examine Police Services   During the 1960s and early 1970s, considerable turmoil existed throughout the country related to issues of police and race relations, corruption, and use of force. During that period, five national Blue Ribbon Commissions—ad hoc, short-term investigations of law enforcement—were initiated to examine various aspects of police services and the criminal justice process (Walker & Macdonald, 2009). Each commission captured its findings in a written report that included recommendation for reform:

- The President's Commission on Law Enforcement and Administration of Justice was influenced by urban racial turmoil. An outgrowth of its report published in 1967 and 1968 was the Safe Streets Act of 1968 and the Law Enforcement Assistance Administration, which provided significant funding for police-related programs.

2 ▪ The National Advisory Commission on Civil Disorders (popularly known as the Kerner Commission) was also inspired by the riots and other disorders in many U.S. cities in the summer of 1967. Its report examined patterns of disorder and prescribed responses by the federal government, the criminal justice system, and local government.

3 ▪ The National Commission on the Causes and Prevention of Violence was established after the assassinations of Martin Luther King, Jr., and Robert Kennedy in 1968. Its report, "To Establish Justice, To Insure Domestic Tranquility," was published in 1969.

4 ▪ The President's Commission on Campus Unrest was established following student deaths related to protests at Kent State and Jackson State universities in 1970.

5 ▪ The National Advisory Commission on Criminal Justice Standards and Goals issued six reports in 1973 in an attempt to develop standards and recommendations for police crime control efforts.

In response to the negative police image that emerged during the 1960s, several departments across the country established programs to enhance their relationships with the communities they served. These programs included public-relations programs, community-relations programs, and crime prevention programs.

Efforts to Enhance Relations between the Police and the Community To avoid confusion, it is helpful to distinguish among public relations, community relations, and human relations because these terms are used frequently throughout this text and in other literature on policing.

▪ **Public relations**: Efforts to enhance the police image—"We'll tell you what we're doing, but leave us alone to fight crime"
▪ **Community relations**: Efforts to interact and communicate with the community—team policing, community resource officers, and school resource officers
▪ **Human relations**: Efforts to relate to and understand other people or groups of people—the focus of Section II

Public-relations efforts are usually one-way efforts to raise the image of the police. These efforts by police departments include hosting departmental open houses and providing speakers for school and community events. Many police departments have established a public-relations office or division and have assigned specific officers to the public-relations effort. Such efforts reflect the growing recognition by police administrators that they need public support.

In the past several decades, especially in the late 1970s and also as a result of the widening gap between the police and the public, many police departments began community-relations programs. Unlike public-relations efforts, which were primarily one-to-one communications and often media generated, community-relations programs sought to bring the police and the community

public relations
Efforts to enhance the police image. See also *community relations*.

community relations
Efforts to interact and communicate with the community—team policing, community resource officers, and school liaison officers. See also *public relations*.

human relations
Efforts to relate to and understand other individuals or groups.

closer through isolated police tactics such as team policing and community resource officers. Efforts to enhance community relations also frequently involved citizens through crime prevention programs.

Crime Prevention Programs Crime prevention programs that enlist citizens' aid include Operation Identification programs, neighborhood- or block-watch programs, and home and automobile security programs. Such programs, which continue to be strategies used in many community policing efforts, are discussed in detail in Section III.

The Law Enforcement Assistance Administration Another response to the negative image of the police was the establishment of the Law Enforcement Assistance Administration (LEAA) in 1968. Over the next several years, LEAA provided billions of dollars to the "war on crime," funding studies and programs for law enforcement. LEAA awarded more than $9 billion to state and local governments to improve police, courts, and correctional systems; to combat juvenile delinquency; and to finance innovative crime-fighting projects. Tens of thousands of programs and projects were supported with LEAA funds, and millions of hours were applied to identify effective, efficient, and economical ways to reduce crime and improve criminal justice. Although the consensus among law enforcement officials today is that LEAA was mostly mismanaged, there was also a very positive aspect of LEAA known as the Law Enforcement Education Program (LEEP), which provided thousands of officers with funding for higher education.

The Courts The courts also had a major impact on criminal justice during the 1960s. Several legal decisions limited police powers and clarified the rights of the accused. The exclusionary rule, established in *Weeks v. United States* (1914), mandated that federal courts must refuse to consider evidence obtained by unreasonable, and therefore unconstitutional, search and seizure, no matter how relevant the evidence was to the case. In 1961, *Mapp v. Ohio* extended the exclusionary rule to every court and law enforcement officer in the country.

In 1963, in *Gideon v. Wainwright* the Supreme Court ruled 9 to 0 that the due process clause of the Fourteenth Amendment requires states to provide free counsel to indigent (impoverished) defendants in all felony cases. Another landmark case came the following year in *Escobedo v. Illinois* (1964), when the Court ruled that if individuals confess without being told of their right to have a lawyer present, the confessions are not legal.

In 1966, this right to have a lawyer present, and at public expense if necessary, and other rights were reaffirmed in what is probably the best-known Supreme Court case to date—*Miranda v. Arizona.* The Court held that evidence obtained by police during custodial interrogation of a suspect cannot be used in court unless the suspect is informed of the following four basic rights—called *Miranda* rights—*before* questioning:

- The suspect's right to remain silent
- The right of the police to use in a court of law any statement made by the suspect

- The suspect's right to have an attorney present during questioning
- The suspect's right to have a court-appointed attorney before questioning if he or she cannot afford one

Another landmark decision was handed down in 1968 in *Terry v. Ohio*. This case established police officers' right to stop and question a person to investigate suspicious behavior and to frisk that person if the officer has reason to believe the person is armed. In delivering the opinion of the Court, Chief Justice Warren stated:

> [W]here a police officer observes unusual conduct which leads him reasonably to conclude in light of his experience that criminal activity may be afoot and that the persons with whom he is dealing may be armed and presently dangerous, where, in the course of investigating this behavior, he identifies himself as a policeman and makes reasonable inquiries, and where nothing in the initial stages of the encounter serves to dispel his reasonable fear for his own or others' safety, he is entitled for the protection of himself and others in the area to conduct a carefully limited search of the outer clothing of such persons in an attempt to discover weapons which might be used to assault him. Such a search is a reasonable search under the Fourth Amendment, and any weapons seized may properly be introduced in evidence against the person from whom they were taken. (*Terry v. Ohio*, 1968)

Other Problems and Challenges during the Progressive Era   Despite the *Terry* decision, reported crime increased and the public's fear of crime intensified. An influx of immigrants added to the problems of major cities. During the 1970s, the widespread closing of mental hospitals and deinstitutionalization of patients with mental illness brought thousands of individuals with psychiatric, psychological, and behavioral disorders and problems into the mainstream of the United States, often without means to support themselves. This, coupled with the return of many Vietnam veterans who found it difficult to reenter society, resulted in a large homeless population.

Another challenge to the effectiveness of the professional model was the Kansas City Preventive Patrol Study. This classic study found that increasing or decreasing preventive patrol efforts had no significant effect on crime, citizen fear of crime, community attitudes toward the police, police response time, or traffic accidents. As Klockars (1983, p.130) noted, "It makes about as much sense to have police patrol routinely in cars to fight crime as it does to have firemen patrol routinely in fire trucks to fight fire."

Many law enforcement officials view the Kansas City Preventive Patrol Study as the beginning of a new era in policing. It was considered by police to be the first experimental design used in policing and, as such, was a landmark. It set the stage for further research in policing and is viewed as the first true movement in the professionalization of policing. Its findings are also controversial. Although there were problems with the research design and implementation of this study, it succeeded in raising questions about many of the assumptions that had long existed regarding policing. It concluded what many police officials already knew but did not want publicized for fear of the impact on police budgets. Other research conducted in the 1970s also questioned police effectiveness:

> Research about preventive patrol, rapid response to calls for service, and investigative work—the three mainstays of police tactics—was uniformly discouraging.

> Research demonstrated that preventive patrol in automobiles had little effect on crime, citizen levels of fear, or citizen satisfaction with police. Rapid response to calls for service likewise had little impact on arrests, citizen satisfaction with police, or levels of citizen fear. Also, research into criminal investigation effectiveness suggested that detective units were so poorly administered that they had little chance of being effective. (Kelling, 1988, p.4)

By the mid-1970s, the general period of reform in policing in the United States had slowed. Many promising reforms, such as team policing, had not caused any major changes. (Chapter 5 discusses team policing and its demise.) The reform movement was called into question by two articles: Herman Goldstein's "Problem-Oriented Policing" in 1979 and James Q. Wilson and George L. Kelling's "Broken Windows" in 1982.

Other reasons for reevaluating police methods were the changing nature of the people who became police and their frustration with the traditional role of the patrol officer. Although patrol was given lip service as the backbone of policing, it was seen as the least desirable assignment. A change was needed at the patrol level to attract more highly educated and less militaristic recruits. The patrol officer had to become more important to the department in accomplishing its mission.

Finally, many businesses and individuals began to hire private security officers to ensure their safety, amidst a growing public perception that the police were unable to "preserve the peace" alone. Whereas some called for greater cooperation between public and private policing, others argued that the public should collaborate with all policing efforts.

A combination of the dissatisfaction with criminal justice and the role of patrol officers, research results, the trend toward private policing, and the writings of Goldstein and Wilson and Kelling led to the third era of policing—the community era.

The Community Era (1980 to Present)

In the 1980s, many police departments began experimenting with more community involvement in the "war on crime." Also during this decade several cities tested Goldstein's problem-oriented approach to policing. The emphasis in many departments began to shift from crime fighting to crime prevention.

According to some historians, the community era had its roots in the Kerner Commission Report, released in February 1968 by the President's National Advisory Committee on Civil Disorder. The report condemned racism in the United States and called for aid to African American communities to avert further racial polarization and violence. Gradually, law enforcement became more responsive to the public's desire for a different kind of policing, and the community era began gaining traction.

The community era goes by many names: community policing, community-oriented policing (COP), neighborhood policing, and the like. Currently the term *community policing* is most commonly used. At the heart of most "new" approaches to policing is a return to the ancient idea of community responsibility for the welfare of society—police officers become a part of the community, not apart from it. A comparison of traditional policing and community policing is made in Table 1.1.

Whereas traditionally policing has been **reactive**, responding to calls for service, community policing is **proactive**, anticipating problems and seeking solutions to them. The term *proactive* is beginning to take on an expanded definition. Not only is it taking on the meaning of anticipating problems, but it is also taking on the Stephen Covey slant, that of accountability and choosing a response rather than reacting the same way each time a similar situation occurs. Police are learning that they do not obtain different results by applying the same methods. In other words, to get different results, different tactics are needed. This is the focus of Chapter 4.

Although community policing is considered innovative, one of its central tenets of involvement with and responsiveness to the community is similar to the principles set forth by Sir Robert Peel in 1829 when he established the London Metropolitan Police. Peel stated: "The police are the public and the

reactive
Responding after the fact; responding to calls for service. The opposite of *proactive*.

proactive
Anticipating problems and seeking solutions to those problems, as in community policing. The opposite of *reactive*.

Table 1.1	Comparison of Traditional Policing and Community Policing	
Question	**Traditional Policing**	**Community Policing**
Who are the police?	A government agency principally responsible for law enforcement.	Police are the public and the public are the police: The police officers are those who are paid to give full-time attention to the duties of every citizen.
What is the relationship of the police force to other public service departments?	Priorities often conflict.	The police are one department among many responsible for improving the quality of life.
What is the role of the police?	Focusing on solving crimes.	A broader problem-solving approach.
How is police efficiency measured?	By detection and arrest rates.	By the absence of crime and disorder.
What are the highest priorities?	Crimes that are high value (e.g., bank robberies) and those involving violence.	Whatever problems disturb the community most.
What, specifically, do police deal with?	Incidents.	Citizens' problems and concerns.
What determines the effectiveness of police?	Response times.	Public cooperation.
What view do police take of service calls?	Deal with them only if there is no real police work to do.	Vital function and great opportunity.
What is police professionalism?	Swift, effective response to serious crime.	Keeping close to the community.
What kind of intelligence is most important?	Crime intelligence (study of particular crimes or series of crimes).	Criminal intelligence (information about the activities of individuals or groups).
What is the essential nature of police accountability?	Highly centralized; governed by rules, regulations, and policy directives; accountable to the law.	Emphasis on local accountability to community needs.
What is the role of headquarters?	To provide the necessary rules and policy directives.	To preach organizational values.
What is the role of the press liaison department?	To keep the "heat" off operational officers, so they can get on with job.	To coordinate an essential channel of communication with the community.
How do the police regard prosecutions?	As an important goal.	As one tool among many.

Source: Malcolm K. Sparrow. *Implementing Community Policing*, U.S. Department of Justice, National Institute of Justice, November 1988, pp. 8–9.

Table 1.2	The Three Eras of Policing		
	Political Era (1840s to 1930s)	**Reform Era (1930s to 1980s)**	**Community Era (1980s to Present)**
Authorization	Politics and law	Law and professionalism	Community support (political), law, and professionalism
Function	Broad social services	Crime control	Broad provision of services
Organizational design	Decentralized	Centralized, classical	Decentralized, task forces, matrices
Relationship to community	Intimate	Professional, remote	Intimate
Tactics and technology	Foot patrol	Preventive patrol and rapid response to calls	Foot patrol, problem solving, public relations
Outcome	Citizen, political satisfaction	Crime control	Quality of life and citizen satisfaction

Source: Based on George L. Kelling and Mark H. Moore. "From Political to Reform to Community: The Evolving Strategy of Police." In *Community Policing: Rhetoric or Reality*, edited by Jack R. Greene and Stephen D. Mastrofski. New York: Praeger Publishers, 1991, pp. 6, 14–15, 22–23.

LO3

The three eras of policing are political, reform, and community. During the political era, the police were decentralized, focused on providing broad social services, and sought an intimate relationship with the community. During the reform era, the police were centralized, focused on crime control, and their relationship with the community they served was professionally remote. During the community era, the police again became more decentralized, focused on the provision of services and quality-of-life issues, and sought to reestablish a close relationship with the community.

public are the police." Policing had strayed so far from Peel's principles during the previous century that the concepts central to community policing seemed fresh.

Highlights of the three eras of policing are summarized in Table 1.2.

Today there is considerable citizen–police interaction and problem solving. Although still resistant to change, police agencies are now more likely to respond to the needs and wishes of the communities they serve. The significant changes in the way police address sexual assault, domestic violence, sexual abuse of children, drunk driving, and missing children attest to this new responsiveness. The public wants the police to be proactive; citizens want police to try to prevent crime in addition to apprehending criminals after they have committed a crime.

However, despite the growth and success of community policing in many jurisdictions, in some areas of the country, the tension between the police and the communities they serve—particularly communities of color—has become palpable. Since the 2012 shooting death of Trayvon Martin, an unarmed 17-year-old African American male who was killed by a neighborhood watch volunteer, several other incidents across the country have involved unarmed Black men dying at the hands of the police, tragedies that have sparked protests, riots, and fear and severely damaged the public's trust in the police. These events will be presented and examined in greater detail later in the text where they are relevant to the topic of discussion.

On December 18, 2014, President Barack Obama signed an executive order establishing the President's Task Force on 21st Century Policing. This Task Force was charged with identifying best practices and offering recommendations on how policing practices can promote effective crime reduction and strengthen community policing as a critical and necessary step toward promoting trust among law enforcement officers and the communities they serve. Findings and suggestions from the Task Force's *Final Report* (2015) will be presented and discussed throughout this text as they apply to the community policing principles being discussed.

FEATURES OF COMMUNITY POLICING

Several major features associated with community policing are regular contact between officers and citizens; a department-wide philosophy and department-wide acceptance; internal and external influence and respect for officers; a well-defined role including both proactive and reactive policing—a full-service officer; direct service—the same officer takes complaints and gives crime prevention tips; citizens identify problems and cooperate in setting up the police agenda; police accountability is ensured by the citizens receiving the service in addition to administrative mechanisms; and the officer is the leader and catalyst for change in the neighborhood to reduce fear, disorder, decay, and crime:

> Community policing goes beyond simply putting officers on foot or bicycle patrols, or in neighborhood stations. It redefines the role of the officer on the street, from crime fighter to problem solver and neighborhood ombudsman. It forces a cultural transformation of the entire department including a decentralized organizational structure and changes in recruiting, training, awards systems, evaluation, promotions, and so forth. Furthermore, this philosophy asks officers to break away from the binds of incident-driven policing and to seek proactive and creative resolution to crime and disorder. (Peak and Barthe, 2009, p.77)

The chief of police is an advocate and sets the tone for the delivery of both law enforcement and social services in the jurisdictions. Officers educate the public about issues (such as response time or preventive patrol) and the need to prioritize services. Increased trust between the police officer and citizens because of long-term, regular contact results in an enhanced flow of information to the police. The officer is continually accessible in person, by telephone, or in a decentralized office with regular visibility in the neighborhood.

Richard Ellis/Getty Images

The Black Lives Matters movement was created by three women as a "call to action" against the widespread anti-Black racism in the United States and the deadly oppression of Blacks not only at the hands of law enforcement but by society at large. Here, citizens in North Charleston, South Carolina, participate in a rally on April 8, 2015, to protest the death of Walter Scott, a Black man who was shot and killed by police officer Michael Slager. Video captured by a bystander showed the white officer shooting Scott as he ran away. Officer Slager was tried for murder in the incident, which ended in a mistrial. A new trial is set to occur as this text goes to press.

Officers are viewed as having a stake in the community. They are role models, especially for youth, because of regular contact with citizens. Influence is from the bottom up—citizens receiving service help set priorities and influence police policy, meaningful organizational change, and departmental restructuring—ranging from officer selection to training, evaluation, and promotion. When intervention is necessary, informal social control is the first choice. Officers encourage citizens to solve many of their own problems and volunteer to assist neighbors. Officers encourage other service providers such as animal control workers, firefighters, and mail carriers to become involved in community problem solving. Officers mobilize all community resources, including citizens, private and public agencies, and private businesses. Success is determined by a reduction in citizen fear, neighborhood disorder, and crime.

Identification and awareness of these features have allowed law enforcement departments nationwide to implement the principles and philosophy of community policing. Also important to understanding community policing is knowledge of the essential elements identified by researchers and practitioners.

ESSENTIAL ELEMENTS OF COMMUNITY POLICING

Three essential elements of community policing are partnerships, problem solving, and organizational change (Morabito, 2010). Partnerships describe the indispensable relationship between the community and law enforcement. Partnerships are central to modern-day policing because they recognize a basic truth—law enforcement cannot do it alone (Peed, 2008). Although partnerships are critical to policing, they must be purposeful, directed toward improving the quality of life through the second essential element of community policing—problem solving—which seeks to reduce problems by addressing their immediate underlying causes (Peed, 2008). However, partnerships and problem solving do not occur on their own but require an active, conscious effort to start them and a continued nurturing to sustain them (Peed, 2008). In other words, without organizational change, problem solving and partnerships will not happen.

Numerous studies have examined community policing and factors that influence the effectiveness of its implementation. Important results include the understanding that the *context of policing* is essential and varies from community to community, meaning there exist myriad ways for the community policing philosophy to be translated into practice. With so much emphasis placed on developing relationships with citizens in the community, it is also vitally important that police–police interactions—elements of traditional policing that are known to add personal value to the job of an officer—are not overlooked or ignored (Lord & Friday, 2008).

Rosenberg, Sigler, and Lewis (2008) examined, over a 19-month period, police officer attitudes toward community policing in Racine, Wisconsin, and found that patrol officers' and investigators' attitudes were less favorable toward community policing concepts, programming, decentralization of substations, and the community policing unit than those of senior command officers and, in some

IDEAS IN PRACTICE

"NEW HAVEN'S TOP COP: 'YOU DON'T KNOW US ANYMORE.'"

By Conor Friedersdorf (*The Atlantic*, November 19, 2015)

New Haven, Connecticut, is a high-crime city that is also home to the Ivy League school, Yale University. As the chief of the New Haven Police Department, Dean Esserman wanted to know what would happen if more cops walked a beat. To find out, he began assigning all rookie officers to daily foot patrols on the same blocks for the first year after graduating from the police academy, and the results were highly favorable. In an article in the *Yale Daily News*, Esserman explained how his new approach aligns with philosophy of community policing:

> What I've come to learn after being a police chief for 25 years in four American cities is that we lost our way. We don't know our own history. But our history has a lot to do with who we are and where I think we need to head.
>
> Before there were police there were constables. And before there were constables there was the night watch. Originally, the police were the citizens that night who were just chosen to walk the street, with a bell, a staff, and a lantern, and look out for the community. The next night another citizen did that job. And no one was paid. It was a caretaker job.
>
> Later, night watchmen became constables, and they got paid. Later still they got trained. And only 100 years later did they become organized police departments. So the truth is that we always were a part of the community....
>
> But the average American police officer doesn't know that history. They don't connect to that history. They connect to the uniform. They connect to the distance and the professionalism and the apartness. So we're trying to return to that....
>
> Every month or two, I bring these young rookies into my conference room alone with the door closed. And we go around the room and I say, "Tell me a story." I've been doing this now for the four years that I've been chief in New Haven. And the stories are always the same. The first week it's a quiet walk. Everybody is kind of eyeballing you and you're eyeballing everybody. By the end of the month you can't get down the block without a half-a-dozen conversations and honking their horns. People know your children's names and you know their children's names.
>
> They know your days off.
>
> By the second or third month I almost always hear this story:
>
> *Chief, you gotta explain this to me, I don't get it. I've walked this beat everyday with my partner for three months. And I say hello to this lady every morning. Yesterday, she asked me if I could stay a minute. She wanted to talk. She told me something horrendous had happened to her three or four months ago. I said, Ma'am, why didn't you tell me then? She said, "Because I didn't know you then, officer."*
>
> And that's when the moment of insight occurs.... The only way you get past that barrier of a uniform or skin color is through relationships. So we have people who don't believe in the New Haven police department, and God knows they don't believe in the chief of police.
>
> But they believe in their cop. That's what we're going back to—we're going back to a cop that has to earn their trust in the neighborhood, and that takes time.

Source: http://www.theatlantic.com/politics/archive/2015/11/new-havaens-top-cop-you-dont-know-us-anymore/416514/

cases, sergeants. Both patrol officers and investigators indicated strained relationships with supervisors and were more supportive of a decentralized organizational structure than were sergeants and senior command officers.

DIMENSIONS OF COMMUNITY POLICING

Maguire and Mastrofski (2000) examined the dimensionality of the community policing movement and found that the number of dimensions underlying it varied significantly according to the source of the data:

- Skolnick and Bayley (1988) described four recurring elements of community policing found internationally: community-based crime prevention, reorientation of patrol activities, increased police accountability, and decentralization of command.

- Bayley (1994) defined community policing using four dimensions: consultation, adaptation, mobilization, and problem solving.
- Bratton (1996) defined community policing as the three *p*s: partnership, problem solving, and prevention.
- Rohe, Adams, Arcury, Memory, and Klopovic (1996) use three dimensions separating community policing from traditional policing: shared responsibility, prevention, and increased officer discretion.
- Roth and Johnson (1997) operationalized community as articulated by the COPS office using four dimensions: problem solving, community partnership building, preventive interventions, and organizational change.
- Maguire and Katz (1997) used four additive community policing indices measuring patrol officer activities, management activities, citizen activities, and organizational activities.

Cordner (1999)explains that community policing began as a vague idea about achieving a two-pronged goal: increasing the positive contact between police and citizens and reducing citizens' fear of crime. After that idea had a chance to swirl for a few years, the concept of community policing settled into a period in which it was viewed as having two primary components: community engagement and problem solving. Cordnerdevised a four-dimensional framework for conceptualizing community policing and determining whether the essential elements are in place.

The Philosophical Dimension

LO4

Community policing is often conceptualized as having four dimensions: philosophical, strategic, tactical, and organizational.

Many advocates of community policing stress that it is a philosophy rather than a program. The three important elements within this philosophical dimension are citizen input, a broadened function, and personalized service. Citizen input meshes well with an agency that is a component of a government "of the people, by the people, for the people (Lincoln's *Gettysburg Address*, 1863).A broadened police function means expanding responsibility into areas such as order maintenance and social services and protecting and enhancing the lives of our most vulnerable citizens: juveniles, the elderly, minorities, the disabled, the poor, and the homeless. The personal service element supports tailored policing based on local norms and values and on individual needs (Cordner, 1999).

The Strategic Dimension

A philosophy without means of putting it into practice is an empty shell. This is where the strategic dimension comes in. This dimension consists of key operational concepts that convert philosophy into action (Cordner, 1999). The three strategic elements of community policing are reoriented operations, a geographic focus, and a prevention emphasis. The reorientation in operations shifts reliance on the squad car to emphasis on face-to-face interactions. It may also include differential calls for service. The geographic focus changes patrol officers' basic unit of accountability from time of day to location. Officers are given permanent assignments, so they can get to know the citizens within their area. Finally, the prevention emphasis is proactive, seeking to raise the status of prevention/patrol officers to the level traditionally enjoyed by detectives.

The Tactical Dimension

The tactical dimension translates the philosophical and strategic dimensions into concrete programs and practices. The most important tactical elements, according to Cordner, are positive interactions, partnerships, and problem solving. Officers are encouraged to get out of their vehicles and initiate positive interactions with the citizens within their beat. They are also encouraged to seek out opportunities to partner with organizations and agencies and to mediate between those with conflicting interests, for example, landlords and tenants, adults and juveniles. The third essential element, problem solving rather than responding to isolated incidents, is the focus of Chapter 4.

The Organizational Dimension

Cordner's fourth dimension, the organizational dimension, is discussed in Chapter 5.

Clearly, just as there is no one definition of community policing that will satisfy everyone, there is no one way to look at how community policing is viewed in practice.

DEMOCRACY AND THE POLICE

Community policing as an operational force grew out of the belief that police agencies in a democratic society should be guided by principles that foster mutual trust and respect between police and the public. Several core principles that guide fair and democratic policing are:

- Engaging the community to create and maintain trust relationships
- Maintaining rights to privacy while protecting national security
- Taking diversity into account when devising policing strategies; diversity includes not only racial and ethnic considerations but also concerns the homeless, released offenders, youths, and immigrant populations.
- Making a commitment to police integrity and combating racially biased policing
- Building successful working relationships between law enforcement and the media
- Encouraging openness and policing innovations through technological and other strategic advances (Mentel, 2008)

Many were skeptical of the durability of the community policing philosophy when the Office of Community Oriented Policing Services (COPS) was created more than 20 years ago. However, time has shown how practical and important this concept is to the mission of law enforcement in the United States, as will be demonstrated throughout the remaining chapters of this text.

COPS—NOT JUST A FAD

NOT JUST A FAD

The COPS Office was created in 1994 as a component of the U.S. Justice Department. The mission of the Office is to advance the practice of community policing. The Office carries out its mission by providing grants and training to tribal, local, and state law enforcement agencies. The funding allows agencies to hire and train officers, to acquire technology, and to develop and test new policing strategies. It also provides community policing training and technical assistance, reaching not only law enforcement officers but state and local leaders and community members.

The Office also maintains an online Resource Information Center that offers publications and training materials on community policing topics.

The COPS Office continues to demonstrate its staying power and its significant financial investment in American law enforcement. Under the American Recovery and Reinvestment Act (ARRA) of 2009, the COPS Office is continuing to provide funding for agencies to hire additional police officers and sheriff's deputies.

The Fiscal Year (FY) 2015 COPS Hiring Program (CHP) made available approximately $113 million in funding to state, local, and tribal law enforcement agencies to hire new and/or rehire career law enforcement officers. To date, the COPS Office has funded the addition of nearly 125,000 officers to more than 13,000 state, local and tribal law enforcement agencies to advance community policing in small and large jurisdictions across the nation.

Source: COPS Web site: http://cops.usdoj.gov/pdf/2015AwardDocs/chp/2015_CHP_PostAward_FactSheet.pdf

SUMMARY

Community policing is a philosophy that promotes organizational strategies that support the systematic use of partnerships and problem-solving techniques to proactively address the immediate conditions that give rise to public safety issues such as crime, social disorder, and fear of crime. Running through definitions of community policing are two basic themes: police–community partnerships and a proactive, problem-solving approach to the police function.

"Modern" policing began with the formation of the London Metropolitan Police, founded by Sir Robert Peel in 1829. Peel's principles emphasized the interdependence of the police and the public as well as the prevention of crime and disorder.

Policing in the United States has had three distinct paradigm shifts, or eras: political, reform, and community. During the political era, the police sought an intimate relationship with the community. During the reform era, the police relationship with the community they served was professionally remote. The professional model emphasized crime control by preventive automobile patrol coupled with rapid response to calls. During the community era, the police sought to reestablish a close relationship with the community.

During the 1960s and 1970s, relations between the police and the public were extremely strained. In an effort to improve relations, many police departments instituted public-relations programs whose goal was to improve the police image. Many departments also began crime prevention programs that enlisted the aid of citizens, including programs such as Operation Identification, neighborhood or block watches, and home and automobile security programs.

Cordner's four dimensions of community policing are the philosophical, strategic, tactical, and organizational dimensions.

DISCUSSION QUESTIONS

1. From the perspective of law enforcement, what are the strengths and weaknesses of each of the three eras of policing? Answer this question from the perspective of a citizen.
2. What lessons should community policing advocates learn from history?
3. Are any community policing strategies being used in your community? If so, which ones?
4. What advantages does community policing offer? Disadvantages?
5. How is the relationship between the police and the public usually portrayed in popular television programs and movies? In the news media?
6. How might the historical role of the police in enforcing slavery in the South and later segregation contribute to present-day police–minority relations?
7. Can you see any evidence of the patronage or spoils system of policing in the 21st century?
8. What is the relationship of community policing to problem-solving policing?
9. Is community policing being implemented in law enforcement agencies in the United States and to what extent?
10. Have you witnessed any examples of the "thin blue line"?

CASES CITED

Escobedo v. Illinois, 378 U.S. 478 (1964)
Gideon v. Wainwright, 372 U.S. 335 (1963)
Mapp v. Ohio, 367 U.S. 643 (1961)

Miranda v. Arizona, 384 U.S. 436 (1966)
Terry v. Ohio, 392 U.S. 1 (1968)
Weeks v. United States, 232 U.S. 383 (1914)

Inside Police Agencies: Understanding Mission and Culture

Learning Objectives

LO1 Understand how police spend the majority of their time.

LO2 Explain how the makeup of the police force has changed in recent years.

LO3 Identify the sources that affect and shape the police image.

LO4 Explain how and why discretion is exercised by police agencies and their officers.

LO5 Recognize when police are authorized to use force and the level and amount of force allowed.

LO6 List and describe the building blocks of ethics.

Key Terms

deadly force
discretion
excessive force
force
less-lethal force
Lucifer effect
mission statement
negative contacts
911 policing
police culture
procedural justice
reasonable force
selective enforcement

The mission statement of a police department is not a one-size-fits-all declaration and must reflect the multiple facets of policing that each jurisdiction values. Law enforcement organizations are charged with performing many duties within the community while effectively adapting to a multitude of situations and surroundings. The fluidity of these job requirements mandates that officers be skilled in delivering a wide range of responses under rapidly changing conditions, responses that might rely on communication skills alone, might require the use of nonviolent tactics, or that warrant the use of deadly force. In all situations, discretion and reason are paramount.

Lately, many stories in the media focus on the worst-case scenario situations involving law enforcement—officer-involved shootings. No one in the field looks forward to being a part of such an event, but all must be prepared for it, should circumstances require such a response. The majority of a police officer's job consists of communicating with the public.

What does not appear in the media very often, not because of the lack of occurrence but from the inability of such "routine" events to spark high ratings, are the stories of police officers who use no force at all in their interactions. For instance, on January 17, 2015, Officer Ruby of the London (Kentucky) Police Department used his discretion in the handling of a shoplifting call at local Kroger Supermarket. When the officer arrived, he found that the man apprehended for shoplifting had stolen baby formula. The suspect, a single father who had fallen on hard times, was unable to pay for baby formula to feed to his very hungry 6-month-old infant. The store manager and the store's loss prevention officer were not interested in a formal prosecution of the suspect, but they felt the need to report it.

As with most decisions in law enforcement, use of police discretion rarely, if ever, involves a Black and White issue. Areas of grey in the decision to arrest are more common than reported. Officer Ruby used his discretion to not arrest this suspect but, instead, to pay for the infant's formula and release the father. Before letting the man leave the supermarket, Officer Ruby gave him information about social workers in the area as well as other community resources available to those experiencing financial hardship.

Upon release, it was reported that the man was very quiet and extremely humble, offering a simple "thank you" and handshake to the officer before leaving with his child. Officer Ruby was quoted as saying, "I think when people look at us, they see just the uniform and just the car, just the tools that we have on our belt. But behind the uniform, I'm a human being and I'm a person out in this community just like any of them. I have a little boy. I'm a father just like that gentleman was. We're not these robots. There's a human behind the badge."

INTRODUCTION

Adhering to professional oaths and codes of conduct is an integral part of policing. One policy of the Commission on Accreditation of Law Enforcement Agencies (CALEA) states: "Any employee, prior to assuming sworn status, will take the oath of office to enforce the laws of the city and state government, and to uphold the Constitution of the United States and the Constitution of the state" (CALEA 1.1.1, *Standards for Law Enforcement Agencies*, 2012). The Maryland oath of office is typical:

> I swear (or affirm) that I will support the Constitution of the United States, and that I will be faithful and bear true allegiance to the State of Maryland and support the Constitution and laws thereof; and that I will, to the best of my skill and judgment, diligently and faithfully, without partiality or prejudice, execute the office of police officer according to the Constitution and laws of this State.

As part of their training, all new Federal Bureau of Investigation (FBI) agents are escorted on a tour through the U.S. Holocaust Memorial Museum in Washington, D.C. to witness what can happen when law enforcement officers waiver from their core values and lose sight of what is right. Following the tour, agents are required to self-reflect and examine what makes them different from the law enforcement officers in Germany who were systematically co-opted by the Nazis. Trainees are asked what they think will keep them anchored so that they do not start down a slippery slope of abusing their power. Answers often range from the Constitution to personal morals and compassion, to upholding the law.

The program, which is called Law Enforcement and Society: Lessons of the Holocaust and is a joint partnership between the Anti-Defamation League and the museum, was developed in 1999 after D.C. Metropolitan Police Chief Charles Ramsey toured the museum and recognized the value of teaching trainees about law enforcement's integral role in the Nazis' rise to power. The FBI Director at that time, Louis Freeh, incorporated the tour into the Bureau's new agent training, and the program's relevance reached new heights following the 9/11 attacks. In 2005, Director Robert S. Mueller asserted, "At a time when law enforcement must be aggressive in stopping terror, these classes provide powerful lessons on why we must always protect civil rights and uphold the rule of law" (Federal Bureau of Investigation, 2010).

Although "police officers" are the professionals entrusted with guarding the Constitution discussed in this chapter, the concepts explained apply equally to those with different titles such as deputies or sheriffs. And although the chapter focuses on police officers as professionals, always remember that police officers are first and foremost people—sons, daughters, mothers, fathers, brothers, sisters, aunts, uncles, neighbors, and friends. They may belong to community organizations, attend local churches, and be active in politics. Their individual attributes greatly influence who they are as police officers.

THE POLICE MISSION

mission statement
A written declaration of purpose.

Why do law enforcement agencies exist? What is their mission? The answer is obvious to those who say the purpose is to catch "bad guys." Others believe the purpose is to prevent crime, maintain order, or protect the public. A **mission statement** is a written declaration of purpose. There are those who believe writing out a mission statement is baloney because it is just words. When one police chief was asked the question, "What is your mission statement?" he responded, "Look at our patch. It says to protect and serve. That's all the mission statement we need." This chief did not believe in a written mission statement. Nonetheless, articulating the reason for an agency's existence helps its members focus on the same goals and determine how to accomplish their purpose.

Mission statements have been described as "instruments of organization communication. They have the ability to shape the attitudes and behavior of individuals in the organization. They also have the ability to shape the perceptions of the public" (DeLone, 2007, p. 218). Mission statements are not necessarily constant or permanent. Many social changes such as the civil rights movement, the Vietnam antiwar demonstrations, the immigration of illegal aliens, and the like have influenced mission statements. DeLone (2007) studied the extent to which the terrorist attacks on September 11, 2001, influenced agencies' mission statements and found that all but one of the reviewed departments changed their mission statements in the wake of the attacks, making the argument that they all experienced forceful environmental incentives to change.

A mission statement is a "road map" that delineates how an agency will arrive at a desired destination. Without it, a law enforcement agency can wander, appearing inconsistent, inefficient, and purposeless. The mission statement defines what the agency's commitment is to the community it serves and how it views its relationship with the community. A mission statement can reveal rather accurately the state of police–community relations. The importance of mission statements is summarized eloquently by Lewis Carroll's Cheshire cat in *Alice in Wonderland:* "If you don't know where you're going, it doesn't matter which way you go."

A mission statement can also focus a police department's energies and resources. Will the department continue to be reactive, focused on fighting crimes that have already occurred, or proactive, focused on identifying problems and attacking them? As Wilson and Kelling (1989, p. 49) note, a community-oriented policing philosophy requires redefining the police mission: "To help the police become accustomed to fixing broken windows as well as arresting window-breakers requires doing things that are very hard for many administrators to do."

The Houston (Texas) Police Department's mission statement embodies these goals: "The mission of the Houston Police Department is to enhance the quality of life in the city of Houston by working cooperatively with the public to prevent crime, enforce the law, preserve the peace, and provide a safe environment." The Aurora (Illinois) Police Department's mission statement reads: "We will enhance the quality of life in Aurora through innovation, partnerships, and dedicated service to our community." Developing a mission statement that reflects an agency's commitment to the community it serves can be the vehicle to positive, meaningful police–community relations as well as to a more effective police department. This mission statement in large part determines where the agency places its priorities. In 2013, approximately 70 percent of all local law enforcement agencies, employing 88 percent of all local police officers, had a written mission statement that included a community policing component (Reaves, 2015).

How are mission statements developed? A committee, composed of members of the community and police officers, assesses various police functions. Why would a law enforcement agency include input from the community when it develops its mission statement? Community input improves police–community relations and increases the likelihood of an agency accomplishing its missions. The public identifies the services it expects from its police department. If those expectations go unmet, the department generally suffers loss of financing and political support as well as increased interference in day-to-day operations.

Some departments also develop a vision statement, which is more philosophical and embodies the spirit of the department. The San Jose (California) Police Department has the following vision statement: "The San Jose Police Department is a dynamic, progressive, and professional organization dedicated to maintaining community partnerships which promote a high quality of life for the City's diverse population. The Department is committed to treating all people with dignity, fairness, and respect, protecting their rights and providing equal protection under the law" (San Jose Police Department, 2016).

From the preceding examples, it is clear that such statements require thought and reflect how a department views itself. Closely related to the mission statement are the goals and objectives set by a department. Programs emphasizing a service philosophy may not sit well with some police officers. For example, in one police department, its Neighborhood-Oriented Policing (NOP) program was perceived as more social work than police work and was referred to as "Nobody on Patrol." To avoid such perceptions, top management should emphasize that the community policing philosophy enhances the ability to detect and apprehend law violators. In fact, community policing is tougher on crime than traditional policing because it relies on citizens helping the police and sharing responsibility for their neighborhood.

Fighting Crime versus Service to the Public

Police departments are often divided on whether their emphasis should be proactive or reactive. Every department will have officers who are incident oriented (reactive) and believe their mission is to do **911 policing**—responding to calls—and may speak disparagingly of the community policing officers as "social workers."

911 policing
Incident-driven, reactive policing.

Is the best police officer the one who catches the most "bad guys"? Certainly police departments will continue to apprehend criminals. The crimes they target may, however, contribute to negative police–community relations. The police usually focus on certain kinds of crime, particularly common crimes such as burglary, robbery, assault, and auto theft. The police expect that offenders who commit these crimes might flee or try to avoid arrest in some other way. Police may need to use force to bring offenders to justice.

Police officers generally do not enforce white-collar crimes. They would not, for example, investigate or arrest a businessperson for insider trading, price fixing, or cheating on income taxes. White-collar crime involves those in business, the professions, or public life—those who tend to be relatively well-to-do, influential people.

Common crimes can conceivably be committed by anyone, rich or poor. The vast majority of these crimes, however, are committed by those from society's lower socioeconomic levels, and the population at or near the poverty level often includes a disproportionate number of minority citizens. As Klockars (1985, p. 57) notes, because the police officers' domain is the streets: "Those people who spend their time on the street will receive a disproportionate amount of police attention ... particularly people who are too poor to have backyards, country clubs, summer homes, automobiles, air conditioning, or other advantages that are likely to take them out of the patrolman's sight."

These facts contribute to the impression that the police are focused solely on the kind of crime poor people and minorities commit and, therefore, that they are hostile to the poor or members of minority groups. This negative impression does little to foster good community relations.

Police work involves much more than catching criminals. It is a complex, demanding job requiring a wide range of abilities. Studies suggest that 80 percent of police officers' time is spent on nonenforcement activities. The vast majority of the problems police attend to are in response to citizen requests for service.

Service to the community includes peacekeeping; preventing suicides; looking for lost or runaway children or vulnerable adults; protecting children and other vulnerable people; maintaining public safety; assisting motorists with disabled vehicles; dealing with emergencies and crisis situations, such as vehicle crashes and natural disasters; delivering death notifications; resolving conflicts; preventing crime; and educating the public.

Community policing emphasizes proactive strategies to help reduce social disorder and crime. Research has found that, on average, 75 percent of a typical police shift is unassigned, with officers spending the majority of unassigned time engaged in self-initiated routine patrol or offering backup rather than engaging in proactive policing activities (Famega, Frank, & Mazerolle, 2005). Furthermore, supervisors' directives often failed to accomplish the goals associated with proactive policing strategies. The researchers suggest that detailed directives based on valid crime analyses can improve patrol officer performance and promote positive outcomes in crime reduction (Famega et al., 2005).

Defining exactly what police work entails is almost impossible. Most would agree, however, that people have always called the police for help. They call not only about criminal matters but also about a variety of situations where they perceive a need for government intervention. The police respond to such calls and usually take whatever action is needed. It has been said that the police are the only social-service agency available 24/7, and they make house calls.

LO1

The majority of police actions have little to do with criminal law enforcement and, instead, involve service to the community.

Police officers are often the first responders in emergencies.

New York Daily News/Getty Images

Neighborhood Cops or Special Ops?

The proactive or reactive controversy can be seen in the existence of two contradictory models in policing: community policing and special weapons and tactics (SWAT) teams. SWAT teams are by nature reactive. The number of SWAT units has grown rapidly, with the majority of departments serving cities with populations of more than 50,000 having SWAT units. In many emergency situations, such teams are indispensable and have saved lives. It is not a question of either–or.

Marcou (2009) contends that SWAT teams are not necessarily reactive and that community-oriented SWAT teams are becoming more proactive in their approach to problem solving. As part of a proactive approach, SWAT team members are establishing partnerships with the community and learning that there are talents and resources outside of the agency at their disposal if needed (Marcou, 2009).

Recall from Chapter 1 the point emphasized by the Community Oriented Policing Services (COPS) Office: "The community policing model balances reactive responses to calls for service with proactive problem solving centered on the causes of crime and disorder."

WHO ARE THE POLICE?

Traditionally, police officers have been a fairly homogeneous group: White, male, with a high school education and a military background. Although the number of women and minorities going into law enforcement has increased over the past several decades, making the police a more heterogeneous group, officers are still primarily White males.

In 2013, 87.8 percent of full-time sworn police officers in the nation were males and approximately 73 percent were White (Reaves, 2015). In 1987, ethnic and racial minorities comprised 14.6 percent of all full-time sworn law enforcement officers, and over the next 25 years minority representation increased 150 percent so that by 2013, more than a quarter (27%) of full-time local police officers were members of a racial or ethnic minority. From 2007 to 2013, the percentage of Black officers remained at about 12 percent, the percentage of Hispanic officers increased from 10.3 percent to 11.6 percent, and the percentage of officers who were members of other minority groups (Asian, Native Hawaiian, or other Pacific Islander; or American Indian or Alaska Native) increased fourfold, from 0.8 percent to 3.0 percent (Reaves, 2015). Police departments in larger jurisdictions were more diverse than those in smaller ones. In 2013, more than 40 percent of officers in jurisdictions with 500,000 or more residents were members of a racial or ethnic minority, compared to fewer than 20 percent officers in jurisdictions with a population of less than 50,000.

Despite some progress in recruiting, women remain significantly underrepresented among the ranks of the police. Although college faculty may be seeing more women in their law enforcement classes, so far that increase has not been reflected in actual numbers hired. Possible reasons for the discrepancy are numerous. Some female law enforcement students become disillusioned by the bias against women in many departments; some conclude that police work does not fit with family life; some see the limited opportunity for promotion. While the percentage of females working in first-line supervisory positions (9.5%) was less than that among sworn personnel overall (12.2%) in 2013, the percentage of female first-line supervisors was more than twice as high in departments serving 250,000 or more residents (15%), compared to departments serving fewer than 50,000 residents (6%) (Reaves, 2015). In addition, an estimated 3 percent of local police chiefs were female, including about 7 percent of the chiefs in jurisdictions with 250,000 or more residents. From these data, it appears that females have more promotional opportunities in larger departments.

Hiring criteria in law enforcement have changed over the past 30 years. Where once new recruits were required to have only a high school diploma or less, today's officers are expected to have some college education. In 2013, the percentage of local police officers employed by a department with a college requirement for new officers (32%) was twice as high as in 1993 (16%). An estimated 15 percent of police departments had some type of college requirement in 2013; 10 percent required a 2-year degree, and 1 percent required a 4-year degree. Nearly one quarter (23%) of officers were employed by a department that required new entry-level officers to have a 2-year degree, compared to 7 percent in 2003. Departments serving a population of 1 million or more (29%) were most likely to require a degree. In smaller population categories, the percentage of departments with a degree requirement ranged from 9 percent in jurisdictions with fewer than 2,500 residents to 20 percent in jurisdictions with 25,000 to 49,999 residents. An estimated 54 percent of departments with a degree requirement considered military service as an alternative (Reaves, 2015).

This evolving standard has, without question, changed the kind of officer getting hired because police officers have traditionally come from the working class and were less likely to have a college education. The majority of officers hired 30 years ago were military veterans, reinforcing the military model in departments. These officers followed rank, took orders without question, and were not encouraged or expected to "think for themselves." Today, most officers hired are not military veterans. In fact, one of the primary paradigm shifts called for in the *Final Report of the President's Task Force on 21st Century Policing* (2015) is for today's police officers and agencies to move from a warrior to a guardian mindset. This shift, according to the Task Force, is crucial in efforts to rebuild fractured relationships between communities and the police and restore public trust in their local law enforcement agencies.

The advent of community policing has caused police departments to look for the type of people who are more likely to be successful at solving problems and building community relationships and who are more service oriented as opposed to adventure oriented. The COPS Office funded several demonstration sites at police departments to help redesign what these agencies were looking for in candidates:

> Some characteristics are commonly identified across sites and create a common core of service-oriented traits. They include integrity, courage, teamwork, people-oriented interpersonal skills that reflect an interest in and an awareness of others, strong communication skills, and a work ethic that demonstrates dedication and responsibility. They also include a measure of emotional health that was variably described as temperament, frustration tolerance, or ability to manage stress. Together, these traits appear to reflect a strong component of emotional intelligence, a dimension that is just now starting to emerge in the literature on the psychological screening of police applicants. (Scrivner, 2006, p. 67)

> Of course, law enforcement candidates today are scrutinized as never before for signs of racial prejudice, drinking problems, drug issues, and other factors that could become liability issues down the road. The background investigations for midsize to larger departments are very rigorous, often to the depth of interviewing neighbors of a recruit's childhood residence, among other things.

LO2

Today police departments have more minority and female officers. The educational level of the officers is much higher, and fewer have military experience. More officers are also as interested in helping people as they are in fighting crime, and greater emphasis is being placed on embracing a guardian mindset, as opposed to a warrior approach to policing.

Such changes in the makeup of the police force are fundamental to the community policing philosophy. Higher levels of officer training and education are considered so important that they form one of the six fundamental pillars identified by the President's Task Force on 21st Century Policing (2015), as shown on the following page. As police departments become more representative of the communities they serve, they will be better able to understand the problems they must address. As officers become better educated, they will be better equipped to devise solutions to community problems.

An obvious defining characteristic of the police—minority or nonminority, male or female, high school education or college degree—is that they have tremendous power over the citizens they serve and protect: "In American society, nothing is more sacred to us than our freedom. And, in an American society, only one segment of that society is given the authority, the power, and

The *Final Report of the President's Task Force on 21st Century Policing* (2015, pp. 51–52) stresses:

> As our nation becomes more pluralistic and the scope of law enforcement's responsibilities expands, the need for more and better training has become critical. Today's line officers and leaders must meet a wide variety of challenges including international terrorism, evolving technologies, rising immigration, changing laws, new cultural mores, and a growing mental health crisis. All states and territories and the District of Columbia should establish standards for hiring, training, and education.
>
> The skills and knowledge required to effectively deal with these issues require a higher level of education as well as extensive and ongoing training in specific disciplines. The task force discussed these needs in depth, making recommendations for basic recruit and in-service training, as well as leadership development in a wide variety of areas:

- Community policing and problem-solving principles
- Interpersonal and communication skills
- Bias awareness
- Scenario-based, situational decision making
- Crisis intervention
- Procedural justice and impartial policing
- Trauma and victim services
- Mental health issues
- Analytical research and technology
- Languages and cultural responsiveness

> ... In addition to discussion of training programs and educational expectations, witnesses at the listening session made clear that new approaches to recruitment, hiring, evaluation, and promotion are also essential to developing a more highly educated workforce with the character traits and social skills that enable effective policing and positive community relationships.
>
> To build a police force capable of dealing with the complexity of the 21st century, it is imperative that agencies place value on both educational achievements and socialization skills when making hiring decisions. Hiring officers who reflect the community they serve is also important not only to external relations but also to increasing understanding within the agency. On the other hand, task force member Constance Rice described the best line officer she knew—White, but better at relating to the African-American community than his Black colleagues. Her recommendation was to look for the character traits that support fairness, compassion, and cultural sensitivity.
>
> The need for understanding, tolerance, and sensitivity to African Americans, Latinos, recent immigrants, Muslims, and the LGBTQ community was discussed at length at the listening session, with witnesses giving examples of unacceptable behavior in law enforcement's dealings with all of these groups. Participants also discussed the need to move towards practices that respect all members of the community equally and away from policing tactics that can unintentionally lead to excessive enforcement against minorities. ...
>
> Though today's law enforcement professionals are highly trained and highly skilled operationally, they must develop specialized knowledge and understanding that enable fair and procedurally just policing and allow them to meet a wide variety of new challenges and expectations. Tactical skills are important, but attitude, tolerance, and interpersonal skills are equally so. And to be effective in an ever-changing world, training must continue throughout an officer's career.

the responsibility to take that freedom away—the police. So, I say to you today that there is *no greater responsibility* than to be entrusted with the freedom of an entire free society" (Walls, 2003, p. 17).

In addition, police may face a life-threatening situation at any time. Their lives may depend on each other. They experience situations others would not be likely to understand. All of the preceding factors influence what has been called the police culture.

THE POLICE CULTURE

Police work is often unpleasant. Police frequently have to deal with ugly situations and antisocial behavior. Police are lied to, spit upon, and sworn at. They see unspeakable atrocities. Because of their shared experiences and unique exposure to their community, many police officers develop a fierce loyalty to each other. This unique conglomeration of organizational values, beliefs, and expectations that is passed on to newcomers in the department is known as the **police culture**.

Goldstein (1990, pp. 29–30) observes:

> The strength of the subculture grows out of the peculiar characteristics and conflicting pressures of the job: the ever-present physical danger; the hostility directed at the police because of their controlling role; the vulnerability of police officers to allegations of wrongdoing; unreasonable demands and conflicting expectations; uncertainty as to the function and authority of officers; a prevalent feeling that the public does not really understand what the police have to "put up with" in dealing with citizens; a stifling working environment; the dependence that officers place on each other to get the job done and to provide for their personal safety; and the shared sense of awareness, within a police department, that it is not always possible to act in ways in which the public would expect one to act.

police culture
The informal values, beliefs, and expectations passed on to newcomers in the department; may be at odds with the formal rules, regulations, procedures, and role authority of managers.

Negative Perceptions of the Police Culture

Although the trend in American society is to celebrate diversity and embrace different cultures, the police culture has allowed itself to be painted in such a negative light that even some of its own members are calling for its abolishment (Oldham, 2006). This is due in part to researchers, many of whom have described a monolithic police culture focused on widely shared attitudes, values, and norms that help manage the strains created by the nature of police work and the punitive practices of police management and supervision (Paoline, 2004). These include a distrust and suspiciousness of citizens and a tendency to assess people and situations in terms of their potential threat (maintaining the edge), a lay-low or "cover-your-ass" orientation to police work, a strong emphasis on the law enforcement elements of the police role, a we-versus-them attitude toward citizens, and a norm of loyalty to their peer group (Paoline, 2004).

Skolnick's classic description, "A Sketch of the Policeman's 'Working Personality'" (1966), included such descriptors as social isolation, solidarity, and authority. Yet even five decades ago, he recognized the officer's desire to work with the community (1966, p.117): "Although the policeman sees himself as a specialist in dealing with violence, he does not want to fight alone. He does not believe that his specialization relieves the general public of citizenship duties. Indeed, if possible, he would prefer to be the foreman rather than the workingman in the battle against criminals."

Solidarity, or loyalty, and secrecy within a police department can result in a code of silence. The code of silence, which is the refusal of police officers to report any misconduct by other officers, has been written about extensively. The National Institute of Ethics conducted the most extensive research ever on the code of silence, involving 3,714 officers and recruits. The results: 70 percent said that a law enforcement code of silence exists and is fairly common throughout the country; 52 percent said that it did not really bother them. Excessive use of force was the most frequent situation in which the code occurred (Trautman, 2000).

This code may result in a "culture of denial," with officers denying incidents of brutality or turning a blind eye to patterns of abuse and encouraging a culture of silence in the face of unethical behavior perpetuated by fellow officers (Futterman, Mather, & Miles, 2007). To understand the power and persistence of the code, consider some observations made over the centuries regarding the nexus between truth, morality, and human action (or inaction):

> *"IT IS NECESSARY ONLY FOR THE GOOD MAN TO DO NOTHING FOR EVIL TO TRIUMPH."*
>
> —*Edwin Burke (1729–1797)*

> *"THE GREAT ENEMY OF TRUTH IS VERY OFTEN NOT THE LIE—DELIBERATE, CONTRIVED, AND DISHONEST—BUT THE MYTH—PERSISTENT, PERSUASIVE, AND REALISTIC."*
>
> —*John F. Kennedy's Yale commencement speech, 1962*

Unfortunately, the code of silence, to whatever extent it exists in a department, is a reality in policing. While the code persists, presumably serving to protect officers and justify their conduct in their quest for justice, it causes irreparable damage to the public's perception of and faith in the police profession.

Positive Perceptions of the Police Culture

Although every profession, including law enforcement, will have "bad people," Oldham (2006, p. 18) asserts that "the law enforcement community is perhaps the best and quickest at culling these types of individuals from the ranks." This outlook suggests a different, positive view of the police culture, that the values of "duty, honor, dedication, and self-sacrifice are not lost on our 'people'" (Oldham, 2006, p. 18).

Researching Police Officer Attitudes

Paoline's research (2004) has called into question the assumptions that have been made about a monolithic police culture. He has studied similarities and differences among contemporary police officer attitudes to locate some boundaries of the occupational culture of law enforcement, with the research examining officers' expectations about citizens, supervisors, procedural guidelines, law enforcement itself, order maintenance, community policing, aggressiveness, and selectivity. The results identified five analytically distinct groups or subcultures of officers that could be expected to form, as shown in Table 2.1.

This research has both positive and negative implications for community policing. While the study shows that not all officers resist a community policing orientation, a number of patrol officers do fail to embrace the order maintenance objectives commonly associated with community policing. In terms of statistically significant mean differences, the most differentiating attitude across the groups was seen in the community policing orientation (Paoline, 2004).

These findings also have important implications for those officers who still hold tight to a warrior mentality, placing a higher value on crime fighting and aggressiveness than on community policing and order maintenance, because in today's social climate, policymakers and the public are growing increasingly intolerant of such an approach to policing. The *Final Report of the President's Task Force on 21st Century Policing* (2015, p. 11) notes:

> How officers define their role will set the tone for the community. As Plato wrote, "In a republic that honors the core of democracy—the greatest amount of power is given to those called Guardians. Only those with the most impeccable character are chosen to bear the responsibility of protecting the democracy." Law enforcement cannot build community trust if it is seen as an occupying force coming in from outside to rule and control the community."

To that end, the Task Force (2015, p. 1) stresses: "Law enforcement culture should embrace a guardian—rather than a warrior—mindset to build trust and legitimacy both within agencies and with the public."

Having looked at some perspectives on police culture, let us now focus on how the public often views the police.

THE POLICE IMAGE

How does the public view the police?

- The handsome, relatively realistic cops of television and movies?
- Unselfish, fearless heroes who protect the weak and innocent?
- Dirty Harrys?
- Hard-hearted, brutal oppressors of the underclass?
- Corrupt abusers of power, who become part of the criminal world?

Our society has varied images of law enforcement professionals. As noted in Chapter 1, that image is greatly affected by how the public perceives the criminal justice system within which the police function. Many Americans believe in an ideal justice system in which fairness and equality are guiding

Attitudes of 5 different types of police officers

Table 2.1 — Attitudinal Expectations for Group Formation

	Group 1: Tough Cops	Group 2: Clean-Beat Crime Fighters	Group 3: Avoiders	Group 4: Problem Solvers	Group 5: Professionals
Citizens	(−) citizens are hostile and uncooperative	(−) citizens are unappreciative	(−) citizens do not understand the police	(+) help citizens get to the root of problems	(+) maintain positive rapport with citizens
Supervisors	(−) supervisors are unsupportive	(−) supervisors are unsupportive	(−) or (+/−) pacify supervisors to keep out of trouble	(+) especially in more community policing departments	(+) value supervisory approval
Procedural guidelines	(−) they do more harm than anything	(1) value these due process safeguards	(−) viewed as obstacles	(−) too restrictive, impede efforts to solve problems	(+) accept the limitations placed on them
Law enforcement	(+) narrow role orientation that only includes law enforcement	(1) very rigid law enforcement orientation	(−) or (+/−) believe in only handling unavoidable (i.e., serious) crimes	(−) or (+/−) not the most important/defining function for an officer	(+) accept this role, though not rigid or inflexible
Order maintenance	(−) if handle, do so informally (not regarded as real police work)	(+) as long as they can handle them formally (i.e., ticket or arrest) as part of role	(−) would only create more work	(+) expansive role orientation in handling citizen problems	(+) value roles beyond crime fighting
Community policing	(−) not real policing	(−) may impede their efforts to fight street crime	(−) would only create more work	(+) expansive role orientation	(++) expansive role orientation
Aggressiveness	(+) believe in aggressive style of patrol, part of image	(+) believe in aggressive style of patrol in controlling all illegality	(+) only increases chances to get into trouble	(−) usually only results in negative consequences for citizens	(−) or (+/−) exception rather than the norm
Selectivity	(+) believe in handling only real (i.e., serious) violations formally	(−) believe in pursuing and handling all forms (i.e., minor and serious) of illegal behavior	(+) believe in handling only unavoidable serious offenses that, if not handled, would bring undue negative attention to them	(+) discretionary informal judgment (over strict law enforcement) valued in handling problems	(−) handle full range of offenses, though do not feel the need to handle all formally (i.e., ticket or arrest)

Note: (+/−) indicates neutral attitudes.
Source: Paoline, Eugene A. III. (2004, June). "Shedding Light on Police Culture: An Examination of Officers' Occupational Attitudes." *Police Quarterly*, 7(2), pp. 205–236, copyright © 2004 by *Police Quarterly*. Reprinted by permission of SAGE Publications.

principles, truth and justice prevail, and the accused is innocent until proven guilty. Law enforcement professionals are part of this idealized vision; many view police officers and sheriff's deputies as unselfish, fearless, compassionate protectors of the weak and defenseless, who can uncover the truth, bring the guilty to justice, and make things "right."

In contrast, others in our society see a criminal justice system that is neither fair nor just. Some individuals point out that the system primarily employs officers who are White, middle-class males. They also believe that some officers abuse their power and, in some cases, also abuse those with whom they come into contact in the line of duty.

Drawing from Gallup Polls conducted between 1977 and 2012, the Bureau of Justice Statistics compared the rating of law enforcement officers' honesty and ethical standards. In 1977, 8 percent of the polled American public rated the police "very high" and 29 percent rated them "high," while 50 percent gave an "average" rating, 9 percent rated the police "low," and 3 percent rated them "very low." In 2001, possibly as a result of 9/11, police were rated "very high" by 23 percent and "high" by 45 percent. Only 1 percent of respondents rated the police "very low" in 2001. By 2012, however, ratings had slid slightly, with police rated "very high" by 14 percent, "high" by 44 percent, "average" by 32 percent, "low" by 7 percent, and "very low" by 3 percent (*Sourcebook of Criminal Justice Statistics Online*, n.d.). A Gallup Poll conducted in December 2015 asked respondents to rate the honesty and ethical standards of police officers on the same 5-point scale. Even in the wake of several high-profile police shootings, 56 percent of those polled rated the police either "high" or "very high" in terms of honesty and ethical standards (Saad, 2015). A salient finding of the poll was that 40 percent of non-Whites rated the honesty and ethical standards of the police as "high" or "very high" in 2015, a considerable increase from the 23 percent who reported this view in 2014.

I wonder what the %s would be today?

Horowitz (2007) notes that while overall satisfaction with the police is generally high, it is not evenly distributed. The first and most critical step in building positive relationships with the community is to understand the nature of this uneven distribution and why some people or segments of the community hold negative views of the police.

An individual's opinion of the police is based on many factors, possibly including television programs, movies, newspapers, magazines, books, the opinions of friends and family, level of education, neighborhood, economic status, disabilities, gender, minority group membership, and—most important—contacts with the criminal justice system. Several National Institute of Justice (NIJ) studies have found that public satisfaction with the police is shaped largely by demographic variables, neighborhood crime conditions, and experiences with officers—whether firsthand or indirect. Race, interestingly, was not found in these studies to be directly related to satisfaction. Although police have no control over the first two factors, they have direct control over the third one: "Treating individuals respectfully and professionally during each encounter can establish, build, and maintain crucial support for the police within the community" (Horowitz, 2007, p. 9). The challenge, therefore, becomes treating every encounter with every individual of the public—whether victim, witness, or suspect—professionally and fairly. **Procedural justice** is the

procedural justice
The idea of being treated fairly during a process or procedure.

idea of being treated fairly during a process or procedure. A positive process experience outweighs a positive outcome. For example, someone who receives a speeding ticket will regard the system favorably if he or she thinks that the outcome is arrived at fairly. Procedural justice facilitates positive police contacts, which builds public trust and enhances police legitimacy.

The concept of procedural justice is at the heart of the philosophical foundation for the Task Force on 21st Century Policing, which is "to build trust between citizens and their peace officers so that all components of a community are treating one another fairly and justly and are invested in maintaining public safety in an atmosphere of mutual respect. Decades of research and practice tell us that the public cares as much about how police interact with them as they care about the outcomes that legal actions produce. People are more likely to obey the law when they believe those who are enforcing it have the right—the legitimate authority—to tell them what to do. Building trust and legitimacy, therefore, is not just a policing issue. It involves all components of the criminal justice system and is inextricably bound to bedrock issues affecting the community such as poverty, education, and public health" (President's Task Force on 21st Century Policing, 2015, p. 5).

The media can greatly affect public opinion. The police image is affected by the manner in which television and newspaper stories present crime and law enforcement activities (Smith, 2011). The average citizen holds many mistaken beliefs about police work because of the proliferation of movies and television shows that "play fast and loose" with the truth, resulting in what is commonly called the *CSI effect*: "The popular crime show *CSI* and its spinoffs set in New York and Miami would have people believe that every police force has at its disposal high-tech gadgetry to solve every crime, as well as a team of experts to follow each case through to its quick and satisfying conclusion. Loyal TV viewers often expect the same from their local cops" (Basich, 2008, p. 55). Improving police–media relations is the focus of Chapter 8.

An additional source of the police image is the folklore surrounding citizen interactions with police. People tend to embellish stories of their contacts with the police. In addition, many stories people tell about contacts with the police are actually not theirs but those of a friend of a friend. Unfortunately, few if any of these stories can be traced to their origins, but in the meantime, police end up with a negative image. Further, police seldom participate in the same social circles in which the stories are recounted and therefore have no means of defending themselves, their co-workers, their departments, or their actions.

Yet another contributor to the police image is the work itself. Police officers are charged with some of society's most distasteful and dangerous tasks and are allowed to use reasonable force to effect arrests. They are even permitted, under strict circumstances, to use deadly force. This ability, however, creates a paradox for the police image—using force to achieve peace. Nonetheless, the nature of police work and the power they are legally permitted to use make the police extremely powerful and contribute to their image.

The police image is further affected by the police uniform and equipment. The uniform most police officers wear is a visible reminder of the authority and power bestowed upon them. In fact, officers know that the uniform plays a major part in their ability to gain cooperation and compliance from the public.

Much of their authority comes simply from what they are wearing. People recognize and react to visible symbols of authority. The police uniform conveys power and authority as well as the stereotypes about police officers. Citizens encountering a police officer in uniform usually cooperate more and curtail their illegal or deviant behaviors. The uniform and its trappings—patches, badges, medals, mace, nightsticks, handcuffs, and guns—can be intimidating and can evoke negative public responses. Reflective sunglasses and tie tacks with handcuffs or guns can add to this negative image.

Officers' behavior also has a direct impact on their image. One behavior that may negatively affect the police image is accepting gratuities, no matter how small, such as free coffee.

The manner in which police exercise their authority also has an impact on the police image. The attitude of law enforcement officers, their education, their personal image of policing, discipline, professionalism, and interaction with the community have an enormous impact on the public's perception of the police.

Seemingly innocent and humorous police novelty items have caused major confrontations between police and the communities they serve. Some police product companies produce calendars, posters, T-shirts, and mugs that support or make light of police brutality. Although these items are most always meant to be humorous, they can be immensely destructive to police–community relations because the public often does not share the same sense of humor. Particularly offensive examples include slogans such as "Brutality, the fun part of police work" and takeoffs on the *Dirty Harry* line, "Go ahead, make my day."

A case in point: In the early 2000s, an African American suspect died in police custody as the result of a carotid hold applied by police officers during a struggle. In response to the African American community's anger and concern, the chief of police issued an order prohibiting the carotid hold. Already in severe conflict with their chief over several other issues, two officers produced and sold T-shirts within the department that said, "Don't choke 'em, smoke 'em." The T-shirts went on sale the day of the suspect's funeral. It is not difficult to understand how destructive this was to the police image and community relations in that city as well as in other cities where the media reported these events.

> **LO3**
> The police image is affected by individual backgrounds, the media, and citizens' personal experiences with the criminal justice system. The police image is also shaped by appearance and police actions.

In contrast to this unfortunate incident is the Hug-a-Bear Program that many departments now use. Plush teddy bears are used to calm traumatized children that officers encounter in the course of fulfilling their duties. The bears, sometimes donated to the department by community organizations, are often carried in patrol cars and have been invaluable at accident scenes, in child-abuse situations, and at the scene of fires. Programs such as this can reduce the effect of negative contacts people may have with the police.

Personal Contacts

Although the public has many stereotypes of the police, those stereotypes are shattered or reinforced each time a citizen has personal contact with a police officer. Each individual police contact can have a positive or negative impact on police–community relations because personal contact with the police is an important determinant of citizens' attitudes. The unfortunate reality is that many people have police contact only when something goes wrong in their lives. Citizens commonly interact with the police when they receive a traffic citation, have an illegally parked vehicle towed, have a loud party terminated, have been victimized, discuss a child who is in trouble with the law, have a domestic "disagreement" broken up, are arrested for driving while intoxicated (DWI) or some other offense, or receive a death notification. Many more possible scenarios in which citizens become angry or disillusioned occur daily because of the actions police officers must take to perform their duties. And while officers have many opportunities to assist citizens and be a positive presence in the community, much of what they must do causes people unhappiness, a mix that leads the public to have a "love–hate relationship" with police. **Negative contacts** are unpleasant interactions between the police and the public. These contacts may or may not relate to criminal activity but they can contribute to a negative police image and difficulty in maintaining good community relations.

A meta-analysis of 27 recently published studies that examined overall citizen satisfaction with law enforcement found that the strongest factor influencing citizen satisfaction with, and trust in, the police was experiencing a negative contact with police, either personally or having heard from a family member or close friend about the encounter (Johnson, 2015). Interestingly, while the research showed that those who had experienced such a negative interaction were significantly more likely to possess highly negative attitudes toward all police officers, experiencing a positive contact had a minimal influence on increasing a citizen's overall satisfaction with police (Johnson, 2015).

negative contacts
Unpleasant interactions between the police and the public; may or may not relate to criminal activity.

Being arrested is without question one of the most negative contacts a citizen can have with police. Arrestees may be combative, verbally abusive, or try to bite, kick, spit on, or otherwise lash out at the arresting officer. Considering that many arrest situations are witnessed by curious onlookers, it is vital that officers maintain professionalism during these encounters—a negative contact with an individual citizen need not spread into a negative contact involving numerous bystanders as well.

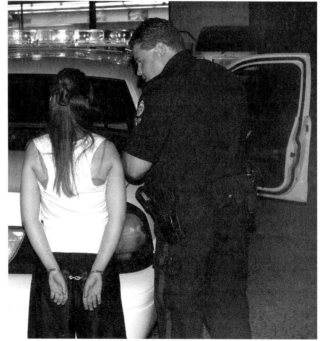

Jack Dagley Photography/Shutterstock.com

For the most part, the police have no way to eliminate negative contacts and still perform their duties. A major challenge of law enforcement is to build good community relations despite the often adversarial nature of the job. The fact that many negative contacts take place between police and noncriminal individuals, the so-called average citizens, makes the task especially difficult.

More positive contacts are needed. For example, the Fremont (Nebraska) Police Department has put a new spin on the phrase "gotcha." In Fremont, officers observing young people doing something good (e.g.,, wearing a bike helmet or picking up litter) give out tickets for soda and French fries at local fast-food restaurants. This works best for bike patrol officers.

A study of the attitudes of African American, Hispanic, and White residents of Chicago before and after encounters with the police found that, contrary to previous research, direct contact with police during the past year did not change attitudes, but vicarious experience (hearing about someone else's good or bad encounter with the police) did predictably influence attitudes (Rosenbaum, Schuck, Costello, Hawkins, & Ring, 2005). This research revealed that people's initial attitudes about police play a "critical role" in shaping their judgments of subsequent direct and indirect experiences as well as their future attitudes and that having only one or two police-initiated contacts does not considerably influence the generally relatively stable attitudes people hold toward the police. The conclusion is that a negative attitudinal predisposition provokes a negative police response (Rosenbaum et al., 2005).

Public Expectations

Skogan (2005) describes four expectations of citizens, all of which are elements of procedural justice. First, they want to be able to explain their situation to the police. Second, they want the police to be unbiased, neutral, objective, evenhanded, and fair. Third, they want to be treated with dignity and respect and have their rights acknowledged. Fourth, they want the police to consider their needs and concerns about their well-being. Despite these findings, the reality is often different.

Otherwise law-abiding citizens who receive traffic tickets or who are arrested for a DWI episode often believe they should be excused and that the police should concentrate on "real" criminals. Many police officers feel that citizens want the law enforced to the letter except when it comes to themselves. The public commonly demands that the police crack down on criminals, on drunk drivers, and even on traffic violators. For many police departments, the majority of their complaints involve traffic problems. Citizens often demand that police enforce speed laws near their homes. Inevitably, when the police respond by issuing citations to violators, some of those who want the laws to be strictly enforced are ticketed; they often feel betrayed and angry. Somehow they see their own violation of the speed law as different from that of teenagers or "outsiders," and they feel they deserve a break. Most police officers have been asked: "Why don't you spend your time catching real criminals instead of picking on citizens?"

Citizens become incensed when crime flourishes and hold the police responsible for combating crime. They hear it constantly referred to as a "war on crime" or "war on drugs," and since 9/11 a "war on terrorism," which demands an all-out attack by police on criminals and terrorists. Like American soldiers in Vietnam, however, the police are fighting a war they cannot win because it requires assuming social responsibilities that belong to politicians rather than to police. Klockars (1991, p. 244) also holds this view:

> The fact is that the "war on crime" is a war police not only cannot win, but cannot in any real sense fight. They cannot win it because it is simply not within their power to change those things—such as unemployment, the age distribution of the population, moral education, freedom, civil liberties, ambitions, and the social and economic opportunities to realize them—that influence the amount of crime in any society. Moreover, any kind of real war on crime is something no democratic society would be prepared to let its police fight. We would simply be unwilling to tolerate the kind of abuses to the civil liberties of innocent citizens—to us—that fighting any kind of a real war on crime would inevitably involve.

In addition, when citizens have a problem, they expect the police to help resolve it. In fact, police sociologist Egon Bittner (1974) states that we have police for just that reason—because "something-ought-not-to-be-happening-about-which-something-ought-to-be-done-NOW!" The NOW portion of Bittner's explanation refers to the police's unique ability to use force to correct a situation. Klockars (1985) notes that Bittner purposely did not refer to the situation as illegal because the police are called on in many situations that do not involve an illegality. Bittner left the purpose of police involvement wide open: Something ought to be done. What actions, if any, the police take in response to citizens' requests is usually up to the individual officer's discretion.

POLICE DISCRETION

discretion
Freedom to make choices among possible courses of action or inaction, for example, to arrest or not arrest.

The police have awesome discretionary power—to use force, to remove people's freedom by arresting and jailing them, and even to take someone's life. **Discretion** is the ability to act or decide a matter on one's own. Everett (2006, p. 10) defines *discretion* as using "professional judgment to choose from alternative courses of action."

LO4

Each agency exercises discretion when it establishes its mission, policies, and procedures. Each officer exercises discretion when deciding whether to issue citations or make arrests when laws are violated. Community policing emphasizes wider use of officer discretion.

Police use discretion because no set of policies and procedures can prescribe what to do in every circumstance. Indeed, as Chief Justice Warren Burger once acknowledged: "The officer working the beat makes more decisions and exercises broader discretion affecting the daily lives of people every day and to a greater extent than a judge will exercise in a week." The International Association of Chiefs of Police (IACP) "Police Code of Conduct" states: "A police officer will use responsibly the discretion vested in his position and exercise it within the law. The principle of reasonableness will guide the officer's determinations, and the officer will consider all surrounding circumstances in determining whether any legal action will be taken" (IACP, 2008, p. 112).

Martinelli (2011, p. 61) stresses: "Police discretion involves legal, educated decision-making processes. ... Though there are many factors to consider regarding officer discretion, personal biases, prejudices, and values are not to be employed in this decision-making process." Officers make their choices based on a variety of reasons:

- Is there evidence to prove a violation in court?
- Will a good purpose be served by arrest or citation, or is police contact sufficient to end the violation?
- What type of crime and suspect are involved?
- What circumstances exist at the time?

Clearly, police agencies and officers have broad discretion in deciding which laws to enforce, under which circumstances, and against whom. Some believe the law should be enforced consistently and in every instance. Most officers, however, believe that such police action would soon be unacceptable, far too harsh, and virtually impossible. For example, officers would probably not arrest a stranded motorist in a blizzard who, in danger of freezing to death, breaks into an alarmed commercial building. Nor would they be likely to arrest a driver who develops chest pain and breathing difficulty and drives through a stop sign in an attempt to maneuver off the road. In these cases the value of police discretion, or **selective enforcement**, is apparent. It makes sense to most people not to enforce the letter of the law.

selective enforcement
The use of police discretion, deciding to concentrate on specific crimes such as drug dealing and to downplay other crimes such as white-collar crime.

Police discretion may also pose a problem for police, however, because citizens know that officers can act subjectively. The person an officer tickets or arrests may feel discriminated against. The public is also concerned that discretion gives the police too much freedom to pick and choose when and against whom they will enforce the law. Citizens worry that discretion allows the police too much room to discriminate against some and overlook the violations of the wealthy and powerful.

The police are not the only players in the criminal justice system to exercise discretion. Prosecutors exercise discretion when determining priorities for prosecution and in plea negotiations. Judges exercise discretion in preliminary hearings, exclusionary rulings, and sentencing. Parole boards, parole officers, probation officers, corrections officials, and prison guards also exercise discretion.

Reasons for Police Discretion

Police departments are bureaucracies subject to rules and regulations that may contribute to irrational and inappropriate behavior. Such regulations limit an officer's ability to use common sense or act in a humane way in certain situations. Such limitations subject the officer to critical media coverage and adverse public opinion. For example, the police strictly upheld the law and towed a car containing a crying and screaming girl who was paraplegic because the vehicle was parked 15 minutes too long in a restricted zone. Millions of Americans and Canadians who viewed this episode on national television were incensed by the police's chosen "by the book" course of action.

Discretion is necessary for a number of reasons. The statute books are filled with archaic or ambiguous laws. Some laws are almost never enforced, and no one expects them to be. There are not enough police to act on every violation. They must select which laws they will enforce. Police prioritize the offenses on which they act. Crime is of more concern than a violation of a regulation, and felonies are a greater threat than misdemeanors. The police act accordingly. Discretion is important to maintaining good community relations. If the police were to enforce the letter of the law, community resentment would soon follow.

Changes in Police Discretion

Community standards influence how the police enforce laws. In most urban areas, significant changes have occurred over the past several decades regarding drunk driving, and law enforcement has responded to the increased public awareness of the dangers of drunk driving by routinely arresting and charging violators. Whereas driving under the influence was once given little attention by the public or the police, this violation is now rarely overlooked. Agencies and their officers have a mandate from the public to strictly enforce DWI laws. Thus, police discretion in this area is limited.

A similar change has occurred regarding public tolerance of domestic violence. Once among the laws the public knew police would not enforce, laws against spouse beating and the physical and sexual abuse of children are now strictly upheld, bringing again a significant change in police discretion.

Community policing has also had a great impact on police discretion. Officers are trusted to use good judgment in everyday activities with fewer limits and restricting rules. Community policing functions well when officers have the discretion to make the decisions necessary to help solve community problems. Officers working in the community are usually more informed about the problems and community members and are often more connected and trusted by community members. However, the increased officer discretion necessary for community policing is a concern to many police administrators who fear loss of control of their officers.

In *Terry v. Ohio* (1968), the Supreme Court recognized the role that discretion plays in policing. It granted police authority to stop and question people in field interrogations. Research has found this tactic to significantly reduce crime.

The Downside of Police Discretion

Officers usually work independently without direct supervision and have tremendous power to decide what action they will take, who they will arrest, and which laws they will enforce: "Police decisions not to invoke the criminal process largely determine the outer limit of law enforcement. ... These police decisions, unlike their decision to invoke the law, are generally of extremely low visibility and consequently are seldom the subject of review. Yet an opportunity for review and appraisal of nonenforcement decisions is essential to the functioning of the rule of law in our system of criminal justice" (Goldstein, 2004, p. 77).

Abuse of Discretion

In the wake of the August 2014 shooting death of Michael Brown by Ferguson (Missouri) police officer Darren Wilson, the U.S. Department of

Justice (DOJ) launched an investigation into the policies and practices of the Ferguson Police Department. The investigation revealed critical insight into the operations of the police department, including the approach to law enforcement and the policing culture it created. Among the many findings, the Justice Department learned that the Ferguson police chief had been under constant pressure from city officials to increase revenue through enforcement activity. Ferguson city officials budgeted for increased revenue each year by raising the amount of municipal fines and fees, and they kept close watch on whether the police department was delivering. Following is an excerpt from the Justice Department's final report pertaining to the effect of police discretion when it is abused (United States Department of Justice, 2015, pp. 81–82):

Exercise of Discretion, Even When Lawful, Often Undermines Community Trust and Public Safety

Even where lawful, many discretionary FPD enforcement actions increase distrust and significantly decrease the likelihood that individuals will seek police assistance even when they are victims of crime, or that they will cooperate with the police to solve or prevent other crimes. Chief Jackson told us "we don't get cooperating witnesses" from the apartment complexes. Consistent with this statement, our review of documents and our conversations with Ferguson residents revealed many instances in which they are reluctant to report being victims of crime or to cooperate with police, and many instances in which FPD imposed unnecessary negative consequences for doing so.

In one instance, for example, a woman called FPD to report a domestic disturbance. By the time the police arrived, the woman's boyfriend had left. The police looked through the house and saw indications that the boyfriend lived there. When the woman told police that only she and her brother were listed on the home's occupancy permit, the officer placed the woman under arrest for the permit violation and she was jailed. In another instance, after a woman called police to report a domestic disturbance and was given a summons for an occupancy permit violation, she said, according to the officer's report, that she "hated the Ferguson Police Department and will never call again, even if she is being killed."

In another incident, a young African-American man was shot while walking on the road with three friends. The police department located and interviewed two of the friends about the shooting. After the interview, they arrested and jailed one of these cooperating witnesses, who was 19 years old, on an outstanding municipal warrant.

We also reviewed many instances in which FPD officers arrested individuals who sought to care for loved ones who had been hurt. In one instance from May 2014, for example, a man rushed to the scene of a car accident involving his girlfriend, who was badly injured and bleeding profusely when he arrived. He approached and tried to calm her. When officers arrived they treated him rudely, according to the man, telling him to move away from his girlfriend, which he did not want to do. They then immediately proceeded to handcuff and arrest him, which, officers assert, he resisted. EMS and other officers were not on the scene during this arrest, so the accident victim remained unattended, bleeding from her injuries, while officers were arresting the boyfriend. Officers charged the man with five municipal code violations (Resisting Arrest, Disorderly Conduct, Assault on an Officer, Obstructing Government Operations, and Failure to Comply) and had his vehicle towed and impounded. In an incident from 2013, a woman sought to reach her fiancé, who was in a car accident. After she refused to stay on the sidewalk as the officer ordered, she was arrested and jailed. While it is sometimes both essential and difficult to keep distraught family from being in close proximity to their loved ones on the scene of an accident, there is rarely a need to arrest and jail them rather than, at most, detain them on the scene.

Rather than view these instances as opportunities to convey their compassion for individuals at times of crisis even as they maintain order, FPD appears instead to view these and similar incidents we reviewed as opportunities to issue multiple citations and make arrests. For very little public safety benefit, FPD loses opportunities to build community trust and respect, and instead further alienates potential allies in crime prevention.

Among the investigation's conclusions was that bias played a clear role in how Ferguson police exercised their discretion and that training was required to educate officers on how stereotypes and implicit bias can infect police work, what negative impacts profiling has on public safety and crime prevention, and how procedural justice and police legitimacy relate to community trust, police effectiveness, and officer safety. The report stressed (2015, p.6): "The City must replace revenue-driven policing with a system grounded in the principles of community policing and police legitimacy, in which people are equally protected and treated with compassion, regardless of race."

Discretion and the Police Image

Unless the police exercise their discretion with care, the community may complain about an actual or perceived abuse of power or discrimination in the way police enforce the law. If the community believes the police overlook violations committed by a certain segment of society or strictly enforce laws against another, severe community-relations problems will develop, as was seen in the events that transpired in Ferguson, Missouri.

A police agency's policies, procedures, and priorities and the manner in which it equips and assigns its officers indicate how that agency will exercise discretion. Individual officers have the greatest amount of discretion. Police officers have wide discretion in matters of life and death, honor and dishonor in a tension-filled, often hostile, environment. In addition, within the police bureaucracy, discretion increases as one moves down the organizational hierarchy. Thus, patrol officers—the most numerous, lowest ranking, and newest to police work—have the greatest amount of discretion. All officers should be acutely aware of the power they wield and the immense impact the exercise of discretion has on the community and the police–community relationship.

Although officers often operate independently, it is important to remember that the community watches how officers perform their duties. The public notes how and when officers enforce the law. Citizens may form opinions about their police department and about all officers in that department based on an individual officer's actions. Perhaps the most critical discretionary decision an officer can make is when and how much force to use.

USE OF FORCE

The International Association of Chiefs of Police (IACP) defines **force** as "that amount of effort required by police to compel compliance from an unwilling subject." Managing and applying force is one of the most important, complex, pressing issues in modern law enforcement: "The use of force—including deadly force—is at once *necessary* to achieve law enforcement goals and *contrary* to the core mission to protect life. ... This awesome power to use force against the citizenry comes with a great responsibility to use it only when necessary and justified" (Ederheimer and Johnson, 2007, p. 1).

force
That amount of effort required by police to compel compliance from an unwilling subject.

Police officers are trained and equipped to overcome the resistance they can expect to encounter as they perform their duties. Criminals are often likely to try to evade arrest and require the police to find and forcibly take them into custody. Police also deal with noncriminal situations that can require overcoming resistance, such as mentally ill individuals who are behaving dangerously and may require forceful intervention.

The use of force by the police encompasses a wide range of possible actions, from the officer's mere presence to the use of deadly force. The police presence affects a majority of citizens. The police uniform and squad cars are symbols of the officer's power to enforce the law and bring violators to justice, by the use of force if necessary. The visual image of power and authority created by the uniform and equipment facilitates the officer's ability to gain public compliance. The police image is also affected, either positively or negatively, by whether a department develops an authority-heavy image. Care must be taken not to develop such an intimidating image that it alienates the community.

Use-of-Force Continuums

The use of force can thought of as existing along a continuum, with no physical force used with a cooperative person, to ordinary force used with a person who is resisting, to extraordinary force used with a person who is assaultive. Force continuums were developed by law enforcement trainers in the 1960s and, since then, dozens of continuums have been created. Some agencies use a straight-line continuum while others have adopted a circular continuum to counter criticism that straight-line models imply that force must be applied in a linear progression. An online search will reveal myriad different use-of-force continuums.

Although many departments still use such continuums to train their officer how to apply force and escalate or de-escalate in response to a subject's behavior, the current trend has police agencies moving away from the training in and use of such continuums. At a recent national conference titled "Re-engineering Use of Force," it was shown that these continuums are falling out of favor amidst a growing understanding that the use of force cannot be measured and applied in such a mechanical way. Departments have begun to realize that, instead of relying on continuums that teach officers to match their tactics to a specific level of suspect resistance, they must train their officers to evaluate the entire situation and make reasonable, comprehensive decisions on which approach and tactics to use based on the circumstances at hand (Police Executive Research Forum, 2015).

Reasonable Force

reasonable force
Force no greater than that needed to achieve the desired end.

Reasonable force is force no greater than that needed to achieve the desired end. The landmark case that established what constitutes reasonable force is *Graham v. Connor* (1989), in which the Supreme Court held:

> The calculus of reasonableness must embody allowance for the fact that police officers are often forced to make split-second judgments—in circumstances that are tense, uncertain, and rapidly evolving—about the amount of force that is necessary in a particular situation. ... The reasonableness of a particular use of force must be judged from the perspective of a reasonable officer on the scene, rather than with the 20/20 vision of hindsight.

LO5

Although officers are authorized to use force, including deadly force, they must use only that level and amount of force *reasonably* necessary to accomplish a legitimate law enforcement objective.

The *Graham* Court listed four factors against which an officer's actions must be measured: (1) the immediate threat of serious physical harm to the officer or others; (2) the degree to which the situation is tense, uncertain, and rapidly evolving; (3) the nature of the crime at issue; and (4) whether the subject is resisting arrest or attempting to evade arrest by flight. The ruling in *Graham* is broad and favors police officers, considering numerous factors that continuums do not. In *Graham*, the Court held that the calculation of reasonableness under the Constitution "is not capable of precise definition or mechanical application."

Most citizens understand and support law enforcement officers' obligations to enforce the law and to use appropriate force when necessary. All officers have a duty to the profession to encourage public support by professional behavior respectful of each citizen's rights. Sometimes, however, public support of the police does not exist in a community. Lack of support may be the result of the unique characteristics of coercion. It may be that the public does not think that the actions of their police officers are ethical, or the citizens may even perceive the police as evil.

Wargo (2006) observes: "It is rare when a social scientist actually embraces theologically loaded words like 'good' or 'evil.' Yet this is exactly what Zimbardo explores." Philip Zimbardo has researched extensively the transformation of good people into evil, what he calls the **Lucifer effect**[1]. Zimbardo, who conducted the 1971 Stanford Prison Experiment, states: "We imagine a line between good and evil, and we like to believe that it's impermeable. We are good on this side. The bad guys, the bad women, they are on that side, and the bad people never will become good, and the good never will become bad. I'll say today that's nonsense" (Wargo, 2006). Zimbardo's research proved that the line is permeable and that ordinary, good people can be transformed into perpetrators of evil. Zimbardo also suggests that this change can go beyond the individual to administrative evil, which

Lucifer effect
The transformation of good people into evil.

---

[1] Lucifer was God's favorite angel who fell from grace and ultimately became Satan.

describes a systemic culture of unethical behavior that is able to grow and persist within an organization when leaders allow corruption and immoral conduct to go unchecked.

Excessive Force

The IACP defines **excessive force** as "the application of an amount and/or frequency of force greater than that required to compel compliance from a willing or unwilling subject." Excessive force is synonymous with police brutality.

From 2002 to 2011, an average of 44 million people age 16 or older had one or more face-to-face contacts with police each year in the United States (Hyland, Langton, & Davis, 2015). Of those who had contact, 1.6 percent had force used or threatened against them during their most recent contact. The majority (75%) of the people who had force used or threatened against them thought the force, whether verbal or physical, was excessive, although an exact definition of *excessive* was not specified. Of those who experienced force, 87 percent did not believe the police acted properly (Hyland et al., 2015).

Controversy on the use of force by police is almost always discussed in terms of police brutality, which is considered a problem by a large segment of the public. The extent of the problem of excessive force is perceived differently among urban and suburban, rich and poor, and minority and majority populations. Valid reasons exist for why different people have different perceptions of the problem. One reason is that the job the police are required to do differs from community to community.

Citizens in White suburban areas are more likely to see the police in more positive circumstances when they report a crime and have been victimized; when they need assistance after an automobile crash or in a medical emergency; when their child is lost or when their car has run out of gas; and when they have locked themselves out of a car or home—or want their home watched. In each scenario, the police are there to lend assistance. Citizens in suburban areas may never see a police officer use force. The most negative experience they are likely to have with a police officer is receiving a traffic ticket.

Because the police must intervene in crimes where apprehension is likely to be resisted, most of their enforcement efforts are directed toward "common" criminals. In contrast, white-collar criminals are unlikely to flee or resist; they tend to see their situation as a legal dilemma to be won or lost in court. White-collar criminals are relatively wealthy and have a career and a place in the community; they have too much to lose to simply flee. Thus, because police enforcement efforts focus on common criminals, who are frequently poor, use of force by the police will most commonly be directed against this part of the population, often in socioeconomically disadvantaged neighborhoods.

When people from these widely separated communities talk about the police, it seems as though they are speaking of entirely different entities. On the one hand, police may be referred to as brutal, racist aggressors, whereas on the other hand, they may be described as professional, helpful, efficient protectors. Which is the true picture of the police?

excessive force
Force greater than that reasonably necessary to accomplish a legitimate law enforcement purpose.

Less-Lethal Force

less-lethal force
Force that has less potential for causing death or serious injury than do traditional tactics.

When an increased level of force is necessary but deadly force is too extreme, there now exists a variety of **less-lethal force** alternatives that allow the application of force that has less potential for causing death or serious injury than do traditional tactics. Options for controlling a suspect with less-lethal force are verbal or visual management of the scene; empty-hand control and take-down procedures; physical restraints (e.g., handcuffs, flexcuffs); aerosols (e.g., Mace, CN and CS tear gas, oleoresin capsicum [OC] pepper spray); impact weapons (e.g., batons, projectile launchers such as beanbags and flexible baton rounds); K-9s; capture nets; and electronic control devices (ECDs), alternately called conducted energy devices (CEDs), such as the TASER.

Debate has centered over the terminology applied to these weapons— should they be called *less than lethal*, *less lethal*, *defensive*, *intermediate*, or something else? Some use-of-force experts prefer the term *less lethal* to *less than lethal* because of liability implications and misrepresentation of a weapon's lethality. Whatever term is used, it must be recognized that many of these alternatives *can* cause death. Although officers acknowledge the fatal possibilities that may accompany the use of less-lethal force, at times officers are justified in using force they *know* will likely result in a subject's death.

Deadly Force

deadly force
Any force that can reasonably be expected to cause or is intended to cause death or serious physical injury.

Although definitions vary among jurisdictions, **deadly force** is generally defined as "any force that can reasonably be expected to cause death or serious bodily injury." The landmark Supreme Court case concerning deadly force is *Tennessee v. Garner* (1985), a case stemming from a 1974 incident in which a Memphis police officer shot and killed an unarmed 15-year-old boy who was fleeing the police after having stolen $10 in money and jewelry from an unoccupied home. The officer testified that he had shot the boy to prevent him from escaping, an act allowed under Tennessee law. In delivering the opinion of the Court, Justice White stated:

> This case requires us to determine the constitutionality of the use of deadly force to prevent the escape of an apparently unarmed suspected felon. We conclude that such force may not be used unless it is necessary to prevent the escape and the officer has probable cause to believe that the suspect poses a significant threat of death or serious physical injury to the officer or others.

The Supreme Court ruled that the Tennessee "fleeing felon" statute was unconstitutional because it authorized use of deadly force against unarmed fleeing suspects who posed no threat to the officer or third parties. This ruling also invalidated similar laws passed in almost half of the states that allowed police officers to use deadly force to prevent the escape of a suspected felon.

It is worth noting that no federal agency currently keeps track of the number of persons killed by police officers. While the Federal Bureau of Investigation (FBI) and Bureau of Justice Statistics (BJS) each make attempts to track the number of deaths caused by officers, police agencies are not required to report such data, and analysis has found that departments that voluntarily do so appear to report only 25–50 percent of the actual fatalities they had.

The Violent Crime Control and Law Enforcement Act of 1994 requires the DOJ to "acquire data about the use of excessive force by law enforcement officers" and "publish an annual summary of the data acquired," and the BJS is the arm of the DOJ charged with the collection, analysis, and dissemination of information regarding the operation of justice systems at all levels of government, including police use of excessive force. However, this mandate was never carried out, and prior to the 2014 events in Ferguson, no federal agency, including the BJS, possessed a reliable system for tracking police use of force incidents (Ramsey, 2015).

Following the shooting death of Michael Brown and the riots in Ferguson, journalists with the Washington Post, seeking information and insight about police use of force and finding none available from official government sources, undertook a project to create a log of every fatal police shooting that occurred in the United States during 2015. The year-long study, which documented a total of 965 people fatally shot by the police in 2015, found that the vast majority of those shot and killed fell into one or more of three categories:

- They were armed
- They were suicidal, experiencing a mental crisis, or displayed other symptoms of mental illness
- They fled when they were ordered by police to stop (Kindy, Fisher, Tate, & Jenkins, 2015)

In contrast, the journalists found that the type of high-profile incidents that have sparked protests and riots in many U.S. communities—most often involving White police officers killing unarmed Black men—constituted less than 4 percent of on-duty fatal police shootings during 2015 (Kindy et al., 2015).

Since Ferguson, the BJS has recommitted itself to tracking not only police killings but all uses of force by police in the process of arrest. The FBI has also made such data collection a top priority and plans to unveil a revised tracking system in 2017. Efforts are also underway at nongovernmental entities to gather data about police behavior. In 2013, even before Ferguson, the National Science Foundation (NSA) had funded a project called the Justice Database, which was developed by the Center for Policing Equity (CPE) and located at the University of California, Los Angeles (UCLA) to monitor police behavior, including stops and use of force, and explore racial disparities in policing. To date, more than 40 police departments and law enforcement agencies across the country have signed on to report data (Ramsey, 2015).

Use of Force Incidents Contributing to the Erosion of Public Trust in the Police

Although tension between the police and some of the communities they serve is nothing new in this country, recent years have seen a more widespread unraveling of public trust in the police, fueled primarily by several high-profile incidents in which Black men lost their lives at the hands of White law enforcement officers. Following is a brief listing of some of the incidents that have contributed to the erosion of public trust in the police, particularly in communities of color:

- July 17, 2014 (Staten Island, New York)—Eric Garner, a 43-year-old Black man with asthma, was illegally selling untaxed cigarettes on a sidewalk in New York City. He was unarmed. Three NYPD officers tried to arrest him and Garner resisted. He was placed in a choke hold, a move that violated NYPD's use of force policy. Garner gasped repeatedly during the choking, straining to tell officers that he couldn't breathe. He died a short time later. A Staten Island grand jury reviewed the case, including a video of the incident taken by a witness, and decided to not indict any of the officers involved in Garner's death. In February 2016, a federal grand jury began hearing evidence on the case.

- August 9, 2014 (Ferguson, Missouri)—Michael Brown, an 18-year-old, unarmed Black man, was walking down the street at night and had an encounter with police officer Darren Wilson, who was White. During the encounter, Wilson shot and killed Brown. On November 29, 2014, a grand jury decided not to indict the officer in Brown's death.

- April 9, 2015 (North Charleston, South Carolina)—Walter Scott, a 50-year-old, unarmed Black man, was shot and killed by Officer Michael Slager, who was White, during a daytime traffic stop for a broken tail light. Scott tried to run away, presumably because he was delinquent in child support payments, and was shot eight times in the back. A bystander captured part of the encounter on his cell phone. Slager was indicted for murder and his trial is set to begin October 31, 2016. The incident prompted the police chief in North Charleston to order body cameras for every officer the next day.

- April 12, 2015 (Baltimore, Maryland)—Freddie Gray, a 25-year-old Black man, was arrested on the street for possession of an illegal weapon and placed in a police van for transport to jail. Either during the arrest or after he was placed in the van, his spine was severed. Gray died on April 19, 2015. Six Baltimore police officers, three White and three Black, were charged and will be tried separately. Several videos have emerged of the arrest and of activity when the van made stops along the way to the jail.

- November 15, 2015 (Minneapolis, Minnesota)—Jamar Clark, a 24-year-old Black man, was involved in an altercation with two White officers and, during the incident, was shot and killed. Clark was unarmed at the time, although several reports suggest he had tried to grab one of the officer's service weapons during the incident. The county attorney declined to use a grand jury and, after reviewing all of the evidence that would have been submitted to a grand jury, announced that no charges would be filed against the two Minneapolis police officers involved.

Re-Engineering Training on Police Use of Force

It is no secret or surprise that police use of force is currently a very hot topic. Most everyone—police professionals, policymakers, and the public—recognize and agree there exists a critical need to address how today's officer are trained to use force. Chuck Wexler, executive director of the Police Executive Research Forum (PERF), observes (2015, p. 3):

TECHNOLOGY IN COMMUNITY POLICING

BODY CAMERAS

The use of body-worn cameras by police officers has become a much debated topic. A 2013 survey of police departments revealed that approximately 75 percent did not use this technology (Miller & Toliver, 2014). However, following the events in Ferguson and Staten Island and the grand juries' decisions in both cases to not indict the officers involved in the deaths of two civilians, the call to outfit all officers nationwide with body cameras gained considerable momentum. In fact, on December 1, 2014, a mere 2 days before the grand jury in New York announced its decision to not indict NYPD Officer Daniel Pantaleo for using a fatal chokehold on Eric Garner, President Obama had pledged $263 million in federal funding to enable police agencies to purchase body-worn cameras and improve their training in use-of-force incidents ("Considering Police Body Cameras," 2015).

An article in the *Harvard Law Review* examines the contours of the body-camera debate, including the benefits and drawbacks, and suggests recommendations for implementing this technology to ensure that the use of such cameras does serve the purpose of increasing transparency and officer accountability and, ultimately, public trust in the police. The article cautions that agencies should not be too quick to rush into adopting this technology because once it is deployed, it is "increasingly difficult to have second thoughts or to scale back" ("Considering Police Body Cameras," 2015, p. 1817):

This widespread galvanization over body cameras exemplifies the human tendency, in times of tragedy, to latch on to the most readily available solution to a complex problem.

But ... body cameras are a powerful—and indiscriminate—technology. Their proliferation over the next decade will inevitably change the nature of policing in unexpected ways, quite possibly to the detriment of the citizens the cameras are intended to protect. ... [P]roper implementation of this new policing tool requires careful consideration of current policy proposals, rather than the rapid, reactionary adoptions currently taking place nationwide. Their adoption should also not be used as an excuse to stifle continued conversation about the root causes of police violence and fractured community relations, as body cameras alone will never be the hoped-for cure-all. (pp. 1796–1797)

Over the past year, the policing profession has been shaken by controversies over the deaths of Eric Garner, Michael Brown, Tamir Rice, Walter Scott, Antonio Zambrano-Montes, and many others. I don't know anyone who would dispute that the reputation of American policing has suffered from these incidents. ...

[We] need to rethink the training the police officers receive on de-escalation strategies and tactics. As we look back at the most controversial police shooting incidents, we sometimes find that while the shooting may be legally justified, there were missed opportunities to ratchet down the encounter, to slow things down, to call in additional resources, in the minutes *before* the shooting occurred.

A conference was held on May 7, 2015, bringing together nearly 300 police chiefs and other law enforcement executives, federal government officials, academicians and researchers, and representative from police agencies in the United Kingdom, to share their views about police use-of-force training and brainstorm ways to reengineer this crucial aspect of the police mission. One of the key results of that day-long discussion was the need to recruit officers who are suited to the mission of policing and to weed out candidates who think policing is all about weapons. The "warrior vs. guardian" theme was pervasive in many of the conference participants' statements. Chief Joseph Price from Leesburg, Virginia, shared this perspective (PERF, 2015, p. 29):

> When you ask police officers why they chose to become an officer, most of them say they wanted to help people and help their community. This is consistent with the guardian mindset.
>
> So how did we become warriors? I think it's partly because political leaders have put us in wars—the war on drugs, the war on crime, the war on terror, the war on gangs. Police chiefs didn't come up with those names; they were coined by political leaders.
>
> We need to change that mindset, to teach officers that at times they may need to fight like a warrior, but most of the time they need to have the mindset of a guardian. A warrior comes in, takes over, does what he needs to do, and leaves. That's not what we want our cops to do. We want our cops to be part of that community and to solve problems—not *for* the community, but *with* the community.
>
> Many inappropriate uses of force result from officers thinking, "I can't back down; I need to win at all costs." But that's not smart policing or effective tactics. We need to do a better job of training officers to control their adrenaline and try to defuse physical confrontations.

Another police chief, David Rausch from Knoxville, Tennessee, observed that changing terminology can help officers make better decisions about when and how to use force (PERF, 2015, p. 30): "Our police department changed the term 'use-of-force report' to 'response to resistance report.' And since we made that change, we have seen a decline in uses of force. 'Use of force' sounds aggressive. By changing the terminology, it tells our officers that the only time it is acceptable to use force is when you are responding to resistance. If you are responding to resistance, it's not an attack. That goes along with the guardian concept."

Another theme to emerge from the conference was the need for a culture of ethics and professionalism to permeate recruit training. Bill O'Toole, director of the Northern Virginia Criminal Justice Training Academy (PERF, 2015, p. 63), offered a viewpoint critical of current training methods that model militaristic communication styles as they give recruits the misplaced idea that harshness is preferred or required when communicating on the job:

> For nine years, we've been telling our recruits that two things matter most: "Your safety, and our integrity." That became our mantra. But now we're going to change that, and tell recruits that what matters most is an unwavering commitment to the sanctity of human life, followed by your safety and our integrity. ...
>
> We've had discussions about police culture. When I was 21, I joined the Army for military police training, so I could get a veteran's preference to get into the policing profession. And that was my first exposure to training. We were often demeaned, dehumanized, spoken down to, subjected to profanity, and it didn't seem to make sense, but it was military training and I figured there was probably some purpose to it. I've seen this same type of training rearing its ugly head at some academies, or with some instructors, or even within some agencies,

thinking that this military model is going to "toughen somebody up." I think this philosophy of training is completely wrong for law enforcement academies.

I feel very strongly about the importance of our instructors modeling the same behaviors that we want our recruits to exhibit when they interact with the public after they graduate. So when we ask, "Where can we start," our starting point is in developing and maintaining the right training culture—an ethical and professional environment for training.

ETHICAL POLICING

To maintain the public trust, police must be men and women of good character who hold foremost the ideals of fairness and justice. The manner in which police use their discretion to enforce the law and solve problems determines whether the public views the police as ethical.

The Building Blocks of Ethics

Ethics is a multifaceted system of moral principles built on "a foundation of lesser but equally important individual components, each with their own unique well-defined meaning" (Borrello, 2005, p. 65). Together these components provide a framework for what is considered to constitute ethics.

> **LO6**
> The six commonly recognized building blocks of ethics are integrity, honesty, values, standards, courage, and civility.

Integrity   Ethics includes integrity, that is, doing right when no one is watching. Ethical integrity is paramount in a profession endowed with power, authority, and discretion, and thus, it is the most important value a law enforcement officer can have: "Everything in law enforcement works outward and upward from the foundation of integrity" (Lohner, 2011, p. 20). Police integrity can be defined as "the normative inclination among police to resist temptations to abuse the rights and privileges of their occupation" (National Institute of Justice, 2005, p. 2).

Integrity can be explained through the analogy of a balloon that is filled with all of the components of ethics and then tied. If tied properly, the balloon would be airtight, complete, uncompromised—it would have integrity. If that balloon were left unattended for a year, it might be half its original size, having lost its integrity. Unfortunately, even unnoticeably, this is what happens to some police officers over time (Borrello, 2005). Officers who start their careers with unimpaired integrity, if left alone or unsupervised, not held accountable, ignored, untrained, or unrewarded for ethical behavior, may lose their integrity. Integrity can become compromised in many ways: accepting a free meal, being part of the code of silence, calling in sick when healthy, failing to ticket a friend who is driving excessively over the speed limit. Whatever form it takes, compromising integrity is often the first step toward corruption.

Honesty   Honesty is acutely similar to integrity, synonymous with credibility, and is the foundation on which to develop trust. Honesty is what keeps an officer from padding his or her expense account. It is what makes officers write truthful incident reports and testify accurately on the witness stand.

Consider the case of a 3-year police officer in a large urban police department who came under investigation for logging out for an unauthorized coffee break during a follow-up investigation. When questioned, he denied taking the unauthorized break, not knowing another officer had seen him take it. Rather than facing minor disciplinary actions, he was terminated for his lie. Statistically, departments across the country are experiencing higher rates of termination for honesty issues than ever before (Sutton, 2005).

Values   "A value is simply a belief or philosophy that is meaningful to us. Our values serve as a measure to determine what is important and this determination often controls our behavior" (Borrello, 2005, p. 66). If officers value the friendship of their peers more than they value honesty, and if a peer does something unethical, the code of silence is likely to flourish.

Standards   Standards establish a baseline to guide officers as to what they should or should not do. Most police departments have set standards that officers are expected to meet. Policies and procedures are written standards officers are expected to meet or exceed. These are often used in evaluating officers' performance.

Courage   Ethical courage is "being confronted with a difficult problem and making the right decision despite potentially adverse personal or professional consequences" (Borrello, 2005, pp. 67–68). It is being willing to break the code of silence. It is being willing to speak up when a new policy seems not in the best interests of the community. Ethical survival requires officers to prepare their psyche with the same vigor they use to prepare for tactical survival (Sutton, 2005).

Civility   Politeness and respect are vital attributes for police officers. One of the most common citizen complaints against police officers is that the officer was sarcastic, rude, or impatient. However: "The true test of civility for police officers is found in its application to those who don't seem to deserve it or who make it hard to be nice" (Borrello, 2005, p. 58).

Ethics in the Field

The ethical way to act is not always clear. Unfortunately, the police have often not been given appropriate guidance in ethical decision making. Given the complexities of enforcing the law in an increasingly diverse population, it is inadequate to teach rookie officers the technical skills of policing and then send them into the community under the assumption they will do the "right thing."

A move toward higher ethical standards is perhaps reflected by the decision of many police departments to require their police officers to have a college education. There is also an increasing need to begin a dialogue within the police community on ethics—what ethical behavior is and how to achieve it in the profession.

One simple adage, set forth several decades ago by Blanchard and Peale (1988, p. 9), might serve as a starting point for a discussion on ethics: "There is no right way to do a wrong thing." They (p. 20) suggest three questions that can be used as personal "ethics checks".

- Is it legal?
- Is it balanced?
- How will it make me feel about myself?

The first question should pose little problem for most officers. The focus of the second question is whether the decision is fair to everyone involved, in the short and long term. Does the decision create a win–win situation? The third question is perhaps the most crucial. Would you mind seeing your decision published in the paper? Would you feel good if your friends and family knew about your decision? Ethical behavior by individual officers and by the department as a whole is indispensable to effective police–community partnerships.

Ethical Dilemmas

Ethical dilemmas are often rooted in the ends-versus-means controversy. If officers consider their mission to lock up the bad guys, whatever they have to do to obtain a conviction can be justified: excessive force to get a confession, planting evidence, lying in court—the ends justify the means used to accomplish them. Quinn (2005, p. 27) cautions that at some point in time officers are going to "walk with the devil" to get the job done:

> Every day is a new challenge, and ethical police conduct is often an uphill battle. Even the best of cops have days when they want to give up and do whatever it takes to put a child molester, baby murderer, or other lowlife in prison. When you sit inches away from these scum and they brag about the truly horrific things they have done to an innocent it's easy to abide by the Code—if that's what it takes. When the evidence isn't perfect, you just use a little creative report writing and this guy will never harm another person again. Illegal searches, physical abuse, or even perjury, you know you will be in the company of many good cops who have done the same. But are they really good cops? (pp. 13–14)

Sutton (2005) describes how a police sergeant bolstered the strength of a case against a major narcotics trafficker by claiming in his report that narcotics found in the suspect's residence were discovered after a search warrant had been issued. The truth was that the evidence was discovered during a protective sweep before any warrant was issued. Sutton (2005, p. 64) observes that the officer's motives were noble: "He wanted justice to prevail in a case where the suspect was clearly guilty—but by lying, he violated his oath of office." The ends do not justify the means.

Another source of ethical dilemmas is that police officers are often granted special privileges and allowed exceptions to the law. They can exceed speed limits and violate traffic laws to enforce the law. They can carry concealed weapons and own or have access to weapons that are restricted to citizens. Sometimes this leads new recruits to receive a message that says they are above the law.

Police Corruption

Closely related to unethical behavior, as a result of believing that the ends justify the means or that a police officer is above the law, is actual corrupt behavior. Since policing began, corruption in law enforcement has been a problem. It often begins with small, seemingly benign, actions that officers have little difficulty justifying, such as accepting free coffee. Figure 2.1 illustrates how such justifications can escalate, with loyalty overcoming integrity and then entitlement overcoming accountability.

The continuum of compromise has sometimes been referred to as a "slippery slope." This parallels the broken windows theory of crime that if little signs of disorder are ignored, more serious indications of disorder and crime may flourish.

Research by Son and Rome (2004) found that nearly 70 percent of police officers in their study personally observed someone in their department accepting free coffee or food or speeding unnecessarily. They note that to most officers, such conduct probably constituted what they called "approved deviance." Nearly one-third of the officers reported seeing police officers displaying a badge to avoid a traffic citation while off duty and sleeping while on duty. These behaviors were also usually considered minor. More serious and clearly unacceptable forms of conduct were much less frequently observed.

Research has examined how approved deviance evolves among officers, in an effort to understand the forces and processes that pull rookies into a police subculture where ethically questionable conduct is accepted. Results of such

Figure 2.1	The Continuum of Compromise

Honest Cop

1st Stop	*A perceived sense of victimization*—First development of "us vs. them" mentality and that the only people they can trust are other "real" cops, not administration.
2nd Stop	*Loyalty vs. integrity*—Early exposure to such statements as "How will the department find out about it if we all hang together?"
3rd Stop	*Entitlement vs. accountability*—Officers may develop a sense of entitlement, that they are above the law and "deserve special treatment," allowing both on- and off-duty officers to operate on the belief that many of the rules don't apply to them.
4th Stop	*Acts of omission*—When officers do not do things for which they are responsible. Can include selective nonproductivity (limiting traffic enforcement, ignoring certain criminal violations), avoidance of getting involved, and doing just enough to "get by." Can also allow officers to rationalize not reporting another officer's corrupt behavior.
5th Stop	*Administrative acts of commission*—Rather than just omitting duties and responsibilities, officers begin to commit administrative violations. Breaking small rules may lead to bigger violations, including carrying unauthorized equipment or weapons, engaging in prohibited pursuits, drinking on duty, or firing warning shots. For most officers, this is the extent of their journey down the compromise continuum with departmental sanctions the only risk they will face at this point.
6th Stop	*Criminal acts of commission*—Similar to administrative acts but consequences go beyond reprimands and suspension. The officer would be fired and criminally charged for these acts, such as throwing away evidence, embellishing payroll records, or purchasing equipment with money seized from a drug dealer. The officers justifies it with, "What the hell, we put our lives on the line, and they owe us." When stealing seized assets, the officer says, "It's not like real theft, where there's a real victim. Nobody is getting hurt but the dopers, so what's the big deal?"

Corrupt Cop

Source: Based on Kevin M. Gilmartin and John J. Harris (1998, January). "The Continuum of Compromise." *The Police Chief*, pp. 25–28.

studies have found that newer officers were more willing to admit to witnessing unethical acts committed by fellow officers than were those with more time on the job: "One conclusion would be that the [greater the] length of time an officer is exposed to this socialization process, the greater its impact. When this loyalty to the subculture becomes too strong, the solidarity that follows can adversely affect the ethical values of the officers. The typical 'us versus them' mentality creates an allegiance to the members stronger than that to the mission of the department or even the profession. ... [C]onflicts can and will arise when personnel face a choice between what may be ethically right and their devotion to the other members" (Martin, 2011, p.15). The importance of management and of ethical officers within the department in curbing corruption cannot be underestimated. Among the most important forms of corruption is adherence to the code of silence.

The scandals that rocked the Los Angeles Police Department illustrate the emphasis on ends over means and on the code of silence. Hundreds of criminal convictions may be questioned because of a police-corruption scandal involving allegations of officers framing innocent people, lying in court, and shooting unarmed suspects.

Investigative Commissions

Historically, law enforcement administrators or local officials have responded to police corruption scandals by calling for investigative commissions, as discussed in Chapter 1. Many police chiefs or politicians convene an investigative commission or board of inquiry following a scandal. For example, the Knapp Commission, convened in 1972 by Mayor John Lindsay, was a response to alleged corruption in the New York City Police Department. This commission uncovered widespread corruption. However, 20 years later, the Mollen Commission found many of the same corruption issues had resurfaced.

The scandal involving the videotaped beating of Rodney King resulted in the Christopher Commission. A new chief was appointed who implemented many of the reforms recommended by the commission, but they were not institutionalized. Because these reforms were never made permanent, the corruption eventually returned in the form of the Rampart scandal, which led to formation of yet another commission, the Rampart Board of Inquiry.

The lesson to be learned from the investigative commissions is that too often implemented reforms are only temporary: Departments did not internalize the reforms so that with the passage of time, or once the chief left, the officers reverted to their "corrupt behavior."

Police corruption is an issue to be faced and dealt with. In a department where corruption is tolerated, the public trust will fade. "Ethics is our greatest training and leadership need today and into the next century. In addition to the fact that most departments do not conduct ethics training, nothing is more devastating to individual departments and our entire profession than uncovered scandals or discovered acts of officer misconduct and unethical behavior" (International Association of Chiefs of Police, n.d., p. 1).

IDEAS **IN PRACTICE** POLICE COMPLAINTS

The London Police Web site on making police complaints provides a good example of how to gain public trust by helping take the mystery out of making complaints against the police. The site lets people know how to complain, what will happen, and so on. The site also has a link for officers with information about what happens if someone complains about them.

In the United States, many departments are not very forthcoming about the complaint procedure. They make the complaining party work to find out how to complain; make it intimidating by insisting the complaints be made in person, rather than by phone or in writing; assert that complaints cannot be made on someone else's behalf; and so on. The result: Many people do not complain because they are frightened or intimidated about what will happen.

The Independent Police Complaints Commission (IPCC) became operational on April 1, 2004. It is a new nondepartmental public body funded by the Home Office, but by law entirely independent of the police, interest groups, and political parties, and whose decisions on cases are free from government involvement. The IPCC has a legal duty to oversee the whole of the police complaints system, created by the Police Reform Act of 2002. The IPCC's aim is to transform the way in which complaints against the police are handled, making sure that complaints against the police are dealt with effectively. The IPCC sets standards for the way the police handle complaints, and when something has gone wrong, they help the police learn how to improve the way they work.

Complainants

This section tells complainants all they need to know about making a complaint against the police and the procedures that need to be followed. This page provides information on:

- Who can make a complaint.
- The different ways in which a complaint can be made.
- How to appeal to the IPCC if the person making the complaint is dissatisfied with the way the complaint was handled.

A downloadable complaint form is also available.

Information for Police

This section contains information for police officers and police staff who might be:

- Handling a complaint from a member of the public.
- The subject of a complaint.
- Making a complaint.

This page also explains the role and responsibility of police authorities and how the IPCC is working with different organizations to improve the police complaints system.

Source: Independent Police Complaints Commission (IPCC): http://www.ipcc.gov.uk/complaints

SUMMARY

A mission statement is a written declaration of purpose. Departments must find in their mission a balance between fighting crime and providing service to the public. The majority of police actions have nothing to do with criminal law enforcement but involve service to the community.

Today police departments have more minority and female officers. The educational level of the officers is much higher, and fewer have military experience. More officers are also as interested in helping people as they are in fighting crime and greater emphasis is being placed on embracing a guardian mindset, as opposed to a warrior approach to policing.

Solidarity (loyalty) and secrecy within a police department can result in a code of silence. Such a code has a negative impact on the police image. The police image is affected by individual backgrounds, the media, and citizens' personal experiences with the criminal justice system. The police image is also shaped by appearance and police actions. Negative contacts are unpleasant interactions between the police and the public. They may or may not involve criminal activity.

People expect the law to be enforced except when enforcement limits their own behavior. The police are placed in the dilemma of being expected to win the wars on crime, drugs, and terrorism but are given no control over the causes of these problems. The police cannot win these wars alone. People also expect the police to help them when they have a problem or when someone else is causing a problem.

Each agency exercises discretion when it establishes its mission, policies, and procedures. Each officer exercises discretion when deciding whether to issue citations or make arrests when laws are violated. Community policing emphasizes wider use of officer discretion. Although officers are authorized to use force, including deadly force, they must use only that level and amount of force *reasonably* necessary to accomplish a legitimate law enforcement objective.

Police discretion and authority to use power are balanced by the responsibility to act ethically. Six recognized building blocks of ethics are integrity, honesty, values, standards, courage, and civility.

DISCUSSION QUESTIONS

1. What is the image of the police in your community? What factors are responsible for this image? Could the police image be made more positive?
2. What expectations do you have of law enforcement agencies?
3. Does police discretion frequently lead to abuse of alleged perpetrators?
4. Does the image of law enforcement affect officers' ability to get the job done?
5. How do you explain the development of the two contradictory models in policing: community-oriented policing (COP) and special weapons and tactics (SWAT) teams? Can they coexist?
6. What should be a department's ideal balance between fighting crime and service to the community?
7. What challenges do you think exist in shifting the police from a warrior to a guardian mindset?
8. Have you witnessed police exercise their discretion? How did it impress you?
9. Do you think mission statements are valuable for an organization, or are they only window dressing? How do they affect the organization? Compare the Los Angeles Police Department's mission statement with what appears to be the reality. Does this work?
10. What decisions commonly made by police officers involve ethical considerations?

CASES CITED

Graham v. Connor, 490 U.S. 386 (1989) Page 50
Tennessee v. Garner, 471 U.S. 1 (1985) 52

Deadly Force

↳ Reasonable Force

Terry v. Ohio, 392 U.S. 1 (1968) 15, 46
Police use of discretion

Understanding and Involving the Community

LO1 Explain how U.S. citizens established the "public peace."

LO2 Define *community*.

LO3 Understand what the broken windows phenomenon refers to.

LO4 List what community demographics includes.

LO5 Identify the significant demographic trends shaping the U.S. population.

LO6 Compare and contrast the power structures that typically exist within a community.

LO7 Summarize the ways in which citizens and communities have been involved in community policing.

Key Terms

bifurcated society
broken windows phenomenon
charge bargaining
community
community justice
demographics
displacement
diversion
formal power structure
heterogeneous
homogeneous
incivilities
informal power structure
NIMBY syndrome
plea bargaining
privatization
social capital
social contract
syndrome of crime
tipping point
White flight

In the summer of 2016, Chicagoans living in the Englewood neighborhood, a community identified by the *Chicago Tribune* newspaper as the sixth most dangerous in the city, suffered a rash of drive-by shooters and gang fights. One victim of this violence was 34-year-old Lucille Barnes, a young mother who had attempted to break up a fight between two youths. As retribution for her involvement between the two, she was killed in a drive-by shooting.

Englewood resident Tamar Manasseh was fed up with the senseless deaths of young and old occurring in her neighborhood, which had seen a record year for violence and had tallied 1,200 shootings even before the start of the calendar summer. Outraged by the news of Barnes' death, Manasseh and others in this community decided it was time to take back their streets. Wanting Barnes's death to be remembered more as a rallying cry than daily media coverage, Manasseh founded Mothers and Men against Senseless Killings (M.A.S.K.), a community watch program to supplement Chicago Police Department officers who were patrolling their block. Three days after Barnes was murdered on the corner of 75th Street and Stewart Street, M.A.S.K. members donned pink shirts that read "Moms on Patrol" and started handing out free hugs and free freshly grilled food, along with much needed motherly encouragement, an effort that brought many curious onlookers to the area. From 4:00 to 8:00 p.m., M.A.S.K. members fed, played with, and hugged anyone who passed by their corner. Mothers who participated in the program loved being involved because they could keep an eye on the streets while also being aware of where their kids were. Instead of fighting one another as enemies, kids played and established relationships. Moms were able to provide meals to those on need.

The organization reestablished some of the unification that, at one point in time, seemed like it was lost forever.

Since M.A.S.K. established itself on the corner, there have been no shootings, fist fights, or killings near that location. The organization has grown exponentially, no longer comprised only of mothers but now also including concerned fathers in the neighborhood. News of M.A.S.K.'s success has also sparked interest outside of Chicago, with branches of the organization now established in Evansville, Indiana and Staten Island, New York.

When asked the meaning of the word *community*, many individuals will give different interpretations as to the definition. Just as varied as the explanations of the word's meaning, are the differences in the inhabitants who comprise the population in question. There have been many approaches to pinpointing the composition and the temperament of a community. In the following chapter, one will discover no matter the demographics or the size, all are necessary to protect.

INTRODUCTION

The opening sentence of the American Creed, adopted by the House of Representatives on April 3, 1918, uses language attributed to Abraham Lincoln in his address at Gettysburg on November 19, 1863: "We here highly resolve that these dead shall not have died in vain; that this nation, under God, shall have a new birth of freedom; and that government of the people, by the people, and for the people, shall not perish from the earth." The philosophy implicit in the American Creed is central to the concept of "community" in the United States. Each community is part of a larger social order.

In the United States, individual freedom and rights are balanced with the need to establish and maintain order. The United States was born out of desire for freedom. In fact, former President Jimmy Carter noted: "America did not invent human rights. In a very real sense, it is the other way around. Human rights invented America."

The importance of individual rights to all citizens is a central theme in the following discussion of community. Citizens have established a criminal justice system in an effort to live in "peace," free from fear, crime, and violence. As the gatekeepers to the criminal justice system, the police have an inherent link with the public, as expressed by Sir Robert Peel in 1829: "Police, at all times, should maintain a relationship with the public that gives reality to the historic tradition that the police are the public and the public are the police; the police being the only members of the public who are paid to give full-time attention to duties which are incumbent on every citizen in the interests of community welfare and existence."

LO1

The U.S. Constitution and Bill of Rights, as well as federal and state statutes and local ordinances, establish the "public peace" in the United States.

social contract
A legal theory that suggests that for everyone to receive justice, each person must relinquish some individual freedom.

To ensure the peace, U.S. citizens have also entered into an unwritten social contract. The **social contract** provides that for everyone to receive justice, each person must relinquish some freedom. In civilized society, people cannot simply do as they please. They are expected to conform to federal and state laws as well as to local rules and regulations established by and for the community in which they live. Increased mobility and economic factors have weakened the informal social contract that once helped to keep the peace in our society. As a result, the police, as agents of social control, have had to fill the breach, increasing the need for law-abiding citizens to join with the police in making their communities free from fear, drugs, crime, and terrorism.

COMMUNITY DEFINED

What does the word *community* bring to mind? To many people, it conjures up images of their hometown. To others, it may bring images of a specific block, a neighborhood, or an idyllic small town where everyone knows everyone and they all get along.

community
The specific geographic area served by a police department or law enforcement agency and the individuals, organizations, and agencies within that area; also refers to a feeling of belonging—a sense of integration, a sense of shared values, and a sense of "we-ness."

Community has been defined as a group of people living in an area under the same government. Community can also refer to a social group or class having common interests. Community may even refer to society as a whole—the public. This text uses a specific meaning for community: **Community** refers to the specific geographic area served by a police department or law enforcement agency and the individuals, organizations, and agencies within that area.

Police officers must understand and be a part of this defined community if they are to fulfill their mission. The community may cover a very small area and have a limited number of individuals, organizations, and agencies; it may be policed by a single officer. Or the community may cover a vast area and have thousands of individuals and hundreds of organizations and agencies and be policed by several hundred officers. Although police jurisdiction and delivery of services are based on geographic boundaries, a community is much more than a group of neighborhoods administered by a local government. The schools, businesses, public and private agencies, churches, and social groups are vital elements of the community. Also of importance are the individual values, concerns, and cultural principles of the people living and working in the community and the common interests they share with neighbors. Where integrated communities exist, people share a sense of ownership and pride in their environment. They also have a sense of what is acceptable behavior, which makes policing in such a community much easier.

LO2

Community refers to a specific geographic area served by a police department or law enforcement agency and the individuals, organizations, and agencies within that area. Community also refers to a feeling of belonging—a sense of integration, a sense of shared values, and a sense of "we-ness."

Research strongly suggests that a *sense of* community is the glue that binds communities to maintain order and provides the foundation for effective community action. It also suggests that shared values, participation in voluntary associations, spiritual or faith-based connectedness, and positive interaction with neighbors indicate a strong sense of community and correlate with participation in civic and government activities (Correia, 2000).

Social Capital

A community might also be looked at in terms of its social capital, or the strength and resilience of its social fabric. Coleman (1990, p. 302) developed this concept, which he defined as: "A variety of different entities having two characteristics in common: They all consist of some aspect of a social structure, and they facilitate certain actions of individuals who are within the structure." Coleman saw the two most important elements in social capital as being trustworthiness—or citizens' trust of each other and their public institutions—and obligations—that is, expectation that service to each other will be reciprocated.

Social capital can be found at two levels: local and public. *Local social capital* is the bond among family members and their immediate, informal groups. *Public social capital* refers to the networks tying individuals to broader community institutions such as schools, civic organizations, churches, and the like as well as to networks linking individuals to various levels of government—including the police.

A study using Community Action Support Teams (CASTs) examined the community factors affecting social capital in six cities: Hayward, California; Davenport, Iowa; Ann Arbor, Michigan; Sioux City, Iowa; Pocatello, Idaho; and Ontario, California. Data came from self-administered mail surveys, direct observations, and interviews. Of the 22 hypotheses tested, seven were supported by the data (Correia, 2000, pp. 34–35):

1. Trust in others depends on the level of safety an individual feels in his or her environment. Therefore, the higher the levels of perceived safety, the higher the levels of local social capital will be.

2. The lower the levels of physical disorder, the higher the levels of perceived sense of safety will be.

3. Females will hold lower levels of perceived safety than males.

4. The higher the levels of public social capital, the higher the levels of collective action will be.

5. The more individuals trust one another, the more likely they will be to engage in collective activities. Consequently, the higher the level of local social capital, the higher the level of engagement in collective action will be.

6. The more individuals trust one another, the more likely they will be to interact. Therefore, the higher the levels of local social capital, the higher the levels of neighboring activity will be.

7. The higher the levels of civic activity, the higher the levels of public social capital will be.

However, sociologists have been describing for decades either the loss or the breakdown of "community" in modern, technological, industrial, urban societies such as ours.

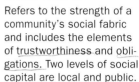

social capital
Refers to the strength of a community's social fabric and includes the elements of trustworthiness and obligations. Two levels of social capital are local and public.

Lack of Community

Community implies a group of people with a common history and understandings and a sense of themselves as "us" and outsiders as "them." Unfortunately, many communities lack this "we-ness." In such areas, the police and public may have a "them-versus-us" relationship. Areas requiring the most police attention are usually those with the fewest shared values and a limited sense of community. When citizens are unable to maintain informal social control, the result is social disorganization and a greater need for formal social control measures (i.e., the police). All entities within a community—individuals as well as organizations and agencies—must work together to keep that community healthy. Such partnerships are vital because a community cannot be healthy if unemployment and poverty are widespread; people are hungry; health care is inadequate; prejudice separates people; preschool children lack proper care and nutrition; senior citizens are allowed to atrophy; schools remain isolated and remote; social services are fragmented and disproportionate; and government lacks responsibility and accountability.

Social capital must exist for citizens to engage in community efforts (Correia, 2000). The implications of this significant finding are discussed in Chapter 5. However, in some instances, government policies may destroy social capital. Major freeways may physically divide neighborhoods. At the local level, budget cuts in schools may result in the elimination of sports or music programs, activities that have been shown to encourage civic engagement.

Broken Windows An interesting theory of the causes of crime and neighborhood decline is the analogy used in Wilson and Kelling's classic article, "Broken Windows" (1982, p. 31):

> Social psychologists and police officers tend to agree that if a window in a building is broken and is left unrepaired, all the rest of the windows will soon be broken. This is as true in nice neighborhoods as in run-down ones. Window-breaking does not necessarily occur on a large scale because some areas are inhabited by determined window-breakers whereas others are populated by window-lovers; rather, one unrepaired broken window is a signal that no one cares, and so breaking more windows costs nothing. (It has always been fun.)

Wilson and Kelling based their broken windows theory, in part, on research done in 1969 by a Stanford psychologist, Philip Zimbardo. Zimbardo arranged to have a car without license plates parked with its hood up on a street in the Bronx and a comparable car parked on a street in Palo Alto, California. The car in the Bronx was attacked by vandals within 10 minutes, and within 24 hours it had been totally destroyed and stripped of anything of value. The car in Palo Alto sat untouched. After a week, Zimbardo took a sledgehammer to it. People passing by soon joined in, and within a few hours that car was also totally destroyed. According to Wilson and Kelling (1982, p. 31): "Untended property becomes fair game for people out for fun or plunder, and even for people who ordinarily would not dream of doing such things and who probably consider themselves as law-abiding."

LO3

The **broken windows phenomenon** suggests that if it appears "no one cares," disorder and crime will thrive. In other words, there exists a long-term indirect link between disorder enforcement and a reduction in serious crime.

broken windows phenomenon
Suggests that if it appears no one cares about the community, as indicated by broken windows not being repaired, then disorder and crime will thrive.

Ingram Publishing/Getty Images

Wilson and Kelling's broken windows theory holds that signs of vandalism and general urban decay indicate that no one cares about a community and that this neighborhood will tolerate crime and disorder.

Broken windows and smashed cars are visible signs of people not caring about their community. Other less subtle signs include unmowed lawns, piles of accumulated trash, and graffiti, often referred to as **incivilities**. Incivilities include rowdiness, drunkenness, fighting, prostitution, abandoned buildings, litter, broken windows, and graffiti. Incivilities and social disorder occur when social control mechanisms have eroded. Increases in incivilities may increase the fear of crime and reduce citizens' sense of safety. Citizens may physically or psychologically withdraw, isolating themselves from their neighbors. Or increased incivilities and disorder may bring people together to "take back the neighborhood."

incivilities
Occur when social control mechanisms have eroded and include unmowed lawns, piles of accumulated trash, graffiti, public drunkenness, fighting, prostitution, abandoned buildings, and broken windows.

The real-world application to policing of the broken windows theory is often credited to William J. Bratton who, in the early 1980s, was in charge of the Boston transit police. Bratton referenced the broken windows theory when he declared that the primary responsibility of patrol was to keep order in a community and prevent offenses rather than simply responding to serious crimes after the fact. Crime on Bratton's watch dropped by 27 percent and, in 1993, Mayor Rudolph W. Giuliani hired Bratton as New York's police commissioner. Bratton focused on quality-of-life initiatives such as cracking down on panhandling, public drinking, street prostitution, and the like. In the 1990s, New York City led the United States in a nationwide decline in serious crime, crediting "order maintenance."

Criminal justice scholars and practitioners alike noted, however, that crime rates were dropping in cities throughout the country, not just New York City, leading researchers to look more closely at the factors affecting the rise and fall of criminal activity. What was found was that the sharp increase in violent crime that began in the mid-1980s and continued into the early 1990s was linked to the crack cocaine epidemic gripping the nation. Once the crack epidemic subsided, crime rates also declined. This trend was observed in jurisdictions nationwide. It just so happened that in New York City from the mid-1980s to the mid-1990s, those areas that had been targeted to receive the highest doses of broken-windows policing were also the same areas with the biggest crack problem. So when the violent crime rate began to fall in New York City during the 1990s, broken-windows policing was inaccurately credited as the reason for the decline when, in fact, crime would have dropped anyway, as it did in cities throughout the nation, without any broken-policing initiatives (Harcourt & Ludwig, 2006).

Not content to simply write off broken windows policing as ineffective, further research attempted to tease apart the reasons why some departments achieved greater success in reducing crime by targeting disorder issues. A common result to emerge from such studies was that the types of strategies implemented played significant a role in the level of crime reduction. Braga, Welsh, and Schnell (2015) found that policing strategies rooted in place-based, problem-oriented interventions had a positive and statistically significant, modest effect on reducing all types of crime but that no significant overall impact was seen with aggressive, zero-tolerance order maintenance strategies (pp. 580–581):

> The results of our systematic review and meta-analysis suggest that disorder policing strategies generate noteworthy crime control gains. Importantly, these strategies yielded consistent crime reduction effects across a variety of violent, property, drug, and disorder outcome measures. These findings provide support for police paying attention to social and physical disorder when seeking to reduce more serious crimes in neighborhoods. Indeed, beyond broken windows policing, these general ideas support key strategies and tactics employed by a wide range of recent police innovations, such as community policing, problem-oriented policing, third-party policing, and hot spots policing. Police departments should continue to engage policing disorder tactics as part of their portfolio of strategies to reduce crime.

> Perhaps of greatest interest to police leaders and policymakers alike is that the types of strategies used by police departments to control disorder seem to matter. Aggressive order maintenance strategies that target individual disorderly behaviors do not generate significant crime reductions. In contrast, community problem-solving approaches that seek to change social and physical disorder conditions at particular places produce significant crime reductions. These findings suggest that, when considering a policing disorder approach, police departments should adopt a "community coproduction model" rather than drift toward a zero-tolerance policing model, which focuses on a subset of social incivilities, such as drunken people, rowdy teens, and street vagrants, and seeks to remove them from the street via arrest.

The Center for Evidence-Based Crime Policy at George Mason University cautions that broken windows policing, and especially zero-tolerance tactics to minor offenses, carries potentially negative repercussions to police-community relations if the public perceives the strategies as unfair, which may lead to reduced citizen satisfaction and damage to citizens' perceptions about the legitimacy of the police (2013). In light of such research and warnings, many cities are moving away from aggressive enforcement of low-level infractions. For example, in March 2016, the New York Police Department stopped its policy of automatically arresting people caught littering, urinating in public, taking up more than one subway seat at a time, or consuming alcohol in public. Officers will instead be allowed to issue summonses for such minor offenses, a move that will eliminate an estimated 10,000 criminal cases from further bogging down the court system annually (Blake, 2016). Mayor Bill De Blasio noted, "Using summonses instead of arrests for low-level offenses is an intuitive and modern solution that will help make sure resources are focused on our main priority: addressing threats to public safety" (Blake, 2016).

Other Factors Negating a Sense of Community   The increasing diversity within our society can present a challenge to community policing. It is extremely difficult to implement community policing when the values of groups within a given area clash. For example, controversy may exist between gay communities and Orthodox Christian or Jewish communities in the same area. Do each of these communities deserve a different style of policing based on the "community value system"? Do "community" police officers ignore behavior in a community where the majority of residents approve of that behavior but enforce sanctions against the same behavior in enclaves where that behavior causes tension? These are difficult ethical questions.

Another factor that negates a sense of community is the prevalence of violence. We live in a violent society. The United States was born through a violent revolution. The media emphasize violence, constantly carrying news of murder, rape, and assault. The cartoons children watch contain more violence than most adults realize. Children learn that violence is acceptable and justified under some circumstances. Citizens expect the police to prevent violence, but the police cannot do it alone. Individuals must come together to help stop violence and in so doing can build a sense of community. However, if the community is unresponsive, community policing cannot succeed, no matter how hard the police work:

> Ironically, it is difficult to sustain community involvement in community policing. The community and the police may not have a history of getting along in poor neighborhoods. Organizations representing the interests of community members may not have a track record of cooperating with police, and poor and high-crime areas often are not well endowed with an infrastructure of organizations ready to get involved. Fear of retaliation by gangs and drug dealers can undermine public involvement. Finally, there may be no reason for residents of crime-ridden neighborhoods to think that community policing will turn out to be anything but another broken promise. Residents may be accustomed to seeing programs come and go in response to political and budgetary cycles that are out of their control (Skogan, 2004, p. 166).

COMMUNITIES AND CRIME

Although traditional policing has most often dealt with high crime levels by stricter enforcement (zero tolerance), "get-tough" policies, and a higher police presence, police usually have little ability to change things for the better in the long run. Cracking down on crime often results in **displacement**, the relocation of crime and criminals to neighboring areas outside the enforcement zone. The community in which the crackdown occurs may be temporarily safer; however, forced by the increased police presence and increased likelihood of arrest, criminals usually just move their operations, often a few blocks or miles away, making adjacent communities less safe. Policing efforts can develop into an unending game of "cat and mouse."

displacement
The theory that successful implementation of a crime-reduction initiative does not really prevent crime; instead, it just moves the crime to another area.

Community Factors Linked to Causes of Crime

Traditional police tactics often fail because the causes of crime in communities are complicated and linked to a multitude of factors, including environmental design; housing age, type, and density; availability of jobs; residents' level of education; poverty level; family structure; demographics (average age of residents, ethnic and racial makeup of the community); mobility; and perhaps other unidentified factors. Such complicated underlying causes require creative solutions and partnerships. Police who form alliances with organizations and agencies associated with education, religion, health care, job training, family support, community leaders, and members can often affect the underlying factors in criminal behavior and community decay.

A theory called the ecology of crime explains how criminal opportunities are created in neighborhoods. Just like a natural ecosystem, a neighborhood can hold only a certain number of things. Add too many and the system will collapse. This is similar to the **tipping point**, the point at which an ordinary, stable phenomenon can turn into a crisis. For example, a health epidemic is nonlinear—that is, small changes can have huge effects and large changes can have small effects, in contrast to linear situations in which every extra increment of effort will produce a corresponding improvement in result.

tipping point
That point at which an ordinary, stable phenomenon can turn into a crisis.

This principle of nonlinearity is captured in the expression, "That's the straw that broke the camel's back." The principle can be applied to the phenomenon of **White flight**, the departure of White families from neighborhoods experiencing racial integration or from cities experiencing school desegregation. Depending on the racial views of White residents, one White neighborhood might empty out when minorities reach 5 percent of the neighborhood population, whereas another more racially tolerant White neighborhood might not tip until minorities make up 40 or 50 percent. Communities need to recognize when they are approaching the tipping point or the threshold in a given situation.

white flight
The departure of White families from neighborhoods experiencing racial integration or from cities experiencing school desegregation.

A study of whether suburbanization was a cause or a consequence of crime in U.S. metropolitan areas found reciprocating evidence that it was, in fact, both:

> Inner-city crime is a motivating factor for middle-class flight. Therefore, crime is a cause of suburbanization. Movement of the middle and upper classes to the suburbs, in turn, isolates the poor in central-city ghettos and barrios.

Sociologists and criminologists have argued that the concentration of poverty creates an environment within which criminal behavior becomes normative, leading impressionable youth to adopt criminal lifestyles. Moreover, from the perspective of routine-activity theory, the deterioration of social capital in high-poverty areas reduces the capacity for guardianship. Therefore, suburbanization may also cause crime. UCR data and census data shows a positive relationship between suburbanization and metropolitan crime (Jargowsky, 2009, p. 28).

The FBI, through its *Crime in the United States* series, presents annual statistics on crime and cautions that overly simplistic or incomplete analysis of such data can create misleading perceptions. Many variables can significantly affect crime, but some of these variables are not readily measurable or applicable among all locales. Valid and accurate assessment of crime and criminality is possible only with careful study and analysis of the many unique conditions affecting each local jurisdiction. Several factors known to affect the volume and type of crime occurring from place to place include:

- Population density and degree of urbanization
- Variations in composition of the population, particularly youth concentration
- Stability of the population with respect to residents' mobility, commuting patterns, and transient factors
- Modes of transportation and highway system
- Economic conditions, including median income, poverty level, and job availability
- Cultural factors and educational, recreational, and religious characteristics
- Family conditions with respect to divorce and family cohesiveness
- Climate
- Effective strength of law enforcement agencies
- Administrative and investigative emphases of law enforcement
- Policies of other components of the criminal justice system (i.e., prosecutorial, judicial, correctional, and probational)
- Citizens' attitudes toward crime
- Crime reporting practices of the citizenry

Theories of Criminality

Why people commit crime has been debated since crime was first defined. A detailed discussion of the theories of criminality is beyond the scope of this text. Thus, this section will briefly discuss only the major theories.

The classical theory was developed by Italian criminologist Cesare Beccaria (1738–1794) and holds that people are rational and responsible for their acts. People are free agents with free will and commit crimes because they want to. A refinement of the classical theory is the *routine activity theory* developed by Lawrence Cohen and Marcus Felson, which states that crime occurs at the intersection of three variables: the availability of a suitable target (a home or store containing easily sold goods), the absence of a watchful guardian (e.g., homeowners, neighbors, guards, security systems), and the presence of a motivated offender (e.g., unemployed individuals, drug abusers). Routine activity theory gives equal weight to the role of victim and offender and suggests that the opportunity for criminal action depends on the victim's lifestyle and behavior.

Among the leading opponents to the classical theory was Cesare Lombroso (1835–1909), an Italian criminologist who developed the positivist theory which holds that how a person acts is fundamentally the result of genetic predisposition and environmental influences. The positivist theory sees criminals as "victims of society" and of their own biological, sociological, cultural, and physical environments. Some scholars later advanced the positivist view by developing the concept of determinism, which regards crime as a consequence of many factors, including population density, economic status, and the legal definition of crime. This multiple-factor causation theory brought the positivist view into direct conflict with the notion of free will.

Two theories on criminality prevalent in the 21st century are lack of self-control and strain theory. The oft-cited self-control theory of Gottfredson and Hirschi (1990) posits that individuals low in self-control have a greater propensity to commit deviant acts, harkening back to classical theory. Using measures such as number of police contacts, age at first police contact, and number of arrests, researchers Beaver, DeLisi, Mears, and Stewart (2009) found empirical evidence to support the hypothesis that low self-control is consistently related to criminal justice system involvement.

A second theory being actively researched is general strain theory (GTS), harkening back to the positivist view of crime. A leading researcher in this theory, Agnew (2005, p. 3) explains, "A general theory must describe the relationship between those individual traits, family factors, school experiences, peer factors, and work experiences that cause crime. . . . Researchers have increasingly come to argue that the causes of crime have reciprocal effects on one another (e.g., individual traits, influence family experiences, and family experiences influence individual traits." Research by Kaufman (2009) finds strong support for GTS.

Messner and Rosenfeld (2007, p. 7) contend, "The American Dream itself and the normal social conditions engendered by it are deeply implicated in the problem of crime. [The American Dream is] a broad cultural ethos that entails a commitment to the goal of material success, to be pursued by everyone in society, under conditions of open, individual competition." The exaggerated emphasis placed by society on monetary achievement, to the near exclusion of other alternative criteria of success, has promoted an "ends over means" preoccupation with financial wealth and possession of property and eroded the social structures required to restrain criminogenic cultural pressures (Messner & Rosenfeld, 2007, p. 10).

Debate has long swirled around the nature-versus-nurture question: Are criminals born or made? Biological theories operate on the premise that certain variables within a person's biological makeup are correlated with criminality. Biological functions and conditions that have been related to criminal behavior include such variables as brain tumors, disorders of the limbic system, endocrine abnormalities, chromosomal abnormalities, and neurologic dysfunction produced by the prenatal and postnatal experience of infants.

A counterposition to the biological theory is the behavioral or environmental theory, which suggests that criminals are made, not born. Many environmental factors have been identified as contributing to criminality, including poverty, unemployment, the disintegrating family, and drug and alcohol abuse.

Comparisons of groups of criminals with groups of noncriminals have failed to produce any single characteristic that absolutely distinguishes the two groups. However, a growing body of evidence suggests that the forces operating to stimulate criminal behavior may be a complex interaction between predisposing biological or genetic factors and certain environmental agents that trigger criminal tendencies. Thus, in the nature–nurture debate, it is likely that criminal behavior is the result of both heredity and life experiences.

Table 3.1 summarizes the major theories on the causes of crime.

Table 3.1	Review of the Major Theories on the Causes of Crime
Theory	**Major Premise**
Rational Choice	Crime is the product of a conscious decision. Offenders are rational actors who weigh the costs and benefits.
Lifestyle	Crime is one part of a lifestyle that involves other reckless behaviors.
Routine activities	Criminal events occur when motivated offenders come into contact with desirable targets that lack guardianship.
Biosocial Perspective	The propensity for criminal behavior is heritable and interacts with the environment.
Neuroandrogenic	Differences between sexes in crime are caused by hormonal differences.
Biological or genetic	Brain-based differences among individuals cause a variety of problem behaviors. Genetic influences cause differences in traits related to crime.
Psychological	Individual differences in thinking or emotional regulation explain why some people commit crime and others do not.
Personality or trait	Temperamental differences among individuals increase their chance of committing crime.
Cognitive	The manner in which offenders see the world and their tendency to process environmental cues through an aggressive "lens" explain the violent and other antisocial behavior of delinquents and criminals.
Psychodynamic	Early personality development influences the ability of a person to control ego impulses.
Psychopathy	A unique constellation of personality and behavioral characteristics, including a lack of remorse, a lack of conscience, and a parasitic lifestyle, increase the risk of engaging in crime or delinquency.
General strain theory	Youth commit crime when they feel strain, when opportunities are blocked, or when things they value are taken away.
Social Structure	Points to unique aspects of the broader social environment that may be crime producing.
Social disorganization	Neighborhoods characterized by racial heterogeneity, mobility, and female-headed households are criminogenic.
Functionalism	Crime is "normal" and inevitable and serves a purpose in society.
Institutional anomie	Economic stressors degrade normal institutions of social control, including the family.
Informal social control	Rates of crime across neighborhoods reflect differences in collective efficacy, or the ability of communities to informally regulate crime.
Social Learning	Similar to any other behavior, criminal behavior has to be learned. It can be learned in small groups or learned by watching others.

Source: Hess, K. M., Orthmann, C. H., & Wright, J. P. (2013). *Juvenile Justice*, 6e. Belmont, CA: Wadsworth Cengage Learning, p. 84.

COMMUNITY DEMOGRAPHICS

In addition to understanding the complex concept of community, it is important to assess the demographics of the area. The term **demographics** refers to the characteristics of the individuals who live in a community.

Although people generally assume that the smaller the population of a community, the easier policing becomes; this is not necessarily true. Small communities generally have fewer resources. The demands of being the sole law enforcement person in a community—in effect, being on call 24 hours a day—may be difficult to manage. A major advantage of a smaller community is that people know each other. A sense of community is likely to be greater in such communities than in large cities such as Chicago or New York.

When assessing law enforcement's ability to police an area, density of population is an important variable. Studies have shown that as population becomes denser, people become more aggressive. In densely populated areas, people become more territorial and argue more frequently about "turf." Rapid population growth can invigorate a community or it can drain its limited resources. Without effective planning and foresight, rapid population growth can result in serious problems for a community, especially if the population growth results from an influx of immigrants or members of an ethnic group different from the majority in that area.

The community's vital statistics are extremely important from a police–community partnership perspective. What is the average age of individuals within the community? Are there more young or elderly individuals? How many single-parent families are there? What is the divorce rate? What is the common level of education? How does the education of those in law enforcement compare? What is the school dropout rate? Do gangs operate in the community? What is the percentage of latchkey children? Such children may pose a significant challenge for police.

Income and income distribution are also important. Do great disparities exist? Would the community be described as affluent, moderately well off, or poor? How does the income of those in law enforcement compare to the average income? Closely related to income is the level of employment. What is the ratio of blue-collar to professional workers? How much unemployment exists? How do those who are unemployed exist? Are they on welfare? Do they commit crimes to survive? Are they homeless? Are there gangs?

The ethnic makeup of the community is another consideration. Is the community basically homogeneous? A **homogeneous** community is one in which people are all quite similar. A **heterogeneous** community, in contrast, is one in which individuals are quite different from each other. Most communities are heterogeneous. Establishing and maintaining good relations among the various subgroups making up the community is a challenge. Usually one ethnic subgroup will have the most power and control. It is helpful if police officers come from all groups, including the dominant one and smaller ones.

For example, the neighboring cities of Brooklyn Park and Brooklyn Center, Minnesota, experienced a 150-percent increase in foreign-born residents between 1990 and 2000, evolving rapidly from fairly homogenous communities to cities with populations reaching 40 to 50 percent diversity

---

demographics
The characteristics of a human population or community.

LO4

Demographics include a population's size, distribution, growth, density, employment rate, ethnic makeup, and vital statistics such as average age, education, and income.

homogeneous
Involving things (including people) that are basically similar, alike; the opposite of *heterogeneous*.

heterogeneous
Involving things (including people) that are unlike, dissimilar, different; the opposite of *homogeneous*.

(Ankerfelt, Davis, & Futterer, 2011). By 2008, this area, often referred to as "the Brooklyns," had become home to what is estimated to be the largest population of Somali and Liberian civil war refugees in the United States. In addition, the prospect of affordable housing and job opportunities has drawn other African, Hispanic, Eastern European, and Asian refugees and immigrants to these cities, demographic changes that have prompted local law enforcement agencies to seek more ethnically diverse recruits: "The fact that the police departments have multicultural police cadets speaks volumes to community members whose race, background, and ethnic status may previously have been a cause for misunderstanding between them and the police. ... To date, six diverse individuals representing a multitude of nationalities have been selected to enroll as police cadets. ... [and] two Liberian and Hmong cadets have completed officer training" (Ankerfelt et al., 2011, p. 27).

Many police agencies are having difficulty hiring new officers who could enhance the diversity of their force and make their departments more representative of the communities they serve. Some departments have turned to hiring immigrants who are legal residents of the United States and who have legal status to work but are not yet citizens. Some departments require that noncitizens hired must become citizens within a certain period of time. The Colorado State Patrol has had success hiring noncitizens to fill difficult positions that require living and working in remote locations in Colorado. Others agencies that allow hiring of noncitizens include the Chicago Police Department, the Boulder (Colorado) Police Department, and several cities in California. The Nashville (Tennessee) Police Department hires U.S. military veterans who are noncitizens.

The demographics of our country are undergoing rapid transformation. Data from the U.S. Census Bureau indicate that as of July 17, 2016, the U.S. population was 324,031,581, and increasing by one person every 11 seconds, after factoring in births, deaths, and migration (U.S. Census Bureau, 2016). The total U.S. population is projected to grow by more than 98 million between 2014 and 2060, or an average of 2.1 million people each year, reaching a total just under 417 million in 2060 (Colby & Ortman, 2015).

Although the overall population growth rate of the country is projected to slow over the next four decades due to declining fertility rates and a modest decline in the rate of international migration, the growth of the foreign-born segment of the population is expected to exceed that of native-born individuals, leading to an increasing share of the future U.S. population that is foreign born. The racial and ethnic composition of the U.S. population is projected to continue becoming increasingly diverse and by 2044, the United States is projected to become a plurality nation. While the non-Hispanic White-alone population will still be the largest, no race or ethnic group is projected to have greater than a 50 percent share of the nation's total. The child population within the United States is even more diverse and is projected to experience the majority–minority crossover in 2020 (Colby & Ortman, 2015). Figure 3.1 shows the racial and ethnic composition of the United States in 2000 and the projected composition in 2050.

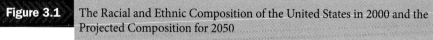

Figure 3.1 The Racial and Ethnic Composition of the United States in 2000 and the Projected Composition for 2050

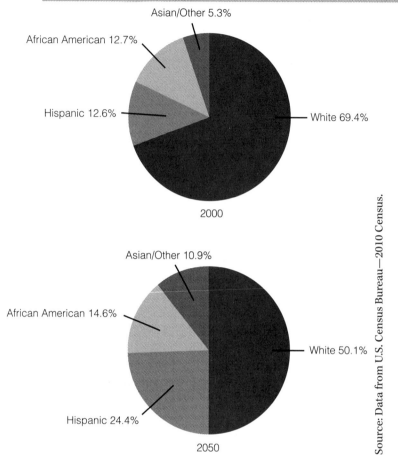

Note: White, Black, and Asian/Other categories exclude Hispanics, who may be of any race. The Asian/Other category includes American Indians, Eskimos, Aleuts, and Pacific Islanders. Totals may not add up to 100 because of rounding.

Data from the Pew Research Center show that more Mexicans are leaving the United States than have migrated here since the end of the Great Recession, resulting in a net loss of 140,000 people of Mexican origin between 2009 and 2014 (Gonzalez-Barrera, 2015). However, in 2013, 28 percent of all U.S. immigrants came from Mexico, allowing it to retain its status as the largest birth country among the U.S. foreign-born population and the largest source of unauthorized immigrants. While the immigration rate from Mexico has been falling, the influx of immigrants from Asia—both legal and illegal—has increased considerably. According to one study by the Migration Policy Institute, the number of unauthorized immigrants from Asia, mainly from India, China, and South Korea, increased 202 percent from 2000 to 2013, and Asians now comprise roughly one-third of the U.S. foreign-born population (Rosenblum & Soto, 2015).

In addition to an increasing racial and ethnic diversity, the U.S. population is projected to continue aging, reflected in the growth of the percentage of the population that is in the older ages. Over the next two decades, the aging of the baby boomers will drive up the ranks of the native population at ages 65 and over, and by 2030, 20 percent of the U.S. population is projected to be 65 and older (Colby & Ortman, 2015). From 2014 to 2060, the percentage of the U.S. population under age 18 is projected to decline from 23 percent to 20 percent, and the work-age population is also expected to decrease from 62 percent to 57 percent during the same time interval.

Another demographic trend in the United States is a widening of the gap between those with wealth and those living in poverty. The middle class is shrinking, and the gap between the "haves" and the "have-nots" is widening, resulting in a **bifurcated society**.

ORGANIZATIONS AND INSTITUTIONS

In addition to understanding the demographics of the community and being able to relate to a great variety of individuals, community policing officers must also be familiar with the various organizations and institutions within the community and establish effective relationships with them. A strong network of community organizations and institutions fosters cohesiveness and shared intolerance of criminal behavior and encourages citizens to cooperate in controlling crime, thereby increasing the likelihood that illegal acts will be detected and reported. These networks and partnerships are essential because no single organization or group is able to address all the problems and concerns of a community alone. All the organizations and groups working beyond their individual capacity are unable to do more than apply localized, specific Band-Aid solutions to all of the community problems.

A good relationship between the schools in the community and the police is vital to maintaining order. Other organizations and institutions with which police officers should interact effectively include departments of human services, health care providers, emergency services providers, and any agencies working with youth. Communities may also have libraries, museums, and zoos that would welcome a good relationship with the police.

THE PUBLIC–PRIVATE POLICING INTERACTION

Historically, public and private police have seen themselves as being in competition. Police often view private security employees as poorly trained, poorly paid individuals who could not land a police job. Names such as "rent-a-cop" and "cop-in-a-box" add to this negative perception. However, private security plays a major role in safeguarding Americans and their property, with an estimated 85 percent of critical U.S. infrastructure protected by private security companies. And as police departments nationwide continue to grapple with budget cuts and other resource deficits, citizens are turning more and more to private policing agencies to safeguard their businesses and communities.

The need for public and private police forces to establish good working relationships was recognized by the National Institute of Justice in the

LO5

Significant demographic trends shaping the population in the United States include an increasing ethnic and racial minority population and the ending of White dominance; an increasing number of legal and illegal immigrants; an increase in the elderly population; and a shrinking of the middle class.

bifurcated society
The widening of the gap between those with wealth (the "haves") and those living in poverty (the "have-nots"), with a shrinking middle class.

early 1980s when it began urging cooperation between the agencies and established the Joint Council of Law Enforcement and Private Security Association. The International Association of Chiefs of Police (IACP) has also recognized this need for cooperation by establishing a Private Sector Liaison Committee (PSLC). Indeed, many communities and police departments are using **privatization**, contracting with private security agencies or officers to provide services usually considered to be law enforcement functions.

privatization
Using private security officers or agencies to provide services typically considered to be law enforcement functions.

Private police present a more cost-effective way to protect assets because they typically cost less than public officers and are more plentiful in number. The most recent available data from the Bureau of Labor Statistics (BLS) indicates that in May 2015, protective services occupations employed 3.35 million people nationwide, and the average annual salary across this broad job-related group was $44,610. Within this category, police and sheriff's patrol officers numbered 653,740 and earned an average $61,270 each year, whereas security guards numbered 1,097,660 and earned an average $28,460 annually and private detectives and investigators numbered 30,460 and made an average $52,840 per year (Bureau of Labor Statistics, 2016).

The Office of Community Oriented Policing Services (COPS) is committed to promoting law enforcement–private security (LE–PS) partnerships and has sponsored several projects aimed at identifying and analyzing such collaborations. The Office of COPS (n.d.) notes:

> Cutting-edge technology, information sharing, and personnel resources are just a few of the benefits that private security brings to these partnerships. . . . Unfortunately, misperception of private security can sometimes be a factor in hindering strong partnerships with law enforcement.

> The private security field, in fact, is much more diverse than what many may imagine. Annually, it spends more than $100 billion on security products and services. In contrast, federal, state, and local law enforcement spend less than half that amount. Additionally, many private security employees are experts in technology, fraud, and forensics investigation and often hold professional certifications and advanced degrees.

> Private security and public law enforcement share many of the same goals: preventing crime and disorder, identifying criminals, and ensuring the security of people and property. As there are two private security practitioners for every one sworn law enforcement officer, effective partnerships can act as a much needed force multiplier.

Some areas of cooperation between police and private security are investigating internal theft and economic crimes, responding to burglar alarms, examining evidence from law enforcement in private crime labs, conducting background checks, protecting VIPs and executives, protecting crime scenes, transporting prisoners, moving hazardous materials, and controlling crowds and traffic at public events. Other likely areas for privatization include public building security, parking enforcement, public parks patrol, animal control, public housing development patrol, applicant screening, and civilian fingerprinting.

THE POWER STRUCTURE

In addition to considering the role private security might play in community policing, the power structure within the community must be considered. Most communities have both a formal and an informal power structure.

The public can usually readily identify the formal power structure. Often policy decisions made at the federal and state levels directly affect local decisions. In addition, federal and state funding can directly influence local programs. In contrast, the public often cannot as readily identify the informal power structure, which includes banks, real estate companies, and other large and influential businesses in a community. The informal power structure is not merely a few people controlling the masses; rather, the control groups are entire subcultures that influence other subcultures. It has been alleged that 400 families control the wealth of the United States, affecting every other subculture. Awareness of the way informal groups, especially wealthy and political groups, exercise their ideologies is important. Knowing how informal group pressure is forced into an organization's formal structure is key to understanding why the community at large often conflicts with the criminal justice system.

Wilson and Kelling (1982, p. 34) suggest: "The essence of the police role in maintaining order is to reinforce the informal control mechanisms of the community itself. The police cannot, without committing extraordinary resources, provide a substitute for that informal control." Law enforcement personnel must understand the different subgroups within their jurisdiction and the power struggles that occur among them. They must also be aware of this reality: Democracy does not always ensure equality.

> **LO6**
>
> A community's **formal power structure** includes divisions of society with wealth and political influence: federal, state, and local agencies and governments, commissions, and regulatory agencies. The **informal power structure** includes religious groups, wealthy subgroups, ethnic groups, political groups, and public interest groups.

formal power structure
Includes divisions of society with wealth and political influence such as federal, state, and local agencies and governments, commissions, and regulatory agencies.

informal power structure
Includes religious groups, wealthy subgroups, ethnic groups, political groups, and public interest groups.

THE CRIMINAL JUSTICE SYSTEM

Many people equate policing or law enforcement with the criminal justice system when, in fact, it is only one part of this system. The other two components, courts and corrections, are much less visible in most communities. Because the police are the most visible component of the system, however, they often become "the criminal justice system" in the eyes of the community.

In the criminal justice process, the role of law enforcement is to prevent, detect, or act on reports of law violations, to apprehend suspects reasonably believed responsible for such violations, and to bring those suspects or defendants before a court of law. The court then assesses the charge and the evidence as presented by both the prosecution, for which the police officer may be a witness, and the defense to determine the defendant's guilt or innocence. The offender, if found guilty of the charge, may be sentenced by the court to confinement in a correctional facility or be allowed to return to the community under supervision.

This three-part system provides a procedure of checks and balances intended to ensure that no person is accused of a crime and then deprived of freedom without every reasonable step being taken to guarantee fairness and equity throughout the process, guarantees consistent with the Fourteenth

Amendment requirements of the "due process" and "equal protection" clauses. The courts are often criticized by the public as being the weak link in the criminal justice process, letting too many offenders "off easy" and allowing wealthy defendants to buy their way out of convictions. Those who criticize judges usually do so based on whether they agree with a judge's procedures and sentencing practices. Critics must remember, however, that the system is designed to work the way it does. After all, if we assumed that everyone arrested by the police is guilty of a crime, there would be no need for prosecutors, judges, juries, or courtrooms. The accused could be taken directly to prison.

Many people have a limited understanding of the role that the courts and corrections play in crime control. Indeed, at times various components of the criminal justice system seem to work against each other. When the perception or the reality is that criminals are not being convicted or are being released early from prison, some people demand more police and ask why they are not doing their job.

Members of the law enforcement community often become frustrated by such attitudes and incidents. Decisions made in court can discourage officers, who may become cynical and wonder why they work so hard to make arrests when they see cases dismissed or plea-bargained. Officers may also become frustrated when those who are convicted are given a light sentence or probation. Officers may be further aggravated by what they view as inadequacies of the corrections system, aware of the many career criminals whose behavior has not improved even after they have been through prison, probation, parole, halfway houses, and rehabilitation programs. Officers are not alone in their disappointment, however. The public, too, can be frustrated by the performance of the courts and corrections.

The public may have a negative opinion of the courts because of their failure to process cases promptly, their inconsistency in plea bargaining, and the long tenure accorded to judges. Many believe that the courts provide "assembly-line" justice and the legal process is filled with delays. Aspects of the correctional system that have impeded good public relations include failures to reform offenders, the early release of recidivists, and the growing prison population.

To help overcome negative opinions and improve public relations, agencies within the criminal justice system are now actively seeking partnerships with others in the community. Many communities now have community prosecution, community courts, community corrections, and even **community justice**. What constitutes good criminal justice administration is open to debate.

Numerous controversial issues related to the effectiveness of the criminal justice system affect police–community partnerships, including plea and charge bargaining, diversion, sentencing, rehabilitation, community alternatives to prisons, victims' rights, and capital punishment. Although many issues are outside police officers' appropriate sphere of action, they affect the system as a whole. Therefore, police officers need to be aware of these issues and their potential impact.

community justice
An ethic that transforms the aim of the justice system into enhancing community life or sustaining communities; partnerships between the formal criminal justice system, the private sector, and community groups to promote public safety and enhance quality of life in the community.

Plea bargaining and **charge bargaining** are legal negotiations between the prosecutor and the defense lawyer or the defendant to reach an agreement or compromise that avoids a court trial, conserving time and expense. The former involves negotiating how a defendant will plead to a specific charge, and the latter refers to negotiating the charge itself. An estimated 90 to 95 percent of cases are disposed of through plea and charge bargaining, not by court trial (Devers, 2011; Mangino, 2014). **Diversion** is a system operating in most states that removes juvenile status offenders and delinquents from the jurisdiction of the courts, when possible. This practice evolved because once offenders are labeled as juvenile delinquents, they may act out and perpetuate that negative role. Many individuals in the justice system consider this being "soft" on crime.

Within the courts, judges often have considerable discretion in sentencing. When the community perceives sentences as too lenient, it sparks controversy. Police officers often believe that sentences are too light for serious crimes. Issues within the corrections component of the criminal justice system include locating alternative correctional facilities within the community. These alternatives become especially controversial when a community must determine the location of the facilities. Citizens often have the **NIMBY syndrome**—that is, "not in my backyard."

A growing number of people are protesting the treatment of victims by the criminal justice system. The law enforcement community has responded to this protest in a number of ways, as discussed in Chapter 7. In addition, the debate continues on the merits and effectiveness of capital punishment as a deterrent to crime and a form of retribution.

Another controversial issue in the criminal justice system is that it has operated reactively, concentrating its efforts on fighting crime to keep the "public peace" and allowing police officers to function as armed social workers. Many believe the system has been shortsighted, focusing almost exclusively on detecting individual offenses and specific ways to eliminate each crime instead of concentrating on developing strategies to proactively attack the syndromes of crime. A **syndrome of crime** is a group of signs, causes, and symptoms that occur together to foster specific crimes. The syndromes of crime are central to problem-oriented policing, discussed in detail in Chapter 4.

CITIZEN INVOLVEMENT IN THE LAW ENFORCEMENT COMMUNITY

Once upon a time, when food resources in a village were seemingly gone, a creative individual—knowing that each person always has a little something in reserve—proposed that the community make stone soup. After setting to boil a single, simple, easy to find, albeit nutritionally void, ingredient—a stone—people in the community were asked if they had "just a little something" to improve the soup. One person found a carrot, another brought a few potatoes, another brought a bit of meat, and so on. When the soup was finished, it was thick and nourishing. Such is the situation in our communities today. Because resources are stretched to the limit, people tend to hold on to their time, talent, or money. These self-protective actions leave most groups without enough

plea bargaining
Legal negotiations between the prosecutor and the defense lawyer or the defendant to reach an agreement on how a defendant will plead to a specific charge, thus eliminating the time and expense of a trial.

charge bargaining
Legal negotiations between the prosecutor and the defense lawyer or the defendant to reach an agreement or compromise on the charge(s) the defendant will plead guilty to, thus avoiding a court trial, conserving time, and reducing expense.

diversion
The practice of removing juvenile status offenders and delinquents from the jurisdiction of the courts, when possible, in an effort to avoid stigmatization and further criminalization.

NIMBY syndrome
"Not in my backyard"; the idea that it is fine to have a halfway house—across town, not in my backyard.

syndrome of crime
A group of signs, causes, and symptoms that occur together to foster specific crimes.

resources to effectively handle community problems and have led many to suggest that it is perhaps time to adopt the "stone soup" stance of cooperation.

Community members have a high interest level in their local police departments and have been involved in a variety of ways for many years. This involvement, although it establishes important contact, should not be mistaken for community policing. It usually does not involve the partnerships and problem-solving activities of community policing.

Civilian Review Boards

The movement for citizen review has been a major political struggle for more than 40 years and remains one of the most controversial issues in police work today. Nonetheless, citizen oversight exists as an established feature within the world of U.S. policing, and there are currently more than 200 such entities throughout the country with varying powers to investigate and punish officers (Kaste, 2015).

Supporters of civilian review boards believe it is impossible for the police to objectively review actions of their colleagues and emphasize that the police culture demands that police officers support each other, even if they know something illegal has occurred. Opponents of civilian review boards stress that civilians cannot possibly understand the complexities of the policing profession and that it is demeaning to be reviewed by an external source.

Currently, most departments handle officer discipline internally, with department personnel investigating complaints against officers and determining whether misconduct occurred.

In Favor of Civilian Oversight   Citizens who demand to be involved in the review process maintain that internal police discipline is tantamount to allowing the "fox to investigate thefts in the chicken coop." According to these citizens, police protect each other and cover up improper or illegal conduct. Citizens believe that this perpetuates abuses and sends a message to brutal officers that their behavior will be shielded from public scrutiny.

In some larger cities, police have lost the power to investigate complaints against fellow officers. The trend is toward more openness and citizen involvement in these matters. Officers should assume they will be required to be more accountable for their actions. Officers may be held to a higher standard and will need to be prepared to justify their use of force in certain situations.

In Opposition to Civilian Oversight   Theoretically, citizen review boards offer an efficient and effective means of identifying officer misdeeds and reconciling them to the satisfaction of the community at large. However, although civilian review boards may be good in theory, they are often poor in reality. They frequently fail to operate objectively, lack impartial or specialized agents to conduct essential investigations, and are devoid of any enforcement power needed to carry out their recommendations. Furthermore, some people who volunteer to serve on a board are not necessarily representative of the community and, in many cases, are "vocal rabble-rousers" who wish to impose their values on the community. Some boards require police officials to sit on them as members, which may cause the perception of impartiality. Opponents to civilian review boards cite such shortcomings as reasons to do without these ineffectual entities.

Police often maintain it would be unfair to allow those outside police work to judge their actions because only police officers understand the complexities of their job and, in particular, how and when they must use force. They stress that few citizens understand such concepts as "command presence" and "verbal force," which are so often necessary in high-risk encounters. As one police sergeant put it: "The public should walk a mile in our combat boots before they judge us." Opponents also argue that police should have full responsibility for managing their own conduct just as other professionals such as physicians and lawyers do.

Striking a Balance   Successful resolution of this issue requires that the concerns of both the community and the police be addressed. The desired outcome would be that the police maintain the ability to perform their duties without the fear that they will be second-guessed, disciplined, or sued by those who do not understand the difficulties of their job. Successful oversight agencies do not simply investigate complaints; they proactively seek the underlying causes of police misconduct or problems.

The President's Task Force on 21st Century Policing considers the issue of oversight so important that is it identified as a "best practice" and highlighted as one of the main pillars necessary for strengthening community policing and trust among law enforcement officers and the communities they serve (2015, p. 26):

> **2.8 Recommendation: Some form of civilian oversight of law enforcement is important in order to strengthen trust with the community. Every community should define the appropriate form and structure of civilian oversight to meet the needs of that community.**
>
> **Many, but not all, state and local agencies operate with the oversight or input of civilian police boards or commissions. Part of the process of assessing the need and desire for new or additional civilian oversight should include input from and collaboration with police employees because the people to be overseen should be part of the process that will oversee them. This guarantees that the principles of internal procedural justice are in place to benefit both the police and the community they serve.**
>
> **We must examine civilian oversight in the communities where it operates and determine which models are successful in promoting police and community understanding. There are important arguments for having civilian oversight even though we lack strong research evidence that it works. Therefore, we urge action on further research, based on the guiding principle of procedural justice, to find evidence-based practices to implement successful civilian oversight mechanisms.**
>
> **As noted by witness Brian Buchner at the Policy and Oversight Listening Session on January 30:**
>
> > **'Citizen review is not an advocate for the community or for the police.**
> > **This impartiality allows oversight to bring stakeholders together**

> **to work collaboratively and proactively to help make policing more**
> **effective and responsive to the community. Civilian oversight alone**
> **is not sufficient to gain legitimacy; without it, however, it is difficult,**
> **if not impossible, for the police to maintain the public's trust'.**

Two action items the Task Force suggests are for the National Institute of Justice (NIJ) to expand its research agenda to include civilian oversight and for the COPS Office to provide technical assistance and collect best practices data from existing civilian oversight efforts to help other jurisdictions create these structures, potentially with some matching grants and funding (2015, p. 26).

Citizen Patrol

Community policing is rooted in law enforcement's dependence on the public's eyes, ears, information, and influence to exert social control. In some communities, citizens' attempts to be those eyes and ears have emerged in the form of citizen patrols. Some citizen patrols have formed as part of partnerships with the local police department, some independent of police partnerships, and some in the face of police opposition. It is difficult for citizen volunteers, especially those in citizen patrols formed in spite of police opposition, to win the respect, trust, and support of the police, who often have strong opinions about civilian involvement in what they consider police business or see citizens as critics of department efforts.

The Alliance of Guardian Angels, an organization that bills itself as serving communities, is controversial. Headed by a high-profile figure, Curtis Sliwa, the Angels go to communities having street crime problems and offer to patrol the streets and make citizen arrests. The members all wear red berets and are usually unarmed. Typically, citizens approve of the Guardian Angels, who they think are making their community safe. Local police, however, are not usually happy to have the Guardian Angels in their communities, often viewing them as untrained vigilantes who do not know the community, often provoke incidents, and sometimes use physical force.

Citizen patrols are not new. The sheriffs' posses that handled law enforcement in America's Wild West have evolved to present-day citizen patrols, reserve police programs, and neighborhood-watch groups. Many of the citizen patrols established throughout the country focus on the drug problem. For example, the Fairlawn Coalition in Washington, DC, established nightly patrol groups to walk the streets of Fairlawn and act as a deterrent to drug trafficking. Wearing bright orange hats, the citizen patrols drove drug dealers from their positions simply by standing out on the streets with them and later by bringing in video cameras, still cameras, and much publicity. The citizen group decided not to invite the Guardian Angels or Nation of Islam to help them, fearing their aggressive tactics could escalate into violence. They chose instead to include men and women aged 40 and older to create a presence on the street but to pose no threat to the physical well-being of dealers.

The Blockos in Manhattan, New York, used a similar approach. To combat street-level drug dealing in their middle-class neighborhood, residents held some meetings and decided to go out into the street as a group and stand near the dealers. They also had a graphic artist provide posters to announce their meetings, and a member persuaded the *New York Times* to publish a story on their efforts.

Another tactic was used in Manhattan by a group called 210 Stanton, referring to the address of a building that was headquarters of a major drug-selling operation. Community patrol officers guarded the entrances to the building, requiring all visitors to sign in. If the visitors were going to the apartment where the drug dealing was occurring, officers accompanied them. In addition, information provided by residents helped solidify the case against the resident of the apartment where most of the drug dealing was taking place. Search warrants were issued, charges filed, and the resident convicted.

In Arizona, ranchers near the Mexican border have formed the American Border Patrol (ABP), a citizens' patrol group whose goal is to help the official U.S. Border Patrol by finding and detaining illegal immigrants crossing into America from Mexico. They claim to have apprehended and turned over about 10,000 illegal immigrants to the Border Patrol in the past 8 years. Federal law enforcement agencies are not enthusiastic about the patrols. The U.S. Border Patrol does not comment on the matter but clearly is against any citizen activities beyond observing illegal activity and calling them for help.

Some citizen groups have exchange programs to reduce the chance of retribution by local drug retailers. Such exchange programs provide nearby neighborhoods with additional patrols while reducing the danger. Local dealers are less likely to recognize a vigil-keeper who lives in another neighborhood.

Town watch or neighborhood watch programs, while not necessarily the same as community patrols, often evolve from the watch programs. Approximately 20,000 town watches, comprised of roughly 5 million volunteers, currently exist throughout the nation. Their popularity has grown as police budget cutbacks have increased. According to the executive director of the National Association of Town Watches, citizens should always keep two critical things in mind: Do not get physically involved if you witness a crime and the only "weapon" you should carry is a cellphone—to call 911 and possibly document an event with video (Tribune News Service, 2012). The tragic event that took place on February 26, 2012, in Sanford, Florida, in which 28-year-old George Zimmerman shot and killed 17-year-old Trayvon Martin, underscores the danger of mixing weapons with neighborhood watch. Although Martin was unarmed, Zimmerman claimed he felt threatened by the teen and, under Florida's "stand your ground" law, shot Martin in self-defense. Zimmerman was arrested and charged with second-degree murder but was later acquitted.

Citizen Police Academies

Another type of community involvement is through citizens' police academies (CPAs) designed to familiarize citizens with law enforcement and to keep the department in touch with the community. Police academies, which are popular with police departments and citizens, have the benefit of building community support for law enforcement and of helping citizens understand the police. The typical agenda of a police academy is shown in Table 3.2.

In 1985, Orlando, Florida, hosted its first CPA and reports that it was an immediate success. Since that time more than 1,000 community-oriented citizens have graduated from the program. The program is free of charge and offered twice a year. The class lasts for 12 to 14 weeks and is held for 3 hours in the evening. Topics include uniformed patrol, special operations, criminal investigation, and youth and criminal law. The CPA also offers elective field trips to the jail and

Table 3.2 ▷▷▷	Typical Agenda of a Citizen Police Academy	
EVANSTON, ILLINOIS, POLICE DEPARTMENT		
12-WEEK COURSE OVERVIEW		
Independent	**Week 7**
• 4-Hour Ride-Along	• Use of Force
• 3-Hour Observation in 911 Communications Center	• Shoot/Don't Shoot
Week 1	**Week 8**
• History of the Police Department	• Drug Investigations
• Department Overview, Station Tour	• Gang Investigations
Week 2	**Week 9**
• Role of Prosecutor	• Juvenile Investigations
• Distinction between Civil and Criminal Law	• Drug Abuse Resistance Education (D.A.R.E.)
• Court System	**Week 10**
• Laws on Search and Seizure	• Community-Oriented Policing/Problem Solving/Community Strategies
• Citizens' Role in the Criminal Justice System	• Overview of Community Policing
• Mock Trial	• Problem-Solving Unit
Week 3	• Problem Solving
• Patrol Procedures	• Office of Professional Standards
• Concept of Preventive Patrol, Reactive vs. Proactive	**Week 11**
• Beat Boundaries, Motor and Foot Patrol	• Police Survival Skills
• Traffic Enforcement	• Martial Arts Demonstration
Week 4	**Week 12**
• Domestic Violence	• Welcome and Opening Remarks
• Youth Services	• Chief of Police Remarks
• Victim Services	• Keynote Speaker
Week 5	• Class Representative Speaker
• Evidence Technicians	• Presentation of Certificates, Class Photo, Distribution of Jackets
• Collection of Evidence	• Refreshments
• Demonstration of Crime Scene Processing	
• Fingerprinting Demonstration on Class Volunteers	
Week 6	
• Role of the Investigator	
• Major Case Investigation	
• The Use of Evidence	
• Crime Scene Processing	

Source: http://www.cityofevanston.org/police/citizen-police-academy/course-overview

a ride-along with a uniformed patrol officer. In 2000, the department hosted its first CPA for senior citizens, held at one of the senior centers during the day.

The Arlington (Texas) Police Department began a CPA for Spanish-speaking residents in 1999 and has since developed an 8-week Asian CPA designed to teach Asian residents how the department functions. Detectives explain how investigations are conducted for homicides, robberies, wrecks, juvenile crimes, and gangs.

The Palm Beach (Florida) Police Department has a Teen Police Academy for students ages 13 to 16. The program includes classroom instruction, hands-on training, and field trips. Many departments around the country have developed similar programs.

In addition to regular CPAs and CPAs for seniors, teens, and specific ethnic groups, some departments have developed alumni CPAs. Any of these endeavors can result in a large pool of willing volunteers for police department projects.

Research has found that a CPA can improve the image of the police and increase the public's willingness to cooperate (Brewster, Stoloff, & Sanders, 2005). A survey of 92 graduates from one CPA found that citizens were more educated about law enforcement, more realistic in their evaluation of media accounts, and more willing to volunteer for police projects.

Citizen Volunteers

Volunteers supplement and enhance existing or envisioned functions, allowing law enforcement professionals to do their jobs more effectively (Kolb, 2005). Volunteers can provide numerous benefits to a department, including maximizing existing resources, enhancing public safety and services, and improving community relations. Other services that volunteers may provide include fingerprinting children, patrolling shopping centers, checking on homebound residents, and checking the security of vacationing residents' homes. Clerical and data support, special event planning, search and rescue assistance, grant writing, and transporting mail between substations also can be done by volunteers.

Volunteers in Police Service (VIPS) is one of five Citizen Corps partner programs. The International Association of Chiefs of Police (IACP) manages and implements the VIPS program in partnership with, and on behalf of, the White House Office of the USA Freedom Corps and the Bureau of Justice Assistance, Office of Justice Programs, U.S. Department of Justice. The VIPS program provides support and resources for agencies interested in developing or enhancing a volunteer program and for citizens who wish to volunteer their time and skills with a community law enforcement agency. The program's ultimate goal is to enhance the capacity of state and local law enforcement to utilize volunteers.

Use of volunteers is increasing in law enforcement departments across the country. To date, more than 2,100 law enforcement agencies across the country have been tapping into the services of more than 244,000 volunteers to perform task ranging from checking the security of the residences of citizens who are out of town to assisting with solving cold cases (IACP, 2011).

Although establishing and maintaining a volunteer program is not cost free, the return on the investment can be substantial (Kolb, 2005). For example, the San Diego Police Department, in 2004, reportedly spent about $585,000 on the staffing, equipment, and management of its four volunteer programs but estimates the value of the hours contributed by volunteers at more than $2.65 million (Kolb, 2005). In another example, the Billings (Montana) Police Department was helped by volunteers doing computer work at what it estimated to be a billable value of $30,000 (Kingman, 2005). A survey by the IACP shows that VIPS programs are funded through numerous structures, including federal grants (25%), in-kind donations (16%), line item agency budgets (15%), community and corporate grants (9%), monetary donations (8%), other miscellaneous funding sources (9%), and various combinations of the preceding (18%) (IACP, 2011).

It is important to note that citizen involvement in understanding and helping to police their communities is very important, but it, in itself, is not community policing. At the heart of the community policing, philosophy is an emphasis on partnerships and on problem solving, the dual focus of the remainder of the text.

IDEAS **IN PRACTICE** — NATIONAL CRIME PREVENTION COUNCIL'S TEENS, CRIME, AND THE COMMUNITY (TCC)

Teens, Crime, and the Community is a program that believes smarter youth make safer communities. Through a combination of education and service-learning, the Teens, Crime, and the Community (TCC) initiative has motivated more than one million young people to create safer schools and communities. TCC increases social responsibility in teens, educates them about the law, reduces their potential for victimization, and engages them in making their homes, schools, and communities safer.

TCC Components

Two programs are administered under the TCC initiative:

- Community Works, a comprehensive, law-related, crime prevention curriculum
- Youth Safety Corps, the club component of the TCC initiative.

Community Works educates students about the costs and consequences of crime, their rights and responsibilities as citizens, and their ability to bring about meaningful change through advocacy and service. Community Works' 11 core lessons teach students how to examine violence and law-related issues in the context of their schools and communities and apply what they learn to real-life circumstances. Twenty additional lessons tackle important youth-related issues including underage drinking, handguns and violence, substance abuse and drug trafficking, gangs, dating violence, conflict management, and police–youth relations.

Youth Safety Corps (YSC) provides youth interested in public safety and crime prevention (such as students who have completed a *Community Works* course) an opportunity to engage in ongoing, active participation in crime prevention. Young people partner with school resource officers, school personnel, and community volunteers to assess and analyze the safety and security issues within their schools and communities that contribute to youth violence and victimization. YSC teams then address those physical and social safety issues by implementing projects, such as painting over graffiti on the walls of a school, developing presentations to teach children about bullying, or surveying students about their attitudes toward underage drinking.

Adults who work with youth can facilitate a Community Works program, a Youth Safety Corps program, or both. Both Community Works and Youth Safety Corps have been successfully implemented as separate programs in school and community settings. However, Community Works and Youth Safety Corps work best together to provide an opportunity for the continual development of knowledge and skills. Youth further develop their understanding of crime and their skills to stay safe through Community Works, and they learn leadership and team-building skills by continuing to respond to their community's various safety needs with Youth Safety Corps. Youth master knowledge and skills when knowledge is reinforced and skills are practiced and applied.

The complementary goals and service project components of Community Works and Youth Safety Corps give youth the opportunity to participate in a comprehensive initiative that provides a framework to foster resiliency and help youth develop their leadership potential.

Source: 2016 National Crime Prevention Council. http://www.ncpc.org /programs/teens-crime-and-the-community/about-tcc

SUMMARY

The U.S. Constitution and Bill of Rights, as well as federal and state statutes and local ordinances, establish the "public peace" in the United States. The social contract provides that for everyone to receive justice, each person must relinquish some freedom.

Community refers to the specific geographic area served by a police department or law enforcement agency and the individuals, organizations, and agencies within that area. Community also refers to a feeling of belonging—a sense of integration, a sense of shared values, and a sense of "we-ness." The broken windows phenomenon suggests that if it appears "no one cares," disorder and crime will thrive. In other words, there exists a long-term indirect link between disorder enforcement and a reduction in serious crime.

In order to understand a community, police must know about its demographics. Demographics include a population's size, distribution, growth, density, employment rate, ethnic makeup, and vital statistics such as average age, education, and income. Significant demographic trends shaping the population in the United States include an increasing ethnic and racial minority population and the ending of White dominance, an increasing number of legal and illegal immigrants, an increase in the elderly population, and a shrinking of the middle class.

Organizations and institutions can play a key role in enhancing community safety and quality of life. Operating within each community is a power structure that can enhance or endanger police–community relations. The formal power structure includes divisions of society with wealth and political influence: federal, state, and local agencies and governments, commissions, and regulatory agencies. The informal power structure includes religious groups, wealthy subgroups, ethnic groups, political groups, and public interest groups.

Controversial issues in the criminal justice system that affect police–community partnerships include plea bargaining, diversion, sentencing, rehabilitation, community alternatives to prisons, victims' rights, and capital punishment.

Citizen involvement in the law enforcement community and in understanding policing has taken the form of civilian review boards, citizen patrols, citizen police academies, ride-alongs, and similar programs.

DISCUSSION QUESTIONS

1. How would you describe your community?

2. What instances of broken windows have you seen in your neighborhood? Other neighborhoods?

3. Can you give examples of the NIMBY syndrome?

4. What major changes have occurred in your community in the past 10 years? In your state?

5. Who is included in the power structure in your community?

6. What barriers hamper community involvement in poor neighborhoods?

7. How extensively are the services of private security used in your community? Do they cooperate with or compete against the local police?

8. Do you favor the use of civilian review boards? Why or why not?

9. Which seems more "just" to you: retributive justice or restorative justice?

10. What factors are most important in establishing a "sense of community"?

Problem Solving: Proactive Policing

Learning Objectives

LO1 Explain how problem solving requires changes in the ways police treat incidents.

LO2 Compare and contrast efficiency and effectiveness, noting which one community policing emphasizes.

LO3 Identify the first step in a problem-solving approach.

LO4 Describe the four stages of problem solving used in the SARA model.

LO5 Summarize the purpose and goal of the DOC model.

LO6 Explain what the focus of crime mapping is.

Key Terms

analysis (in SARA)
assessment (in SARA)
DOC model
effectiveness
efficiency
entrapment
geographic information system (GIS)
geographic profiling
hot spots
impact evaluation
incident
least-effort principle
magnet phenomenon
mediation
problem-oriented policing (POP)
problem-solving approach
process evaluation
qualitative data
quantitative data
response (in SARA)
routine activity theory
scanning (in SARA)

Halloween celebrations in Madison, Wisconsin, have historically been impressive 3-day festivities, culminating on the Saturday closest to Halloween, and encompassing the area from the University of Wisconsin all the way to the state capitol via State Street. What began in the late 1970s as a community celebration had developed in recent years into a chaotic and disorderly event with rampant underage drinking and property destruction. When the traditional Madison Halloween festivities began to take on a more criminal atmosphere, the Madison Police Department (MPD) turned to the SARA model of problem solving—scanning, analysis, response, assessment—to identify underlying incidents that inspired the appearance of criminality in certain hot spots.

Scanning for the problem zone during the festivities was primarily on State Street, the main thoroughfare connecting the University of Wisconsin-Madison to the state capitol. Here, the MPD used data captured through police officer body cameras and other cameras posted throughout the event area to determine that the source of the criminality was primarily intoxicated 18–25 year old White males who were associated with the university. In the analysis portion of the exercise, the MPD found that these individuals were often responsible for bringing alcohol to the event, that not all of the trouble makers were arrested, those individuals who were arrested were not immediately removed from the scene, there was no official time determined for concluding the event, and that there was inadequate police coverage to effectively regulate the area.

In response to these problems, the MPD and surrounding community decided to improve police reaction in the following ways: hold discussions with community groups concerning behavioral expectations during the event, effectively establish the date of the event, increase police staff, modify the arrest policy, establish a logistics team to remove offenders from the area, increase lighting, remove potential targets or objects that could be used to cause property damage, enforce a glass ban limited to the time and place, utilize GIS technology to evaluate hot spots, and determine an ending time for the event with a concluding activity (i.e., concert) to make it easier to officially terminate the event.

Upon assessment of the event with the suggested improvements, MPD found there were many indicators marking the Halloween celebration as a success. Community leaders reported a decrease in property damage, injuries to event attendees were lessened, no police officers reported injuries, hot spots were effectively targeted, and partygoers dispersed at the planned time. Arrests still occurred, but they were conducted in a far more efficient manner.

Using a problem-oriented policing approach, the Madison Police Department was able to restore its traditional community event from one of chaos to one of controlled entertainment. For police departments to be effective, innovative thinkers are necessary to integrate minor changes for major results.

INTRODUCTION

problem-solving approach
Involves proactively identifying problems and making decisions about how best to deal with them.

A **problem-solving approach** involves identifying problems and making decisions about how best to deal with them. A basic characteristic of community policing is that it is proactive rather than reactive, meaning it involves recognizing problems and seeking their underlying causes.

To illustrate, a man and his buddy, who could not swim, were fishing on a riverbank when a young boy floated past, struggling to stay afloat. The fisherman jumped in and pulled the young boy from the water. He resumed his fishing, but within a few minutes another person came floating by, again struggling to stay afloat. Again, the fisherman reacted by jumping in and pulling the person to safety. He then resumed his fishing and again, within minutes, another person came floating by. The fisherman got up and started heading upstream. His buddy called after him, "Where are you going?" To which the fisherman replied, "I'm going to find out who's pushing all these people into the river!" It is usually more effective to get to the source of a problem rather than simply react to it.

AP Images/Gary Kazanjian

Families living in poverty may find themselves trapped by their economic circumstances, unable to afford to move away from threatened neighborhoods. Although law enforcement cannot be expected to solve all of a community's problems, a proactive response to a neighborhood's social challenges, and an effort to partner with other community agencies, can help thwart future crime and disorder issues.

WHAT IS PROBLEM-ORIENTED POLICING?

Herman Goldstein, a pioneer of problem-oriented policing (POP), is credited with coining the term and describes it as follows:

> Problem-oriented policing is an approach to policing in which discrete pieces of police business (each consisting of a cluster of similar incidents, whether crime or acts of disorder, that the police are expected to handle) are subject to microscopic examination (drawing on the especially honed skills of crime analysts and the accumulated experience of operating field personnel) in hopes that what is freshly learned about each problem will lead to discovering a new and more effective strategy for dealing with it. Problem-oriented policing places a high value on new responses that are preventive in nature, that are not dependent on the use of the criminal justice system, and that engage other public agencies, the community and the private sector when their involvement has the potential for significantly contributing to the reduction of the problem. Problem-oriented policing carries a commitment to implementing the new strategy, rigorously evaluating its effectiveness, and, subsequently, reporting the results in ways that will benefit other police agencies and that will ultimately contribute to building a body of knowledge that supports the further professionalization of the police[1]. (Goldstein, 2001)

Eck and Spelman (1987, p. xv) define **problem-oriented policing (POP)** more concisely as "a departmental-wide strategy aimed at solving persistent community problems. Police identify, analyze, and respond to the underlying circumstances that create incidents."

problem-oriented policing (POP)
A department-wide strategy aimed at solving persistent community problems by grouping incidents to identify problems and to determine possible underlying causes.

[1] Source: Reprinted by permission of the POP Center.

To fully understand problem-oriented policing, one must have a grasp of how a *problem* is defined.

Problem Defined

Goldstein (1990, p. 66) defines a problem as "a cluster of similar, related, or recurring incidents rather than a single incident, a substantive community concern, and a unit of police business." Identifying the problems in a community allows police to focus their efforts on addressing the possible causes of such problems.

A variation on this definition is that "a problem is a recurring set of related harmful events in a community that members of the public expect the police to address" (Clarke and Eck, 2005, p. 26). This definition draws attention to the six required elements of a problem captured by the acronym CHEERS: *c*ommunity, *h*arm, *e*xpectation, *e*vents, *r*ecurring, and *s*imilarity.

Community includes individuals, businesses, government agencies, and other groups. Only some community members need to experience the problem. *Harm* can involve property loss or damage, noise complaints, or serious crime. Illegality is not a required characteristic of problems (Clarke & Eck, 2005). *Expectation* should never be presumed but must be shown through such processes as citizen calls, press reports, or other means. *Events* must be discrete, describable incidents; most are brief. *Recurring* events—that is, events that happen more than a few times—may be symptomatic of acute or chronic problems. An acute problem appears suddenly and may dissipate quickly, even if nothing is done. Or it may become a chronic problem, persisting for a long time if nothing is done. *Similarity* means the recurring events must have something in common—for example, the same type of victim, same location, same time, similar circumstances, or the like. Common crime classifications are usually not helpful.

From Incidents to Problems

Goldstein (1990, p. 20) was among the first to criticize the professional model of policing as being incident driven: "In the vast majority of police departments, the telephone, more than any policy decision by the community or by management, continues to dictate how police resources will be used." The primary work unit in the professional model is the **incident**—that is, an isolated event that requires a police response. The institution of the 911 emergency call system has greatly increased the demand for police services and the public's expectation that the police will respond quickly.

incident
An isolated event that requires a police response; the primary work unit in the professional model.

Goldstein (1990) asserts that most policing efforts are directed at improving the overt, offensive symptoms of a problem. He suggests that police are more productive if they respond to incidents as symptoms of underlying community problems.

During the past quarter century, law enforcement agencies around the country have combined the operational strategies of community-oriented policing and problem solving to address crime and quality-of-life issues.

Throughout this text, references to community policing infer that problem solving is involved.

Although problem solving may be the ideal, law enforcement cannot ignore specific incidents. When calls come in, most police departments respond as soon as possible. Problem solving has a dual focus. First, it requires that incidents be linked to problems. Second, time devoted to "preventive" patrol must be spent proactively, determining community problems and their underlying causes.

Regardless of whether police officers respond to incidents, seek symptoms of problems, or both, the public can help or hinder their efforts. Police and community members must discuss and agree to any community involvement program before it is adopted. At times, well-meaning individuals and community groups, acting unilaterally, can actually interfere with a police effort and cause unnecessary destruction, injury, and even death.

The dual themes of this book are the manner in which police can form effective partnerships with the community to address the issues of crime and disorder and the necessity of a problem-solving approach to such issues. Like any response, the problem-solving process will not always result in success. In fact, mistakes should be expected and seen as learning opportunities. If no mistakes are made, then little problem solving is taking place.

> **L01**
>
> Problem-solving policing requires police to group incidents and identify the underlying causes of problems in the community.

Problem-Oriented Policing and Community Policing

Problem solving has been one of the three key components of community policing since it was introduced, but confusion between problem-oriented policing and community policing occasionally exists; some practitioners view the two as opposing approaches, while others equate community policing and problem solving. As Wilson and Kelling (1989, p. 49) explain: "Community-oriented policing means changing the daily work of the police to include investigating problems as well as incidents. It means defining as a problem whatever a significant body of public opinion regards as a threat to community order. It means working with the good guys, and not just against the bad guys."

The importance of problem-oriented policing to community policing is evidenced by the launching and funding of the Center for Problem-Oriented Policing (POP Center) by the COPS Office and its partners. All police can benefit from a POP approach, including those who embrace community policing, because the two approaches are compatible.

Although Goldstein has suggested that community involvement is a positive development, he believes problem-oriented policing relies mostly on police participants. In addition, Goldstein's model emphasizes problem solving over partnerships. The differences between community policing and problem-oriented policing are summarized in Table 4.1.

THE POP CENTER

The mission of the Center for Problem-Oriented Policing is to advance the concept and practice of problem-oriented policing in open and democratic societies. It does so by making readily accessible information about ways in which police can more effectively address specific crime and disorder problems.

The Center for Problem-Oriented Policing is a non-profit organization comprising affiliated police practitioners, researchers, and universities dedicated to the advancement of problem-oriented policing.

Since the publication of the first POP Guide in 2001, over 900,000 copies of the POP guides and other POP Center publications have been distributed by the U.S. Department of Justice Office of Community Oriented Policing Services (COPS Office) to individuals and agencies throughout the world. POP Center materials are also widely used in police training and college courses.

Launched in 2003, the POP Center Web site has provided innovative learning experiences, curriculum guides, teaching aids, problem analysis tools, and an immense range of information to its users. Among the many ongoing accomplishments of the POP Center Web site are:

- Tens of thousands of visitors to the POP Center Web site read and download its content each month.
- The POP Center Web site was awarded the 2005 APEX Grand Award for Publication Excellence in Web & Intranet Sites. Wrote the judges: "Superbly researched and written reports clearly convey useful, actionable information in this easily-navigable, well-designed site."
- The POP Center Web site was awarded a League of American Communications Professional 2005 Spotlight Award for Web sites.

Source: http://www.popcenter.org/about/
Reprinted by permission of the POP Center.

Table 4.1	Selected Comparisons between Problem-Oriented Policing and Community Policing Principles	
Principle	**Problem-Oriented Policing**	**Community Policing**
Primary emphasis	Substantive social problems within police mandate	Engaging the community in the policing process
When police and community collaborate	Determined on a problem-by-problem basis	Always or nearly always
Emphasis on problem analysis	Highest priority given to thorough analysis	Encouraged, but less important than community collaboration
Preference for responses	Strong preference that alternatives to criminal law enforcement be explored	Preference for collaborative response with community
Role for police in organizing and mobilizing community	Advocated only if warranted within the context of the specific problem being addressed	Emphasizes strong role for police
Importance of geographic decentralization of police and continuity of officer assignment to community	Preferred, but not essential	Essential
Degree to which police share decision-making authority with community	Strongly encourages input from community while preserving ultimate decision-making authority to police	Emphasizes sharing decision-making authority with community
Emphasis on officers' skills	Emphasizes intellectual and analytic skills	Emphasizes interpersonal skills
View of the role or mandate of police	Encourages broad, but not unlimited, role for police, stresses limited capacities of police, and guards against creating unrealistic expectations of police	Encourages expansive role for police to achieve ambitious social objectives

Source: Michael S. Scott. *Problem-Oriented Policing: Reflections on the First 20 Years.* Washington, DC: U.S. Department of Justice, Office of Community Oriented Policing Services, 2000, p. 99.

In Summary: The Key Elements of Problem-Oriented Policing

Problem-solving experts have identified the following key elements of POP (Eck & Spelman, 1987; Scott & Goldstein, 1988; Goldstein, 1990):

- *Group incidents as problems.* A problem, rather than a crime, a case, a call, or an incident, is the basic unit of police work.

- *Focus on problems of concern to the public.* A problem is something that concerns or causes harm to citizens, not just the police. Things that concern only police officers are important, but they are not problems in this sense of the term.

- *Focus on substantive problems as the heart of policing.* Addressing problems means more than quick fixes; it means dealing with conditions that create problems.

- *Use systematic inquiry.* Police officers must routinely and systematically analyze problems before trying to solve them, just as they routinely and systematically investigate crimes before making an arrest. Individual officers and the department as a whole must develop routines and systems for analyzing problems. Make full use of the data in police files and the experience of police personnel.

- *The analysis of problems must be thorough but it may not need to be complicated.* This principle is as true for problem analysis as it is for criminal investigation.

- *Avoid using overly broad labels in grouping incidents, so separate problems can be identified.* Problems must be described precisely and accurately, and specific aspects of each problem must be identified. Problems often are not what they first appear to be.

- *Identify multiple interests in any one problem and weigh them when analyzing the value of different responses.* Problems must be understood in terms of the various interests at stake. Individuals and groups of people are affected in different ways by a problem and have different ideas about what should be done about the problem.

- *Capture and critique the current response.* The way the problem is currently being handled must be understood and the limits of effectiveness must be openly acknowledged in order to come up with a better response. Acknowledge the limits of the criminal justice system as a response to problems.

- *Encourage a broad and uninhibited search for solutions.* Initially, any and all possible responses to a problem should be considered so as not to cut short potentially effective responses. Suggested responses should follow from what is learned during the analysis. They should not be limited to, nor rule out, the use of arrest.

- *Adopt a proactive stance.* The police must proactively try to solve problems rather than just react to the harmful consequences of problems.

- *Strengthen the decision-making processes and increase accountability.* The police department must increase police officers' freedom to make or participate in important decisions. At the same time, officers must be accountable for their decision making.

- *Evaluate results of newly implemented responses.* The effectiveness of new responses must be evaluated, so these results can be shared with other police officers and so the department can systematically learn what does and does not work[2].

Finally, the experts acknowledge that while it is acceptable to take some risks in responding to problems, effectiveness must be sought as the ultimate goal.

BEING EFFICIENT AND EFFECTIVE

A problem-solving approach to policing was developed partially in response to concerns for efficiency and effectiveness. Wilson and Kelling (1989, p. 46) illustrate the consequences when emphasis is placed on efficiency:

> The police know from experience what research by Glenn Pierce, in Boston, and Lawrence Sherman, in Minneapolis, has established: Fewer than 10 percent of the addresses from which the police receive calls account for more than 60 percent of those calls. If each call is treated as a separate incident with neither a history nor a future, then each dispute will be handled by police officers anxious to pacify the complainants and get back on patrol as quickly as possible. . . .
>
> A study of domestic homicides in Kansas City showed that in eight out of ten cases the police had been called to the incident address at least once before; in half the cases they had been called five times or more.

efficiency

Minimizing waste, expense, or unnecessary effort; results in a high ratio of output to input; doing things right.

effectiveness

Producing the desired result or goal; doing the right things.

Efficiency involves minimizing waste, expense, or unnecessary effort. Efficiency is doing things right. The police in the preceding studies were very efficient, responding promptly and dealing with the problem, usually to the citizen's satisfaction. But were they effective? And if they are not effective, efficiency does not really pay off. Making the same efficient responses to the same location is *not* really efficient. The response needs to be effective as well.

Effectiveness is a measure of how well the response produces the desired result or goal. Effectiveness is doing the right thing. Ideally, both efficiency and effectiveness are present in policing. There can be effectiveness without efficiency, but there cannot be efficiency without effectiveness, because any effort that does not achieve the desired goal is wasted.

LO2

Efficiency, doing things right, has been the traditional emphasis in law enforcement. Effectiveness, doing the right things, is the emphasis in community policing. Effectiveness should produce an increase in efficiency, because officers are proactively solving problems rather than simply reacting to them.

Police, along with other emergency services, face an inherent contradiction between effectiveness and efficiency. There must be enough staff available to respond to emergencies quickly at all times. Having this capacity, however, means that a number of personnel must have a substantial amount of slack time. Without slack time, all personnel may be busy when emergencies occur, reducing response effectiveness. Unfortunately, too often police departments have emphasized efficiency—for example, rapid response to calls, number of citations issued, and the like—rather than effectiveness, or what will produce the desired outcomes of the department.

Across the country, most police departments respond in a timely manner to every call for service. Just one example of this policy illustrates how efficiency can overshadow effectiveness as well as the magnet phenomenon.

---

[2] Source: Adapted from Scott & Goldstein (1988). Reprinted by permission of the POP Center.

The **magnet phenomenon** occurs when a phone number or address is associated with a crime simply because it was a convenient number or address to use.

Addressing Substantive Problems

Traditionally, police have responded to incidents, handled them as effectively as possible, and then moved on to the next call. This fragmented approach to policing conceals patterns of incidents that may be symptomatic of deeper problems: "The first step in problem-oriented policing is to move beyond just handling incidents. It calls for recognizing that incidents are often merely overt symptoms of problems" (Goldstein, 1990, p. 33).

A focus on substantive problems (effectiveness) rather than on the smooth functioning of the organization (efficiency) is a radical change and difficult for some departments to make. Those departments that have made the shift in focus have achieved excellent results.

LO3
The first step in problem solving is to group incidents as problems.

Common Mistakes in Problem Solving

Recall the statement made earlier in the chapter: The problem-solving process will not always result in success, and mistakes should be expected and seen as learning opportunities. If no mistakes are made, then little problem solving is taking place. Some mistakes, however, can and should be avoided because they signal procedural problems and inefficiencies that impede actual forward progress in solving a problem. For example, common mistakes in problem solving include spending too much energy on unimportant details, failing to resolve important issues, having a closed mind, being secretive about true feelings, and not expressing ideas. Other mistakes commonly made during problem solving include making multiple decisions about the same problem, finding the right decision for the wrong problem (i.e., dealing with symptoms rather than causes), failing to consider the costs, delaying a decision, and making decisions while angry or excited. When evaluating a decision made during a problem-solving brainstorming session, ask: Is the decision consistent with the agency's mission, goals, and objectives? Is it a long-term solution? Is it cost-effective? Is it legal, ethical, and practical? Is it acceptable to those responsible for implementing it?

THE SARA MODEL: A FOUR-STAGE PROBLEM-SOLVING PROCESS

The basic elements in a problem-solving approach combine steps a police department can take and theoretical assumptions to make the steps work. Many departments have developed problem-solving approaches that incorporate these basic elements. One of the best known problem-solving approaches is the SARA model, a four-stage problem-solving process first used in the Newport News (Virginia) Police Department (Eck & Spelman, 1987).

Scanning refers to identifying recurring problems and prioritizing them to select one problem to address. The problems should be of concern to the public as well as the police. At this stage, broad goals may be set.

LO4
The four stages of the SARA problem-solving model are scanning, analysis, response, and assessment.

analysis (in SARA)
Examines the identified problem's causes, scope, and effects; includes determining how often the problem occurs and how long it has been occurring, as well as conditions that appear to create the problem.

response (in SARA)
Acting to alleviate the problem, that is, selecting the alternative solution or solutions.

assessment (in SARA)
Refers to evaluating how effective the intervention was; was the problem solved?

qualitative data
Examine the excellence (quality) of the response, that is, how satisfied were the officers and the citizens; most frequently determined by surveys, focus groups, or tracking complaints and compliments.

quantitative data
Examine the amount of change (quantity) as a result of the response; most frequently measured by before-and-after data.

2nd **Analysis** examines the identified problem's causes, scope, and effects. It includes determining how often the problem occurs, how long it has been occurring, and what conditions appear to create the problem. Analysis also should include potential resources and partners who might assist in understanding and addressing the problem.

3rd **Response** is acting to alleviate the problem—that is, selecting the alternative solution or solutions to try. This may include finding out what other communities with similar problems have tried and with what success and looking at whether any research on the problem exists. Focus groups might be used to brainstorm possible interventions. Experts might be enlisted. Several alternatives might be ranked and prioritized according to difficulty, expense, and the like. At this point, goals are usually refined and interventions implemented.

4th **Assessment** refers to evaluating the effectiveness of the intervention. Was the problem solved? If not, why? Assessment should include both qualitative and quantitative data. **Qualitative data** examine the excellence (quality) of the response—that is, how satisfied were the officers and the citizens? This is most frequently determined by surveys, focus groups, or tracking complaints and compliments. **Quantitative data** examine the amount of change (quantity) as a result of the response. This is most frequently measured by before-and-after-response data.

The SARA model of problem solving stresses that there are no failures, only responses that do not provide the desired goal. When a response does not give the desired results, the partners involved in problem solving can examine the results and try a different response. Other communities might benefit from what was learned.

Scanning and Analysis

Scanning and analysis are integrally related. The sources for analyzing a community's problems provide the basis for analysis. Potential sources of information for identifying problems—beyond the internal sources of patrol, investigations, vice, communications, and records, the crime analysis unit, the chief's office, and other law enforcement agencies—include elected officials, local government agencies, community leaders, business groups, schools, neighborhood-watch groups, newspapers, and other media and community surveys. Comprehensively analyzing a problem is critical to the success of a problem-solving effort. Effective, tailor-made responses cannot be developed unless one knows what is causing the problem (Office of Community Oriented Policing Services, 2011).

This step in the SARA model is often skipped for a variety of reasons. Sometimes it is because at first the nature of the problem seems obvious or because there is pressure to solve the problem immediately. Taking the time for analysis may be seen as too time consuming without producing tangible results, especially when responding to calls seems to preclude this type of activity. If not done, however, there is a chance of addressing a nonexistent problem or of applying ineffective solutions.

The COPS Office (Office of Community Oriented Policing Services, 2011, p. 14) suggests: "The first step in analysis is to determine what information is needed. This should be a broad inquiry, uninhibited by past perspectives. Questions should be asked whether or not answers can be obtained. The openness and persistent probing associated with such an inquiry are not unlike the approach that a seasoned and highly regarded detective would take to solve a puzzling crime: reaching out in all directions, digging deeply, asking the right questions."

The problem analysis triangle (sometimes called the crime triangle) illustrates how crime or disorder results when (1) likely offenders and (2) suitable targets come together in time and space (3) in the absence of capable guardians (recall the routine activity theory discussed in Chapter 3). These three elements comprise the core of the triangle. Offenders can sometimes be controlled by other people, called handlers. Targets and victims can sometimes be protected by other people, called guardians. And places are usually controlled by certain people, called managers. These three control mechanisms comprise the outer perimeter of the crime triangle. Effective problem solving requires understanding how offenders, targets/victims, and places are or are not effectively controlled.

Problem solvers are advised to discover as much as possible about all three sides of the triangle as they relate to the problem by asking about each side: Who? What? When? Where? How? Why? and Why not?

Studies have shown that a small number of victims account for a large amount of crime and that effective interventions targeted at repeat victims can significantly reduce crime. Researchers in England found that victims of burglary, domestic violence, and other crimes are likely to be revictimized very soon after the first victimization—often within a month or two. Data from one study of residential burglary in West Yorkshire, England, showed that burglary victims were four times more likely than nonvictims to be victimized again, and the majority of repeat burglaries occurred within 6 weeks of the first (Office of Community Oriented Policing Services, 2011). To address this problem, the local police division tailored a three-tiered response to repeat burglary victims, based on the number of times their homes had been burglarized. Initial evaluation of the response indicated that residential burglaries had decreased by more than 20 percent with no crime displacement to adjacent neighborhoods. Recall from Chapter 3 that displacement is the theory that successful implementation of a crime-reduction initiative does not really prevent crime. Instead, it just moves the crime to the next block, neighborhood, or city. Police databases are not designed to track repeat victims, so police in the West Yorkshire project had some difficulty tracking repeat victims.

To assist in problem analysis, the Newport News (Virginia) Police Department developed a problem analysis guide that lists topic headings police should consider in assessing problems. Their problem analysis guide highlights the complex interaction of individuals, incidents, and responses occurring within a social context and a physical setting. The problems that Newport News police identified and their ways of approaching them are discussed later in the chapter.

Responses by Law Enforcement

Numerous studies, as well as simple observation, make clear that there is great variety in the way different officers respond to the same type of incident or problem. However, many police responses are fairly routinized and follow a rather uniform pattern that has been established over time by the specific agency or unit in which the officer works (Goldstein & Susmilch, 1981). The most prevalent law enforcement response to identified problems is generally increased use of conventional strategies such as enforcement and patrol (Bichler & Gaines, 2005).

Assessing Responses to Problems

Eck asserts that the assessment stage actually starts at the beginning of the process: "The evaluation builds throughout the SARA process, culminates during the assessment, and provides findings that help you determine if you should revisit earlier stages to improve the response" (2002, p. 6). Figure 4.1 illustrates the problem-solving process and evaluation.

Two types of evaluations should be conducted: **Process evaluation** determines if the response was implemented as planned, and **impact evaluation** determines if the problem declined (Eck, 2002). Table 4.2 provides guidance in interpreting the results of process and impact evaluation.

Several nontraditional measures will indicate if a problem has been affected by the interventions (Eck, 2002, p. 27):

- Reduced instances of repeat victimization
- Decreases in related crimes or incidents
- Neighborhood indicators
  - increased profits for legitimate businesses in target area
  - increased use of area/increased (or reduced) foot and vehicular traffic

process evaluation
Determines if the response was implemented as planned.

impact evaluation
Determines if the problem declined.

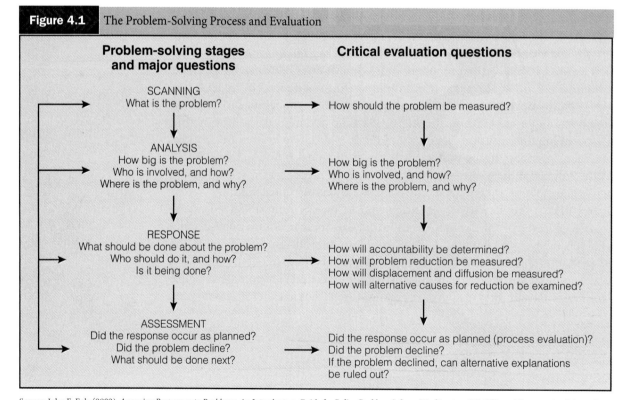

| Figure 4.1 | The Problem-Solving Process and Evaluation |

Source: John E. Eck. (2002). *Assessing Responses to Problems: An Introductory Guide for Police Problem-Solvers.* Washington, DC: Office of Community Oriented Policing Services, p. 6.

Table 4.2	Interpreting Results of Process and Impact Evaluations		
		Process Evaluation Results	
		Response implemented as planned, or nearly so	Response not implemented, or implemented in a radically different manner than planned
Impact Evaluation Results	Problem declined	A. Evidence that the response caused the decline	C. Suggests that other factors may have caused the decline, or that the response was accidentally effective
	Problem did not decline	B. Evidence that the response was ineffective, and that a different response should be tried	D. Little is learned; perhaps if the response had been implemented as planned, the problem would have declined, but this is speculative

Source: John E. Eck. (2002). *Assessing Responses to Problems: An Introductory Guide for Police Problem-Solvers.* Washington, DC: Office of Community Oriented Policing Services, p. 10.

- increased property values
- improved neighborhood appearance
- increased occupancy in problem buildings
- less loitering
- fewer abandoned cars
- less truancy
- Increased citizen satisfaction regarding the handling of the problem, which can be determined through surveys, interviews, focus groups, electronic bulletin boards, and the like
- Reduced citizen fear related to the problem

CRITICAL THINKING WHAT WOULD YOU DO?

For years, a convenience store across the street from a high school had been a magnet for high school students during the three lunch periods at the open-campus school. The store complained of disturbances, thefts, and intimidation of customers. Other businesses complained about "spillover" from student gatherings that affected their businesses. The grocery store experienced shoplifting; the dry cleaner had students smoking in the back of his building; and they all complained about drug sales at the bus stop at that intersection. Nearby residential neighbors complained about cigarette butts and empty soda cans littering their yards after lunch each day. Everyone disliked the loud music played on car stereos throughout the lunch periods. Every day one or more people called the police department to complain. And every day the police department dispatched one or two squad cars.

Often the squads reported everything was quiet when they arrived. Lunchtime had ended, and the students had returned to school. Or if there was still a problem, the students scattered when they saw the police, and no action was necessary. Nearly every school day, for years, these same calls came into the police department. The police response was polite and quick. By police department standards, their response was efficient. By neighborhood standards, the police response was completely ineffective.

What Would You Do?

? Using the SARA model, how would you approach this problem? Outline what you would do at each step of the process. Be prepared to explain why your recommended action is not the typical reactive police response.

TECHNOLOGY IN COMMUNITY POLICING

ENHANCING COMMUNITY POLICING THROUGH GPS TRACKING TECHNOLOGY

The Redlands (California) Police Department (RPD) has implemented a GPS tracking program as a way to address community crime trends and strengthen the public's trust that the police are dedicated to addressing all levels of crime. The ultimate goal of the program is to enhance RPD's community policing efforts and promote police legitimacy.

The problem facing RPD was how to respond to citizens' concerns about property theft and revictimization, considering that research has found that those who have been crime victims once have a higher likelihood of being victimized again:

> The majority of Redlands residents' and business owners' criminal concerns seem to focus around their fear that their property will be stolen when they are not home, when their business is closed, or when their vehicles are left unattended. . . . [E]ven when property is protected by cameras and alarms, criminals often are successful in stealing the targeted items. . . .
>
> When residents and business owners become victims of property crime, there is a natural fear that the criminals will

return and re-victimize them, not to mention the disgust that they feel knowing that somebody violated their personal space. In the past, first responders have been limited to simply making suggestions on how victims can harden the target or install security measures to deter the suspects from returning. . . .

Now, when patrol and community service officers conduct the initial crime investigation, they can offer victims the opportunity to partner with the police department and set up a specialized electronic stakeout in an attempt to apprehend the suspects who victimized them.

Suspects often return to the same location to commit additional crimes, or they may share their success with other people who are intent on driving up the crime rates. In many of the arrests made by RPD, detectives have learned the suspects arrested during the tracker activations were responsible for the crime that initiated the tracker deployment.

Since the program began, RPD has acquired 27 motion-activated GPS tracking devices, 20 of which were purchased with asset forfeiture funds and seven of which were privately funded. Deployment of these GPS tracking devices has led to 140 arrests for crimes involving armed robbery, vehicle burglary, commercial burglary, bike theft, laptop theft, metal theft, and theft from a cemetery. While such arrests are a tangible measure of the program's success, the more valuable result is the appreciation expressed by the community's residents and business owners and the empowerment citizens feel by partnering with law enforcement in an effort to keep the community safe and crime free, partnerships that have enhanced community policing and promoted police legitimacy. The GPS tracking program is now being replicated at police departments across the nation.

Source: Office of Community Oriented Policing Services. (2015, May). "Enhancing Community Policing through GPS Tracking Technology." *Community Policing Dispatch, 8(5)*. Retrieved July 20, 2016 from http://cops.usdoj.gov/html/dispatch/05-2015/enhancing_cp_through_gps.asp

The SARA Model in Action

The Herman Goldstein Award for Excellence in Problem-Oriented Policing was established in 1993, honoring Professor Herman Goldstein for conceiving and developing the theory of problem-oriented policing. This award is given to innovative, effective POP projects that have demonstrated measurable success in reducing specific crime, disorder, or public safety problems. The Herman Goldstein Award is discussed in more detail later in this chapter.

The 1998 award winner was Operation Cease Fire, Boston Police Department (Brito & Allan, 1999, pp. 328–339). This classic exemplary model has had a tremendous impact on police departments across the country, being replicated and adapted nationwide.

Scanning   In 1987, Boston had 22 victims of youth homicide. In 1990, that figure had increased 230 percent to 73 victims. Police were responding to six or seven shootings every night and were becoming overwhelmed. For many of Boston's youths, the city had become a dangerous, even deadly, place. This situation led to the formation of a gun project working group.

The working group's line-level personnel believed the gun violence problem was a gang problem, because most victims and offenders were gang members and because the worst offenders in the cycle of fear, gun acquisition, and gun use were gang members. Another aspect of the problem identified was that many of the involved youths were not "bad" or inherently dangerous but were participating because gang membership had become a vital means of self-protection.

Analysis   A team of Harvard University researchers framed the relevant issues in gun-market terms. Gun trafficking and other means of illegal firearm acquisition represented the supply side, whereas fear and other factors potentially driving illicit gun acquisition and use represented the demand side. Research techniques included geographic mapping of youth homicides, gathering of criminal histories of youth homicide victims and offenders, analyzing the gun market using Boston Police Department and Bureau of Alcohol, Tobacco, and Firearms gun recovery and tracing data, and collecting hospital emergency room data. Key findings of this research included the following:

- Most youth gun and knife homicides and woundings occurred in three specific neighborhoods.
- Of the 1,550 firearms recovered from youths, 52.1 percent were semiautomatic pistols.
- Trace analysis revealed that 34 percent of traceable firearms recovered from youths were first sold at retail establishments in Massachusetts.
- Of all traceable guns recovered from youths, 26 percent were less than 2 years old and, thus, almost certainly trafficked rather than stolen.
- Nearly 20 percent of all guns recovered from youths had obliterated serial numbers, suggesting they were relatively new "trafficked" guns.
- Of the 155 youth gun and knife homicide victims, 75 percent had been arraigned for at least one offense in Massachusetts courts.
- Boston had roughly 61 gangs with 1,300 members in the three high-risk neighborhoods previously identified. Although this represented less than 3 percent of the youths ages 14 to 24 in these neighborhoods, these gangs were responsible for at least 60 percent of Boston's youth homicides.

Response   The working group devised a two-pronged response known as Operation Cease Fire. The first prong involved mounting a direct law enforcement attack on illicit gun trafficking by (1) using trace information to identify gun traffickers and (2) systematically debriefing gang offenders facing serious charges for violent, drug, and other crimes.

The second, and perhaps more important, prong involved creating a powerful deterrent to gang-related violence by making clear to youths that future violence would result in a certain and severe crackdown on the gang and impose "costs" on the entire gang, not just the shooter. Such "costs" might include cash-flow problems caused by street-drug market disruption, arrests from outstanding warrants, the humiliation of strict probation enforcement, and possibly severe sanctions brought by federal involvement. The working group's familiarity with local gangs enabled them to link, with a high degree of accuracy, a particular act of violence to a certain gang relatively quickly and dispense sanctions swiftly. Operation Cease Fire transformed the police response to violence, turning uncertain, slow, and often mild responses into ones that were certain, rapid, and of whatever severity the working group deemed appropriate.

Assessment In the first 2 years of Operation Cease Fire, youth homicides dropped roughly 70 percent. Between 50 and 60 percent of the residents in the three identified high-risk neighborhoods felt satisfied that the Boston Police Department was doing all it could to reduce area crime, and more than 33 percent of those residents reported a great deal of confidence in the department's ability to prevent crime (an increase from the 1995 average of 10 percent). Citywide, 76 percent of residents felt safe alone in their neighborhoods at night, compared with 55 percent in 1995. Perhaps the most significant result was that 88 percent of residents said they would be willing to work with each other and police to reduce and prevent crime—a noteworthy result because Operation Cease Fire not only achieved its goal but did so ethically.

LO5

The **DOC model** (dilemmas–options–consequences) challenges officers to carefully consider their decisions and the short- and long-term consequences of those decisions. The goal is to fuse problem solving and morality.

DOC model

Dilemmas–Options–Consequences challenges officers to carefully consider their decisions and the short- and long-term consequences of those decisions, with the goal of fusing problem solving and morality.

MAKING ETHICAL DECISIONS

Ethical policing is essential if law enforcement is to rebuild and maintain the public's trust. Choosing an ethical course of action often requires comprehensive and purposeful thought and can be facilitated by using the DOC model.

After a dilemma is identified, an action is needed, leading to the options phase and questions such as: What are my options? Am I considering all options? Am I being open-minded and creative? Do my options rely on only me, or could I use a resource or someone's help? Whose?

For each choice, officers must assess the consequences by asking: What happens because of my choice? What if I do nothing? Who is affected by what I do? How? Will I protect myself? Will I protect the quality of life and dignity of others? Will I preserve my moral and ethical integrity? What are the short-term effects? What are the long-term effects?

Ethical concerns can arise even in successful and popular police operations, such as stings. Sting operations and ethics are interconnected. Although sting operations have been used for over 40 years, artful deceptions and undercover operations have been used for as long as policing has existed (Newman & Socia, 2007). Since being introduced in the United States in the 1970s, modern sting operations have been justified as an effective, less forceful way to catch criminals as well as to collect evidence needed to convict them. The ethical challenge most often brought against sting operations is that stings are simply another form of lying, which is morally wrong, period

(Newman & Socia, 2007). Detractors question whether such deception is ethically worse if the deceiver is a government official.

Stings also carry the potential for entrapment issues, with offenders claiming they were tricked into committing a crime. **Entrapment** is an act of government agents to induce a person to commit a crime that is not normally considered by the person for the purpose of prosecuting that person. Many Supreme Court cases have dealt with the issue of entrapment and have led to rulings that help define the boundaries for law enforcement. In _Sorrells v. United States_ (1932), the Supreme Court stated: "Society is at war with the criminal classes, and the courts have uniformly held that in waging this warfare the forces of prevention and detection may use traps, decoys and deception to obtain evidence of the commission of a crime." In _United States v. Russell_ (1973) the Court held: "There are circumstances when the use of deceit is the only practicable law enforcement technique available. It is only when the government's deception actually implants the criminal design in the mind of the defendant that the defense of entrapment comes into play."

Police defend stings with two arguments: (1) The benefits of a successful sting far exceed the ethical cost of using deception and (2) Deception is "soft" coercion compared with other types police are authorized to use.

In addition to considering the ethics involved in problem solving, community policing officers often find they must rely on their skills in mediation as well.

> **entrapment**
> An act of government agents to induce a person to commit a crime that is not normally considered by the person for the purpose of prosecuting that person.

MEDIATION AS A PROBLEM-SOLVING TOOL

Research shows that many calls for service involve landlord/tenant disputes, loud parties, rowdy teens, traffic complaints, and even domestic calls not requiring law enforcement intervention. But police traditionally use enforcement strategies such as rapid response and random patrol to address these problems.

Mediation, sometimes called alternative dispute resolution (ADR), is shared problem solving by parties in dispute guided by a neutral person:

> Community mediation offers constructive processes for resolving differences and conflicts between individuals, groups, and organizations. It is an alternative to avoidance, destructive confrontation, prolonged litigation, or violence. It gives people in conflict an opportunity to take responsibility for the resolution of their dispute and control of the outcome. Community mediation is designed to preserve individual interests while strengthening relationships and building connections between people and groups, and to create processes that make communities work for all of us[3]. (National Association for Community Mediation, n.d.)

> **mediation**
> The intervention of a third party into an interpersonal dispute, where the third party helps disputants reach a resolution; often termed alternative dispute resolution (ADR).

In some instances, the mediator might be a police officer. Changing roles from law enforcer authority to a partner in conflict resolution requires skills different from those many officers are accustomed to using. If a police officer is the mediator, mediation may provide a short-term solution, but this is often

---

[3] Source: Reprinted by permission of the National Association for Community Mediation.

the result of the perceived coercive power of the mediating officer (resolve this, or else …).

The community mediation program strategy, while not typically a police initiative, is one that can solve community problems and result in time savings for the police. Community mediation provides an alternative to neighbors taking legal action against each other when minor issues arise. If they cannot settle a dispute between themselves, police are often called, and court action, lawsuits, and even relocation can follow. In rare cases, matters can escalate to include retaliation and violence. Mediation programs offer guidance from professionally trained and certified mediators to help conflicting parties reach agreement. Police involvement is often simply referral.

PROBLEM-SOLVING POLICING, CRIME-SPECIFIC PLANNING, AND CRIME ANALYSIS

To maintain effective police–community partnerships, police must also fulfill their crime-fighting role. Police can approach this role with many of the problem-solving skills just discussed, using crime-specific planning, a more precise strategy than POP in that it considers underlying problems categorized by type of offense. Crime-specific planning involves reviewing the following factors:

- *The offense:* Seriousness, frequency of occurrence, susceptibility to control, whether a crime of opportunity or calculation, the modus operandi, and any violent characteristics present
- *The target:* Property taken or damaged, when attacked, how attacked, where located, number of potential targets in area, accessibility, transportation patterns surrounding the target
- *Impact:* On the community, public concern, drain on resources of the criminal justice system
- *Response:* Of the victim, the community, the criminal justice system

Traditionally, crime-specific planning involved only the first two factors. The last two factors have been added as a result of the community policing philosophy.

A careful analysis of these factors provides the basis for problem solving and deriving alternatives for approaching each specific crime problem.

Goldstein has argued that problem-oriented policing depends crucially on the availability of high-level analytic capacity in the department. Clarke and Eck (2005, p. 5), likewise, note: "A fully effective police agency must take advantage of the details of crime situations to reduce crime opportunities. Crime analysts have important roles in applying both elements—focusing with precision using their analytical methods, and helping to craft appropriate police tactics that fit the details of problems they have uncovered. This makes the 21st century the century of crime analysis in policing." White (2008, p. 1) describes the framework of crime analysis:

> The theoretical framework of problem-oriented policing has evolved steadily over the past few decades and it has become increasingly clear how much the approach depends for its success on the careful analysis of data about crime

problems. Indeed, problem-oriented policing and data analysis are highly interdependent. A framework for problem-oriented policing is of little use if good data are not available and, similarly, complex data about crime problems require a meaningful framework for analysis. In fact, methods of capturing and analyzing data about crime problems have rapidly developed at the same time as advances have been made in the theory of problem-oriented policing agenda. Computerized crime data and geographic information systems (GISs) are just two examples.

Assistance is available to agencies developing crime analysis units from the International Association of Crime Analysts (IACA), an advocacy group promoting professional standards, practical educational opportunities, and an international network for the standardization of analytic techniques. Also of assistance to crime analysis is computer software that provides probability assessments.

USING TECHNOLOGY FOR PROBLEM SOLVING

Technology has become an indispensable tool for law enforcement. Computers can greatly assist departments using the SARA model for problem solving. In the scanning phase, crime analysis can use information from the Records Management System (RMS) to identify problems. Computer Aided Dispatch (CAD) can identify locations getting repeat calls for police service. Likewise, databases, charts, graphs, and spreadsheets can identify similarities in incidents indicating a need for problem solving. Basic analysis can also be done with computerized data, including CompStat, crime mapping, geographic information systems (GISs), geospacial statistical analysis, and geographic profiling.

CompStat

CompStat, short for computer statistics or comparative statistics, originated in the New York City Police Department in 1994 under the leadership of then-commissioner William Bratton. CompStat is a progressive, goal-oriented, information-driven police management strategy based on four core components: (1) accurate and timely collection of crime data and intelligence analysis, (2) rapid deployment of personnel and other resources, (3) effective tactics and strategies to address crime and disorder problems, and (4) relentless follow-up, assessment, and accountability (Jang, Hoover, & Joo, 2010).

The crime control strategies that form the foundation of CompStat policing include hot-spot policing, problem-solving approaches, and broken windows enforcement (Jang et al., 2010). The CompStat model embraces the broken windows philosophy by taking a zero-tolerance approach to even minor infractions and offenses, under the premise that a police focus on improving social disorder and quality of life issues can ultimately impact and reduce serious crime. Research has found, however, that while the CompStat approach can be effective in reducing property crime and total index crime rates, it does not significantly reduce violent crime rates (Jang et al., 2010).

Serpas and Morley (2008, p. 60) assert that CompStat has revolutionized crime fighting in this country, making communities safer and enhancing the accountability and empowerment of patrol officers. The Columbia (South Carolina) Police Department, for example, has successfully implemented CompStat, which they credit with enhancing teamwork in the department, improving relationships with neighboring law enforcement agencies and community organizations, and increasing the number of arrests while significantly reducing the level of crime in the city (Crisp & Hines, 2007).

Wintersteen (2007, p. 56) provides additional support for CompStat, citing the results of its implementation in Paradise Valley, Arizona:

- Crime down 20 percent in 2005 compared with 2003
- Crime down 38 percent in 2006 compared with 2003
- Collisions down 16 percent in 2005 compared with 1997, despite increased traffic and more distraction factors

Not everyone finds CompStat effective and ethical, and care must be taken to ensure that this technology is not allowed to diminish the appropriate and necessary application of officer discretion or to form the basis for illegal productivity goals and quotas. For instance, some departments are facing harsh criticism for using CompStat to increase their numbers of summonses, stop-and-frisks, and arrests while constricting the ability of officers to make decisions and exercise discretion (Kates, 2012). In New York City, where the CompStat model was born, police leaders came under censure for the application of the strategy and its related "stop and frisk" initiative that allowed police officers to temporarily detain, question, and, if necessary, pat down those they saw behaving suspiciously. While the "stop and frisk" tactic was intended to serve as a preventive dragnet to capture people who posed a public threat— those carrying concealed weapons, drugs, or both—it was far more effective in snaring those engaged in minor infractions and who presented little, if any, danger to public safety through their actions. Critics of the tactics argue that the hard-line stance against low-level offenses has "wreaked havoc on a generation of young black and Latino men, whose lives have been altered by the kind of penny-ante arrests that are a hallmark of the [broken windows] theory" (Bruinius, 2014). In 2013, a federal judge ruled NYPD's "stop and frisk" dragnet tactic unconstitutional, calling it a form of racial profiling. As mentioned in Chapter 3, NYPD has since stopped its aggressive enforcement of minor "nuisance" infractions.

Crime Mapping

"Crimes are human phenomena; therefore, their distribution across the landscape is not geographically random" (Rossmo, 2005, p. 1). Maps that show where crimes have occurred can help direct police resources to locations where they are most needed and enable law enforcement to protect citizens more effectively. Mapping crime has evolved from using color-coded pushpins to user-friendly mapping software, designed to examine and predict crime and criminal behavior. Traditional density mapping allows departments to visualize how crime is distributed throughout the jurisdiction and to detect patterns or trends along various corridors, within certain neighborhoods, or as associated with other geographical features. Such mapping allows departments to more readily identify **hot spots**, or areas where incidents of crime and disorder tend to cluster in close proximity to one another. Mapping can also reveal *hot dots*, or specific addresses of persistent calls for police service. These maps, such as the one shown in Figure 4.2, help law enforcement administrators direct patrols to areas where they are most needed—"putting cops on the dots."

Given that prevention is one of the primary goals of proactive policing, hot spots enforcement may provide police with a new way to break the vicious cycle of crime. In 2005 and 2006, the Police Executive Research Forum (PERF) surveyed police to identify the most widely used antiviolence strategy and found that the highest-ranking program cited (63% of the respondents) was hot spot enforcement: "In general, hot spot enforcement refers to police efforts to identify the location—a residence, a store, a nightclub, or other particular address; a street corner; a city block; a neighborhood—that generates the most calls to 911 or other indicators of criminal activity. Then, police analyze the types of crimes being committed at each hot spot and devise ways of reducing the crime. ... [N]early 9 out of 10 agencies use hot spots enforcement efforts directed either at larger hot spot areas like neighborhoods, smaller hot spot places like intersections, or both" (PERF, 2008, p. 3).

Several theories of crime and disorder concentration exist to explain different types of crime phenomena that occur at different geographic levels,

hot spots
Areas where incidents of crime and disorder tend to cluster in close proximity to one another.

LO6
Crime mapping changes the focus from the criminal to the location of crimes—the hot spots and hot dots where most crimes occur.

| **Figure 4.2** | Hot Spot Map |

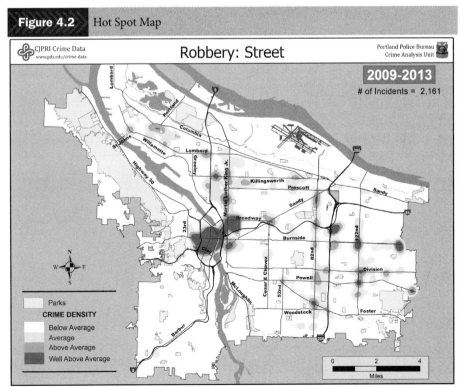

Source: Portland State University

helping the police interpret the data and determine which responses are most appropriate (Eck, 2005). *Place theories* deal with crimes that occur at the lowest level of analysis—specific places or *hot dots*—and explain why crime events occur at specific locations. These locations usually are represented on maps as dots. Police action at this level is very precise—for example, warrants.

Street theories look at hot spots at a slightly higher level such as streets or blocks—for example, a prostitution stroll. These hot spots are represented on maps as straight, bent, or curved lines. Police action is still quite precise—for example, they may focus on concentrated patrolling as well as changing traffic and street patterns.

Neighborhood theories deal with large areas such as square blocks, communities, and census tracts. Hot spots in these areas are represented by two-dimensional shapes such as ellipses, rectangles, and other polygons. Relevant police action might include engaging residents in collective action against crime and disorder.

Other large area theories look at crime patterns on the city level, multijurisdictional level, or multistate level and, although interesting, are less useful for local police agencies (Eck, 2005). Table 4.3 provides more detail regarding hot spots and mapping.

Mapping hot spots and using incident-based deployment has been used to address public safety issues such as traffic crashes. One jurisdiction with several miles of major interstate highway running through the city used mapping to identify the specific corridor of hot spot crash activity that was costing millions of dollars and several hundred injuries every year. Armed with that data, the department mobilized a unit for interstate traffic enforcement and crash reduction and was able to remedy a problem area in their community (Hoelzer & Gorman, 2011).

Recognizing that the majority of calls for police service—around 70 percent by some estimates—are for noncriminal matters, some departments have begun to use mapping to address, assess, and enhance the police response to other types of issues, such as locating lost children or elderly residents suffering from Alzheimer's disease, and improving surveillance and protection

Table 4.3	Hot Spot Concentrations, Evidence, Theory, and Causes		
Concentration	**Hot Spot Depiction**	**Action Level**	**Action Examples**
Place—at specific addresses, corners, or other places	Points	Place, corner	Nuisance abatement, hot spot patrols
Among victims	Points, lines, and areas depending on the nature of concentration	High-risk targets and potential victims	Developing networks among potential victims, repeat victimization programs
Street—along streets or block faces	Lines	Streets, highways	Concentrated patrolling of specific streets, traffic reengineering
Area—neighborhood areas	Ellipses, shaded areas, and gradients	Large areas	Community partnerships, neighborhood redevelopment

Source: Eck, John E. (2005, August). "Crime Hot Spots: What They Are, Why We Have Them, and How to Map Them." In *Mapping Crime: Understanding Hot Spots*, edited by John E. Eck, et al., pp. 1–15. Washington, DC: National Institute of Justice. (NIJ 209393).

efforts around critical infrastructure in a post-9/11 era (Markovic & Scalisi, 2011). Many departments map field contacts in addition to locations at which officers provide services such as "well-being checks."

In addition to identifying hot spots, mapping is also routinely used to track registered sex offenders in communities. Information from mapping is often enhanced by geographic information systems (GISs).

Geographic Information Systems

A **geographic information system (GIS)** enhances traditional mapping by adding information from various other databases. For example, modern GIS software can generate maps that correlate crime with vacant housing units, parks, or schools; income level of a census tract; patterns of car thefts; and locations of chop shops.

"Because police solutions to crime are necessarily about where crime takes place, the ability to visualize and analyze geographic patterns becomes paramount" (Peed, Wilson, & Scalisi, 2008, p. 24). Advancements in GIS technology continue to help crime analysts improve their ability to assemble and integrate demographic, economic, and social data to create new units of analysis that model human behavior more accurately.

geographic information system (GIS)
Creating, updating, and analyzing computerized maps.

Geospacial Statistical Analysis

Geospacial statistical analysis takes GIS technology a step further by allowing analysts to identify areas within the community that are statistically similar to locations where prior incidents have occurred and, thus, at increased risk for future incidents: "Ultimately, this approach enables law enforcement to act proactively to prevent crime and influence outcomes" (McCue, 2011, p. 4).

Drawing on environmental criminology and the principle set forth in the **routine activity theory**—that crime occurs at the intersection of a motivated offender, a suitable target, and an absent or ineffective guardian—geospacial statistical analysis helps law enforcement understand and identify the specific jurisdictional characteristics that either attract or deter crime to their area. This information-based response represents a game-changing shift in police operations by allowing law enforcement to create customized solutions to particular crime problems and, ultimately, keep their communities safer (McCue, 2011).

routine activity theory
Principle of environmental criminology that states crime occurs at the intersection of a motivated offender, a suitable target, and an absent or ineffective guardian.

Geographic Profiling

Geographic profiling takes crime-mapping technique and turns them inside out by using a complex mathematical algorithm and the locations of past crimes to calculate probabilities of a suspect's residence: "Geographic profiling is a technique that can help identify the likely area where a serial offender resides, or other place (e.g., work, girlfriend's place) that serves as an anchor point or base of operations" (National Institute of Justice, 2009).

Dr. Kim Russmo, a former police detective from Vancouver, Canada, first proposed the concept of geoprofiling (or geographic profiling) in his doctoral

geographic profiling
A crime-mapping technique that takes the locations of past crimes and, using a complex mathematical algorithm, calculates probabilities of a suspect's residence.

thesis while at British Columbia's Simon Fraser University. His concept was eventually packaged commercially by Environmental Criminology Research, Inc., into a software program called Rigel and has been used by police agencies worldwide, including the Federal Bureau of Investigation; the Bureau of Alcohol, Tobacco, Firearms, and Explosives; and Scotland Yard. Other major software programs being employed by police agencies to perform geographic profiling tasks are CrimeStat and Dragnet.

Geographic profiling can help prioritize suspect lists, direct stakeouts, and conduct neighborhood canvasses. In March 2008, the Office of Community Oriented Policing Services (COPS) and the National Institute of Justice (NIJ) launched the first issue of *Geography and Public Safety*, dealing with applied geography for the study of crime and public safety, providing a valuable new resource for law enforcement in all capacities and ranks, from patrol to special investigations, from front-line officers to police chiefs.

A similar popular approach to geographic profiling is a psychological theory called the **least-effort principle**, which posits that criminals tend to commit crimes a safe distance away from their residence yet still within a zone where they feel comfortable and familiar. The related distance-decay concept holds that "people, including criminals, generally take more short trips and fewer longer trips in the course of their daily lives, which may include criminal activities" (Harries, 1999, p. 152). Combining these two concepts allows analysts to use multiple incidents that are traceable to a perpetrator to significantly narrow the search area for the criminal's residence. In this process, key locations are weighted and then geocoded onto a map, producing a three-dimensional "jeopardy surface" of peaks and valleys, color ramped to highlight the most likely area where the criminal lives.

Geographic profiling can be used as the basis for several investigative strategies, including suspect and tip prioritization, address-based searches of police record systems, patrol saturation and surveillance, neighborhood canvasses and searches, DNA screening prioritization, Department of Motor Vehicle searches, postal/zip code prioritization, and information-request mailings. It is important to stress that geographic profiling does not solve cases; rather, it provides a method for managing the large volume of information usually generated in major crime investigations. It should be regarded as one of several tools available to detectives and is best used in conjunction with other police methods. Geographic crime patterns are clues that, when properly decoded, can be used to point in the offender's direction.

The National Institute of Justice (2009) cautions: "Though there have been anecdotal successes with geographic profiling, there have also been several instances where geographic profiling has either been wrong on predicting where the offender lives/works or has been inappropriate as a model. Thus far, none of the geographic profiling software packages have been subject to rigorous, independent, or comparative tests to evaluate their accuracy, reliability, validity, utility, or appropriateness for various situations."

least-effort principle
Concept proposing that criminals tend to commit acts of crimes within a comfort zone located near but not too close to their residence.

PROBLEM SOLVING AT WORK

The theoretical foundation of problem solving in Newport News, Virginia, was discussed earlier. During the problem-identification process, several problems became evident (Eck & Spelman, 1987). The Newport News police categorized the problems, so they could be analyzed. The way the department addressed the problem of commercial burglaries illustrates the problem-solving approach. The patrol officers surveyed the area and found that some major streets had been barricaded as a result of a major highway construction project. This resulted in limited vehicle traffic, limited police patrol at night, and a large increase in nighttime burglaries. To alleviate these problems, patrol officers were instructed to leave their squads and patrol the area on foot at night. The officers also persuaded the merchants to clean up the piles of trash and debris that could easily conceal the burglars' activities.

Besides dealing with the environment, Sergeant Quail, the officer in charge, also analyzed the specific problem (Eck & Spelman, 1987). He collected reports of burglaries committed in the area and plotted them on a detailed map to identify geographic patterns. He also recorded a description of the suspects, time of commission, type of property taken, and similar information on a specially designed form to identify the modus operandi and repeat offender patterns. Finally, suspecting that some offenders were using vacant apartments located above some of the businesses to conceal stolen property, he began to investigate this possibility.

This resulted in the apprehension of several burglars and a decrease in the burglary rate. When construction was completed and the barriers removed, burglaries decreased further, so Sgt. Quail developed a policy on and procedure for allowing police and city agencies to communicate better about construction projects, street closings, and potential burglary problems.

Promising Practices from the Field

The Center for Problem-Oriented Policing provides on its Web site (www.popcenter.org) myriad examples of case studies and a variety of problem-specific guides to help police formulate effective responses to crime and disorder problems in their communities. The COPS Office Web site (www.cops.usdoj.gov) also contains numerous examples of promising practices in problem solving. Two examples follow from the POP Center's Web site.

Peoria, Illinois—Nuisance Houses   Peoria is a diverse community with an urban center (population approximately 115,000) ringed by various suburban neighborhoods, the entire metropolitan area home to more than 370,000 people. The largest city on the Illinois River, Peoria had begun to experience an uptick in nuisance behaviors that were negatively impacting the quality of life (QOL) in many neighborhoods. Chronic nuisance activities, such as noise and loud music, littering, loitering, disorderly conduct, and general antisocial behavior by unsupervised youth, were found to occur around a select few, known problem households or retail businesses. A more serious crime affecting Peoria residents' QOL was illegal drug trafficking, and the Peoria Police Department (PPD) had begun to notice that the areas most plagued by open air drug markets were the same areas where other nuisance behaviors were most prevalent. The PPD took a problem-solving approach to finding a solution to identify and combat nuisance properties, with a secondary motive being to clean up more serious crime in the process.

The department decided to try parking an unmanned squad car in front of problem properties in an effort to curb nuisance and criminal behavior, but such an untended vehicle proved an easy target for vandalism. During PPD's first attempt at this tactic, in which the squad was placed in front of a suspected drug house, the car was so badly damaged that it was no longer drivable and had to be towed from the neighborhood:

> Someone had gone to a considerable amount of trouble to convey just how strongly they objected to a police car being parked at that particular spot.... Initially there was some sentiment [at PPD] that our experiment was a failure and that it was an embarrassment for the Department to allow this to happen in a public place and worse, to have to haul the car away with a tow truck in full view of the entire neighborhood. It was not unreasonable to come away with the perception that the bad guy won. This was especially true since early intelligence indicated that it was the drug dealer himself who damaged the car. Through discussion, an entirely different theory emerged. Perhaps the damaged car was proof that the experiment was a success. Perhaps it demonstrated that the drug dealers were extremely unhappy about a police car being parked in front of their house. If this were true, the problem was not tactic, it was the tool we were using. We needed to find a way to have the same affect, without having to tow another squad car (Burke & Hermacinski, 2011, pp. 5–6).

A better solution was found in an old armored car that had been donated to the department several years earlier by Brink's. Originally intended for tactical operations, the vehicle had never been put to use and was sitting idle. With a few modifications to harden vulnerabilities (e.g., installation of headlight and taillight screens to keep them from being smashed; a locking fuel cap; a padlocked hood; and foam-filled tires to prevent them from going flat), the armored truck was transformed into a fortified surveillance vehicle dubbed "the Armadillo." A surveillance system, consisting of five infrared cameras capable of providing 360-degree coverage, was mounted on the top to both document illegal activities in the area and deter vandalism to the vehicle itself. Emergency lights were mounted on the roof to make it even more conspicuous. A digital recorder with a removable hard drive was mounted inside the cab. Finally, large gold lettered decals were placed on all sides of the Armadillo that read, "Peoria Police Nuisance Property Surveillance Vehicle":

> In addition to dissuading illegal activity, the vehicle offers a few side benefits that have nearly overshadowed the primary goals. When problems are quickly addressed with the Armadillo, citizens feel a sense of security and relief. The moment the Armadillo arrives in front of a problem property, it says two things very distinctly. It says to the law abiding, good people in the area, "we have heard your complaints and we want to help you stop the chaos." It says to the thugs and the miscreants, "You have dedicated your time to make life miserable for your neighbors we will now dedicate our time to give you a taste of what that feels like." (Burke & Hermacinski, 2011, pp. 7–8)

The PPD deployed the Armadillo for its first real test on July 10, 2008 and has since received overwhelmingly positive feedback from citizens. Requests for its presence have exceeded their ability to deploy it, and they have since acquired a second Armadillo. All requests for the Armadillos are vetted by a nuisance abatement officer using criteria that include drug trafficking complaints, code enforcement complaints, traffic violations, chronic police crime reports, excessive calls for service, and quality-of-life issues such as loitering and loud music. Once a property is assessed as being "a cancer to the neighborhood," the Armadillo is parked there for 3 to 5 days and the property owner or landlord is notified of the reason for the Armadillo's deployment.

Positive results of the Armadillo project include crime reduction and a long-term decrease in calls for service at nuisance properties and surrounding residences, restoration of peace and quiet in troubled neighborhoods, increased citizen satisfaction at the ability of the PPD to respond quickly and immediately deploy the Armadillo, and greater landlord involvement in dealing with problem tenants (Burke & Hermacinski, 2011). An additional benefit is that the project takes very few man-hours to operate.

Charlotte-Mecklenburg, North Carolina—Storage Facility Burglaries In 2005, the Charlotte-Mecklenburg area experienced a 28 percent increase in commercial burglaries. Seven percent of these burglaries occurred at mini-warehouse or storage facilities, most of which involved multiple units within one facility, with an average of 3.5 victims per incident. A sergeant and two detectives from the Charlotte-Mecklenburg Police Department (CMPD) were assigned to initiate a problem-solving effort to address the storage facility burglaries.

The detectives began by reviewing all 99 of the burglary reports from 2005, which involved a total of 291 individual victims and noted that most of the 75 storage facilities in the jurisdiction did not have significant burglary problems. When crime mapping was applied, no correlation was found between the location of a facility, the occurrence of burglary at the facility, and the level of crime in the surrounding neighborhood. Furthermore, no reliable patterns were detected regarding the kinds of property being targeted. When the detectives conducted on-site visits to each facility in an effort to identify variances in design, policy, and practice that might account for different levels of victimization, they discovered that the use of disc-style locks seemed to be the most effective measure for securing individual storage units. The only facility that required customers to use disc locks on its units had not suffered a single burglary incident.

The CMPD designed an experiment to test the hypothesis that the use of disc locks would substantially reduce the occurrence of burglary. Three locations were selected: two storage facilities that would suggest, but not require, that customers use the disc locks, and the one facility that already required the use of the locks. The police department purchased the disc locks for use in the study and launched the initiative on July 1, 2006. The detectives also worked with the mini-storage industry and area owners to develop a "best practices" guide that addressed measures such as performing background checks on customers, educating renters on burglary prevention, restricting customer access to times when on-site managers were present, encouraging the use of disc locks, improving lighting, using surveillance cameras, and providing police with the access codes to enter the facilities.

At the end of the test period, results were assessed and found to be positive. The facilities involved in the study realized a 58 percent reduction in the number of reported burglary incidents from the previous year and a 69 percent reduction in the number of individual burglarized units during the 1-year test. Highlighting the protective advantage of the disc locks was the fact that one incident at one of the test facilities involved entry into 26 separate storage units, none of which was secured by a disc lock. This single burglary incident accounted for 79 percent of that facility's burglaries during the test period. Also during the test period, facilities that were not involved in the study experienced a 39 percent increase in the number of reported burglary incidents and a 45 percent increase in the number of individual units burglarized.

(Adapted from Karin Schmerler, Matt Perkins, Scott Philips, Tammy Rinehart, and Meg Townsend. (2011, July). *Problem-Solving Tips: A Guide to Reducing Crime and Disorder through Problem-Solving Partnerships*, 2nd ed. Washington, DC: Office of Community Oriented Policing Services. Retrieved July 20, 2016 from http://www.popcenter.org/library/reading/pdfs/ProbSolvTips_2ed.pdf)

The Herman Goldstein Award Projects

Several award projects have been implemented to recognize individual agencies' and communities' efforts at curbing local crime and disorder through problem-oriented policing. Two of the better known awards are the Herman Goldstein Award and the Tilley Award.

Herman Goldstein Award   First introduced in 1993, the Herman Goldstein Award recognizes outstanding police officers and police agencies—both in the United States and around the world—that engage in innovative and effective

 IDEAS IN PRACTICE   HALLOWEEN ON STATE STREET

One of the 2008 winners of the Herman Goldstein Award was the Madison (Wisconsin) Police Department's Halloween on State Street. In 2002 this traditional Halloween street event erupted into a riot involving disorderly behaviors, extensive criminal damage, assaults, injured officers, and looting of businesses. An annual problem-solving project was thereafter designed to prevent injury and property damage and instill peace. Repeated analysis of video clips, officer observations, and GIS analysis implicated problems with crowd movement; synthesis of arrest data showed the arrestees were 18- to 25-year-old males from Wisconsin and surrounding states, had university affiliation, and were disproportionately legally intoxicated. The response was guided by what had been used in other locations experiencing similar problems

and by models of crowd behavior and theory. Stability was restored with policing responses, a fully gated event area with a fee assessed for admission, and entertainment on several stages. At the conclusion of the event, the fencing was adjusted and police were used to facilitate crowd movement away from problem areas. Halloween-related arrests decreased significantly over a 2-year period, most notably for alcohol and disorderly conduct. Crowd attendance stabilized to safe levels. Injuries to attendees and officers all but disappeared. In recent years, little or no property damage has occurred and the impact to the surrounding neighborhoods has been minimized.

Source: http://www.popcenter.org/library/awards/goldstein/2008/08-34(F).pdf

problem-solving efforts and achieve measurable success in reducing specific crime, disorder, and public safety problems. This international competition is named after the founder of POP, University of Wisconsin Professor Emeritus Herman Goldstein, and is administered by the Center for Problem-Oriented Policing. (The award program was administered by the Police Executive Research Forum, or PERF, from 1993 to 2003; www.policeforum.org.)

The Center for Problem-Oriented Policing has assembled a panel of seven judges, made up of experienced researchers and practitioners, who select a small number of finalists from among award submissions and, finally, the winner. Submissions usually come from the United States, Canada, the United Kingdom, and Australia. The judges consider a number of factors in their selections, including the depth of problem analysis, the development of clear and realistic response goals, the use of relevant measures of effectiveness, and the involvement of citizens and other community resources in problem resolution. Police agencies whose projects successfully resolve any type of recurring community problem that results in crime or disorder are eligible to compete for the award. The number of submissions is 50 to 70 per year, and of those roughly 5 to 10 per year are selected as finalists (Center for Problem-Oriented Policing, 2012a)[4].

Tilley Award   The Tilley Award was set up by the U.K. Home Office Policing and Reducing Crime Unit (now the Crime and Policing Group) in 1999 to encourage and recognize good practice in implementing POP. The award, funded by the Home Office, pays for winners to attend the Annual International Problem-Oriented Policing Conference in San Diego, and winners usually have the opportunity to present their projects at the conference. The prizes are presented at the annual U.K. National Problem-Oriented Policing Conference. The award is open to all U.K. police forces (Center for Problem-Oriented Policing, 2012b)[5].

 **IDEAS IN PRACTICE**   NUISANCE ABATEMENT IN WASHINGTON PARK—MILWAUKEE, WISCONSIN

The Milwaukee (Wisconsin) Police Department (MPD) was named one of two U.S. finalists for the 2015 Herman Goldstein Award. MPD teamed with a neighborhood coalition called the Washington Park Partners in an effort to abate nuisance properties and improve the built environment. Following is an excerpt from their application summary:

> The Washington Park neighborhood, located on the city of Milwaukee's near west side, is home to numerous engaged residents, business owners, and organizations, all organized through a neighborhood coalition named the Washington Park Partners. However, like many central city neighborhoods, Washington Park also struggles with decades of systematic disinvestment and

associated decline. In fact, Washington Park is one of the three most affected Milwaukee neighborhoods from the recent foreclosure/housing crisis. Numerous boarded up, dilapidated properties have spread throughout the neighborhood and seriously destabilized a number of Washington Park blocks. Through receipt of a three year federal investment in the form of a FY12 Byrne Criminal Justice Innovation (BCJI) Grant from the US Department of Justice, the Milwaukee Police Department and community partners convened to develop comprehensives strategies to address drivers of crime, which includes nuisance property issues and foreclosed property

(Continues)

---

[4] Source: Reprinted by permission of the POP Center.

[5] Source: Reprinted by permission of the POP Center.

IDEAS **IN PRACTICE**

NUISANCE ABATEMENT IN WASHINGTON PARK—MILWAUKEE, WISCONSIN (*Continued*)

mitigation and shall be the basis for this submission (see appendix L for BCJI Initiative details). Analysis of the problem revealed multiple factors, including:

- Resident survey and focus group feedback on the need to address absentee or non-owner occupied housing units
- Review of recent "scattered site" housing development efforts (in Washington Park and throughout the city) that left individual home owners without integration opportunities with their neighbors and broader community
- City-owned receipt of tax foreclosures (along with privately held foreclosures) that remained uninhabited and boarded for significant periods of time, attracting prolonged criminal activity
- A neighborhood home-ownership rate of under 50%

Through regular BCJI team meetings, a coordinated, multi-faceted approach to this problem was developed. Through training provided by the Local Initiatives Support Corporation (LISC)—Milwaukee, in partnership with National LISC's Community Safety Initiative, Milwaukee Habitat for Humanity staff, MPD officers and BCJI partners became skilled on Crime Prevention Through Environmental Design (CPTED) principles and the need to focus on resident feedback for community safety planning. This work initially focused on one residential block that formed the basis for future strategic interventions across the neighborhood. Additional developments to date include:

- Targeted, block-by-block, address specific interventions by law enforcement in identified neighborhood hot spots, informed by community partner input
- MPD personnel included in new homeowner training for Milwaukee Habitat for Humanity owners
- Formation of a neighborhood Landlord Alliance, to engage property owners in the larger community
- From 2013 to 2014, a drop in Part I neighborhood crime by 11.5% and hot spots experiencing a 23.7% percent decrease

SUMMARY

Problem-solving policing requires police to group incidents and identify the underlying causes of problems in the community. The magnet phenomenon occurs when a phone number or address is associated with a crime simply because it was a convenient number or address to use. One concern of a problem-solving approach is differentiating between efficiency and effectiveness. Efficiency, doing things right, has been the traditional emphasis in law enforcement. Effectiveness, doing the right things, is the emphasis in community policing. Effectiveness should produce an increase in efficiency, because officers are proactively solving problems rather than simply reacting to them.

The first step in problem solving is to group incidents as problems. The four stages of the SARA problem-solving model are scanning, analysis, response, and assessment. Problem analysis considers the individuals involved, the incidents, and the responses.

The DOC model (dilemmas–options–consequences) challenges officers to carefully consider their decisions and the short- and long-term consequences of those decisions. The goal is to fuse problem solving and morality.

Crime-specific planning uses the principles of problem solving to focus on identified crime problems. Crime mapping changes the focus from the criminal to the location of crimes—the hot spots and hot dots where most crimes occur.

DISCUSSION QUESTIONS

1. How do you approach problems? Do you use a systematic approach?

2. Problem solving can take more time than the traditional approach to policing. Which is more effective? More efficient? More expensive? Explain your answers.

3. Does your department use problem solving? Is the department proactive or reactive?

4. Does your law enforcement agency employ anyone to specifically conduct crime analysis?

5. What difficulties can you foresee for a department that uses problem-solving techniques?

6. How do problem solving and crime-specific planning differ?

7. Some officers have resisted implementing problem-solving strategies. Why do you think that is?

8. In what kinds of problems do you think a problem-solving approach would be most effective?

9. What is the relationship between community-oriented policing and problem-oriented policing?

10. How might computers help police in their problem-solving efforts?

CASES CITED

Sorrells v. United States, 287 U.S. 435 (1932)
United States v. Russell, 411 U.S. 423 (1973)

page 109 strings are okay
109 strings cannot be used to entrap

Implementing Community Policing

In the Southeast section of Los Angeles exists a neighborhood called Watts, well-known for gang violence and drug distribution. The police officers patrolling the public housing projects in Watts are hoping to change the perception of the Los Angeles Police Department (LAPD) by using their new and improved community policing strategies. By making more buddies than arrests, the department is gambling on improving the long-held negative perception of police by people living in their districts.

Prior to the implementation of the revamped community policing tactics, the LAPD was primarily known for the Rodney King beating and the Rampart Division police scandal. On March 3, 1991, the department was rocketed into the national discussion of police brutality when a video was released showing four police officers repeatedly beating a seemingly lifeless Black suspect. The Community Resources against Street Hoodlums unit of the Rampart Division created a criminal subculture within the department known for selling narcotics, frame ups, brutality, and attempted murders. With these two events still very fresh in the minds of many Watts residents, it is no surprise that building trust has been a challenge between the police and this community.

The LAPD is hoping that implementation of these new community policing tactics will make it easier to build trust between law enforcement and neighborhood tenants. For LAPD Chief Charlie Beck, community policing programs offer more transparency into the police department's mission and operations. The police department offers numerous community policing programs to attract a variety of residents throughout the surrounding districts. Citizens can engage in the Community Police Academy, become active members on the community advisory boards, become reserve officers, belong to Neighborhood Watch, or participate as block captains. LAPD has also trained interested citizens on how to respond to domestic violence incidents and how to help provide mediation and community referral services to the victim.

Youth, a primary demographic in implementing a community policing philosophy, can also participate with the LAPD through traditional programs such as D.A.R.E, Police Activity League, and a Community Police Academy geared toward kids. Other more innovative programs are also offered to help build trust of the police among the community's young people, such as a jeopardy program targeting youths at risk for gang culture, a magnet school offering a rigorous high school curriculum geared to those interested in future law enforcement careers, and offering any university criminal justice student an internship through which to learn about police administrative functions.

Many in the Los Angeles community appreciate the new and improved tactics deployed by the LAPD to garner the trust of the citizens they serve. Although not a perfect organization, the past chapters of corruption are being rewritten to reflect a more modern department interested in reform and public confidence. By improving relationships among community members, the LAPD is hoping to continue in its success with its community policing programs.

INTRODUCTION

You have looked at the philosophy of community policing and at the key players—politicians, business people, faith-based organizations, civic organizations, the schools, the community, and the police. You have also considered a basic component of community policing—problem solving. The challenge is to move from theories about using problem-solving techniques and partnerships to actual implementation.

CHANGE

It has been said that nothing is constant except change. Nonetheless, police administrators, supervisors, and even line personnel frequently resist change in any form and prefer the status quo. Change is occurring, however, and will continue to occur. Police departments can resist, or they can accept the challenge and capitalize on the benefits that may result. Issues requiring departments to change include technological advances; demographic changes; fiscal constraints; shifting values; the need to do more with less; heightened media coverage of police misconduct; and citizen fear of crime, disorder, violence, gangs, and terrorism.

Change does take time. Traditions die hard. Most police officers will find proposed changes to their culture extremely threatening. The police culture is a tremendously strong force. However, when contemplating the challenges of change, one must remember that a huge ship can be turned by a small rudder. It just takes time and steadfast determination.

Efforts to implement significant changes in policing, of any kind, have encountered severe difficulties. Frontline police services are "notoriously" resistant to change. Most officers usually are not seen as they perform their duties. In the field, they exercise discretion in applying whatever model of policing their department uses. They are also accustomed to changing fads, fancies, and directives from their superiors and so are often cynical about what the "dream factory" (headquarters) is asking from them. Unsympathetic officers will often comply as minimally as possible with such changes, ignoring "new-fangled" ideas and continuing to deliver the policing they feel appropriate, thus subverting new thinking from within. In addition, high rates of senior staff turnover, external political pressures, and traditional performance measurements can inhibit efforts to implement change (Newburn, 2008).

Five concerns that have most strongly influenced the development of problem-oriented policing and, by implication, community policing are (Goldstein, 1990, p. 14):

1. The police field is preoccupied with management, internal procedures, and efficiency to the exclusion of appropriate concern for effectiveness in dealing with substantive problems.

2. The police devote most of their resources to responding to calls from citizens, reserving too small a percentage of their time and energy for acting on their own initiative to prevent or reduce community problems.

3. The community is a major resource with an enormous potential, largely untapped, for reducing the number and magnitude of problems that otherwise become the business of the police.

4. Within their agencies, police have readily available to them another huge resource: their rank-and-file officers, whose time and talents have not been used effectively.

5. Efforts to improve policing have often failed because they have not been adequately related to the overall dynamics and complexity of the police organization. Adjustments in policies and organizational structure are required to accommodate and support change.

It is also helpful to be familiar with five categories of "adopters" to expect within any organization, as Figure 5.1 shows.

The *innovators* are risk takers. They embrace uncertainty and change. The *early adopters* are opinion leaders, the ones to whom others come for advice. The *early majority* accept new ideas slightly ahead of the majority. The *late majority* are more skeptical. They can be persuaded but usually require a great deal of peer pressure. The *late adopters* are the most difficult to convince. They tend to be suspicious of all innovations. Recognizing these individual characteristics may be helpful in developing strategies to "sell" community policing to the troops.

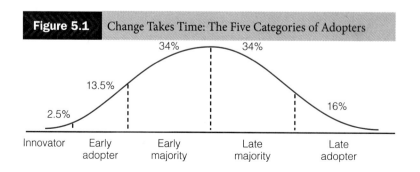

Figure 5.1 Change Takes Time: The Five Categories of Adopters

Some changes have already occurred within many departments that should make the transition to community policing easier, including better-educated police officers who are less inclined to accept orders unquestioningly; more diversity within the police ranks; and a shift in incentives with intrinsic, personal worth–type rewards becoming as important as extrinsic, monetary rewards. Other changes are needed to move from the traditional, reactive, incident-driven mode of policing to the proactive, problem-solving, collaborative mode typical of community policing.

Before change to community policing can occur, management must know specifically what changes are needed. Some changes basic to implementing the community policing philosophy have already been briefly described in Chapter 2.

How these changes fit into the transition from a philosophy to practice will become evident as the chapter progresses.

LO1

Community policing will require a change in management style, mission and vision statements, departmental organization and community mobilization efforts, the agency's strategic plan and strategies to implement, hiring and promoting practices, and training.

Change Management and Management Styles

Three core components of community policing have been identified, the first two of which—community partnerships and problem solving—have already been discussed. The third component—change management—requires departments to recognize that forging partnerships with the community and adopting a problem-solving approach will necessarily bring about a change in the organizational structure of policing. To be effective, this change must be properly managed, including recognizing the need for change, communicating a clear vision that change is possible and desirable, identifying the specific steps required for positive change to occur, developing an understanding of and embracing the benefits of change, and fostering an organization-wide commitment to change (Davis, 1998). Change management also requires recognizing the importance of organization-wide support for community policing, including support in terms of how calls for service are managed (McEwen, Spence, Wolff, Wartell, & Webster, 2003). In essence, **change management** is the development of an overall strategy that examines the present state of the organization, envisions the future state of the organization, and devises the means of moving from one to the other.

change management
The development of an overall strategy to examine the present state of an organization, envision the future state of the organization, and devise a means of moving from one to the other.

Although the term *management* is pervasive in the literature seeking to guide departments in their move toward implementing community policing, the importance of *leadership* in this transition cannot be overlooked. A successful transition process requires the commitment of a leader who is open, willing to make change, and supports decisions with steadfastness and energy (Community Policing Consortium, 2000).

Yet another change is that community policing usually requires a different management style. The traditional autocratic style effective during the industrial age will not have the same effect in the 21st century. One viable alternative to the autocratic style of management is participatory leadership. In **participatory leadership,** each individual has a voice in decisions, but top management still has the ultimate decision-making authority. What is important is that everyone has an opportunity to express their views on a given issue or problem:

participatory leadership
A management style in which each individual has a voice in decisions, but top management still has the ultimate decision-making authority.

Consultative, democratic, or participative leadership has been evolving since the 1930s and 1940s. Democratic leadership does not mean that every decision is made only after discussion and a vote. It means rather that management welcomes employees' ideas and input. Employees are encouraged to be innovative. Management development of a strong sense of individual achievement and responsibility is a necessary ingredient of participative or consultative leadership.

Democratic or participative managers are interested in their subordinates and their problems and welfare. Management still makes the final decision but considers the input from employees. (Hess, Orthmann, & LaDue, 2016, p. 68)

Table 5.1 compares the authoritarian and participatory styles of management.

"As the lines of demarcation between leader and follower continue to blur, empowering strategies and inclusive decision-making styles will not just be recommended practices; they will be essential competencies of police leadership" (Wuestewald & Steinheider, 2006b, p. 32). Barriers to participative or shared leadership include a dysfunctional relationship between the administration and the union, apathy and nonparticipation, hidden agendas and informal leaders, lack of communication, and a power culture that will not let go of the status quo (Broken Arrow Police Department Leadership Team, 2006, p. 37). Wuestewald and Steinheider (2006a, p. 53) note: "Probably the most difficult aspect of undertaking a participative approach to management is for senior executives to make the personal commitment to accept the decisions of others."

vision
Intelligent foresight; starts with a mental image that gradually evolves from abstract musings to a concrete series of mission statements, goals, and objectives.

Creating Vision and Mission Statements

The leader must also have a vision for the department and the community. **Vision** might be thought of as intelligent foresight. This vision should include the essential elements of the community policing philosophy: problem solving, empowerment, forming community partnerships, and being

Table 5.1	Authoritarian and Participatory Leadership Styles Compared
Authoritarian (Mechanistic) Style	**Participatory (Organic) Style**
Response to incidents	Problem solving
Individual effort and competitiveness	Teamwork
Professional expertise	Community orientation; ask customers what they want
Go by the "book"; decisions by emotion	Use data-based decision making
Tell subordinates	Ask and listen to employees
Boss as patriarch and order giver	Boss as coach and teacher
Maintain status quo	Create, innovate, experiment
Control and watch employees	Trust employees
Reliance on scientific investigation and technology rather than people	Reliance on skilled employees—a better resource than machines
When things go wrong, blame employees	Errors mean failed systems/processes—improve them
Organization is closed to outsiders	Organization is open

Source: From HESS/ORTHMANN/LADUE, *Management and Supervision in Law Enforcement*, 7E, p. 69.

proactive—making preventing crime as important as enforcing the law. Examining the department's past for strengths and weaknesses, successes and failures is an important step in creating a vision for the future.

The vision for each department will be different. It must be tailored to reflect the personnel within the department and the community the department serves. A vision should be something that everyone involved can buy into and feel a part of. This means involving leaders from within the department and the community from the beginning of the transition. The CPC recommends the entire workforce be directly involved in the envisioning and planning processes; at the very least, a cross section of the workforce representing all ranks or grades and incorporating sworn, unsworn, and civilian personnel and their respective union representatives should be involved (Florida Regional Community Policing Institute, 2004).

Union support for community policing is absolutely necessary. Without it—or worse, with open opposition—the risk of failure is high. Union leadership has tremendous influence over its members, who will likely follow the lead of union officials. Unions are concerned about issues they perceive as affecting officers negatively, including the likelihood of permanent shifts and area assignments, concern that COP may negatively affect the union contract, the perceived increase of power and influence the community will have in department matters, the potential that citizen review boards may be formed under community policing, the perceived softening of the police image, officer safety concerns, and the concern of officers being held responsible for the crime that occurs in their assigned area.

Agencies with unions can take the opportunity to form partnerships within by inviting union leaders to participate in the process. Having been elected by their membership, they will have the advantage of not being seen as management's hand-selected few.

The CPC also recommends that those who have been identified as antagonistic to the change process be deliberately co-opted. They cannot be ignored because they will not go away. Actively seek ways to avert their antagonism (Florida Regional Community Policing Institute, 2004).

Once the vision is articulated, it should be translated into a mission statement, as discussed in Chapter 2. The development of a mission statement is important for any organization, but it is critical in developing and implementing community policing. Its importance cannot be overstated. Again, the mission statement must be something everyone can buy into and feel a part of. Once the vision and mission statements have been articulated, the next step is to conduct a needs assessment.

Assessing Needs

The needs assessment is critical to the successful implementation of community policing and should include not only the department but also the community of which it is a part.

Analyzing the Department   The first step in needs assessment is to analyze the department's organization.

L02

The traditional law enforcement organization design has been that of a pyramid-shaped hierarchy based on a military model. However, the pyramid might be inverted to implement community policing, as shown in Figure 5.2.

Figure 5.2 Typical Police Department Management Structure and an Inverted Pyramid

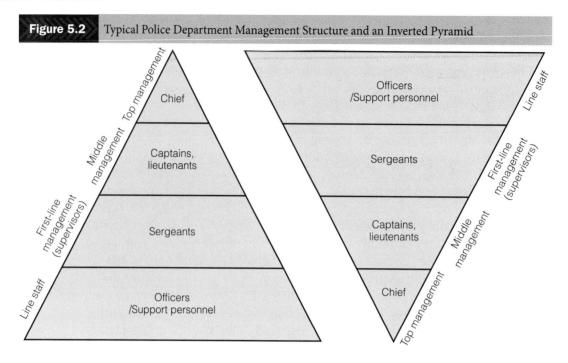

Under a traditional police management structure, command officers and supervisors have complete authority over subordinates, and they have little tolerance for ideas originating at the bottom of the pyramid. Communication flows downward through the bureaucratic chain of command. This bureaucratic organizational structure worked well for decades. Recently, however, it has been called into question, with many looking to corporate America as a more appropriate organizational model.

To remain competitive, business and industry are undergoing extensive changes in organization and management styles. Law enforcement agencies also face the need for change to meet the competition of private policing. The private police industry employs nearly three times more people than does public law enforcement and outspends police by more than 73 percent (Harr & Hess, 2010). In addition, an estimated 85 percent of U.S. businesses and infrastructure are protected by private security. Some states have given them police powers.

Law enforcement agencies must compete not only with private police but also for the college graduates now entering the workforce. In addition, like business, many departments are turning to a **flat organization**: fewer lieutenants and captains, fewer staff departments, fewer staff assistants, more sergeants, and more patrol officers. Typical pyramid-organization charts will have the top pushed down and the sides expanded at the base.

Progressive businesses are restructuring top-heavy organizations, pushing authority and decision making as low as possible. Successful businesses concentrate on soliciting ideas from everyone in their organization about nearly every aspect of their operation. This approach can be applied to policing, especially in small departments. If officer retention is to be maintained and loyalty

flat organization

Unlike a typical pyramid organization chart, the top is pushed down and the sides are expanded at the base. In a police department, this means fewer lieutenants and captains, fewer staff departments, and fewer staff assistants but more sergeants and more patrol officers.

and morale preserved and heightened, officers must be **empowered**—that is, given authority and enabled to make decisions.

The operating principle of **decentralization** goes hand-in-hand with empowerment by pushing decision-making authority and autonomy as far down the management hierarchy as possible, to the rank where information is plentiful, typically at the level of the patrol officer:

> Decentralization is … closely linked to the implementation of community policing. … More responsibility for identifying and responding thoughtfully to community problems is delegated to individual patrol officers, who are encouraged to take the initiative in finding ways to deal with the problems of the communities in which they are operating. The consequence of this kind of decentralization is not only that the organization can become more proactive and more preventive, but also that it can respond to different sized problems. (National Research Council, 2004, p. 88)

Some ways to measure implementation of decentralization include participatory management initiatives, identification of community zones, use of bicycle and/or foot patrol, evaluation of policies and procedures, and improved citizen confidence in the patrol officers with whom they most often interact.

In summary, departments that have successfully implemented community policing have made several organizational changes:

- The bureaucracy is flattened and decentralized.
- Roles of those in management positions change to leaders and mentors rather than managers and supervisors.
- Patrol officers are given new responsibilities and empowered to make decisions and problem solve with their community partners.
- Permanent shifts and areas are assigned.

The department's organization should be carefully analyzed to identify barriers within the agency likely to impede the community policing initiative. This needs assessment should also consider external constraints controlled by others outside the department such as finance and budgeting, hiring rules, and state-mandated training programs. In addition to analyzing the department, the community being served must also be analyzed.

Analyzing the Community   Law enforcement agencies can learn the views of their community and at the same time let citizens know that their opinions matter. Interviews of community leaders and focus groups can be useful, but they are limited to one segment of the community or a small group of people. Polls and surveys have also become popular ways to get a better idea of the views of a much larger segment of the population.

The following three questions were asked of Chicago residents in a survey regarding the quality of police service (Skogan, 2004b, p. 75):

1. How responsive are the police in your neighborhood to community concerns? Do you think they are [very responsive to very unresponsive]?

empowered
Granting authority and decision making to lower-level officers.

decentralization
An operating principle that encourages flattening of the organization and places decision-making authority and autonomy at the level where information is plentiful, usually at the level of the patrol officer.

2. How good a job are the police doing in dealing with the problems that really concern people in your neighborhood? Would you say they are doing a [very good job to poor job]?

3. How good a job are the police doing in working together with residents in your neighborhood to solve local problems? Would you say they are doing a [very good job to poor job]?

A community survey might also offer police an opportunity to find out how citizens perceive crime and disorder problems in their community, posing questions such as the following: How do you perceive crime in our community? Has crime affected you personally? Are you aware of any problems in your neighborhood? Do you have any concerns about your safety while walking in your neighborhood?

At the heart of the community policing philosophy is the recognition that the police can no longer go it alone—if they ever could. They must use the eyes, ears, and voices of law-abiding citizens. A starting point is to analyze the community's demographics, as described in Chapter 3, including how much social capital is available for community policing efforts. Communities in which social capital is low but levels of community-oriented policing activity is high often perceive officers as facilitators who engage citizens in helping to alleviate complex social problems. However, in areas with high levels of both social capital and community policing, COP is more likely to be seen as a true partnership, a collaborative effort in which citizens and police work together to develop and implement effective problem-solving activities to improve the residents' quality of life (Correia, 2000). Thus, COP activity may be driven more by community factors than by factors internal to police organizations.

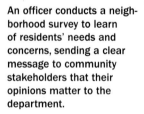

An officer conducts a neighborhood survey to learn of residents' needs and concerns, sending a clear message to community stakeholders that their opinions matter to the department.

AP Images/ALEX BRANDON

Police must develop a comprehensive picture of their community. They can do this through surveys and direct interactions with citizens. How community members respond when asked what problems they think the police should focus on and what solutions they would suggest can help the department meet the community's needs. Surveys ask for input from everyone instead of just the few citizens who are the most involved. Although usually a small number of leaders attend community meetings, the challenge is to reach beyond them to the average citizen. A survey is one answer; it offers some confirmation that community leaders are representing the needs and interests of their community. It would be enlightening to conduct a similar survey with police officers and their managers. Such shared information could go far in building trust among line officers, managers, and citizens.

The Bureau of Justice Statistics (BJS) and the Office of Community Oriented Policing Services (COPS) have available for local law enforcement agencies a computer software package designed to help conduct public opinion surveys about how well the police are doing their jobs. While conducting needs assessments, attention should be paid to who might be community leaders to enlist in the community policing initiative.

According to Correia (2000, p. 56): "It appears that the number of participants actively engaged in a community policing program is not as important as the character of the individuals participating. A 'critical mass' of individuals with high levels of social engagement may be more effective in solving a community's problems than a large number of individuals with low levels of social cohesion." A critical mass in physics is the smallest amount of a fissionable material that will sustain a nuclear chain reaction. In the context of community policing efforts, a **critical mass** is the smallest number of citizens and organizations needed to support and sustain the community policing initiative.

Once the needs assessment has been conducted, the next step is to develop a blueprint—that is, to do some strategic planning.

Strategic Planning

Strategic planning is long-term, large-scale, future-oriented planning. It begins with the vision and mission statements already discussed. It is grounded in those statements and guided by the findings of the needs assessment. From that point, specific goals and objectives and an accompanying implementation strategy and time line are developed. What looks like a straightforward process can turn extremely difficult as dilemmas arise and threaten the plan. Among the most predictable are the resistance to change and fear of the unknown that will be played out in the department and in the community. This resistance is also one of the most serious and difficult issues to be faced in a transition.

The strategic plan is long range. Departments do not successfully implement community policing in a year or two. It takes time—sometimes a decade or longer—for most departments to fully implement it. Again, all interested parties should be allowed input into the strategic plan.

critical mass
The smallest number of citizens and organizations needed to support and sustain the community policing initiative.

LO3
To best support and sustain the community policing initiative, it may be more important and effective for COP agencies to target a critical mass of individuals—a small number of highly socially engaged citizens and organizations—than to try to mobilize the entire community.

strategic planning
Long-term, large-scale, futuristic planning.

The Durham (New Hampshire) Police Department used a 1-day planning session to develop its strategic plan (Kurz, 2006). The department wanted to reach the widest possible audience and at the same time limit the group to a reasonable size. They sent invitations to members of the town council, the chamber of commerce, the school board, the ecumenical council, the high school's student senate, district court judges, chairpersons of town boards, members of organizations with a history of community commitment (e.g., the Lions, the Rotary Club), area clergy, defense attorneys, business leaders, media representatives, and student senators and officials from the University of New Hampshire.

The eight long-term objectives (5-year plan) that came out of the planning session were: (1) reduce the incidence of crime, (2) increase quality of service and customer satisfaction, (3) increase availability of grants and alternative funding sources, (4) maintain status as a nationally accredited law enforcement agency, (5) implement a comprehensive equipment replacement program, (6) provide high-quality training for all agency personnel, (7) increase the diversity of agency personnel, and (8) maintain an acceptable workload for police officers (Kurz, 2006, pp. 7–8). For each long-term objective, the plan identified a performance indicator, target dates for achievement of a series of short-term goals, and a list of strategies the department would use to achieve the objective.

At the end of each year, progress toward accomplishing the vision, mission statement, goals, and objectives should be measured. This may require a change in how performance usually has been assessed. Historically, police have measured their failures—the number of crimes committed—and successes— the number of arrests made. Such statistics are relatively easy to gather and to analyze. Assessing the effectiveness of crime prevention efforts, however, is much more difficult. How does a department measure reduced fear of crime, or satisfaction with police service, or the number of victimizations that did not happen? Nonetheless, as the CPC notes: "What gets measured gets done."

In addition to having a realistic time line, the strategic plan must also be tied to the agency's budget. Without the resources to implement the activities outlined in the long-range plan, they are not likely to be accomplished. Again, the transition will take time and, in some instances, additional resources.

Developing Strategies

Hundreds of strategies have been developed to implement community policing. Among the most common are use of foot, bike, and horse patrols; block watches; newsletters; community surveys; citizen volunteer programs; storefronts; special task units; and educational programs. Another common strategy is to assign officers to permanent beats and teach them community organizing and problem-solving skills. Some communities help teach landlords how to keep their properties crime free. Many communities encourage the development of neighborhood organizations, and some have formed teams (partnerships); for example, code and safety violations might be corrected by a team consisting of police, code enforcers, fire officials, and building code officers. Other communities have turned to the Internet to connect with their citizens.

The Los Angeles Police Department (LAPD) added a blog (Web log) to its popular Web site in 2006 that gives real-time, unfiltered information directly to the public (Los Angeles Police Department, 2006). Through the blog, the department can directly address rumors or misunderstandings that exist among the public or that are voiced by the media. The site also gives the department a chance to promote the good work of the officers and civilian employees, whose efforts often go unrecognized. The LAPD Web site registers about 1 million hits a day and 30 million each month. Naturally, smaller departments would not expect such impressive results, but even the smallest communities might find a computer-savvy citizen to volunteer to set up and manage a Web site for the department.

"What works?" "Has somebody tried ...?" "What can we do about ...?" "Why can't we ...?" Such questions are being asked by communities nationwide as they tackle the challenges of reducing violence, drugs, and other crimes and improving homeland security.

Section III describes numerous strategies that have been used throughout the country as departments move toward community policing.

> **LO5**
> The most important consideration in selecting strategies to implement community policing is to ensure that the strategies fit a community's unique needs and resources.

Hiring and Promoting ~~Start~~

Recruiting and selecting personnel are among the most important considerations in successfully implementing the community policing philosophy. Picking suitable, adaptable, self-disciplined recruits from the start is far preferable to overhauling and training officers lacking these characteristics (Haberfeld, 2006). Goldstein believes police agencies that hold tight to the traditional "crime fighting" model of policing will have difficulty transitioning to new ways of doing the job, stating: "Of all the changes required, redefining the role of rank-and-file police officers is the most important and has the greatest implications for the future of policing" (Community Policing Consortium, n.d.). Officers for the 21st century working in a department that has made the transition to community policing will need different attitudes and skills than those used in the past:

> One frequently discussed way to boost organizational support for community policing over time is to recruit and train a "new breed" of officer. In addition to the skills and abilities traditionally associated with success in police work, community policing demands above-average skills in verbal and written communication, the ability to work closely with people from all walks of life, and a strong desire to develop skills in conflict resolution and creative problem solving through collaboration. The challenge for police departments is to reach out and attract individuals who might otherwise not think of police work, such as persons in education and social work fields. (Connors & Webster, 2001, p. 93)

In a characteristic-based job analysis of what recruits should look like to do community policing effectively, several core competencies were identified, including (1) social competence, (2) teamwork, (3) adaptability/flexibility, (4) conscientiousness/dependability, (5) impulse control/attention to safety, (6) integrity/ethics, (7) emotional regulation and stress tolerance, (8) decision making and judgment, (9) assertiveness/persuasiveness, (10) avoidance of substance abuse and other risk-taking behaviors, and (11) commitment to service/social concern (Scrivner, 2006). In addition, the President's Task Force on 21st Century Policing has advanced a recommendation to recruit and hire officers who possess character traits that support fairness, compassion, and cultural sensitivity, the qualities that fit the "guardian" mindset (2015).

In addition to hiring officers who fit the community policing philosophy, departments are increasingly hiring for diversity: "Hiring officers who reflect the community they serve is important not only to external relations but also to increasing understanding within the agency" (President's Task Force, 2015, p. 51). *Diversity* encompasses not only race and gender, but also language, life experience, religious beliefs, sexual orientation, and cultural background

Regarding race, the number of minority officers has increased over the past quarter century, particularly in larger agencies serving more highly populated jurisdictions. In 2013, 27 percent of full-time sworn police officers were members of a racial or ethnic minority, an increase of 150 percent since 1987, when minorities comprised 14.6 percent of sworn officers (Reaves, 2015). Currently, more than two in five officers in jurisdictions with 500,000 or more residents are members of a racial or ethnic minority, compared to fewer than one in five officers in jurisdictions with a population of less than 50,000. Despite progress, a lack of diversity remains the norm for hundreds of police departments across the country, and recruiting and retaining minority officers remains a challenge for most departments (Peak, 2014): "One of the first facts people noticed after a white police officer killed Michael Brown, an unarmed black teenager in Ferguson, Mo., was that only three of the 53 cops on the local force were black. That's nowhere near the city's racial composition, where two-thirds of residents are African-American." Overcoming the negative perceptions of law enforcement held by many residents in communities of color is a complicating factor in recruiting for diversity. Sherrilyn Ifill, president of and director-counsel for the NAACP Legal Defense and Educational Fund, Inc., shared at a listening session for the President's Task Force on 21st Century Policing this perspective of youth in poor communities:

> By the time you are 17, you have been stopped and frisked a dozen times. That does not make that 17-year-old want to become a police officer . . . . The challenge is to transform the idea of policing in communities among young people into something they see as honorable. They have to see people at local events, as the person who lives across the street, not someone who comes in and knows nothing about my community (2015, p. 11).

Delores Jones-Brown, a former prosecutor and professor at John Jay College of Criminal Justice in New York, expresses a similar sentiment, acknowledging that racial minorities often do not sign up as police recruits because "they don't want to become part of [what's seen as] the problem" (Peak, 2014).

Many now advocate a community policing approach as the best way to change such negative perceptions and improve the diversity of the applicant pool.

The International Association of Chiefs of Police (IACP) launched a Web-based recruiting site called DiscoverPolicing.org in November of 2008. In February 2009, the IACP won the Interactive Media Award's Best in Class for the Web site. The site was honored specifically for excellence in recruiting (Matrix Group, 2009). DiscoverPolicing.org is a central hiring place designed to recruit the right kind of officers who reflect community diversity.

Agencies also seek candidates with the skills to complement their community policing and intelligence-oriented policing styles. DiscoverPolicing.com seeks to correct the pervasive, completely inaccurate image of the law enforcement profession fostered by the media and popular culture. The site contains information on all aspects of law enforcement careers: benefits, kinds of agencies and job opportunities, skills and abilities needed, and information about hiring and training. The site also has links and contact information for agencies in all 50 states, allowing applicants to connect with hiring agencies (Kohlhepp & Phillips, 2009).

In areas where the available pool of candidates is limited and force numbers need to be increased, some departments lower their standards, sacrificing quantity for quality.

Training

Training is critical for a successful transition to community policing. Unfortunately, when departments are faced with budget cuts and diminishing resources, training is often one of the first areas to be sacrificed (Skogan, 2004a). The President's Task Force on 21st Century Policing identifies "Training and Education" as one of the six main "pillars" crucial to rebuilding public trust and restoring police legitimacy:

> Though today's law enforcement professionals are highly trained and highly skilled operationally, they must develop specialized knowledge and understanding that enable fair and procedurally just policing and allow to meet a wide variety of new challenges and expectations. Tactical skills are important, but attitude, tolerance, and interpersonal skills are equally so. And to be effective in an ever-changing world, training must continue throughout an officer's career (2015, p. 52).

For departments to which a community policing is a new paradigm, training must be provided to all personnel at all levels to explain the change process and reduce fear and resistance. Necessarily, training must explore the community policing philosophy and the planning process to encourage all stakeholders to participate. However, such training should *not* be the spearhead of change.

Many efforts have been made to place training at the leading edge of change in both the public and private sectors. Much time and energy are expended in such efforts, but, no matter how effective the training, it will be neutralized if what is learned is inconsistent with practices and procedures occurring in the department. As the community policing philosophy takes hold in a department, officers will be more receptive to the training they will need to be effective community policing officers.

LO6

Among the most important areas to include in training are communication skills, problem-solving skills, and leadership skills.

Communication skills are the focus of Section II. Problem-solving skills were discussed in Chapter 4.

Once hired, new recruits are almost always trained by partnering them with seasoned officers for a few months. It is common for these training officers to influence recruits and their work for the rest of their careers. Most often, the influence includes strong pressure to adopt traditional policing methods and thinking. Recruits are frequently told to "forget what you learned in the academy." No matter what education and training the recruit had prior to hiring, it is frequently replaced with the methods and values of senior officers.

The COPS Office, in conjunction with the Reno (Nevada) Police Department and the Police Executive Research Forum (PERF), has developed a model Police Training Officer (PTO) program that incorporates contemporary adult educational methods and a version of problem-based learning. The 15-week program begins with a 1-week integration period followed by four 3-week phases: nonemergency incident response, emergency incident response, patrol activities, and criminal investigation. A week between the second and third phase is devoted to mid-term evaluation. The last week is devoted to final evaluation.

During each phase, journals (not part of the evaluation) are kept and neighborhood portfolio exercises are completed. The neighborhood portfolio exercises are designed to give trainees a sense of the community as well as to develop community contacts. Each phase also includes weekly coaching and training as well as problem-based learning exercises. Assessment of the programs shows that is has produced outstanding results (Nelson, 2004, p. 15): "New officers enter the field with problem-solving skills that are rarely seen at that career level. New officers also display remarkable leadership and a willingness to work as partners with the local community to fight crime and disorder."

The COPS Office has also funded a network of Regional Community Policing Institutes (RCPIs) across the country to help local law enforcement agencies meet their community policing training needs. RCPIs train not only officers but citizens in the community and government leaders as well, reaching more than 70,000 individuals each year and offering information on topics such as counterterrorism and homeland security, human trafficking, gangs, school safety, Internet predators, meth labs, domestic violence, cultural diversity, ethics and integrity, rural community policing, community partnerships, technology for community policing, and more (Office of Community Oriented Policing Services, 2006).

AN EXAMPLE OF A STRATEGIC PLAN TO IMPLEMENT COMMUNITY POLICING

The Columbia (South Carolina) Police Department's 2015–2019 Strategic Plan, an excerpt of which is shown in Figure 5.3, sets forth the agency's direction for a 5-year period and lists its mission, vision, values, and goals as well as initiatives, plan elements, and strategies. Following is a portion of the Columbia Police Department's Strategic Plan. To view the entire plan, visit their Web site https://www.columbiasc.net/depts/headlines/cpd_strategicplan_2015-2019_web.pdf.

Figure 5.3	The Columbia, South Carolina, Police Department's 2015–2019 Strategic Plan

INTRODUCTION

The **Columbia Police Department's 2015–2019 Strategic Plan** sets forth our direction for the next five (5) years.
Our goals are focused on 4 key areas:

1. Staffing and facilities
2. Professional development
3. Policing
4. Equipment and technology

MISSION, VISION, AND CORE VALUES

Mission Statement: The Columbia Police Department will provide professional and ethical service in protection of our citizens while preventing crime and reducing the fear of crime through problem solving partnerships.
We will accomplish our mission by:

- Solving crimes
- Meeting the expectations of our community
- Building and maintaining public trust
- Reducing victimization
- Demonstrating fiscal responsibility
- Upholding the constitutional rights of our citizens
- Enforcing the law with integrity, fairness and compassion

Vision Statement: Through our steadfast commitment to policing excellence, the Columbia Police Department will be transformed to exhibit the innovation, engagement and professionalism of an exceptional organization whose workforce truly reflects the values and diversity of the City of Columbia.

Core Values:
Professionalism
Integrity
Diversity
Service orientation
Fairness
Courage
Collaboration
Communication

POLICING IN THE 21ST CENTURY CHALLENGES AND OPPORTUNITIES

Organizational Transformation, Accountability & Transparency
To accomplish our mission, we must have the trust and confidence of the citizens we serve. To that end, we will employ many initiatives to further build and maintain public trust and confidence. These initiatives will improve our ability to be more accountable, transparent and self-monitoring.

Some of the initiatives highlighted in our strategic plan include:

- Establishing a Discipline Review Board to review completed internal investigations of complaints against CPD officers;
- Publishing an Annual Internal Affairs Report to provide citizens with an overview of police department internal affairs activities, along with supporting data and information;
- Developing an annual CPD report to provide citizens with an overview of police operations; and
- Enhancing processes to more effectively track and report information related to officer-involved shootings.

Community Policing – Refocusing on Community Needs and Relationships
Our strategic plan serves to reinforce the tenets of community policing: community partnerships, using problem solving to address crime systematically, and organizational transformation of the police department and its employees to enhance the effectiveness of these efforts.

Key community policing strategies include:

- Making long-term assignments of police officers in city neighborhoods to further facilitate police-community relationships;
- Building and cultivating relationships with community stakeholders to identify public safety needs and develop problem solving strategies; and
- Expanding the use of evidence based and data driven strategies, such as Crime Prevention Through Environmental Design, to prevent and reduce crime.

Source: Adapted from Columbia Police Department. *2015-2019 Strategic Plan.* http://www.columbiasc.net/depts/city-council/docs/2015/2015_council_
committees/public_safety_committee/cpd_strategic_plan.pdf

LESSONS LEARNED FROM TEAM POLICING

Scott (2000, p. 97) provides a look at team policing and its influence on community policing after some 20 years have passed:

> Team policing, a loose collection of ideas about how the police might more effectively serve the public, is, in hindsight, seen as the precursor to contemporary community policing methods. Several key people, like Patrick Murphy, who advocated team policing methods also would later advocate community policing. Many U.S. police agencies tested and implemented team policing in its various forms in the 1970s and 1980s. . . . A number of large and medium-sized police agencies can today attribute geographic decentralization of their operations to team policing initiatives. The decentralization of *authority,* however, which was central to team policing's underlying theories, proved more threatening to many police executives, and did not survive as well as *geographic* decentralization.

Few people today have declared team policing either an unqualified success or an unqualified failure (Walker, 1993). There is general consensus today that team policing might have been a bit ahead of its time but that many of its premises were and remain sound and that it had sufficient appeal both to the community and to rank-and-file police officers. Indeed, several core features of team policing, such as stability of geographic assignment, unity of command, interaction between police and community, geographic decentralization of police operations, despecialization of police services, greater responsiveness to community concerns, some decentralization of internal decision making, and at least some shared decision making with the community, are in place in many of today's police agencies. Even when these features fall short of what some might consider optimal, most police managers generally consider them desirable almost 30 years after the advent of team policing.

Walker (1993) suggests that those implementing community policing should take some lessons from what was learned from the team policing programs instituted during the mid-1960s to mid-1970s. Both community policing and team policing had a neighborhood focus, decentralized decision making, community input, and a new police role. The basic goals of community policing differ radically from those of team policing, however, with community policing rejecting the crime-attack model in favor of an emphasis on order maintenance and quality-of-life problems. In addition, the team policing effort faced several major obstacles, including opposition from middle management, who feared losing their power of authority to officers of lower ranks; resentment by officers who felt the more nebulous "team" approach actually created disparate and unfair workloads; and shortcomings with communications technology, as dispatch was routinely unable to contact officers whose duties took them outside the boundaries of their team beat (Walker, 1993). Perhaps the most important lesson to be learned from team policing, however, was that unclear definitions of goals and roles held the greatest potential to thwart the successful implementation of community policing. Because community policing represents a radical redefinition of the traditional police role—from that of crime fighter to problem solver and public service provider—it requires resocializing not only the officers involved but also the public they serve (Walker, 1993).

LO7

Both community policing and team policing have a neighborhood focus, decentralized decision making, community input, and a new police role. The basic goals of community policing differ radically from those of team policing, however, with community policing rejecting the crime-attack model in favor of an emphasis on order maintenance and quality-of-life problems. The most important lesson to be learned from team policing is the problem associated with unclear definition of goals.

BENEFITS THAT MIGHT BE ACHIEVED FROM COMMUNITY POLICING

The benefits of implementing community policing are numerous, to the department, to individual officers, and to the community at large. Community policing brings police closer to the people, building relationships between police and community and among community members themselves. As police interaction with the community becomes more positive, productive partnerships are formed and community and officer leadership skills are developed. Citizens see that problems have solutions, and this gives citizens courage to tackle other community issues. As citizens feel more empowered to get involved, prevention and detection of crime increases, leading to reduced fear of crime in the community and improved quality of life. Reduced levels of crime allow more police resources to be allocated to services that have the greatest impact on the quality of community life. Making effective use of the talents and resources available within communities further extends severely strained police resources. Community policing also provides real challenges for officers, making them more than "order takers and report writers," which leads to increased job satisfaction among officers.

RESISTANCE TO COMMUNITY POLICING

Despite the many advantages and benefits presented by the community policing approach, resistance will be encountered. Managers should anticipate and prepare for resistance and the changes that accompany the transition to the community policing philosophy.

Consider the following analogy: A professional truck driver does not drive his 50-ton trailer-truck the same way he drives a sports car. In the truck, he corners more slowly and avoids braking sharply; otherwise, the trailer's momentum could cause the truck to overturn or jackknife. Police organizations also have considerable momentum, and many officers find a high degree of comfort in sticking to the status quo.

Kennedy (2006, p. 164) observes: "Law enforcement likes enforcing the law." And, as are most humans, police are creatures of habit. Law enforcement officers most readily accept change in small, incremental doses, including "innovations that require the least radical departures from their hierarchical paramilitary organizational structures, continue incident-driven and reactive strategies, and maintain police sovereignty over crime issues. In its most basic form, hot spots policing simply concentrates traditional enforcement activity at high crime places" (Braga & Weisburd, 2007, p. 17). Other strategies, such as pulling levers or broken windows policing, also appeal to police because they permit officers to use mostly traditional tactics but deploy them in new ways that provide greater efficiency, effectiveness, and, consequently, better results. It is, therefore, not surprising that strategies calling for the greatest changes in existing police practices and structures are the most difficult to implement. Nonetheless, research has found that police attitudes have been gradually changing toward the adoption of new strategies, with officers' views towards the community and problem-oriented policing philosophy becoming more positive (Braga & Weisburd, 2007).

IDEAS **IN PRACTICE** — ALISON NEIGHBORHOOD INITIATIVE

(Category: Population over 250,000—Waterloo Regional Police Service, Ontario, Canada)

Population Served: 500,000

In 2006 when the chief of the Waterloo Regional Police Service (WRPS) received a letter from a Muslim resident titled, "Unrest in the Community," that described a crisis due to ethnic tensions in Cambridge, Ontario, Canada, a catalyst was launched. That catalyst inspired police and community members to overcome barriers and learn the power of collaboration and the value of small change. The police collaborated with Muslim community leaders, the Cambridge YMCA, Waterloo Regional Housing, and the City of Cambridge to create a long-term plan that aimed to develop relationships based on trust and inclusivity, to create training opportunities around cultural diversity, and to maintain a safe community.

The WRPS wanted the Muslim community to feel confident the police would respond to their concerns, would involve them in the investigative process, and would be sensitive to their cultural heritage. WRPS hoped to change the negative perception the community may have had about the police because of the way the police were perceived in their countries of origin.

Because this initiative created an equal partner with the Muslim community, this initiative had support from the rest of the community.

In 2009, a collaborative event took place at the Islamic Center as a sign of the new partnership, the badging of new police recruits. At this event, two student winners presented their inspiring essays on "What Do Police Officers Bring to Our Community?" The news of this event brought such a stream of letters of support from the community that they were able to fund an outreach coordinator. WRPS realized that the police are not experts at everything, and there are many people with talents, skills, and connections that can be used when developing and implementing an action plan. However, the most important lesson WRPS learned was that they have a great deal more to learn from the community, and they will keep adapting their agency to the needs of the community.

Source: *IACP Community Policing Awards (Sponsored by Cisco): 2011 Winners and Finalists.* San Jose, CA: Cisco Systems, Inc. 2011. Retrieved August 2, 2016, from http://www.iacpcommunitypolicing.org/download/brochure_C02-690744_FINAL.pdf

---

LO8

Impediments to COP implementation include:

- Organizational impediments—resistance from middle management, line officers, and unions; confusion about what COP is; problems in line-level accountability; officers' concerns that COP is "soft" on crime; lack of COP training
- Union impediments—resistance to change, fear of losing control to the community, resistance to increased officer responsibility and accountability, and fear that COP will lead to civilian review boards
- Community impediments—community resistance, community's concern that COP is "soft" on crime, civil service rules, pressure to demonstrate that COP reduces crime, and lack of support from local government
- Transition impediments—balancing increased foot patrol activities with maintaining emergency response time

PITFALLS TO AVOID

Common pitfalls in making the transition to community policing include unrealistic expectations and focusing on short-term instead of long-term results; adopting a task force approach; resisting the move toward community empowerment; taking advantage of the position; and misrepresenting an inadequate program as legitimate in order to receive funding.

One pitfall is the common expectation that implementing a new strategy such as community policing, highly touted as an effective method of crime reduction, will have immediate and measurable results. It may have immediate results—but not the ones citizens were expecting. Ironically, increased citizen vigilance and reporting, although a desirable and positive outcome of successful community policing, may initially indicate an *increase* in crime and lead to disappointment and widespread skepticism regarding community policing's effectiveness. Such misunderstandings, generated by ambiguous promises, can sabotage a department's efforts to build the relationships with citizens necessary for community policing. Before making predictions and promises regarding community policing's long-term benefits, make sure everyone understands the possible short-term outcomes.

Another pitfall is management's inability to gain the commitment of the entire organization by encouraging officers to become specialists instead of generalists. This often occurs when an agency adopts a specialized unit approach, isolating acceptance of the philosophy to those in the community policing unit. Such separation and isolation marginalizes the community policing approach and essentially dooms the initiative to failure. The area of crime prevention in agencies has almost always been the responsibility of specialized units. This usually resulted in a shift in thinking of officers, such that they felt preventing crime was the job of those few personnel assigned to the unit. It is not uncommon for an officer, when asked by a citizen how to prevent being burglarized, for example, to respond by telling the citizen to contact someone in the crime prevention unit.

There has also been a tendency for officers not assigned to specialized units to minimize such units' importance, claiming their own assignment was "real police work" and everything else was essentially unimportant. In some cases, officers assigned to special units became discounted and ignored by their colleagues as irrelevant and not part of the group.

ADVANTAGES AND DISADVANTAGES OF IMPLEMENTATION MODELS

Many agencies have numerous specialized units, so it is understandable that when they seek to implement community policing they do so by creating specialized community policing agencies (Scheider, 2008). Other agencies use community policing generalists, assigning responsibility for community policing to all officers, and still others use a combination of these two approaches (hybrid).

Community Policing Specialists

Having dedicated officers assigned full time to community policing has several advantages:

- Officers have sufficient time to devote to proactive problem-solving and partnership-building efforts.
- It is easier for agencies to develop the knowledge and skills needed to maximize efforts.
- The visibility of community policing activities both within the department and in the community is increased.

Specialized units, however, also have disadvantages, such as causing resentment among other officers who believe the units receive special treatment and their activities are not real police work (calling them "grin and wave squads"). Further, specialized units might lead the majority of officers to believe they are not responsible for developing partnerships, using problem-solving activities, or paying attention to community relations. Such units also limit the number of officers receiving community policing training, making it unlikely that community policing will grow beyond the special unit.

Community Policing Generalists

Community policing advocates (such as the COPS Office) generally support the agency-wide implementation of community policing, seeing community policing as a philosophy that should influence all aspects of police work. Adopting a community policing generalist model removes potential tension between a special unit and the other officers. This model also has other advantages: It emphasizes proactive problem solving and partnership development to all officers and builds these activities into their jobs.

- It applies community policing principles to all aspects of police business, including routine patrol, investigations, arrests, and traffic stops.
- It increases the potential scope and breadth of community policing efforts and facilitates its eventual institutionalization.

A disadvantage of the generalist model is that it can result in a watered-down version of community policing (more community relations than community policing), with officers devoting limited time to partnership building and problem solving. If officers do not see such activities as integrated into their current duties, they might see them as extra work and resist implementing them. In fact, officers often report they have insufficient time for community policing and will resist agency-wide implementation. Finally, it can be difficult for large agencies to provide adequate training to large enough numbers of officers to fully implement the community policing philosophy. To overcome concerns, some agencies have implemented a community policing model combining the specialized and generalist models.

Hybrid Approaches

Some agencies have formed special community policing units while encouraging all officers to participate in their efforts. For example, a special unit might engage in in-depth problem-solving efforts for a precinct or an entire city, but at the same time, agency leaders may make it clear that some problem-solving activities are expected of *all* officers focused on a specific neighborhood or even a single address. All officers are encouraged to rely on the special unit for help in implementing their own community policing efforts. Finally, all officers can receive appropriate training in community policing tailored to their positions.

EVALUATING PROGRESS

Without specifying desired outcomes as part of the strategic plan, the community policing initiative could be reduced to another series of community relations exercises rather than the anticipated cultural, organizational, and structural changes achieved through community policing in partnership and problem solving. Recall from Chapter 4 that the SARA (scanning, analysis, response, and assessment) model of problem solving shows that there are no failures, only responses that do not provide the desired goal. Remember also from Chapter 4 the mental lock: "To err is wrong." Avoid this thinking trap by understanding that risk-taking is a necessary part of progress and that erring is wrong only if you fail to learn from your "mistake." Edison is quoted as saying he did not fail 25,000 times to make a storage battery. He simply knew 25,000 ways *not* to make one.

Evaluating progress can take many forms. It should have been built into the strategic plan in concrete form. Which goals and objectives have been met? Which have not? Why not? The evaluation might also consist of conducting a second needs assessment of both the department and the community a year later to determine whether needs are being better met. It can be done through additional surveys and interviews assessing reduced fear of crime and improved confidence in police. Are citizens making fewer complaints regarding police service? Are officers filing fewer grievances?

> **LO9**
> When evaluating, failures should be as important as successes—sometimes more important—because a department learns from what does not work.

Evaluating effectiveness is difficult. Police have long been able to evaluate their efficiency by looking at police activity—what police do rather than what effect it had. It is far easier to look at numbers—crime reports filed, arrests made, tickets issued, drugs seized—than to measure how problems have been solved. Measuring effectiveness requires careful consideration of performance indicators and establishment of realistic and meaningful measures. Performance indicators must be responsive to community concerns, and output measures must reflect the ability of the police to adapt and mobilize their efforts to diagnose and solve community problems (Community Policing Consortium, 2000).

SUMMARY

Community policing will require a change in management style, mission and vision statements, departmental organization and community mobilization efforts, the agency's strategic plan and strategies to implement, hiring and promoting practices, and training. A department's vision should include the essential elements of the community policing philosophy: problem solving, empowerment, forming community partnerships, and being proactive—making preventing crime as important as enforcing the law.

A needs assessment should include not only the department but also the community of which it is a part. The traditional law enforcement organization design has been that of a pyramid-shaped hierarchy based on a military model. However, the pyramid might be inverted to implement community policing. Another change might occur in leadership style, with a preference for participatory leadership, where each individual has a voice in decisions but top management still has the ultimate decision-making authority.

To best support and sustain the community policing initiative, it may be more important and effective for COP agencies to target a critical mass of individuals—a small number of highly socially engaged citizens and organizations—than to try to mobilize the entire community.

The strategic plan should include community partnerships and problem solving as well as any needed cultural and organizational changes in the department. It should also include a realistic time line and ways to assess progress. It must also be tied to the department's budget. The most important consideration in selecting strategies to implement community policing is to ensure that the strategies fit the community's unique needs and resources.

Training is also critical for a successful transition to community policing. However, do *not* make training the spearhead of change. Among the most important areas to include in training are communication skills, problem-solving skills, and leadership skills.

Those implementing community policing should take some lessons from what was learned from the team policing programs instituted during the mid-1960s to mid-1970s. Both community policing and team policing have a neighborhood focus, decentralized decision making, community input, and a new police role. The basic goals of community policing differ radically from those of team policing, however, with community policing rejecting the crime-attack model in favor of an emphasis on order maintenance and quality-of-life problems. The most important lesson to be learned from team policing is the problem associated with unclear definition of goals. Managers should anticipate and prepare for resistance to the community policing philosophy and the changes that accompany the transition. They should also be aware of and try to avoid common pitfalls in making the transition to community policing, including unrealistic expectations and focusing on short-term instead of long-term results; adopting a task force approach; resisting the move toward community empowerment; taking advantage of the position; and misrepresenting an inadequate program as legitimate to receive funding.

Impediments to COP implementation include organizational, union, community, and transition impediments. Organization impediments may include resistance from middle management, line officers, and unions; confusion about what COP is; problems in line-level accountability; officers' concern that COP is soft on crime; and lack of COP training. Union impediments may include resistance to change, fear of losing control to the community, resistance to increased officer responsibility and accountability, and fear that COP will lead to civilian review boards. Community impediments may include community resistance, community's concern that COP is "soft" on crime, civil service rules, pressure to demonstrate COP reduces crime, and lack of support from local government. Transition impediments may include balancing increased foot patrol activities with maintaining emergency response time.

When evaluating, failures should be as important as successes—sometimes more important—because a department learns from what does not work.

DISCUSSION QUESTIONS

1. What do you consider the greatest obstacles to implementing community policing?

2. If you had to prioritize the changes needed to convert to community policing, what would your priorities be?

3. Find out what your police department's mission statement is. If it is not community policing focused, how would you revise it?

4. How would you determine whether community policing efforts are working?

5. Why might citizens not want to become involved in community policing efforts?

6. Why is a diverse law enforcement agency important? What ideas do you have for recruiting with this in mind?

7. How would you go about assessing your community's needs regarding efforts to reduce crime and violence?

8. Are there conflicting groups within your "community"? Does one group have more political power than another?

9. Can you explain why some police officers oppose community policing?

10. Name at least three attributes that would indicate a job candidate might be a good fit for a department engaged in community policing.

ADDITIONAL RESOURCES

COPS Office (Department of Justice)
    www.cops.usdoj.gov
Justice Information Center
    www.justiceinformationcenter.us

Police Executive Research Forum
    www.policeforum.org
Upper Midwest Community Policing Institute
    www.umcpi.org

Building Relationships and Trust

Jim West/Alamy Stock Photo

With the basic background supplied in Section I, you are ready to look at the interaction occurring between the police and the public they serve and protect. At the most basic level, police–community relations begin with one-on-one interaction between an officer and a citizen.

The section begins with a discussion of the communication skills needed to interact effectively with citizens, including with the increasingly diverse populace of the United States and with victims and witnesses (Chapter 6). Next, building partnerships with key stakeholders and selling the concept of community policing, both internally and externally, are explored (Chapter 7). The section concludes with a look at building partnerships with the media and how the media can also collaborate in selling the concept (Chapter 8).

Although these crucial components of community policing are discussed separately, overlap often exists.

149

Communicating with a Diverse Population

Learning Objectives

LO1 Explain the communication process.

LO2 Identify the barriers to communication that police officers often confront.

LO3 Summarize the dilemma law enforcement officers sometimes face when interacting with immigrants.

LO4 Explain the difference between prejudice and discrimination.

LO5 Identify the disabilities police officers frequently encounter when interacting with citizens.

LO6 List the special challenges posed by persons suffering from Alzheimer's disease.

LO7 Explain why effective communication with victims of and witnesses to crime is essential.

Key Terms

acculturation
Alzheimer's disease (AD)
Americans with Disabilities Act (ADA)
assimilation
attention-deficit hyperactivity disorder (ADHD)
bias
communication process
crack children
crisis behavior
EBD
ethnocentrism
fetal alcohol syndrome (FAS)
implicit bias
jargon
kinesics
nonverbal communication
posttraumatic stress disorder (PTSD)
poverty syndrome
racial profiling
stereotyping

New York City is America's most populous city. With such a diversity of cultures, it is no wonder the city's police force is leading the field in improving communication among their 2,981,544 foreign-born citizens. To say that communication within this unique microcosm of a city is crucial to effective law enforcement is an understatement. By using technology, along with increasing diversity among their ranks, the department has had far-reaching success among the numerous populations residing in New York's five boroughs.

NYPD has always been the standard bearer when it comes to communication with diverse populations. The precinct receptionist program started in 1968, in which bilingual citizens were actively recruited to assist in interpretation, has now blossomed into routinely supporting federal law enforcement agencies when they are in need of interpretative assistance. The NYPD wants to ensure that all citizens are treated with civility. Therefore, respectful communication where understanding can be reached among all parties has become a priority. Their creation of the New Immigrant Outreach Unit, Executive Order 41, and Language Access Plan has been largely applauded by the communities in which they patrol.

The New Immigrant Outreach Unit has allowed the police department to network with newest additions to the various immigrant communities in which they are sworn to protect. Because these communication contacts are also foreign born, they are familiar with the anxieties and other issues new immigrants face. These individuals build trust with the new migrant and help build a bilingual foundation within the community that can benefit law enforcement. By networking in such a manner, the police can monitor the growth and any new public safety concerns within the community, while also being able to provide links to social services an immigrant culture might need.

Executive Order 41 is another initiative to build trust and foster communication between foreign-born communities and law enforcement. This piece of legislation mandates that police are not allowed to inquire as to an individual's immigration status. Thus, regardless of whether the individual is a victim or a witness to a crime, the police cannot request that person's status.

In addition to the increased diversity and legislation, the NYPD has also substantially invested in their Language Access Plan. The Language Line technology allows for free language interpretation within the many boroughs. Street supervisors, department wide, have been handed one of the many 35,000 smartphones with the downloaded Language Line customized app. This groundbreaking technology allows access to numerous interpreters, at any point in time during patrol, who can speak 1 of 50 languages. While the department's officers and their 72 language capabilities are impressive, it is comforting for the new immigrants to have access to their individual dialect through Language Line. This technology not only brings security to the foreign-born population within the city, it also encourages trust between the diverse population and law enforcement.

INTRODUCTION

Effective communication with the public is vital to good police–community relations. In fact, at the heart of police–community relations are the one-on-one interactions between an officer and a citizen: "Communication is essential to the development of partnerships that make community policing an effective strategy for ensuring public safety. Community policing programs, in which law enforcement officers partner with community members to identify and solve problems, cannot work well when officers and residents fail to understand each other" (Shah & Estrada, 2009, p. 5). Effective communication becomes even more challenging as our society becomes more diverse, requiring an understanding not only of the communication process but also of the differences among individuals that affect communication.

Keep in mind while reading this chapter that although various groups are presented separately to keep the discussion organized, in real life individuals can rarely be so neatly compartmentalized. Americans embody every overlapping combination of diversity characteristics imaginable—from the young Hispanic girl who is deaf, to the middle-aged Jewish man who is homeless, to the elderly Black woman with bipolar disorder.

THE COMMUNICATION PROCESS

Communication is basically the transfer of information.

Communication involves transferring thoughts from one person's mind to another's. The people involved, the accuracy of the message in expressing the sender's thoughts, and the channel used all affect communication. A simplified illustration of the process is shown in Figure 6.1.

The sender encodes the message in words—spoken or written—and then transmits the message by phone, by texting, by fax, by letter, in person, or in some other way. The receiver decodes the message. The receiver may then provide the sender with some kind of feedback indicating the message has been received. Many factors will influence the message. Important individual characteristics in communication include the sender's and receiver's age, education, gender, values, emotional involvement, self-esteem, and language skills.

Surprisingly, police departments rarely train their officers in communication skills. Many police managers erroneously assume that the people they hire know how to communicate. The Rand report, "Training the Twenty-First Century Police Officer: Redefining Police Professionalism for the Los Angeles Police Department," notes: "To communicate effectively is to be skilled in the overt and the subtle, to make one's intentions known whether the recipient is deaf, unable to understand English, mentally handicapped, enraged,

L01

The **communication process** involves a sender, a message, a channel, a receiver, and, sometimes, feedback.

communication process

Involves a sender, a message, a channel, a receiver, and, sometimes, feedback.

Figure 6.1 The Communication Process

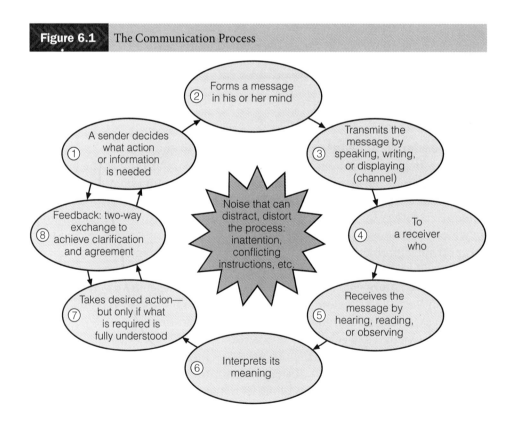

under the influence of drugs or alcohol, or simply unfamiliar with normal police procedure" (Glenn et al., 2003, p. 120). Skilled officers can communicate effectively even when they are under tremendous stress. The skill is critical for successfully gaining compliance or cooperation from subjects and for managing situations where arrest, search and seizure, or use of force scenarios that are "intricately related" are required.

Nonetheless, "Tactical communications as currently taught are too limited in scope and poorly integrated with other instruction. Officers need to learn how, when, and with what type of person certain communication techniques are more effective. This is particularly important when deadly force might be applied. A person who does not understand English or a person with a mental illness might inadvertently send aggressive signals to the officer. The officer needs to be adept at selecting from and effectively applying various modes of communication, verbal and nonverbal, under conditions of extreme stress" (Glenn et al., 2003, p. 136).

The late Dr. George Thompson, the name behind the effective and popular police training company the Verbal Judo Institute, asserted that the use of courtesy and respect is the safest and most powerful way for police officers to interact with even dangerous or explosive members of the public (2009). Thompson, a college English professor who became a police officer, called the technique *tactical civility*. According to Dr. Thompson, when officers respond to verbal attacks in kind, they give up their own personal and professional power and allow themselves to be controlled by others. A display of anger also reveals weakness and indecision, something most officers cannot afford to show in public. If officers react with rudeness or threatening comments, they put the other person on notice of pending attack, a tactical mistake.

Thompson recommended officers not give such an early warning but just remain civil, get tough if necessary, and return to civility. Politeness does not equal weakness, but the other person may mistake it for that, causing him or her to play into an officer's hands. An officer who can maintain a courteous manner, even in the face of extreme rudeness, will only benefit from such self-control, particularly down the road when an encounter may be brought into court or scrutinized by a supervisor or internal affairs (IA) division. Regardless of the temptation: "Don't use words that will betray you later" (Thompson, 2009).

Community policing can only work if officers handle people with dignity and respect. This mandate often becomes more challenging in those neighborhoods where residents live in fear of crime and are reluctant to "get involved" if they see something that requires a police response: "The people in affluent, successful America do not want a police presence, except indirectly. The people who *need* us bar their windows and hope for the best" (Thompson, 2006). The "gap" between the police and many areas in the community needs to be eliminated. If that gap can be closed, offenders have nowhere to commit their crimes. In communities where people see the police as guardians, they work in concert with the police to "take out the bad guys."

In a democracy, an effective police force requires the consent and cooperation of the citizens (Giles, Fortman, Dailey, Barker, & Hajek, 2005). When that consent and cooperation exist, witnesses to crimes willingly come forward with information; citizens are more likely to follow police directives in an emergency; and citizens are also more likely to support the police legislatively—for example, in increasing funding for police departments.

How can that consent and cooperation be achieved? Research has found that police are most likely to obtain cooperation if they engage in *process-oriented policing*—that is, they are attentive to the way they treat people, behaving in ways that positively influence the degree to which people perceive the procedures used as fair. In other words, police must adhere to the principles of procedural justice.

Several elements influence people's judgments regarding fairness of procedures (Skogan & Frydl, 2004). One key element is participation; procedures are perceived as fairer if people are allowed to explain their situation. A second key element is neutrality. Evidence of evenhandedness and objectivity increases perceived fairness. Third, people value being treated with dignity and respect. Finally, people perceive procedures as being fairer when they trust the motives of decision makers.

Nonverbal Communication and Body Language

nonverbal communication

Includes everything other than the actual words spoken in a message, such as tone, pitch, and pacing.

Treating people fairly with dignity and respect involves not only the words officers speak but also their nonverbal messages. **Nonverbal communication** includes everything except the actual words spoken in a message, such as tone, pitch, and pacing. Body language refers to messages conveyed by facial expressions and how a person moves. To test the power of body language, consider what the following actions say about a person:

- Walking—fast, slow, stomping
- Posture—rigid, relaxed
- Eye contact—direct, indirect, shifting
- Gestures—nod, shrug, finger point
- Physical spacing—close, distant

Police officers' nonverbal communication was discussed in Chapter 2. Officers communicate with the public most obviously through the uniforms they wear and the equipment they carry. Other forms of body language are equally important. How officers stand, how they look at those to whom they are talking, whether they smile or frown—all convey a message.

Eye contact is a powerful nonverbal communication tool. Eye contact inspires trust and shows confidence, even if it is merely the illusion of confidence. It can buy you time if you are caught off guard and need to form a response. Eye contact quietly keeps control while deftly wielding power.

Usually, police officers want to convey the impression that they "know their way around." However, this may actually interfere with effective communication. When interviewing a truthful witness, police officers may want to modify their body language and soften their language. A relaxed manner may result in more in-depth communication and better understanding.

In addition to understanding nonverbal messages, many police officers develop an ability to interpret body language, also called **kinesics**, to such an extent that they can tell when a person is lying or about to become aggressive or flee. This is what some call a "sixth sense," and it alerts officers when something is not as it appears or when someone is suspicious, untruthful, afraid, or hesitant.

Criminals are often apprehended because an officer thought they looked suspicious or because something did not feel right about a traffic stop or other contact. Many law enforcement officers develop an uncanny ability to spot stolen cars in traffic based on a driver's actions and driving maneuvers. Officers also learn to read their own hunches. Acting on a hunch can save lives. Police officers can tell story after story of nagging and intuitive feelings on which they acted.

kinesics
The study of body movement or body language.

Barriers to Communication

Law enforcement officers must be aware of communication barriers that exist in the increasingly diverse society of the United States. Two critical barriers to communication are language barriers and cultural barriers.

In the United States, more than 60 million people (21%) aged 5 and older speak a language other than English at home, and for 62 percent of this group, that language is Spanish (Ryan, 2013). More than half (58.2%) of the individuals who speak another language at home report that they speak English "very well," while 15.4% reported their ability to speak English as "not well," and 7 percent reported that they spoke no English at all. A significant percentage of the population is classified as limited-English proficient (LEP), meaning they have a limited ability to speak, read, write, or understand English (Shah & Estrada, 2009). The increasing numbers of LEP individuals living in the United States means that the majority of law enforcement agencies nationwide now have daily contact with people who do not speak English.

The implications for law enforcement are substantial, as the failure to communicate effectively can be disastrous in a variety of police functions from the routine to the deadly. It can compromise the integrity of the judicial process, interfere with crime control, and undermine the core purpose of police work (Venkatraman, 2006). In addition, federal law requires police departments to address the language barrier. Title VI of the Civil Rights Act of 1964 (42 U.S.C. § 2000d et seq.) and Executive Order 13166 mandate that all agencies that receive federal funding must provide meaningful access to people who have limited English proficiency. Failure to do so could constitute discrimination on the basis of national origin.

The spoken language is not the only barrier. Gestures can also be misinterpreted. For example, making the A-okay sign (a circle with the thumb and forefinger) is friendly in the United States, but it means "you're worth zero" in France, Belgium, and many Latin American countries. The thumbs-up gesture meaning "good going" in the United States is the equivalent of an upraised middle finger in some Islamic countries. The amount of eye contact also varies with different racial and ethnic groups. For example, in the United States, Caucasians maintain eye contact while speaking about 45 percent of the time,

African Americans about 30 percent, Hispanics about 25 percent, and Asians about 18 percent.

Cultural differences can present numerous barriers and challenges to effective communication. Many new immigrants have a limited understanding of the role of police and how officers expect people to behave during routine encounters. For example, when police in El Salvador make a traffic stop, it is customary for the driver to get out of the car and approach the officer. In some countries, it is common for men to keep their wallets in their socks. However, in the United States, these behaviors—walking toward an officer without being directed to or reaching toward a sock when asked for identification—can easily be misinterpreted by an officer as threatening and may lead the officer to use force on the person. "If a language barrier further impairs clear communication, the situation could escalate dangerously" (Lysakowski, Pearsall, and Pope, 2009, p. 5).

In some Asian cultures, only the oldest family member will deal with the police on behalf of the entire family. But older Asian immigrants are also the least likely in the family to speak English. The only way for officers to communicate, in many cases, is by using one of the elder's grandchildren as an interpreter, which the elder usually considers to be a loss of face.

Communication can also be hindered by the fear and distrust of government that immigrants may bring with them based on experiences with police in their homelands: "Many immigrants—refugees, especially—come from places where police are corrupt and abusive. In Lowell, Massachusetts, for example, many residents in the large Cambodian population fled the Khmer Rouge regime and genocide. People who have experienced civil war, genocide, and martial law may have difficulty trusting that the police are there to help" (Lysakowski et al., 2009, p. 4). Immigrants may also be fearful that reporting any crime victimization to police may bring scrutiny to their immigration status, or the status of their family members or neighbors.

Lack of time is another barrier to effective communication. Police officers and citizens are busy. Often, neither the officer nor the citizen wants to take the time to communicate fully and to establish high empathy. Bad timing can also interfere with communication. Police officers frequently are interrupted by calls for service and need to cut short conversations with others.

jargon
The technical language of a profession.

The use of jargon, the technical language of a profession, is another barrier to communication. Law enforcement has its own special terminology—for example, alleged perpetrator, modus operandi, and complainant. Officers should avoid using such terms when talking with the public.

Lack of feedback can also reduce effective communication. The old adage sums up this problem well: I know that you believe that you understand what you think I said, but I am not sure you realize that what you heard is not what I meant.

A failure to listen is one of the most common and most serious barriers to effective communication. Our educational system concentrates on the communication skills of reading and writing. Some time is devoted to speaking, but little or no time is devoted to listening. It is simply assumed that everyone knows how to listen.

Law enforcement officers need to receive information more than they need to give it. A major portion of their time is spent receiving information for forms and reports, taking action in arrests, eliciting information in interviews and interrogations, and many other duties requiring careful listening. As important as listening is, many people lack good listening skills.

Listening skills *can* be improved. The effective communicator is skilled not only at speaking (or writing) but also at listening (and reading). In addition, the effective communicator recognizes personal biases likely to occur in a society as diverse as the United States.

> **LO2**
>
> Police officers may have more barriers to communication because of the image they convey, their position of authority, and the nature of their work. Other barriers include lack of time, use of police jargon, lack of feedback, and a failure to listen.

Facing the Challenge of Diversity

Keeping the peace and serving and protecting a society as diverse as the one in the United States presents an extreme challenge to police officers. To meet the challenge, police might consider the following guidelines:

- Each person is, first and foremost, an individual.
- Each group, whether racial, ethnic, religious, or socioeconomic, consists of people who share certain values. Knowing what these values are can contribute greatly to effective police–community interactions.

CRITICAL THINKING — WHAT WOULD YOU DO?

A woman executive at a shopping center discovered a minor theft of company property from her company car. The car had been parked outside a police office where several traffic officers took breaks between shifts. The office was not accessible to the public but had an identification sign on the locked door.

The woman knocked on the door and asked the sergeant who opened it who was responsible for watching the parking area. She also commented on the officers she could see sitting inside the room and suggested they were not doing their jobs. The officers in the room stopped talking with each other and turned their attention to the conversation at the office door.

The sergeant and the woman never got around to discussing the missing item. Instead he responded to her comments with questions. "What do you mean by that?" "What are you trying to say?" She left to tell her supervisor, refusing to file a police report. She soon returned, however, and encountered another officer just outside the office. Their conversation, later characterized as "heated" by witnesses, centered on the woman's suggestion that the officers should do more to prevent theft in the parking lot. She implied they were lazy and shirked their responsibilities.

At this point the woman asked to file a police report, and the officer asked her to enter the police office with him to do so. They entered the office, but when the officer suggested they enter a private office away from the hubbub of the break area, she refused to do so. She later said the officer intimidated her by slamming drawers, moving quickly, and ordering her into the room. She feared being alone with him.

The officer's perception of the incident was entirely different. He commented that the woman had a "chip on her shoulder" and an "attitude." She was demanding, and dealing with her was "impossible."

After refusing to enter the office to file the report, the woman sat down on a chair in the break area. She was told to either go into the other room and file the report or to leave. When she refused to do either, she was escorted from the office and left outside the locked doors. The woman filed a complaint against the police department.

With better communication, this problem and thousands like it could be avoided.

What would you do?

[?] Understanding the principles of effective communication, how could this situation have been handled differently by the sergeant who first spoke with the woman? As the police chief who received the woman's complaint, what would you recommend to your officers regarding communicating with the public in situations such as these?

- Each group can contribute to making the community safer.
- Communication skills are vital. Empathy, listening, and overcoming language barriers are crucial to implementing the community policing philosophy.
- An awareness of personal prejudices and biases can guard against discrimination. An awareness of the language used to talk about different groups is extremely important.

The term *minority,* for example, has subtle secondary, if not caste-status, implications that are the opposite of the implications of *majority,* which is frequently a polite code word for "White." *People of color* also places distance between those so designated and Caucasians. Officers should consider the terms they use and how they might be perceived by those being labeled. Of course, in an emergency, when officers need to communicate with each other rapidly, a descriptive term such as *Black* or *White* is appropriate and, indeed, necessary for a rapid response. It is important for officers to know when to use certain terms.

ETHNIC DIVERSITY: A NATION OF IMMIGRANTS

Dealing effectively with diversity is important to community policing because community outreach, communications, trust, and activism are all necessary to community partnerships, and none of these can be achieved without accepting—indeed, embracing—diversity. Culture is a collection of artifacts, tools, ways of living, values, and language common to a group of people, all passed from one generation to the next. Diversity is most obvious and sometimes most problematic when groups with different "ways of living" coexist in the same community. The culture provides a framework or worldview, a lens through which events are seen and interpreted. **Ethnocentrism** is the preference for one's own way of life over all others. People are naturally attracted to others who are similar to themselves because they feel less uncertain about how similar people will respond to them and more certain about the likelihood that similar people will agree with them. Ethnocentricity and segregation are consequences of a desire to avoid uncomfortable uncertainty.

The sociologic literature on ethnic and racial diversity contains three theories on the consequences of two or more cultures inhabiting the same geographic area: assimilation, cultural pluralism, and cultural conflict. These are not mutually exclusive and may occur at the same time, creating problems for the transition to community policing.

Assimilation theorists suggest that our society takes in or assimilates various cultures. Assimilation, also referred to as **acculturation**, was, indeed, what happened among the early colonists. Initially, the colonists came from various countries with different religions. They settled in specific geographic areas and maintained their original culture—for example, the Pennsylvania Dutch.

Over time, the triple forces of continued immigration, urbanization, and industrialization turned the United States into a "melting pot" with diverse cultures from the various colonies merging. The melting pot was accomplished relatively painlessly because of the many similarities among the colonists.

ethnocentrism
The preference for one's own way of life over all others.

assimilation
Occurs when a society takes in or assimilates various other cultures to become a "melting pot." Also called *acculturation*.

acculturation
Occurs when a society takes in or assimilates other cultures. Also called *assimilation*.

They looked quite similar physically; they valued religion and "morality"; most valued hard work; and, perhaps most important, there was plenty of land for everyone. The "homogenization" of the United States was fairly well accomplished by the mid-1800s. The formerly distinct cultures blended into what became known as the American culture, a White, male-dominated culture of European origin.

Unfortunately, the colonists excluded the Native Americans. Like animals, they were herded onto reservations. Native Americans have only recently begun to enter into the mainstream of American life. Some Native Americans do not want to be assimilated, seeking instead to maintain their culture and heritage. The same is true of many African Americans. Consequently, cultural diversity will continue to exist in the United States. Assimilation does not always occur.

An alternative to assimilation is *cultural pluralism*, with diverse cultures peacefully coexisting. One example of cultural pluralism is found in Native American culture. There are more than 450 recognized tribes and bands of Native Americans in this country, with populations ranging from less than 100 to more than 100,000. Before colonization of the United States, the tribes had distinct territories, languages, and cultures. Later, as the settlers took their lands, Native Americans joined together in self-defense. Today, Native Americans are often referred to as a single entity, although the individual tribes still maintain their unique identities.

Cultural pluralism is particularly noticeable when new immigrants arrive in the United States. Often, instead of attempting to assimilate into the mainstream of U.S. culture, immigrants seek out and live near others from their homelands, forming Chinatowns; Little Italys; Little Havanas; Little Greeces; and, most recently, Hmong and Somali communities. This has resulted in what is sometimes referred to as the *hyphenated American:* for example, the Italian-American man, the Polish-American woman, the African-American doctor, the Asian-American professor, and so forth.

Cultural pluralism rests on the assumption that diverse cultures can coexist and prosper; but peaceful coexistence is not always the reality. The *cultural conflict theory* suggests that diverse cultures that share the same territory will compete with and attempt to exploit one another. Such cultural conflict was common between the early settlers and the Native American tribes. Conflict was also common between the White immigrants and the more than 6 million slaves imported from Africa between 1619 and 1860. The hostile treatment of Japanese Americans during World War II was rooted in cultural conflict. Following Japan's attack on Pearl Harbor, many U.S. citizens saw Japanese Americans as a national threat. More than 110,000 Japanese Americans, the great majority of whom were American-born citizens, were forced by the government to sell their homes and businesses and then were placed in internment camps.

Cultural conflict can currently be seen in growing tensions between specific ethnic groups as they compete for the limited remaining resources available. In Minnesota, for example, a controversial law permits only Native Americans to harvest wild rice or spear fish. The Mille Lacs band of Chippewa has sued the state of Minnesota, claiming treaty rights allow them to fish outside their reservation without state regulation. Native Americans are also lobbying to be allowed to take motorboats into wilderness areas to enhance their guide business.

The Immigration Issue

The words that appear at the base of the Statue of Liberty once reflected a welcoming philosophy of a country developed in large part by immigrants, primarily of European descent.

> *"GIVE ME YOUR TIRED, YOUR POOR,*
> *YOUR HUDDLED MASSES YEARNING TO BREATHE FREE,*
> *THE WRETCHED REFUSE OF YOUR TEEMING SHORE,*
> *SEND THESE, THE HOMELESS, TEMPEST-TOST TO ME,*
> *I LIFT MY LAMP BESIDE THE GOLDEN DOOR!"*
>
> —*Emma Lazarus*

Today the situation has changed.

Polls find that Americans are increasingly concerned about immigration, with a growing number of respondents believing that immigrants are a burden to the country, taking jobs and housing and straining our health and educational systems. Recall from Chapter 3 the discussion about national demographics and our rapidly changing population. Census projections estimate that the number of people living in the United States who are born here will increase by 62 million (22%) between 2014 and 2060, while the foreign-born population is projected to increase by 36 million (85%) during the same time period: "The foreign born, because its rate of growth is projected to outpace that of natives, is expected to account for an increasing share of the total population, reaching 19 percent in 2060, up from 13 percent in 2014" (Colby & Ortman, 2015, p. 2).

It is not the numbers alone that alarm many Americans, however, but the fact that millions of immigrants are in the country illegally. The Department of Homeland Security (DHS) estimates that the number of unauthorized resident immigrants in the United States in January 2010 was 10.8 million, the same number as the previous year but less than the 11.8 million estimated in January 2007 (Hoefer, Rytina, & Baker, 2011). The DHS defines an unauthorized resident immigrant as a foreign-born noncitizen who is not a legal resident. Most unauthorized residents either entered the country without inspection or were admitted temporarily and stayed beyond the date they were required to leave.

DHS data indicate that the national unauthorized resident population grew by 27 percent between 2000 and 2010 and that, of all unauthorized immigrants residing in the United States in 2010, 62 percent had originally come from Mexico (Hoefer et al., 2011). Increased efforts to secure our borders seem to be producing results, however, and the largest wave of immigration in history from a single country to the United States appears to have come to a standstill: "After four decades that brought 12 million current immigrants—most of whom came illegally—the net migration flow from Mexico to the United States has stopped and may have reversed" (Passel, Cohn, & Gonzalez-Barrera, 2012, p. 1). Indeed, a new report citing data from the 2014 Mexican National Survey of Demographic Dynamics (ENADID) indicates that approximately 1 million Mexicans and their families, including children born in the United States, returned to Mexico in the years between 2009 and 2014. During the same time period, U.S. Census figures indicate that an estimated 870,000 Mexicans immigrated to the United States, resulting in a net loss of about 140,000 people of Mexican origin from our nation over a recent 5-year period (Gonzalez-Barrera, 2015). Public opinion polls reveal that while most citizens continue to support tightened border security and tough measures to crack down on illegal immigration, they also are increasingly supportive of creating better pathways to citizenship for those who are in the United States illegally (Pew Research Center, 2011).

Communicating with New Immigrant Populations

Not since the early 20th century has the United States experienced such a large increase in immigration, and never in our country's history has the immigrant population been so diverse and geographically dispersed. Police agencies nationwide are having unprecedented contact with immigrants—as victims, witnesses, suspects, and potential officer recruits—thus, building trust and rapport with these communities has become a vital task.

However, as already discussed, officers face numerous barriers to effective communication with new immigrants, including language and communication barriers, cultural misunderstandings, an imported distrust of police and judicial systems carried over from countries of origin, and fear that contact with police could lead to deportation. These barriers have prompted many agencies to examine and rethink how they police immigrant communities because these areas often present greater challenges in terms of gaining the trust of community residents. Without trust, it is difficult for law enforcement to engage people in the types of partnerships needed for effective community policing (Khashu, Busch, & Latif, 2005).

Promising practices undertaken by the Lexington (Kentucky) Division of Police to help bridge the language divide existing between officers and new immigrants included drawing upon the expertise of an academic institution to fine-tune its language learning programs and partnering with other law enforcement agencies to provide hands-on cultural training for officers (Shah & Estrada, 2009). Knowing another language can be a lifesaver. For example, in one incident, an officer in Washington, DC, conducting a late-night stop in a Spanish-speaking neighborhood, knew enough Spanish to understand when the driver instructed a passenger in Spanish to shoot the officer when he got close. The officer called for backup and ordered the occupants out of the car. When one suspect opened fire, the officer was prepared and shot back (Venkatraman, 2006).

In an effort to improve relations between new immigrant communities, the Vera Institute began working with the New York Police Department, organizing working groups with representatives from New York City's Arab, African, and emerging Latin American immigrant communities. A series of facilitated forums focused on such topics as the relationship between the police and the community; the community's crime, safety, and policing needs and concerns; and strategies for improving police–community relations. They also tested several initiatives, including developing fact sheets for police officers and coordinating public education and outreach campaigns on legal rights and responsibilities, reporting crimes, and police procedures. According to the institute, by cultivating alternative communication channels such as the police–immigrant working group forums, the project demonstrated new, more effective, more culturally sensitive ways to reach out to and serve New York City's immigrant communities.

LO3

A dilemma facing law enforcement regarding the immigration issue is whether police can build trusting partnerships with immigrant communities if they are also to gather intelligence and enforce immigration law.

The 9/11 attacks sent "shock waves" through local and federal law enforcement agencies and Arab-American communities alike. Law enforcement's role in immigration enforcement was stepped up, and their interactions with people of Arab descent became much more intense (Henderson, Ortiz, Sugie, & Miller, 2006). Before the attacks, Arab Americans were "largely unnoticed in the fabric of American life," but after the attacks, these persons found themselves at the center of attention that was mostly unwelcome. The Vera Institute tried to build relationships with Arab-American communities and found that the number-one barrier, as perceived by community leaders, police personnel, and Federal Bureau of Investigation (FBI) personnel, was distrust of law enforcement. Of the top six solutions mentioned for overcoming barriers to working together, "improving or initiating communication and dialogue" was the most commonly suggested solution by police and FBI personnel. Improving or initiating communication and dialogue was the second most commonly suggested solution by community leaders, with cultural awareness training being the most commonly suggested (Henderson et al., 2006).

Some jurisdictions are tapping the cultural resources of their communities to tackle trust issues as well as communication barriers by encouraging citizens from diverse ethnicities to join the ranks of their reserve units. For example, in Dearborn, Michigan, where more than 30 percent of the residents are Arab American, the police department actively promotes and supports a reserve officer program in which 7 of the 33 volunteer reserves are from the Arab-American community (Haddad, 2011). In addition, 8 of the 25 youth participants in the Dearborn Police Department's Explorer program are from the Arab-American community. Such efforts have proven quite effective in helping the police build inroads and relationships with members of the increasingly diverse community (Haddad, 2011).

Recognizing Prejudice and Discrimination

Communication is also a key factor in recognizing one's own and others' biases and prejudices.

No one can be completely objective. Everyone, consciously or unconsciously, has certain preferences and prejudices. Consequently, it is critical to recognize prejudices and stereotypes to avoid discrimination.

A *prejudice* is a negative judgment not based on fact; it is an irrational, preconceived negative opinion. Prejudices are often associated with a dislike of a particular group, race, or religion. They represent overgeneralizations and a failure to consider individual characteristics.

Prejudice is also referred to as **bias**, a belief that inhibits objectivity. Taken to an extreme, a bias becomes hatred. It is important for law enforcement to understand bias and its extreme form—hate—to deal with bias and hate crimes, discussed in Chapter 14 . Prejudices or biases are the result of overly general classification or stereotyping.

Stereotyping assumes that all people within a specific group are the same and necessarily possess the same characteristics; they lack individuality. Many people stereotype police officers based on what they see on television—scenes showing cops in car chases and shootouts. Officers are not shown standing on the street corner in late January directing traffic after a car crash or being tended to at the medical center because they were bitten on the arm by a prostitute who resisted arrest.

Police officers may also stereotype those with whom they come in contact. In the traditional mode of policing, officers spend a considerable amount of time dealing with criminals and their victims. Some officers may begin to categorize certain types of individuals as perpetrators. Police officers focus so much attention on crime that they may develop a distorted view of who the "bad guys" are. Generalizing from a few to the many is a serious problem for many police. It is a very natural tendency to stereotype people, but it is a tendency that can be fatal to effective communication.

Preconceived ideas about a person's truthfulness or "worth" can result in strained relationships with individuals and little or no interchange of ideas. The very language used to refer to others can interfere with communication. For example, would you rather be called a "cripple" or a "person with a disability"?

Much attention is currently being focused on what has been identified as **implicit bias**, or the unintentional, subconscious associations every individual makes among groups of people and stereotypes about those groups. Decades of research in psychology and neurology support the conclusion that all people, even those who are well-intentioned and unequivocally reject bigotry, possess implicit biases based simply on exposure to or insulation from the social world around them. The National Initiative for Building Community Trust and Justice (2015, p. 1) observes: "Under certain conditions, those automatic associations can influence behavior, making people respond in biased ways even when they are not explicitly prejudiced."

On one level, the human brain operates on an implicit system designed to be "reactive rather than reasoned," allowing quick generalizations and mental shortcuts. This "thinking without thinking" was labeled by journalist Malcolm Gladwell as "blink." Biases that are unconscious or implicit cause "blink responses" that influence a person's choices and actions without that person consciously thinking or deciding to act a certain way (Fridell, 2011).

Implicit bias, although an unavoidable part of human nature, is malleable and can be changed. Initiatives to achieve fair and impartial policing (FIP), a movement that forms a cornerstone of procedural justice, assert that through training and policy review, the negative impacts of implicit bias can be reduced, with biased associations being gradually unlearned and replaced with nonbiased ones (Dasgupta, 2013). In other words, officers can be taught how to identify their "blink responses" and pause their decision making long enough to form a reasoned, rather than reactive, response. Thus, training

bias
A prejudice that inhibits objectivity; can evolve into hate.

stereotyping
Assuming all people within a specific group are the same, lacking individuality.

implicit bias
The unintentional, subconscious associations every individual makes among groups of people and stereotypes about those groups.

officers to recognize and modify their implicit biases can help improve how they interact with increasingly diverse populations. Based on the science of bias, the FIP perspective reflects a new way to approach the issue of biased policing and reveals that it is not, as many argue, caused by widespread racism in policing but is instead a manifestation of subconscious biases that can impact the perceptions and behavior of even well-intentioned people, including police officers (Fridell, 2015).

Prejudices may lead to discrimination, which can be manifested in two ways: (1) Some individuals or groups may be treated preferentially or (2) persons of equal stature may be treated unequally. Illegal unequal treatment may be based on race, religion, sex, or age.

L04

Prejudice is an attitude; discrimination is a behavior.

This difference between attitude and overt behavior was summed up by English Justice Cyril Salmon when he passed sentence on nine youths convicted of race rioting in 1958: "Think what you like … But once you translate your dark thoughts into savage acts, the law will punish you, and protect your victim." Unfortunately, prejudices may result in racism.

Racism For the community policing philosophy to become a reality, racism, wherever it exists, must be recognized and faced. Racism is a belief that a human population having a distinct genetically transmitted characteristic is inferior. It also refers to discrimination or prejudice based on race. The racist idea that some groups (ethnic groups) are somehow genetically superior to others has no scientific basis.

The issue of racism as it relates to community policing is multifaceted and extremely emotionally charged. Furthermore, racism flows in both directions between the police and the citizens within the communities they serve. Some officers make the critical mistake of trying to achieve rapport by using terminology they hear members of a minority group using among themselves.

In February 2015, James B. Comey, director of the Federal Bureau of Investigation, delivered a speech at Georgetown University addressing the complicated relationship between law enforcement and the diverse communities they serve. It was the first time an FBI director had spoken publicly about the racial divide between law enforcement and communities of color. Saying that law enforcement has made mistakes that it needs to acknowledge, including its part in helping to maintain the status quo of the racial laws and discriminatory policies of the past, Comey urged honest conversation between the races to bridge the divide. He included a defense of police officers who are mostly good people but who have become cynical because of the tough job they do.

After the deaths of Michael Brown and Eric Garner, the protests that followed, and the killings of two NYPD officers, Comey had asked his staff how many Blacks are killed by police in this country every year and was shocked to learn that no one had an answer because neither the FBI nor any other federal agency was keeping accurate statistics on the number of police shootings in the country. Comey has since taken steps to correct that data deficit and has vowed that the FBI will begin keeping those records in 2017. Although police agencies are not required to report such information to the FBI, departments have agreed to make an effort to compile a record as accurately as possible of the number of people killed by police each year. Comey's speech, while too lengthy to reprint here, can be found on the FBI's Web site (Comey, 2015).

Racial Profiling   Using certain extralegal racial characteristics, such as skin color, as indicators of criminal activity is **racial profiling**. The contention that police single out subjects based solely on the color of their skin is a serious concern for any department engaged in such a practice and for the credibility of the police profession as a whole.

The *Sourcebook of Criminal Justice Statistics* (University at Albany, n.d.) states: "It has been reported that some police officers or security guards stop people of certain racial or ethnic groups because these officials believe that these groups are more likely than others to commit certain types of crimes." It then asks those surveyed if they believe such racial profiling is widespread in three specific circumstances: at motor vehicle stops, at airport security checkpoints, and in shopping malls (to prevent theft). Fifty-three percent believed racial profiling was widespread during motor vehicle stops; 49 percent believed it was widespread in shopping malls; and 42 percent believed it was widespread at airport security checkpoints. In all three circumstances, Blacks and Hispanics saw racial profiling as more widespread than Whites perceived it to be. A more recent poll shows that 70 percent of Americans oppose the police practice of racial profiling, while 25 percent support the practice (Ekins, 2014).

The "veil-of-darkness method" has been proposed as an innovative and low-cost approach to test for racial profiling in a department's traffic stop practices. This method uses changes in natural lighting to establish a benchmark for stop data, the basic premise being that during nighttime hours, traffic officers possess a degraded ability to discern motorists' race; therefore, stop patterns at night represent a presumptively race-neutral benchmark. The hypothesis is that if a comparison of daytime stops to nighttime stops reveals no statistically significant difference regarding the race of the drivers involved, there is no racial bias by the traffic unit in determining which vehicles to pull over (Worden, McLean, & Wheeler, 2012).

Prior to the September 11, 2001, attacks on the World Trade Center and the Pentagon, the practice of racial profiling was being denounced by one police chief after another across the country. Suddenly, after the attacks, the debate was renewed, as police chiefs tried to decide if racial profiling was not only necessary but also the only sensible thing to do in view of the threat to the United States and its citizens. With the heightened threat of more terrorist attacks, people who appeared to be of Arab or Middle Eastern descent began reporting that they had been singled out for stops, questioning, searches, or arrests solely on the basis of their appearance. In some areas of the country, it seems that motorists of certain racial or ethnic groups are being stopped more frequently by police; oftentimes, the drivers claim, it is for no apparent reason.

However, profiles of certain serial crimes have been used for decades. Police have relied on profiles of drug couriers and serial rapists. Many practitioners argue that race is often part of a perpetrator's description and that to deny police this information because it might offend someone's sense of political correctness does a great disservice to law enforcement.

racial profiling
A form of discrimination that singles out people of racial or ethnic groups because of a belief that these groups are more likely than others to commit certain types of crimes. Race-based enforcement is illegal.

[handwritten margin note: if # of night = day stops - theory says no racial profiling exists for traffic stops.]

Racial Disparity in the Criminal Justice System   Closely related to the issue of racial profiling is the issue of whether our criminal justice system discriminates against racial minorities, resulting in a disproportionate number of members of minority groups being incarcerated. Indeed, 44 percent of Americans believe the criminal justice systems treats Black and Hispanic citizens less fairly than White Americans (Ekins, 2014). Although "Equal Justice under Law" is the foundation of our legal system and is carved on the front of the U.S. Supreme Court building, racial disparity is an unfortunate reality of the criminal justice system for both juveniles and adults. Although it is clear that minorities are overrepresented in the justice system, the more salient question is whether this represents racial discrimination.

Many discussions of racial discrimination are muddied because of failure to differentiate between *discrimination* and *disparity* (Walker, Spohn, & DeLone, 2012). Whereas discrimination refers to unfair, differential treatment of a particular group, disparity refers simply to a difference and does not necessarily involve discrimination. In criminal justice, the critical distinction is between legal and extralegal factors. *Legal factors* are those criteria that provide a legitimate basis for action by a criminal justice official, such as the witnessed commission of a crime, the seriousness of the offense, and an offender's prior criminal record. *Extralegal factors,* on the other hand, fall outside the scope of legitimacy for taking an enforcement action and include a person's race, ethnicity, gender, socioeconomic status, and lifestyle (Walker et al., 2012). Disparity in the racial composition of individuals involved in the criminal justice system—either as victims or offenders—is likely a result of numerous factors related to socioeconomics, education, employment, and other areas in which minorities are at a disadvantage. Controversy continues as to whether this is evidence of discrimination or disparity.

Strategies to Overcome Barriers Based on Racial and Ethnic Diversity   Various strategies have been proposed to help agencies attack bias and overcome racial or ethnic barriers between the police and the community. Some are very general, whereas others are quite specific.

One of the first steps to take is implementing a zero-tolerance policy for bias within police ranks and publicizing that philosophy. Another strategy is to develop an outreach effort to diverse communities to reduce victimization by teaching them practical crime prevention techniques. A critical part of this effort involves training and education for both the police and citizens, as well as the formation of key partnerships between law enforcement and community groups.

Police must often rely on the services of translators, interpreters, community liaisons, religious leaders, and other trusted members of an ethnic community to develop an effective crime prevention program for that group. Schools can also assist by including crime prevention techniques in classroom instruction and special English as a Second Language classes.

Ethnic or racial diversity is usually visually obvious, but other forms of diversity within the United States may also pose a challenge to law enforcement and community policing, including religious and socioeconomic diversity.

RELIGIOUS DIVERSITY

Many of those who came to America in the 1600s did so to escape religious persecution, and the colonists' desire for religious freedom is evident in our Bill of Rights. The First Amendment protects, among other freedoms, freedom of religion. The First Amendment was drafted and adopted to protect the establishment and practice of different religious communities in the early colonies: Congregationalism in New England, Quakerism in Pennsylvania, and Catholicism in Maryland. Over the years, these distinctions have become much less important, with the term *Christian* taking on the meaning of a melting pot for people of similar religious beliefs. However, religious tension still exists between many Christians (the majority religious group) and those of Jewish faith (the minority religious group). Anti-Semitism is a problem in some communities and may result in hate crimes.

Religious diversity continues to increase, presenting unique challenges to community policing efforts aimed at enhancing citizens' levels of trust, communication, and activism. For example, in our post-9/11 society, Arab mericans have been increasingly discriminated against because of their religious beliefs, or their perceived beliefs. Although often considered a monolithic group, Arab Americans come from 22 different Arabic-speaking countries, and whereas the media and many non-Arabs usually associate them with Islam, in actuality an estimated two-thirds are Christian: "Prior to September 11, 2001, Arab Americans went largely unnoticed in the American mainstream. The relative scarcity of academic research on Arab Americans and the fact that the U.S. Census only began keeping information on people of Arab descent in 2000 are both evidence of their low profile" (Henderson et al., 2006, p. 5).

Since 9/11, the seemingly continuous media stream of news about terrorist acts committed by Islamic extremists has fueled a fear among citizens in many western nations. Americans now have a heightened sense of vigilance not only at home but also while traveling abroad. However, amidst this uncertainty and fear lies a critical distinction being made between Muslim people and the Muslim religion of Islam, a difference born out in various polls. A recent Brookings Institution survey found that while 61 percent of Americans had an unfavorable attitude toward Islam, 46 percent had a unfavorable view toward Muslims. When viewed from the flip side, only 37 percent of Americans had a favorable view of Islam, while 53 percent had a favorable view of Muslims (Telhami, 2015).

An interesting extrapolation of this data shows that the majority of those people polled who know some Muslims, even if not well, reported a positive views of Muslims, a finding that is consistent regardless of political views. For example, 22 percent of Republicans who do not know any Muslims have a favorable view, while 51 percent of Republicans who do know some Muslims expressed positive views, and 59 percent of Republicans who know some Muslims well had favorable views (Telhami, 2015). These findings seem to expose some truth to the notion that people fear what they do not know or understand and further underscore the critical importance of building relationships between citizens who, despite broadly diverse religious beliefs, are all Americans.

SOCIOECONOMIC DIVERSITY

Even the casual observer recognizes social and economic differences in the United States. Sociologists usually divide individuals within the United States into three basic classes, based primarily on income and education: the lower, middle, and upper classes. These basic classes may be further subdivided. As noted, the middle class is shrinking, and the gap between the rich and the poor has become wider, resulting in tension.

The Lower Socioeconomic Class

Poor people have more frequent contact with the criminal justice system because they are on the streets and highly visible. A poor person who drives an old car may get a repair ticket, whereas a wealthier person is more likely to drive a newer car not requiring repairs. In addition, the repair ticket issued to the poor person is likely to be a much greater hardship for that person than a similar ticket would be to someone in the middle or upper classes.

Immigrants and certain races and ethnic groups are frequently equated with poverty and crime in an interaction described as the poverty syndrome. The **poverty syndrome** includes inadequate housing, inadequate education, inadequate jobs, and a resentment of those who control the social system.

poverty syndrome
Includes inadequate housing, education, and jobs and a resentment of those who control the social system.

The Homeless   Carrying their worldly goods and camping everywhere from laundry rooms to train and bus stations, the homeless pose a challenge for law enforcement. Even before the foreclosure crisis and economic recession that hit our country in 2008, homelessness was a national crisis, with an estimated 2.5 to 3.5 million Americans experiencing homelessness each year (National Law Center on Homelessness and Poverty, 2011). An annual point-in-time (PIT) estimate of individuals and families experiencing homelessness identified 610,042 people on the streets or in shelters on a single night in January 2013 (United States Interagency Council on Homelessness, 2013). Approximately two-thirds (65%) of those counted were sheltered, meaning they were sleeping in emergency shelters or transitional housing. The other one-third (35%) were sleeping in other places not meant for human habitation, such as in their cars, on the streets, or in abandoned buildings. Nearly two-thirds (64%) of the people experiencing homelessness on a single night were individuals, and the other one-third (36%) were people in families. In many cases, homelessness is temporary; people who are homeless 1 month may not be the following month. Thus, it is difficult to accurately measure the number of homeless on any given day.

Many of those who are homeless are women and children, veterans, alcoholics, drug addicts, and mentally impaired persons. Police need to balance the safety and other needs of the homeless with the need to protect the public from interference with its rights. The needs of the homeless are as varied as the people who comprise this group. Besides needing the obvious—a place to live and an income to support themselves—other needs include better nutrition; medical care; clothing; substance abuse and mental health treatment; and, especially for children, an education.

Ted Soqui/Corbis Historical/Getty Images

As with other diversity issues, training can be a valuable step toward improving police relations with a community's homeless population.

In a study on homeless children, the National Center on Family Homelessness found that 1 in 30 children in America experienced homelessness in 2013—a total of about 2.5 million youths (*America's Youngest Outcasts,* 2014): "Children experiencing homelessness are among the most invisible and neglected individuals in our nation. Despite their ever-growing number, homeless children have no voice and no constituency. Without a bed to call their own, they have lost safety, privacy, and the comforts of home, as well as friends, pets, possessions, reassuring routines, and community. These losses combine to create a life-altering experience that inflicts profound and lasting scars" (p. 10). For many children, the mental and physical stress of being homeless spawns a host of other difficulties:

> The impact of homelessness on the children, especially young children, is devastating and may lead to changes in brain architecture that can interfere with learning, emotional self-regulation, cognitive skills, and social relationships (p. 7)....

> Children experiencing homelessness face additional risks associated with residential instability, hunger insecurity, and often unremitting stress. These children commonly witnessed violence in their family and community, and are frequently separated from primary caregivers. Without the comfort, responsiveness, support, structure, and guidance from their caretakers during times of stress, these children are likely to feel less safe and to manifest more symptoms [of behavioral problems]. (*America's Youngest Outcasts,* 2014, p. 83)

Although being homeless is not a crime, the activities of some homeless people do violate laws and local ordinances. Such activities include public drunkenness; public urination and defecation; loitering; trespassing; panhandling; littering; disorderly conduct; or more serious offenses such as vandalism, theft, and assault. Cities across the nation have tried numerous legislative and other tactical measures in their efforts to eliminate or minimize the problems presented by the homeless:

- Anticamping laws that make sleeping in public places illegal and in some cases make it illegal to possess camping equipment in the city
- Laws against soliciting employment in public places
- Removal of park benches
- Locking public restrooms
- Laws prohibiting providing food to homeless people
- Curfews for homeless people
- Laws against sitting, lying, or sleeping on sidewalks

Critics of these common "tactical" efforts contend that such practices criminalizing homelessness fail to address the underlying causes of homelessness and, instead, make the problem worse by moving people away from services: "When homeless persons are arrested and charged under these ordinances, they may develop a criminal record, making it more difficult to obtain the employment and/or housing that could help them become self-sufficient" (*Homes Not Handcuffs*, 2009, p. 11).

More than a handful of communities across the country have enacted outright bans or placed extreme restrictions on providing food to the indigent and homeless. Lawsuits continue to be filed, with courts deciding in favor of cities in some cases and against them in other rulings. Thus, no consensus can be found among court rulings to date regarding the constitutionality of feeding bans. Other criminalization measures, however, have been found to violate the civil rights of homeless persons.

In *Pottinger v. City of Miami* (1992), a U.S. district court judge found the city's practice of conducting "bum sweeps" (i.e., making minor arrests of transients and confiscating and destroying the property of the homeless) was a violation of their constitutional rights. The central question in this case was whether the government can lock up a person for being outside when that person has no place to go. Noting that there were roughly 6,000 homeless people in Miami but fewer than 700 shelter spaces, the court held that the criminalization of essential acts performed in public, when there was no alternative, violated the plaintiffs' rights to travel and due process under the Fourteenth Amendment, and the right to be free from cruel and unusual punishment under the Eighth Amendment.

In October 2005, the city of St. Louis, Missouri, agreed to settle a lawsuit filed against it by 25 homeless and impoverished people who claimed they were illegally "swept" from the downtown area and jailed prior to the city's Fourth of July celebration in 2004 (*Johnson v. Board of Police Commissioners,* 2004). The city, the police department, and the Downtown Partnership— all named defendants in the case—shared in paying a combined $80,000 in damages to the plaintiffs, $20,000 of which was to go toward meals and other services for the area's homeless. Following the settlement, the police department implemented several changes in the way it addressed the homeless issue, such as avoiding arresting homeless people or removing them from downtown areas without probable cause that a crime had been committed; instituting a policy where, under most circumstances, a summons to court is issued for "quality-of-life" violations rather than arrest; emphasizing to officers that an "individual's residential status (homeless or nonhomeless) is not to be considered in any of [their] decisions"; and affirming that begging is not a crime if it is not "aggressive" (*A Dream Denied,* 2006, p. 42).

Further complicating interactions with those who are homeless is the fact that they are often victims rather than perpetrators of crime. Between 1999 and 2010, hundreds of homeless people were attacked and killed, and many such attacks go undocumented: "Homeless people are treated so poorly by society that their attacks are often forgotten or unreported" (National Coalition for the Homeless, 2010, p. 11). In 2010 alone, 113 attacks on homeless individuals resulted in 24 deaths. And since 1999, the National Coalition for the Homeless has documented 1,184 acts of violence against the homeless, of which 312 led to the death of the victim (National Coalition for the Homeless, 2012).

As with other diversity issues, training for officers can be a valuable step toward improving relations with a community's homeless population. Unfortunately, many departments do not provide the means, training, or tools necessary for officers to successfully reach out to the community's homeless. However, in jurisdictions where police are trained and empowered to address the issue of homelessness, their intervention can benefit both the homeless and the neighborhood. A New York City police officer, Fran Kimkowski, developed an innovative approach to the homeless problem for a group of men who were homeless in the Long Island City section of Queens, New York. Assigned to calm the fears of residents when the Salvation Army opened a shelter for homeless veterans in the neighborhood, Kimkowski wanted to show the residents that the homeless men could and would contribute to the community if given a chance. She organized V-Cops, a group of homeless veterans who volunteer to help prevent crime in the neighborhoods. Partnerships to address the issue of homelessness are also discussed in Chapter 7.

The Powerful and Connected

At the opposite end of the socioeconomic scale are powerful, privileged, and politically connected people. In the traditional role of crime fighter, the police seldom interact with the upper class, but when they must, problems can arise. One of the most common issues occurs when officers provide accommodation and/or special treatment to powerful people in those rare circumstances when one might be arrested. Such special treatment often results in public outrage and bad press for the police department involved, and yet, it happens time and again. Much of the public assumes such actions to be the norm and imagines that many in this category are never arrested in the first place unless it is unavoidable.

In community policing, the personal and financial resources of those in the public eye and upper socioeconomic level can be invaluable. A population's socioeconomic profile can reveal much about the balance of power within a community.

PERSONS WITH DISABILITIES

When people think of "cultural diversity," they typically think of racial, ethnic, religious, or socioeconomic differences among citizens. However, a significantly large "minority" group in the United States, an estimated 36 million noninstitutionalized people, consists of individuals with physical or mental disabilities. The U.S. Census Bureau estimates that about 12 percent of Americans have cognitive or mental disabilities, a figure likely to rise as the population ages and baby boomers grow older. These are populations that provide even more diversity and challenge to community policing efforts.

Understanding Physical and Mental Disabilities and the Americans with Disabilities Act

A police officer asks a woman to perform some field sobriety tests. She cannot do so even though she is not under the influence of any drug, including alcohol. Another person ignores the direct order of a police officer to step back on the sidewalk. Yet another person approaches an officer and attempts to ask directions, but his speech is so slurred he is unintelligible. These common occurrences for police officers can often be misinterpreted. In each of the preceding instances, the individual interacting with the officer has a disability: a problem with balance, a hearing impairment, and a speech disability. A disability is a physical or mental impairment that substantially limits one or more of a person's major life functions. This includes people with mobility disabilities; mental illnesses; mental retardation; epilepsy or other seizure disorders; and speech, hearing, and vision disabilities.

Greater recognition of this "minority" came on July 26, 1990, when then-President Bush signed into law the **Americans with Disabilities Act (ADA)**, calling it "another Independence Day, one that is long overdue." The ADA guarantees that persons with disabilities will have equal access to any public facilities available to persons without disabilities.

Americans with Disabilities Act (ADA)
Legislation signed in 1990 that guarantees that persons with disabilities will have equal access to any public facilities available to persons without disabilities.

In addition, the ADA affects virtually everything that law enforcement officers do—for example, receiving citizen complaints; interrogating witnesses; arresting, booking, and holding suspects; operating phone (911) emergency centers; providing emergency medical services; enforcing laws; and various other duties ("Justice Department Offers Local Police Guidance for Complying with ADA," 2006, p. 2). The ADA does not, however, grant special liberty to individuals with disabilities in matters of law, nor does it dictate that the police must take a "hands off" approach toward people with disabilities engaged in criminal conduct or those posing a direct threat to the health or safety of others or to him- or herself.

Because the ADA guarantees access to government services, it helps build partnerships for community policing. Under the ADA, all brochures and printed material must be available in Braille or on audiotape if requested. To include people with disabilities in community partnerships, the police must be able to communicate with them and should conduct their meetings in barrier-free places.

Many people in our communities have made treatment of those with disabilities a priority and are available and willing to work with law enforcement agencies to ensure that people with disabilities are treated respectfully and protected from those who would victimize them. The outcome of increased awareness and service in this area will not only make police officers' jobs easier when they encounter people with disabilities but will also help reduce their fear and vulnerability. The focus on those with disabilities will make the community a better and safer place for everyone and help to build police–community relations.

Frequently Encountered Disabilities

It is fairly common for on-duty police officers to encounter individuals who seem confused, are unable to communicate, or who otherwise exhibit behavior that is inappropriate to the time and/or place.

Sometimes the cause of such behavior is intoxication or use of illegal drugs, but other times the behavior results from a medical condition. Some of these incidents occur when an individual is experiencing a seizure, either as a result of epilepsy, diabetes, or a consequence of drug use or some other medical problem. To a first responder who has not been trained to recognize such conditions, an epileptic seizure may be mistaken for a drug- or alcohol-induced stupor because the person may have incoherent speech and a glassy-eyed stare and may be wandering aimlessly. Regardless of the cause, a seizure is a disabling and involuntary condition that requires an appropriate police response, including the recognition that the individual involved is unable to make conscious decisions or respond to directions from a police officer (Epilepsy Foundation, n.d.).

> **LO5**
> Disabilities police officers frequently encounter include mobility impairment, vision impairment, hearing impairment, impairment as a result of epilepsy, and mental or emotional impairment.

Mental Disabilities

Individuals with mental or emotional disabilities, in contrast to the preceding disabilities, pose a significant challenge to community policing efforts. Historically, society institutionalized people who were mentally ill or intellectually disabled. In the mid-1960s, however, treatment in the community replaced institutionalization. *Deinstitutionalization* refers to the release into society of thousands of individuals who were mentally ill or intellectually disabled so that such persons could be cared for by family or a special network of support services. This was the result of several factors, including development of medications to control mental illness; research showing that people who were institutionalized did not receive adequate treatment and could do better in the community; federal programs to build and operate mental health centers; and patients' rights litigation and state legislation.

Community-based mental health service rests on the premise that people have the right not to be isolated from the community simply because they have a mental illness or disability. This premise works only if a support system for them exists. Unfortunately, the network of support services has developed slowly. As a result, thousands of people who have mental illness or are intellectually disabled are homeless and living on the street, and thousands more are living with families who are ill equipped to provide the necessary care and assistance.

Mental Illness   Mental illness has been defined as a biopsychosocial brain disorder characterized by dysfunctional thoughts, feelings, and/or behaviors that meet diagnostic criteria (Cordner, 2006). It includes schizophrenia, major depression, and bipolar disorder; obsessive–compulsive disorder; and posttraumatic stress disorder. Mental illness is not, in and of itself, a police problem but rather a medical and social services problem. However, police officers frequently encounter people with mental illness—about 5 percent of U.S. residents have serious mental illness, and 10 to 15 percent of incarcerated individuals have severe mental illness (Cordner, 2006).

Problems associated with mental illness often become police problems, including crimes, suicides, disorderly behavior, and a variety of calls for service. Unfortunately, the traditional police response to people with mental illness has often been "ineffective and sometimes tragic" (Cordner, 2006). Mental illness should not be confused with crisis behavior. **Crisis behavior** results when a person who is not mentally ill has a temporary breakdown in coping skills. Anyone can suffer from a crisis.

crisis behavior
Results when a person has a temporary breakdown in coping skills; not the same as mental illness.

The people that police encounter who are mentally ill frequently lack social support, are difficult to manage, and may have complications such as alcohol or drug abuse. Often people who feel threatened by the strange behavior of a person who is mentally ill may call the police to handle the problem. Officers become involved with people who are mentally ill because the police are the only responders who have around-the-clock, mobile emergency response capacity, as well as the authority to detain and arrest persons and use force when needed. When police are called to manage people who are mentally ill, the behaviors they most frequently encounter are bizarre, unusual, or strange conduct; confused thoughts or actions; aggressive actions; or destructive, assaultive, violent, or suicidal behavior. Suicide is 1 of the 10 leading causes of death in the United States and is the second leading cause of death for people ages 15–34 (National Institute of Mental Health, 2015). The National Institute of Mental Health (NIMH) has estimated that more than 90 percent of people who kill themselves have a diagnosable mental disorder, most commonly a depressive disorder or a substance abuse disorder. In 2014, poisoning was the most common suicide method for females and firearms were the most frequent for males (Curtin, Warner, & Hedegaard, 2016).

Suicide by cop (SBC), a method in which a person engages in actual or apparent danger to others in an attempt to get oneself killed or injured by law enforcement, is a well-recognized phenomenon and a troubling trend. One study of officer-involved shootings (OISs) found that 36 percent of OIS incidents resulted from SBC situations, confirming the growing incidence of this method of suicide (Mohandie, Meloy, & Collins, 2009). Furthermore, of all SBC incidents examined during the study, the subject was killed 97 percent of the time. Even more troubling is data showing a one-in-three chance that someone other than the suicidal individual will be injured or killed during an SBC incident (Mohandie et al., 2009).

It is important to note that the California Court of Appeals ruled, in *Adams v. City of Fremont* (1998), that officers are not legally obligated to intervene on behalf of a suicidal individual if officers feel their own safety is in jeopardy. The court's opinion stated, in part: "We hold that police officers responding to a crisis involving a person threatening suicide with a loaded firearm have no legal duty under tort law that would expose them to liability if their conduct fails to prevent the threatened suicide from being carried out."

One natural outgrowth of a mental health system that withholds needed treatment until a person with a mental illness becomes dangerous is that police officers and sheriff's deputies are forced to become frontline mental health workers. The safety of both law enforcement officers and citizens is compromised when law enforcement responds to crises involving people with severe mental illnesses who are not being treated (Treatment Advocacy Center, 2006). In many cases, however, a patient who was receiving treatment for mental illness either voluntarily stopped taking their medication or their plan had lapsed (Moore, 2006).

In one case, police shot and killed a suspect who had just robbed a gas station. The suspect turned out to be a mentally disturbed female with whom the police had dealt over the past year. After robbing the gas station, she ordered the clerk to call 911 and stayed there until he did. The confrontation and subsequent shooting seemed orchestrated, forced by the depressed, suicidal woman. She claimed to have a gun, threatened to shoot the officers, and advanced toward one with an object in her hand. The object turned out to be a comb. This is a tragic situation where a person who is suicidal arranges to die at the hands of the police.

Departments must train officers to deal with these types of crisis situations and make the necessary resources available (Scoville, 2010). Many departments are developing Crisis Intervention Teams (CIT) to improve their service and response to events and incidents involving unique populations such as the mentally ill. The CIT model, which was developed in Memphis, Tennessee, in 1988, combines police officers with mental health professionals and includes extensive training to help improve the ability of officers to recognize symptoms of a mental health crisis, enhance officers' confidence in addressing such an emergency, and reduce inaccurate beliefs about mental illness. The development of a CIT goes well beyond police training to focus, instead, on building relationships between law enforcement and the mental health community in an effort to improve the effectiveness of the response to mental health 911 calls. The goal of CIT training is to equip officers with the skills needed to safely deescalate situations involving people with mental illness who are in crisis (Hill, Guill, & Ellis, 2004).

Law enforcement members of a CIT team learn that people who are severely mentally ill need an entirely different approach; an entirely different voice tone, voice volume, and personal space; and both observational and questioning skills (*Tactical Response* Staff, 2006). Highlighting the critical need for these skills, the President's Task Force on 21st Century Policing recommends (2015, p. 56):

> POSTs should make Crisis Intervention Training (CIT) a part of both basic recruit and in-service officer training. . . . It has been found that after completing CIT orientation, officers felt encouraged to interact with people suffering a mental health crisis and to delay their "rush to resolution." Dr. Randolph Dupont, Chair of the Department of Criminology and Criminal Justice at the University of Memphis, spoke to the task force about the effectiveness of the Memphis Crisis Intervention Team (CIT), which stresses verbal intervention and other de-escalation techniques. Noting that empathy training is an

important component, Dr. Dupont said the Memphis CIT includes personal interaction between officers and individuals with mental health problems. Officers who had contact with these individuals felt more comfortable with them, and hospital mental health staff who participated with the officers had more positive views of law enforcement. CIT also provides a unique opportunity to develop cross-disciplinary training and partnerships.

Intellectual Disability   Another challenging and frequently misunderstood mental disability that police encounter is intellectual disability, which is often, and incorrectly, equated with mental illness. Intellectual disability, the nation's fourth-ranking disabling condition, affects 3 percent of the U.S. population and encompasses disabilities that arise when normal intellectual development fails to occur. Unlike mental illness, intellectual disability is permanent. It is diagnosed when three criteria exist: (1) significant subaverage general intellectual functioning (as measured by IQ tests); (2) resulting in, or associated with, defects or impairments in adaptive behavior, such as personal independence and social responsibility; (3) with onset by age 18.

People with intellectual disability are usually aware of their condition and may be adept at concealing it. Thus, it may be more difficult to recognize an intellectual disability than a mental illness. Communication problems, interaction problems, inability to perform tasks, and personal history can help officers make this determination.

AGE DIVERSITY

Yet another communication challenge is posed when police officers must interact with those who are much older or much younger than they are. Law enforcement officers deal with individuals of all ages and must be able to communicate effectively with them. At midyear 2015, more than one-fifth (21.1%) of the U.S. population was younger than 5 or age 65 and older (United States Census, 2015). Although it is rare for most people in these age groups to be involved in criminal behavior, they are among the most vulnerable of our populations and, because of that, police officers will have considerable contact with them. Most contact will take the form of providing assistance and protecting their welfare.

The Elderly and Communication Challenges

As the baby-boom generation ages and general life expectancies increase, the age structure of the United States is projected to change substantially. The first of the baby-boom generation began turning 65 in 2011, and by 2030 the entire boomer cohort (19.6% of the entire U.S. population) will be aged 65 or older. The U.S. Census Bureau predicts that by 2050, more than 20 percent, or more than 86 million people, will be of age 65 and older (Colby & Ortman, 2015).

Many individuals aged 65 and older do *not* consider themselves elderly and, in fact, are in better physical and mental condition than other individuals much younger than they are. Police officers need to understand and empathize with the physical and emotional challenges of the aged, so they may deliver the best possible service.

Older people tend to admire and respect authority and are often grateful for any help the police may offer. They are usually in contact with the police if they become victims of crime, are involved in an automobile crash, or are stopped for a traffic violation. Many older people have serious medical problems for which they may require emergency medical assistance. In fact, more than half of the U.S. population older than 65 is disabled in some way.

Some older people suffer from **Alzheimer's disease (AD)**, a progressive, irreversible, and incurable disease of the brain that adversely affects behavior. An estimated 5.4 million Americans have AD, the vast majority (5.2 million) of whom are age 65 and older (Alzheimer's Association, 2016). Nearly half (45%) of all people aged 85 and older have developed AD, and considering that the number of Americans surviving to age 80 and beyond is expected to grow dramatically due to advances in medicine and medical technology, as well as social and environmental conditions, it is very likely that future police officers will encounter during their careers an increasing number of citizens with this type of dementia.

Alzheimer's disease (AD)
A progressive, irreversible, and incurable brain disease with no known cause that affects more than 5 million elderly Americans; the classic symptom is memory loss.

Alzheimer's disease afflicts people of all social, economic, and racial groups. Officers should know the symptoms, the most classic of which is gradual loss of memory. Other symptoms include impaired judgment, disorientation, personality change, decline in ability to perform routine tasks, behavior change, difficulty in learning, loss of language skills, and decline in intellectual function. A number of behavior patterns common to patients with AD may bring them to the attention of police officers.

Data indicate that an estimated 125,000 people with AD or a similar condition wander from the safety of their home every year and are unable to find their way back (Schafer & McNiff, 2011). In addition to missing-person calls, other incidents that may bring Alzheimer's patients or those with general dementia into contact with the police include driving and traffic difficulties (getting lost, "losing" their car, running out of gas, causing crashes, or leaving the scene of a crash because they forgot it happened), false reports to 911, indecent exposure, shoplifting, cooking accidents, trespassing, overdoses, choking, homicide, suicide, abuse or neglect, and other types of victimization (Schafer & McNiff, 2011).

LO6
People with AD may wander or become lost, engage in inappropriate sexual behavior, lose impulse control, shoplift, falsely accuse others, appear intoxicated, drive erratically, or become victims of crime. Many symptoms of AD and intoxication are identical: confusion and disorientation; problems with short-term memory, language, sight, and coordination; combativeness and extreme reactions; and loss of contact with reality.

People afflicted with AD may become victims of crime because they are easy prey for con artists, robbers, and muggers. Also, police may become aware of patients with AD as a result of legal actions such as evictions, repossessions, and termination of utility service as a result of the patients' forgetfulness or inability to make payments.

The Helmsley Alzheimer's Alert Program, started in 1991, provides information on missing patients to public safety agencies. When a person with AD is reported missing, the Alzheimer's Association sends an alert with identifying information to a fax service that transmits it simultaneously to hundreds of locations, including police, hospital emergency rooms, and shelters. When the patient is found, another fax is sent to inform the agencies that the search is over.

The Young and Communication Challenges

A frequently overlooked segment of the population important to community policing implementation is youths. Just *who* is classified as a youth is established by state statutes and varies in age from 16 to 18 years. Because youths lack economic and political power, their problems and concerns may not receive the attention they deserve. But our nation's future depends on the values they form—they are the future decision makers of our country.

Most young people (95%, according to FBI statistics) have not been in trouble with the law. The overwhelming majority of "good kids" should not be forgotten in community policing efforts. They can be valuable as partners in problem solving and, if provided opportunities to become active in areas of interest to them, will most likely continue to be good citizens. And almost certainly some juveniles have been arrested multiple times, so that the actual percentage of youths who have been arrested is even lower than it appears at first glance. The youth who do have contact with police due to status offending, delinquency, or other antisocial conduct are discussed in greater detail in Chapter 12 . Here the discussion focuses on youth with special needs, who may not necessarily come into police contact but are at a higher risk to do so because of their various disabilities or disorder—conditions that often present communication challenges to responding officers. Youths with special needs include those who are emotionally/behaviorally disturbed; who have specific learning disabilities; who have an attention-deficit disorder; or who have behavior problems resulting from prenatal exposure to drugs, including alcohol, or to human immunodeficiency virus (HIV).

EBD
Emotionally/behaviorally disturbed.

Emotionally/behaviorally disturbed children, often referred to as **EBD**, usually exhibit one or more of the following behavioral patterns: severely aggressive or impulsive behavior; severely withdrawn or anxious behavior such as pervasive unhappiness, depression, or wide mood swings; or severely disordered thought processes reflected in unusual behavior patterns, atypical communication styles, and distorted interpersonal relationships.

Parents and teachers in some communities have expressed concerns that children labeled as EBD have fewer coping skills to deal with police contacts than other children and may be traumatized by such contacts. A large percentage of youths suspected of crimes are EBD, and that condition is one cause of their unlawful behavior. It is impossible, however, to arrange for an EBD specialist to be present at all police contacts because a majority of contacts are unplanned events that occur on the street.

Attention-deficit hyperactivity disorder (ADHD)

A common disruptive behavior disorder characterized by heightened motor activity (fidgeting and squirming), short attention span, distractibility, impulsiveness, and lack of self-control.

Attention-deficit hyperactivity disorder (ADHD) is one of the most common disruptive behavior disorders in youths, with an estimated 5 to 10 percent of all children having it. Occurring four times more often in boys than girls, ADHD is characterized by heightened motor activity (fidgeting and squirming), short attention span, distractibility, impulsiveness, and lack of self-control. (*Note:* The disorder of being easily distracted *without* the presence of hyperactivity is ADD, or simply attention-deficit disorder. The two disorders, ADHD and ADD, are commonly confused and the terms used interchangeably; the absence of hyperactivity is the primary distinguishing feature between them.) Children with ADHD may do poorly in school and have low self-esteem. Although the condition often disappears by adulthood, by then those who had ADHD as children may have other behavior problems, including drug abuse, alcoholism, or personality disorders.

Other children may present special challenges because of some form of specific learning disability (SLD), also known simply as a learning disability (LD), which is a disability category the federal government uses to define "a complex cluster of lifelong neurobiological disorders that can severely interfere with a person's ability to acquire competency in one or more of the following areas:

- Oral language (listening, speaking, understanding)
- Reading (decoding or phonics, word knowledge, comprehension)
- Written language (spelling and written expression)
- Mathematics (computation, problem solving)
- Executive functioning (planning, decision making, reasoning, organization, remembering, interpreting)
- Socialization (interpreting social situations, appropriate social interactions)" (Association for Children with Learning Disabilities, 2016)

Data from the National Institutes of Health indicate that roughly 15 percent of the U.S. population—one in seven Americans—has some type of SLD. SLDs, many of which occur before birth while the brain is forming, can severely interfere with a person's ability to interpret what is seen and heard or to process information, even though many people with SLDs possess the intellectual capacity to learn (Association for Children with Learning Disabilities, 2016). SLDs do not include learning problems that result from visual, hearing, or motor handicaps, intellectual disability, or emotional disturbance.

Symptoms of learning disabilities include short attention span; poor memory; difficulty following directions; disorganization; inadequate ability to discriminate between and among letters, numerals, or sounds; poor reading ability; eye–hand coordination problems; and difficulties with sequencing. Such children are often discipline problems, are labeled "underachievers," and are at great risk of becoming dropouts.

Although SLDs are usually discussed in an educational context, the effects of these deficits extend to all facets of life, including work. Characteristics that may bring a youth with a learning disability into conflict with the law include responding inappropriately to a situation; saying one thing and meaning another; forgetting easily; acting impulsively; needing immediate gratification; and feeling overly frustrated, which results in disruptive behavior. Those who interact with such children need to be patient and communicate effectively. Youths with learning disabilities look like their peers. Inwardly, however, most are very frustrated, have experienced failure after failure, and have extremely low self-esteem. When these types of disabilities go undiagnosed or are inappropriately treated, the consequences to the individual can be severe, greatly decreasing their ability to succeed in school, the workplace, and life in general.

Prenatal exposure to drugs can also cause serious problems. The term **crack children** is sometimes used to refer to children exposed to cocaine while in the womb. They may exhibit social, emotional, and cognitive problems. Children who were exposed to drugs prenatally may also have poor coordination, low

crack children
Children who were exposed to cocaine while in the womb.

tolerance levels, and poor memory. Police officers should be aware of these symptoms and recognize that they reflect a condition over which the youth has limited or no control.

fetal alcohol syndrome (FAS)
The leading known cause of mental retardation in the Western world; effects include impulsivity, inability to predict consequences or to use appropriate judgment in daily life, poor communication skills, high levels of activity, distractibility in small children, and frustration and depression in adolescents.

Another pressing problem is that of **fetal alcohol syndrome (FAS)**, the leading known cause of intellectual disability in the Western world. FAS effects include impulsivity; inability to predict consequences or to use appropriate judgment in daily life; poor communication skills; and high levels of activity and distractibility in small children and frustration and depression in adolescents.

Yet another group of at-risk children who present special problems to law enforcement are children prenatally exposed to HIV. Such children may have an intellectual disability, language delays, gross- and fine-motor skill deficits, and reduced flexibility and muscle strength.

Children with special needs are likely to be in contact with the police, and many may become status offenders, committing offenses based on age such as underage smoking or drinking or violating curfews. Others may become more serious offenders, as discussed in Chapter 12 . Youths with special needs may also be at greater risk for joining gangs, as discussed in Chapter 13 .

VICTIMS AND WITNESSES

A final population presenting communication challenges are victims of and witnesses to criminal acts.

> *"IF YOU HAVEN'T BEEN THERE, YOU DON'T KNOW THE FEELINGS OF EMPTINESS AND FEAR AND HOW IT CHANGES YOUR LIFE. I WAS IN A STATE OF SHOCK. I WALKED AROUND IN A DAZE FOR WEEKS. I WASN'T FUNCTIONING. NO ONE REALLY UNDERSTOOD HOW I FELT."*
> —*Sherry Price, Rape Victim*

Understanding others is particularly important in police work. Understanding others does not, however, mean that you sympathize with them or even that you agree with them. *Sympathy* is an involuntary sharing of another person's feelings of fear, grief, or anger. *Empathy* is an active process involving trying to *understand* another person's feelings. Empathy requires effective communication skills.

L07
It is essential for law enforcement officers to communicate effectively with victims and witnesses because they are a major source of common crime information known to law enforcement.

Results of Being Victimized

People who become victims of crime often come out of the experience feeling victimized by both the perpetrator and the system. The entire criminal justice system is focused on the criminal. Victims are sometimes blamed for being victimized and many times are left in the dark about progress on their case. Perpetrators, on the other hand, have an attorney representing them every step of the way, ensuring that their rights are not violated. Many victims are shocked to learn that the prosecutor represents the state, not the victim. If the crime was a violent one, victims are often frightened, traumatized, and feel very much alone. They may suffer physical injury, financial and property losses, emotional distress, and psychological trauma.

Some suffer from **posttraumatic stress disorder (PTSD)**, a persistent reexperiencing of a traumatic event through intrusive memories, dreams, and a variety of anxiety-related symptoms.

Nonreporting of Victimization

Many victims feel it is their civic duty to report victimization and hope doing so will bring offenders to justice. Others report crimes simply because they want to recover their property or file an insurance claim. In the absence of such motivators, however, a large percentage of robberies, aggravated assaults, burglaries, and rapes go unreported to the police. Victims may consider the matter private, feel ashamed, or believe the police will be unable to do anything. In the case of victims of sexual assault, they often feel they will not be believed and all too frequently, they are right.

When crime is underreported, the police do not know there is a problem or may think it is only a minor problem. They do not have a true picture of the situation, which makes it difficult to problem-solve effectively.

Some victims and witnesses fear threats or retaliation from the offender(s). Many victims of violent crimes are warned by their attackers that going to the police will result in dire consequences for either the victims themselves or people they care about.

One reason gangs flourish is that they operate through intimidation, both inside and outside of court. Police must often deal with courtroom intimidation. Sometimes the court is packed with gang members who give threatening looks and suggestive signals to witnesses. Some departments counter this tactic by taking classes of police cadets into the courtroom. Confronted with this law enforcement presence, gang members often give up and leave. It is important for law enforcement to encourage reporting crime by reassuring victims and witnesses they will be protected against threats, intimidation, or reprisals by the victimizers.

Assisting Victims

Society has made progress in assisting victims of crime. In 1981, then-President Ronald Reagan proclaimed National Victims of Crime Week, putting the full weight and influence of his office behind the victims' movement. Since then, a variety of organizations and programs have been created to help victims.

Organizations   Providing help to crime victims originated as a grassroots effort in the 1960s and 1970s to help battered women and victims of sexual assault. Organizations dedicated to helping victims include the National Organization for Victim Assistance (NOVA), founded in 1976; the Office for Victims of Crime (OVC), founded in 1984; and the National Victim Center, founded in 1985.

Other victim organizations have been formed, including Mothers against Drunk Driving, Students against Destructive Decisions, Parents of Murdered Children, the National Organization of Victim Assistance, and Victims for Victims. In addition, victim compensation laws and victim advocacy and

posttraumatic stress disorder (PTSD)

A persistent reexperiencing of a traumatic event through intrusive memories, dreams, and a variety of anxiety-related symptoms.

protection programs attempt to address what is widely perceived as the system's protection of the accused's rights to the victim's detriment.

Programs Implemented   Numerous programs also have been implemented to help victims deal with the financial and emotional fallout of victimization. The two main types of programs provided for victims are victim compensation programs and victim/witness assistance programs. *Victim compensation programs* help crime victims cope with crime-related expenses such as medical costs, mental health counseling, lost wages, and funeral or burial costs. *Victim/witness assistance programs* provide services such as crisis support, peer support, referrals to counseling, advocacy within the justice system, and, in some cases, emergency shelter. Crime victim compensation programs have been established in every state. Programs are based on identified needs of victims and witnesses.

Victims' Bill of Rights   Victims and witnesses have two basic rights: the right to obtain certain information from the criminal justice system and the right to be treated humanely by the system. Most victims' bills of rights include both informational and participatory rights. They commonly require the victim to be informed about available financial aid and social services, as well as the whereabouts of the accused; advised of case status and scheduling; protected from harassment and intimidation; provided with separate waiting areas during the trial; and granted a speedy disposition of the case and return of property held as evidence.

Police officers can help victims by letting them know their rights, including the right to become active in the case processing and to prepare a victim impact statement (VIS). They can also tell victims what services are available.

Some departments are using innovative approaches to reach out to victims and maintain lines of communication. For example, in some lower-income communities where few residents can afford telephone service, cellular phone links have been established to help crime victims reach the police. Cell phones have no lines to cut and can be preprogrammed with 911 and the general information number of the police department, but all other calling capability can be locked out. An example of how communications are maintained with prior victims is seen in Jefferson County, Kentucky, where the Victim Information and Notification Everyday (VINE) system automatically alerts victims with a telephone call when an inmate is released from custody. VINE could serve as a national model for using technology.

Agencies That Can Assist

Agencies usually included in a victim/witness assistance referral network are community groups, day care centers, domestic violence programs, food stamp distribution centers, job counseling and training programs, mental health care programs, physical health care programs, private sector allies, private and community emergency organizations, rape crisis centers, unemployment services, victim assistance or advocacy organizations, victim compensation boards, volunteer groups, and welfare agencies.

The Direction of Victims' Rights and Services in the 21st Century

Examples of "promising practices" transforming victim services include children's advocacy centers; community criminal justice partnerships; crisis response teams; technologies to benefit crime victims (such as VINE); community police, prosecutors, and court programs; initiatives of allied professionals (such as partnerships between criminal justice agencies, schools, the medical and mental health communities, religious communities, and the business community); comprehensive victim service centers; and specialized programs for diverse crime victims (including disabled victims and victims of gang violence).

SUMMARY

The quality of police–community relations depends on effective communication. The communication process involves a sender, a message, a channel, a receiver, and, sometimes, feedback. Important individual characteristics in communication include age, education, gender, values, emotional involvement, self-esteem, and language skills. Two critical barriers to communication in a diverse society are language barriers and cultural barriers. Police officers may have more barriers to communication because of the image they convey, their position of authority, and the nature of their work. Other barriers include lack of time, use of police jargon, lack of feedback, and a failure to listen.

A dilemma facing law enforcement regarding the immigration issue is whether police can build trusting partnerships with immigrant communities if they are also to gather intelligence and enforce immigration law. One challenge facing our increasingly diverse society is discrimination. It is critical to recognize prejudices and stereotypes to avoid discrimination. Prejudice is an attitude; discrimination is a behavior.

Disabilities police officers frequently encounter include mobility impairment, vision impairment, hearing impairment, impairment as a result of epilepsy, and mental or emotional impairment. An epileptic seizure may be mistaken for a drug- or alcohol-induced stupor because the person may have incoherent speech and a glassy-eyed stare and may be wandering aimlessly. Another population the police encounter daily is the elderly, people aged 65 and older, who may be victims of Alzheimer's disease (AD). People with AD may wander or become lost, engage in inappropriate sexual behavior, lose impulse control, shoplift, falsely accuse others, appear intoxicated, drive erratically, or become victims of crime. Many symptoms of AD and intoxication are identical: confusion and disorientation; problems with short-term memory, language, sight, and coordination; combativeness and extreme reactions; and loss of contact with reality.

Young people are a frequently overlooked segment of the population important to implementing community policing. Youths with special needs include those who are emotionally/

behaviorally disturbed (EBD); who have specific learning disabilities; who have an attention- deficit disorder; or who have behavior problems resulting from prenatal exposure to drugs, including alcohol, or to human immunodeficiency virus (HIV).

Finally, it is essential for law enforcement officers to communicate effectively with victims and witnesses because they are a major source of common crime information known to law enforcement.

DISCUSSION QUESTIONS

1. In what ways might a person become a victim and need assistance from the police?
2. What role do euphemisms ("soft" words) play in communication?
3. In what ways might the general public be perceived as "customers" of a police department? What implications does this have?
4. How diverse is your community?
5. Have you ever tried to communicate with someone who does not speak English? What was it like?
6. How would you describe the American culture?
7. Would you favor eliminating the word *minority* when talking about diversity? If so, what term would you use instead?
8. Do you consider yourself "culturally literate"? Why or why not?
9. Have you encountered instances of racism? Explain.
10. Have you or someone you know ever been a victim of crime? Was the crime reported to the police, and if not, why?

CASES CITED

Adams v. City of Fremont, 80 Cal. Rptr. 2d 196 (1998)
Johnson v. Board of Police Commissioners, 351 F. Supp. 2d 929 (E.D. Mo. 2004)
Pottinger v. City of Miami, 76 F.3d 1154 (11th Cir. 1996)

[Handwritten annotations:]

Page 174 - Officers not obligated to intervene in suicide attempts if they fear for their own life.

Page 170 - "Bum sweeps" violate the 8th + 14th Amendments

Page 170 - Homeless cannot be swept off the streets

Building Partnerships: A Cornerstone of Community Policing

CHAPTER 7

Learning Objectives

LO1 Explain why police seek to partner with the community.

LO2 Identify the four dimensions of trust.

LO3 Explain how beats should be assigned to foster partnerships.

LO4 Identify the common criticisms of community policing partnerships and how they can be addressed.

LO5 Identify the key collaborators with whom police should partner to fulfill a community justice mission.

LO6 Summarize the restorative justice approach.

LO7 Explain why it can be more difficult for police to build partnerships in a lower-income neighborhood.

Key Terms

call management
call stacking
collaboration
community justice
criminogenic needs
dynamic risk factors
restorative justice
stakeholders
static risk factors
TRIAD
working in "silos"

Distrust and rolling tensions ruled the streets of Ferguson, Missouri, in late summer 2014. The frustration of racial disparities involving the interactions between police officers and the Black community exploded after the August 9 shooting of Michael Brown, an unarmed Black teenager, by Darren Wilson, a White officer, an incident that propelled the small town of about 22,000 people into the national spotlight. Ferguson is an overwhelmingly White suburb in the major metropolitan area of St. Louis, Missouri, which is 70 percent Black. After the shooting, the community deteriorated into confrontation and violence. Needless to say, amicable talks and community building were the last things on the minds of Ferguson's residents and local law enforcement.

That was until U.S. Attorney General Eric Holder announced the creation of the National Initiative for Building Community Trust, a program that provided grants to help train police officers and local community members on ways to reduce racial bias. In addition to building trust and reducing prejudice between the police and citizen, the organization sought to further educate the public on fairness within the criminal procedure. Finally, this organization was tasked with training law enforcement officers and community members—two seemingly rival groups—proper methods for reconciling differences and ways to reduce tension through honest and frank conversation. Instead of allowing grievances to boil over into violence through this communication, the discussions would allow the opportunity for misconceptions to be resolved and trust to be restored.

Academics, faith-based leaders, law enforcement professionals, community leaders, and civil right advocates came together to provide training and education to police officers and community residents, serving as the building blocks that would form the nation's new cornerstone in community policing. Instead of the stoned wall that once stood to keep selective groups out of the conversation, there now existed an all-inclusive wall promoting bias reduction partnerships.

INTRODUCTION

In community policing, the term *partnerships* refers to the collaboration that takes place between police officers, community members and groups, other government agencies, nonprofits, service providers, private businesses, the media, and other stakeholders. These partnerships require a policing perspective that is far broader than the standard law enforcement emphasis. Through these collaborations, the police become an integral part of the community culture and acquire an outlook that recognizes the value of activities that contribute to the orderliness and well-being of a neighborhood (Bureau of Justice Assistance, 1994). In turn, the community is able to assist in defining future police priorities and in allocating resources:

> Community policing, recognizing that police rarely can solve public safety problems alone, encourages interactive partnerships with relevant stakeholders. The range of potential partners is large and these partnerships can be used to accomplish the two interrelated goals of developing solutions to problems through collaborative problem solving and improving public trust. The public should play a role in prioritizing public safety problems. (Office of Community Oriented Policing Services, 2009, p. 5)

Community partnerships with various stakeholders are crucial for police agencies serious about community policing. Community policing cannot succeed without them. Traditional policing expected the community members to remain in the background. Crime and disorder were viewed as police matters, best left to professionals. That meant most citizen–police interactions were *negative contacts*. After all, people do not call the police when things are going well. Consequently, a citizen's only opportunity to interact with officers was as a victim of crime, as an involved party in some other emergency situation, or as the subject of some enforcement action such as receiving a traffic ticket.

Some people may question why the police would consult the public about setting police priorities and why officers would ask citizens to work with them to solve neighborhood problems. Some feel that the police are paid to deal with crime and disorder and should not expect communities to take any responsibility or do their job for them. The reality is that the police cannot effectively do the job we need them to do by themselves. Much of the information and resources they need lie in the communities they serve. Comparisons can be made to what we have learned from the medical profession. Most people understand that doctors cannot keep us well unless we take some responsibility for our own health by exercising, eating healthy, watching our weight, and avoiding tobacco. Just as we can have an impact on our own personal health and safety, we can have an impact on our community's health and safety.

The benefits to all stakeholders of participating in a partnership include:

LO1

Partnerships usually result in a more effective solution to a problem because of the shared responsibilities, resources, and goals.

- A sense of accomplishment from bettering the community
- Gaining recognition and respect
- Meeting other community members
- Learning new skills
- Fulfilling an obligation to contribute

CORE COMPONENTS OF PARTNERSHIPS

Partnerships are often referred to as collaborations. **Collaboration** occurs when several agencies and individuals commit to work together and contribute resources to obtain a common goal. Figure 7.1 illustrates the core components of a partnership or collaboration.

Stakeholders

Partnerships are made up of **stakeholders**, those people who have an interest in what happens in a particular situation. This might include school board members, business leaders, elected officials, neighborhood-watch and block clubs, community activists, the attorney general, trade organizations, social service organizations, federal law enforcement agencies (e.g., Federal Bureau of Investigation; Drug Enforcement Administration; Bureau of Alcohol, Tobacco, Firearms, and Explosives; United States Immigration and Customs Enforcement), the media, private foundations, and other charitable organizations. For example, a project to reduce thefts from cars on a college campus could involve stakeholders from several groups: students,

collaboration
Occurs when a number of agencies and individuals make a commitment to work together and contribute resources to obtain a common, long-term goal.

stakeholders
Those people who have an interest in what happens in a particular situation.

Figure 7.1	Core Components of a Successful Collaboration/Partnership

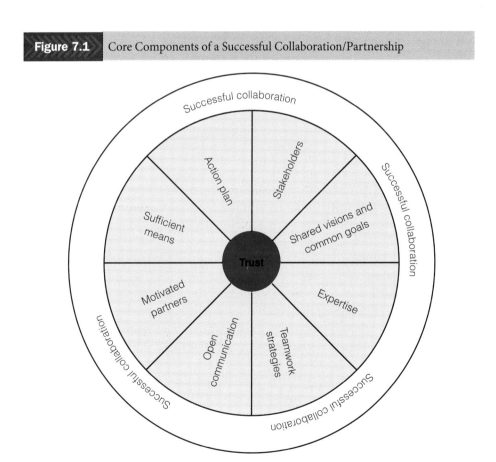

Source: Tammy A. Rinehart, Anna T. Laszlo, and Gwen O. Briscoe, *Collaboration Toolkit: How to Build, Fix and Sustain Productive Partnerships* (Washington, DC: U.S. Department of Justice, Office of Community Oriented Policing Services, 2001), 7.

administrators, professors, the facilities and maintenance departments, and police. Stakeholders will change depending on the problem being addressed, but when possible the collaboration should reflect the diversity of the community.

Active Community Involvement

Community policing relies on active community involvement, recognizing that such involvement gives new dimension to crime control activities. While police continue to handle crime fighting and law enforcement responsibilities, the police and community work together to modify conditions that can encourage criminal behavior. The resources available within communities allow for an expanded focus on crime prevention activities.

Patrol officers are the primary providers of police services and have the most extensive contact with community members. In community policing efforts, they provide the bulk of the community's daily policing needs and are assisted by immediate supervisors, other police units, and appropriate government and social agencies. Upper-level managers and command staff are responsible for ensuring that the entire organization backs the patrol officers' efforts.

Effective community policing depends on optimizing positive contact between patrol officers and community members. Patrol cars are only one method of conveying police services. Police departments may supplement automobile patrols with foot, bicycle, scooter, and horseback patrols and add mini-stations to bring police closer to the community. Regular community meetings and forums will afford police and community members an opportunity to air concerns and find ways to address them. Once the stakeholders are enlisted in partnerships, the focus becomes building trust among all collaborators.

Building Trust

Establishing and maintaining mutual trust is a central goal of community policing and community partnership. Indeed, *trust* exists at the center of Figure 7.1, binding all of the core components of successful partnerships together.

Police have long recognized the need for cooperation with the community. In the fight against serious crime, police have encouraged community members to come forth with relevant information. In addition, police have spoken to neighborhood groups, participated in business and civic events, worked with social agencies, and taken part in educational and recreational programs for school children. Special units have provided a variety of crisis intervention services.

So then how do the cooperative efforts of community policing differ from the actions that have taken place previously? These actions include helping accident or crime victims, providing emergency medical services, helping resolve domestic and neighborhood conflicts (e.g., family violence, landlord–tenant disputes, or racial harassment), working with residents and local businesses to improve neighborhood conditions, controlling automobile and pedestrian traffic, providing emergency social services and referrals to those at risk (e.g., adolescent runaways, the homeless, the intoxicated, and the mentally ill), protecting the exercise of constitutional rights (e.g., guaranteeing a person's right to speak and protecting lawful assemblies from disruption), and providing a model of citizenship (helpfulness, respect for others, honesty, and fairness). Although these are all services to the community, none are true partnerships, which require sharing of power and responsibility to identify and respond to problems.

Nonetheless, these services are important because they help develop trust between the police and the community. This trust will enable the police to gain greater access to valuable information from the community that could lead to the solution and prevention of crimes, will engender support for needed crime control measures, and will provide an opportunity for officers to establish a working relationship with the community. The entire police organization must be involved in enlisting community members' cooperation in promoting safety and security.

It is no surprise that the public's trust in police has been shaken in recent years by the high-profile shootings of Black men, many of whom were unarmed, by White officers. These events have driven a deep wedge between many communities of color and the police forces sworn to protect and serve them. Rebuilding damaged public trust in local police is no easy task, yet it is so crucial that it forms one of the fundamental pillars outlined in the *Final Report of the President's Task Force on 21ˢᵗ Century Policing* (2015, p. 1): "Trust between law enforcement agencies and the people they protect and serve is essential in a democracy. It is key to the stability of our communities, the integrity of our criminal justice system, and the safe and effective delivery of policing services." To this end, the task force recommends the following action item (2015, p. 15): "Law enforcement agencies should create opportunities in schools and communities for positive nonenforcement interactions with police. Agencies should also publicize the beneficial outcomes and images of positive, trust-building partnerships and initiatives."

> **LO2**
> Four dimensions of trust are shared priorities, competency, dependability, and respect.

[handwritten margin note: 4 Parts of Trust 1. Shared Priorities 2. Competency 3. Dependability 4. Respect]

IDEAS IN PRACTICE BUILDING PARTNERSHIPS AND TRUST

It's important that police departments encourage individual officers to establish community relationships and partnerships, and even become community leaders. The support and encouragement from command staff and supervision make a huge difference in an individual officer's ability and willingness to go above and beyond—to truly be community police officers. But to get proactively involved in their community, they must also have the ability to identify a need and find a solution by being given the time and opportunity to do so.

An example of this kind of community involvement is the Evansville (Indiana) Police Department's handling of a problematic basketball event. According to Chief Bill Bolin, "The annual Evansville Dust Bowl basketball tournament had become known for violence and ended a few years ago after a person was shot and killed at the event. Last winter, I was approached by the head of the local NAACP and the leaders of a group called Young & Established about partnering with them to bring the event back. I saw this as great community outreach opportunity to partner with the tournament, rather than perform a strictly enforcement role during the event. I am proud to say our officers and even the city prosecutor played in the tournament this year and it went off without a hitch."

(Continues)

IDEAS **IN PRACTICE**

BUILDING PARTNERSHIPS AND TRUST (*Continued*)

Examples like the Evansville police department's approach to the basketball tournament not only prevent problems, but enhance the trust of the community simply by having officers engage in a non-enforcement capacity. And there are many other examples of how police officers around the United States have built trust and established ongoing community relationships just by taking the steps to address an issue that is important to that community.

Here is another example, which I witnessed firsthand in Hawthorne, California, where the Los Angeles Kings ice hockey team practices. I and other Hawthorne Police Department (HPD) officers noticed that none of our local kids played ice hockey because of its expense. So with the blessing of the department, we set out to change that. We contacted Matt Langen from the National Hockey League Players Association and applied for the "Goals and Dreams" grant, which provides free equipment to deserving organizations. After explaining that Hawthorne police officers would be volunteering to teach the kids how to play, 20 sets of equipment were donated to the project. HPD officers also raised enough money to pay for ice rink rental for eight weeks, and the "Hawthorne Force" Ice Hockey program was born.

At first, there was some apprehension on the part of the families, who are mostly Latino and African American. But when the parents saw the same police officers who patrolled the streets teaching their six- to eight-year-olds how to ice skate and become comfortable with the officers, they did too. The kids trusted the officers and everyone bonded over the success of the team. These youngsters were doing something they had never been able to even contemplate before, all because of the efforts of police officers and the support of the police administration.

Now, two years later, the program has more than 80 kids on six teams, all coached by volunteer officers who take pride in the kids, the parents, and the community. The parents support and trust the officers and have a great relationship with the HPD. What's more, the program has been replicated by police; one example is Ville Deux-Montagnes, Québec, Canada, and it continues to grow, helping police officers bond with communities through sports.

Chief Robert Fager of the HPD sums up the value of this kind of engagement best: "To think that societal relationships are a secondary priority in running a public safety organization is professional suicide. Law enforcement is built upon the trust and needs of its

U.S. Department of Justice-Community Oriented Policing Services

community—and with the advent of social media and information access, that community can be national in scope. Our department's contemporary philosophy integrates direct interaction with our citizenry through community forums, youth scholastic and sports partnerships, no-cost driver safety and basic first-aid classes, and our personal pride—Coffee with a Cop.

"In essence, create offerings that move or attract people, then invest your staff in it. Not only do you derive true-value feedback, but moreover, you literally reintroduce police officers and citizens to each other, with no overtone, and allow them to reinvigorate the common goal of a safer, more enriched community."

These trust-building non-enforcement activities cost little in terms of money, time, or effort, but they pay huge dividends in public safety. All you need do is encourage your officers to get out of their cars some time and go into a church, mosque, or community center and just talk to people. Officers will usually find a warm welcome and will often learn something new about people. What's more, those people will learn something new about police officers. And that is how relationships are started—with a simple handshake and a smile. It's time to get engaged.

SOURCE: Excerpt from Cognac, C. (2015, June). "Ready, Set, Engage! Ideas and Options for Community Engagement and Partnership Building." *Community Policing Dispatch*, 8(6). Retrieved August 10, 2016, from http://cops.usdoj.gov/html/dispatch/06-2015/community_engagement_and_partnership_building.asp

Building trust will not happen overnight; it will require ongoing effort. But trust must be achieved before police can assess community needs and construct the close ties needed to engender community support. The use of unnecessary force and arrogance, aloofness, or rudeness at any level of the agency will dampen the willingness of community members to ally themselves with the police. In addition, how officers have been traditionally assigned needs to be changed.

Assignments That Foster Partnerships

The goal of community policing is to reduce crime and disorder by carefully examining the characteristics of problems in neighborhoods and then applying appropriate problem-solving remedies. However, when officers' assignments continually change, there is little or no chance for them to develop the relationships and trust with citizens that is needed for community policing to occur. Likewise, communities are not given the opportunity to get to recognize and know officers who work in their neighborhoods.

"Beats should be configured in a manner that preserves, as much as possible, the unique geographical and social characteristics of neighborhoods while still allowing efficient service" (Bureau of Justice Assistance, 1994, p. 13). Officers who have permanent assignments become experts about their beats. Beat officers know the community leaders, businesspeople, school personnel, and students. They know the crime patterns and problems and have the best chance to develop partnerships for problem solving. Community members will become accustomed to seeing the permanent beat officers working in the community.

This increased police presence is an initial move in establishing trust and serves to reduce fear of crime among community members, which, in turn, helps create neighborhood security. Fear must be reduced if community members are to participate actively in policing. People will not act if they feel that their actions will jeopardize their safety.

> **L03**
> Traditional shift and beat *rotation* works to the detriment of building partnerships. To facilitate the fostering of police–community partnerships, patrol officers should be given responsibility for a permanent beat consisting of a small, well-defined geographic area.

A Shared Vision and Common Goals

Although the delivery of police services is organized by geographic area, a community may encompass widely diverse cultures, values, and concerns, particularly in urban settings. A community consists of more than just the local government and the neighborhood residents. Churches, schools, hospitals, social groups, private and public agencies, and those who work in the area are also vital members of the community. In addition, those who visit for cultural or recreational purposes or provide services to the area are also concerned with the safety and security of the neighborhood. Including these "communities of interest" in efforts to address problems of crime and disorder can expand a community's resource base.

Concerns and priorities will vary within and among these communities of interest. Some communities of interest are long lasting and were formed around racial, ethnic, or occupational lines or a common history, church, or school. Others form and re-form as new problems are identified and addressed. Interest groups within communities can be in opposition to one another— sometimes in violent opposition. Intracommunity disputes have been common in large urban centers, especially in times of changing demographics and population migrations.

These multiple and sometimes *conflicting interests* may impede establishing a common vision and shared goals and require patrol officers to function not only as preservers of law and order but also as skillful mediators. For example, a community group may oppose certain police tactics used to crack down on gang activity, which the group believes may result in discriminatory arrest practices. The police must not only protect the rights of the protesting group but must also work with all community members involved to find a way to preserve neighborhood peace. For this process to be effective, community members must communicate their views and suggestions and back up the negotiating efforts of the police. In this way, the entire community participates in the mediation process and helps preserve order. The police must encourage a spirit of cooperation that balances the collective interests of all citizens with the personal rights of individuals. To this end, the effective formation of partnerships requires the police to recognize both the conflicts and the commonalities that exist within the community.

The Remaining Core Components of Successful Partnerships

The remaining components, although vital, are not described, either because they are self-explanatory or because they have been discussed elsewhere in the text.

CRITICISMS OF PARTNERSHIPS

Partnerships are time consuming and therefore cost money. Most police agencies do not have extra personnel available for community policing–type projects. Many departments are 911 driven. Officers respond to one call after another and have a difficult time keeping up with the demand for service. When would they have the time to meet with stakeholders and develop plans to solve problems?

LO4

Criticism of the partnerships in community policing usually centers on time and money.

Working as partners with the community may take time and cost more in the short run, but continuing to treat the symptoms without solving the problem has its own long-term costs. It will mean responding again and again to the same calls, often involving the same people, and using temporary tactics to temporarily resolve problems. One way many departments free up time for officers to problem-solve and partner with community members is to manage the volume of 911 calls and to ultimately reduce the number of calls through effective call management or call reduction.

MAKING TIME FOR PARTNERING AND PROBLEM SOLVING: CALL MANAGEMENT

In most departments, calls for service determine what police officers do from minute to minute on a shift. People call the police to report crime, ask for assistance, ask questions, get advice, and many other often unrelated requests. Police departments try to respond as quickly as possible, and most have a policy of sending an officer when requested. However, through effective call management or call reduction, departments can free up time for partnerships without incurring additional expense.

When using **call management** or call reduction, departments take a fresh look at which calls for service require the response of one or more officers and, regardless of past practice, which do not. In call management, calls are prioritized based on the department's judgment about the emergency nature of the call (e.g., imminent harm to a person or a crime in progress), response time, need for backup, and other local factors. Priority schemes vary across the country, but many have four or five levels.

Call management usually involves **call stacking**. A computer-aided dispatch system is used to rank calls. Nonemergency, lower-priority calls are held (stacked), and higher-priority calls always receive attention and response ahead of the stacked calls. Using an officer to take telephone reports of none-mergency, low-priority calls is one change that has helped. Reports of minor thefts occurring days or even months in the past and made for insurance purposes are an example of incidents that could be handled completely by phone.

Similar results can be obtained by taking reports by appointment. If the reporting party is willing, an appointment can be set up to have an officer take a report at a time that is less busy for the department but still convenient for the caller. Many people find this method agreeable. Certain kinds of reports can be made on an agency's Web page, by mail, or by fax. Figure 7.2 illustrates the type of intake and response common in call management.

Another method of call management is to have civilian employees handle certain calls that do not involve dangerous situations, suspects, or investigative follow-up. These calls might include reports of abandoned vehicles, complaints about animals, bicycle stops, building checks, burglary, criminal mischief, funeral escorts, lost and found property, park patrol, parking issues, paperwork relays, runaways, subpoena service, theft, traffic crashes (with no injuries), traffic control, vandalism, and vehicle lockouts. However, police unions may take issue with such an approach unless reserve officers are used.

Call management may also involve dealing with the 911 system, which was set up for emergency calls for assistance. However, large numbers of callers, as many as 50 to 90 percent by some estimates, use 911 to ask for information or to report nonemergency situations (Office of Community Oriented Policing Services, 2007). Most agencies field hundreds or even thousands of phone calls a year from citizens seeking information, often unrelated to police services. Keeping the public informed in other ways, such as on a Web site or through newspapers and newsletters, about city policies, services, and procedures and when and when not to call police can reduce the volume of calls.

call management

Calls are prioritized based on the department's judgment about the emergency nature of the call (e.g., imminent harm to a person or a crime in progress), response time, need for backup, and other local factors.

call stacking

A process performed by a computer-aided dispatch system in which none-mergency, lower-priority calls are ranked and held or "stacked" so that the higher priorities are continually dispatched first.

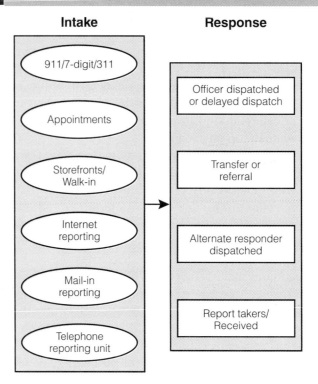

Figure 7.2 Call Management Intake and Response

Source: Tom McEwen, Deborah Spence, Russell Wolff, Julie Wartell, and Barbara Webster, *Call Management and Community Policing: A Guidebook for Law Enforcement* (Washington, DC: U.S. Department of Justice, Office of Community Oriented Policing Services, February 2003), 12.

People call the police for nonpolice matters for a variety of reasons: because they do not know who can help; because they believe the police know or should know the answers to all questions; because they know the phone number (911); and because, no matter what day of week or time of day it is, they know the phones will be answered. Every 911 call center fields calls asking why the electricity is out, what the weather conditions or driving conditions are, when the snowplows will start plowing, what time the shopping center opens, what time the neighborhood-watch meeting begins, what the driving directions are to a distant state, what the juvenile curfew hours are, where to pay a utility bill, and why there is no stop sign or semaphore at a certain location. Calls reporting pothole locations or complaining about raccoons, deer, and other wildlife—and even about noisy church bells—are clogging 911 lines across the country.

A growing number of cities across the United States are implementing 311 call centers, at which trained employees field a wide range of questions from citizens or forward requests to an appropriate agency. The 311 system diverts nonemergency calls from 911 and is increasingly viewed as a tool to enhance citizen access to government services and expand the original police nonemergency role. Three-one-one advances the community policing mission by providing an avenue through which citizens can share information with law enforcement and report quality-of-life issues before they escalate into more serious crime and disorder problems, taking a public service approach that reflects the nation's move toward community-oriented government (Office of Community Oriented Policing Services, 2007).

Three-one-one systems are not without drawbacks. Disadvantages include high implementation costs, lack of caller ID or location identifiers for 311 as are provided by most 911 systems, failure to record information, underuse of neighborhood policing resources, and a common dispatch policy for both 311 and 911 (Mazerolle, Rogan, Frank, Famega, & Eck, 2005).

Results of a 311 Call System in Baltimore

Baltimore has implemented a 311 nonemergency call system to reduce the response burden on police and improve the quality of policing. Researchers note a 34-percent total reduction in calls to 911 (Table 7.1) and widespread community acceptance of 311 as an alternative number (Mazerolle et al., 2005, p. 3). Most low-priority calls have moved from 911 to 311. Certain types of calls in particular migrated from 911 to 311, such as reports of larceny, parking violations, and loud noise complaints.

Not all of the results of the study were positive, however. The number of priority 1 calls *increased* by more than 27 percent after the 311 system was introduced. Researchers believe this increase was unrelated to implementing the system, because their analysis showed that priority 1 calls for specific categories of serious crime had begun to increase several months before the 311 system was installed.

The large reduction in priority 5 calls to 911 was partly offset by an increase in nonemergency calls referred to other city agencies. Citizens may have stopped calling the police about priority 5 matters because the department stopped dispatching patrol cars in response to these calls after introducing 311.

Table 7.1	The Impact of 311 on Calls to the Police			
Pre-311 Implementation		**Post-311 Implementation**		
Call Priority	**911 Only**	**911 Only**	**311 Only**	**911 + 311**
1	417,728	470,263	62,534	532,797
2	902,565	633,706	184,931	818,637
3	415,133	177,967	138,722	316,689
4	201,043	66,169	103,878	170,047
5	111,500	375	50,454	50,829
Total	2,047,969	1,348,480	540,519	1,888,999

Note: Preintervention period was 730 days, from October 1, 1994, to October 1, 1996, excluding February 29, 1996, (leap year). Postintervention period was 730 days, from October 2, 1996, to October 1, 1998.

Source: Alberto R. Gonzales, Tracy A. Henke, Sarah V. Hart. *Managing Calls to the Police with 911/311 Systems*. Washington, DC: U.S. Department of Justice, Office of Justice Programs, February 2005, p. 3. https://www.ncjrs.gov/pdffiles1/nij/206256.pdf.

Unrecorded calls were estimated to be about 8 percent more frequent after the introduction of 311. This small but significant increase may have resulted from a greater inclination by 311 operators to handle calls about nonpolice matters without recording them.

Online Reporting

Another way to make time for partnerships and problem solving is to have complainants report priority 5 calls online. A Web search of "citizen online reporting" will reveal the hundreds, if not thousands, of jurisdictions that make this reporting avenue available to local residents. Minneapolis, Minnesota, for example, has an e-report Web site. When people sign on, they are cautioned that the site is not monitored 24 hours a day and that, before they begin, they should make sure they do not need a police officer to take the report. The site also directs them to call 911 immediately if:

- A crime is in progress.
- Someone is hurt or threatened.
- They can provide information about someone who may have committed a crime.

The e-report site then asks specific questions such as who is reporting the incident, what happened, where it happened, and the like. Data from dispatch and online reports can be of great assistance in a department's problem-solving efforts and can inform the agency on communities and organizations that might benefit most from partnership efforts.

KEY COLLABORATORS: COMMUNITY JUSTICE

Police departments should identify and partner with local key collaborators and be certain they are included in community policing efforts.

LO5

Key collaborators who should not be overlooked in forming partnerships include prosecutors, courts, corrections, other government agencies, private security providers, victims, volunteers, and even such groups as taxi drivers.

community justice
Partnerships between the formal criminal justice system, the private sector, and community groups to promote public safety and enhance quality of life in the community.

The trend to involve the community is affecting all aspects of the justice system, with many researchers and practitioners advocating the move toward community justice. **Community justice** is broadly defined as partnerships between the formal criminal justice system, the private sector, and community groups to promote public safety and enhance quality of life in the community: "Community justice is rooted in the actions that citizens, community organizations, and the criminal justice system can take to control crime and social disorder. Its central focus is community-level outcomes, shifting the emphasis from individual incidents to systemic patterns, from individual conscience to social mores, and from individual goods to the common good" (Karp & Clear, 2000, p. 324). Berman and Anderson (2010) note that the essence of community justice can be boiled down to two ingredients: partnerships and problem solving. However, "No criminal justice agency—not police, not courts, not prosecutors, not probation, not parole, not the defense bar—can hope to build partnerships or solve neighborhood problems without investing significant time and energy in engaging the community" (Berman & Anderson, 2010, p. 1). Because different communities have different problems, which warrant different responses, each community's path toward community justice will be individualized; there is no one-size-fits-all.

Community justice has its roots in restorative justice, which can be traced back to the code of Hammurabi in 2000 BCE. This type of justice holds offenders accountable to the victim and the victim's community rather than to the state. Rather than seeking retribution (punishment), **restorative justice** seeks restitution—to repair the damages as much as possible and to restore the victim, the community, and the offender. Under common law, criminals were often required to reimburse victims for their losses. Beginning in the 12th century, however, under William the Conqueror, crimes were considered offenses against the king's peace, with offenders ordered to pay fines to the state, a tradition that was brought to the United States. In the 1970s, reformers began trying to change the emphasis of the criminal justice system from the offender back to the victim. The Victim Witness Protection Act of 1982 marked the reemergence of the victim in the criminal justice process.

restorative justice
Seeks not retribution (punishment) but, rather, restitution, to repair the damage of crime as much as possible and to restore the victim, the community, and the offender.

The Centre for Justice and Reconciliation (2016) states: "Restorative Justice is a theory of justice that . . . is best accomplished through cooperative processes [i.e., partnerships] that allow all willing stakeholders to meet, although other approaches are available when that is impossible. This can lead to transformation of people, relationships and communities."

In addition to reorienting the goals of justice to be more inclusive of victims and the community, one of the guiding principles of restorative justice is that stakeholders share responsibilities for achieving justice through partnerships for action. Table 7.2 summarizes the differences between the traditional retributive approach to justice and restorative justice.

LO6
Restorative justice advocates a balanced approach to justice that involves offenders, victims, local communities, and government to alleviate and repair the harm caused by crime and violence and to maintain peaceful communities.

The most common forms of restorative justice that occur through court sanctioning via sentences include restitution (payments to victims) and community service. Other restorative justice practices include victim impact statements, family group conferences, sentencing circles, and citizen reparative boards.

In the United States, the community justice emphasis has influenced prosecutors, courts, and corrections.

Table 7.2	Paradigms of Justice—Old and New
Old Paradigm/Retributive Justice	**New Paradigm/Restorative Justice**
1. Crime defined as violation of the state	Crime defined as violation of one person by another
2. Focus on establishing blame, on guilt, on past (did he/she do it?)	Focus on problem solving, on liabilities and obligations, on future (what should be done?)
3. Adversarial relationships and process normative	Dialogue and negotiation normative
4. Imposition of pain to punish and deter/prevent	Restitution as a means of restoring both parties; reconciliation/restoration as goal
5. Justice defined by intent and by process; right rules	Justice defined as right relationships; judged by the outcome
6. Interpersonal, conflictual nature of crime obscured, repressed; conflict seen as individual versus State	Crime recognized as interpersonal conflict; value of conflict recognized
7. One social injury replaced by another	Focus on repair of social injury
8. Community on sidelines, represented abstractly by state	Community as facilitator in restorative process
9. Encouragement of competitive, individualistic values	Encouragement of mutuality

(Continued)

Table 7.2	Paradigms of Justice—Old and New (*Continued*)
10. Action directed from state to offender: • Victim ignored • Offender passive	Victim's and offender's roles recognized in both problem and solution: • Victim rights/needs recognized • Offender encouraged to take responsibility
11. Offender accountability defined as taking punishment	Offender accountability defined as understanding impact of action and helping decide how to make things right
12. Offense defined in purely legal terms, devoid of moral, social, economic, political dimensions	Offense understood in whole context—moral, social, economic, political
13. "Debt" owed to state and society in the abstract	Debt/liability to victim recognized
14. Response focused on offender's past behavior	Response focused on harmful consequences of offender's behavior
15. Stigma of crime unremovable	Stigma of crime removable through restorative action
16. No encouragement for repentance and forgiveness	Possibilities for repentance and forgiveness
17. Dependence on proxy professionals	Direct involvement by participants

Source: Howard Zehr. *Journal of Community Corrections* (formerly *IARCA Journal*) Volume 4 Number 4, March 1991, p. 7. Civic Research Institute, Inc. Used by permission of Civic Research Institute, publisher of *Journal of Community Corrections*, official journal of the International Community Corrections Association, formerly the International Association of Residential and Community Alternatives.

Community Prosecutors

As community policing evolves, new collaborations continue to emerge. Including the prosecutor as a partner is one collaboration gaining popularity, and for good reason. Community members' concerns are often not murder or robbery but the types of things that contribute to neighborhood decline and fear of crime, such as abandoned buildings, heavy neighborhood traffic, or street-drug dealing. These neighborhood stability issues are frequently addressed by police, but prosecutors tend to see them as a low priority: "Community prosecution seeks to change the traditional orientation of prosecutors by more fully integrating them into the community and removing barriers between the office and those it is designed to serve" (Cunningham, Renauer, & Khalifa, 2006, p. 203).

Community prosecution builds on the 1980s innovations of community policing and has steadily gained popularity throughout the country (Wolf, 2006). Similar to community policing, community prosecution focuses not on specific cases but on community issues and problems, often involving quality-of-life issues. The community prosecution philosophy calls on prosecutors to take a proactive approach and think of themselves as problem solvers "who seek not only to prosecute individual offenders but also develop lasting solutions to public-safety problems" (Campbell & Wolf, 2004, p. 1). When prosecutors become involved as partners in community policing, they attend neighborhood meetings, ride with officers on their beats, and get a completely different view of the issues and incidents that devastate communities and breed more crime and disorder. Three defining characteristics of community prosecution are:

- the development of partnerships with a variety of government agencies and community-based groups

- the use of varied enforcement methods, such as problem-solving techniques, to address crime and public safety issues
- the involvement of the community (Fanflik, Budzilowicz, & Nugent-Borakove, 2007)

With community prosecutors, police can strengthen the enforcement value and the services they provide (Jansen & Dague, 2006). The similarities between community prosecution and community policing are many, and, as Table 7.3 illustrates, the operational elements of *community* are what enable community prosecution to work well in conjunction with community policing.

Many local district attorneys' offices report having adopted a "community prosecution" approach to crime control. Data from the Bureau of Justice Statistics indicate that, during 2005, two-thirds of all prosecutors' offices used tools other than traditional criminal prosecution to address community problems, and more than half sought input from the community to identify problem areas or information about crime (Perry, 2006). City attorneys' offices are also beginning to recognize the value of working with law enforcement and the community to develop creative solutions to livability issues. The nontraditional tools prosecutors are now aggressively using include nuisance abatement; drug-free and prostitute-free zones; landlord–tenant laws; truancy abatement; graffiti cleanup; and community courts, including several types of specialized courts (Wolf & Worrall, 2004).

Community Courts

A recent alternative to the traditional courtroom is the community court, a neighborhood-focused court that offers an immediate, visible response to low-level, quality-of-life offenses that disrupt and degrade the community and provides an efficient way to process the most frequent types of complaints. With their origins in community policing and problem-oriented policing, community courts are a natural extension of the community justice movement and bridge the gap between the justice system and the local neighborhoods

Table 7.3	Operational Elements of Community	
	Community Policing	**Community Prosecution**
Partnerships	The active enlistment of nonpolice individuals and agencies, public as well as private, in address[ing] community security programs	Partnerships between the prosecutor, law enforcement, public and private agencies, and the community
Problem Solving	Remedying conditions that generate crime and insecurity, involving conditions-focused prevention at local levels	Varied prevention, intervention, and enforcement methods (e.g., use of tools other than criminal prosecution to address problems)
Community Involvement	Asking communities regularly and systematically what their security needs are and how the police might more effectively meet them	Inclusion of the community's input into the criminal justice system, including the courtroom

Source: Fanflik, P. L.; Budzilowicz, L. M.; & Nugent-Borakove, M. E. (2007, October). *Managing Innovation: A Closer Look at Community Prosecution Management Issues.* Alexandria, VA: National District Attorneys Association, American Prosecutors Research Institute.

they serve by (1) bringing new resources from both inside and outside the justice system to bear on local crime and disorder issues and (2) applying problem-solving strategies to the complex issues that face state and local courts (Doniger, 2009).

The first community court was launched in 1993 in midtown Manhattan to target quality-of-life offenses such as graffiti, illegal vending, prostitution, fare beating, vandalism, and shoplifting. At the time, court dockets were overflowing with such misdemeanor cases, which limited the overburdened traditional court to either sentencing offenders to a few days of jail time or disposing of cases with no sentence at all—responses that communicated to the victims, community, and offenders that these offenses were not taken seriously. The Midtown Community Court, however, marked a "bold departure from 'business as usual' in the court system," by dispensing a combination of punishment and treatment, sentencing low-level offenders to pay back the neighborhood through visible community restitution projects while simultaneously providing services for issues such as substance abuse, addiction, unemployment, lack of job skills, and homelessness—problems commonly identified as the underlying sources of criminal behavior (Lang, 2011, p. 3). Data show the innovative approach has made a positive impact. For example, in 2009, only 50 percent of defendants processed through the traditional downtown criminal courts completed their community service mandates, whereas 87 percent of the Midtown-processed defendants completed their court-ordered mandates (Lang, 2011). Figure 7.3 illustrates case flow and interventions at the Midtown Community Court.

Although community courts have traditionally been thought of as neighborhood courts, they can be equally effectively when used to process cases from an entire city or county (Schweig, 2014). Consider the Red Hook Community Justice Center in Brooklyn, New York, which was launched in June 2000 and was the first multijurisdictional community court in the United States. Located in a geographically and socially isolated neighborhood that is home to one of New York's oldest and largest public housing developments, Red Hook seeks to advance a coordinated response to local problems such as drugs, crime, and landlord–tenant disputes. A single judge hears neighborhood cases from three police precincts, in which approximately 200,000 people live, that under ordinary circumstances would go to three different courts—Civil, Family, and Criminal. The Red Hook judge has a wide range of sanctioning and service option at his disposal, including community restitution projects, educational workshops, GED classes, short-term psychoeducational groups, and long-term treatment (e.g., drug treatment, mental health counseling, and trauma-focused psychotherapy). Red Hook staffs an on-site clinic with social service professionals who use trauma- and evidence-informed approaches to assess and connect court clients to appropriate services. The Justice Center also strives to connect court-involved youth to strengths-based programming, including art projects and peer education programs (Center for Court Innovation, n.d.). Among the documented results of Red Hook are the following:

Figure 7.3 Summary of Case Flow and Interventions at the Midtown Community Court

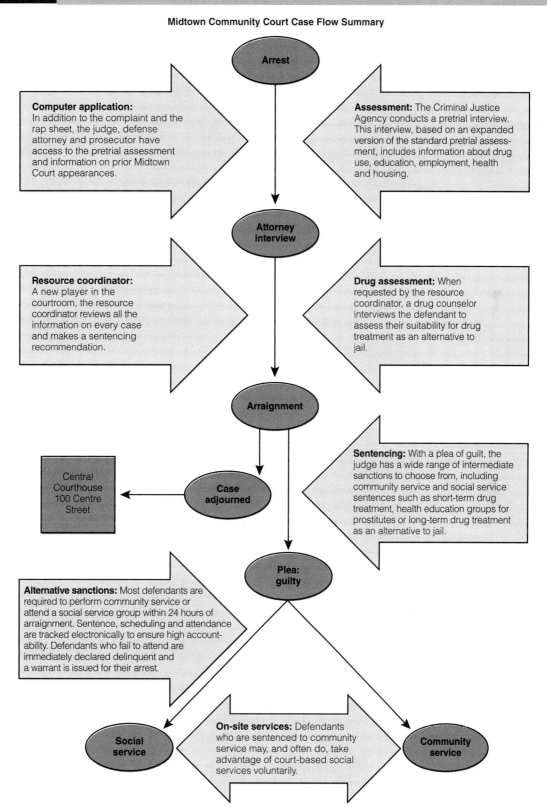

Midtown Community Court Case Flow Summary

Arrest

Computer application: In addition to the complaint and the rap sheet, the judge, defense attorney and prosecutor have access to the pretrial assessment and information on prior Midtown Court appearances.

Assessment: The Criminal Justice Agency conducts a pretrial interview. This interview, based on an expanded version of the standard pretrial assessment, includes information about drug use, education, employment, health and housing.

Attorney interview

Resource coordinator: A new player in the courtroom, the resource coordinator reviews all the information on every case and makes a sentencing recommendation.

Drug assessment: When requested by the resource coordinator, a drug counselor interviews the defendant to assess their suitability for drug treatment as an alternative to jail.

Arraignment

Central Courthouse 100 Centre Street

Case adjourned

Sentencing: With a plea of guilt, the judge has a wide range of intermediate sanctions to choose from, including community service and social service sentences such as short-term drug treatment, health education groups for prostitutes or long-term drug treatment as an alternative to jail.

Plea: guilty

Alternative sanctions: Most defendants are required to perform community service or attend a social service group within 24 hours of arraignment. Sentence, scheduling and attendance are tracked electronically to ensure high accountability. Defendants who fail to attend are immediately declared delinquent and a warrant is issued for their arrest.

Social service

On-site services: Defendants who are sentenced to community service may, and often do, take advantage of court-based social services voluntarily.

Community service

Source: Eric Lee and Jimena Martinez. *How It Works: Summary of Case Flow and Interventions at the Midtown Community Court.* New York: Center for Court Innovation, 1998, p. 4.

- *Caseload:* The Red Hook Community Justice Center handles approximately 3,000 misdemeanor criminal cases, 11,000 summonses, 500 housing court cases, and 175 juvenile delinquency cases each year. Of the criminal cases, the most frequent charges are drug possession, minor assault, traffic violations, public drinking, and trespassing.

- *Reduced Incarceration:* Red Hook has achieved a 50 percent reduction in the use of jail in misdemeanor cases.

- *Reduced Recidivism:* Adult defendants handled at Red Hook were 10 percent less likely, and juvenile defendants were 20 percent less likely, to commit new crimes than offenders who were processed through traditional court.

- *Fairness:* More than 85 percent of criminal defendants report that their cases were handled fairly by the Justice Center. These results were consistent regardless of defendant background (e.g., race, sex, education) or case outcome.

- *Increased Alternative Sentences:* Seventy-eight percent of offenders were sentenced to community or social service, compared with 20 percent of offenders in comparable cases who were processed at the regular criminal courthouse in Brooklyn.

- *Accountability:* Compliance rates with Red Hook court orders average 75 percent, which is 50 percent higher than compliance rates achieved by comparable courts.

- *Increased Public Trust:* Approval ratings of police, prosecutors, and judges have increased threefold since Red Hook opened.

- *Decreased Levels of Fear:* Since 1999, the percentage of Red Hook residents who say they are afraid to go to the parks or subway at night has dropped 42 percent.

- *Public Support:* A door-to-door survey found that 94 percent of local residents support the community court, compared to only 12 percent of local residents who rated local courts favorably before Red Hook opened.

- *Community Restitution:* Each year, sentenced passed by the Justice Center contribute roughly 70,000 hours of community service to Red Hook, which translates to more than $500,000 worth of labor, based on the minimum wage.

- *Cost Savings:* Taxpayers saved an estimated $5,000 per defendant in avoided victimization costs relative to similar cases processed through traditional misdemeanor court.

- *Recognition:* The Red Hook Community Justice Center has served as a model nationally and internationally, including replications in New York, Dallas, Hartford, Portland, Seattle, Newark, Liverpool (England), Melbourne (Australia), and Vancouver (Canada). The project has received numerous awards, including national prizes from the National Criminal Justice Association, the American Bar Association, and the Rudy Bruner Foundation. In addition, the Justice Center was the subject of an acclaimed PBS documentary, Red Hook Justice (Center for Court Innovation, n.d.).

Community courts are as diverse as the communities they serve—some handle only criminal offenses such as stalking, auto theft, and assault, and others accept a wider variety of criminal and noncriminal offenses, from truant youth and landlord–tenant conflicts, to environmental code violations, drug addiction, chronic homelessness, shoplifting, vandalism, and sex trafficking (Lang, 2011). Despite their diversity, community courts share a common set of core principles and practices, including (Lang, 2011, pp. 3–4):

- *Enhanced Information:* Using better staff training (about complex issues like drug addiction and mental illness) combined with better information (about defendants, victims, and the community context of crime) to help improve the decision making of judges, attorneys, and other justice officials
- *Community Engagement:* Engaging citizens to help the justice system identify, prioritize, and solve local problems
- *Collaboration:* Bringing together justice players (such as judges, prosecutors, defense attorneys, probation officers, and court managers) and potential stakeholders beyond the courthouse (such as social service providers, residents, victims groups, schools) to improve inter-agency communication, improve trust between citizens and government, and foster new responses to problems
- *Individualized Justice:* Using evidence-based risk and needs assessment instruments to link offenders to individually tailored community-based services (e.g., job training, drug treatment, safety planning, mental health counseling) where appropriate
- *Accountability:* Employing community restitution mandates and regular compliance monitoring—with clear consequences for noncompliance—to improve the accountability of offenders
- *Outcomes:* Collecting and analyzing data on an active and ongoing basis—measuring outcomes and process, costs, and benefits—to evaluate the effectiveness of operations and encourage continuous improvement

While taking many forms, all community courts address local public safety issues by promoting community collaboration, creative partnerships, innovative programs, alternatives to incarceration, and respectful treatment of defendants. The goals community courts work toward are tangible—improved neighborhood safety, lower levels of public fear, decreased crime and disorder, greater accountability for low-level offenders, and increased public confidence in the justice system.

By year end 2010, 37 community courts were operating in jurisdictions throughout the country, and more communities were planning to install such courts (Lang, 2011). More information about community courts is available from the Center for Court Innovation at www.courtinnovation.org.

Community courts are a type of specialized court under the larger umbrella of *problem-solving courts,* which includes other specialized courts such as drug, domestic violence, gun, and mental health courts. Problem-solving courts subscribe to the philosophy that it is no longer sufficient for judges to simply process and adjudicate offenders, but that through their dispositions judges must also strive to ameliorate conditions conducive to crime and disorder, reduce recidivism, improve public confidence in the justice system, and prevent crime in the future (Wolf, 2007). Several shared principles distinguish problem-solving courts from the conventional approach to case processing and case outcomes in state courts (Berman & Feinblatt, 2001, pp. 131–132):

- *Case Outcome:* Problem-solving courts seek to achieve tangible outcomes for victims, for offenders, and for society, including reductions in recidivism, reduced stays in foster care for children, increased sobriety for addicts, and healthier communities.

- *System Change:* Problem-solving courts promote reform outside of the courthouse as well as within it. For example, family treatment courts that handle cases of child neglect have encouraged local child welfare agencies to adopt new staffing patterns and to improve case management practices.

- *Judicial Authority:* Problem-solving courts rely on the active use of judicial authority to solve problems and to change the behavior of litigants. Instead of passing off cases to other judges, to probation departments, or to community-based treatment programs, judges at problem-solving courts stay involved with each case throughout the post-adjudication process. Drug court judges, for example, closely supervise the performance of offenders in drug treatment, requiring them to return to court frequently for urine testing and courtroom progress reports.

- *Collaboration:* Problem-solving courts employ a collaborative approach, relying on both government and nonprofit partners (criminal justice agencies, social service providers, community groups, and others) to help achieve their goals. For example, many domestic violence courts have developed partnerships with batterers' programs and probation departments to help improve the monitoring of defendants.

- *Nontraditional Roles:* Some problem-solving courts have altered the dynamics of the courtroom, including, at times, certain features of the adversarial process. For example, at many drug courts, judges and attorneys (on both sides of the aisle) work together to craft systems of sanctions and rewards for offenders in drug treatment. And by using the institution's authority and prestige to coordinate the work of other agencies, problem-solving courts may engage judges in unfamiliar roles as conveners and brokers.

Community Corrections

The third component of the criminal justice system, corrections, also is an often-overlooked partner in the community policing effort. The movement toward community-based corrections has been growing steadily since the 1970s, when states, facing overcrowded correctional facilities strained beyond their intended capacities, began passing community corrections acts as ways to divert nonviolent, first-time offenders from the traditional path of incarceration. While the increased use of community corrections may have started as a way to ease prison crowding, further research has bolstered the movement by providing evidence that the "get tough," "lock 'em up and throw away the key" approach popular during the 1980s and 1990s was not only expensive and ineffective at reducing crime but was actually counterproductive and, in many cases, made offenders *more* likely to commit crime upon their release.

Several scientifically validated risk-assessment tools have been developed to objectively predict how likely an individual is to reoffend and then categorize them as low-, medium-, or high-risk offenders. Such tools commonly assess an offender's **dynamic risk factors**, also called **criminogenic needs**, which are those characteristics or variables that can be changed, such as drug addiction, antisocial attitudes and values, the tendency to hang out with criminal peers, family dysfunction, and unemployment. This is in contrast to **static risk factors**, which cannot be changed, such as an offender's prior criminal record. Research shows that appropriate interventions that target criminogenic needs can reduce, often significantly, the likelihood of recidivism. However, research has also shown that low-risk offenders who are sentenced to the same programs and interventions as medium- and high-risk offenders and are treated more harshly than is needed, based on their assessed risk, actually recidivate *more* often than other low-risk offenders who receive more appropriate treatment. This means the system actually does more harm than good when it applies a "one size fits all" method to handling offenders (Council of State Governments Justice Center, 2013). Such empirical evidence has spurred the growth of various community correctional interventions in an effort to better address different offenders' criminogenic needs.

Community corrections, also called intermediate sanctions, usually has included a range of correctional alternatives existing along a continuum of increasing restriction and control—from day fines to forfeiture, restitution, community service, intensive supervision programs, house arrest, day reporting centers, and residential community centers—which are tougher than conventional probation but less restrictive and costly than imprisonment. Traditionally, the task of administering these correctional alternatives has fallen almost exclusively on those internal stakeholders within corrections— probation and parole officers.

Whereas it is one thing to conduct correctional activities outside the confines of barred institutions, it is quite another to actively draw the community and other external stakeholders into the corrections process. As with the overall movement of community justice, this has become the new paradigm in community corrections, which requires a complicated interplay among judicial and correctional personnel from related public and private agencies, human services organizations, citizen volunteers, civic groups, and faith-based organizations. And because community corrections agencies, like all other justice agencies, are experiencing somber budget realities that require them to do more with less, partnerships have become more important than ever to achieving successful reentry outcomes (Matz, DeMichele, & Lowe, 2012).

Probation is, by far, the most commonly imposed form of community corrections. At yearend 2014, an estimated 4,708,100 adults (persons age 18 and older) were under community supervision, 3,864,100 (82%) of which were probationers (Kaeble, Maruschak, & Bonczar, 2015). In addition, nearly 400,000 juveniles were also under some type of probationary supervision (Sickmund, Sladky, & Kang, 2015). Consequently, partnerships between police and probation officers hold great potential to benefit a large number of offenders within

dynamic risk factors

Those characteristics or variables that can be changed, such as drug addiction, antisocial attitudes and values, the tendency to hang out with criminal peers, family dysfunction, and unemployment; also called *criminogenic needs*.

criminogenic needs

Those characteristics or variables that can be changed, such as drug addiction, antisocial attitudes and values, the tendency to hang out with criminal peers, family dysfunction, and unemployment; also called *dynamic risk factors*.

static risk factors

Those characteristics or variables which cannot be changed, such as an offender's prior criminal record.

the criminal justice system and, ultimately, significantly affect public safety levels within a community. Indeed: "The combination of community supervision and community-oriented policing is a match that needs to occur. Of utmost importance, the partnership has the potential to enhance public safety by suppressing criminality, addressing neighborhood problems, increasing interagency information sharing, and assisting reentry" (Matz et al., 2012).

One type of partnership that has proved successful is that between individual patrol officers and probation officers in the same neighborhood. Probation officers who ride along with patrol officers can often spot probationers violating a condition of their probation, and the officer can make an immediate arrest. Or the probation officer can talk with the offending probationer, letting him or her know that the illegal activities will no longer go unnoticed. For communities embattled in the gang–drug–gun issue, partnerships between police and corrections officers can prove beneficial. One effort to reduce gun crime across the country has been the Project Safe Neighborhoods (PSN) initiative, a task force idea based on the successful Operation Ceasefire implemented in Boston during the mid-1990s. Under Operation Ceasefire, police and probation and parole officers partnered to proactively search for individuals thought to be at high risk of illegal possession of firearms, jointly conducted nighttime home visits of these individuals, and gathered and shared intelligence to vigorously enforce the conditions of probation to ensure offender compliance. It is worth noting that the Supreme Court ruling in *United States v. Knights* (2001) upheld the constitutionality of warrantless searches of probationers' or parolees' homes based on "reasonable suspicion" or "reasonable grounds" by either probation or parole officers or the police.

An early police–probation/parole partnership aimed at addressing gang-related violence was Boston's Operation Night Light, which was developed in the early 1990s. Under this program, police and probation or parole officers would share intelligence and conduct joint patrols, which often focused on increased suppression tactics (e.g., curfews and association restrictions for gang members) in an effort to keep gang violence and juvenile recidivism under control. Although rigorous research on the effects of this program are lacking, and numerous problems were identified (such as issues regarding jurisdictional boundaries and overreliance on suppression and deterrence to the exclusion of treatment), it did pave the way for other police–community corrections partnerships.

For example, the American Probation and Parole Association (APPA), in recognizing the potential benefits of police–probation/parole partnerships, developed the C.A.R.E. model, which not only supports the Project Safe Neighborhoods (PSN) initiative but also serves as an extension of the Office of Juvenile Justice and Delinquency Prevention's (OJJDP) Comprehensive Gang Model (Matz et al., 2012). Similar to the SARA model of problem solving, the C.A.R.E. model consists of four primary components: (1) **C**ollaboration, (2) **A**nalysis, (3) **R**eentry, and (4) **E**valuation. Notably, the first step is forming collaborations, or partnerships, between justice agencies and various community, social service, and faith-based organizations. These partners then identify and analyze specific local problems, formulate appropriate reentry programs that take into account each offender's criminogenic needs, and evaluate the results of these interventions. The ultimate goal of the C.A.R.E. initiative is to enable gang-affiliated probationers and parolees to separate themselves from the gang lifestyle with the help of such expanded partnerships, which can provide educational assistance, vocational training, and substance abuse treatment (Matz et al., 2012).

Police–probation partnerships may also include sharing probation or parole data for use in law enforcement geographic information systems (GIS) or CompStat databases to build criminal cases targeting serious offenders.

Philadelphia has forged a partnership between its Adult Probation and Parole Department and local police to address the growing violence in the city and attempt to gain control over increasing numbers of weapons violations. A unique feature of this effort is involving a research partner through the University of Pennsylvania's Department of Criminology: "A statistical model began to emerge from Penn's preliminary analysis of our data and from their mapping of the variables determined to be of interest. We named this model PROBE-Stat, articulating a mission statement to unite community supervision agencies and academic criminology in a data-driven partnership to prevent crime, especially serious violence, committed by and against offenders under court supervision in the community" (Malvestuto & Snyder, 2005, p. 2).

Other Government Agencies

Criminal justice agencies are not the only local government agencies responsible for responding to community problems. Partnering with other city and county departments and agencies is important to problem-solving success. Sometimes described as **working in "silos,"** local government agencies and departments have traditionally worked quite independently of each other. Under community policing, appropriate government departments and agencies are called on and recognized for their abilities to respond to and address crime and social disorder issues.

Fire departments, building inspections agencies, health departments, street departments, parks and recreation departments, and child welfare agencies frequently are appropriate and necessary stakeholders in problem-solving initiatives: "Elected officials have an important role to play in close coordination with their law enforcement executive, to make the community policing philosophy and the strategies it encourages work best and potentially expand beyond law enforcement" (Chapman & Scheider, 2006, p. 4).

State and federal agencies may also be of assistance, including the Federal Bureau of Investigation (FBI), the Drug Enforcement Administration (DEA), the U.S. attorney in the region, the state attorney, the state criminal investigative agency, and the state highway department.

One partnership between the COPS Office, the FBI, and the Bureau of Justice Assistance (BJA) of the U.S. Department of Justice was formed to enhance counterterrorism training and technical assistance to state, local, and tribal law enforcement. The FBI and COPS are delivering the BJA-funded State and Local Anti-Terrorism Training (SLATT) through the COPS network of local

working in "silos"
Occurs when agencies with common interests work independently with no collaboration.

Regional Community Policing Institutes (Office of Community Oriented Policing Services, 2004). COPS has expanded its partnership with the FBI and BJA by developing counterterrorism roll call training programs for line officers, in which short segments on various aspects of counterterrorism are presented to officers during their roll calls.

Private Security Providers

Since September 11, 2001, law enforcement and private security organizations have been under pressure to not only provide traditional services but also to contribute to the national effort to protect the homeland from internal and external threats:

> Despite their similar interests in protecting the people of the United States, the two fields have rarely collaborated. In fact, through the practice of community policing, law enforcement agencies have collaborated extensively with practically every group but private security. By some estimates, 85 percent of the country's critical infrastructure is protected by private security. The need for complex coordination, extra staffing, and special resources after a terror attack, coupled with the significant demands of crime prevention and response, absolutely requires boosting the level of partnership between public policing and private security (Office of Community Oriented Policing Services, 2004, p. 1).

Recognizing a need for collaboration between private policing and public policing, the International Association of Chiefs of Police held a summit in early 2004 to discuss possible collaborations between public and private police around the issue of terrorism. Their goal is to develop a national strategy to build such partnerships between federal, state, tribal, and local public sector police agencies and private security agencies. The focus of such partnerships will be terrorism prevention and response. The summit was supported by the COPS Office. The summit also looked at the differences in such collaborations, and some are significant, including differences in the screening, hiring, training, and responsibilities of private security and public police officers.

Some areas of cooperation are investigating internal theft and economic crimes, responding to burglar alarms, examining evidence from law enforcement in private crime labs, conducting background checks, protecting VIPs and executives, protecting crime scenes, transporting prisoners, moving hazardous materials, and controlling crowds and traffic at public events.

Two forces driving the increased partnerships between public and private police are the proliferation of cybercrime and the need for specialized knowledge for crime investigation (Dodge, 2006). The expanding responsibilities of private security include surveillance, investigation, crowd control, prison escorts, court security, guarding and patrolling, proactive crime prevention, risk management and insurance assessment, weapons training, crime scene examination, and forensic evidence gathering.

Volunteers

The use of citizen volunteers by police departments has increased significantly in recent years. Volunteers help leverage existing resources while simultaneously enhancing public safety. Volunteer programs not only allow agencies and officers to focus on policing and enforcement functions by providing supplemental and/or support services, these partnerships also create valuable ties between law enforcement and the community. Partnering with volunteers was discussed in detail in Chapter 3.

Before leaving the discussion of volunteers, however, take a brief look at a unique partnership that aims to address the criminal victimization of our nation's older population. The American Association of Retired Persons (AARP), the International Association of Chiefs of Police (IACP), and the National Sheriffs' Association (NSA) have adopted a joint resolution and formed a partnership called **TRIAD** to provide specific information such as crime prevention materials (brochures, program guides, and audiovisual presentations on crime prevention and the elderly), policies, exemplary projects relating to the law enforcement response to the older community, and successful projects involving the formation of senior advisory councils to advise departments on the needs of seniors. TRIAD also trains police about aging, communication techniques with elderly citizens, victimization of the elderly, and management programs using older volunteers. TRIAD has been identified as a concrete example of community policing. Leadership is provided by an advisory group of older persons and those providing services to the elderly called Seniors and Law Enforcement Together (SALT).

TRIAD
A three-way partnership among the American Association of Retired Persons (AARP), the International Association of Chiefs of Police (IACP), and the National Sheriffs' Association (NSA) to address criminal victimization of older people.

BUILDING PARTNERSHIPS IN A VARIETY OF NEIGHBORHOODS

The effective mobilization of community support requires different approaches in different communities. Establishing trust and obtaining cooperation are often easier in middle-class and affluent communities than in poorer communities, where mistrust of police may have a long history.

Building bonds in some neighborhoods may involve supporting basic social institutions (e.g., families, churches, schools) that have been weakened by pervasive crime or disorder. The creation of viable communities is necessary if lasting alliances that nurture cooperative efforts are to be sustained. Under community policing, the police become both catalysts and facilitators in the development of these communities.

LO7
Building partnerships in lower-income neighborhoods may be more difficult because often there are fewer resources and less trust between the citizens and law enforcement.

A PARTNERSHIP TO PREVENT STALKING

Data from the Bureau of Justice Statistics indicate that an estimated 14 in every 1,000 persons age 18 or older are victims of stalking during any given 12-month period. About half (46%) of stalking victims experience at least one unwanted contact per week, and 11 percent of victims said they had been stalked for 5 years or more. Approximately one in four stalking victims reported some form of cyberstalking, such as e-mail (83%) or instant messaging, and 46 percent of stalking victims felt fear of not knowing what would happen next (Baum, Catalano, Rand, & Rose, 2009). Many incidents of stalking are not reported to law enforcement because victims feel it is a private or personal matter, or they report it to another official (40.3%). The next most frequent reason for nonreporting is that the victim feels it is not important enough to report or that he or she does not think a crime has occurred (38.4%) (Baum et al., 2009).

Stalking is a complex and unique crime, making it more difficult to recognize, investigate, and prosecute. The factors that make stalking unique are, first, that the crime is committed repeatedly against the same victim. Second, these victims suffer extreme fear, and with good reason. Stalking victims are frequently severely injured, some fatally, by their stalkers. Stalkers, as a group, are highly motivated offenders, are especially determined to commit these crimes, and are difficult to deter. Protection orders, conviction, and even incarceration may not be sufficient to stop them, as some offenders are able to continue stalking, in some form, even from prison.

Like most police agencies in the United States at the end of the 20th century, the Philadelphia (Pennsylvania) Police Department (PPD) had no protocols or procedures for handling stalking cases. Acknowledging the need to increase officers' ability to recognize and respond to stalking crimes, the PPD agreed in 2000 to pilot test the National Center for Victims of Crime's Model Stalking Protocol (Velazquez, Garcia, & Joyce, 2009). With the goals of training the officers and developing a specific protocol on stalking, the PPD took a community policing approach to form key partnerships, beginning with a survey of the department's 7,000 officers. The survey found that officers were not knowledgeable about stalking, had not been trained in stalking, did not perceive it as a problem, and consequently were not providing the service victims deserved.

The department decided to process all stalking cases through one division during the pilot program. They first coordinated their efforts internally, and then they invited several community victim service agencies and the district attorney's office to serve as partners. All partners had representatives at the planning meetings.

The first step was training. The PPD developed a day-long training program and trained about 75 domestic violence detectives, victim assistance officers, victim assistance organizations, and the district attorney's office on stalking. All officers in the division attended a 1-hour training session on how to recognize and respond to stalking. An invitation to attend was extended to all interested officers in the entire department, to signal how important the department viewed stalking offenses.

Project leaders then developed a stalking policy for the department, and in preparation for taking the project department-wide, they conducted train-the-trainer training. With funding from the U.S. Department of Justice's Office on Violence against Women, the PPD trained 700 first-line supervisors who, in turn, trained the officers they supervised. The training covered the interrelated crimes of domestic violence, sexual assault, and stalking. It also covered the new protocol in detail, including patrol procedures and individual officer responsibilities.

Although a formal program evaluation has not been done yet, the initiative has had positive effects, according to department leaders, who cite significant increases in the number of stalking and stalking-related investigations and in the quality of affidavits and arrest warrants. Training has eliminated many misconceptions officers held about the law, the process, and the willingness of prosecutors to pursue felony charges. Training has also resulted in the department being added to a judge's study group that reviews domestic violence-related cases and shares information that helps protect victims.

All partners in the initiative are now able to provide accurate and consistent information about stalking. The department provides officers with stalking tip cards to carry. In addition, the PPD has started a 24-hour hotline that is answered 7 days a week by partner agencies. With operators fluent in both English and Spanish, the hotline is able to assist victims of stalking, domestic assault, and sexual assault.

A new partnership with the probation department has also been developed. Police officers and probation officers make unscheduled visits to people who are on probation for domestic-related offenses. These unannounced visits are designed to check that offenders are not in violation of their probation and, in the case of those who have an order of protection against them, the visits provide an additional layer of security to victims.

The PPD, the fourth largest in the United States, with 7,000 officers, is a big ship to turn. Not every officer is on board yet with the idea that stalking is important or that the new protocol is useful, but department leaders believe that such buy-in will come as they continue to demonstrate their own steady, visible support of the importance of stalking and the protocol and procedures now in place (Velazquez et al., 2009).

 IDEAS IN PRACTICE   CITYWIDE VANDALS TASK FORCE

Based in Brooklyn, with a satellite command in… Manhattan, the Citywide Vandals Task Force is charged with the responsibility of tracking and preventing vandalism in all boroughs. The unit is under the direction of Commanding Officer, Captain Elwood Selover. The unit falls under the direction of the Transit Bureau, and with good reason. "Though there are many vandals who do not 'tag' in the subways," explained Captain Selover, "[t]he transit system is still at the heart of the graffiti culture. We address this crime aggressively throughout the five boroughs, but effectively combating graffiti in the City means being able to do so in the subway system."

Part of battling graffiti is educating people; explaining how it hurts a community, and disabusing them of the idea that it is a victimless crime. Members of the Task Force regularly speak at Community Board meetings, schools, and other venues, about how the task of keeping parks, streets, and subways clear of graffiti goes a long way to cleaning up or outright preventing more serious and dangerous problems. Also on the syllabus is help in identifying signs that one's child may be getting drawn into the graffiti culture. Parents sometimes dismiss their children's actions as normal adolescent behavior when they are in fact signs of more nefarious associations. The Task Force, in partnership with the Chief of Department's Office, and the Community Affairs Bureau, has put out a pamphlet to aid in this venture, and continues to look for new and better ways to incorporate every stakeholder in the battle against graffiti.

The officers assigned to the Vandals Task Force possess a passion for their work that is matched only by the commitment of the Department to ensure that we are relentless in our efforts to battle graffiti. The

(*Continues*)

IDEAS **IN PRACTICE** CITYWIDE VANDALS TASK FORCE *(Continued)*

majority of the unit functions in a patrol capacity; they have directed patrols and daily assignments. The Task Force members are dispatched in plainclothes, across the city, to target the areas hardest hit by vandals. They keep tabs on what is happening on the street, and parlay this information into arrests or more comprehensive investigations.

One of the subunits within the Task Force is the School Conditions Apprehension Team. They are specifically assigned to work with the myriad schools in the City to help identify and prevent graffiti vandalism. This reorganization has helped facilitate the more effective utilization of resources owing to the fact that the majority of those perpetrating this crime are youths.

Updating the Graffiti Offender Data Base and utilizing its myriad features to identify perpetrators and solidify cases are just some of the ways by which the Task Force accomplishes its mandate.

Tracking and nabbing the City's most industrious and destructive offenders has become a priority for the Task Force. Using conventional investigative skills, as well as a recently updated graffiti offender data base, officers can track and net those who wreak the most havoc on our City. The data bank allows officers from across the City to contribute to the effort. Offenders arrested for graffiti are brought to the attention of the Task Force and their arrest information is entered along with a mug shot and a photo of the damage caused. But an arrest is not required for the data bank to be utilized. A complaint made regarding graffiti is forwarded to the Citywide Vandals Task Force; that information is entered as well. This vigilance allows officers to match a number of identical "tags" to compile stronger cases against the offenders, to hold them responsible when they are eventually arrested.

"Tags" are like signatures, the vandals do them the same way each time. For them it is a matter of being recognized; they want people to know that each successive "tag" was made by the same person. Fortunately this enables the Task Force to work with the DA's office to compile cases and enhance arrests.

The Worst of the Worst book is constantly reviewed and Captain Selover is briefed on the updates enabling the Task Force to use the book as a key tool in its Anti-Graffiti offensive. Along with the database, the Task Force has put together a "Worst of the Worst" book, a sort of vade mecum of the 100 or so graffiti vandals that the Task Force has identified as the top menaces. This book is packed with information on each offender detailing their area of operation, tags, pedigree information, and more. The Graffiti Coordinators in each patrol precinct have a copy and use [their copies] as tools to keep this crime in check. The Task Force is intent upon furthering the crime decline in the City and is, by far, one of the Department's best weapons in doing so. Their efforts have helped transform New York's reputation back into one [of] the preeminent travel destination[s] in the world.

Source: New York City Police Department. (2016). *Crime Prevention: Citywide Vandals Task Force. New York*, NY: Author. Retrieved August 12, 2016, from http://www.nyc.gov/html/nypd/html/crime_prevention/citywide_vandals_taskforce.shtml

SUMMARY

Partnerships usually result in a more effective solution to a problem because of the shared responsibilities, resources, and goals. The benefits to all stakeholders of participating in a partnership include a sense of accomplishment from bettering the community, gaining recognition and respect, meeting other community members, learning new skills, and fulfilling an obligation to contribute. A partnership will only be successful, however, if trust exists between and among partners. Four dimensions of trust are shared priorities, competency, dependability, and respect.

Traditional shift and beat rotation works to the detriment of building partnerships. To facilitate the fostering of police–community partnerships, patrol officers should be given responsibility for a permanent beat consisting of a small, well-defined geographic area.

Demands on police from one community of interest can sometimes clash with the rights of another community of interest. Such conflicting interests may impede establishing a common vision and shared goals. When forming partnerships, the conflicts within communities are as important to recognize as the commonalities. Criticism of the partnerships in community policing usually centers on time and money.

Key collaborators who should not be overlooked in forming partnerships include prosecutors, courts, corrections, other government agencies; private security providers; victims; volunteers; and even such groups as taxi drivers. The trend to involve the community is affecting all aspects of the justice system, with many researchers and practitioners advocating the move toward community justice, which has its roots in restorative justice. Restorative justice advocates a balanced approach to justice that involves offenders, victims, local communities, and government to alleviate and repair the harm caused by crime and violence and to maintain peaceful communities.

Building partnerships in lower-income neighborhoods may be more difficult because often there are fewer resources and less trust between the citizens and law enforcement.

DISCUSSION QUESTIONS

1. What are the most important factors that lead you to trust another person? To distrust someone?
2. Discuss the pros and cons of using volunteers in a law enforcement agency.
3. Select a campus problem you feel is important and describe the partners who might collaborate to address the problem.
4. Why are permanent shift and area assignments for officers important in community policing?
5. Why is trust an issue between police and residents of low-income neighborhoods?
6. What are the main criticisms or arguments against having police involved in community policing partnerships?
7. What strategies can help free up time for officers' involvement in partnerships?
8. Explain the difference between community courts and traditional courts.

CASE CITED

United States v. Knights, 534 U.S. 112 (2001)

Forming Partnerships with the Media

LO1 Explain what the common goal of the police and the media is and why the police–media relationship can be called symbiotic.

LO2 Identify the amendment that protects freedom of the press.

LO3 Identify what amendment guides the police in their relationship with the media.

LO4 Explain some legitimate reasons for not giving information to the media.

LO5 Identify the factor found in a police–media relationship survey that most affect the relationship.

LO6 Summarize how officers can improve relations with the media.

LO7 Understand why partnerships with the media are critical to the successful implementation of community policing.

CSI effect
news media
   echo effect
perp walks
PSAs
public information
   officer (PIO)
soundbites
symbiotic

Police use media in many ways while performing their daily operations, from more traditional formats such as newspaper, radio, or television, to newer social media outlets such as Facebook, Instagram, and Twitter. Staying connected with the media allows police to share information with the public and vice versa on issues related to missing persons, crime suspects, investigations, and general safety matters. Media, particularly social media, allow a level of transparency into police work that did not exist previously, transparency that can reinforce the relationship with the public and build trust from the community.

A story that has recently rocked the digital and traditional forms of media is the epidemic of creepy clown sightings across the country. These sightings have fueled the nation's coulrophobia, the fear of clowns, and have resulted in an onslaught of calls to police for incidents related to clown sightings, encounters, and threats. To those not fearful of clowns, these stories seem trivial. However, the epidemic and the fear across the country in relation to these masked marauders, who are often juveniles, are causing quite a stir in law enforcement and leading to clown bans across communities nationwide.

There are many examples of where juveniles have used social media to threaten schools and communities. In Virginia, a 13-year-old female contacted a clown via social media to organize a plot to murder her teacher. There are reports of some adults who, seeking an excuse to get out of social obligations, have fabricated being accosted by knife-wielding clowns. While the vast majority of these clown-related incidents are pranks and without true merit, they still create enough community angst that the local police are called in to respond.

Police must keep media on their proverbial duty belt to promote communication with and build trust among the citizens in their communities. Regardless of the significance of the story or the importance of the information conveyed through social or traditional media avenues, law enforcement's partnership with the media is crucial to the furtherance of community policing.

INTRODUCTION

The media can be a powerful ally or a formidable opponent in implementing the community policing philosophy. Positive publicity can enhance both the image and the efforts of a department. Conversely, negative publicity can be extremely damaging. Therefore, police agencies can and should make every effort to build positive working partnerships with the media.

The public's fascination with crime is evident in the popularity of such reality shows as Cops, The First 48, Vegas Strip, and dozens of other criminal justice-themed broadcasts. In fact, some of these shows go beyond just reporting what the police are doing and actually get involved as crime-fighting extensions of law enforcement, engaging the television-viewing public by reenacting crime events and displaying suspects' faces on millions of screens across the world.

Perhaps the most well-known police–media partnership is the one behind the hugely successful weekly television show *America's Most Wanted,* which ran for 25 years, from 1988 to 2013. Hosted by John Walsh, whose son Adam was kidnapped and murdered in 1981, the show produced results immediately. Four days after the show debuted, the first fugitive featured on the program was caught, and by the time the final episode ran, the show had helped catch 1,203 fugitives, including 17 people who had been placed on the FBI's Most Wanted list (Cochran, 2013). The show aired in countries all over the world, and 43 arrests of fugitives featured on the show have taken place outside of the United States. Believing in the power of the media to help law enforcement locate and capture criminals, Walsh campaigned for another television show and, in 2014, began appearing on CNN's *The Hunt*, which is similar to America's Most Wanted.

Police departments and individual officers need the media. The media can shape public opinion, and most police agencies are concerned about their public image. Administrators know that crime and police activities are covered by the media regardless of whether the police provide reporters with information. Most police departments understand that the level of police cooperation will ultimately affect how the public views the police. At the same time, reporters rely on the police for information.

> **LO1**
> The police and members of the media share the common goal of serving the public. The police and the media also share a **symbiotic** relationship; they are mutually dependent on each other.

symbiotic
Describes a relationship of mutual dependence upon each other.

BALANCING VARIOUS LEGAL RIGHTS AND INTERESTS

Understanding the relationship between the police and the media starts with being aware of the competing interests held by each entity, including what legal rights the media has in carrying out its mission and how those rights can be at odds with the constitutional obligations of the police.

> **LO2**
> The First Amendment to the U.S. Constitution guarantees the public's right to know—that is, freedom of the press.

The First Amendment and Freedom of the Press

The First Amendment to the U.S. Constitution states: "Congress shall make no law … abridging the freedom of speech or of the press." The free flow of information is a fundamental right in our society.

In fact, our society deems the public's right to know so important that the media operate without censorship but are subject to legal action if they publish untruths. The courts have usually stood behind journalists who act reasonably to get information, but they also have upheld the privacy protections fundamental under the Fourth Amendment.

Police beat reporters are often eager and aggressive in carrying out their duty to inform the public. Anxious to do well and to be the first with information, they gather and publicize police and crime news as much as they can. The police beat is a high-visibility beat, considered a prestigious assignment by many newspapers and television stations and is, therefore, sought by the experienced, aggressive reporters. Coverage of crime events also draws increased viewership and readership, prompting many news organizations to give "top billing" to such stories.

The Media's Impact on Public Perception   Although keeping the public informed about situations affecting their individual and community's safety is an important and valuable service, the priority and emphasis placed on these stories often confuse the public about the true extent of crime and inflate the general level of fear people feel regarding their chances of personal victimization. For example, a study by criminal justice researchers at Portland State University found that local media in the Portland area devote a disproportionate amount of coverage to "individual criminal events, particularly crimes that involve atypical victims and offenders or severe acts of violence" (Brown, 2015). This steady diet of negative news has the effect of "normalizing" crime to the point that the American public often believes, incorrectly, that violent crime is widespread and rising and that their communities are increasingly unsafe. However, official statistics indicate violent crime has been steadily declining over the past two decades. "The media does provide a great source of information. However, it is essential to recognize that it does have some level of power over our perceptions and we must look for facts before jumping to conclusions" (Brown, 2015).

The Media's Impact on the Criminal Justice System   Acknowledging the power of the media to shape public perception, some have also speculated that the media, through their coverage of isolated, high-profile cases, can influence the operations of the criminal justice system and even the disposition of individual cases, a phenomenon called the **news media echo effect**. Much like a pebble thrown into a pond, the impact of a highly publicized case has a rippling effect that spreads throughout the judicial system and affects the entire process—that is, defendants in a similar crime category as one recently publicized may be treated differently within the criminal justice system from the way they would have been treated had such a high-profile case not preceded theirs.

Popular media, such as crime dramas, are also impacting the criminal justice system by creating certain beliefs within the general public which, in turn, can influence police operations. For example, New York City Police

news media echo effect The theory that the media have the power, through their coverage of isolated, high-profile cases, to influence the operations of the criminal justice system and even the disposition of individual cases.

Commissioner Ray Kelly has noted a growing expectation among juries to see video footage in criminal trials, including recordings of interviews and interrogations. In a speech, Kelly called it part of the "CSI effect." Recall from Chapter 2 that the **CSI effect** is a phenomenon created when the viewing public believes that every police force has access to the same high-tech crime-solving gadgets they see on popular police television shows. Kelly notes such shows have "helped fuel an assumption that these tools are a given in law enforcement" (Goldman, 2012).

The media have been aided in their quest for newsworthy information through the passage of some legislation, including the Freedom of Information Act (FOIA), which establishes the presumption that the records of the agencies and departments of the U.S. government are accessible to the people. The "need to know" standard has been replaced by a "right to know" standard, with the government having to justify keeping certain records secret. Exceptions include when the national security is involved, if an investigation's integrity might be compromised, or when the privacy rights of individuals might be violated.

In addition, every state has a public records law that specifies what information a law enforcement agency must release, what information must not be released, and what is discretionary. Such laws are enacted to protect the rights of citizens under suspicion of breaking the law, as guaranteed by the Sixth Amendment.

> **CSI effect**
>
> A phenomenon created when the viewing public believes that every police force has access to the same high-tech crime-solving gadgets they see on popular police television shows

The Sixth Amendment, Suspects' Rights, and Criminal Investigations

The Sixth Amendment to the U.S. Constitution establishes that "in all criminal prosecutions, the accused shall enjoy the right to a speedy and public trial, by an impartial jury of the state and district wherein the crime shall have been committed."

In addition to ensuring these rights, police officers are also responsible for investigating the crimes that suspects are accused of committing. Law enforcement officers sometimes view reporters as an impediment to fulfilling their duties. Officers often try to protect information they deem imperative to keep out of the media and may, therefore, be at odds with reporters. Such conflicts arise when police try to prevent public disclosure of information that may tip off a criminal of impending arrest, make prosecution of a particular crime impossible, or compromise the privacy rights or safety of a victim or witness. Reporters are eager to do well on their assignments, whereas officers try to avoid weakening their case and getting reprimanded for being too open with the media. The parties' conflicting interests may result in antagonism.

Of special concern are information leaks from within the department. Sometimes those who leak information are showing off how much they know, but the results can devastate an investigation.

Much concern centers on how pretrial publicity by the media might influence potential jurors, particularly in high-profile cases, such as the

> **L03**
>
> The Sixth Amendment guarantees suspects the right to a fair trial and protects defendants' rights.

Boston marathon bombing trial of Dzhokhar Tsarnaev and the trial of Aurora, Colorado movie theater shooter James Holmes. Critics of pretrial dissemination of information by the media contend that such publicity leads to a defendant being unfairly tried in the court of public opinion prior to his or her constitutionally guaranteed fair trial by an impartial jury. "Requests to limit pretrial publicity, whether coming from a prosecutor or defendant, often argue that the broad scope of pretrial coverage means that potential jurors will draw their own conclusions about the defendant based on media coverage, not evidence vetted by and arguments made in a procedurally oriented court of law" (Tricchinelli, 2013). However, studies have found that pretrial media coverage has little, if any, effect on juries, and the Supreme Court has held that jurors' exposure to media accounts of a crime does not, in itself, deprive a defendant of his or her due process rights: "Prominence does not necessarily produce prejudice, and juror *impartiality*, we have reiterated, does not require *ignorance*." Nonetheless, trial court judges retain the authority to impose media bans and gag orders if they determine such measures necessary to preserving a defendant's constitutional rights (Tricchinelli, 2013).

Victim Privacy Rights

As mentioned, the Freedom of Information Act (FOIA) protects the privacy rights of some people, such as sex crime victims. However, amid the shock and confusion that often occur immediately after a crime, victims may easily be caught off guard by aggressive media personnel and may unwittingly put themselves or the investigation at risk by agreeing to an interview.

In addition, the Office for Victims of Crime (OVC) has created a new online Directory of Crime Victim Services, which links crime victims and victim service providers to contact information for assistance 24/7. Searchable by location, type of victimization, agency type, and available services, OVC's online directory is becoming the best resource for finding crime victim assistance (http://ovc.ncjrs.gov/findvictimservices/).

To help victims and witnesses protect their own rights, as well as safeguard the criminal investigation, some departments have begun distributing media relations advisory cards (see Figure 8.1). Such cards, however, have caused concern among some journalists, who contend the advisories will interfere with news gathering. Members of the Society of Professional Journalists (SPJ), a group that includes a wide range of media professionals, said the practice could negatively affect whether immigrants and those who do not know their rights decide to speak with reporters.

Not surprisingly, this opposing perspective often generates substantial conflict between the media and the police, which can contaminate an agency's efforts to fulfill its community policing mission. The Wisconsin Department of Justice, Crime Victim Services "Rights and Services for Crime Victims and Witnesses" brochure provides the following information for victims on dealing with the media (n.d., p. 13):

Figure 8.1	Media Advisory Card for Crime Victims and Witnesses

Source: Used by permission of the Fairfax County Police Department.

In high profile cases, dealing with the media can add stress to you and your family. Many victims and family members of victims have found it helpful to have one family member or a family friend assigned to handle all contacts with the media. No matter who responds to media requests, you should know that you can:

- Decline an interview (even if you have given other interviews).
- Agree to an interview, but refuse to answer certain questions.
- Select a time and place for interviews. You may protect the privacy of your home by giving interviews elsewhere or providing your point of view through a spokesperson and/or a written statement.
- Protect children from interviews. A child may be re-traumatized by having to talk to the media.
- Request offensive photos not be printed or aired.
- Grieve in private and ask reporters, photographers, or others to respect your privacy.
- Demand a retraction or correction of inaccurate reporting.
- Request to be treated with dignity and respect at all times.

CRITICISM OF THE MEDIA

Journalists are sometimes criticized for giving fame to infamous criminals, such as the Columbine High School killers or the Boston Marathon bombers, while victims remain overlooked and obscure. As Shakespeare wrote: "The evil that men do lives after them; the good is often interred with their bones." Some have expressed concern that the detailed and sensationalist media coverage following mass shootings and other terroristic events might feed a vicious cycle of copycat effects, in which mentally unbalanced individuals seek to carry out horrific acts of violence in the hopes of seeing their name and "work" make the headlines. In acknowledging that news reports of such events do have value and play a role in keeping the public informed, one sociologist has cautioned: "It's important to recognize that such incidents are not mono-causal, and sensational news coverage is, increasingly, part of the mix of events that contributes to these rampages. We need to figure out how to balance the public interest in learning about a mass shooting with the public interest in reducing copycat crime" (Tufekci, 2012). Suggested guidelines to reduce the "incentive" for copycat crime include:

- Withholding by law enforcement of any details regarding the method and manner of the killings
- The prompt shut down of any social media accounts held by the suspected killer(s)
- Not immediately naming or profiling the killer(s)
- Ceasing the practice of interviewing survivors in the immediate aftermath of the event, when they are most vulnerable (Tufekci, 2012)

At a news conference following the mass shooting at Pulse Night Club in Orlando, Florida, on June 12, 2016, which left 49 people dead, FBI Director James Comey made an off-the-cuff policy decision to not identify the gunman by name, stating, "Part of what motivates sick people to do this kind of thing is some twisted notion of fame or glory, and I don't want to be part of that for the sake of the victims and their families, and so that other twisted minds don't think that this is a path to fame and recognition" (Tucker, Freking, & Sullivan, 2016). Although the FBI has noted that there has been no formal policy change in how authorities address suspected terrorists when speaking publicly, Comey's statement was indicative of the rising concern among many, including law enforcement and public policy experts, that extensive media publicity given to lone-wolf killers will inspire others to carry out violent attacks.

Another criticism, according to some researchers, is that political leaders and law enforcement officials use the media to serve propaganda functions in the state's ideological machinery and to promote their "law-and-order" crime control agendas. They influence public perception of crime by filtering or screening the information provided to the media and, therefore, share responsibility with the media for the misleading depictions of crime and crime policy.

Marcus Yam/Los Angeles Times/Getty Images

Lieutenant Mike Madden of the San Bernadino (California) Police Department addresses the media following the deadly mass shooting and attempted bombing on December 2, 2015, that left 14 people dead and another 22 seriously wounded. The two suspects in the case, who were killed by police shortly after the incident, were a married couple later described as homegrown violent extremists.

Such influence undermines the efforts of community policing by diminishing the importance of and need for partnerships between law enforcement and the community to effectively address crime. In addition to heavily influencing the public's perception of crime, the media also play a significant role in how the public views the criminal justice system, including law enforcement.

CONFLICT BETWEEN THE MEDIA AND THE POLICE

The news media and the police are two powerful forces in our society that depend on one another but are often hostile toward and mistrust each other. A workshop held to bring law enforcement and media personnel together to air grievances, discuss issues of common concern, and generally get to know one another better so that the two groups could work more effectively together revealed their different perspectives. A major theme among media participants was their need to get information from law enforcement in a timely manner to keep the public informed, as the public has a right to know. One area of contention between the two groups, however, was *when* the public has the right to know, with the police commonly expressing that they were more interested in doing their job than in giving the media a story (Parrish, 2012). Nonetheless, an important part of the community policing job is communicating with the public through the media, and the media are often in a position to help police reach vital sources of information about crime within the community. Nonetheless, conflict continues because significantly different perspectives exist between the police and the media concerning what the priorities should be for officers in "doing their jobs."

Sources of Conflict

Conflict between the media and the police may arise from a variety of sources, but perhaps the most basic are competing objectives, contradictory approaches to dangerous situations, and stereotyping.

Competing Objectives A fundamental source of conflict is the competing objectives of the media and the police. The First Amendment guarantee of freedom of the press is often incompatible with the Sixth Amendment guarantee of the right to a fair trial and protection of the defendant's rights. This leads to a basic conflict between the public's right to know and the individual's right to privacy and a fair trial.

To do their job, members of the media need information from the police. Journalists say they have problems obtaining information they are entitled to because the police refuse to provide it. In some cases, reporters believe they have been singled out by the police for "punishment" in response to a negative story about the police. Reporters tell of police who restrict information, refuse requests for interviews, disregard reporters' deadlines, hang up the phone on reporters, provide inaccurate information, play dumb, or even blackball a particular reporter in retaliation for a story they did not like.

Indeed, some police agencies or officers who have had negative experiences with the media or believe they have been tricked into releasing information do react by becoming uncooperative, by not giving information to which the news media is entitled, by playing favorites among reporters, and even by lying. However, this behavior only aggravates an already difficult relationship.

Motivated by a desire to protect their case and the privacy of those involved, police complain that the media is critical and biased against the police; that reporting is often inaccurate; that journalists lack sensitivity, especially toward victims; and that the news media releases sensitive material and betrays the trust of officers.

One point of contention concerns "off the record" comments some public officials are inclined to make to reporters. Many have been unpleasantly surprised to find that they have been quoted in the next edition of the newspaper or online. Officers must learn to say only that which they can accept attribution for and are prepared to read or hear reported in the media. To speak to a reporter "off the record" does not guarantee the information will not be reported. It may, in fact, make it more likely to be reported. Because different reporters have different definitions of what it means to speak "off the record," an officer faced with such a situation should first ask the reporter, "What do you mean by that?"

In some cases, reporters promise to keep information "off the record" when they have no authority to do so. Although many media professionals do respect "off the record" information, they may misquote, which can cause significant problems and additional conflict. Law enforcement agencies should also be aware that the media may sometimes distort information received from the police department for a political purpose.

As discussed, the way the public views crime and the police depends in large part on what the media report. Although many police officers are keenly aware of the conflict between themselves and the media, they often do not understand how the need to withhold information contributes to the conflict and the resulting negative coverage or what they and their department can do to alleviate the problem. Officers must remember, however, that the media consist of businesses in fierce competition with each other for readers, listeners, and viewers. What officers may consider sensationalism, reporters might consider the competitive edge.

Contradictory Approaches to Dangerous Situations   Another source of conflict between law enforcement and the media is the danger members of the media may expose themselves to in getting a story and the police's obligation to protect them. As with that of the general public, the safety of the media at crime scenes, riots, or potentially dangerous situations is important. Although most reporters and photographers will not cross yellow police tape lines, many are willing to risk a degree of personal safety to get close to the action.

If a situation is unfolding and the police and the media are both on the scene, officers should not order journalists to stay away—a red flag to most reporters. Instead, officers, better trained at reading dangerous situations, should urge reporters and photographers to leave an area if they deem it unsafe and tell them why, not just shout, "Get out of here!" This is especially true if citizens are allowed to be in the area but the media is moved away (Parrish, 2012).

Penny Parrish, at the time a television news director whose crew was attacked during a riot, talked with police after the incident. The officers said they knew their first responsibility was to secure the area and calm things down, but they also felt responsible for the safety of the media, and it angered them that the media were "stupid" enough to be in the middle of the riot. The crew was told to leave and was doing so when attacked. Despite their alleged dislike of the media, the officers did not want to see the media crew hurt.

One reporter who was injured so severely she was unable to walk for 2 months and eventually left the news business because she was so burdened by stress recalled after the attack: "We were there and they [the rioters] were angry. They saw us more as the arm of the law than as an unbiased journalist" (Krajicek, 2003, p. 4). She said the assault changed her perspective and she began to identify with victims. "We'd cover crime and show the video on the news and not take into consideration the victim's family watching that. I'd feel grief. I'd go home and cry myself to sleep at night." She now frequently shows video footage of her attack and its aftermath to journalism students. "I like to let young wanna-be reporters see what they are up against" (Krajicek, 2003, p. 4).

To avoid similar scenarios, police should meet with local media representatives to discuss rules of safety, so they might, together, develop a general policy. This should be done before an incident arises. It might boil down to deciding the media have the right to make decisions about their own well-being but that officers will issue warnings to try to ensure the safety of news crews.

The issue of media crew safety, and whether the police are responsible for that safety, remains a big issue. However, the International Association of Chiefs of Police's Model Media Policy states that the media cannot be kept from an area based *solely* out of concern for their safety (Parrish, 2012).

Most jurisdictions now differentiate between access at a crime scene and access at a natural disaster. Journalists are often given better access to areas ravaged by fires, storms, or floods. They help to inform the public regarding the disaster areas where they themselves cannot reach. For example, when wildfires ravaged areas of Colorado, families relied on local television footage to find out whether or not their homes were still standing.

Another important issue, according to Parrish (2012), is live media coverage of major incidents, such as hostage situations. Although police agencies should still urge the media to refrain from airing live pictures showing the location of officers at a scene, the greatest danger of live photos or video now comes from social media. Citizens with cell phones often capture incidents as they happen and post them immediately on social networking sites, actions that can endanger officers and citizens alike. Officers should be aware of the power of social media and how it impacts their jobs, incidents, and agencies, and all agencies should have a social media policy covering both on-duty and off-duty use (Parrish, 2012).

Stereotyping   Stereotyping is a dangerous habit and can greatly impede good working relationships between law enforcement and members of the media. Although it happens to both the police and the media, by each other as well as by the general public, it is important for officers and reporters to see each other as individuals. Both work under the U.S. Constitution and, thus, need to open the lines of effective communication and work together for the public good.

Understanding differences in personality can help build effective relationships between individual police officers and individual media personnel and greatly reduce the barriers between the two professions. There can and must be a trust factor for this to be effective. For example, a radio newscaster who has the trust of the police department can be given confidential information, knowing that he or she will not release it until given the go-ahead. This one-on-one relationship can be of value to law enforcement and to the media.

Dissolving stereotypic views of each other is a significant step toward changing a dysfunctional conflict between the police and the media into a healthy, beneficial conflict.

Benefits of Conflict

Conflict between the police and the media is necessary because each must remain objective and able to constructively criticize the other when needed. Conflict need not be dysfunctional. In fact, healthy conflict between the media and the police is necessary and beneficial. Conflict can stimulate people to grow and change. It can diffuse defensiveness if those in conflict recognize that their roles are, by definition, conflicting yet complementary. Better understanding of each other may lead to a cooperative effort to serve the public.

Most large law enforcement agencies recognize that a cooperative relationship with the media is to their benefit. Many have developed media policies that set forth for officers exactly what may and may not be released to the media, how information will be released, and by whom.

GENERAL POLICIES AND PROTOCOL FOR MEDIA RELATIONS

Most agencies have developed written policies governing release of information to the media. These policies recognize the right of reporters to gather information and often direct officers to cooperate with the media. Parrish, one of the authors of the Model Media Policy of the International Association of Chiefs of Police, says policies are important to guarantee consistency in the manner in which information is disseminated to media (2012).

Being Professional When Interviewed

Officers who encounter and release information to the media are expected to display the highest level of professionalism because not only will their message be relayed to the public but so will their image and, by reflection, the image of their department. Consequently, many agencies have specific policies and protocols to guide officers during media interviews.

Parrish (2012) cautions that police often respond too quickly when they get a request for an interview, saying "yes" or "no" rather than buying some time and finding out just who will be doing the interviewing, what the subject(s) will be, and what the deadline is. Parrish notes that the closer the deadline is, the more frantic and pushy journalists may become. Although an interview should be a positive opportunity for the police to relay an important message to the community, such deadline pressure from the media can turn the situation into a negative, embarrassing, and potentially case-jeopardizing debacle for the unprepared interviewee.

Parrish (2012) suggests that officers who are interviewed should learn to speak in **soundbites**, very short sentences containing solid information. Most television interviews run only 7 to 12 seconds. The most important information should be put up front. However, this often requires telling a story in reverse, giving the conclusion before the background information leading up to it, an interview technique that usually requires practice to master. To develop a strong soundbite, the officer to be interviewed should write out the main points to be conveyed and then reverse the order of them, placing the "final," and usually most important, piece of information at the beginning to create "a perfect soundbite" (Donlon-Cotton, 2006, p. 22).

> **soundbites**
> Good, solid information stated briefly, that is, within 7 to 12 seconds.

Officers should also avoid using "no comment" and instead provide a truthful explanation of why they cannot respond. "No comment" implies there *is* a story. Alternatives to "no comment" might be, "This matter is currently under investigation, and it would be premature to discuss anything more at this point," or "Making that information available at this time would jeopardize this active investigation," or, simply, "I am not authorized to comment on that at this time."

The media knows that bad relations with the police can result in limited access to police information. Cooperation and mutual trust benefit both the media and the police.

Lying to the Media

Lying to the media is always a bad idea, as is making promises that you cannot keep or misleading reporters. Such actions usually haunt the individual officer or the agency in the form of negative press or lack of media cooperation when the police need help. It is better to honor commitments to the media and be straightforward when information is to be released.

Agencies and officers who deceive the media are at great risk of losing public confidence. On the very rare occasion when it becomes necessary to lie to the media, such as when it is needed to save a life or protect public safety, after the need to lie has passed, the department should explain why lying was necessary and, perhaps, apologize.

Who Can Speak for the Department?

The nature of police business often requires the delicate handling and release (or retention) of information, and it is frequently difficult and time consuming, particularly for larger agencies, to keep all officers equally informed about which details of a case may be provided to the media. Some police departments feel comfortable allowing any member to talk to the media and provide information. However, the trend, particularly for larger departments, is to designate a **public information officer (PIO)** to communicate with the media, as a PIO is trained in public relations and tasked with providing consistent, accurate information while controlling leaks of confidential or inaccurate details and managing controversial or negative situations to the department's benefit.

Desirable traits of a PIO include strong community ties and the ability to communicate clearly in a way that promotes the agency's mission. It is not necessary that a PIO be a police officer, but it helps if the PIO has a solid understanding of police operations. Public speaking and writing skills are also important (Morley & Jacobson, 2007). PIOs must be prepared to respond to three broad categories of questions the media typically asks during crises or other high-profile events, as illustrated in Figure 8.2.

public information officer (PIO)

An officer trained in public relations and assigned to disseminate information to the media, thereby providing accurate, consistent information while controlling leaks of confidential or inaccurate information and managing controversial or negative situations to the department's benefit.

Policies Regarding Photographing and Videotaping

They say a picture is worth a thousand words. Talking with reporters is one thing, but allowing the media to photograph or shoot video at crime scenes is something quite different because police must follow important Fourth Amendment constraints. Furthermore, although prohibiting cameras may give the impression that the police have something to hide, people not involved in an investigation must not be allowed to contaminate the crime scene. As a result, many departments have policies in place regarding the use of cameras at crime scenes.

Indeed, the popularity of television shows where camera crews ride along with officers as they patrol the community and respond to calls is evidence of the public's fascination with such activities.

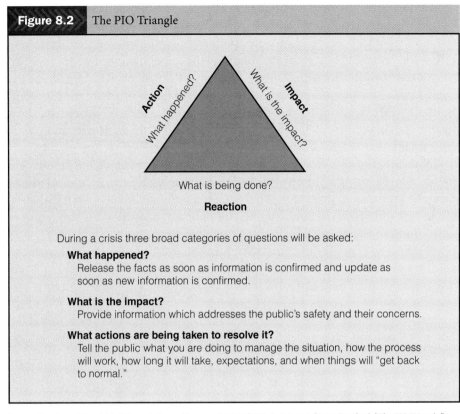

| **Figure 8.2** | The PIO Triangle |

During a crisis three broad categories of questions will be asked:

What happened?
Release the facts as soon as information is confirmed and update as soon as new information is confirmed.

What is the impact?
Provide information which addresses the public's safety and their concerns.

What actions are being taken to resolve it?
Tell the public what you are doing to manage the situation, how the process will work, how long it will take, expectations, and when things will "get back to normal."

Source: Courtesy of Ronald G. Edmond, Group Manager, NSEMP/EML. In Buice, E. (2003, October). "The PIO Triangle." *Law and Order*, p. 32.

TECHNOLOGY IN COMMUNITY POLICING

PIOs AND DIGITAL MEDIA

Advances in communications technology have brought both new capabilities and new challenges to PIOs and the law enforcement departments they work for. The rapid rise and spread of tools such as Facebook, Twitter, Nixle, RSS feeds, and YouTube have had a profound impact on the digital news environment, and today's PIOs must embrace and become proficient at using such technology to promote and control their messages or they risk becoming obsolete.

Source: Davis, P. (2010, July). "The PIO and Today's Digital News Environment." *FBI Law Enforcement Bulletin*, pp. 1–8.

Perp walks, another once-common police practice where suspects were paraded before the hungry eyes of the media, have also fallen on shaky legal ground. Although the public likes to see the "bad guys" apprehended and facing trial, if the perp walk is conducted before the trial, what happens to a core principle of the criminal justice system that a defendant is innocent until proven guilty?

perp walk
The police practice of parading suspects before the media, often simply for the publicity provided by news media coverage.

This nearly century-old tradition may not see much action in the 21st century. As with media ride-alongs, courts have begun ruling that perp walks violate a suspect's right to privacy. Many jurisdictions have suspended the practice of perp walks, whereas others await rulings by the appellate courts.

Another problem with allowing cameras at crime or accident scenes is viewed not from the police perspective but from that of the victim or complainant, who might not want themselves, their family members, or their home to be on someone's video, documentary, or TV series. However, nobody has a right to expect privacy in a public place.

Police officers should also be aware of the news system called "file video" or "file photos," where pictures are kept indefinitely and can be reused at any time. For example, in one case a photographer arranged to go with a squad on a high-risk entry into a crack house. The police department let the reporter come along to get some video of how they were working to curb drug traffic in the city. The reporter did the story, and the police were pleased with the resulting public image. Two years later, one officer involved in the high-risk entry unit faced an indictment by a federal grand jury for police brutality. The reporter mentioned to his boss that they had video of this officer breaking into the home of some poor Black citizens on the north side. The editors decided that was just what they needed for the story, and the video the police had at one time encouraged the media to take was used against the officer.

UNDERSTANDING AND IMPROVING RELATIONS WITH THE MEDIA

> **LO5**
> A police–media relationship survey found that the factor most affecting this relationship was accessibility to police data and personnel.

Police need to understand that the media are facing some of the same challenges law enforcement is facing, especially cutbacks and being asked to do more with less.

The media also usually work under extreme time pressure and under the public eye. Seldom do journalists bungle a story intentionally. They are often uninformed about how their reporting may affect a case and are often also under extreme pressure to get the story submitted before a deadline. Reporters, particularly rookies or those new to the police beat, may be ignorant of law enforcement procedures and of Sixth Amendment requirements. Journalists must often fashion a complicated investigation or series of events into a paragraph-long news story or a 15- to 20-second story at the top of the hour. Furthermore, they commonly work under severe deadline pressure.

> **LO6**
> To improve police–media relations, journalists should be informed of a department's policies and procedures regarding the media and crime scenes. Officers should avoid police jargon and technical terminology and respect reporters' deadlines by releasing information in a timely manner so that the news media has a chance to fully understand the situation.

Inviting local newspaper and broadcast reporters to enroll in a citizens' police academy or participate in ride-along programs are ways to improve relationships and enhance the media's understanding of what police work involves. Conversely, police officers could benefit from learning more about the media and their mission and responsibilities. Officers must remember that reporting is a highly competitive business.

A good rapport with the media can also help the police department accomplish its mission because improved media relations lead to improving community relations. As stated earlier, the media are often the primary link between the law and the citizenry. To reach the community, the victims of crime, and possible witnesses, the police must first reach the media.

IDEAS IN PRACTICE IMPROVING MEDIA RELATIONS

A large police department is finding a simple idea successful—breaking bread with media members who cover it each day. Twice each year the Prince George's County, Maryland, Police Department's (PGPD) Media Relations Division (MRD) hosts a media breakfast. Reporters and assignment editors sit down for a meal with the agency's chief and executive command staff. Of course, PGPD provides food, but, more important, its personnel share positive stories about the agency and build mutually beneficial relationships.

MRD has hosted these breakfasts since 2012. In years past many personnel felt that PGPD did not get adequate coverage in the news. With a focus on transparency, the agency has transformed its relationship with the media. Two former journalists lead MRD with a commitment to ensure that the various media outlets report PGPD's news fairly and accurately. The MRD team knows there is a wealth of positive, impactful stories to tell about the department.

PGPD held the most recent media breakfast on March 17, 2015, at its Aviation Unit hangar. A large turnout from both the agency's command staff and the media attended, including representatives from local television affiliates, radio stations, and print agencies. After brief introductions department personnel started rolling out new and positive story ideas. The Aviation Unit commander explained new technology featured on PGPD's helicopter that will help in the search for missing persons. A handler from the K-9 Section introduced three new dogs. A Traffic Enforcement Unit representative spoke about the department's efforts to arrest drunk drivers, using beer goggles as a visual aid; the entertaining show-and-tell helped promote that evening's St. Patrick's Day DUI checkpoint. Several commanders of various investigative units also pitched story ideas, including one involving a significant breaking-and-entering arrest.

As PGPD officials hoped and anticipated, media personnel covered the stories. Representatives from one major newspaper have planned to participate in a ride along with the K-9 Unit, one television station featured a story about the upcoming Young Adult Citizens Police Academy, and a leading radio station highlighted PGPD's new aviation technology. Not only did the agency benefit but the community enjoyed positive stories about its police department.

The media breakfast's face-to-face interaction did more than facilitate beneficial news stories. It helped foster a strong, respectful relationship between PGPD and the media. Of course, from time to time the news about the department will be negative. In those instances the agency will address concerns transparently. But, the breakfast allowed personnel to interact with media representatives in a relaxed atmosphere, shake hands, and put faces to names. This interaction put PGPD in a position to raise concerns about a particular story to a news director or ask a reporter to hold a report that could jeopardize an ongoing investigation.

Media representatives seemed to enjoy the breakfast meeting, as well. Most of the reporters and assignment editors lingered after it ended to chat with the command staff and members of MRD. Attendees sent several complimentary tweets. One well-respected veteran from the Washington, D.C., news market commented that more police departments should follow PGPD's lead and invite the media to similar meet-and-greet events. Hopefully, other law enforcement agencies will.

Source: Cotterman, C. (2015, September 8). "Focus on Media Relations: A Recipe for Success with News Outlets." *FBI Law Enforcement Bulletin.* Retrieved August 18, 2016, from https://leb.fbi.gov/2015/september/focus-on-media-relations-a-recipe-for-success-with-news-outlets

The media can also be of assistance in public education programs. For example, an agency in California wanted to increase the accuracy of citizens' reports of suspicious and criminal activities. They enlisted the aid of the local newspaper to run a public announcement about what to include in suspect and vehicle descriptions.

In Chicago, the police use the media in their crime prevention efforts. The Federal Communications Commission (FCC) requires all media to set aside airtime or publication space for community projects. This is another excellent avenue for law enforcement agencies to convey educational messages to the residents of their communities.

One tool that can help community policing achieve its mission through the media is the seasonal press release, designed to proactively address specific

Figure 8.3	Seasonal News Release Ideas

Seasonal news release ideas

June/July/August
- Travel safety tips
- Teen curfew information
- Fireworks safety tips
- Bicycle safety
- Swimming safety
- Boating safety
- Drunk driving information
- Fishing and hunting laws and safety tips
- TV violence information
- Graffiti information and prevention

August
- Truancy sweeps
- Latchkey children safety tips

October
- Halloween safety tips

November/December/January
- Shopping safety
- Home invasion
- Drunk driving information and statistics

Anytime
- Car theft prevention (don't leave car keys in car, etc.)
- Phone safety
- Scams
- Safety at ATMs
- Internet safety tips
- Bioterrorism information
- Check and credit card fraud
- Babysitter tips
- Walking at night
- Car jacking prevention

Source: Christy Whitehead. "Seasonal Press Releases." *Law and Order*, June 2004, p. 21.

crime and disorder issues that routinely occur at certain times of the year. For example, when children are out of school on summer break, bicycle safety, water safety, and curfews become bigger issues than they are during the winter. Similarly, over the holidays, shoppers, who are often hurried and distracted, should be reminded how to stay safe in parking lots or how to keep their gift-laden homes from becoming the targets of thieves. Figure 8.3 provides some seasonal news release ideas.

STRATEGIES FOR DEVELOPING PARTNERSHIPS WITH THE MEDIA

Recall from Chapter 1 the definition of community policing: a philosophy that emphasizes working proactively with citizens to reduce fear, solve crime-related problems, and prevent crime. It is a collaborative effort founded on close, mutually beneficial ties between the police and the people. There is no more effective or efficient way for law enforcement to forge a relationship with the community than to partner with the media. Community leaders, key elected officials, church leaders, school boards, parent–teacher association members, philanthropists, and local celebrities often maintain contact with media sources. These people could be brought together through a police–media partnership to sponsor or support crime prevention activities in the community.

Ride-Along Programs for the Media

Parrish (2012) suggests that one of the most effective ways for police and media to better understand each other is to use a ride-along program:

> Police managers should spend a shift riding with a reporter or a photographer—not as part of a story but as a way to get to know the individual and better understand the job of a journalist. Reverse ride-alongs are also important with police managers accompanying a reporter or photographer on a story.

> Many police agencies allow the media to ride with officers for stories on topics such as DUI enforcement. The end result is that the public learns about police programs, and the media get to know officers as individuals.

> Recently, some agencies are inviting the media to "embed" with officers on high-profile events such as protests. The Philadelphia, Miami, and Sacramento police departments are among the agencies who have tried this. The police often end up with pictures and video of arrests that can be used to show what really happened on the street. Many cases of police brutality went away when defendants saw the video.

Such partnerships with the media are not entirely new. For example, the McGruff "Take a Bite Out of Crime" national media campaign, created by the Ad Council for the National Crime Prevention Council, Crime Stoppers, and other crime prevention media collaborations have existed for decades.

The "McGruff" National Media Campaign

McGruff, the crime dog, is to law enforcement what Smokey the Bear is to the National Forest Service. The McGruff National Media campaign, also known as the "Take a Bite Out of Crime" campaign, is aimed at promoting citizen involvement in crime prevention activities through public service announcements, or **PSAs**.

PSAs
Public service announcements.

McGruff was conceived in 1978, when the Advertising Council, Inc., accepted a mission to develop a public education campaign, supported by the U.S. Department of Justice, to help the nation's citizens learn ways to prevent crime. Through the volunteered time and talent of 19 agencies, which formed the nucleus of the Crime Prevention Coalition of America, McGruff the Crime Dog and his slogan, "Take A Bite Out Of Crime," were born. The first McGruff PSAs were developed in 1979 and premiered in February 1980. Today the National Crime Prevention Council manages the National Citizens' Crime Prevention Campaign, of which McGruff is a featured character (National Crime Prevention Council, 2016):

> Over the years, McGruff has made thousands of appearances at community and school events and on radio and television. His messages have changed from urging personal, family, and home security to more broadly based crime

prevention concerns. In 1984, the U.S. Postal Service released a first-class postage stamp bearing McGruff's likeness. By the mid-1980s, McGruff was encouraging people to join Neighborhood Watch and clean up streets and parks so they'd be less inviting for criminals. During the mid-1990s, the Campaign addressed the effects of gun-related violence on children. Current issues include volunteering, bullying, Internet safety, and identity theft. And McGruff will soon tackle cyberbullying and telemarketing fraud against seniors.

While national media campaigns have shown considerable success, local efforts to enjoin the media in the police effort to prevent crime have generally been lacking. There are, of course, exceptions. For example, in Cleveland, Ohio, the mayor obtained sponsorship of a local television and radio station to publicize the city's gun exchange, violence reduction, and crime prevention initiatives. The television station not only helped to announce these very successful initiatives, it also operated the telephone banks for donations.

Law enforcement officials in San Antonio, Texas, invited prominent local media figures to participate in a city crime prevention commission. By involving the media in the panel's deliberations and programs, the department

McGruff, the crime dog, helps teach citizens how to "take a bite out of crime."

Source: National Crime Prevention Council. McGruff the Crime Dog* is a registered mark of the National Crime Prevention Council.

created a partnership that generated positive media coverage and provided free broadcast equipment and facilities for public service announcements and other programming.

The Utah Council for Crime Prevention also invited local media personnel to serve on the council's board, a collaboration resulting in locally produced television documentaries and public service announcements, as well as other activities raising public awareness of crime prevention throughout the state.

The Knoxville (Tennessee) Police Department (KPD) Public Information Office conducts periodic meetings with local media outlets to address concerns, answer questions, and get feedback on how to better serve the community through the release of pertinent public safety information. As part of this effort to enjoin the media in their mission to deliver quality community policing services to the residents of Knoxville, the KPD Public Information Office operates a Code-a-Phone system, a network of 30 mailboxes on a taped news line that is accessible to the media from any phone. KPD PIOs provide regular updates each day at 6:00 A.M. and then throughout the day as events warrant (Knoxville Police Department, n.d.).

Crime Stoppers

Crime Stoppers began in September 1976 and is a nonprofit program involving citizens, the media, and the police. Local programs offer anonymity and cash rewards to people who furnish police information that leads to the arrest and indictment of felony offenders. Each program is governed by a local board of directors made up of citizens from a cross-section of the community, the businesses of the community, and law enforcement. The reward money comes from tax-deductible donations and grants from local businesses, foundations, and individuals.

When a crime-related call is received by Crime Stoppers, it is logged in with the date, time, and a summary of the information given by the caller. Callers are given code numbers to be used on all subsequent calls by the same person regarding that particular case. Each week, one unsolved crime is selected for special treatment by the media. Over 1,000 programs throughout the United States, Canada, Australia, England, and West Africa are members of Crime Stoppers International. Statistics posted on the home page of the Crime Stoppers USA Web site (www.crimestoppersusa.com) are updated monthly and indicate that, as of August 1, 2016, the program has resulted in 695,862 arrests, including arrests for 9,250 homicides; 1,036,810 cases cleared; more than $105 million in rewards paid; more than $1.1 billion in recovered property; and more than $3 billion worth of drugs seized.

MARKETING COMMUNITY POLICING

Chermak and Weiss (2006) studied the police–media relationship and identified strategies law enforcement agencies can use to market community policing initiatives to the public, offering the following recommendations:

- Law enforcement agencies should implement and devise broad marketing strategies to increase public awareness and involvement in community policing activities.

IDEAS **IN PRACTICE**   STRATEGY: MEDIA CAMPAIGNS ABOUT COMMUNITY STANDARDS FOR TOLERANCE

Strategy

Using media resources as an education vehicle builds awareness about diversity and decreases prejudice.

Crime Problem Addressed

Demographic studies show that the United States is becoming more diverse. Members of minority groups form the majority of the population in more than fifty American cities. The change in population has increased bias-related crimes. Awareness programs create understanding, and this understanding builds a community of people who respect one another's differences.

Key Components

This strategy uses all forms of media, but primarily television and newspapers. The purpose is to educate viewers and readers and present information on other cultures, religions, and races; program content also promotes critical thinking about prejudices. The media cosponsor community events focusing on reducing prejudice and cover the events for the community. Examples of media programming are live specials and festivals, documentaries, and PSAs.

Key Partners

The key partners are local media talents, educators, community members, and people in the private sector. The most important partnership is with a television station that agrees to provide both air time and technical and production support. Leaders of various racial, religious, and ethnic groups and local organizations should agree to act as consultants and proponents of the program. Furthermore, teachers receive training from the programming on how to teach and deal with diversity in the classroom. This project requires willingness to participate and active input from all of the partners.

Potential Obstacles

Soliciting the media requires an effective campaign by community leaders to convince the media and the public that bias crimes are a problem that affects the entire community.

Signs of Success

Spreading information via the media is an efficient and influential method to reach a large audience. The Anti-Defamation League's Boston office successfully implemented "A World of Difference" (AWOD) program, which links media and educational resources to develop diversity awareness programming. Several of the programs that evolved from this project are now used in diversity awareness and anti-prejudice training sessions for more than 110,000 elementary and secondary school educators, for college students on more than 400 campuses, for more than 70,000 employees in a variety of workplaces, for law enforcement professionals, and for community organizations. AWOD has expanded internationally to Germany, South Africa, and Russia following invitations from those three countries.

Applying the Strategy

The Anti-Defamation League in Washington, D.C., together with WUSA-TV, created a local AWOD campaign focusing on multicultural education training for teachers. Task forces of community leaders and local educators ensured that the materials addressed the concerns and needs of the greater Washington metropolitan area. In addition to live specials, documentaries, PSAs, and a special news series, there were several programs concentrating on the campaign. Because WUSA used the campaign as a guide for much of its programming, the anti-prejudice, pro-acceptance message permeated the fabric of the community.

Source: National Crime Prevention Council. (2016). *Strategy: Media Campaigns about Community Standards for Tolerance.* Gambrills, MD: Author. Retrieved August 18, 2016, from http://www.Ncpc.Org/Topics/Hate-Crime/Strategies/Strategy-Media-Campaigns-About-Community-Standards-For-Tolerance

- Law enforcement agencies will need to increase the amount of personnel and monetary resources to more effectively market community policing in the news and in the community.
- The media and community policing training curriculum will have to be broadened to include a discussion of more effective ways to market community policing.
- Research has to be conducted that can effectively evaluate whether implementing a broad marketing strategy is effective.

Among the options available to police departments are positive media stories (free advertising); a Web site sharing department information; social networking sites; blogs; email press releases; marketing alliances such as citizen police academies, a media academy, participation in committees, and community groups; poster campaigns; public service announcements; and addresses to community groups. All can help raise awareness of and interest in community policing.

Increasingly, police and fire departments are using social networking to disseminate information to the public. Hundreds of police departments across the country now maintain a presence on Facebook, with hundreds more subscribing to Twitter and other social media venues. Public safety officials are finding the use of sites to be not only speedy but also a convenient way to distribute news media releases, AMBER Alerts, road closings, and suspect descriptions. The Boca Raton (Florida) Police Department uses Facebook, MySpace, and Twitter to communicate with residents. When Lakeland (Florida) Police received a report of an explosive device on the roof of a city parking garage, they sent a squad to investigate and they posted a notice on Twitter. "We think the police department has an obligation to get information out to the community through whatever means or mechanisms we have at our disposal," said Lakeland Police Assistant Chief Bill LePere. "Traditional media releases, expecting the local print media to pick it up and run it in the newspaper tomorrow, is 24 hours too late" (France, 2009).

LO7

As police departments adopt the community policing philosophy and implement its strategies, public support is vital. The media can play an important role in obtaining that support—or in losing it.

A comprehensive discussion of marketing techniques available to police departments is beyond the scope of this text. Numerous resources in this area are available. Marketing community policing is important in efforts to make neighborhoods safe and to prevent or reduce crime. It is interesting that publicity about policing efforts has been shown to also have a deterrent effect on crime.

SUMMARY

One important group with which the police interact is the media. The police and members of the media share the common goal of serving the public. They share a symbiotic relationship; they are mutually dependent on each other. The First Amendment to the U.S. Constitution guarantees the public's right to know—that is, freedom of the press. The Sixth Amendment guarantees suspects the right to a fair trial and protects defendant's rights. The differing objectives of these amendments may lead to conflict between the media and the police. Police may need to withhold information from the media until next of kin are notified, in the interest of public safety, or to protect the integrity of an investigation.

Another source of conflict between the media and the police is the danger in which members of the news media may place themselves when trying to obtain a story. To help ensure the safety of media personnel at explosive situations, police should meet with media representatives to explain the safety rules *before* an incident arises. Conflict need not be dysfunctional. In fact, healthy conflict between the media and the police is necessary and beneficial. If lying to the media might save a life or protect the public safety, after the need to lie has passed, the department should explain why lying was necessary and, perhaps, apologize.

A step toward improved media relations is to recognize why reporters may foul up a story. Reporters may bungle a story because of ignorance, oversimplification, or time constraints. A police–media relationship survey found that the factor most affecting this relationship was accessibility to police data and personnel.

To improve police–media relations, journalists should be informed of a department's policies and procedures regarding the media and crime scenes. Officers should avoid police jargon and technical terminology and respect reporters' deadlines by releasing information in a timely manner so the news media has a chance to fully understand the situation.

As police departments adopt the community policing philosophy and implement its strategies, public support is vital. The media can play an important role in obtaining that support—or in losing it.

DISCUSSION QUESTIONS

1. What examples are you aware of where the police lied to the media? Were they justified in doing that?

2. Does your police department have a public information officer?

3. How fairly do you feel the media in your community report crime and violence? Collect three examples to support your position.

4. How fairly do you feel national media (radio, television, magazines, newspapers) cover crime and violence? Collect three examples to support your position.

5. What might make good topics for PIOs during crime prevention week?

6. Why is it important to remember that journalism is a for-profit business?

7. Do you feel the media are sometimes insensitive to victims and could also be part of the second injury of victimization? If so, can you give examples?

8. What media are available in your community to inform the public of police department operations?

9. Which media do you feel have the most impact on the public?

Community Policing in the Field: Collaborative Efforts

The Office of Community Oriented Policing Services (COPS) leads in the efforts to implement community policing throughout the country. The COPS Office defines community policing as "a policing philosophy that promotes and supports organizational strategies to address the causes and reduce the fear of crime and social disorder through problem-solving tactics and police–community partnerships."

The director of the COPS Office is Ronald L. Davis, who was appointed by Attorney General Eric Holder in November 2013 and in December 2014, was chosen by President Obama to serve as the Executive Director of the newly created President's Task Force on 21st Century Policing. Prior to becoming the COPS Director, Davis served 8 years as Chief of Police of East Palo Alto, California, and 20 years with the Oakland, California, Police Department. Davis was recognized for his innovative community policing efforts and for working collaboratively with the community to dramatically reduce crime and violence in a city once named as the murder capital of the United States.

Community policing focuses on crime and social disorder through the delivery of police services that include aspects of traditional law enforcement, as well as prevention, problem solving, community engagement, and partnerships. The community policing model balances reactive responses to calls for service with proactive problem solving centered on the causes of crime and disorder. Community policing requires police and citizens to join together as partners in the course of both identifying and effectively addressing these issues.

As explained in the previous section, communities consist of individuals, organizations, businesses, agencies, the media, citizen groups, schools, churches, and police departments. Effective interactions with the members of ethnic and cultural minorities,

AP Images/Reed Saxon

the disabled, the elderly, the young, crime victims and witnesses, and the media are critical to developing projects and programs to meet a community's needs.

This section begins by describing early experiments in crime prevention and community policing strategies (Chapter 9). It then looks at efforts to address crime, disorder, and fear concerns at the neighborhood level (Chapter 10). Next is a discussion of strategies to combat the drug problem (Chapter 11) and partnerships to involve youths and to make our nation's schools safer (Chapter 12). This is followed by discussions regarding the challenges presented by gangs (Chapter 13), strategies to understand and prevent violence (Chapter 14), and efforts to understand and prevent terrorism (Chapter 15). The section concludes with a look at what research reveals about the effectiveness of various strategies, including where efforts might be focused in the future (Chapter 16).

AP Images/Shelby Mack

Early Experiments in Crime Prevention and the Evolution of Community Policing Strategies

Learning Objectives

LO1 Know what the most commonly implemented crime prevention programs have traditionally been.

LO2 Identify what the most common strategies used in community policing have traditionally been.

LO3 Explain what was demonstrated in the Flint, Michigan Neighborhood Foot Patrol Program.

LO4 Summarize the characteristics of several exemplary police–community strategies.

LO5 List the impediments that might hinder implementing community policing.

Key Terms

CPTED
dark side of crime
empirical study
Guardian Angels
qualitative
     evaluations

COMMUNITY POLICING IN THE FIELD: COLLABORATIVE EFFORTS

The most commonly implemented crime prevention programs nationwide include increased street lighting, property identification programs, and citizen patrol projects such as neighborhood and block watch programs. While these programs may be effective at reducing overall fear of crime for citizens, critical assessment of these measures often fails to produce any evidence to support the overall effectiveness of the program in deterring criminal behavior.

As an example, many organizations, such as the Los Angeles Police Department, refer to neighborhood watch programs as "the cornerstone of [their] crime prevention strategy," yet such programs have generally been found to be effective less than 10 percent of the time. Reasons for ineffectiveness include low participation of citizens, individuals and neighborhoods dropping out of the program once it has begun, and lack of funding. While only 1 in 10 neighborhood watch programs appear to be effective, a thorough strategic watch agenda, including methods to ensure active participation and preliminary program assessments measures, are cornerstones to program effectiveness.

One such program in the Kings Villages Apartment Complex in Northwest Pasadena, California, has been able to reduce fear of crime, the incivilities that invite crime, and the overall crime rate in a small area of their city. The program was organized and led by an 80-year-old immigrant from Panama and a 65-year-old blind man who was a survivor of gang-related violence while in his twenties. The group started small and through the effort of friends, supporters, and the local police, grew to become one of the more effective neighborhood watch programs in the state. The incivilities are gone, nearly 100 percent of gang-related graffiti has been removed, and groups have been organized to clean up the streets, efforts that have reduced the overall burglaries, larcenies, homicides, and drug-related arrests over a short time. The crime that flourished, when gangs and drug dealers controlled the streets prior to the program's inception, has been driven out and the area once again belongs to the law-abiding residents of Kings Villages Apartments.

INTRODUCTION

Community involvement with and assistance in accomplishing the mission of law enforcement is becoming widely accepted. The change toward community involvement is illustrated in a change in the Portland (Oregon) Police Department's mission statement. The old mission statement proclaimed:

> The Bureau of Police is responsible for the preservation of the public peace, protection of the rights of persons and property, the prevention of crime, and the enforcement of all Federal laws, Oregon state statutes, and city ordinances within the boundaries of the City of Portland.

The new mission, in contrast, is:

> The mission of the Portland Police Bureau is to reduce crime and the fear of crime. We work with all community members to preserve life, maintain human rights, protect property and promote individual responsibility and community commitment.

The change from traditional policing to community involvement does require many chiefs of police and their officers to take risks. Are the results of the shift toward community policing worth the risks? This chapter reviews experiments conducted across the country to answer this question. Although this chapter may appear somewhat dated, it is a necessary addition to document efforts during the past decades to improve crime prevention strategies and to involve citizens in such efforts. Many lessons were learned from the experiments of this time period.

TRADITIONAL APPROACHES TO CRIME PREVENTION

L01

Among the most commonly implemented crime prevention programs have been street lighting projects; property marking projects; security survey projects; citizen patrol projects; and crime reporting, neighborhood-watch, or block projects.

When crime prevention became popular in the late 1960s and early 1970s, many communities undertook similar types of programs. These programs have continued into the 21st century.

Claims of success should be carefully examined. Critics often say that the evaluations are flawed. Indeed, research within communities is extremely difficult because:

- Measuring what did not happen is nearly impossible.
- Crime is usually underreported.
- A reduction in reported crime could be the result of the crime prevention program or because the responsible criminal or criminals have left town, gone to jail on some other charge, died, and so on.

- Crime can be influenced by everything from seasonal and weather changes, school truancy rates, and the flu, to road construction or even a change in a bus stop location. A drop in the crime rate does not necessarily mean a crime prevention program is working.

In addition, many of these programs are evaluated by people who have no training or experience in appropriate research methods; consequently, they sometimes produce flawed results. Some also argue that crime is not prevented by programs like Neighborhood Watch; instead, they argue, crime is displaced to neighborhoods where the residents are not as likely to report suspicious activity to the police.

Use of crime data to evaluate crime prevention projects poses special problems. Crime data, obviously, are limited to reported crimes. Practitioners are aware of the **dark side of crime**—that is, the huge amount of crime that is unreported. When projects are instituted to enlist the community in preventing crime, the citizens' heightened awareness and involvement often result in an *increase* in reported crime, but this does not necessarily mean that crime itself has actually increased.

dark side of crime
The large amount of crime that goes unreported.

As you read this chapter, consider the difficulties in evaluating crime prevention projects or, indeed, any project involving many diverse individuals and problems.

Street Lighting Projects

Since ancient times, lighting has been one means to deter and detect crime. Street lighting projects aimed at crime prevention through environmental design (CPTED) are important elements in a community's crime suppression efforts. Most street lighting projects seek to improve not only the likelihood of deterring and detecting crime but also the safety of law-abiding citizens. Available research indicates that street lighting does not decrease the incidence of crime in participating target areas but that it is useful to reduce citizens' fear of crime and increase their feelings of security.

Property Identification Projects

Often referred to as "Operation Identification" or "O-I" projects, property identification aims to deter burglary and, when deterrence fails, return stolen property if it is recovered. Most property identification projects provide citizens with instructions, a marking tool, and a unique number to be applied to all valuable items within a household. Stickers are provided to homeowners to display on windows and doors warning possible burglars that the residents have marked their valuables and they are on record with the police. In addition to its deterrent effect, the property identification program also helps police track the source of stolen goods and return stolen property to its rightful owners.

It is sometimes difficult to get people to participate in such programs. In addition, although the burglary rate may drop for those enrolled in the program, it may not drop citywide. There is no evidence available to suggest a difference in the number of apprehended or convicted burglars in communities that do or do not participate in these types of programs.

Crime Prevention Security Surveys *START*

Crime prevention user and security surveys are also usually an integral part of projects that focus on the environmental design of facilities and "target hardening" as a means to deter or prevent crime. Such surveys can reveal opportunities for improvement or indicate that people are afraid to visit a particular place because of high levels of victimization due to low lighting or because such locations are isolated, confining, or deserted. Surveys used to determine the effectiveness of the existing environmental design are usually conducted by police officers specially trained in this area. They perform comprehensive on-site inspection of homes, apartments, and businesses. Of particular interest are doors, windows, locks, lighting, and shrubbery that might be used to a burglar's advantage. The officer suggests specific ways to make a location more secure. Zahm (2007) explains the approach typically taken in CPTED:

CPTED

Crime Prevention through Environmental Design—altering the physical environment to enhance safety, reduce the incidence and fear of crime, and improve the quality of life.

Crime prevention through environmental design (**CPTED**) is an approach to problem solving that asks what is it about this location that places people at risk, or that results in opportunities for crime? In other words, *why here*? Three case examples will illustrate this point:

Case #1: Custodial workers routinely find evidence of smoking, drinking, and vandalism in a high school lavatory.

Why here? The lavatory is in an isolated area of the building, adjacent to a ticket booth and concession stand that are active only during athletic events. The school's open lunch policy allows students to eat anywhere on campus, while monitors are assigned only to the cafeteria.

CPTED response: A lock is installed on the lavatory door, and it remains locked unless there is an athletic event. The open lunch policy has been revised: Students are still allowed to leave the cafeteria but must eat in designated areas, and a faculty member is charged with patrolling these areas during lunch periods.

Case #2: The back wall of a building in an office center is repeatedly tagged with graffiti.

Why here? The taggers have selected an area that is out of the view of passers-by: a rear corner location where two buildings come together at the end of a poorly lit service lane. Visibility is further reduced by hedges at the site's perimeter. Businesses in the office center are open from 9 A.M. to 5 P.M. during the week; however, the tagged building is next to a roller skating rink where activity peaks at night and on weekends.

CPTED response: Hedges are trimmed and wall-mounted light fixtures installed along the service lane, with motion detection lighting in the problem area. The skating rink agrees to change to a "no re-admission" policy to keep skaters inside the building and away from the office property.

Case #3: ATM patrons at a bank are being robbed after dark.

Why here? The bank is situated along a commercial strip in a neighborhood with vacant properties and abandoned businesses. The ATM is in the front corner of the bank building, and the drive-through teller windows are at the side of the building, around the corner from the ATM. Robbers hide in the darkened drive-through teller area and attack unsuspecting ATM users after they complete a transaction.

CPTED response: The bank installs a fence at the corner of the building, creating a barrier between the ATM and the drive-through teller area.

In each of these case examples, asking *why here?* reveals that opportunities for crime and other problems arise out of a variety of environmental conditions related to the building, the site, and the location, and how the place is used. Solving a problem thus requires a detailed understanding of both crime and place, and the response should consider one of the three objectives of crime prevention through environmental design: control access, provide opportunities to see and be seen, or define ownership and encourage the maintenance of territory. … Crime Prevention through Environmental Design is an approach to problem solving that considers environmental conditions and the opportunities they offer for crime or other unintended and undesirable behaviors. …

CPTED emerged out of research on the relationship between crime and place, theories known variously as environmental criminology, situational prevention, rational choice theory, or routine activities theory, among others. Each theoretical approach focuses on the crime event and how a criminal offender understands and uses the environment to commit a crime.

CPTED is unusual when compared with some police activities because it encourages prevention and considers design and place, while policing has traditionally valued an efficient and effective response to incidents, and identifying and arresting offenders.

Citizen Patrol Projects

Many variations of citizen patrol exist in the United States. Some are directed at a specific problem such as crack houses and the sale of drugs in a neighborhood. Others are aimed at general crime prevention and enhanced citizen safety. Citizen patrols may operate throughout a community or may be located within a specific building or complex of buildings such as tenement houses. The most successful patrols are affiliated with a larger community or neighborhood organization, sustain a working relationship with law enforcement, and are flexible enough to engage in non–crime prevention activities when patrolling is patently unnecessary.

One hazard of citizen patrols is the possibility of vigilantism, which has a long, often proud, history in the United States and, indeed, in the history of law enforcement and criminal justice. Now this hazard is quite serious because of the increase of readily available handguns in our country.

Guardian Angels
Private citizen patrols who seek to deter crime and to provide a positive role model for young children.

Probably the best-known citizen patrol is the **Guardian Angels**, a group of private citizens who seek to deter crime and to provide a positive role model for young children. The Guardian Angels began in 1979 in New York City and conducted safety patrols on the subways and streets of New York. After several years, Guardian Angels groups formed in other large cities throughout the United States and elsewhere, although their membership and activities have dwindled in recent years.

Citizen volunteers even patrol the Internet. The largest online safety group is WiredSafety (www.wiredsafety.org), a nonprofit organization with more than 9,000 volunteers worldwide. Calling itself a cyber-neighborhood watch, WiredSafety provides help for online victims of cybercrime and harassment and assists law enforcement anywhere in the world in preventing and investigating cybercrimes through its affiliate organization (www.wiredcops.org). Volunteers are trained how to patrol the Internet in search of child pornography, child molesters, and cyberstalkers.

Citizen Crime Reporting, Neighborhood, or Block Programs

Citizen crime reporting programs (CCRPs) help to organize neighborhoods as mutual aid societies and as the eyes and ears of the police. Thousands of neighborhood-watch programs exist throughout the United States, and many describe them as the backbone of the nation's community crime prevention effort as they serve to increase surveillance, reduce criminal opportunities, and enhance informal social control.

Usually local residents hold meetings of such programs in their homes or apartments. During the meetings, neighbors get to know each other and what is normal activity for their neighborhood. They receive educational information about crime prevention from the local police department and are told how to contact the police if they see something suspicious. Signs are posted throughout the neighborhood warning possible offenders of the program. Often the programs provide safe houses for children to use if they encounter danger on their way to or from school.

Some programs work to enhance citizens' reporting capability. Whistle Stop programs, for example, provide citizens with whistles, which they can blow if they are threatened or see something requiring police intervention. Anyone hearing the whistle is to immediately call the police. Whistle Stop programs are the modern-day version of the "hue and cry." Other programs have implemented special hotlines whereby citizens can call a specific number with crime information and perhaps receive a monetary reward.

Very few of the programs concentrate on only the "neighborhood watch." Crime prevention efforts such as Project Operation Identification and home security surveys are by far the most common activities of neighborhood-watch programs. Street lighting programs, crime tip hotlines, and measures to address physical environmental concerns are also quite common. Regardless of the activities incorporated, neighborhood-watch programs have been assessed through meta-analysis as being associated with reductions in crime (Holloway, Bennett, & Farrington, 2008).

 **IDEAS IN PRACTICE** FIGHTING FORECLOSURE PROBLEMS IN MANHATTAN, ILLINOIS

Following is an example of how police in one community tackled the problem of foreclosed properties. By encouraging frequent collaboration between stakeholders, engaging in problem-solving policing, and building trust with the community, local police were able to effectively monitor foreclosed properties with the goals of preserving property values and preventing the foreclosure-related crime that had affected nearby cities, thus preserving quality of life for their citizens.

Fighting Foreclosure Problems in Manhattan, Illinois

Problem properties create more than just an eyesore. They act as a drain on police resources, create hazardous environments, and lessen the quality of life for neighbors and community residents.

The Village of Manhattan, Illinois, is a residential community of about 6,897 people south of Chicago. It has more than doubled in size since 2000. With larger nearby towns facing serious foreclosure problems, Manhattan's police department and village administrators decided to take preventive action before their problem grew too large to control.

The village created a database, updated weekly, of all properties in the various stages of foreclosure. Using the database as a guide, the police department,

code compliance office, public works department, and finance department are responsible for a four-point approach to tracking and securing foreclosed structures: monitoring and securing the buildings; enforcing city codes; shutting off water service; and placing liens, if necessary, on delinquent accounts. Law enforcement officers regularly monitor the vacant houses, check for signs of vandalism, and conduct outreach to neighbors in adjacent properties through a Neighborhood Watch program.

Village officials and the Manhattan Police Department have considered these efforts a success. After checking all vacant structures, Manhattan police found that 27 percent of the area's vacant houses were not locked. They secured the houses and, using their monitoring system, identified additional potential problem properties. Since the initiative was put into place, one concerned neighbor alerted the authorities about a distressed homeowner who was illegally stripping his house and selling all valuable construction material and appliances on Craigslist.

Source: Mentel, Z. (2009, July). "Shutting the Door on Foreclosure and Drug-Related Problem Properties: Two Communities Respond to Neighborhood Disorder." *Community Policing Dispatch, The e-Newsletter of the COPS Office*, Vol. 2, Issue 7. Retrieved September 1, 2016, from http://www.cops.usdoj.gov/html/dispatch/July_2009/communities_respond.htm

Special Crime Watch Programs

In addition to the traditional types of crime watch programs commonly implemented throughout the country, some communities have developed more specialized types of crime watch programs such as mobile crime watch, youth crime watch, business crime watch, apartment watch, realtor watch, and carrier alert.

Honolulu's mobile crime watch enlists the aid of motorists who have cell phones. Volunteers attend a short orientation that trains them to observe and report suspicious activity. Participants also receive Mobile Watch decals for their vehicles. They are advised to call 911 if they hear screaming, gunshots, breaking glass, or loud explosive noises or if they see someone breaking into a house or car, a car driven dangerously or erratically, a person on the ground apparently unconscious, anyone brandishing a gun or knife, or an individual staggering or threatening others.

The volunteers are also trained to recognize and report other unusual behaviors such as children appearing lost; anyone being forced into a vehicle; cars cruising erratically and repetitively near schools, parks, and playgrounds;

TECHNOLOGY IN COMMUNITY POLICING

NEXTDOOR

A crime spree had struck the quiet residential neighborhood of Grandview, Arizona, a suburb of Phoenix. During a three-month time span, 25 homes were burglarized, with many break-ins happening while the homeowners were away for only a few hours. Although the police took reports and looked into the incidents, scant evidence existed and no arrests were made, so the residents took to the Internet to share information and stir up leads:

> They crowdsourced details of the crimes on Nextdoor.com, a private social network for urban neighborhoods, and began

noticing patterns. The burglars would wait to see a homeowner leave and then enter the house and stuff a pillowcase with high-value items like jewelry, guns and cameras before slinking out. Sometimes, they'd hit as many as three houses in a day.

The residents started a virtual neighborhood watch using Nextdoor, sending out detailed alerts about any suspicious cars or people and essentially live-blogging strangers' movements throughout the 1 square-mile area. . . .

The National Sheriff's Association is working on an app that will help neighborhood watch members share real-time video surveillance footage shot on a smartphone with law enforcement and with each other. The hope is that the program will shorten response times between when civilians believe they've witnessed something suspicious and when police respond.

As of June 2016, the Nextdoor social network was being used by more than 100,000 neighborhoods throughout the country.

Source: Kelly, H. (2014, May 16). "Hyperlocal Apps Help Residents Fight Crime." CNN.com. Retrieved September 1, 2016, from http://www.cnn.com/2014/05/14/tech/social-media/neighborhood-watch-apps-nextdoor/

a person running and carrying something valuable; parked, occupied vehicles at unusual hours near potential robbery sites; heavier than normal traffic in and out of a house or commercial establishment; someone going door-to-door or passing through backyards; and persons loitering around schools, parks, or secluded areas or in the neighborhood.

Most successful community-based programs that focus on crime prevention or safety issues have a close partnership with law enforcement. The community and law enforcement have vital components to offer each other, making cooperation between the two highly desirable. It is difficult to imagine, for instance, an effective community-based crime watch program without input or cooperation from the local police agency. Crime watch programs are built on the premise of mutual aid—citizens, police, and police foundations working together.

OTHER EFFORTS TO ENHANCE CRIME PREVENTION

Continuing the community crime prevention momentum generated during the 1960s and 1970s, new programs were initiated during the 1980s and 1990s to encourage citizens to play an active role in reducing crime in their own neighborhoods. These initiatives have included National Night Out; the creation of organizations focused on crime prevention, such as Crime Stoppers and Mothers Against Drunk Driving (MADD); and the expanded use of volunteers.

National Night Out

National Night Out (NNO) is a program that originated in 1984 in Tempe, Arizona. Held annually on the first Tuesday of August, this nationwide program encourages residents to turn on their porch lights, go outside, and meet their neighbors in an effort to build stronger, more vigilant communities that are more resistant to crime and disorder. Neighborhood-watch programs are encouraged to plan a party or event during NNO.

Since 1984, when 2.5 million people in 23 states gathered for the first NNO, the event has grown significantly. In 2015, more than 38.3 million people in 15,728 communities from all 50 states, U.S. territories, Canadian cities, and military bases worldwide participated in NNO (National Association of Town Watch, 2015). In addition to the traditional "outside lights and front porch" vigils, many communities have expanded their NNO activities to include block parties, safety fairs, youth events, cookouts, parades, festivals, and visits from local law enforcement, fire/rescue personnel, and other local officials. Some neighborhoods also use NNO as an opportunity to collect food for the local food shelf or "gently worn" clothing for a local shelter for homeless people or battered women.

Organizations Focused on Crime Prevention

Community organizations encourage citizens to play an active role in reducing crime in various ways. Among the most visible organizations focused on crime are citizen crime prevention associations, Crime Stoppers, and MADD. Crime Stoppers was discussed in Chapter 8.

AP Images/Olivia Nisbet

Police officers, state police, and city officials meet on the Massachusetts Avenue Bridge to kick off National Night Out with a "Hands Across the River" event in Boston. Officers visit all 11 police districts in the Boston area to give Community Service Awards to residents who have helped fight crime in their neighborhoods.

Citizen Crime Prevention Associations   The many activities undertaken by citizen crime prevention associations include paying for crime tips; funding for police and community crime prevention programs; supporting police canine programs; raising community awareness through crime prevention seminars, newsletters, cable TV shows, and booths; providing teddy bears for kids; raising money through sources such as business contributions, membership fees, charitable gambling, and sales of alarms and mace; and funding specific programs such as rewards to community members who call the hotline with crime information.

Mothers Against Drunk Driving   MADD is a nonprofit, grassroots organization whose membership is open to anyone: victims, concerned citizens, law enforcement officers, safety workers, and health professionals. MADD was founded in California in 1980 after Candy Lightner's 13-year-old daughter was killed by a hit-and-run driver. The driver had been out of jail on bail for only 2 days for another hit-and-run drunk-driving crash. He had three previous drunk-driving arrests and two convictions, but he was allowed to plea bargain to vehicular manslaughter. His 2-year prison sentence was spent not in prison, but in a work camp and later a halfway house.

The most frequently committed violent crime in the United States is alcohol-impaired driving, which claimed just under 10,000 lives in 2014—an average of one every 53 minutes—and injured approximately 290,000 more (Blincoe, Miller, Zaloshnja, & Lawrence, 2015; MADD, 2016). Thus the mission of MADD is to stop drunk driving and to support victims of this violent crime. MADD seeks to raise public awareness through community programs such as Operation Prom/Graduation, their poster/essay contest, their "Tie One on for Safety" Project Red Ribbon campaign, and a Designated Driver program. Their national newsletter, "MADD in Action," is sent to members and supporters. MADD also promotes legislation to strengthen existing laws and adopt new ones. In addition, MADD provides victim services. Annual candlelight vigils are held nationwide to allow victims to share their grief with others who have suffered loss resulting from drunk driving.

Using Volunteers

Many police departments make extensive use of volunteers, as was discussed in Chapter 7. Volunteers may serve in a crime prevention capacity as reserve officers, auxiliary patrol, or community service officers or on an as-needed basis.

Reserve officers, auxiliary patrol, or community service officers (CSOs) usually wear uniforms and badges but are unarmed. However, in some departments, reserve officers are armed and receive the same training as sworn officers. They are trained to perform specific functions that assist the uniformed patrol officers in crime prevention efforts, such as watching for suspicious activity and providing crime prevention education at neighborhood-watch meetings, civic groups, churches, and schools.

EARLY EMPIRICAL STUDIES OF COMMUNITY POLICING

During the 1980s, many programs were adopted by departments moving toward community policing. Also during this time, many departments began experimenting with a variety of community policing strategies. As evidenced by numerous empirical studies, some strategies were successful; others were not. An **empirical study** is based on observation or practical experience. Greene and Taylor (1991, pp. 206–221) describe studies of community policing in major cities throughout the country, including Flint, Newark, Oakland, San Diego, Houston, Boston, and Baltimore County.

empirical study
Research based on observation or practical experience.

Flint, Michigan, Neighborhood Foot Patrol Program

The classic Neighborhood Foot Patrol Program of Flint, Michigan, was conducted from January 1979 to January 1982. It focused on 14 experimental neighborhoods to which 22 police officers and 3 supervisors were assigned. The officers were given great discretion in what they could do while on foot patrol, but communication with citizens was a primary objective.

The Flint study tried to document what police did on foot patrol and how that differed from motorized patrol (Mastrofski, 1992, p. 24):

> Looking at the department's daily report forms, the researchers found that foot officers reported many more self-initiated activities—such as home and business visits and security checks—than police in cars. Officers on foot averaged much higher levels of productivity across most of the standard performance measures: arrests, investigations, stopping of suspicious persons, parking citations, and value of recovered property. The only category in which motor patrol officers clearly outproduced their foot patrol counterparts was in providing miscellaneous services to citizens.

According to citizen surveys (Trojanowicz, 1986), 64 percent were satisfied with the project and 68 percent felt safer. When asked to compare foot patrol and motorized patrol officers, citizens rated the foot patrol officers higher by large margins in four of the six areas: preventing crime, encouraging citizen self-protection, working with juveniles, and following up on complaints. Motorized patrol officers were rated superior only in responding to complaints. In addition, in the foot patrol neighborhoods, crime rates were down markedly and calls for service were down more than 40 percent.

No statistical tests were done, however, and results across the 14 neighborhoods varied greatly. Therefore, the results should be interpreted with caution. In addition, problems were encountered in the Flint Foot Patrol Program. For example, because the program was loosely structured, some officers were not accountable, and their job performance was poor. Nonetheless, according to Skolnick and Bayley (1986, p. 216):

> Foot patrol… appears from our observations and other studies to generate four meritorious effects. (1) Since there is a concerned human presence on the street, foot patrol is more adaptable to street happenings, and thus may prevent crime

LO2
The most common strategies traditionally used in community policing were foot patrol, newsletters, and community organizing.

L03

The Flint Neighborhood Foot Patrol Program appeared to decrease crime, increase general citizen satisfaction with the foot patrol program, reduce citizens' fear of crime, and create a positive perception of the foot patrol officers.

before it begins. (2) Foot patrol officers may make arrests, but they are also around to give warnings either directly or indirectly, merely through their presence. (3) Properly carried out, foot patrol generates goodwill in the neighborhood, which has the derivative consequence of making other crime prevention tactics more effective. This effectiveness in turn tends to raise citizen morale and reduce their fear of crime. (4) Foot patrol seems to raise officer morale.

First Newark, New Jersey, Foot Patrol Experiment

The original Newark Foot Patrol Experiment was done between 1978 and 1979 and addressed the issues of untended property and untended behavior. This experiment used 12 patrol beats. Eight of the beats, identified as using foot patrol, were divided into pairs, matched by the number of residential and non-residential units in each. One beat in each pair dropped foot patrol. An additional four beats that had not previously used foot patrol added foot patrol officers. As in the Flint experiment, officers had great flexibility in their job responsibilities while on foot patrol.

In areas where foot patrol was added, residents reported a decrease in the severity of crime and evaluated police performance more positively. Business owners, however, believed that street disorder and publicly visible crime increased and reported that the neighborhood had become worse. Pate (1986, p. 155) summarizes the results of the first experiment:

> The addition of intensive foot patrol coverage to relatively short (8- to 16-block) commercial/residential strips during 5 evenings per week over a 1-year period can have considerable effects on the perceptions of residents concerning disorder problems, crime problems, the likelihood of crime, safety, and police service. Such additional patrol, however, appears to have no significant effect on victimization, recorded crime, or the likelihood of reporting a crime.

> The elimination of foot patrol after years of maintenance, however, appears to produce few notable negative effects. Similarly, the retention of foot patrol does not prove to have notable beneficial effects.

Second Newark, New Jersey, Foot Patrol Experiment

A second foot patrol experiment was conducted in Newark in 1983 and 1984. This experiment used three neighborhoods and a control group (which received no "treatment") and included a coordinated foot patrol, a cleanup campaign, and distribution of a newsletter. Only the coordinated foot patrol appeared to reduce the perception of property crime and improve assessments of the police. The cleanup effort and newsletter programs did not affect any of the outcome measures studied, nor did they reduce crime rates.

Oakland, California, Foot Patrol Program

In 1983, Oakland assigned 28 officers to foot patrol in its central business district. In addition, a Report Incidents Directly program was established whereby local businesspeople could talk directly to the patrol officers about any matters that concerned them. Mounted patrols and small vehicle patrols were also used.

The crime rate dropped in the Oakland treatment area more than citywide declines, but again, no statistical tests were reported for this experiment.

San Diego, California, Community Profile Project

San Diego conducted a community profile project from 1973 to 1974 designed to improve police–community interactions. Twenty-four patrol officers and three supervisors were given 60 hours of community orientation training. The performance of these officers was compared with 24 other patrol officers who did not receive the training, and the officers who received the training were found to have become more service oriented, increased their non–law enforcement contacts with citizens, and had a more positive attitude toward police–community relations. The project did not consider the effect of community profiling on crime or on citizens' fear of crime.

Houston, Texas, Fear-Reduction Project

Like the second Newark experiment, Houston conducted a fear-reduction experiment between 1983 and 1984, testing five strategies: a victim recontact program following victimization, a community newsletter, a citizen contact patrol program, a police storefront office, and a program aimed to organize the community's interest in crime prevention.

The victim recontact program and the newsletter of the Houston Fear-Reduction Project did not have positive results. In fact, the victim recontact program backfired, with Hispanics and Asians experiencing an increase in fear. Contact was primarily with White homeowners rather than minority renters. The citizen contact patrol and the police storefront office did, however, result in decreases in perceptions of social disorder, fear of personal victimization, and the level of personal and property crime. The police storefront officers developed several programs, including monthly meetings, school programs, a fingerprinting program, a blood pressure program, a ride-along program, a park program, and an anticrime newsletter (Skogan & Wycoff, 1986).

Boston Foot Patrol Project

In 1983, Boston changed from predominantly two-officer motorized patrol to foot patrol and shifted the responsibilities of the foot patrol and motorized one-officer patrol to less serious crimes and noncrime service calls. The experiment studied 105 beats to determine whether high, medium, low, unstaffed, or no change in foot patrol affected calls for service by priority. Violent crimes were not affected by increased or decreased foot patrol staffing. After the department shifted to foot patrol, the number of street robberies decreased but the number of commercial robberies increased.

Baltimore County Citizen Oriented Police Enforcement Project

The Baltimore Citizen Oriented Police Enforcement (COPE) Project, started in 1981, focused on the reduction of citizens' fear of crime. This problem-oriented project focused on solving the community problems of fear and disorder that lead to crime: "'Citizen Oriented Police Enforcement' officers would engage in intensive patrol, develop close contacts with citizens, conduct 'fear surveys' (door-to-door canvassing to identify concerns), and use any means within their power to quell fear" (Taft, 1986, p. 10).

Baltimore County's COPE Project reduced fear of crime by 10 percent and crime itself by 12 percent in target neighborhoods. It also reduced calls for service; increased citizen awareness of and satisfaction with the police; and improved police officer attitudes.

Summary and Implications of the Early Experiments

There is considerable inconsistency in findings across the preceding studies regarding both fear of crime and actual crime rates. Regarding fear of crime, the first Newark project observed a reduction and the second Newark project showed a reduction in the panel analysis (where the data were analyzed by individuals responding) but did not show a reduction in the cross-sectional analysis (where the data were analyzed by area rather than by individuals responding). The Houston study had the opposite results: a reduction in fear in the cross-sectional analysis but not in the panel analysis. In the Flint study, citizen perceptions of the seriousness of crime problems increased. In Baltimore County, fear of crime declined slightly. The San Diego, Oakland, and Boston programs did not consider fear of crime. Thus, the conclusion to be made at that time was that there was no consistent evidence to support the hypothesis that foot patrol reduces fear of crime (Greene & Taylor, 1991).

Inconsistent findings were also reported regarding crime rates. The Oakland study was the only one to demonstrate a reduction, but no statistical treatment was done. Again, the conclusion was: "Clearly, these studies do not point to decreases in crime or disorder as a consequence of community policing or foot patrol" (Greene & Taylor, 1991, p. 216).

Wycoff (1991), however, took an opposing view by stating that the fear-reduction studies conducted in Houston and Newark "provide evidence of the efficacy of what the authors referred to as 'community-oriented' policing strategies for reducing citizen fear, improving citizens' attitudes toward their neighborhoods and toward the police, and reducing crime."

Criticism has been leveled at these early experiments for their flawed research designs and lack of rigorous statistical analysis, with subsequent studies (discussed shortly) aiming to improve the methodology and empirical integrity of research efforts.

Fear-Reduction Strategies Experiments Compared

Wycoff (1991, pp. 107–108) summarizes the seven strategies tested in the Newark and Houston experiments as follows:

Newsletters (Houston and Newark). These were tested with and without crime statistics. They were police produced and provided residents of the test area with information about crime prevention steps they could take, the police department, and police programs in their area.

Victim recontact (Houston). Patrol officers made telephone contact with victims to inform them of the status of their case, inquire whether they needed assistance, offer to send crime prevention information, and ask whether victims could provide additional information.

Police community station (Houston). A neighborhood storefront operation was conducted by patrol officers. The station provided a variety of services for the area.

Citizen contact patrol (Houston). Officers concentrated their patrol time within the target area where they made door-to-door contacts, introducing themselves to residents and businesspeople and asking whether there were any neighborhood problems citizens wished brought to the attention of the police.

Community organizing (Houston). Officers from the Community Services Division worked to organize block meetings attended by area patrol officers. They organized a neighborhood committee that met monthly with the district captain and developed special projects ("safe" houses for children, identifying property, and a cleanup campaign) for the area.

Signs of crime (Newark). This program focused on social disorder and conducted "random intensified enforcement and order maintenance operations" (e.g., foot patrol to enforce laws and maintain order on sidewalks and street corners, radar checks, bus checks to enforce ordinances and order, enforcement of disorderly conduct laws to move groups off the street corners, and road checks for DWI, improper licenses, or stolen vehicles). Addressing physical deterioration involved an intensification of city services and the use of juvenile offenders to conduct cleanup work in the target areas.

Coordinated community policing (Newark). This was the "kitchen sink" project that included a neighborhood community police center, a directed police–citizen contact program, a neighborhood police newsletter, intensified law enforcement and order maintenance, and a neighborhood cleanup.

Reducing Fear of Crime with Video Surveillance of Public Places

Many studies have tried to determine if closed-circuit television (CCTV) in public places reduces the fear of crime in those who use the areas. These studies looked at whether consumer buying increases in areas with CCTV systems; the basis was the belief that an area benefits from a positive economic impact when people feel safer. Although the findings are mixed, they generally show a somewhat reduced level of fear of crime among people in CCTV areas but *only* if those surveyed were aware they were in an area under surveillance. Most of the studies found that less than half of the interviewees were aware that they were in a CCTV area. Reduced fear of crime may increase the number of people using an area, and this, in turn, may increase the level of natural surveillance. It may also encourage people to be more security conscious (Ratcliffe, 2006). Because of this, relying on CCTV to reduce fear of crime may require a significant and ongoing publicity campaign.

One unintended consequence of using CCTV is the possibility of a negative public response to the cameras' existence (Ratcliffe, 2006, pp. 5–6):

> In one survey, one-third of respondents felt that one purpose of CCTV was "to spy on people." In other surveys, some city managers were reluctant to advertise the cameras or have overt CCTV systems for fear they would make shoppers and consumers more fearful. In other words, it is hoped that most citizens will feel safer under the watchful eye of the cameras, but CCTV may have the reverse effect on some people.

> Remember that the primary crime prevention mechanism appears to work by increasing a perception of risk in the offender. With their reluctance to advertise the system, some city managers may be inadvertently reducing the cameras' effectiveness. By failing to advertise the cameras' presence, fewer offenders will be aware of the system and so will not perceive an increase in risk. On the whole, however, the public appears to be strongly in favor of a properly managed surveillance system for public areas.

OTHER CRIME PREVENTION PROGRAM STUDIES IN THE 1980S

Several communities conducted crime prevention studies in the 1980s. Studies in Seattle, Portland, and Hartford focused on citizen efforts to prevent residential crime; the study in Portland also focused on preventing crime in and around commercial establishments. Two studies examined the media and crime prevention: the McGruff national media campaign and the effectiveness of anticrime newsletters. Evaluations of these studies generally show positive results and support the conclusion that community crime prevention programs can be effective in reducing crime and fear of crime, improving citizens' quality of life, and enhancing the economic viability of urban neighborhoods and commercial locations (Heinzelmann, 1986).

The Seattle Program

The Citywide Crime Prevention Program (CCPP) of Seattle, described by Lindsay and McGillis (1986), focused on residential burglaries and used property identification, home security checks, and neighborhood block watches to significantly reduce the residential burglary rate as well as the number of burglary-in-progress calls.

Fleissner, Fedan, and Klinger (1992, p. 9) note: "When citizens and police in South Seattle banded together to fight crime, quarterly crime statistics showed dramatic improvements in the quality of life. Citizen activity spread in the city's other three police precincts; now community policing is a going concern throughout Seattle—a citywide success."

Not only did the burglary rate drop significantly but burglary-in-progress calls to police rose significantly in treatment areas, and the quality of these calls was relatively high in that most provided sufficient suspect information as to allow police to make subsequent arrests (Lindsay & McGillis, 1986).

The Portland Program

Portland also instituted a burglary prevention program, which included providing citizens with information about locks, alarms, outside lighting around entrances, removal or trimming of hedges, and precautions to take while on vacation (Schneider, 1986). The program also encouraged citizens to mark property with identification numbers. Door-to-door canvassing and a heavy emphasis on neighborhood rather than individual protection were important components of the program.

Data analysis revealed that Portland's higher crime areas went from a residential burglary rate that exceeded 20 percent annually—meaning more than one in five homes could expect to be burglarized at least once each year—to a burglary rate of approximately 8 percent for households participating in the prevention program (Schneider, 1986). There was also noted, however, a class bias in program participants, with those who attended meetings, engraved their property, and displayed the decals tending to be of a higher socioeconomic status (Schneider, 1986).

The Hartford Experiment

The Hartford Experiment used a three-pronged approach to reduce crime and the fear of crime: changing the physical environment, changing the delivery of police services, and organizing the citizens to improve their neighborhoods. This experiment centered on the interdependence of citizens, the police, and the environment: "The approach focuses on the interaction between human behavior and the (physically) built environment. It was hypothesized that the proper design and effective use of the built environment can lead to a reduction in crime and fear" (Fowler & Mangione, 1986, p. 80).

The program was based on four previous research efforts. First was that of Jacobs (1961), which found that neighborhoods that were relatively crime free had a mix of commercial and residential properties, resulting in many people on the streets and a great opportunity for police surveillance. In addition, a community with such mixed-use property tended to have residents who cared about the neighborhood and watched out for each other.

Angel (1968) described similar findings in his concept of "critical density," which states that if quite a few people are present on the most frequently used streets, they will serve as deterrents to burglary. In addition, Newman's classic work (1972) suggests that crime can be reduced by redesigning buildings to increase the number of doorways and other spaces that could be easily observed. Finally, Repetto (1974), like Newman, found that opportunities for surveillance could reduce crime and, like Jacobs, that neighborhood cohesiveness could have the same result.

Based on this research, the Hartford Experiment focused on Asylum Hill, a residential area a few blocks from the central business district of Hartford that was rapidly deteriorating. It was found that because of the high rate of vehicle traffic, residents did not use their yards and felt no ties to the neighborhood. The physical design of the neighborhood was changed to restrict through traffic and visually define the boundaries of the neighborhood. Cul-de-sacs were built at a few critical intersections, and some streets were made one way.

A second change in the neighborhood involved patrol officer assignments. Instead of rotating assignments within a centralized department, Hartford began using a decentralized team of officers assigned permanently to the Asylum Hill area. Finally, the Hartford Experiment helped organize the neighborhood, including the establishment of block watch programs, recreational programs for youths, and improvements for a large neighborhood park.

As a result of these changes, residents began coming outside to enjoy their neighborhood more, spending more time walking, using the nearby park, and relaxing in their front yards, both during the day and in the evening (Fowler & Mangione, 1986).

Researchers caution that these types of crime control programs must be tailored to fit the particular set of circumstances found in an individual neighborhood: "What one would want to derive from the Hartford Project is not a program design, but rather an approach to problem analysis and strategies to affect them" (Fowler & Mangione, 1986, p. 106).

LATER STUDIES OF FOOT PATROL PROGRAMS

As discussed, earlier studies of foot patrol programs were criticized because of various methodological shortcomings. Several recent studies have met with more encouraging results, as departments have begun to incorporate data analysis of crime types and locations into their foot patrol strategies (Craven, 2009).

San Francisco Police Department Foot Patrol Program

One such recent study of foot patrol was conducted at the San Francisco (California) Police Department (SFPD) and is reported on by Rosenfeld (2008). Among the key findings were:

- The SFPD committed significant resources to foot beat staffing. The number of hours dedicated to foot beats during the first 6 months of 2007 totaled 83,475, representing an 86 percent increase when compared to the same time period in 2006.

- Foot patrols increase the community's perception of safety. Eighty-two percent of those responding to the telephone survey and 73 percent of those responding to the written survey felt safer as a result of foot patrols.

- Both police staff and the community widely accept foot patrols. Seventy-nine percent of the SFPD respondents believe foot patrols are an effective tool for the department. Correspondingly, 90 percent of the community member respondents believe foot patrols are a necessary tool for the SFPD to use in addressing crime and quality of life issues.

Philadelphia Foot Patrol Experiment

The Philadelphia Foot Patrol Experiment has garnered attention lately for its focus on place-based policing, showing that when police resources are directed at hot spots, or those geographic locations where crime incidents tend to cluster, foot patrol can indeed have a net positive effect on reducing crime, particularly violent crime (Ratcliffe, Taniguchi, Groff, & Wood, 2011). The concept of spatial dosage, whether pertaining to the number of officers patrolling a certain area or the geographic extent of one patrol beat, was identified as a salient variable in whether foot patrol could effectively reduce violent crime.

EARLY EFFORTS USING THE MEDIA IN CRIME PREVENTION

Two different approaches to using the media have also been extensively studied: the "McGruff" media campaign and police–community anticrime newsletters. The McGruff "take a bite out of crime" campaign was discussed in detail in Chapter 8. Barthe (2006, pp. 30–31) describes how printed materials such as police–community anticrime newsletters and brochures can help in crime prevention efforts:

> Ease of production and low distribution costs make fliers and leaflets favorites of police departments and other crime prevention agencies. Using readily available desktop publishing software, an agency can create a cost-effective publicity campaign. Police officers can deliver the material door-to-door or place it on car windshields.

> Mailings can also be an effective way to reach people with crime prevention messages. Some studies have shown newsletters and brochures to be effective ways to spread crime prevention information, but such media do not always produce the intended result. In the early 1980s, the Houston Police Department failed to reduce residents' fear of crime by distributing newsletters containing local crime rates and prevention tips. In Newark, New Jersey, the police department used a similar strategy. While people liked receiving the newsletters, they rarely read them.

> General publicity campaigns aimed at victims have had limited effectiveness. A 4-month national press and poster campaign tried to educate people about the importance of locking their parked cars, but it failed to change people's behavior. Another campaign used posters and television spots to remind people to lock their car doors, but it also proved ineffective. These studies demonstrate that people often pay little attention to crime prevention messages. A common reason given is that potential victims do not feel that it concerns them. For instance, domestic violence awareness campaigns have to compete with the possibility that women do not want to see themselves as victims.

QUALITATIVE EVALUATIONS AND SALIENT PROGRAM FEATURES

Qualitative evaluations are more descriptive and less statistical than empirical studies. One large-scale qualitative evaluation, undertaken by the National Symposium on Community Institutions and Inner-City Crime Project, sought to identify model programs for reduction of inner-city crime. Almost 3,500 national organizations, criminal justice scholars, and federal, state, and local

qualitative evaluations
Assessments that are more descriptive and less statistical than empirical studies; the opposite of quantitative evaluation.

government agencies were asked to recommend outstanding local programs. The result was the identification of approximately 1,300 programs. Each was sent a request for detailed information, and 350 (27%) responded. From these, 18 were selected for site visits. Although each program was unique, they shared some common characteristics (Sulton, 1990).

Many of the programs focus on specific social problems of inner-city residents, problems that were "identified as correlates with, if not causes of, inner-city crime, such as emotional or family instability, lack of education, absence of vocational skills, unemployment, drug and alcohol abuse, juvenile gangs, and sexual abuse and exploitation" (Sulton, 1990, p. 10). The programs have a clear focus, a clear audience, and a clear idea of how to proceed.

On a much smaller scale, but equally instructive, is the Newport News (Virginia) Police Department's reliance on data to identify a problem and to evaluate a solution:

> Local hunters and other gun owners held target practice at an excavation pit. Officer Hendrickson found that between April and September one year, the department had been called 45 times to chase away shooters and that the problem had existed for at least 15 years. Most of the calls had come from a couple whose nearby home was bullet-riddled and who thought the police were doing a good job because each time they chased away the shooters.

> Officer Hendrickson interviewed shooters and learned that most were soldiers from nearby Fort Eustis; many others were sent to the pit by gun shop owners. The officer also determined the pit was close enough to a highway to make any firearms discharge there illegal. Deciding to use education backed by legal sanctions, he first photographed the damage and other evidence, which he used to persuade a judge to give anyone convicted once of illegal shooting a suspended sentence and a small fine; a second offense would result in confiscation of the weapon and a jail sentence. The officer obtained from the property owners permission to arrest on their property and the same from the C & O Railroad for shooters crossing the tracks to reach the pit. He also wrote a pamphlet defining the problem and the department's intended enforcement action, and distributed it to the military base and all area gun shops. Finally, he had "No Parking—Tow Zone" signs erected on the shoulder where most shooters parked.

> The results were simple. Officers issued 35 summonses to shooters in September, 15 in October, and the last on November 12. The pit soon became so overgrown that it was uninviting for target practice. (Adapted from Guyot, 1992, p. 321)

IMPEDIMENTS TO COMMUNITY POLICING REVISITED

Success in the preceding incident and others might indicate that community policing and problem-solving policing would be readily accepted by law enforcement officials and the communities they serve. Such acceptance is not, however, always the case because of several impediments (Skogan, 2004, pp. 162–167):

LO4

Eighteen model programs shared the following characteristics. The programs:

- Focused on causes of crime.
- Built on community strengths.
- Incorporated natural support systems.
- Had an identifiable group of clients.
- Targeted those who were less affluent.
- Had clearly stated goals and well-defined procedures.
- Had sufficient resources.
- Had a strong leader.

Impedimente

- Making community policing an overtime program
- Making it a special unit
- Shortchanging the infrastructure
- Resistance in the ranks
- Resistance by police managers
- Resistance by police unions
- Resistance by special units
- Competing demands and expectations
- Lack of interagency cooperation
- Problems evaluating performance
- Unresponsive public
- Nasty misconduct
- Leadership transitions

Recall from Chapter 5 the challenges facing implementation of community policing:

- Resistance by police officers
- Difficulty involving other agencies and organizing the community
- Reluctance of average citizens to participate, either because of fear or cynicism

Resistance to change is common, especially in a tradition-oriented profession such as law enforcement, but it does not account for all the problems police departments have in implementing community policing. A former police officer and current assistant professor at South Carolina University School of Law believes that the pervasive use of the term *police warrior* and perpetuation of the "warrior mindset" is causing many of the problems between police officers and the communities they serve: "Though adopted with the best of intentions, the warrior concept has created substantial obstacles to improving police/community relations. In short, law enforcement has developed a 'warrior' problem. . . . Law enforcement training and tactics reflect the warrior concept, identifying aspects of modern policing that, if not addressed, will continue to prevent or undermine efforts to improve public perceptions of police legitimacy. I join a growing chorus of voices contending that it is the Guardian, not the Warrior, that offers the appropriate metaphor for modern officers" (Stoughton, 2015).

One challenge is that projects were usually established as special units that some saw as elite: "The perception of elitism is ironic because community policing is meant to close the gap between patrol and special units and to empower and value the rank-and-file patrol officer as the most important agent for police work" (Sadd & Grinc, 1996).

Another substantial impediment is how to respond to calls for service. A potential conflict exists between responding to calls for service and community policing efforts, because calls for service use much of the time needed for problem identification and resolution efforts. The unpredictability of calls for service presents management problems for agencies wanting to implement community policing strategies. Departments must set their priorities and

L05

Impediments to implementing innovative community-oriented policing include:

- The powerful pull of tradition.
- Substantial segments of the public not wanting the police to change.
- Unions that continue to be skeptical of innovation.
- The high cost of innovation.
- Lack of vision on the part of police executives.
- Police departments' inability to evaluate their own effectiveness (Skolnick & Bayley, 1986).

determine how to balance calls for service (reactive) with a problem-oriented approach (proactive). As stressed throughout this text, the one-on-one interaction between police officers and the citizens they serve is critical.

Some simple services that police departments might provide for the community cost little and require limited personnel. For example, relatively inexpensive efforts to enhance community safety through crime prevention might include conducting monthly meetings, meeting with school administrators, conducting fingerprinting programs, participating in athletic contests, publishing newsletters, and providing ride-alongs. Other services, however, may be relatively expensive and require many officers.

Whatever the cost to implement, community policing appears to offer a realistic approach to reducing violence, crime, and the drug problem. The remaining chapters discuss several approaches to community policing and problem solving to address these issues.

A FINAL NOTE: THE IMPORTANT DISTINCTION BETWEEN PROGRAMS AND COMMUNITY POLICING

It must be stressed that programs identified throughout this chapter are not examples of community policing programs *per se*, although community policing may incorporate the use of these and other strategies. Too many police officials think that because they have a neighborhood-watch program or a ride-along program they are doing community policing. In fact, some police chiefs and sheriffs state with pride that they are deeply involved in community policing because they have a DARE program. Community policing is an overriding philosophy that affects every aspect of police operations; it is not a single program, or even a hundred programs. Such programs, particularly in isolation, are more community relations or even public relations, not community policing.

SUMMARY

Crime prevention became popular in the late 1960s and early 1970s, with many communities taking an active role. Among the most commonly implemented crime prevention programs have been street lighting projects; property marking projects; security survey projects; citizen patrol projects; and crime reporting, neighborhood-watch, or block projects. Specialized crime watch programs include mobile crime watch, youth crime watch, business crime watch, apartment watch, realtor watch, and carrier alert.

Continuing the community crime prevention momentum generated during the 1960s and 1970s, new programs and organizations were initiated during the 1980s and 1990s to encourage citizens to play an active role in reducing crime in their own neighborhoods. Among the most visible organizations focused on crime are citizen crime prevention associations, Crime Stoppers, and MADD. Many police departments also expanded their use of volunteers, who may serve in a crime prevention capacity as reserve officers, auxiliary patrol, or community service officers or on an as-needed basis.

The most common components of community policing experiments have been foot patrol, newsletters, and community organizing. Several empirical studies in the 1980s assessed the effectiveness of community policing efforts. The Flint Neighborhood Foot Patrol Program appeared to produce a decrease in crime, an increase in general citizen satisfaction with the foot patrol program, a decline in the public's fear of crime, and a positive perception of the foot patrol officers.

In the first Newark Foot Patrol Experiment, residents reported positive results, whereas business owners reported negative results. The second Newark Foot Patrol Experiment included a coordinated foot patrol, a cleanup campaign, and distribution of a newsletter. Only the coordinated foot patrol was perceived to reduce property crime and improved assessments of the police.

The Oakland program, using foot patrol, mounted patrol, small vehicle patrol, and a Report Incidents Directly program, resulted in a substantial drop in the rate of crime against persons and their property. The San Diego Community Profile Project provided patrol officers with extensive community-orientation training. These officers became more service oriented, increased their non–law enforcement contacts with citizens, and had a more positive attitude toward police–community relations.

The victim recontact program and the newsletter of the Houston Fear-Reduction Project did not have positive results. In fact, the victim recontact program backfired, with Hispanics and Asians experiencing an increase in fear. Contact was primarily with White homeowners rather than minority renters. The citizen contact patrol and the police storefront office did, however, result in decreases in perceptions of social disorder, fear of personal victimization, and the level of personal and property crime.

The Boston Foot Patrol Project found no statistically significant relationship between changes in the level of foot patrol provided and the number of calls for service or the seriousness of the calls. Baltimore County's COPE Project reduced fear of crime by 10 percent and crime itself by 12 percent in target neighborhoods. It also reduced calls for service; increased citizen awareness of and satisfaction with the police; and improved police officer attitudes.

Other studies have reviewed the effectiveness of community crime prevention efforts. The Seattle Citywide Crime Prevention Program, using property identification, home security checks, and neighborhood block watches, significantly reduced the residential burglary rate as well as the number of burglary-in-progress calls. The Portland antiburglary program also succeeded in reducing the burglary rate for those who participated. The Hartford Experiment restructured the physical environment, changed the way patrol officers were assigned, and organized the neighborhood in an effort to reduce crime and the fear of crime.

The criminal justice system includes law enforcement, the courts, and corrections. What happens in each component of the criminal justice system directly affects the other two components. Consequently, a coordinated effort among law enforcement, courts, and corrections is required to effectively deal with the crime problem and to elicit the support of the community in doing so. Model court programs also involving the police include a community dispute resolution center and a deferred prosecution/first offenders unit.

The effectiveness of the media in assisting crime prevention efforts is another evaluation focus. Eighteen model programs identified by the National Symposium on Community Institutions and Inner-City Crime Project shared the following characteristics: The programs (1) focused on causes of crime, (2) built on community strengths, (3) incorporated natural support systems, (4) had an identifiable group of clients, (5) targeted those who were less affluent, (6) had clearly stated goals and well-defined procedures, (7) had sufficient resources, and (8) had a strong leader.

Impediments to implementing innovative community-oriented policing include the powerful pull of tradition; substantial segments of the public who do not want the police to change; unions that continue to be skeptical of innovation; the cost of innovation; lack of vision on the part of police executives; and police departments' inability to evaluate their own effectiveness.

DISCUSSION QUESTIONS

1. Why is it difficult to conduct research on the effectiveness of community policing?

2. Which studies do you think have the most value for policing in the next few years? Which studies have the most promise?

3. Why would a police department want to reduce fear of crime rather than crime itself?

4. Which of the fear-reduction strategies do you believe holds the most promise?

5. What do you think are the most reasonable aspects of the crime prevention through environmental design (CPTED) approach?

6. Do you think that victims who ignored the CPTED approach to crime prevention are culpable?

7. Has your police department conducted any research on community policing or crime prevention efforts? If so, what were the results?

8. What do you think are the most important questions regarding police–community relations that should be researched in the next few years?

9. How much of a police department's budget should be devoted to research? Which areas should be of highest priority?

ADDITIONAL RESOURCES

Every interest organization has a Web page on the Internet, including several federal agencies. A search using the terms *community policing* or *crime prevention* will yield a tremendous amount of current information. Many organizations offer expertise in building partnerships and provide a variety of publications, training, and services that can strengthen local efforts. A sampling follows.

Bureau of Justice Assistance Clearinghouse, Box 6000, Rockville, MD 20850; (800) 688–4252

Center for Community Change, 1000 Wisconsin Avenue NW, Washington, DC 20007; (202) 342–0519

Citizens Committee for New York City, 305 7th Avenue, 15th Floor, New York, NY 10001; (212) 989–0909

Community Policing Consortium, 1726 M Street NW, Suite 801, Washington, DC 20006; (202) 833–3305 or (800) 833–3085

National Center for Community Policing, School of Criminal Justice, Michigan State University, East Lansing, MI 48824; (517) 355–2322

National Crime Prevention Council, 1700 K Street NW, 2nd Floor, Washington, DC 20006-3817; (202) 466–6272

National Training and Information Center, 810 North Milwaukee Avenue, Chicago, IL 60622–4103; (312) 243–3035

Police Executive Research Forum, 2300 M Street NW, Suite 910, Washington, DC 20006; (202) 466–7820

Safe Neighborhoods and Communities: From Traffic Problems to Crime

Learning Objectives

LO1 Explain the role crime prevention plays in community policing.

LO2 Identify what is usually at the top of the list of neighborhood concerns and what behaviors are involved.

LO3 Summarize what engineering and enforcement responses can address the problem of speeding in residential areas.

LO4 List how various community policing efforts have addressed citizens' fear of crime.

LO5 Understand the three primary components of CPTED and how CPTED directly supports community policing.

LO6 Describe the two side effects of place-focused opportunity blocking efforts.

LO7 Define the risk factor prevention paradigm.

LO8 Know what partnerships have been implemented to prevent or reduce crime and disorder.

Key Terms

cocoon neighborhood watch
contagion
diffusion
opportunity blocking
place
risk factor prevention paradigm
synergism
target hardening
traffic calming

In 1992, Oakland County, Michigan, experienced a population increase for which the city was not adequately prepared to handle. While industry boomed and the population grew, roadway congestion and safety became two primary areas of concern, leading many residents to turn to their community leaders for resolutions to these problems. A solution was found in a technology relatively new to the United States: adaptive traffic signaling. The program, which was imported from Austria, uses machine vision technology to determine when traffic concerns are present and innovative computer software to adjust traffic signals in an attempt to regulate traffic flow and reduce congestion.

The primary goals of the Adaptive Traffic Signaling campaign were to reduce traffic congestion, decrease the number of accidents, improve traffic flow, quicken the response to motorist concerns, and increase the overall safety of vehicular and pedestrian travel. Recent research by the Texas A&M Transportation Institute estimates that by 2020, the average driver will waste nearly 45 hours and 25 gallons of gas because of roadway delays due to traffic congestion. After adjusting for population growth, U.S. citizens as a group will waste nearly 9 million hours merely sitting in traffic.

The use of new technologies, such as adaptive traffic signaling strategies, has allowed for a reduction in traffic congestion and motor vehicle crashes, while creating much safer pedestrian travel in areas such as Oakland County. The strategy uses sensors, much like those used with motion sensor lighting, to detect when a vehicle or vehicles are approaching a roadway. Based on precalculations, the sensors can relay data that determine which lights will remain or turn green. The process includes the use of electromagnetic loops in the pavement, as well as cameras, to adjust for a heavy flow of traffic. This tool has proven to be extremely useful in the Oakland County, Michigan, area for strategic events, including the numerous high school, college, and professional sporting events in the area. These updated strategies have been much more effective than the outdated strategies to control traffic throughout much of the United States that still use predetermined traffic signal patterns for traffic control. Beyond the obvious lack of frustration by drivers, the practice is seen as more environmentally friendly, better for business and economics, and, most importantly, much more safe for citizens in the community.

The use of adaptive signaling in the Oakland County, Michigan, was funded primarily by federal grants and was of little expense to local taxpayers.

However, the benefits to the average citizen were priceless. Overall motor vehicle accidents in the areas where the new technologies were installed decreased by nearly 60 percent, with violent crashes decreasing by 50 percent. Higher rates of driver satisfaction, lower incidents of road rage, and lower rates of pedestrian-related accidents were evident after the installation of new technologies.

INTRODUCTION

Community policing stresses using partnerships and problem solving to address making neighborhoods and communities safer, including looking at concerns related to traffic, at neighborhood disorder, at crime, and at the fear of crime. Many Americans, including many police, believe traffic problems and crime prevention are solely the responsibility of law enforcement. When crime surges in a community, the usual public response is to demand the hiring of more officers. Citizens often believe that a visible police presence will deter and reduce crime, even though most studies indicate this is not the case. For example, the classic Kansas City Preventive Patrol Experiment found overwhelming evidence that decreasing or increasing routine preventive patrol within the range tested had no effect on crime, citizen fear of crime, community attitudes toward the police on the delivery of police services, police response time, or traffic accidents. In 1975, the FBI's Uniform Crime Report noted:

> Criminal justice professionals readily and repeatedly admit that, in the absence of citizen assistance, neither more manpower, nor improved technology, nor additional money will enable law enforcement to shoulder the monumental burden of combating crime in America.

The advent of community policing and partnerships is often credited with the dramatic decrease in crime witnessed in the late 1990s (Rosen, 2006). Despite predictions that a significant crime wave would occur in the 1990s as a result of the increase in the population of youth and young adults (a "boom" that never materialized), the United States experienced the longest and deepest decline in crime since World War II. Some scholars have speculated that these drops in the crime rate may have resulted from modest improvements in policing. During the 1990s, the New York Police Department (NYPD), for example, increased its workforce by 35 percent (13,000 people), changed its management style, and engaged in more aggressive police work, particularly in public-order offenses. By 2016, the NYPD had approximately 34,500 sworn officers.

Other variables that may have contributed to a decrease in the crime rate are the booming economy, a drop in the high-risk (teens to young adult) population, and an increase in the number of people in prison. Research, however, has been unable to consistently demonstrate a clear correlation between these variables and the crime rate, as it is noted that the drop in the youth population and an increase in the incarceration rate also occurred in the 1980s when crime across the country soared.

Furthermore, and in contrast to what was happening in the United States, Canada experienced a 30-percent drop in violent crime during the 1990s at a time when the country's prison population was declining, there were fewer officers on the street, and the economic gains were moderate. Therefore, from these contrasting scenarios and societal variables, the difficulty in determining the causes of fluctuating crime rates becomes apparent.

In 2005 and 2006, it appeared that the downward trend in violent crime rates of the 1990s was over. Violent crime was growing at an alarming rate. The FBI reported the largest single-year-percentage increase in violent crime in 14 years. At the Police Executive Research Forum (PERF) National Violent Crime Summit in August 2006, 170 representatives—mayors, police chiefs, and public officials—from more than 50 cities met to discuss the gathering storm of violent crime sweeping through our nation's communities. The information they shared was sobering. Murder was up 27.5 percent in the first 6 months of 2005 in Boston, 27 percent in Memphis, and 25 percent in Cincinnati. Robbery was up in even more startling numbers. Even communities with relatively low crime rates saw significant increases in 2005 and early 2006.

Police chiefs pointed to gangs, violent criminals returning from prisons, drug trafficking, and juveniles with easy access to guns as the forces behind the uptick in violent crime. Others, such as Mayor Douglas Palmer of Trenton, New Jersey, suggested that the focus on homeland security and fighting terrorism had taken resources away from hometown security and local crime prevention efforts (Rosen, 2006). Additional factors identified by PERF summit participants as contributing to the increasing violent crime trend included a decrease in police department staffing levels; decreased federal involvement in crime prevention and community policing; a strained social service community, educational system, and criminal justice system, particularly courts and corrections; the glamorization of violence and the "thug" pop culture; and the phenomenon of crime becoming "a sport" (Rosen, 2006, p. 9).

In discussing ways to stem the potential tide of increasing violent crime, participants in the summit were reminded of the crime wave that gripped the country during the late 1980s and early 1990s and how that situation was turned around. Los Angeles Police Chief William Bratton recalled the Omnibus Crime Bill of 1994, with its emphasis on community policing and problem solving, and how efforts then were focused on the holistic treatment of a community, an approach that, by all accounts, significantly helped reduce crime in the late 1990s (Rosen, 2006).

Then, in 2007, violent crime rates once again began to trend downward across the country, with the biggest declines observed in the largest cities, suggesting that the rising rates of 2005 and 2006 were merely an anomaly. And while it may be hypothesized that big cities are doing better because they have more resources and more advanced policing methods, criminologists do not know for sure what factors have accounted for the differing rates.

In all, violent crime rates in 2007 fell 1.4 percent and property crime rates fell 2.1 percent. In 2008, the United States entered a recession and a time when most experts expected crime to rise. However, for reasons that have yet to be identified or explained, crime continued to fall. In 2014, the estimated number of violent crimes in the nation decreased 0.2 percent when compared with 2013 data, and property crimes decreased by 4.3 percent, marking the 12th straight year the collective estimates for these offenses declined. Preliminary data for 2015 showed an uptick in violent crime in several large cities but a decrease in property crimes nationwide (Federal Bureau of Investigation, 2016). As this text goes to print, it remains unclear as to whether this increase in violent crime marks the beginning of an ongoing trend or whether it is merely another anomaly such as that observed a decade earlier.

Whatever the reasons for the overall declining crime rate over the past two decades, the importance of getting the community involved in staving off local crime and disorder is clear. The broad nature of policing in the 1990s highlighted the critical contributions that citizens and community agencies and organizations can make to combat crime. For communities to thrive, citizens need to have a sense of neighborhood and work together as a team. The resulting synergism can accomplish much more than isolated individual efforts. **Synergism** occurs when individuals channel their energies toward a common purpose and accomplish together what they could not accomplish alone.

The technical definition of synergism is "the simultaneous actions of separate entities which together have greater total effect than the sum of their individual efforts." A precision marching band and a national basketball championship team are examples of synergism. Although there may be some outstanding solos and a few spectacular individual "dunks," it is the total team effort that produces the results.

The police and the citizens they serve must realize that their combined efforts are greater than the sum of their individual efforts on behalf of the community. When police take a problem-solving approach to community concerns and include the community, what they are doing often falls under "crime prevention."

Community policing and crime prevention are, however, distinct entities. Further, crime is usually not the greatest concern of a neighborhood—traffic-related problems are of greater concern because they affect all citizens daily. A note: The discussion of domestic violence in this chapter is relatively brief. Domestic violence is most certainly a crime, but the discussion of community policing and domestic violence is placed later in the text (Chapter 14), where violence is discussed in depth.

synergism
Occurs when individuals channel their energies toward a common purpose and accomplish what they could not accomplish alone.

L01
Crime prevention is a large part, in fact a cornerstone, of community policing.

TRAFFIC ENFORCEMENT AND SAFETY

The United States is a highly mobile nation, with motor vehicle travel being the primary means of transportation. Citizens consider it a *right* to drive their vehicles, although it really is a privilege, and they resent any limitations imposed on this "right." At the same time, however, they expect local and state governments to keep the roadways in good condition and the police to keep traffic moving. The ease with which drivers can travel safely is considered to be a vital attribute of a prosperous and livable community (Maggard & Jung, 2009). Mark Marshall, past president of the International Association of Chiefs of Police (IACP), put the importance of traffic enforcement and safety into perspective when he stated: "I believe that it is no exaggeration to say that few duties of the law enforcement community affect the quality of life of our citizens as significantly as the rendering of quality police traffic services" (Marshall, 2011, p. 6).

Preliminary data reported by the U.S. Department of Transportation's National Highway Traffic Safety Administration (NHTSA) indicate that motor vehicle traffic deaths increased by 7.7 percent in 2015 (NHTSA, 2016a). In addressing this rise in fatalities, NHTSA Administrator Dr. Mark Rosekind observed, "As the economy has improved and gas prices have fallen, more Americans are driving more miles. But that only explains part of the increase. Ninety-four percent of crashes can be tied back to a human choice or error, so we know we need to focus our efforts on improving human behavior while promoting vehicle technology that not only protects people in crashes, but helps prevent crashes in the first place." Driver behavior that contributes to traffic crashes includes drunk, drugged, distracted and drowsy driving; failure to use safety features such as seat belts and child seats; and speeding.

Speeding in Residential Areas

Studies have shown that traffic-related issues continue to top the list of citizens' complaints to police (Casstevens, 2008). Data from NHTSA consistently show that speeding is one of the most prevalent factors contributing to traffic crashes. In 2010, speeding was identified as a contributing factor in nearly one-third (32%) of all fatal crashes, and 86 percent of speeding-related fatalities in 2010 occurred on roads that were not Interstate highways (NHTSA, 2012a).

Speeding in residential areas raises concern over the safety of children, pedestrians, and bicyclists and increases the risk of vehicle crashes as well as the seriousness of injuries to other drivers, passengers, pedestrians, and bicyclists struck by a vehicle. In many cities, "traffic calming" has been the response. **Traffic calming** devices, such as speed bumps and traffic circles (roundabouts), are intended to slow traffic in residential areas and are popular in communities where residents believe the measures make children safer and neighborhoods quieter.

Aggressive enforcement of speed limits may seem to run counter to community policing efforts to establish rapport with citizens. Nonetheless, NHTSA data indicate that of the 10,591 speeding-related traffic fatalities that occurred across the United States in 2009, 12 percent happened at speeds of less than 35 miles per hour (mph) and another 19 percent resulted from crashes occurring at speeds of 35–40 mph (NHTSA, 2012b). Such figures underscore the reality that speeds that are common in residential areas may still produce fatalities should a vehicle strike a pedestrian, bicyclist, or even another motorist.

Most speed-reduction enforcement efforts focus on highway or main thoroughfare speeding and aggressive driving, although broad public education campaigns can also have a positive effect on reducing speeding through residential areas. The Governors Highway Safety Association (GHSA) report

---

LO2

Traffic problems top the list of concerns of most neighborhoods and communities. Concerns include speeding in residential areas, street racing, red-light running, impaired drivers, and nonuse of seat belts.

---

traffic calming

Describes a wide range of road and environmental design changes that either make it more difficult for a vehicle to speed or make drivers believe they should slow down for safety.

Speeding and Aggressive Driving (2012, p. 4) highlights the continued role that speeding plays in traffic fatalities and makes several recommendations to the states and the NHTSA to address the problem:

- States should explore addressing speed concerns through aggressive driving enforcement since the driving public believes that aggressive driving is a serious threat to their safety.

- Speed concerns can also be addressed through targeted enforcement in school and work zones, which are additional enforcement strategies supported by the public.

- The National Highway Traffic Safety Administration (NHTSA) should sponsor a national high visibility enforcement campaign and support public awareness efforts to address the issues of speed and aggressive driving.

- NHTSA should promote best practices in automated enforcement strategies.

- NHTSA should sponsor a *National Forum on Speeding and Aggressive Driving*, similar to efforts undertaken in 2005, to bring together experts to review and update effective tools and strategies states can employ to reduce speed and aggressive driving.

Closely related to the challenge of preventing speeding is the challenge of preventing street racing.

Street Racing

Street racing of automobiles has been an American tradition since the early 1950s, and probably many years before. Although no national database currently tracks the number of lives lost every year to illegal street racing, an Internet search of "street racing crashes" provides ample evidence, stories, and images of the deadly results of these activities. Too often those injured or killed are innocent bystanders and other motorists who are at the wrong place at the wrong time. Some jurisdictions, such as Los Angeles, have formed task forces to address the growing problem of street racing and the crashes and fatalities that sometimes result from such activities (Martinez, 2016). Officers note that

> **L03**
>
> *Engineering responses* to speeding include using traffic calming, posting warning signs and signals, conducting anti-speeding public awareness campaigns, informing complainants about actual speeds, and providing realistic driver training. *Enforcement responses* to reduce speeding include (1) enforcing speeding laws, (2) enforcing speeding laws with speed cameras or photo radar, (3) using speed display boards, (4) arresting the worst offenders, and (5) having citizen volunteers monitor speeding (Scott, 2001b).

TECHNOLOGY IN COMMUNITY POLICING

HOW TECHNOLOGY IS MAKING NEIGHBORHOOD TRAFFIC WORSE: THE WAZE APP

The double-edged sword of technology has created a safety hazard for some communities, which has, in turn, become an issue for police as well. Consider, for example, the traffic app Waze, used by motorists in Los Angeles seeking alternative routes for congested freeways, routes that often take them through residential neighborhoods. One resident expresses the following concern: "Logically speaking, people using shortcuts are likely to be in a hurry and people in a hurry are likely to be speeding. Moreover, people using mobile apps are likely to be juggling hand-held devices while people living on quiet streets are less likely to be vigilant in watching out for traffic" (Thornton, 2015).

social media is often involved, not only as a way for racers to boast about their skills and share information about where races are happening but also for racers and spectators alike to communicate about which areas to avoid because of an active police presence. Monitoring social media can help alert officers to where these events are taking place.

Red-Light Running

Red-light running is a common occurrence and can be deadly. The Insurance Institute for Highway Safety (IIHS) reports that in 2014, 709 people were killed and an estimated 126,000 were injured in crashes that involved red-light running (IIHS, 2016). Studies have found that the majority of those killed are not the red-light runners themselves but occupants in other vehicles, passengers in the car that ran the red light, bicyclists, or pedestrians.

In Phoenix, Arizona, a group of parents formed the Red Means Stop Coalition after their sons and daughters were hit by red-light runners. The group works alongside local police departments, the governor's highway safety office, and local corporations to elevate the issue of red-light running prevention in the press and among elected and public officials. Similar traffic safety groups across the United States complement the efforts of law enforcement officials by informing the public of the red-light running problem and focusing on driver behavior changes.

Because it is impossible for police to monitor every intersection with a stoplight, cameras are helping fill the void. A study by the IIHS found that red-light cameras reduce the fatal crash rate caused by red-light runners by 21 percent. Further evaluation of the use of such devices in 79 large cities throughout the country showed that red-light camera programs saved nearly 1,300 lives through 2014 and that shutting down such programs increased the rate of fatal red-light-running crashes by 30 percent (IIHS, 2016).

TECHNOLOGY IN COMMUNITY POLICING

RED-LIGHT CAMERAS

Automated red-light cameras are being used in many jurisdictions to address the problem of red-light running. Since the 1990s, when the technology was first introduced as a low-cost way to police intersections, red-light cameras have become increasingly popular and, as of July 2012, approximately 555 communities throughout the United States were using them (IIHS, 2011).

In June 2007, Springfield, Missouri, installed red-light cameras at selected intersections as part of their "respect red" drivers' education campaign. A vocal minority of residents were highly critical that such "Big Brother" technology was being used simply as a way to generate revenue from unsuspecting drivers—a complaint commonly heard among red-light camera opponents in other cities. However, nearly 3 years after the cameras were activated, the program was $33,000 in the red:

> Fortunately for the city, making money was never the goal. Improving safety was, and by that measure, the cameras were a success. City officials say their data show red-light

running crashes decreased both at camera-equipped intersections and city-wide. Citations fell 36 percent to an average of 1.05 a day per camera.

Springfield traffic engineer Jason Haynes says the fact that the program didn't make money helped to maintain community support.

Source: Insurance Institute for Highway Safety. (2011, February 1). "City Uses Cameras as Safety Tool, not Moneymaker." *Red Light Running Kills, Status Report*, Vol.46, No.1, pp. 1–2, 6–7.

Use (or Nonuse) of Seat Belts

Recent data from the National Occupant Protection Use Survey (NOPUS), conducted annually by the National Center for Statistics and Analysis of the National Highway Traffic Safety Administration indicate that an estimated 88.5 percent of Americans wore their seat belts while riding in or driving a vehicle in 2015, a number statistically unchanged from 86.7 percent in 2014 (Pickrell & Li, 2016). Seat belt use has increased steadily since 1994, when 58 percent of passenger vehicle occupants reportedly wore seat belts, and has been accompanied by a steady decline in the percentage of unrestrained passenger vehicle (PV) occupant fatalities during daytime. The 2015 NOPUS also found the following:

- Seat belt use for occupants in the West is higher than in the other regions: Northeast, Midwest, and South in 2015.

- Seat belt use continued to be higher in the States in which vehicle occupants can be pulled over solely for not using seat belts ("primary law States") as compared with the States with weaker enforcement laws ("secondary law States") or without seat belt laws.

- Seat belt use for occupants in passenger cars increased significantly from 88.1 percent in 2014 to 90.3 percent in 2015.

- Seat Belt use for occupants in pickup trucks increased significantly from 77.2 percent in 2014 to 80.8 percent in 2015.

The NHTSA estimates that safety belt use at rates higher than the 90 percent level prevents 15,700 fatalities and 350,000 serious injuries each year. The country also saves about $67 billion in economic costs of fatalities and injuries from motor vehicle crashes.

Strategies used to encourage seat belt use vary from incentives for safe driving to mandatory use policies and fines for failure to buckle up. "Click It or Ticket," an annual nationwide, short-duration, high-visibility seat belt enforcement program, is an example of the latter. Officers in participating agencies are asked to focus on seat belt compliance and ticketing of violators. At the same time, federal funding pays for advertising that highlights the program and seat belt safety. The enforcement includes surveys that measure "before and after" seat belt use, seat belt checkpoints, saturation patrols, fixed patrols, and extensive media coverage. Agencies are encouraged to create partnerships with the media and other community organizations. These partners have conducted child/family vehicle check-up clinics, assisted at child seat checkpoints, attended the department's Click It or Ticket news conference, and assisted with public education.

Impaired Drivers

Decades ago, drunk driving was not considered the crime that it is today. Now, crashes caused by alcohol-impaired driving are treated as violent crimes. NHTSA data show that alcohol-impaired driving fatalities increased by 3.2 percent from 2014 to 2015, accounting for 29 percent of overall motor vehicle fatalities that year (NHTSA, 2016b). It is also recognized that driving under the influence of drugs, whether illegal or prescription, is also a form of impaired driving.

A study by the NHTSA found that alcohol use by drivers was clearly associated with elevated risk of crash involvement. In this study, drivers with a breath alcohol concentration (BAC) of 0.08 (the per se legal limit in every state) were four times more likely than sober drivers to be involved in a crash, and drivers with BAC levels at 0.15 had 12 times the risk for crashing (Compton & Berning, 2015). The study also examined the potential for a number of drugs to impair driving ability. Marijuana (THC) was the only single category of drug for which study findings reached statistical significance. A caveat: Although drivers who tested positive for THC were overrepresented in the crash-involved population, when demographic factors (such as age and gender) and alcohol use were controlled, the study found no increase in the crash risk associated with THC use.

Responses to address the drunk driving problem include legislation (lowering the legal limit for per se violations), strict enforcement by police, curtailing driving privileges, sanctioning convicted drunk drivers by requiring installation of electronic ignition locks that prevent intoxicated drivers from operating their vehicles, monitoring drunk drivers, providing public education, providing alternative transportation and environmental design, and locating licensed establishments in areas that reduce the need for patrons to drive. As of August 2005, laws setting a legal blood alcohol content (BAC) of .08 have taken effect in all 50 states, the District of Columbia, and Puerto Rico, an effort that took nearly 20 years of work by proponents.

Some of the most promising and potentially effective approaches to eliminating drunk driving have come through improvements in technology for monitoring a driver's BAC, such as ignition interlocks, passive alcohol sensors, and Secure Continuous Remote Alcohol Monitor (SCRAM) devices. Passive alcohol sensors (PASs) help agencies to work more effectively in enforcing driving while intoxicated (DWI) restrictions, as research shows the use of a PAS can increase the detection of unlawful BAC by about 50 percent at checkpoints and by roughly 10 percent on routine patrols (Dewey-Kollen, 2006).

Emerging technologies include infrared sensing that enforcement officers can use to help determine an offender's alcohol content level, devices that can detect subdural blood alcohol concentrations through a driver's hand placed on the steering wheel, and algorithms to detect a vehicle's weaving so an officer can determine if the driver is impaired. Another device still in the research phase is the Driver Alcohol Detection Systems for Safety (DADSS), which would prevent drunk drivers from starting their vehicles. The DADSS project was authorized by Congress in 2012, and in 2013 the NHTSA formed a partnership agreement with 15 major auto manufacturers to continue research, with their goal to have an implementable technology by 2020 (NHTSA, 2015). The NHTSA does not intend for DADSS to be mandatory for all vehicles but, rather, an option or upgrade, particularly for commercial vehicles and those driven by teenagers (Kauffman, 2015). Although opposition to the technology exists, it has also found widespread support from many groups, including Mothers Against Drunk Driving (MADD). MADD National President Colleen Sheehey-Church has stated: "For 35 years, MADD has worked to stop the horrible crime of drunk driving. This technology represents the future, when one day drunk driving will be relegated to the history books. While we still have a lot of work to do, we are closer than ever to eliminating drunk driving."

Police Pursuits

Data from the NHTSA reveal that more people are killed every year by police pursuits than by floods, tornados, hurricanes, and lightning combined (Ingraham, 2015). An average of one person a day dies in the United States as a result of a police pursuit. Some of these high-speed chases careen through local streets and neighborhoods as the suspect desperately tries to escape capture. As with persons killed by red-light runners, many of those killed during police chases are people other than the driver who is being pursued, including occupants of other cars, bicyclists, pedestrians, and passengers in the vehicle being chased. According to NHTSA records, more than 11,500 people died between 1979 and 2013 as a result of a police pursuit (Frank, 2015b). However, further investigation into these statistics shows that inconsistent coding practices and other methodological discrepancies have led to a significant underreporting of these deaths, with some sources estimating the chase-related fatalities are understated by nearly 31 percent (Frank, 2015a).

It might surprise many to learn that these high-risk pursuits are often precipitated by rather low-level offenses. Analysis of nearly 8,000 high-speed police chases documented in the International Association of Chiefs of Police (IACP) database found that the overwhelming majority of pursuits (91%) were initiated in response to a nonviolent crime. The event responsible for the largest number of police pursuits was a simple traffic infraction (42%). Pursuit of a stolen vehicle accounted for 18 percent of the chases, and 15 percent of police pursuits involved a suspected drunk driver (Ingraham, 2015).

Safe Communities

Nine agencies within the U.S. Department of Transportation (DOT) are working together to promote and implement a safer national transportation system by combining the best injury prevention practices into the Safe Communities approach to serve as a national model. The NHTSA defines a *safe community* as "a community that promotes injury prevention activities at the local level

TECHNOLOGY IN COMMUNITY POLICING

STARCHASE: THE END OF HIGH-SPEED POLICE PURSUITS?

As police departments nationwide seek safer ways to capture suspects who flee, a company called StarChase has devised a product it hopes will help agencies achieve their goal. With the StarChase technology, officers can fire small, adhesive-coated GPS-equipped projectiles from the grill of their squad car at a suspect's vehicle and then track its movement, eliminating the need for dangerous high-speed pursuits. The company's president boasts that their product has had "zero fatalities, zero injuries, zero property damage and zero liability" (CBS News, 2016). With training, officers are expected to be able to hit the targeted suspect vehicle 75 percent of the time, although certain weather conditions, such as rain, hinder the ability of the projectiles to stick. In December 2015, the Milwaukee, Wisconsin, Police Department implemented a trial of the StarChase system and, through 28 successful deployments, 17 people were arrested and 26 stolen cars were recovered. More than 50 police departments across the country currently use StarChase.

Source: CBS News, 2016.

to solve local highway and traffic safety and other injury problems. It uses a 'bottom up' approach involving its citizens in addressing key injury problems" (NHTSA, n.d.). According to the Safe Communities Web site, safe communities have six elements. A safe community:

- Uses an integrated and comprehensive injury control system with prevention, acute care, and rehabilitation partners as active and essential participants in addressing community injury problems.

- Has a comprehensive, community-based coalition/task force with representation from citizens; law enforcement; public health, medical, injury prevention, education, business, civic, and service groups; public works offices; and traffic safety advocates that provides program input, direction, and involvement in the Safe Community program.

- Conducts comprehensive problem identification and uses estimating techniques that determine the economic costs associated with traffic-related fatalities and injuries within the context of the total injury problem.

- Conducts program assessments from a "best practices" and a prevention perspective to determine gaps in highway and traffic safety and other injury activity.

- Implements a plan with specific strategies that addresses the problems and program deficiencies through prevention countermeasures and activities.

- Evaluates the program to determine the impact and cost benefit where possible.

CRITICAL THINKING

Residents of a neighborhood in the city where you work as a patrol officer have persistently complained about cars speeding through their neighborhood streets. Although efforts to impact the speeding problem by issuing citations have made the situation somewhat better, it is only a temporary fix; drivers begin to speed through the neighborhood again once the police move on to another problem area. Your sergeant has asked you to lead a team of three other patrol officers to problem-solve this situation with the goal of helping residents feel safe on their streets once again. This neighborhood has:

- many families with young children and pets
- an elementary school
- a senior living complex with independent living apartments and also an assisted living wing and a nursing home
- three busy controlled intersections with small businesses, banks, a library, and a post office
- a neighborhood park with no parking lot

The sergeant has asked you to be creative and to partner with the appropriate stakeholders. You are allowed to request whatever resources you need, but remember: Simply writing more tickets has not solved the speeding problem. The residents will be looking to you to provide leadership in trying some new things.

What would you do? Use the SARA model to improve this problem.

? Prepare a report showing how you addressed each of the steps in the SARA model of problem solving, who you added to your team from outside the police department, and how you will know if your solutions are working. Include a map of the area with your report, showing the busy intersections, the park, and other busy locations such as the library, post office, etc. Indicate on the map where most of the speeding has been taking place as well as any car crashes that have occurred.

A patrol officer helps a girl through a bike safety course designed to teach children how to control their bikes, avoid obstacles, and properly use their brakes. Bicycle safety classes can significantly reduce incidents of child injury.

AP Images/John Lovretta

ADDRESSING DISORDER CONCERNS

In addition to traffic concerns, citizens are often more concerned about minor offenses (disorders) than they are about crime and violence in their communities. Neighborhood and business district improvements such as cleaning up trash, landscaping, and planting flowers can serve as a focus for community organizing and help residents take pride in their neighborhoods. Key partnerships in beautification projects include police departments, the public works staff, the business community, and residents. These partnerships can also be expanded to help fight crime and to reduce the fear of crime.

Addressing disorder goes far beyond beautification, however. Allowing neighborhood disorder to go unchecked creates an advertisement that no one in the area cares what happens (Recall the discussion of "broken windows" in Chapter 3). This condition attracts more disorder, crime, criminals, and other destructive elements. When communities begin to clean up the neighborhood, report crime, improve security, look out for each other, and work cooperatively, crime and disorder problems begin to disappear. Many of the topics in this chapter describe how *broken windows* get fixed and, as a result, how neighborhoods improve.

ADDRESSING CRIME AND THE FEAR OF CRIME

A major goal of community policing is to reduce not only crime itself but also the *fear* of crime so that citizens will be willing to join together to prevent crime.

Video Surveillance of Public Places

An increasingly popular approach to reduce crime and the fear of crime is video surveillance of public places. Video cameras connected to closed-circuit television (CCTV) can be used as a tool for "place management," for providing medical assistance, or for gathering information. Strategically placed cameras can be used to monitor traffic flow, public meetings, or demonstrations that may require additional police resources. The devices can also be a community safety feature, allowing camera operators to contact medical services if they see someone suffering from illness or injury as a result of criminal activity or noncrime medical emergencies. In addition, cameras can be used to gather intelligence and monitor known offenders' behavior in public places—for example, shoplifters in public retail areas (Ratcliffe, 2011).

According to the Center for Problem-Oriented Policing, use of CCTV can prevent crime by creating a deterrent to potential offenders who are aware of the cameras' presence. A key element in such prevention through deterrence, however, rests on adequate signage and recognition by the public that they are under surveillance. If offenders are unaware they are being watched, or if they are under the influence of drugs or alcohol and, thus, "altered" to the point where they do not care that they are being monitored, the deterrent value of CCTV is significantly diminished (Ratcliffe, 2011).

CCTV can also impact crime by helping police detect crimes in progress and provide visual identification of offenders for later arrest and prosecution. The value of this tool in this capacity is dependent, however, on how rapidly police can respond to incidents identified by camera operators.

Fake, or decoy, cameras are also used to create the illusion that people are being monitored. For example, the public transportation systems in some communities have installed both active and dummy cameras on board their bus fleet to enhance the public's perception of widespread surveillance capabilities. Augmenting the deterrent impact and crime prevention value through the use of such tactics is a concept referred to as a diffusion of benefits (Ratcliffe, 2011). Despite these numerous benefits, video surveillance can have unintended consequences.

Unintended Consequences of Video Surveillance   Among the unintended consequences of video surveillance are displacement, increased suspicion or fear of crime, and increased reported crime.

Displacement occurs when offenders, aware of the surveillance cameras, simply move their activity to another area out of camera sight. However, general crime prevention literature suggests that the amount of crime displaced rarely matches the amount of crime reduced. Video surveillance may also force offenders to be more imaginative and diversify operations.

Another concern is that the public may respond negatively to the cameras. Results of one survey showed that one-third of respondents felt one purpose of the cameras was to spy on people. Other surveys showed some city managers were reluctant to advertise the cameras or have the cameras very visible for fear they would make shoppers and consumers more fearful (Ratcliffe, 2011). Ironically, although it is hoped that most citizens would feel safer under the watchful eye of the cameras, the surveillance may have the reverse effect on some people.

A third concern is that reported crime rates will increase for some offenses with low reporting rates such as minor acts of violence, graffiti tagging, and drug offenses. The public needs to be prepared for the fact that the increase in recorded crime does not reflect an increase in actual crime.

Public Concerns Regarding Video Surveillance In addition to concerns about these potential unintended consequences, the public may be concerned about privacy issues.

As noted in the discussion of using cameras to detect red-light runners, civil liberties unions often object to video surveillance, claiming it is an invasion of privacy and citing the Fourth Amendment's prohibition against unreasonable search and seizure. However, the Fourth Amendment protects *people*, not *places.* The Fourth Amendment does not protect people in clearly public places where there is no expectation of privacy. However, as Ratcliffe (2011, p. 34), points out: "The public is unlikely to support CCTV if there is a risk that video of them shopping on a public street when they should be at work will appear on the nightly news." He suggests that a policy be established covering when recorded images are to be released to the police, media, or other agencies in the criminal justice system. He further recommends that video footage not be released for any reason other than to enhance the criminal justice system.

Evaluation of Video Surveillance Establishing whether video surveillance reduces crime is difficult because this problem-oriented solution is seldom implemented without incident or without other crime prevention measures being initiated simultaneously. In addition, as noted, use of video surveillance may inadvertently increase the crime rate, especially for offenses with low reporting rates.

Research results are mixed, with some studies finding video surveillance to be effective against property crime and less effective against personal crime and public order offenses. Other studies report mixed results regarding reducing fear of crime. Several studies produced inconclusive results. Ratcliffe (2011, pp. 22–23) reports the following general findings:

- CCTV is more effective at combating property offenses than violent or public order crime (though there have been successes in this area).
- CCTV appears to work best in small, well-defined areas (such as public car parks).
- The individual context of each area and the way the system is used appear to be important.
- Achieving *statistically significant* reductions in crime can be difficult (i.e., crime reductions that clearly go beyond the level that might occur as a result of the normal fluctuations in the crime rate are difficult to prove).
- A close relationship with the police appears important in determining a successful system.
- There is an investigative benefit to CCTV once an offense has been committed.
- CCTV appears to be somewhat effective in reducing fear of crime but only among a subset of the population.

USING ADVANCING TECHNOLOGY TO FIGHT CRIME

In addition to using video surveillance in public places, numerous types of technology are also being used to fight and, in some instances, prevent crime. Although it is not new, crime mapping technology is often the first step in proactive policing to identify hot spots. As discussed in Chapter 4, hot spots are areas where incidents of crime and disorder tend to cluster in close proximity to one another. Most veteran police officers are keenly aware of those areas in their beats that tend to be troublesome. However, in an effort to help the community formulate responses, law enforcement executives and crime analysts who are not on the streets patrolling beats can also identify hot spots by using maps and geographic information systems, and statistical tests (National Institute of Justice, 2010):

Maps and Geographic Information Systems

Analysts can create a variety of maps that visualize different aspects of a particular location. Density maps, for example, show where crimes occur without dividing a map into regions or blocks; areas with high concentrations of crime stand out.

Analysts use geographic information systems (GIS) to combine street maps, data about crime and public disorder, and data about other features such as schools, liquor stores, warehouses, and bus stops. The resulting multidimensional maps produce a visual display of the hot spots. The GIS places each crime within a grid system on a map and colors each cell based on how many incidents occurred in that area.

Although high-crime areas may often be defined as hot spots based on past experiences of officers or the characteristics of those areas, GIS allows law enforcement agencies to more accurately pinpoint hot spots to confirm trouble areas, identify the specific nature of the activity occurring within the hot spot, and then develop strategies to respond.

Statistical Tests

Analysts can use statistical software to determine whether an area with a high number of crimes is a hot spot or whether the clustering of those crimes is a random occurrence. CrimeStat III and GeoDa are two computer software programs for hot spot analysis.

- **CrimeStat III.** CrimeStat is a spatial statistical program used to analyze the locations of crime incidents and identify hot spots.
- **GeoDa.** The GeoDa Center for Geospatial Analysis and Computation at Arizona State University develops state-of-the-art methods for geospatial analysis, geovisualization, geosimulation, and spatial process modeling and implements them through software tools.

Biometric identification systems are also becoming more sophisticated, widely available, affordable, and useable. Biometrics can use one or more of several different physical and/or behavioral characteristics such as fingerprints and palmprints; hand and finger geometry; facial recognition; iris and retinal scans; voice identification; and DNA analysis (*National Science and Technology Council*, 2011).

Following are examples of other technologies being used by police departments across the country (Police Executive Research Forum, 2012):

- In Camden, New Jersey, gunshot detection technology is being used to immediately alert police to the exact location of shots being fired. Since installing the system in a location with the highest number of calls for service and crimes involving firearms, the department has learned that roughly one-third of the shootings in that area went unreported.

- In Minneapolis, Minnesota, police are testing video analytics, the automated analysis of video feeds that can trigger alerts based on criteria specified by the police. For example, the system can be programmed to monitor the feed from a camera at a train station and send an alert if an object resembling a backpack is abandoned on a platform.

- In Arlington, Texas, the police department reviews social media accounts of active duty officers as well as applicants going through the recruiting and hiring phases. The agency notes that posts in such forums, as well as the friends one has, speak to one's character and give the agency a better idea about whether a candidate has the qualities they are looking for in officers. If a pattern of behavior or posts raises concerns, the agency makes a point to dig a little deeper during the background investigation.

TECHNOLOGY IN COMMUNITY POLICING

MOBILE MULTIMODAL BIOMETRICS

In the decade since the 9/11 terrorist attacks, new emphasis has been placed on biometrics and priority given to making that technology more accessible to those on the front lines of national security efforts:

Very small, smartphone-based mobile devices with biometric capabilities are also in early development at this point. The familiar form factor of a handheld device is leading to increased acceptance by law enforcement for suspect identification in the field (early adoption at this point).... The new mobile biometric devices allow first responders, police, military, and criminal justice organizations to collect biometric data with a handheld device on a street corner or in a remote area and then wirelessly send it for comparison to other samples on watch lists and databases in near real-time.

Identities can be determined quickly without having to take a subject to a central facility to collect his or her biometrics, which is not always practical.

Source: National Science and Technology Council. (2011, September). *The National Biometrics Challenge*. Washington, DC: Author, Subcommittee on Biometrics and Identity Management. Retrieved September 14, 2016, from https://www.fbi.gov/file-repository/about-us-cjis-fingerprints_biometrics-biometric-center-of-excellences-biometricschallenge2011.pdf

A March 2011 survey of law enforcement agencies revealed (*Police Executive Research Forum*, 2012):

- 71 percent of responding agencies reported having in-car video recording capability, and 25 percent of all the responding agencies have video cameras in *all* of their police cars.

- 23 percent of the responding agencies reported that they are able to stream video feeds from fixed surveillance cameras into police vehicles.

- 71 percent of the responding agencies said they use license plate readers (LPRs) that can automatically scan hundreds of vehicle tags per hour and trigger alerts—for example, when the device spots a stolen vehicle or a vehicle registered to a person who is the subject of an arrest warrant.

- 83 percent of responding agencies reported using global positioning system (GPS) devices to track the movements of criminal suspects, and 69 percent reported using GPS to determine the location of police vehicles. Tracking police vehicles can be useful for quickly dispatching officers who are closest to a crime scene, identifying the location of an officer who is injured and needs assistance, and managing officer deployments.

A caution: Agencies must be aware that the use of technology is becoming increasingly scrutinized by the courts as a potential Fourth Amendment search issue. In *United States v. Jones* (2012), the Supreme Court held that placing a GPS tracker on a suspect's car was a search and required a warrant. More recently, the Court delivered a similar ruling in *Torrey Dale Grady v. North Carolina* (2015), affirming that the government's attachment of a tracking device to a person, a car, or any other personal effect amounts to a search and is, thus, protected by the Fourth Amendment.

The PERF survey also revealed that social media and Web sites are transforming the way law enforcement agencies communicate with the community, with 74 percent of surveyed agencies reporting they use Facebook, 57 percent use Twitter, 34 percent use YouTube, and 34 percent use Nixle (*Police Executive Research Forum,* 2012). Social media not only helps police receive tips and other information from the public but can also help in criminal investigations; 89 percent of agencies reported monitoring social media to identify investigative leads, such as reviewing the Facebook or Twitter pages of known or suspected gang members for current photos and other incriminating information posted about illegal activity. Despite these notable benefits of social media to law enforcement, such technology has also presented challenges. For example, 57 percent of the responding agencies said they already have experienced disputes or controversies regarding officers' personal postings on social media sites (Police Executive Research Forum, 2012).

Although new technologies continue to be developed and applied to policing, other crime prevention methods rely on more conventional, low-tech measures such as locks, lights, and community links—all common elements in crime prevention through environmental design, or CPTED.

CRIME PREVENTION THROUGH ENVIRONMENTAL DESIGN

In 1971, C. Ray Jeffrey coined the phrase *Crime Prevention Through Environmental Design (CPTED)*, and since then, it has become a popular strategy for dealing with crime with some proven successes. According to this approach, the "proper design and effective use of the built environment can lead to a reduction in the fear and incidence of crime and an improvement in the quality of life" (Crowe, 2000). CPTED focuses on reducing crime opportunities and on promoting positive social behavior but does not attempt to change the motivation of individual perpetrators.

CPTED has three major components: target hardening, changes to the physical environment, and community building. **Target hardening** refers to making potential objectives of criminals more difficult to obtain. The three main devices used for target hardening are improved locks, alarm systems, and security cameras. Most people do not object to locks and alarm systems properly used, but some have "Big Brother" concerns about surveillance cameras.

target hardening
Refers to making potential objectives of criminals more difficult to obtain through the use of improved locks, alarm systems, and security cameras.

Changes to the physical environment often include increased lighting, which has been a means of increasing security for centuries. Other changes usually involve removing items that give potential offenders the ability to hide—for example, dense vegetation, high shrubs, walls, and fences.

Community building, the third element of CPTED, can have the greatest impact on how individuals perceive the livability of their neighborhood. Community building seeks to increase residents' sense of ownership of the neighborhood and of who does and does not belong there. Community building techniques can include social events such as fairs or neighborhood beautification projects.

In addition to the trio of major components, CPTED is defined by five underlying principles: natural surveillance, access management, territoriality, physical maintenance, and order maintenance (Centers for Disease Control and Prevention, 2016). The Centers for Disease Control and Prevention (CDC) is studying how these principles of CPTED can be applied to school violence prevention, focusing on three geographic areas of schools: grounds, buildings, and interiors:

1. *Natural surveillance* refers to the placement of physical features that maximize visibility. Example: The strategic use of windows that look out on the school entrance so that students can see into the school and know that others can see them.

2. *Access management* involves guiding people by using signs, well-marked entrances and exits, and landscaping. It may also include limiting access to certain areas by using real or symbolic barriers. Example: Landscaping that reduces access to unsupervised locations on the school grounds.

3. *Territoriality* is defined by a clear delineation of space, expressions of pride or ownership, and the creation of a welcoming environment. Example: Motivational signs, displays of student art, and the use of school colors to create warmth and express pride.

4. *Physical maintenance* includes repair and general upkeep of space. Example: Removing graffiti in restrooms in a timely manner and making the necessary repairs to restrooms, light fixtures, and stairways to maintain safety and comfort.

5. *Order maintenance* involves attending to minor unacceptable acts and providing measures that clearly state acceptable behavior. Example: Maintaining an obvious adult presence during all times that student's transition from one location to another.

> **L05**
>
> CPTED has three major components: target hardening, changes to the physical environment, and community building. By emphasizing the systematic analysis of crime in a particular location, CPTED directly supports community policing by providing crime prevention strategies tailored to solve specific problems.

Applying the principles of CPTED can potentially benefit schools by:

- Creating a warm and welcoming environment
- Fostering a sense of physical and social order
- Creating a sense of ownership by students
- Sending positive messages to students
- Maximizing the presence of authority figures
- Minimizing opportunities for out-of-sight activities
- Managing access to all school areas

The CDC notes: "Environmental design alone will not prevent all violent acts within schools. However, CPTED is a promising prevention strategy that, if shown to be effective, may lead to reducing fear among students and teachers, to more positive social interactions, and to safer schools" (CDC, 2016).

Glass doors or doors with windows right next to them present an easy access opportunity for burglars.

altrendo images/Juice Images/Getty Images

The Importance of Place   Eck (1997) has studied the importance of place to crime and disorder, noting that most places do not have crime while, conversely, most crime is concentrated in and around a small number of places. Eck's definition of **place** is specific: "A place is a very small area reserved for a narrow range of functions, often controlled by a single owner and separated from the surrounding area." This concept of place is similar to that of a hot spot.

Eck theorizes that preventing crime at these high-crime places can bring about a significant reduction in the total crime throughout the nation and suggests that **opportunity blocking**—changes to make crime more difficult, riskier, less rewarding, or less excusable—may have a greater direct effect on offenders than other crime prevention strategies. Eck notes two side effects from place-focused opportunity blocking efforts.

Displacement, in which offenders simply change the location of their crimes, has been discussed as a potential negative of prevention efforts. However, concern about displacement may cause a benefit of prevention efforts to be overlooked—that is, diffusion. **Diffusion** of prevention benefits occurs when criminals believe that the opportunity blocking of one type of criminal activity is also aimed at other types of criminal activity. For example, when magnetic tags were put in books in a university library, book theft declined, as did the theft of audiotapes and videotapes, which were not tagged. According to Eck (1997): "Diffusion is the flip side of the coin of crime contagion. **Contagion** [emphasis added] suggests that when offenders notice one criminal opportunity they often detect similar opportunities they have previously overlooked. Crime then spreads. The broken window theory is an example of a contagion theory. Thus under some circumstances offenders may be uncertain about the scope of prevention efforts and avoid both the blocked opportunities and similar unblocked opportunities. When this occurs, prevention may spread."

place

A very small area reserved for a narrow range of functions, often controlled by a single owner and separated from the surrounding area.

opportunity blocking

Changes to make crime more difficult, risky, less rewarding, or less excusable; one of the oldest forms of crime prevention.

diffusion

Occurs when criminals believe that the opportunity blocking of one type of criminal activity is also aimed at other types of criminal activity.

contagion

Suggests that when offenders notice one criminal opportunity they often detect similar opportunities they have previously overlooked; crime then spreads; the broken window theory is an example.

The Risk Factor Prevention Paradigm   Risk factors have been broadly defined as "those characteristics, variables, or hazards that, if present for a given individual, make it more likely that this individual, rather than someone selected from the general population, will develop a disorder" (Mrazek & Haggerty, 1994, p. 127). As Shader (2002, p. 1) explains:

> In recent years, the juvenile justice field has adopted an approach from the public health arena in an attempt to understand the causes of delinquency and work toward its prevention (Farrington, 2000). For example, the medical community's efforts to prevent cancer and heart disease have successfully targeted risk factors (Farrington). To evaluate a patient's risk of suffering a heart attack, a doctor commonly asks for the patient's medical history, family history, diet, weight, and exercise level because each of these variables has an effect on the patient's cardiac health. After this risk assessment, the doctor may suggest ways for the patient to reduce his or her risk factors. Similarly, if a youth possesses certain risk factors, research indicates that these factors will increase his or her chance of becoming a delinquent. A risk assessment may aid in determining the type of intervention that will best suit the youth's needs and decrease his or her risk of offending. Farrington (2000) calls this recent

LO6

Two side effects of place-focused opportunity blocking efforts are displacement of crime and diffusion of prevention benefits.

The **risk factor prevention paradigm** seeks to identify key risk factors for offending and then implement prevention methods designed to counteract them.

risk factor prevention paradigm
Seeks to identify key risk factors for offending and then implement prevention methods designed to counteract them.

movement toward the public health model the "risk factor paradigm," the basic idea of which is to "identify the key risk factors for offending and tool prevention methods designed to counteract them."

National Emphasis on Community Policing and Crime Prevention

Although community policing occurs on the local level, it often takes funding from the federal level to get programs off the ground and flying or to keep them going after they have become established. To encourage jurisdictions across the country to make the paradigm shift to community policing, several national organizations have been created that offer financial support, training opportunities, and other types of resources. Two federal programs established within the Department of Justice focus on community policing and crime prevention.

The Office of Community Oriented Policing Services The Violent Crime Control and Law Enforcement Act of 1994 authorized $8.8 billion over 6 years for grants to local police agencies to add 100,000 officers and promote community policing. To implement this law, Attorney General Janet Reno created the Office of Community Oriented Policing Services (or COPS Office) in the Department of Justice. Although originally the COPS Office was designed to go out of business after 6 years, its success at increasing the numbers of police officers across the country and in raising awareness of community policing resulted in Congress extending the life of the agency.

COPS provides grants to tribal, state, and local law enforcement agencies to hire and train community policing professionals, acquire and deploy cutting-edge crime-fighting technologies, and develop and test innovative policing strategies. COPS-funded training helps advance community policing at all levels of law enforcement—from line officers to law enforcement executives—as well as others in the criminal justice field. In the two decades since its inception, the COPS Office has invested approximately $14.7 billion to add officers to the nation's streets and schools, enhance crime-fighting technology, support crime prevention initiatives, and provide training and technical assistance to help advance community policing. The programs and initiatives developed have provided funding to more than 13,000 of the nation's 18,000 law enforcement agencies. Through these efforts, the COPS Office has helped create a community policing infrastructure across the nation (Office of Community Oriented Policing Services, 2015).

Approximately 81 percent of the nation's population is served by law enforcement agencies practicing community policing. Because community policing is by definition inclusive, COPS training also reaches state and local government leaders and the citizens they serve. This broad range of programs helps COPS offer agencies support in virtually every aspect of law enforcement.

The Community Policing Consortium Another organization that provides assistance is the Community Policing Consortium, a partnership of five police organizations: the International Association of Chiefs of Police (IACP), the

National Organization of Black Law Enforcement Executives (NOBLE), the National Sheriffs' Association (NSA), the Police Executive Research Forum (PERF), and the Police Foundation (PF). The consortium, funded and administered by COPS within the Department of Justice, provides training throughout the United States, particularly to agencies that receive COPS grants. The training materials emphasize community policing from a local perspective, community partnerships, problem solving, strategic planning, and assessment. Their quick-read periodicals, *The Community Policing Exchange, Sheriff Times*, and the *Information Access Guide,* relate real-life experiences of community policing practitioners across the country.

The Weed and Seed Program   Until recently, a third federal initiative was the weed and seed program, launched in 1991 with three sites. Over its 20-year life span, the program grew to include 300 sites nationwide, ranging in size from several neighborhood blocks to several square miles, with populations ranging from 3,000 to 50,000. The program, which was not funded in 2012, strategically linked concentrated, enhanced law enforcement efforts to identify, arrest, and prosecute violent offenders, drug traffickers, and other criminals operating in the target areas and community policing (weeding) with human services—including after-school, weekend, and summer youth activities; adult literacy classes; and parental counseling—and neighborhood revitalization efforts to prevent and deter further crime (seeding).

The Weed and Seed Data Center noted that four fundamental principles underlie the Weed and Seed strategy: collaboration, coordination, community participation, and leveraging of resources. And although funding for the national program has been discontinued, countless Weed and Seed initiatives have taken hold in local jurisdictions across the country, many of which continue to be funded year after year as municipalities realize the benefit of such programming to the quality of life in their communities.

Partnerships to Prevent or Reduce Crime and Disorder

The specific needs of communities across the country, and the crime and disorder problems that plague them, are as diverse as the communities themselves. One strength of community policing is being able to adapt to these specific community needs and find creative solutions to each area's unique problems. The discussion now turns to examine various partnerships that have been formed to address specific crime and disorder problems experienced by jurisdictions throughout the United States.

ADDRESSING SPECIFIC PROBLEMS

As has been stressed throughout this text, problem solving is a key component of community policing. An invaluable resource for communities engaged in problem solving is the Center for Problem-Oriented Policing, a nonprofit organization comprising affiliated police practitioners, researchers, and universities dedicated to the advancement of problem-oriented policing. Its mission is to advance the concept and practice of problem-oriented policing in open

LO8
Partnerships to prevent or reduce crime and disorder include business anticrime groups, local government–community crime prevention coalitions, community coalitions, grassroots organizations, and landlords and residents in public housing using advances in technology and celebrating community successes.

and democratic societies. It does so by making readily accessible information about ways in which police can more effectively address specific crime and disorder problems.

Another invaluable resource is the COPS Office, introduced earlier. This office has published a series of problem-oriented guides, which focus on understanding and preventing specific community problems. Several of the most recent guides are cited in the following discussion. The COPS Office also provides funding for community policing initiatives and hiring and provides training through its regional community policing institutes.

Preventing Burglary in Public Housing

Public housing complexes, because of the density of people with common access to buildings, often show higher than average crime rates (Eck, 1997). Restricting pedestrian access and movement is key to reducing burglary in such places. A second strategy is target hardening by providing locks and improved security to access points. A third approach is to make burglary targets unattractive to offenders. Focusing on residences with previous burglaries is effective, as is focusing on residences surrounding burgled dwellings, as data show that locations that have been targeted once for crime are often hit again later (Eck, 1997). Focusing only on those living around at-risk places rather than an entire neighborhood is called **cocoon neighborhood watch**.

cocoon neighborhood watch

Focusing on only those living around at-risk places rather than an entire neighborhood.

Preventing Burglary and Theft at Construction Sites

Construction site burglary has been recognized as a significant problem in the United States and elsewhere in the world, with an estimated $1 billion to $4 billion worth of materials, tools, and construction equipment stolen every year in the United States alone (Boba & Santos, 2006). The National Equipment Register (NER), which helps law enforcement track down stolen equipment, reports more than 11,000 pieces of equipment were stolen in 2013 (Strawn, 2014). It is recommended that police establish cooperative working relationships with builders and that builders, in turn, share information about burglary problems and patterns, local building practices, and loss prevention efforts (Boba & Santos, 2006). If it can be established that certain houses are at high risk for victimization, response measures can be concentrated at those locations.

Specific responses to reduce construction site burglary include improving builder practices: limiting the number of construction sites supervised, coordinating delivery and installation, screening and training workers and subcontractors, limiting the hiring of subcontractors, having a tracking system for tools, encouraging hiring loss prevention personnel, hiring on-site private security patrols, and establishing an employee hotline to report crime.

Target hardening measures are also recommended, including improving lighting, installing and monitoring closed-circuit television, installing alarm systems, using portable storage units, installing fencing, marking property, installing global positioning satellite locater chips, and displaying crime prevention signage (Strawn, 2014). Other high-tech ways to protect equipment and control construction site theft are to install geo-fencing and radio frequency identification (RFID) systems, use equipment with keyless ignition/transponder chip keys, and monitor the site through drone surveillance (iSqFt, 2016).

Preventing Theft of and from Vehicles

Thefts of and from vehicles might be prevented by hiring parking attendants, improving surveillance at deck and lot entrances and exits, hiring dedicated security patrols, installing and monitoring CCTV systems, improving the lighting, securing the perimeter, installing entrance barriers and electronic access, and arresting and prosecuting persistent offenders.

Many police departments furnish citizens with information on how to prevent auto theft. Information may be provided in the form of pamphlets, newspaper stories, public service announcements on television, or speeches to civic organizations. The two main messages of anti–car theft programs are to not leave the keys in the car ignition and to lock the car.

These messages are conveyed in a variety of ways, from stickers on dashboards to posters warning that leaving keys in the ignition is a violation of the law if the car is parked on public property. In addition, leaving one's keys in the ignition is an invitation to theft, could become a contributing cause of some innocent person's injury or death, and could raise the owner's insurance rates.

New York City has developed a voluntary anti–auto theft program that enlists the aid of motorists. The Combat Auto Theft (CAT) program allows the police to stop any car marked with a special decal between 1 A.M. and 5 A.M. Car owners sign a consent form affirming that they do not normally drive between 1 A.M. and 5 A.M., the peak auto theft hours. Those who participate in the program waive their rights to search and seizure protection.

Preventing Robberies at Automated Teller Machines

Automated teller machines, or ATMs, were first introduced in the late 1960s in the United States and now can be found almost everywhere. However, bank customers sometimes trade safety for convenience because the most recently available data show the overall rate of ATM-related crime is between one per 1 million and one per 3.5 million transactions (Scott, 2001a; Weider, 2013). Scott (2001a) presents the following general conclusions about ATM robbery:

- Most are committed by a lone offender, using some type of weapon, against a lone victim.
- Most occur at night, with the highest risk between midnight and 4 A.M.
- Most involve robbing people of cash after they have made a withdrawal.
- Robberies are somewhat more likely to occur at walk-up ATMs than at drive-through ATMs.
- About 15 percent of victims are injured. The average loss is between $100 and $200.

Specific responses to reduce ATM robberies include altering lighting, landscaping, and location; installing mirrors on ATMs; installing ATMs in police stations; providing ATM users with safety tips; installing CCTV; installing devices to allow victims to summon police during a robbery; and setting daily cash withdrawal limits (Scott, 2001a).

Preventing Witness Intimidation

People who are witnesses to or victims of crime are sometimes reluctant to report criminal offenses or to assist in their investigation. This reluctance may be in response to a perceived or actual threat of retaliation by the offender(s) or their associates. Dedel (2006) points out that historically witness intimidation is most closely associated with organized crime and domestic violence, but recently it has occurred in investigations of drug offenses, gang violence, and other types of crime.

An effective strategy to prevent witness intimidation usually requires multiagency partnerships including the police, prosecutors, and other agencies such as public housing, public benefits, and social service agencies. The strategy should also consider how to limit liability should the witness actually be harmed. Dedel (2006) suggests liability can be limited in several ways:

- Taking reports of intimidation seriously and engaging in the defined process for protecting witnesses
- Promising only those security services that can reasonably be provided
- Documenting all offers of assistance and all efforts to protect witnesses, along with the acceptance or refusal of such assurance
- Making sure witnesses understand the circumstances under which protections will be withdrawn and documenting all decisions to withdraw security

Specific responses to reducing intimidation by protecting witnesses include minimizing the risk of identification witnesses face when reporting crime or offering statements; protecting the anonymity of witnesses; using alarms and other crime prevention devices; reducing the likelihood of contact between witnesses and offenders; transporting witnesses to and from work and school; supporting witnesses; keeping witnesses and defendants separated at the courthouse; and relocating witnesses, either temporarily, for a short term, or permanently through the Federal Witness Security Program (Dedel, 2006).

Strategies to deter intimidators include admonishing them and explaining the laws concerning intimidation, requesting high bail and no-contact orders, increasing penalties for intimidation, and prosecuting intimidators. Increasing patrols in a targeted area or compelling witnesses to testify is usually ineffective. Most states have material witness laws that allow the arrest and detention of a person who refuses to provide information in court. Dedel (2006, p. 32) recommends: "Because of concerns for the rights of victims and the lack of proof that compelling witnesses to testify is effective, this should be the option of last resort."

Preventing Identity Theft

Americans worry more about becoming a victim of identity theft than they do about any other crime, including terrorism and murder (*Sourcebook of Criminal Justice Statistics Online*, 2011). Data from the Bureau of Justice Statistics (BJS) indicate that an estimated 17.6 million Americans, or roughly 7 percent of U.S. residents age 16 or older, were victims of identity theft in 2014 (Harrell, 2015). Most (86%) of the cases of identity theft involved the misuse of an existing credit card or bank account, approximately 4 percent of victims had their personal information stolen and used to open a new account or for other fraudulent activity, and 7 percent of victims experienced multiple types of identity theft during the most recent incident, findings that were similar to those reported in 2012 (Harrell, 2015).

The majority of U.S. residents (85%) reported taking actions to prevent identity theft, including checking credit reports, shredding documents with personal information, and changing passwords on financial accounts. Most victims of identity theft discovered the crime when their financial institution contacted them about suspicious activity (45%) or when they noticed fraudulent charges on their account (18%), most did not know how the offender obtained their information, and almost all (9 in 10) knew nothing about the offender. Four commonly recognized types of identity theft are described in Figure 10.1.

Until recently, victims had great difficulty in getting reports of identity theft from the police. However, in response to growing media coverage and congressional testimony concerning identity theft, the IACP adopted a resolution in 2000 urging all police departments to provide incident reports and other assistance to identity theft victims. In fact, the Federal Trade Commission (FTC) has issued a memorandum to all police officers stating that, under the federal Fair Credit Reporting Act (FCRA), a detailed police report

Figure 10.1	The Four Types of Identity Theft	
	Financial Gain	**Concealment**
High Commitment (lots of planning)	*Organized:* A fraud ring systematically steals personal information and uses it to generate bank accounts, obtain credit cards, etc. *Individual:* The offender sets up a look-alike Internet Web site for a major company; spams consumers, luring them to the site by saying their account information is needed to clear up a serious problem; steals the personal/financial information the consumer provides; and uses it to commit identity theft.	*Organized:* Terrorists obtain false visas and passports to avoid being traced after committing terrorist acts.* *Individual:* The offender assumes another's name to cover up past crimes or avoid capture over many years.
Opportunistic (low commitment)	An apartment manager uses personal information from rental applications to open credit card accounts.	The offender uses another's name and ID when stopped or arrested by police.

*An Algerian national facing U.S. charges of identity theft allegedly stole the identities of 21 members of a Cambridge, Massachusetts, health club and transferred the identities to one of the people convicted in the failed 1999 plot to bomb the Los Angeles International Airport.

Source: Graeme Newman. *Identity Theft.* Washington, DC: Community Oriented Policing Services Office, 2004.

is required before victims of identity theft can claim certain rights under the law (Federal Trade Commission, n.d.). By law, a victim can only assert his or her rights if the police report specifies which accounts and information on the credit report resulted from the identity theft. The FTC has made available online an ID Theft Complaint form to help police gather all of the victim's information required by law.

Addressing Domestic Violence

Domestic disputes are some of the most common calls for police service. Many domestic disputes do not involve violence, but the COPS Office has a guide discussing those that do (Sampson, 2007). The guide helps police analyze and respond to their local problem.

In the United States, domestic violence accounts for about 20 percent of the nonfatal violent crime women experience. Through the community policing philosophy and its practices, some law enforcement agencies are seeking to improve their effectiveness in dealing with the problem of domestic violence by forming police–community partnerships to enhance their response options. PERF, with funding from the COPS Office, explored the nature, function, and impact of such police–community partnerships. The research shows that partnerships between the police and community residents and agencies have improved the way agencies communicate with each other and the way they focus their energies on improving the safety of victims of domestic violence. This publication highlights such initiatives around the country that can be replicated to better address domestic violence.

Preventing Street Prostitution

Street prostitution is a sign of neighborhood disorder and attracts strangers, drug dealers, pimps, and other criminals into a neighborhood. Prostitutes, often addicted to drugs and/or infected with the human immunodeficiency virus (HIV) or other sexually transmitted diseases (STDs), wait on street corners for customers from more orderly and affluent neighborhoods, who cruise the streets and frequently assume any females they see to be prostitutes. Women residents of the neighborhood become afraid to wait for a bus or walk to a store. Parents do not want their children exposed to the problem and worry about the dangerous trash (used condoms and needles) left on public and private property. Whereas prostitution has often been a low priority for police, it is a high-priority issue for affected neighborhoods (Scott & Dedel, 2006b).

Traditional responses have been largely ineffective. Basically consisting of arrest and prosecution, they include neighborhood "sweeps," in which as many prostitutes as possible are arrested and sporadic arrests of "johns" are conducted. Community policing has spawned a multitude of other responses, many of which have proved more effective. Some responses include establishing a very visible police presence; holding public protests against prostitution; educating and warning prostitutes and clients; targeting the worst offenders; obtaining restraining orders against prostitutes; suspending government aid to prostitutes; imposing curfews on prostitutes; exposing clients

CRITICAL THINKING

The Center for Problem-Oriented Policing has an excellent scenario in which to put your SARA problem-solving skills to use to address a fictitious but realistic situation involving street prostitution. Your task will be to analyze and correctly assess the unique issues in a community and then assemble the most appropriate responses. The module, accessible at http://www.popcenter.org/learning/prostitution/intro/default.cfm, was written by Michael Scott and Bob Heimberger and developed by the SUNY Professional Development Program and will take 1–2 hours to complete successfully.

In this module, you will assume the role of a public safety consultant to the mayor. Your task is to define the prostitution problem in Central City and present a plan for dealing with it. In Part 1, you must thoroughly analyze the problem. If your analysis is sufficient, you will be allowed to proceed to Part 2 and given the go-ahead to develop your plan. During the process, you will have two budgets allocated, one for your analysis (Part 1), and one for your response plan (Part 2). Your spending will be tracked and displayed.

Source: Scott, M., & Heimberger, B. (n.d.). *Street Prostitution Interactive Module.* Albany, NY: Center for Problem-Oriented Policing.

to humiliating publicity; notifying those with influence over a client's conduct (employers, spouses, etc.); restricting a client's ability to drive by vehicle confiscation or drivers license revocation; helping prostitutes to quit; encouraging prostitutes to report serious crime; providing prostitutes with information about known dangerous clients; diverting traffic by closing alleys, streets, and parking lots; providing enhanced lighting; securing abandoned buildings; and holding property owners responsible when their property is being used for prostitution (Scott & Dedel, 2006b).

As more and more police departments develop their own Web sites, many are posting online photos of Johns and others involved in the prostitution trade. For example, the Canton (Ohio) Police Department's Web site posts numerous photos, preceded by this statement:

> The following individuals were arrested by the Canton Police Department and convicted in Canton Municipal Court for either soliciting for prostitution or patronizing prostitution. This service is provided as a deterrent to prostitution in Canton, Ohio. Our citizens deserve an environment that promotes health, safety, and stability.

Preventing Assaults in and Around Bars

Assaults in and around bars are a frequent problem in large cities as well as small towns. Most of these assaults are alcohol-related, but some are not. The majority occur on weekend nights at a relatively small number of places (Scott & Dedel, 2006a).

In addition to alcohol, factors that contribute to aggression and violence in bars include the type of establishment, the concentration of bars, the closing time, aggressive bouncers, a high proportion of young male strangers, price discounting of drinks, continued service to drunken patrons, crowding and lack of comfort, competitive situations, a low ratio of staff to patrons, lack of good entertainment, unattractive décor and dim lighting, tolerance for disorderly conduct, availability of weapons, and low levels of police enforcement and regulation.

An effective strategy to address the problem of violence in and around bars requires a broad-based coalition incorporating the interests of the community, the bars, and the government (Scott & Dedel, 2006a). In addition, any response strategy should address as many identified risk factors as possible, such as the practices of serving and patterns of consumption, the physical comfort of the environment, the overall permissiveness of the environment, and the availability of public transportation to disperse crowds after bars have closed. Scott and Dedel (2006a) recommend combining two groups of responses to address the problem: (1) responses to reduce how much alcohol patrons drink and (2) responses to make the bar safer.

Reducing Alcohol Consumption Alcohol consumption can be reduced by establishing responsible beverage service programs including monitoring drinking to prevent drunkenness, promoting slower drinking rates, prohibiting underage drinking, providing reduced-alcohol or nonalcoholic beverages, requiring or encouraging food services with alcohol services, and discouraging alcohol price discounts. Additional measures include establishing and enforcing server liability laws and reducing the concentration or number of bars (Scott & Dedel, 2006a).

Making Bars Safer Bars can be made safer by training staff to handle patrons nonviolently; establishing adequate transportation; relaxing or staggering bar closing times; controlling bar entrances, exits, and immediate surroundings; maintaining an attractive, comfortable, entertaining atmosphere; establishing and enforcing clear rules of conduct for bar patrons; reducing potential weapons and other sources of injury; communicating about incidents as they occur; and banning known troublemakers from bars.

Preventing Robbery of Taxi Drivers

The Occupational Safety and Health Administration (OSHA) has warned of the dangers of driving a taxi, noting that cab driving is among the top 10 occupations with the highest rates of homicide and nonfatal assaults and that cabbies are 60 times more likely than those working in other jobs to be killed on duty (Kloberdanz, 2016). According to the National Institute for Occupational Safety and Health (NIOSH), cab drivers have a higher risk of injury and murder on the job than those employed as police or security guards, mainly because of risk factors such as working alone with the public, handling cash, and working at night in high-crime areas. Random stabbings, shootings, and assaults are common hazards for taxi drivers, with records showing 700 cabbies were killed on duty between 1992 and 2006 (Kloberdanz, 2016).

OSHA recommendations for cab drivers, which include many of the safety measures advocated by the International Taxi Drivers Safety Council, are to install safety shields between the front seat and the back passenger area; equip cabs with silent alarms and "bandit lights," which are illuminated devices mounted outside of the cab to alert the police or others that the cab driver is in trouble; installing surveillance cameras inside the cab; equipping taxis with GPS tracking systems; implementing a cashless fare system that requires riders to pay with credit or debit cards to deter robberies; and using a Caller ID system to allow cab companies to identify the location of fares (Kloberdanz, 2016).

Additional strategies to keep taxi drivers safe focus on cabbie practices such as controlling who gets into the taxi, directing passengers to particular seats in the cab, finding out the destination before moving, sharing destination information with others, putting additional people in the cab, setting rules and asking those who do not meet them to get out, trying not to provoke passengers, knowing where to go for help late at night, allowing others to see inside the cab, limiting where the cab will make a drop off, staying in the cab unless it is safe to get out, and limiting injury when a robbery occurs by simply handing over the money and not fighting back (Smith, 2005).

Police practices might also help to prevent taxi driver robberies, including targeting repeat offenders and authorizing police stops without reasonable suspicion or probable cause if the drivers have signed an authorization to do so.

Finally, industry rules, regulations, and practices might include controlling the environment around taxi stands, eliminating passenger and driver conflict over money, setting driver competency standards, running driver safety training programs, screening passengers by the dispatching company, and exempting drivers from seat belt use.

Preventing Violent Confrontations with People with Mental Illness

The importance of communicating effectively with individuals who are mentally ill and partnering with mental health professionals was discussed in Chapter 6. Among the most important partners in working with violent individuals who are mentally ill is the mental health community, including emergency hospitals to which police may take those in crisis. It is widely recognized that traditional police responses to violent individuals are often not effective with those who are mentally ill. Among the responses suggested are training generalist police officers; providing more information to patrol officers; using less-lethal weapons; deploying specialized police officers as members of a crisis intervention team (CIT); or deploying specialized nonpolice responders. Whichever approach is selected, training of police officers is a crucial element in achieving a successful response and is most effective when it includes consultation with mental health professionals and other social service providers (Tucker, Van Hasselt, Vecchi, & Browning, 2011).

A partnership approach to dealing effectively with violent individuals who are mentally ill should involve stakeholders—for example, initiating assisted outpatient treatment, establishing crisis response sites, establishing jail-based diversion, and establishing mental health courts.

Preventing Crimes against Businesses

The annual cost of crime against business is in the billions of dollars. Such victimization hurts business owners, employees, neighbors, customers, and the general public (Chamard, 2006). One way to address the problem of crimes against businesses is to develop police–business partnerships. Such partnerships can take a variety of forms, ranging from an individual business working with the police to address a specific problem to an area-wide partnership including businesses from a particular geographic location. The partnerships can also be issue specific or business specific. One of the most common police–individual business partnerships involves police assisting retailers in preventing shoplifting.

Police–Individual Business Partnerships to Prevent Shoplifting   Shoplifting might be prevented by improving store layout and displays, upgrading security, establishing early warning systems (to notify other stores about shoplifters), banning known shoplifters, installing and monitoring CCTV systems, using electronic article surveillance (EAS), and attaching ink tags to merchandise.

With EAS, a tag is attached to each piece of merchandise. When a person pays for an article, the tag is deactivated and removed by a checkout clerk. Tags that have not been removed or deactivated are detected at store exit gates, and an alarm is sounded. Ink tags, rather than setting off an alarm if not removed, ruin the merchandise to which they are attached when the offender tries to remove them.

Area-Specific Police–Business Partnerships   One approach to area-specific police–business partnerships is the business improvement district (BID), a consortium of property and business owners who voluntarily pay a special assessment in addition to their regular taxes. The funds from the special assessment are spent on beautification, security, marketing, or whatever the membership decides is needed to enhance the viability of the area. Goals usually include raising the standards of public spaces; reducing crime, social disorder, and the fear of victimization; improving public transportation; generating sales and revenues for area businesses; and increasing the number of local jobs. The United States has an estimated 2,000 BIDs (Chamard, 2006). Although no solid research has been conducted, anecdotal evidence suggests this approach holds promise.

Issue-Specific Police–Business Partnerships   Issue-specific partnerships focus on a certain type of crime or a particular situation, often a public order problem such as public drinking or panhandling that has reached the point where intervention is required (Chamard, 2006). Such partnerships need not last after the specific problem has been solved.

Business-Specific Police–Business Partnerships   Business-specific partnerships are often formed in response to an outbreak of crimes targeting a particular type of business such as robberies of banks or convenience stores (Chamard, 2006). Others are formed to address specific chronic problems such as safety in public parking lots and garages.

IDEAS IN PRACTICE

IDENTITY THEFT AND FRAUD PREVENTION PROGRAM

Beaverton, Oregon, Police Department Wins Webber Seavey Award

The Webber Seavey Award recognizes innovative police programs from around the world and is co-sponsored by the International Association of Chiefs of Police (IACP) and Motorola, Inc.

The Beaverton, Oregon, Police Department began its identity theft and fraud prevention program in 2003, after analyzing the increasing case load they were seeing. Identity theft and fraud cases were up 54 percent over the previous 4 years, similar to what police departments all over the country were experiencing. Beaverton police applied for and won a $238,375 federal grant from the Department of Justice to tackle the community's identity theft problem. They formed a planning committee, which decided to direct their efforts toward enhanced investigations, helping victims, and educating the public on protecting themselves from these crimes.

"The department formed a Special Enforcement Unit and during its first 2 years, members of the unit made 494 fraud-related arrests, prevented the loss of more than $701,000 from citizens and businesses, and recovered $33,170," said Michelle Harrold, a management analyst with the Beaverton police.

Partnerships for this initiative also included a banking industry group to help police solve a case involving more than $126,450, and a marketing firm to assist in outreach.

Careful to make their efforts proactive, the department provided targeted training to officers and volunteers to enable them to assist victims of identity theft and fraud. They also developed identity theft and fraud prevention literature that officers gave out to residents and local businesses, and they posted prevention information and tips on their Web site. "The team really hit the streets and worked with our local retailers to try to change habits that put their businesses at risk," Harrold said.

The police department conducted free workshops and educational seminars for the community. Some seminars were designed especially for the business community in an effort to make them more aware of business practices that put them and their customers at risk.

Because thieves often search recycling and garbage for personal identifying information of potential victims, community members were informed that shredding sensitive documents with a cross-cut shredder is a good preventative practice. The department recommended shredding paper containing personal information such as credit card statements, financial statements, preapproved credit card offers, old tax documents, checks, and household bills.

Going a step further, the police department provided free document shredding events for the public at which a commercial-sized shredding truck was available. Participants were allowed to bring up to three boxes of documents, per vehicle, to be shredded and were encouraged, at the same time, to bring canned food to donate to the Oregon Food Bank.

"We need to compliment the community for working with us. The key to our success is it's an ongoing program," said Beaverton Police Chief David Bishop.

Sources: The Bureau of Justice Statistics; the International Association of Chiefs of Police (IACP) Web site (http://www.theiacp.org); Christina Lent, "Police ID Theft Work Earns International Recognition," *Beaverton Valley Times*, October 26, 2006; David G. Bishop, "Identity Theft and Fraud Prevention Program," *The Police Chief*, May 2007.

PARTNERSHIPS IN ACTION AGAINST CRIME AND DISORDER

Partnerships across the country are working on reducing crime and disorder, some focusing on one specific area, and others taking more comprehensive approaches.

Norfolk, Virginia, cut homicides by more than 10 percent and has reduced overall crime rates citywide by 26 percent and in some neighborhoods by as much as 40 percent. A good share of the credit goes to Police Assisted Community Enforcement (PACE), a crime prevention initiative that works neighborhood by neighborhood in conjunction with teams of social, health, and family services agencies (the Family Assistance Services Team, or FAST) and public works and environmental agencies (Neighborhood Environmental Assistance Teams, or NEAT) to cut through red tape and help residents reclaim their neighborhoods (National Crime Prevention Council, 1995).

The Minnesota Crime Prevention Association enlisted the support of families, public officials, and 45 statewide and local organizations, including schools and churches, to wage a campaign against youth violence. Actions ranged from encouraging children and parents to turn off violent television shows to providing classroom training in violence prevention (National Crime Prevention Council, 1995).

In Trenton, New Jersey, a partnership of schools, parents, city leaders, and others led to a Safe Haven program in which the schools in the neighborhood became multipurpose centers after school hours for youth activities including sports, crafts, and tutoring. Children have flocked to the centers as a positive alternative to being at home alone after school or being at risk on the streets (National Crime Prevention Council, 1995).

Crime near a college campus in Columbus, Ohio, became an opportunity for a partnership formed by the City of Columbus, the State of Ohio, Ohio State University, the Franklin County Sheriff, and the Columbus Police. The Community Crime Patrol puts two-person, radio-equipped teams of observers into the neighborhoods near the campus during potential high-crime hours. A number of these paid, part-time observers are college students interested in careers in law enforcement (National Crime Prevention Council, 1995).

In Danville, Virginia, a partnership approach to working with public housing residents resulted in a 53-percent reduction in calls about fights, a 50-percent reduction in domestic violence calls, and a 9-percent reduction in disturbance calls. The Virginia Crime Prevention Association worked with the Danville Housing Authority to bring public housing residents, local law enforcement, social services, and other public agencies together into an effective, problem-solving group. Residents were at the heart of the group, identifying problems that were causing high rates of aggravated assault in the community and working to provide remedies such as positive alternatives for youths and social services and counseling for adults and children. Residents developed a code of conduct for the community, spelling out expectations for the behavior of those who live there (National Crime Prevention Council, 1995).

Boston's Neighborhood Justice Network, in partnership with the Council of Elders, the Jewish Memorial Hospital, the Boston Police Department, the Department of Public Health, and the Commission on Affairs of the Elderly, created a program to help reduce violence and other crimes against older people. It provides basic personal and home crime prevention education, assistance in dealing with city agencies, training in nonconfrontational tactics to avert street crime, and other helpful services that reduce both victimization and fear among the city's older residents (National Crime Prevention Council, 1995).

These are just a few of a wide range of programs designed by community groups that have changed the quality of life in small towns and large cities, in neighborhoods and housing complexes, in schools and on playgrounds. These groups have proved that there is strength in numbers and that partnerships can provide the community basis for correcting the problems and conditions that can lead to crime. They achieved success because the people involved developed the skills to work together effectively.

SUMMARY

Synergism occurs when individuals channel their energies toward a common purpose and accomplish together what they could not accomplish alone. It can greatly enhance community policing efforts to prevent or reduce crime and disorder. Crime prevention is a large part, and in fact a cornerstone, of community policing.

Traffic problems top the list of concerns of most neighborhoods and communities. Concerns include speeding in residential areas, street racing, red-light running, impaired drivers, and nonuse of seat belts.

Engineering responses to speeding include using traffic calming, posting warning signs and signals, conducting anti-speeding public awareness campaigns, informing complainants about actual speeds, and providing realistic driver training. Enforcement responses to speeding include (1) enforcing speeding laws, (2) enforcing speeding laws with speed cameras or photo radar, (3) using speed display boards, (4) arresting the worst offenders, and (5) having citizen volunteers monitor speeding.

Various community policing efforts to reduce citizens' fear of crime have included enhanced foot and vehicle patrol in high-crime neighborhoods, citizen patrols, neighborhood cleanup campaigns, community education and awareness programs, the placement of police substations in troubled neighborhoods, and the installation of closed-circuit video surveillance cameras.

One frequently used strategy is crime prevention through environmental design. CPTED has three major components: target hardening, changes to the physical environment, and community building. By emphasizing the systematic analysis of crime in a particular location, CPTED directly supports community policing by providing crime prevention strategies tailored to solve specific problems. Another approach to crime prevention is focusing on place.

Two side effects of place-focused opportunity blocking efforts are displacement of crime and diffusion of prevention benefits.

The risk factor prevention paradigm seeks to identify key risk factors for offending and then implement prevention methods designed to counteract them. It is useful in identifying strategies that might be effective for a specific community.

Partnerships to prevent or reduce crime and disorder include business anticrime groups, local government–community crime prevention coalitions, community coalitions, cooperation with grassroots organizations, and landlords and residents in public housing using advances in technology and celebrating community successes.

DISCUSSION QUESTIONS

1. What examples of synergy have you been a part of or witnessed?
2. What crime prevention programs are in your community? Have you participated in any of them?
3. Traffic calming techniques have gained wide support from some drivers but, at the same time, the anger of other drivers. What accounts for the differing perspectives?
4. How does CCTV work to prevent crime and reduce fear?
5. What could be the explanation for some CCTV applications not having the desired effect?

6. Name and explain the five principles underlying CPTED.

7. Because taxes pay for police to combat crime, why should citizens get involved?

8. Why is it so difficult to know the reason for rises and declines in crime?

9. Which do you feel merits the most attention from community policing: concerns about disorder, fear of crime, or crime itself?

CASES CITED

Torrey Dale Grady v. North Carolina, 575 U.S. ___ (2015)
United States v. Jones, 565 U.S. ___ (2012)

Community Policing and Drugs

11

Learning Objectives

Learning Objectives

LO1 Identify the drugs considered by the Drug Enforcement Administration to pose the greatest threat in the United States.

LO2 List the seven core components of the national drug control strategy.

LO3 Summarize the strategies that have been implemented to combat the drug problem in neighborhoods.

LO4 Name the federal grant programs aimed specifically at the drug problem.

LO5 Explain how the conservative and liberal crime control strategies differ.

Key Terms

binge drinking

closed drug market

conservative crime control

doctor shopping

drug diversion

gateway theory

liberal crime control

open drug market

In the late 1980s, G. Van Standifer designed a midnight basketball program in an attempt to reduce crime rates and drug-related activities in his community of Glen Arden, Maryland. Using statistics compiled over the recent years, Standifer decided to concentrate his efforts on 14–24-year-old males in the inner-city areas who had, historically, spent the summer months doing little more than finding trouble in the crime-ridden areas of the city. Standifer encouraged local youth to come shoot hoops instead of hanging around on street corners or associating with gang members. The idea was rooted in social control theory, which asserts that if someone becomes attached, involved, and committed to activities that are viewed as protective factors associated with crime, this individual will be less inclined to perpetrate or become a victim of crime.

Standifer's program grew across the United States, harvesting support and funding from local community members and businesses and eventually peaking with a midnight basketball national championship game in 1991. However, opponents of the program viewed basketball as a simple diversion to the overall problem and were reluctant to fund a sports program in efforts to reduce crime. While midnight basketball leagues remained throughout the country for years to follow, the overall appeal and, eventually, the effectiveness of the program took a back seat to other community policing initiatives thought to have greater potential for helping at-risk youth.

One such program was active in San Antonio, Texas, throughout the 1990s, but participation declined due to lack of support. However, with a refocused police department, an energized community, support from local businesses, and a federal grant from the Department of Education, the San Antonio Eastside Promise Neighborhood Midnight Basketball Program reemerged in 2012 in the city's eastside. The rules are simple: If you want to play, you need to stay out of trouble. The program runs from 11 P.M. to 1 A.M. and is focused on keeping 17–23-year old at-risk youth and young adults off the streets. The program has been effective in multiple facets. First, the program's primary goal of keeping at-risk citizens off the streets on the weekends has been largely successful. Second, the program has been able to teach teamwork through mentorships with experienced coaches and group leaders who foster individual support for participants. A third and unexpected benefit involves the increase in spectators, especially teenagers and young adults, who attend the events at times that, according to crime statistics, they would most likely otherwise be on the streets. While the program is experiencing a rebirth in San Antonio and is still in its infant stages, the police department, local businesses, community members, and even the San Antonio Spurs organization have praised the efforts as a way to reduce the drug problem and street-related crime in the area.

INTRODUCTION

The correlation between drugs and crime is well established. Drug users often commit crimes to support their habit. Drug dealers fight territorial wars over the drug market, making neighborhoods hazardous for all residents. Roughly half (51%) of federal inmates in 2010 were serving time for drug offenses, and about 18 percent of those in state prisons were serving time for drug offenses (Guerino, Harrison, & Sabol, 2012). Data from the National Center on Addiction and Substance Abuse show that of the more than 2.3 million people held in our nation's jails and prison, approximately two-thirds meet the medical diagnostic criteria for substance abuse addiction, yet only 11 percent are receiving any type of treatment while serving time behind bars, meaning they will likely continue their drug involvement upon release (National Center on Addiction and Drug Abuse, 2009). It follows that any effort to reduce the drug problem is likely to also reduce crime and disorder in a neighborhood and community.

THE CURRENT DRUG PROBLEM

The extent of the current drug problem is difficult to accurately pinpoint, although several survey tools have been designed to conduct annual assessments in an effort to gain insight into the situation. One such tool is the National Survey on Drug Use and Health (NSDUH), provided by the Center for Behavioral Health Statistics and Quality (CBHSQ), which is part of the Substance Abuse and Mental Health Services Administration (SAMHSA). The NSDUH obtains information on nine categories of "illicit" drugs: marijuana (including hashish), cocaine (including crack), heroin, hallucinogens, and inhalants, as well as the nonmedical use of prescription-type pain relievers, tranquilizers, stimulants, and sedatives. Nonmedical use refers to the use of prescription drugs without a prescription of the individual's own or simply for the experience or feeling the drugs caused. According to the 2014 NSDUH, an estimated 27.0 million people aged 12 or older—or roughly 1 in 10 Americans (10.2 percent)—used an illicit drug at least once in 2014 (CBHSQ, 2015). This estimate is higher than those for every year from 2002 through 2013 and continues to be driven primarily by the use of marijuana (22.2 million users) and nonmedical prescription pain relievers (4.3 million users) (CBHSQ, 2015). The NSDUH also reports that in 2014, approximately 21.5 million people aged 12 or older had experienced a substance use disorder (SUD) within the past year, including 17.0 million people with an alcohol use disorder, 7.1 million with an illicit drug use disorder, and 2.6 million who had both an alcohol use and an illicit drug use disorder.

One of the most reliable sources of information on the drug problem is *Monitoring the Future* (*MTF*), a national survey of drug use presented into two volumes—Volume I addresses drug use among secondary school students, and Volume II covers drug use among college students and adults ages 19–50. *MTF* is now entering its fifth decade, having been launched in 1975, and is funded by the National Institute on Drug Abuse (NIDA), one of the National Institutes of Health, under a series of investigator-initiated, competitive research grants made to the University of Michigan. Interestingly, and some-what in contrast to the findings of the NSDUH that indicate a rise in illicit drug use, the 2015 MTF shows decreasing use of a number of substances among the nation's youth, including cigarettes, alcohol, prescription opioid pain relievers, and synthetic cannabinoids ("synthetic marijuana"). Other drug use remains stable, including marijuana, with continued high rates of daily use reported among 12th graders and an ongoing decrease in the perception of its harm-fulness (Johnston, O'Malley, Miech, Bachman, & Schulenberg, 2016). Other highlights from the 2015 MTF survey include:

- Cigarette and alcohol use reached their lowest levels in the history of the study.
- Binge drinking (described as having five or more drinks in a row within the past 2 weeks) is 17.2 percent among seniors, down from 19.4 percent last year and down from peak rates in 1998 at 31.5 percent.
- Although use of marijuana remained essentially unchanged in 2015, mari-juana attitudes among students continued to move toward greater accep-tance. Perceived risk of smoking marijuana regularly declined in all three grades, significantly so in 12th grade.
- The psychotherapeutic drugs warrant special attention, given that they now make up a significantly larger part of the overall U.S. drug problem than was true 10–15 years ago. This is, in part, because use increased for many prescription drugs over that period, and in part because use of a number of street drugs has declined substantially since the mid- to late-1990s. It seems likely that young people are less concerned about the dan-gers of using these prescription drugs outside of medical regimen because they are widely used for legitimate purposes.
- Amphetamine use without a doctor's orders—currently the second most widely used class of illicit drugs after marijuana—continued a gradual decline in 2015 in all grades, though the 1-year declines did not reach statistical significance.
- Use of narcotics other than heroin without a doctor's orders (measured only in 12th grade) also continued a gradual decline begun after 2009.

- The use of these drugs showed little or no change from 2014 to 2015: hallucinogens, LSD specifically, hallucinogens other than LSD, inhalants, salvia, tranquilizers, cocaine, crack, powder cocaine, heroin use without a needle, methamphetamine, crystal methamphetamine, bath salts, OTC cough and cold medicines used to get high, and the club drugs GHB, Rohypnol, and ketamine.

- Most teens abusing prescription opioids report getting them from friends or family members. However, one-third report getting them from their own prescriptions, underscoring the need to monitor teens taking opioids and evaluate prescribing practices.

The Drug Enforcement Administration (DEA) publishes an annual *National Drug Threat Assessment* (NDTA), a comprehensive strategic summary of the threats posed to our nation's communities by transnational criminal organizations (TCOs) and the illicit drugs they distribute throughout the United States. The NDTA provides policymakers, law enforcement personnel, and prevention and treatment specialists with relevant strategic drug intelligence to help formulate counterdrug policies, establish law enforcement priorities, and allocate resources to the war on drugs. The most recent NDTA reports that more than 120 people die each day in the United States as a result of a drug overdose, and the number of deaths caused by controlled prescription drugs (CPDs) has outpaced those for cocaine and heroin combined (DEA, 2015b). Between late 2013 and 2014, more than 700 deaths across the United States were attributed to one specific CPD, fentanyl and its analogs. Fentanyl, a powerful synthetic opioid (pain killer), is often abused in the same manner as heroin but it is much more potent. Law enforcement agencies have also begun reporting that some opioid CPD abusers are beginning to use heroin as well. For these reasons, the DEA has ranked CPDs and heroin as the most significant drug threats to the United States (DEA, 2015b). Other major threats identified by the DEA are methamphetamine and marijuana.

Controlled Prescription Drugs

LO1
According to the DEA, the drugs currently considered to pose the greatest threat are CPDs, heroin, methamphetamine, and marijuana.

CPDs top the list of drug threats in the United States. More than half (53%) of nonmedical users of CPDs (pain relievers, tranquilizers, stimulants, and sedatives) age 12 years or older report that they got their drugs from a friend or a relative for free, and that most of those friends or relatives had obtained the CPDs from a single doctor (DEA, 2015b). As CPD users become more frequent abusers, they risk exposure to medical health care providers and law enforcement; consequently, CPD users often turn to buying drugs from street dealers or via the Internet. Such third-party sources often acquire their inventory through a variety of diversions tactics, such as doctor shopping, prescription fraud or forgery, employee theft (from pharmacies, hospitals, physician offices, and so on), nontherapeutic prescribing by rogue practitioners, and burglaries or armed robberies of pharmacies and drug distributors (DEA, 2015b).

One source of assistance for law enforcement is RxPatrol, a collaborative effort between the pharmaceutical industry and law enforcement that collects, analyzes, and disseminates pharmacy theft information, serving as a clearing-house of pertinent leads to the law enforcement community.

Although some data show that abuse of CPDs has lessened slightly, a tradeoff has been recognized, as the level of heroin use has begun to rise. Many CPD abusers have turned to heroin as a cheaper alternative to the high price of illicit CPDs or because they have been unable to obtain prescription drugs (DEA, 2015b).

Heroin

Heroin is a central nervous system (CNS) depressant that relieves pain and induces sleep. The drug is derived from the opium gum produced by poppy plants. Opium gum is converted to morphine in labs near the poppy farms, often in Asia and Latin America, and then to heroin in labs within or near the producing country. After importation, drug dealers cut, or dilute, the heroin before selling it to addicts.

According to the DEA, the threat posed by heroin is serious and has been steadily trending upward since 2007, with the population of heroin users doubling in number between 2007 and 2013 (DEA, 2015a). One reason heroin has become so problematic is because it is more pure and less expensive than it has been in the past. Higher purity levels allow users to smoke or snort heroin instead of injecting it, which has contributed to the drug's increasing popularity and attracted a broader, more diverse group of users (DEA, 2015a). Many OxyContin abusers have also migrated to heroin because OxyContin was reformulated to make it more difficult to inhale or inject. Finally, heroin presents a serious threat because it is far more deadly to its user population than other drugs. In 2013, 8,620 people died in the United States from heroin-related overdoses, nearly triple the number in 2010 (DEA, 2015a).

In response to the nationwide rise in overdoses caused by heroin and other prescription pain killers, many law enforcement agencies are now training officers to administer Naloxone, which also goes by the brand name Narcan, a drug that can reverse the effects of opioid overdose if administered in a timely manner. Although emergency medical technicians (EMTs) typically carry Naloxone, police officers often are the first responders in overdose cases. The Bureau of Justice Assistance (BJA) has created the Law Enforcement Naloxone Toolkit; more information about this resource is available on the BJA's National Training and Technical Assistance Center's website (https://www.bjatraining.org/tools/naloxone/Naloxone-Background).

Methamphetamine

Methamphetamine (meth), a stimulant that can be taken orally, smoked, injected, or snorted, has become a significant problem across the country, and its availability continues to increase (DEA, 2015b). According to the 2014 NSDUH, approximately 569,000 Americans use meth in any given month (CBHSQ, 2015). Effects of meth use include anxiety, confusion, insomnia, paranoia, aggression, visual and auditory hallucinations, mood disturbances, and delusions (SAMHSA, 2016). A SAMHSA Drug Abuse Warning Network (DAWN) report showed that hospital emergency room visits related to meth use rose from about 68,000 in 2007 to about 103,000 in 2011, and more than 60 percent of these cases involved the use of methamphetamine with at least one other substance.

The DEA notes that domestic methamphetamine production has decreased significantly since 2010, most likely as the result of several factors, including restrictions on precursor chemicals, such as pseudoephedrine/ ephedrine tablets, in the United States and the increased availability of Mexico-produced methamphetamine (DEA, 2015b). Most of the seized meth labs in 2014 were so-called "one pot" or "shake and bake" laboratories that produced small-quantity batches of methamphetamine, generally 2 ounces or less. The DEA also reports that the concealment of methamphetamine in liquids has increased significantly throughout the United States, especially along the Southwest Border. "Methamphetamine in solution" refers to powdered methamphetamine that is dissolved in water or alcohol (methanol, ethanol, isopropanol) to disguise the drug. Methamphetamine in solution is placed in various consumer products including liquor bottles, detergent bottles, and other commercial product containers that appear to be factory sealed. The most frequently used method of concealment is to place dissolved methamphetamine in nonalcoholic beverage bottles such as soft drinks, sports drinks, juices, and water bottles, which can pose an especially dangerous threat to innocent civilians (DEA, 2015b).

Marijuana

Marijuana is the most commonly used illicit drug in the United States. In 2014, an estimated 22.2 million Americans aged 12 or older (8.4% of the population) were current users of marijuana (CBHSQ, 2015). Furthermore, survey results show that many Americans consider it neither dangerous nor harmful. Although laws regarding marijuana use have changed in several states over the past decade, marijuana remains illegal under federal law in all states and the District of Columbia via the Controlled Substances Act (CSA). The CSA classifies marijuana as a Schedule I drug, meaning that it is categorized as having a high potential for abuse and has no currently accepted medical use in treatment in the United States (Hughes, Lipari, & Williams, 2016).

Despite the federal ban on marijuana, 25 states and the District of Columbia currently have laws legalizing marijuana in some way. For example, several states have decriminalized the possession of small amounts of marijuana and have legalized its use for recreational purposes, and others have passed medical marijuana laws allowing for limited use of cannabis for certain types of medical conditions. It should be noted, however, that federal law prohibits doctors from prescribing marijuana, meaning they can only write a recommendation, not a prescription, for medical marijuana (Governing, 2016).

The increase in marijuana use has impacted public health in communities across the country and placed a significant strain on the U.S. health care system. Research shows that 1 in 11 marijuana users aged 15 or older become dependent on marijuana, resulting in an estimated 4.2 million people who meet the diagnostic criteria for abuse or dependence on marijuana (Hughes et al., 2016). In addition, marijuana use is a leading cause for visits to emergency rooms and is the second leading substance, behind alcohol, for which people receive drug treatment.

Marijuana has often been considered a gateway to drug abuse and addiction, and many drug policies are structured around such a **gateway theory**—that use of milder drugs leads to experimentation with and, consequently, addiction to harder drugs.

Critics of the gateway theory assert that most drug users begin using drugs in their teens or young adult years and suggest that most people who try any drug, even heroin, use it only experimentally or continue use moderately and without ill effects. Research aimed at shedding light on the veracity of this theory is limited, but what evidence does exist suggests that the "gateway" pattern is more likely the product of combined common influences and variables such as drug availability, favorable attitudes toward drug use, and the involvement of friends in drug use than it is indicative of causal effects of specific earlier drug use that promote progression to "harder" drugs (Degenhardt, Dierker, Chiu, Medina-Mora, Neumark et al., 2010). The policy implications of such findings are that any efforts to prevent use of specific "gateway" drugs may not, in themselves, successfully reduce the use of later drugs. Nonetheless, marijuana retains its "gateway" status not because it *will* inevitably lead to addiction but that it *can* lead to addiction (Caulkins, Reuter, Iguchi, & Chiesa, 2005).

A relatively new threat is the emergence of synthetic marijuana, also called spice, K2, or fake weed (NIDA, 2015a). Resembling potpourri and often marketed as "natural herbal incense," synthetic marijuana is a mixture of herbs and spices that is typically sprayed with JWH-018, a synthetic compound chemically similar to tetrahydrocannabinol, or THC, the psychoactive ingredient in marijuana. Spice has become increasingly popular among youth, in part because it is easily available and relatively inexpensive. In fact, synthetic marijuana was added to the *MTF* survey in 2011 and was found to be the second most commonly used illicit drug by 12th graders, after natural marijuana (Johnston et al., 2016). Since that time, use of synthetic marijuana has shown a decline in use among teens, although misperceptions about its risk remain relatively high.

While one reason for spice's growing popularity is the misperception that its "natural" ingredients make this drug harmless, incidents in emergency rooms across the country and calls to police tell a different story. Statistics indicate that emergency room visits nationwide due to synthetic marijuana use went from 13 in 2009 to more than 500 in the first half of 2010 alone (Macher, Burke, & Owen, 2012). In March 2011, the Drug Enforcement Administration (DEA) placed JWH-018 and four other similar compounds used to make synthetic marijuana into Schedule I of the Controlled Substances Act amidst concern over the chemicals' potential for harm, abuse, and addiction and their lack of accepted medical use. Designation as a Schedule I controlled substance makes spice illegal to sell, buy, or possess. Canada, Britain, Germany, France, and Poland have also banned synthetic marijuana (Macher et al., 2012).

gateway theory
Teaches that milder illicit drugs—such as marijuana—lead directly to experimentation with and an addiction to hard drugs such as crack cocaine and heroin.

Drugged Driving

Drug use becomes increasingly problematic when the users get behind the wheel. The 2014 NSDUH showed that 10 million people aged 12 or older reported driving under the influence of illicit drugs during the year prior to being surveyed (CBHSQ, 2015). Men were found to be more likely than women to drive under the influence of alcohol or drugs. Data reveal that after alcohol, the drug most likely to be found in the blood of drivers involved in crashes is marijuana. Research has not, to date, indicated a clear relationship between marijuana use and crash risk, but it is known that the general effects of marijuana use include slowed reaction time, impaired judgment of time and distance, and decreased coordination (NIDA, 2016a). Drivers who are under the influence of cocaine or methamphetamine can be aggressive and reckless behind the wheel, while those who have taken certain kinds of sedatives can experience dizziness and drowsiness. All of these impairments can lead to vehicle crashes.

Prescription drugs are also commonly linked to drugged driving crashes. A 2010 nationwide study of fatal crashes found that nearly half (47%) of drivers who tested positive for drugs had used a prescription drug, compared to 37 percent of those had used marijuana and about 10 percent of those who had used cocaine. The most common prescription drugs found in these drivers were pain relievers (Wilson, Stimpson, & Pagán, 2014).

Underage Drinking

According to the NSDUH, an estimated 8.7 million people aged 12 to 20 reported drinking alcohol the month prior to the survey, including 5.3 million who reported binge drinking and 1.3 million who reported heavy alcohol use (CBHSQ, 2015). Despite the fact that it is illegal for all secondary school students to drink alcoholic beverages, surveys indicate they have considerable experience with it—in 2015, a reported 10 percent of 8th graders, 22 percent of 10th graders, and 35 percent of 12th graders had tried alcohol (Johnston et al., 2016).

binge drinking
Five or more drinks in a row during the previous 2 weeks.

A growing concern is **binge drinking**, or having five or more drinks in a row at least once in the past 2 weeks. Although binge drinking among high school seniors peaked in 1979 along with overall illicit drug use and has shown a relatively steady decline since then, levels still remain concerning among teens today. In 2015, the prevalence of binge drinking among 8th, 10th, and 12th graders was 5 percent, 11 percent, and 17 percent, respectively (Johnston et al., 2016). Heavy drinking generally peaks in the early 20s and recedes with age after that.

The Cost of Substance Abuse

The National Institute on Drug Abuse estimates that drug abuse costs U.S. society more than $700 billion annually in lost work productivity, health care, and criminal justice expenses (NIDA, 2015b). In 2009, the Rand Corporation issued results of a study that examined the cost of the methamphetamine problem alone in the United States. According to the study, which was commissioned by the Meth Project Foundation with support from the National

Institute on Drug Abuse, the cost of the meth problem in 2005 was about $23.4 billion, a figure that included the "burden of addiction," drug treatment costs, premature death (900 premature deaths among users in 2005), resulting crime, costs of arresting and incarcerating drug offenders, lost productivity, expense of removing children from homes of methamphetamine users and paying for foster care, cost resulting from the production of methamphetamine (fires, explosions, etc.) and the injuries to emergency personnel and other victims, and the cost of cleaning up the hazardous waste resulting from the production process (Rand Corporation, 2009).

There is no doubt drug use exacts an increasingly high toll on communities throughout the United States, despite efforts to legislate the problem. Laws aimed at curbing drug use, abuse, and related crime are nothing new. In fact, the United States is approaching the century mark regarding its first official attempt at controlling drug use through law.

THE "WAR ON DRUGS" AND THE NATIONAL DRUG CONTROL STRATEGY

In 1914, the Harrison Act made buying, selling, or using certain drugs illegal. Initially, trafficking in and/or using illicit drugs did not receive much attention. Then, in 1973, President Nixon declared "war" on drugs. Since that time, federal spending on this war against drug smugglers, users, and sellers has increased significantly.

The White House Office of National Drug Control Policy (ONDCP), a component of the Executive Office of the President, was established by the Anti-Drug Abuse Act of 1988. The principal purpose of ONDCP is to establish policies, priorities, and objectives for the nation's drug control program. The goals of the program are to reduce illicit drug use, manufacturing, and trafficking; drug-related crime and violence; and drug-related health consequences. To achieve these goals, the director of ONDCP is charged with producing the National Drug Control Strategy, a strategy that directs the nation's antidrug efforts and establishes a program, a budget, and guidelines for cooperation among federal, state, and local entities.

By law, the director of ONDCP also evaluates, coordinates, and oversees both the international and domestic antidrug efforts of executive branch agencies and ensures that such efforts sustain and complement state and local antidrug activities. The director advises the president regarding changes in the organization, management, budgeting, and personnel of federal agencies that could affect the nation's antidrug efforts, and regarding federal agency compliance with their obligations under the strategy.

Since the first national drug control strategy was published in 1989, variation has been seen in the strategy's goals. The initial strategy focused on reducing the overall level of drug use as well as reducing initiation and use at every level of intensity from casual use to total addiction. Other official objectives have included reduction in hospital emergency room drug-associated admissions, in the import availability and the domestic production of drugs, and in adolescents' approval of drug use. During the 1990s, the goals were simplified to reducing drug use and drug-related consequences (Caulkins et al., 2005).

The *2015 National Drug Control Strategy* aims to reduce drug use and its consequences through innovative, evidence-based public health and safety approaches and focuses on seven core areas (ONDCP, 2015).

We will examine several of these areas as they relate to the efforts of community policing.

L02

The seven core areas of focus of the *2015 National Drug Control Strategy* are:

- Preventing drug use in our communities
- Seeking early intervention opportunities in health care
- Integrating treatment for substance use disorders into health care and supporting recovery
- Breaking the cycle of drug use, crime, and incarceration
- Disrupting domestic drug trafficking and production
- Strengthening international partnerships
- Improving information systems to better address drug use and its consequences

Prevention: Stopping Drug Use Before It Starts

Prevention has been a focus of the National Drug Control Strategy since its inception. The budget for FY 2017 requests $1.5 billion to go toward drug prevention efforts (ONDCP, 2016).

Despite the Supreme Court's approval, most public schools do not randomly test youths involved in extracurricular activities. One program, the Mandatory-Random Student Drug Testing Program, was designed to supplement existing school-based prevention intervention efforts and has two primary goals: (1) deterring students from substance use and (2) identifying students with substance use problems and referring them to counseling or treatment services. To date the program, which was implemented in seven grantee school districts, has shown no statistically significant effects (National Institute of Justice, n.d.).

The DARE Program One key to preventing drug use is education. Probably the most evaluated program is DARE—the Drug Awareness Resistance Education program developed in Los Angeles in 1983. A report on DARE issued by the government's General Accounting Office in the early 2000s concluded that the program had no statistically significant long-term preventive effect on youths' attitudes toward illicit drug use when compared to children who had not been exposed to the program. In 2001, the U.S. Surgeon General categorized it as an "ineffective program."

Based on the shortcomings of the DARE program revealed by extensive research, the curriculum has been completely revised thanks to a $15-million research grant given to the University of Akron by the Robert Wood Johnson Foundation, the largest health philanthropic organization in the world. The new curriculum is undergoing extensive evaluation, and the results are not yet available.

A Reality-Based Approach to Drug Education Many programs use the terms *drug use* and *drug abuse* interchangeably, but teenagers know there is a difference. The gateway theory, a drug education mainstay, argues that using marijuana leads to using "harder" drugs, but there is no evidence of this. Again, teenagers believe they are being told "untruths."

The Safety First reality-based alternative rests on three assumptions: (1) teenagers can make responsible decisions if given honest, science-based drug education; (2) total abstinence may not be a realistic alternative for all teenagers; and (3) use of mind-altering substances does not necessarily constitute abuse.

Life Skills Training   Another approach to preventing substance abuse is to provide students with skills needed to avoid drugs. Research has found that programs that teach middle-school students how to resist peer pressure, to become more assertive, and to make better decisions are the most successful kind of school-based drug use prevention programs (News Medical, 2005). One such program is LifeSkills Training (LST), a research-validated substance abuse program that has been proven to reduce the risks of alcohol, tobacco, and drug abuse and violence. The program reports that students completing the program have cut marijuana use by 75 percent and alcohol use by up to 60 percent. Rather than simply teaching information about drugs, the LifeSkills program consists of three major components covering critical skills dealing with drug resistance, personal self-management, and general social competencies that make it less likely that students will engage in a wide variety of high-risk behaviors (Botvin LifeSkills Training, n.d.).

LifeSkills Training has been cited for prevention excellence by the National Institute on Drug Abuse, the White House Office of National Drug Control Policy, the U.S. Department of Education, the American Medical Association, the Centers for Disease Control and Prevention, the Center for Substance Abuse Prevention, Blueprints for Violence Prevention, the Coalition for Evidence-Based Policy, and the U.S. Department of Justice's Office of Juvenile Justice and Delinquency Prevention.

When prevention efforts fail, other strategies come into play.

Treatment: Healing America's Drug Users

In 2014, an estimated 21.5 million people aged 12 or older were classified as having a substance use disorder (SUD) within the past year, including 17.0 million people with an alcohol use disorder and 7.1 million people with an illicit drug use disorder (CBHSQ, 2015). An estimated 2.6 million people aged 12 or older had both an alcohol use disorder and an illicit drug use disorder in the past year. According to SAMHSA, an SUD occurs when "the recurrent use of alcohol or other drugs (or both) causes clinically significant impairment, including health problems, disability, and failure to meet major responsibilities at work, school, or home" (CBHSQ, 2015, p. 22).

The government's willingness to spend billions of dollars attacking the drug supply, many critics argue, is a costly and ineffective approach to the drug war; the focus, instead, should be on funding drug *treatment* programs (Katel, 2006). In FY 2017, for the first time, the government proposes more funding for demand reduction efforts (treatment and prevention) than those focused on supply reduction (enforcement and interdiction). For FY 2017, the ONDCP has requested $14.3 billion to treat those who have become drug dependent (ONDCP, 2016).

Empirical evidence supports the argument that substance abuse treatment is a sound public investment. According to several conservative estimates, every $1 invested in addiction treatment programs yields a return of between $4 and $7 in reduced drug-related crime, criminal justice costs, and theft alone (NIDA, 2016b). Consider that the average cost for one full year of methadone maintenance treatment is approximately $4,700 per patient, whereas one full year of imprisonment costs approximately $18,400 per person. When savings related to health care are factored in, total savings can exceed costs by a ratio of 12 to 1. Major savings to the individual and to society also come from significant drops in interpersonal conflicts, improvements in workplace productivity, and reductions in drug-related accidents (NIDA, 2016b).

In light of the fact that a high number of defendants entering (and reentering) the juvenile and criminal justice systems have as their only offense drug possession, drug courts have become an increasingly popular alternative for processing these offenders. Drug courts are community-based courts designed to reflect community concerns and priorities, access community resources, and seek community participation and support. Although the structure, scope, and target populations of drug courts vary from one jurisdiction to another, the goals remain the same: to reduce recidivism and substance abuse and rehabilitate participants. By providing drug treatment to offenders as soon as they enter the court system, instead of waiting until they have passed into the correctional component of criminal justice, drug courts have taken quite a different path from traditional court processes.

Estimates cite more than 2,700 drug courts in this country, serving more than 136,000 people (National Association of Drug Court Professionals, 2016). Drug courts generally involve:

- A team effort among judges, prosecutors, defense, treatment providers, case managers, and community resources
- The use of mandatory drug testing to monitor drug use, with treatment beginning shortly after arrest
- Continuous supervision over the recovery process, with progress closely monitored by judges
- Immediate response to program noncompliance
- Incentives to encourage compliance

Studies of drug courts have produced "generally positive" results (Marlowe, 2010; Marlowe & Carey, 2012). A growing body of research serves to document the benefits of drug courts in terms of reduced recidivism and cost-effectiveness. Five separate meta-analyses have found that drug courts significantly reduce crime by an average of 8 to 26 percentage points and that well-administered drug courts reduce crime rates by as much as 35 percent, when compared to traditional case dispositions (ONDCP, 2011). Furthermore, a cost-effectiveness analysis conducted by The Urban Institute found that drug courts yielded $2.21 in benefits to the criminal justice system for every $1 invested and that expanding the program to all at-risk arrestees raises the average return on investment to $3.36 for every $1 spent (ONDCP, 2011).

Drug courts are even more effective when partnered with law enforcement, as stressed by the ONDCP (ONDCP, 2011, pp. 3–4):

> A strong partnership with local law enforcement is a critical component of a successful drug court. Street-level enforcement officers provide a unique perspective and benefit to drug court teams. Law enforcement can improve referrals to the court and extend the connection of the drug court team into the community for further information gathering and monitoring of participants. Law enforcement personnel play important roles not only in the day-to-day operations of the drug court, but also in showing other government and community leaders the public safety efficacy of these courts.

A comprehensive study of the key attributes of successful drug courts reinforces the importance of this relationship. In the 18 adult drug courts studied, researchers found that:

- Having a member from law enforcement on the team was associated with higher graduation rates, compared to teams without a law enforcement member (57% versus 46%).
- Drug court teams that included law enforcement personnel reduced costs an additional 36 percent over the reductions achieved by traditional drug courts.

Law Enforcement: Disrupting the Market

A comprehensive approach to the drug problem includes not only prevention and treatment but also efforts at stopping drug sale and use, the third core component of the national drug control strategy.

Drug Raids   During the 1980s, drug raids made frequent headlines. Tank-like vehicles, SWAT teams, and sophisticated weaponry all have been involved in drug raids, which can be highly successful when used properly.

An Internet search of *drug raid* produced nearly 25 million results, highlighting the magnitude of the drug problem in our society. Many of the search results were newspaper stories of such raids carried out in communities across the country. For example, a 2-day raid across the New York metro area in June 2012 netted 98 people, including three medical practitioners, involved in the illegal sale of prescription painkillers (CBS News, 2012). In another June 2012 raid, DEA agents raided a home in Olathe, Kansas, as part of a federal sweep to extinguish a marijuana ring that spanned from the heartland of America to California. The alleged drug dealer lived in the home with his wife and two children (Townsend, 2012). Hundreds more such stories exist, illustrating how the drug market permeates neighborhoods of all sizes and often involves persons regarded as "upstanding" members of the community.

Surveillance   The purpose of surveillance is to gather information about people and their activities and associates that may help solve a crime. Surveillance can be designed to serve several functions, including gathering information required for building a criminal complaint, verifying a witness's statement

LO3

Law enforcement strategies to deal with the drug problem include drug raids, surveillance, undercover operations, arresting sellers and buyers, and improving intelligence.

about a crime, gaining information required for obtaining a search or arrest warrant, identifying a suspect's associates, observing criminal activities in progress, apprehending a criminal in the act of committing a crime, and making a legal arrest.

A common type of surveillance is the stakeout, a stationary surveillance in which officers set up an observation post and monitor it continuously. Other types of surveillance include aerial surveillance and audio surveillance, wiretapping, video surveillance, and a host of rapidly developing technologies. Before a judge will approve an application for electronic surveillance, those requesting it must show why surveillance is necessary—for example, standard techniques have been tried and have failed.

Previous editions of this text noted how GPS was increasingly being used as a surveillance tool to catch not only drug dealers but also thieves, robbers, sexual predators, and killers, often without a warrant or court order. After all, it is easy for police to attach a GPS device to a car without the driver ever knowing about it. However, the unsanctioned ability of police to use this method of surveillance was brought to a halt in *United States v. Jones* (2012), when the Supreme Court held that using a GPS device to surveil a person constituted a search within the meaning of the Fourth Amendment and, as such, required a warrant. In *Jones*, federal investigators surreptitiously attached a GPS device to suspected drug trafficker Jones's vehicle as a way to monitor the vehicle's movements on public streets. Although a warrant had been obtained, the device was used beyond the approved scope of the warrant. (The warrant authorized installation of the GPS device in the District of Columbia and within 10 days, but agents installed it on the 11th day and in Maryland, and then proceeded to track the vehicle for 28 days.) Investigators used the GPS data to have Jones indicted for drug trafficking conspiracy, and Jones was convicted in the district court, which ruled that the defendant held no expectation of privacy while driving on public streets. Jones appealed, and the DC circuit court reversed, concluding that the warrantless use of the GPS device did, in fact, violate the Fourth Amendment. The U.S. Supreme Court affirmed, with Justice Scalia delivering the opinion of the Court:

> The Fourth Amendment provides in relevant part that, "The right of the people to be secure in their persons, houses, papers, and effects, against unreasonable searches and seizures, shall not be violated." It is beyond dispute that a vehicle is an "effect" as that term is used in the Amendment. … We hold that the Government's installation of a GPS device on a target's vehicle, and its use of that device to monitor the vehicle's movements, constitutes a "search."

> It is important to be clear about what occurred in this case: The Government physically occupied private property for the purpose of obtaining information. We have no doubt that such a physical intrusion would have been considered a "search" within the meaning of the Fourth Amendment when it was adopted.

This ruling does not mean police cannot use GPS in their investigations, but it does make clear the need for officers to obtain a warrant before applying such surveillance technology. Indeed, a 2011 Police Executive Research Forum (PERF) survey found that most of responding law enforcement agencies (83%)

use global positioning system (GPS) technology to track the movements of criminal suspects (PERF, 2012).

Undercover Assignments Most undercover assignments are used to obtain information and evidence about illegal activity when it can be obtained in no other way. *Light cover* involves deception, but the officer usually goes home at the end of the shift. An example is an assignment where an officer poses as a utility worker or repair person to obtain access to a suspect's home. Often an officer poses as a drug addict to make a drug buy, obtaining evidence to make an arrest. *Deep cover* is much more dangerous but can be very effective. In deep cover, an officer lives an assumed identity to infiltrate a group or organization. No identification other than the cover identification is carried. Communication with the police department is carefully planned.

Regardless of whether the cover used is light or deep, such work requires a "carefully crafted persona and unrelenting self-discipline" (Grossi, 2009, p. 24). The DEA recommends that undercover officers keep their real first names in case they are greeted by someone on the street who does not know they are working undercover. It is also advisable for UC officers to keep their real birth date, so it comes naturally if asked for it.

Some police departments have used *sting operations* during which undercover police agents sell drugs and then arrest those who buy them. These operations have sometimes been criticized as unethical or even an illegal form of entrapment. Police must exercise extreme care if they use such operations as a strategy to reduce the drug problem.

Arresting Dealers The traditional response to users and sellers has been to arrest them when possible. The current antidrug campaign has increasingly focused on a law enforcement model attacking the supply side (traffickers, smugglers, and users) rather than prevention and treatment (Katel, 2006).

Most law enforcement agencies focus efforts on enforcing laws against dealing drugs and increasing prosecution of drug dealers. In addition to being concerned with those who deal in drugs, police officers need to be prepared to manage those who use them.

Arresting Drug Users Arresting users is not without its critics. Hubert Williams, former president of the Police Foundation, suggests: "If we want to use the standard of the number of people we arrest—about 1.7 million people get busted every year—these numbers deal [only] with quantity, not quality. We're busting people for use—not trafficking. We need a new strategy that doesn't focus on the ghetto and the inner city … [one] that brings together intelligence and analyses on the big gangs" (Katel, 2006). Efforts to address the gang problem are the focus of Chapter 13. Indeed, the ONDCP has acknowledged that at the end of the day, we cannot arrest our way out of the drug problem.

Improving Intelligence If police can enlist citizens to provide information about drug dealing to the police, much can be accomplished. Most public housing residents know where drug deals are made. Many also believe, however, that the police either do not care or are actually corrupt because they arrest few dealers. When dealers are arrested, they are often back on the street within hours. Residents should be educated about the difficulties of prosecuting drug dealers and the need for evidence.

Some departments conduct *community surveys* in low-income neighborhoods to learn about how residents view the drug problem. Some departments have established tip lines where residents can provide information anonymously.

Improved reporting can be accomplished in a number of ways, and intelligence can be increased by unusual procedures. Police have been known to interview arrestees to obtain inside information on how certain criminal activities are conducted. In some agencies, arrestees have been interviewed in jail with a jail debriefing form. This information is useful as police continue to document the link between drugs and criminal activity.

Intelligence information can also be improved by facilitating the communication between narcotics investigators and patrol officers. For example, in Atlanta, Georgia, a narcotics supervisor recognized that patrol and narcotics had historically used a different radio frequency and were unable to communicate. The problem was quickly corrected.

Combating Street-Level Narcotics Sales   Citizens know where drug dealing is taking place. If they can be encouraged to report these locations, police can concentrate their efforts on locations receiving the most complaints. Often police officers want to go higher than the street pusher, but they should avoid this temptation. If information regarding someone higher up is obtained, it should be given to the narcotics unit for follow-up. The main purpose of the street-level raids is to respond to citizen complaints and to let them see their complaints being acted on—that is, arrests being made. Officers should know where to search a person being detained on suspicion of possession of drugs. The variety of hiding places for illegal drugs is limited only by the violators' ingenuity. Common hiding places include body orifices, boots, chewing gum packages, cigarettes, coat linings, cuffs, false heels, hair, hatbands, inside ties, lighters, pants, pens and pencils, seams, shoes, shoulder pads, sleeves, and waistbands.

Mazerolle, Soole, and Rombouts (2007, p. 22) summarize the findings from rigorous academic studies evaluating a range of street-level drug law enforcement interventions and conclude: "Police partnerships with a variety of entities (regulators, inspectors, business owners, and local councils) that are community-wide or geographically focused policing approaches to tackling street-level drug market problems are more productive for reducing drug problems than law-enforcement-only approaches focused on hot spots."

Public Housing and the Drug Problem   Various specific strategies have been used to tackle the drug problem in public housing. Often efforts focus on improving the physical environment, limiting entrances, improving lighting, erecting fences, requiring a pass card to gain entrance to the housing, and keeping trash collected.

Another strategy for dealing with the drug problem in public housing projects is for police officers to acquire an understanding of the workings of the local public housing authorities or agencies (PHAs) that manage these complexes. Officers need to work at establishing a relationship with the PHAs and at overcoming the occasional disbelief of management and residents that the police truly want to help. Once this is accomplished, a fact-finding mission should identify key players, provide information about each organization, and determine what programs exist and the participation level.

Next, the specific problem and who is impacted should be identified: What drug or drugs are involved? For whom is this a problem—police, residents, housing personnel, the mayor? Does one problem mask another problem? Then a dialogue should be undertaken with key players to enlist support and mobilize the housing project's residents. Next, a strategy should be developed, including goals, objectives, and tactics that might be used. The strategy should then be implemented, coordinating all available resources, specifying roles for each key player, and determining a time frame. The final step is to evaluate progress. Was the problem improved or changed?

Addressing Drug Dealing in Privately Owned Apartment Complexes Apartment complexes can harbor open or closed drug markets. In an **open drug market**, dealers sell to all potential customers, eliminating only those suspected of being police or some other threat. In a **closed drug market**, dealers sell only to people they know or who are vouched for by other buyers. In apartment complexes, open drug markets pose a greater threat than closed drug markets.

open drug market
Dealers sell to all potential customers, eliminating only those suspected of being police or some other threat.

closed drug market
Dealers sell only to people they know or who are vouched for by other buyers.

Methamphetamine Labs Methamphetamine (meth) labs have three main dangers associated with them: (1) injury from explosions, fires, chemical burns, and toxic fumes; (2) environmental hazards; and (3) child endangerment (Scott & Dedel, 2006):

> **Physical Injury from Explosions, Fires, Chemical Burns, and Toxic Fumes**
>
> Mixing chemicals in clandestine methamphetamine labs creates substantial risks of explosions, fires, chemical burns, and toxic fume inhalation. Those who mix the chemicals (known as "cooks" or "cookers") and their assistants, emergency responders, hazardous material cleanup crews, neighbors, and future property occupants are all at risk from chemical exposure. The long-term health risks such exposure poses are not yet fully known, but one must assume they are significant (2).
>
> Many lab cooks do not take basic lab safety precautions. Using heat to process chemicals poses a higher risk of explosion, although indirect heat in the processing area—such as from smoking, electrical switches, or even equipment-generated friction—can also trigger explosions. In addition, police-forced entry

into labs can cause explosions—some accidental and some triggered by booby traps set by lab operators. (The published literature commonly reports that lab operators are often well armed, but how many shootings occur during lab seizures is unknown.) Despite a decrease in the number of reported fires and explosions over the past few years, the number of police injured when responding to meth- amphetamine labs increased during that time. Poor lab ventilation increases the risks both of explosions and of toxic fume inhalation. On the other hand, good ventilation spreads toxic fumes outside, where they put other people at risk. Heat- ing the chemical red phosphorous can create phosphine, a deadly gas (3).

About three to six people working in clandestine U.S. methamphetamine labs die each year from explosions, fires, or toxic fumes. One out of every five or six labs discovered is found because of an explosion or fire. A survey of those who cook methamphetamine revealed one-quarter had experienced a fire while cooking and, in one-fifth of these, no emergency services were called. Those present tended to leave the premises without warning others, which is particu- larly dangerous in multiunit buildings (4).

Environmental Hazards

Each pound of manufactured methamphetamine produces about 5 to 6 pounds of hazardous waste. Clandestine drug lab operators commonly bury or burn the waste on or near the site, or dump the waste along the road or into streams or rivers. Others pour waste down the drain, place it in household or commer- cial trash, or store it on the property. Dumping toxic waste into trash cans and commercial dumpsters puts sanitation workers at risk. The water used to put out lab fires can also wash toxic chemicals into sewers. In addition, toxic waste can be transferred from surfaces and equipment onto the body and clothing of those in contact with the lab, and can subsequently contaminate other loca- tions. More research is needed to understand this toxic dumping's long-term environmental effects. Residual contamination of the ground, water supplies, buildings, and furniture may last for years (4).

Child Endangerment

Many jurisdictions are now finding that children are commonly exposed to the hazards of clandestine methamphetamine labs. ... Young children frequently put their hands in their mouths, have higher metabolic and respiratory rates than adults, and have developing central nervous systems, all leaving them vulnerable to harm from inhaling, absorbing, or ingesting toxins from chemi- cals. About two-thirds of children found at labs seized by police tested positive for toxic levels of chemicals in their bodies. Others suffer burns to their lungs or skin from chemicals or fire. Some have died in explosions and fires. Many are badly neglected or abused by parents suffering from drug abuse's effects. (Senior citizens whose caretakers are lab operators are similarly vulnerable. Pets, including guard dogs, can also be harmed.) When police agencies start targeting labs for investigation and seizure, social service agencies and family courts should be prepared for increased workloads as well (5).

The Center for Problem-Oriented Policing cautions law enforcement agencies that it is critical that responses be tailored to local circumstances and that each response be based on reliable analysis. In most cases, an effective strategy will involve implementing several different responses. Law enforcement responses alone are seldom effective in reducing or solving the problem. The POP Center (www.popcenter.org) publishes a guide for dealing with meth labs.

Combating Prescription Drug Diversion **Drug diversion** is the rerouting of drugs from legally and medically necessary and authorized uses to uses that are illegal and typically neither medically authorized nor necessary. In 2012, prescribers wrote 82.5 opioid pain reliever (OPR) prescriptions and 37.6 benzodiazepine prescriptions per 100 persons in the United States (Paulozzi, Mack, & Hockenberry, 2014)

> **drug diversion**
> The rerouting of drugs from legally and medically necessary and authorized uses to uses that are illegal and typically neither medically authorized nor necessary.

However, many of these prescribed drugs end up in the hands of those other than the patient to whom the prescription was issued. In 2014, an estimated 6.5 million Americans aged 12 or older—2.5 percent of the population—were current nonmedical users of psychotherapeutic drugs, primarily prescription pain relievers (CBHSQ, 2015).

Teens are increasingly turning from street drugs to prescription drugs to get high because they are easy to get and are often free, with youth often getting prescribed drugs from friends or relatives. New teen users of prescription drugs have caught up with new teen users of marijuana. Youth believe the myth that these prescribed drugs provide a medically safe high, a belief that can have fatal consequences. The rate of drug overdose deaths involving synthetic opioids, a category that includes both prescription synthetic opioids (e.g., fentanyl and tramadol) and nonpharmaceutical fentanyl manufactured in illegal laboratories (illicit fentanyl)—nearly doubled between 2013 and 2014 (Rudd, Aleshire, Zibbell, & Gladden, 2016).

The estimated cost of prescription drug diversion and abuse to public and private medical insurers is more than $72 billion a year, much of which is passed to consumers through higher health insurance premiums. In addition, the abuse of prescription opioids burdens the budgets of substance abuse treatment providers, particularly as there is evidence to suggest prescription opioid abuse might also be contributing to increasing heroin abuse rates in some areas of the country (National Drug Intelligence Center, 2009).

Prescription drug diversion can be propagated by several means, including theft of drugs from pharmacies and health care providers; ordering from rogue Internet pharmacies; through the practice of **doctor shopping**, whereby a patient obtains controlled substances from multiple health care practitioners without the prescribers' knowledge of the other prescriptions already acquired; and by unethical doctors who knowingly and willingly prescribe drugs in exchange for monetary compensation.

> **doctor shopping**
> occurs when a patient obtains controlled substances from multiple health care practitioners without the prescribers' knowledge of the other prescriptions already acquired.

Two organizations available to help law enforcement tackle the problem of prescription drug diversion are the RxPATROL (Pattern Analysis Tracking Robberies and Other Losses) and the National Association of Drug Diversion Investigation (NADDI). RxPATROL maintains a national computer database to help law enforcement solve pharmacy robberies, burglaries, and other major crimes committed in health care facilities. NADDI is a nonprofit organization that provides prescription drug abuse education to law enforcement, regulatory agents, and health care professionals.

TECHNOLOGY IN COMMUNITY POLICING

IDENTIFYING PHARMACY ROBBERS

In the ever-evolving effort to deal with drug-related crime, law enforcement is now collaborating with different national organizations, drug companies, and partners in their own jurisdiction to develop innovative ways to try to deter potential pharmacy robbers and to catch those who do commit such robberies. One innovative, low-cost technology being used in Long Island, New York, is a DNA tracking system developed by Applied DNA Sciences of Stony Brook. With this technology, a pharmacy employee activates a device that sprays a mist at a suspect as he or she exits the pharmacy after a robbery. The colorless, odorless mist is unnoticeable to the suspect but contains plant DNA that is visible under a special light. The presence of this DNA provides strong physical evidence linking a suspect to a crime scene and, thus, makes convicting a suspect much easier.

Source: Jabeen, Amber. 2012. "Using Technology to Combat Pharmacy Robberies." *Community Policing Dispatch* 5 (4). http://cops.usdoj.gov/html/dispatch/04-2012/technology-and-pharmacy-robberies.asp

Strategies to Combat Underage Drinking   Without question, alcohol is the most commonly used and abused drug among our nation's youth. Although the legal drinking age in every state is 21, surveys and studies consistently show that people aged 12 to 20 drink a sizeable amount of all alcohol consumed in the United States (Centers for Disease Control and Prevention, 2015). Excessive drinking causes more than 4,300 deaths among underage youth each year and burdened the United States with $24 billion in economic costs in 2010 (Sacks, Gonzales, Bouchery, Tomedi, & Brewer, 2015). The National Institute on Alcohol Abuse and Alcoholism (NIAAA) states:

> Understanding the scope of alcohol use during the middle- and high-school years, and the associated long-term problems with early drinking, is an important step toward effectively intervening to reduce high-risk drinking and its negative consequences.

> That said, data on alcohol consumption in children younger than age 12 are severely limited because few alcohol consumption surveys include this age group. The available data indicate that between 4 and 10 percent of 4th through 6th graders report having consumed more than just a sip of alcohol, and as many as 60 percent have had some minimal exposure to alcohol, such as a sip from a parent's cup. This early introduction to alcohol, in combination with exposure to parental drinking and alcohol abuse, may put children at higher risk for alcohol-related problems later in life (2014, p. 4).

Although data show that alcohol consumption begins to rise quickly in adolescence in the United States as well as in other high-income countries, surveys have encouraging news. The most recent *Monitoring the Future* shows that in 2015, alcohol use among 10th and 12th graders was the lowest ever reported during the survey's 41 years, and the historic lows were consistent across all categories, including lifetime, annual, 30-day, and binge drinking measures (Johnston et al., 2016).

College students are also an at-risk population for alcohol abuse and related issues, and findings from several surveys indicate that college students drink more heavily than their noncollege peers. In addition, a particularly large number of young people of college age far exceed the standard threshold of "more than five drinks" that defines binge drinking (NIAAA, 2014, p. 4): "Drinking by college students also is associated with increased morbidity and mortality. Alcohol consumption among college students ages 18–24 is associated with unintentional death (an estimated 1,825 students annually), injury (an estimated 599,000 students annually), physical assault (approximately 696,000 students annually), sexual assault (more than 97,000 students annually), health consequences (more than 150,000 students annually), drunk driving (roughly 2.7 million students annually), and alcohol abuse disorders (roughly 20% of college students)."

The City of New Britain, Connecticut, developed a collaborative community response program to combat the underage drinking problem experienced by neighborhoods adjacent to a local university, with complaints ranging from loud, late-night parties to fighting; drinking and driving; excessive traffic and speeding; public urination; broken glass; vandalism (littering, public vomit, parking on lawns); blockage of homeowners' driveways by illegally parked cars; drunken students intimidating and disrespecting neighbors; and occupancy issues related to overcrowded apartment units (*Combating Underage Drinking through a Collaborative Community Response Program*, 2009, p. 3):

> City departments, neighborhood residents, law abiding students, and University officials [had] had increasing difficulty in recent years combating the multiple problems associated with off-campus underage drinking. Underage drinking has led to problem house parties and drinking and driving, in addition to significantly disrupting the local neighborhood surrounding the university. Pervasive underage drinking and associated behaviors have undermined confidence in the police, led to a decline in the quality of life in the neighborhood, and has [con]tributed to the perceived decline in the market value of homes. The intent of the project is to engage the multiple stakeholders in problem solving, to reduce the incidence of aberrant behavior, to promote health and safety by encouraging healthy habits on the part of students, and to restore order in the Belvidere neighborhood surrounding Central Connecticut State University.[1]

A task force coalition was formed comprised of community stakeholders—residents, students, businesses, the media, campus officials, campus police, and local police—with empowerment from both the Mayor of the City of New Britain and the President of Central Connecticut State University (CCSU). A "mutual aid agreement" was drafted to resolve jurisdictional issues between campus and local police that had previously impeded response efforts, and officers from both departments received updated training and education regarding applicable underage drinking laws and party interdiction tactics. House party patrols and DUI checkpoints increased. Educational resources were distributed to CCSU students regarding high-risk versus low-risk drinking, consistent late-night alternative activities,

---

[1] Reprinted by permission of the New Britain, CT, Police Department.

and consistent, constructive late-night activities were made available as an alternative to off-campus drinking parties. Enforcement efforts were stepped up regarding off-campus student misconduct that posed a threat to the health and safety of others. And a federal grant was obtained to cover police overtime (*Combating Underage Drinking through a Collaborative Community Response Program*, 2009).

The collaborative community response achieved positive results, including a 50-percent decrease in campus judicial misconduct cases; a 10-percent reduction in off-campus vandalism and a 60-percent reduction in on-campus vandalism; a decrease in student binge drinking; a 74-percent reduction in hospitalizations related to alcohol intoxication; and positive feedback from residents confirming the significant improvement in quality-of-life in their neighborhood: "Viewing underage drinking as a 'community problem' has led to an overall enhanced sense of responsibility in the Belvidere neighborhood. Such prevention strategies have . . . lowered [students'] overall 'risk profile,' helping to ensure academic success while promoting health and safety on campus and in the surrounding community. These strategies have also helped restore confidence in government services" (*Combating Underage Drinking through a Collaborative Community Response Program*, 2009, p. 21).

LEGISLATION AS A TOOL IN THE WAR ON SUBSTANCE ABUSE

The government has the power to finance the war on drugs by seizing drug traffickers' illegally obtained assets, including cars, weapons, and cash. Among items that have been seized are airplanes, vehicles, radio transmitters with scanners, telephone scramblers, paper shredders, electronic currency counters, assault rifles, and electronic stun guns.

Legislation such as drug abatement statutes is also helping in the war on drugs. Such legislation makes it much easier to shut down crack houses and clandestine drug laboratories. Other legislation is aimed at regulating the sale of cold tablets containing pseudoephedrine, a key ingredient in methamphetamine. Such cold tablets must be locked up, and their sale requires identification and a signature.

In addition to individual counseling approaches that have been demonstrated in numerous experimental studies to reduce alcohol problems, states can play an important role in deterring underage and excessive drinking by passing laws, enforcing compliance, and providing guidance to local communities. Actions states have taken include:

- Enforcement of the legal drinking age of 21 years and laws making it illegal to drive after any drinking if one is under 21 (the law in every state and the District of Columbia).
- Administrative license revocation (the law in 41 states and the District of Columbia).
- Lowering the legal blood alcohol limit to 0.08 percent (the law in every state and the District of Columbia).

- Mandatory screening and treatment of persons convicted of driving under the influence of alcohol (the law in 23 states).
- Primary enforcement of safety belt laws (the law in 32 states and the District of Columbia).

The National Highway Traffic Safety Administration (NHTSA) contends that laws raising the drinking age to 21 led to an immediate decline in crashes of roughly 15 percent, or nearly 1,000 lives saved per year. However, the number of laws, the level of enforcement, and the severity of penalties vary from state to state and, as might be expected, so does the level of drinking. Nonetheless, research continues to show that the federal law not only saves lives but also curbs other hazards of heavy drinking, including dating violence and suicide (DeJong & Blanchette, 2014). Researchers contend that education can help discourage underage drinking as can tougher enforcement of the drinking laws. In addressing some critics' suggestions that the legal drinking age be lowered because alcohol consumption among high school and underage college students is relatively widespread, researcher DeJong notes, "Just because a law is commonly disobeyed doesn't mean we should eliminate it." Clinical trials have shown that when college towns invest greater effort into enforcing the law, and advertise that enforcement effort to students, student drinking decreases (DeJong & Blanchette, 2014).

COLLABORATIVE EFFORTS

Dealing with the substance-abuse problem requires the collaborative efforts of the police, public housing authorities, other agencies, and, most important, the residents themselves.

Empowering Residents

Many police agencies have focused on the broader needs of residents of low-income housing. In Tulsa, Oklahoma, for example, officers believed that limited job opportunities were a problem for youths living in public housing. The officers now steer youths into Job Corps, a training and job service program that is an alternative to the traditional high school. Residents can also be empowered in other ways—for example, by forming associations or holding rallies.

In 2001, a Snohomish County (Washington) deputy introduced Tina Hagget and Susan York to each other. Both lived in neighborhoods plagued by car prowling, speeding, and frenzied traffic associated with drug dealing. The women compared notes and realized the same cars were operating in both neighborhoods, about 5 miles apart. They agreed to partner with law enforcement to stop the drug market in their neighborhood. They learned deputies' names and schedules and contacted them with information, limiting the need to repeatedly explain the problem.

Soon Hagget and York became the unofficial community link between Snohomish County deputies and other neighborhoods struggling against drug crime, sharing their stories, giving advice on what to report to their local authorities, and saving deputies hours of explanations to angry, frustrated residents.

In January 2002, the women attended a Meth Summit sponsored by Snohomish County and volunteered with 10 other citizens and police officers to work on a law enforcement task force exploring options to reduce drug activity in their communities. The result of the task force was Lead On America. The group has published a guide that includes a neighborhood activity log in which residents can describe suspicious vehicles and visitors to the suspect drug house, as well as the signs of a drug house. Figure 11.1 illustrates a portion of the log.

Improving the Physical Environment

Improving indoor and exterior lighting has been successfully used in some projects. Cleanup efforts in trash-strewn lots, which provide easy hiding places for drugs, have also been successful. Some housing projects have developed identification cards for their residents so that outsiders can be readily observed. Others have limited access by reducing the number of entrances and exits. Crime prevention through environmental design (CPTED), as described in Chapter 10, is clearly applicable here.

Just as one of the underlying causes of violence in this country is believed to be the ready availability of guns, another cause commonly acknowledged is the ready availability of drugs, and communities across the country are rallying to stop that flow. In Minneapolis, Minnesota, police and property owners are using black and gold "No Trespassing" signs in inner-city neighborhoods. The signs are part of a program intended to improve residents' security and deter street-level drug dealing by telling officers that they can enter the properties to question loiterers without a call from the property owner. This expands the power of the police greatly and removes from landlords the sometimes-threatening responsibility of signing a citizen's arrest form before the police can act.

The city of St. Paul, Minnesota, also enlisted the aid of residents to forge an alliance to fight drug dealers. The program, called FORCE (Focusing Our Resources on Community Empowerment), centered on getting longtime

Figure 11.1 Neighborhood Activity Log

Neighborhood Activity Log

Never place yourself in any danger trying to gather information. Always call 911 if there is any reason to believe you or someone else is in danger or that there is an in-progress crime being committed.

Date	Start Time	Activity Description	License Number	Vehicle Description	# of Persons	Name or Description of Each Person	End Time	Other	Initial
/ /	: □AM □PM						: □AM □PM		
/ /	: □AM □PM						: □AM □PM		
/ /	: □AM □PM						: □AM □PM		

Source: Cindi Sinnema. "Residents Learn Ways to Best Serve Sheriff's Office in Fight against Meth." *Community Links*, May 2003, 12. Department of Justice.

residents to permit narcotics officers to use their homes to monitor drug sales in the neighborhood. The FORCE team worked with a network of block club leaders to target drug dealers and to force the removal of, or improvements to, ramshackle drug houses. Ramsey County provided child protection services for youths found in drug houses.

Another very successful crime prevention program was developed in Wilson, North Carolina. Their program, "Operation Broken Window," was rooted in the broken window philosophy discussed earlier in this book. One specific block—an open-air drug market widely known as a place where drugs could be easily bought and where undercover police operations had been unsuccessful in reducing the problem—was selected as their "broken window." The Wilson Police Department, using problem-oriented policing as a possible solution, formulated a four-pronged attack: undercover operations; increased uniform police presence with more officers and a satellite police station in the target area; two K-9 units assigned to drug interdiction at the local bus station; and attention to social and environmental conditions. They identified conditions that facilitated drug sales in the target area, cut grass, removed trash, and installed, repaired, or replaced street lights. They inspected buildings for code violations and notified owners to correct the problems. They also boarded up abandoned buildings frequented by drug users. Operation Broken Window was a success. The drug dealers left, and crime rates went down.

In Rialto, California, a successful Operation Clean Sweep was conducted. The department used the SARA model to identify the problem. Their first step was to develop a target list of drug hot spots and dealers. Meetings were held with patrol officers, detectives, and neighborhood-watch groups, which provided valuable, up-to-the-minute insight into activity on the street. This project used small video cameras to record dozens of transactions made by undercover officers in unmarked patrol cars. The drug dealers "sauntered away" after completing their deals, not realizing the drugs they had sold would be taken to the crime lab for evidentiary analysis. The project also involved establishing liaisons with the district attorney and other agencies. Knowing the project would need a multiagency effort to "sweep" those involved in the 89 separate videotaped hand-to-hand narcotics buys, an arrest plan was made

Syracuse Newspapers/S Cannerelli/The Image Works

Oneida City (New York) Police Chief David Meeker, surrounded by members of the New York State Police, the DEA, and the Oneida City Mayor, holds a press conference about the multi-agency investigation that resulted in the seizure of over $56,000 worth of synthetic drugs and about $16,000 in cash and money orders from three stash house shops in Oneida, Lakeport, and Brewerton.

including 15 other agencies. For 3 days, these agencies and the California High-way Patrol helped serve arrest warrants.

In Ocean City, Maryland, a swelling tourist population and inexperienced servers and wait staff led to a major problem for the Ocean City Police Department (OCPD). Underage drinking resulted in crime, injury, and even death for vacationing teenagers, and adults served past the point of intoxication were also a concern. The OCPD created Teaching Effective Alcohol Management (TEAM) to educate seasonal servers and wait staff on examining identification and dealing with intoxicated customers. TEAM incorporated the support of a state alcohol service training agency, the county's licensed beverage association, the local high school Students Against Drunk Driving group, and the Hotel–Motel Restaurant Association.

Training Officers

It is becoming increasingly apparent that the war on drugs is not one that law enforcement can or should tackle alone. Indeed, a paradigm shift is occurring as to how the nation's drug abuse and addiction problems should be handled, which is having an effect on the role police play in handling drug-related crime. Decades of three-strikes laws and "get tough" policies have filled our country's jails and prisons with drug offenders, and many now advocate that drug addiction and the crimes that often attach to addiction should be treated not as a criminal justice problem but, instead, as a public health crisis. To this end, the President's Task Force on 21st Century Policing recommends (2015, pp. 57–58):

> Posts should ensure that basic recruit and in-service officer training include curriculum on the disease of addiction. It is important that officers be able to recognize the signs of addiction and respond accordingly when they are inter-acting with people who may be impaired as a result of their addiction. Science has demonstrated that addiction is a disease of the brain—a disease that can be prevented and treated and from which people can recover. The growing un-derstanding of this science has led to a number of law enforcement agencies equipping officers with overdose-reversal drugs such as naloxone and the pas-sage of legislation in many states that shield any person from civil and criminal liability if they administer naloxone.

> The Obama Administration's drug policy reflects this understanding and em-phasizes access to treatment over incarceration, pursuing "smart on crime" rather than "tough on crime" approaches to drug-related offenses, and support for early health interventions designed to break the cycle of drug use, crime, incarceration, and re-arrest. And the relationship between incarceration and addiction is a significant one. A 2004 survey by the U.S. Department of Justice estimated that about 70 percent of State and 64 percent of Federal prisoners regularly used drugs prior to incarceration.

Comprehensive, Coordinated Community Approaches

The Des Moines (Iowa) Police Department has a community involvement handbook, developed jointly by the police department, the United Way, and more than 35 neighborhood groups. The handbook serves as a source of information as well as a guide for action and is intended to help neighborhood groups become active and start making a difference. Called the "municipal approach," the program has four prongs: community involvement, enforcement, prevention/education, and treatment. Portions of the handbook have been translated into Spanish, Vietnamese, Cambodian, and Laotian. The handbook covers topics such as knowing when to call the police; improving street lighting and residential security lighting; removing trash and litter; cutting down shrubbery; working with landlords and businesses in the area; boarding up abandoned houses; forming neighborhood associations; conducting neighborhood block walks, rallies, and marches; occupying parks and streets; and writing newsletters.

The handbook contains an extensive list of suspicious activity and common indicators of residential drug trafficking that could be of much help to communities seeking to tackle this problem (Figure 11.2).

Figure 11.2 Suspicious Activity and Common Indicators of Residential Drug Trafficking

1. A high volume of foot and/or vehicle traffic to and from a residence at late or unusual hours.

2. Periodic visitors who stay at the residence for very brief periods of time.

3. Alterations of property by the tenants, including the following:

   a. Covering windows and patio doors with materials other than curtains or drapes;

   b. Barricading windows or doors;

   c. Placing dead bolt locks on interior doors; and

   d. Disconnecting fire alarms.

4. Consistent payment of rent and security deposits with U.S. currency, especially small denominations of cash. (Large amounts of 20 dollar bills are commonly seized from drug dealers.)

5. The presence of drug paraphernalia in or around the residence, including, but not limited to, glass pipes, syringes, propane torches, paper or tinfoil bundles, folded shiny-slick paper (snow seals), large quantities of plastic baggies, scales, money wrappers and small glass vials.

6. The presence of unusual odors coming from the interior of the residence, especially the odor of pungent chemical substances and/or burning materials.

7. The presence of firearms, other than sporting firearms, including fully automatic weapons, assault weapons, sawed-off shotguns, machine pistols, handguns, and related ammunition and holsters.

8. The presence of a tenant's possessions and furnishings which are inconsistent with the known income level of the tenant. This would include, but is not limited to, the following:

   a. New and/or expensive vehicles;

   b. Expensive jewelry and clothing; and

   c. Expensive household furnishings, stereo systems and other large entertainment systems.

9. Tenants who are overly nervous and apprehensive about the landlord visiting the residence.

Any of the indicators, by itself, may not be reason to suspect drug trafficking. However, when combined with other indicators, they may be reason to suspect drug trafficking. If you suspect drug trafficking in your neighborhood, please contact the police department.

Source: Des Moines Police. *Drugs: A Municipal Approach, A Community Handbook*, p. 26. Reprinted by permission.

This practical guide might serve as a model for other police departments that wish to involve the community in the fight not only against drugs but also against crime and violence.

Groups that can benefit from a partnership with law enforcement include home/school organizations such as parent–teacher associations; neighborhood associations; tenants' groups; fraternal, social, and veterans' groups; community service clubs (such as Lions, Kiwanis, Jaycees, Rotary); religiously affiliated groups; and associations of homeowners, merchants, or taxpayers.

A Drug Problem in New York City

The following description is from the COPS Web site:

> The Clinton Hill neighborhood had tremendous assets: landmark-worthy brownstone houses, an attractive park, nearby commercial strips, and a hardworking, racially diverse population. A local college added a dependable stream of young consumers to the community's economy. Public signs and well-tended gardens indicated the existence of many block associations and of other civic activism.
>
> The residents' commitment to the community was strong, despite the abandoned and poorly kept rental buildings and high levels of car thefts and break-ins, muggings, and drug activity. As drug dealing increased along a commercial corridor, resident anger at apparent police inaction grew. It took a tragedy to catalyze change.
>
> A local convenience-store owner was murdered in his store, and neighborhood block leaders organized a mass meeting to find out what the police were doing. Unfortunately, residents did not think the police were prepared, and the meeting went poorly. As patrol officers stood in the back of the meeting hall, a yelling match ensued between residents and police department spokespeople. Relations between the two groups were at their worst.
>
> Block leaders reached out to the Neighborhood Anti-Crime Center of the Citizens Committee for New York City, due to its reputation for helping citizens and police get together to take back their neighborhoods. The Citizens Committee dedicated a staff organizer's time to helping the community go through a collaborative problem-solving process. A problem-analysis meeting was scheduled.
>
> Block leaders prepared for the meeting by discreetly inviting a small, core group of concerned residents and identifying specific problem locations, offensive conditions, and past efforts to solve the problems. Due to the rancor between residents and police, residents were urged to conduct this first meeting with limited police presence, so that issues could be aired and strategies developed to improve relations.
>
> The meeting itself was the first positive outcome. Residents invited a couple of trusted community-oriented patrol officers, who helped to discern the nature of the problem. The meeting revealed that there were multiple privately owned, and a few city-owned, problem properties housing drug operations and/or addicts. One multifamily structure was identified as a major drug-dealing center,

impervious to enforcement action for over two decades. It was a fortified drug house. However, much necessary information remained unknown.

The Citizens Committee trained the residents to conduct property research (identifying landlords), and then linked them up with key guardians: the district attorney's narcotics eviction unit; legal technical assistance; the city's housing agency representative, who could work on drug-infested property; and trusted police narcotics investigators, who had good information about specific locations. The Citizens Committee also designed an inside-building survey form and introduced the resident leaders to a Muslim patrol organization, which was invited to visit problem locations in an effort to get more accurate information about the narcotics trade and landlord–tenant issues.

The resident leaders asked these guardians to join them in a collaborative planning meeting, which the Citizens Committee organizer facilitated. The pieces of the puzzle were now assembled, revealing that the police had never been able to get into the significant locations, especially the fortified one, because the landlords either colluded with the dealers or were unresponsive to police department contacts. A combined enforcement and legal strategy was hatched, and subsequent meetings kept everyone informed and on target with follow-up.

The block leaders committed to continued outreach and pressure on those landlords, such as the city itself, who were poorly managing their buildings but not allied with the dealers. And residents continued to provide information.

District Attorney Charles Hynes's office committed to pressing civil charges against landlords if they failed to secure their property appropriately after notification of problems and/or criminal activity. In addition, the community activists recruited a law firm (pro bono) to discuss whether, if criminal enforcement did not pan out, bringing a civil lawsuit for money damages was the best approach—similar to the Oakland Drug Abatement Institute strategy.

As a direct result of the collaborative analysis and meetings, the police received help from other city code-enforcement agencies to execute a new warrant at the most egregious location. Coordination continued between all parties after the search warrant revealed how extensive the drug-dealing operation was at the vacant, privately owned building.

Community members and police attended a housing court hearing and alerted the judge that the landlord's track record of failing to maintain the building warranted a case disposition that would serve community interests. The Clinton Hill neighborhood won. The judge legally bound the landlord to secure the property and maintain it crime-free, and authorized the police to have keys to the premises and check up on the landlord.

The landlord agreed to comply in court but failed to do so. Residents, the police, and the district attorney took the landlord back to court, where the judge ruled against the landlord and granted the police permanent access to the premises for safety inspections. Illegal activity has never resumed at this vacant, and formerly fortified, building.

The community sought to build on this victory to publicize the value of working with the police and others, and to encourage efforts to clean up remaining problem locations. A media event was organized, celebrating everyone's hard work. The first court win proved to be just the beginning, as more buildings were successfully targeted and block leaders and police communicated more openly and consistently.[2]

Editors' note: The Neighborhood Anti-Crime Center of the Citizens Committee for New York City builds community capacity to tackle neighborhood crime problems. In this case, they helped the community collect information from the police, residents, and government agencies and helped the community through a civil-court process. Closing the property made a huge difference in building the community's capacity to take on other problem buildings. This project offers insight into the citizens' perspective on neighborhood crime problems. Citizens sometimes think that if a highly visible crime problem exists in the neighborhood, the police must be allowing it to grow and fester. They may misconstrue police inability to solve a crime problem as collusion in it. This distrust in police must be addressed and worked through for collaborative work between the community and the police to proceed. Oftentimes, in the initial meeting between the community and the police concerning a particular problem, time must be devoted to airing and discussing the community's distrust.

GRANTS TO ASSIST IN IMPLEMENTING SELECTED STRATEGIES

The numerous federal grants available to law enforcement agencies to fund illegal and dangerous drug prevention and abatement efforts have been reduced in recent years, and future funding of other programs is in question. Yet several grants are still available.

LO4

Federal assistance specifically aimed at the drug program is available through the Byrne Justice Assistance Grant, the Drug-Free Communities program, and the Community Oriented Policing program. The Weed and Seed program has been defunded.

The Drug-Free Communities (DFC) Support Program is directed by the White House ONDCP in partnership with the Substance Abuse and Mental Health Services Administration (SAMHSA). In the fall of 2015, ONDCP Director Michael Botticelli announced 697 DFC Support Program grants, totaling $86 million, to providing funding to local community coalitions in their efforts to prevent youth substance use, including prescription drugs, heroin, marijuana, tobacco, and alcohol.

CRIME, DRUGS, AND THE AMERICAN DREAM

Before leaving the subject of community policing and substance abuse, it is appropriate to briefly consider the American Dream. The American Dream has been described as a national ethos of the United States—an established ideal that through hard work and diligence, success and prosperity are available

[2] Narrative prepared by Felice Kirby of the Citizens Committee for New York City, submitted to Rana Kirby as part of an NIJ-sponsored problem-solving project and reprinted—with minor editorial changes—with Kirby's permission.

to all. Crime, drugs, and the American Dream are integrally related. In fact, a drug problem may be the result of the American Dream for many people.

Messner and Rosenfeld (2007, p. x) draw a very distinct correlation between crime and the American Dream: "The American Dream contributes to crime directly by encouraging people to employ illegal means to achieve goals that are culturally approved. It also exerts an indirect effect on crime through its interconnections with the institutional balance of power in society." They suggest:

> **Conservative crime control** [emphasis added] policies are draped explicitly in the metaphors of war. We have declared war on crime and on drugs, which are presumed to promote crime. Criminals, according to this view, have taken the streets, blocks, and sometimes entire neighborhoods from law-abiding citizens. The function of crime control policy is to recapture the streets from criminals to make them safe for the rest of us (104). …

> In contrast to conservative crackdowns on criminals, the **liberal crime control** [emphasis added] approach emphasizes correctional policies and broader social reforms intended to expand opportunities for those "locked out" of the American Dream (107).

These competing interests need to be considered in any strategies used to combat the drug problem in a given neighborhood or community. Messner and Rosenfeld (2007, p. 101) suggest that what is needed is crime reduction through social reorganization: "Crime reductions would follow from policies and social changes that vitalize families, schools, and the political system, thereby enhancing the 'drawing power' of the distinctive goals associated with institutions and strengthening their capacity to exercise social control."

A PROBLEM-SOLVING PARTNERSHIP IN ACTION—ROCKY POMERANCE EXCELLENCE IN POLICING AWARD: OCALA POLICE DEPARTMENT (OCALA, FLORIDA)

The Rocky Pomerance Law Enforcement Excellence Award—named in honor of the late Rocky Pomerance, former police chief of Miami Beach, Florida, and past president of the International Association of Chiefs of Police, who has been recognized as exemplifying the image of an innovative and visionary leader—provides a mechanism for the Florida Police Chiefs Association to recognize member agencies for developing and implementing an innovative approach to policing. In 2010, the Ocala (Florida) Police Department (OPD) was a recipient of this award for its innovative and effective community policing response to the negative impact of open-air drug markets on the local community. The problem-solving strategy implemented by the OPD was the Drug Market Intervention (DMI) Initiative developed by Professor David Kennedy of the John Jay College of Criminal Justice in New York, which proved an effective response to illegal drug markets and their associated crime, violence, and disorder. The following account of the program is adapted from an article (Taylor, 2011) posted on the National Network for Safe Communities (NNSC) Web site.

conservative crime control
Comes down hard on crime; wages "war" on crime and drugs.

liberal crime control
Emphasizes correctional policies and broader social reforms intended to expand opportunities for those "locked out" of the American Dream; wages "war" on poverty and inequality of opportunity.

L05
The conservative camp traditionally wages war on crime and drugs; the liberal camp wages war on poverty and inequality of opportunity.

Problem Identification and Analysis

Drug markets both reflect and exacerbate breakdown in community social control characterized by disorder, crime, and fear of crime. In certain neighborhoods in Ocala, drug dealers and drug buyers had taken over the streets, forcing residents to withdraw.

Many community problems, including the most severe problems with violence and disorder, associated with "the drug problem" are a function of drug *markets*, and particular *forms* of drug markets, rather than with drugs as such. These problems included crime hot spots created by street sales and drug houses; unusable public spaces, for example, sidewalks, parks, and stores; enabling markets for prostitutes and drive-through sex buyers, transients whose presence drives out longtime residents; reduced property values; failed or displaced businesses; eased entry into criminality for young people; and facilitated drug use and addiction. Overt drug markets are areas in which a stranger can readily purchase drugs on the street, in drug houses, from apartments, and the like. Typically, overt markets are located in poorer communities and have clearly defined geographical boundaries.

Unfortunately, these overt markets created strong self-sustaining dynamics. Buyers knew that they could buy in a particular area and sellers know that they could sell there; both continued in the same place despite the risks (i.e. arrest, injury) associated with their illegal behavior. Enforcement and prevention efforts rarely shut down entire markets, which continue to provide attractive venues for new dealers and users returning from jail or prison. The experience of law enforcement is that overt markets, once established, are fiercely resistant to even heavy and sustained attention. Routine drug enforcement is often intrusive with high levels of street stops, vehicle stops, and warrants served on residents, and frequently leads to high levels of arrest, conviction, probation, incarceration, and parole, especially for younger men. In some neighborhoods, a substantial majority of young men end up with criminal records and histories of incarceration or court supervision. Communities frequently resent police practices and the unintended harm that often flows from drug enforcement: criminal records that inhibit people from finishing school, taking entry-level jobs, and pursuing higher education; the sense among young men that arrest and imprisonment are normal or even a rite of passage; parents taken away from the children and families.

Implementation

Rather than focusing on individual drug users and sellers, Drug Market Intervention (DMI) focuses on shutting down drug markets utilizing a multiple-step process:

- **The Identification of Drug Markets:** This was accomplished by mapping drug arrests, Part I crimes, weapons, sexual, and prostitution offenses; reviewing serious crimes within hot spots for a drug connection; and analyzing information from patrol officers, vice/narcotics investigators, informants, and crime tip lines. Six neighborhoods were identified as major overt markets.

- **Identification of Dealers Operating in the Drug Markets:** "Tipping" the market to a closed condition and addressing the small-group/network dynamics that supported offending required identifying and taking out all street-level dealers. To develop the list, vice/narcotics detectives surveyed patrol officers, probation officers, street narcotics officers, and community members; reviewed every arrest report, incident report, and field interview associated with possible dealers; reviewed all known associates; checked suspects' current activities; and generated a list. It was found that only a small number of offenders were driving the problem.

- **Create Deterrence by Banking Cases:** For each drug market, police used ordinary investigative techniques to make cases against each dealer. Undercover officers or confidential informants made buys using digital audio and video surveillance equipment. Volume dealers or violent offenders (those with records of violent or gun crimes, or who were otherwise known to be violent), or those facing a probation or parole revocation or an upcoming court date, were arrested and prosecuted. The cases for low-level dealers without a history of violence were "banked"; that is, taken to the point where a warrant could be signed, and held there. This allowed police to tell dealers that if they continued dealing, they would be arrested immediately and without further investigation, but if they stopped dealing, nothing need happen to them. Banking a case meant that the dealers knew to a certainty ahead of time that they faced whatever inconvenience, expense, and formal penalties their arrests would precipitate. With the charge hanging over their heads, they faced the consequences not just for the single drug transaction (or few drug transactions) for which they could be arrested at the moment, but for *all* transactions they might contemplate while the charge was banked.

- **Identifying "Influentials":** The hope was to enlist those close to the offenders—parents, grandparents, guardians, older members of the communities, ministers, ex-offenders—to create and reinforce positive norms and expectations. The "influentials" were identified in what was, in effect, a parallel investigative phase of the initiative. One or several "influentials" were identified for each dealer—primarily mothers and grandmothers.

- **Organizing Services:** Agencies, volunteer groups, and others that could provide social services and assistance in core areas such as education, housing, employment, food and clothing, drug and alcohol treatment, transportation, and the like were identified and recruited to assist. Resources were reprogrammed, primarily from existing efforts, to support the drug market initiative.

- **Home Visits**—Just weeks prior to the first DMI "Call-In," teams consisting of an Ocala police officer, a service provider, and a respected community leader visited the homes of the identified dealers and their "influentials." They were told that the police had made undercover buys from the dealer; that probable cause existed for an arrest; and that an opportunity to avoid prosecution and an offer of assistance would be discussed at an upcoming meeting that family members and others were encouraged to attend. The offenders received a letter from the police chief inviting them to the meeting with a promise that no one would be arrested that night. Most of these visits went surprisingly well, given the concerns the team had about whether the "influentials" would be receptive to the plan.

- **The Call-In:** The key operational moment in the strategy was the call-in at which law enforcement, community members, and service providers delivered a unified message to dealers in the company of their "influentials." On November 9, 2009, six local drug dealers voluntarily walked into a room amongst a crowd of police and prosecutors, service providers, and community members and were presented with an ultimatum: quit selling drugs or go to prison.

Confronted with photographs, video clips, and binders full of evidence gathered during the course of a long-term undercover operation, the drug dealers were promised they would not be arrested, prosecuted, or jailed if they walked away from the drug dealing life-style. And, if they were willing, job training, educational opportunities, and chemical-dependency treatment would be offered to them. Should they squander the second chance and return to drug dealing anywhere in Marion County, the dealers were told they would feel the full force of the law.

This initiative helped mend broken bridges that existed between law enforcement in Ocala and the community. Law enforcement's willingness not to act on existing cases seemed to make a profound impression on the dealers' families and other community members. Dealers' mothers and families cheered both the community's and law enforcement's messages. Dealers were given an opportunity to immediately meet the service providers following the call-in meeting for the purpose of assessing their various needs and arranging services.

The success of DMI, and ultimately the transformation of neighborhoods in Ocala, rested on the ability to arrange a variety of services, to include drug/alcohol/substance abuse treatment, education, job training, pathways to gainful employment, family counseling, transportation, and ex-offender mentoring. The strategy brings together drug dealers, their families, law enforcement and criminal justice officials, service providers, and community leaders to eliminate overt community drug markets; arrests and prosecutes violent drug dealers; offers non-violent, first-time drug dealers opportunities for education, job training, and other assistance; and establishes clear, predictable, and meaningful consequences for those who return to dealing.

Improvement Process, Results, and Conclusion

After the first year, in one of the six identified drug market neighborhoods, calls for police service dropped 10 percent, police presence increased 104 percent, violent crime decreased 47 percent, and community drug tips increased 16 percent. In another neighborhood, calls for police service dropped 11 percent, police presence increased 62 percent, violent crime decreased 16 percent, and community drug tips increased 40 percent.

The most important benefit of this work is the reconciliation that emerges from the dialogue between the community and police. While numbers are often utilized to gauge change, the true measure of positive change is demonstrated by the "new life" visible in both of these neighborhoods.[3]

SUMMARY

Crime and drugs are clearly linked. According to the DEA, the drugs currently considered to pose the greatest threat are CPDs, heroin, methamphetamine, and marijuana.

The seven core areas of focus of the *2015 National Drug Control Strategy* are preventing drug use in our communities; seeking early intervention opportunities in health care; integrating treatment for substance use disorders into health care and supporting recovery; breaking the cycle of drug use, crime, and incarceration; disrupting domestic drug trafficking and production; strengthening international partnerships; and improving information systems to better address drug use and its consequences.

Law enforcement strategies to deal with the drug problem include drug raids, surveillance, undercover operations, arresting sellers and users, and improving intelligence. In apartment complexes, open drug markets pose a greater threat than closed drug markets.

Federal assistance specifically aimed at the drug problem is available through the Byrne Justice Assistance Grant, the Drug-Free Communities program, and the Community Oriented Policing program. The Weed and Seed program has been defunded.

Crime, drugs, and the American Dream are integrally related. In fact, the drug problem may be the result of the American Dream for many people. How to approach the drug problem is often political. The conservative camp traditionally wages war on crime and drugs; the liberal camp wages war on poverty and inequality of opportunity.

---

[3] Reprinted by permission of the Ocala, Florida, Police Department.

DISCUSSION QUESTIONS

1. What do you see as the relationship between drugs and the American Dream?

2. What programs in your community are directed at the drug problem?

3. Which of the programs discussed in this chapter seem most exemplary to you? Why?

4. Explain how lease enforcement reduces criminal activity in public housing.

5. Some rave party strategies used by police have been criticized as racist. Discuss why some law enforcement responses might be considered racist.

6. Did you receive DARE training as a child? What were your impressions? Do you believe it had any effect on your attitudes and actions regarding drugs?

7. Explain the strategy behind improving the physical environment of a neighborhood or apartment complex. What does that have to do with illegal drug activity?

8. What are the three core principles of the National Drug Control Strategy? Which do you believe to be the most effective? The least?

9. Explain the "gateway" theory of drug use. What is your opinion of the theory?

10. What bar marketing promotions are you aware of that encourage irresponsible drinking?

CASE CITED

United States v. Jones, 565 U.S. _____ 132 S.Ct. 945 (2012)

Bringing Youths into Community Policing

Learning Objectives

LO1 Compare and contrast risk factors and protective factors.

LO2 Identify the federal initiatives aimed at protecting our nation's youth.

LO3 Name the entity that many consider to be the cornerstone of the community.

LO4 Understand how schools should be viewed.

LO5 Explain the "tell or tattle" dilemma.

LO6 Summarize the seven-pronged approach to effective school security.

LO7 Know whether zero-tolerance policies are an effective deterrent to noncon- forming behavior.

Key Terms

bullying
developmental assets
peer child abuse
polyvictimization
protective factor
risk factor
tattling
zero tolerance

Local law enforcement officers who serve Charleston, South Carolina's East Side, which is a predominately low-income African American community, were noticing that many children would run away in fear from the officer patrolling their streets. After homicides would occur, many kids would stand around the perimeter of the yellow caution tape with contempt in their eyes for the police. The youths' disregard and disdain for law enforcement was disheartening to those assigned to the East Side division because many of the officers viewed their primary job as serving and protecting the children who lived in the area. In response to the observable dislike of the police by local youth, the Charleston Police Department (CPD) administration developed Camp Hope, an initiative designed by local police, politicians, academics, and prominent community members to provide outreach to children in an effort to change their negative attitudes and perceptions of local law enforcement.

Instead of being a traditional daytime summer camp, Camp Hope was offered during the evening, when kids were more likely to be lingering around in boredom. Police found that the kids with nothing to do were often from homes in poverty and, lacking any structured activity, were more likely to engage in the local criminal element. By getting involved with police and Camp Hope, these kids found recreation, extracurricular activities, hot meals, field trips, and education in a nonviolent environment. This summer camp relies on police, parents, and local volunteers for its continued success in engaging students with weekly lessons of respect, kindness, attitude, and teamwork.

The idea of youth engagement has been so successful for the CPD that grassroots organizations geared toward children are spreading into surrounding jurisdictions. North Charleston, the scene of the much publicized shooting of Walter Scott, an unarmed Black man, by White police officer, Michael Slager, has seen a dramatic increase in local organizations geared toward engaging children, such as Community Roll Call, Kids and Cops, Operation Safe Summer, and a Cops Athletic Program.

The importance of have a good working relationship between kids and police cannot be overstated. Keeping youth interested in the community's success, as well as their own, makes a community profitable in numerous ways. By improving the civic engagement between police and children, the department increases the odds of improving the relationship with all ages of the community.

INTRODUCTION

Forman (2004, p. 2) contends that community policing will never reach its full potential unless a critical group—youths and young adults—is included in the policing model: "Leaving young people out of [the] model of community policing has tremendous implications. Public safety turns, to a great extent, on what the young do and what is done to them. This is the group most likely to engage in criminal conduct, to be victims of crime, and to be targeted by police." Thus, if community policing is to succeed, it is imperative that the important youth segment of the community not be forgotten. If youths can come to feel a part of their community and their school early on, many future problems might be eliminated.

One of the key recommendations set forth in the *Final Report of the President's Task Force on 21st Century Policing* is for communities to "adopt policies and programs that address the needs of children and youth most at risk for crime or violence and reduce aggressive law enforcement tactics that stigmatize youth and marginalize their participation in schools and communities" (2015, p. 47). The task force notes how a lack in officer training regarding child and adolescent development can leave officers unable to recognize and manage issues involving children's emotional, intellectual, and physical development which can, in turn, lead noncriminal offenses to become escalated into criminal charges.

YOUTH VICTIMIZATION AND DELINQUENCY

A relatively small percentage of youth engage in criminal behavior but many more become victims of crime. Victimization of children, youth, and teens occurs in numerous ways, and some youth experience multiple forms of violence, known as **polyvictimization**. Crimes against young people can range from abuse and neglect to assault and homicide.

polyvictimization
Experiencing multiple forms of victimization (emotional, physical)

Most children and adolescents will experience some form of physical assault during their lifetime. Data from the National Survey of Children's Exposure to Violence (NatSCEV) indicate that in 2011, 41.2 percent of children age 0 to 17 years had been physically assaulted within the previous 12 months (Office for Victims of Crime, 2015). Going beyond the previous year, the survey found that 54.5 percent of children and adolescents age 0 to 17 had experienced some form of physical assault, 24.6 percent were victims of physical intimidation (i.e., physical bullying), 51.8 percent were victims of relational aggression (i.e., emotional bullying), and 10.3 percent were victims of assault with a weapon. Teenagers are particularly at risk for high levels of assault, maltreatment, and property victimization. The NatSCEV shows that, of the U.S. population of 14- to 17-year-olds surveyed in 2011, 69.7 percent had been assaulted, 56.6 percent had experienced a property victimization (including robbery), 41.2 percent had been maltreated, and 27.4 percent had been sexually victimized at some point in their lifetime (Office for Victims of Crime, 2015).

In addition to primary victimization, many youth are exposed to physical and emotional violence in their homes, schools, and neighborhoods. Such exposure to violence increases the probability that a youth will experience other types of violence and future victimization, the effects of which can be cumulative and extremely damaging over time (Office for Victims of Crime, 2015).

Recognizing Risk and Protective Factors

Communities that seek to include youths in their community policing efforts must be aware of the myriad risk and protective factors that play a role in victimization and delinquency. Various definitions of risk factors exist, but in the context of juvenile justice, a working definition of a **risk factor** is a condition, characteristic, or variable that increases the likelihood that a child will become delinquent. Exposure to multiple risk factors can have a cumulative effect, and the relative impact any risk factor has on a child may be either augmented or diminished by the developmental state of that child (Shader, 2002). Conversely, the existence of certain protective factors can work to offset the risk factors and keep a child headed toward a law-abiding adulthood. In general, a **protective factor**, often the opposite of a risk factor, is a condition, characteristic, or variable that increases the likelihood that a child will avoid delinquency. For example, if poor parental supervision is a risk factor, then a high degree of parental monitoring is a protective factor. Truancy is a risk factor; staying in school is a protective factor. Low IQ is a risk factor, high IQ, a protective factor.

Researchers have identified hundreds, if not thousands, of risk factors related to delinquency and have grouped them into five basic domains: individual, family, school, peers, and community. Protective factors also relate to individual characteristics, family, school, peers, and community. The most significant individual risk factor for predicting later delinquency is early antisocial behavior, specifically aggression.

In 2005, the Rand Corporation released a research report, *Stopping Violence before It Starts: Identifying Early Predictors of Adolescent Violence*, which identified several early predictors of middle school students becoming perpetrators of violence in high school. The study showed that the presence of three characteristics in 7th graders made it more likely that a student would frequently resort to overall violence 5 years later: (1) having poor grades, (2) having experienced frequent moves between elementary schools, and (3) exhibiting early deviant behavior. Although these general findings held true for both boys and girls, there were differences. Having low self-esteem and living in a poor neighborhood were additional risk factors for girls, and just being born a boy and going to a school with high drug use were additional risk factors for boys. In addition, boys were more affected than girls by elementary school mobility.

Additional research has found gender-specific risk factors for girls to include early puberty coupled with stressors such as conflict with parents and involvement with delinquent, and often older, male peers (Zahn et al., 2010). The implications of such findings allow practitioners to tailor victimization, delinquency, and violence prevention programs to specific at-risk children. For example, programs may target girls with low self-esteem or boys who move frequently during the elementary school years, as evidence shows these populations may be especially vulnerable to developmental disruptions linked to later delinquency and violence (Rand Corporation, 2005).

risk factor

A condition, characteristic, or variable that increases the likelihood that a child will become delinquent; often the opposite of a *protective factor*.

protective factor

A condition, characteristic, or variable that increases the likelihood that a child will avoid delinquency; often the opposite of a *risk factor*.

LO1

A risk factor is a condition, characteristic, or variable that increases a child's likelihood of becoming delinquent, the impact of which is affected by the child's developmental state. Conversely, a protective factor is a condition, characteristic, or variable that increases the likelihood that a child will avoid delinquency, offsetting any potential risk factors to increase the likelihood a child will reach a law-abiding adulthood.

Key Indicators of Children's Well-Being

In 1994, the Office of Management and Budget (OMB) joined with six other federal agencies to create the Federal Interagency Forum on Child and Family Statistics. Today, the Forum is a collection of 22 federal government agencies involved in research and activities related to children and families. The Forum's annual report, *America's Children: Key National Indicators of Well-Being*, provides a comprehensive summary of three demographic background measures and 41 selected indicators to describe our nation's population of children and depict both the promises and the challenges affecting child well-being in the areas of family and social environment, economic circumstances, health care, physical environment and safety, behavior, education, and health. Additionally, the Forum monitors and reports changes in these indicators over time. Some of the highlights of the 2016 report include (Federal Interagency Forum on Child and Family Statistics, 2016):

- There were 73.7 million children in the United States in 2016, which was 1.3 million more than in 2000. The number of children is projected to be 76.3 million in 2030.

- By 2020, fewer than half of all U.S. children ages 0–17 are projected to be White, non-Hispanic, down from 74 percent in 1980 and 52 percent in 2015. By 2050, only 39 percent of all U.S. children are projected to be White, non-Hispanic.

- In 2014, 69 percent of children ages 0–17 lived with two parents (64% with two married parents and 4% with two unmarried cohabiting parents), 24 percent lived with only their mothers, 4 percent lived with only their fathers, and 4 percent lived without a parent in the household.

- In 2013, about 22 percent of school-age children spoke a language other than English at home.

- In 2013, the adolescent birth rate was 12 per 1,000 adolescents ages 15–17, a record low for the country.

- Twenty percent of all children ages 0–17 (14.7 million) lived in poverty in 2013, down from 22 percent in 2012. This was the first time since 2000 that the child poverty rate declined.

- The percentage of children without health insurance at the time of interview decreased from 14 percent in 1993 to 7 percent in 2013.

- In 2013, over 40 percent of U.S. households (both owners and renters) with children had one or more of three housing problems: physically inadequate housing, crowded housing, or housing cost burden greater than 30 percent of household income. This was down from 46 percent in 2011.

- About 15.8 million children (21% of all children) lived in households that were classified as food insecure in 2013.

- In 2013, the rate of substantiated reports of child maltreatment was 10 per 1,000 children ages 0–17. Younger children were more frequently victims of child maltreatment than were older children. In 2013, there were 24 substantiated child maltreatment reports per 1,000 children under age 1.

- In 2013, 92 percent of young adults ages 18–24 had completed high school with a diploma or an alternative credential such as a General Educational Development (GED) certificate. The high school completion rate has increased since 1980, when it was 84 percent.

The Developmental Asset Approach

"The Asset Approach: Giving Kids What They Need to Succeed" was developed by the Search Institute in Minneapolis, Minnesota. The Search Institute promotes establishing 40 ideals, experiences, and qualities—**developmental assets**—that are associated with reduced high-risk behaviors and increased thriving behaviors (Mannes, Roehlkepartain, & Benson, 2005). These 40 developmental assets are grouped into eight categories that promote (1) support, (2) empowerment, (3) boundaries and expectations, (4) constructive use of time, (5) commitment to learning, (6) positive values, (7) social competence, and (8) positive identity to help youngsters succeed in school and in life.

developmental assets
Forty ideals, experiences, and qualities established by the Search Institute to "help young people make wise decisions, choose positive paths, and grow up competent, caring, and responsible."

Mannes et al. (2005, p. 237) contend: "Developmental assets appear to play an important role in the healthy development of young people across varied life circumstances and in the face of multiple challenges, yet too few youths report experiencing enough of these assets. Young people report having, on average, 19 of the 40 assets." In the communities surveyed, 15 percent of young people had zero to 10 of the 40 assets; 41 percent had 11 to 20 assets; 35 percent had 21 to 30 assets; and only 8 percent had 31 to 40 assets (Mannes et al., 2005). Research found that the presence of fewer than 10 assets was two to five times more powerful in predicting high-risk behaviors than was poverty, supporting the conclusion that the greater the number of developmental assets youth possess, the greater the likelihood they will demonstrate adaptive behaviors such as valuing diversity, maintaining good health, and resisting danger (Mannes et al., 2005).

BUILDING PERSONAL RELATIONSHIPS WITH YOUTH

Building personal relationships with youth is one way police can help youth acquire the assets empirically shown to promote pro-social behavior and attitudes. Action Item 4.7.1 of the *Final Report of the President's Task Force on 21st Century Policing* states: "Communities and law enforcement agencies should restore and build trust between youth and police by creating programs and projects for positive, consistent, and persistent interaction between youth and police (2015, p. 50). Many departments across the country have already developed such programs to allow youth and police officers to get to know and understand each other better. For example, the Kops 'n' Kids program, endorsed by the International Association of Chiefs of Police (IACP), brings together children and officers to have fun rather than to deliver antidrug or anticrime speeches. Officers come with their motorcycles and their K-9s for demonstrations; they share lunch; they form running clubs; they do whatever helps present police as positive role models and build trust with the children.

Many police departments throughout the United States hold an annual Shop with a Cop day in December. One of the largest events takes place in San Diego County, where local, state, and federal law enforcement personnel raise tens of thousands of dollars every year to give underprivileged children a fun day and a brighter holiday season. The San Diego Shop with a Cop is a nonprofit organization, funded by grants and corporate donations. Variations of the Shop with a Cop program exist throughout the country, and some departments have added a back-to-school event in which officers take at-risk children shopping for school supplies. Other police departments treat seriously ill or homeless children to special events, and at least one also gives the parents a $75 grocery gift card.

Noting the unique challenges youth face when encountering the criminal justice system, the President's Task Force on 21st Century Policing recommends that positive, proactive interactions between youth and police be encouraged so as to create the opportunity for coaching, mentoring, and diversion into constructive alternative activities (2015). One example of an effort to strengthen youth–police relations is occurring in Houston, Texas. The Houston Police Department, in partnership with the University of Houston–Clear Lake (UHCL), Texas Southern University, and the Beechnut Academy, launched the Teen and Police Service (TAPS) Academy in January 2012. Funded by a federal grant from the COPS Office, the goal of TAPS is to reduce the social distance between youth and police and increase teens' trust in law enforcement by having officers mentor at-risk youth. The TAPS Academy is structured around an 11-week curriculum and covers topics such as violence, physical and sexual abuse, stalking, domestic trafficking, sexual exploitation, and bullying. Building on the groundwork established by other community policing programs, such as DARE, the TAPS Academy aims to engage specifically with at-risk youth, because this group is least likely to participate voluntarily in other mentoring programs. The academy is designed to help

 IDEAS IN PRACTICE NYPD'S SUMMER YOUTH POLICE ACADEMY

The New York Police Department (NYPD) has implemented a Summer Youth Police Academy program to help build positive relationships between the police agency and the city's young people. The goals of the academy are:

- To enhance responsible citizenship.
- To provide positive interaction with police officers and educate youth about the challenges and responsibility of police work.
- To encourage young people to take part in other youth programs offered by the Police Department such as the Law Enforcement Explorers, Police Cadet Corps, and the Police Athletic League.

The Academy is open to children ages 10 to 16. During the summer of 2015, more than 1,800 youth attended and completed the six-week course.

Sources: New York Police Department. (2016). *Community Programs: Summer Youth Police Academy*. New York, NY: Author. Retrieved October 10, 2016 from http://www.nyc.gov/html/nypd/html/community_affairs/youth_programs_summer_academy.shtml

Marcus, C. R., & Stepansky, J. (2015, August 14). "NYPD Commissioner Bill Bratton Congratulates 1,800 Youth Police Academy Graduates." *New York Daily News*. Retrieved October 11, 2016 from http://www.nydailynews.com/new-york/bratton-congratulates-1-800-nypd-youth-academy-graduates-article-1.2325532

at-risk youth change their behavior, learn responsible decision making, and participate in crime prevention projects. Police mentors, who have received special training to be involved in the TAPS program, are selected to reflect the diversity of the community in which they serve and are chosen because of their desire to create a better life for at-risk teens by helping youth learn better ways to deal with issues they will inevitably encounter (TAPS Academy, 2015). Other cities offering TAPS Academies include Columbus, Ohio; El Paso, Texas; Galveston, Texas; New York City, New York; Richmond, Virginia; Ponce, Puerto Rico; and Tampa, Florida.

PARTNERSHIPS THAT CONNECT YOUTH AND THE COMMUNITY

Partnerships should include youths at all levels of activity, with their roles considered as important as those of adults. A potential obstacle is the attitude of some adult policymakers and leaders that youths are the source of the community's violence problems rather than part of the solution. Forums where youths can present their views can help overcome this bias.

Oakland, California's Teens on Target

In the late 1980s, gun violence was on the rise in Oakland, California, and an increasing number of youth homicides were occurring as the result of heightened gang activity, drug dealing, and racial tensions in the schools and on the streets. In 1989, the nonprofit youth development agency, YouthALIVE!, created the Teens on Target (TNT) initiative, the mission of which was to reduce youth injuries and deaths through peer education, peer intervention, mentoring, and leadership development (Sheppard, 1999). The program is still in operation, training urban youth who live in neighborhoods with the highest rates of violence how to become active advocates for violence prevention.

Metropolitan (DC) Police Department's Youth Advisory Council

The Metropolitan Police Department (MPD) in the District of Columbia started a School Security Division Youth Advisory Council (YAC) in fall of 2002 as a way to include the area youth in community policing and the problem-solving process as well as enable the department to develop partnerships with area youth (Metropolitan Police Department, n.d.). The YAC engages public school students ages 14–18 throughout DC in activities that focus on three basic objectives:

- To expose students to the variety of career paths available
- To provide access to mentors, role models, and internships that can serve as springboards for future career choices
- To offer the opportunity to gain the tools and skills necessary to become successful adults

Monthly meetings include social and educational events and field trips, educational seminars, basic career planning, and special guest speakers who interact with the youth to encourage positive change. Good citizenship is a common topic of discussion among YAC participants, and the citizenship theme changes from year to year. During meetings, students also participate in group-related activities, such as holding elections, planning group activities, problem solving, or a combination thereof. Examples of past activities include (Metropolitan Police Department, n.d.):

- **Beat the Street Program:** A citywide program targeting high crime areas that conducts community awareness activities, provides informational handouts to residents, and coordinates youth activities
- **Police Ride-Alongs and MPD Site Visits:** Allows YAC participants to get a comprehensive look at law enforcement as a possible career path
- **Trip to the Newseum:** Another career path opportunity with a structured itinerary to give YAC students insight into different news-related professions, such as journalism, news reporting, and public speaking
- **College Tours:** Lead YAC participants through a series of college tours, including local institutions and those along the east coast. Before the tour, students attend a college readiness workshop to learn how to stay on track for higher education and employment. During the tour to various colleges, MPD School Resource Officers speak to students about college admission requirements, the application process, financial aid, SAT testing, grade point averages, and housing options.

FEDERAL INITIATIVES

Clearly, the news is not all bad regarding our nation's youth. However, areas of concern do exist, and several federal initiatives have been directed at protecting our country's young people.

The Adam Walsh Child Protection and Safety Act

LO2

Federal initiatives to protect our nation's youths include passage of the Adam Walsh Child Protection and Safety Act, America's Promise Alliance, Project Safe Childhood, and the Safe Start Initiative.

The Adam Walsh[1] Child Protection and Safety Act, also known as the Sex Offender Registration and Notification Act (SORNA), went into effect in 2006 and strengthens the national standards for sex offender registration and notification as well as provides statutory authorization for Project Safe Childhood, described later in this chapter. Of the hundreds of thousands of registered sex offenders nationally, the whereabouts of a large number—approaching 20 percent by some estimates—are currently unknown. The Adam Walsh Act creates stricter requirements for sex offender registration—to prevent offenders from slipping through the cracks and harming children.

---

[1] Adam Walsh was 6 years old in 1981 when he was abducted from a store and brutally murdered. His parents have worked relentlessly since that time to pass this law to protect children from sexual predators. John Walsh, Adam's father, was host of the popular television show *America's Most Wanted*, and now hosts *The Hunt*.

Although SORNA did not create a federal sex offender registry, it did create a new federal felony offense for failing to register as a sex offender and established a baseline sex offender registry standard for all jurisdictions to achieve, while allowing states to enact more stringent requirements if they so desired (McPherson, 2007). The legislation also calls for stricter prison sentences for offenders who fail to register and keep their information current. The offender will be assigned to one of three tiers; the worst offenders will have to check in more frequently, and all offenders have to register in person. In addition, the Act:

- Makes registration as a sex offender a mandatory condition of probation and supervised release.
- Eliminates the statute of limitations for prosecutions of child abduction and felony sex offenses against children.
- Directs the Attorney General to provide technical assistance to jurisdictions to help identify and locate sex offenders relocated due to a major disaster.

All states were required to comply with the Adam Walsh Act by July 2011. However, as of August 2016, only 17 states had substantially complied with SORNA requirements. Some states, including Texas and New York, have officially declined to comply with the Act, even though failure to comply means the loss of 10 percent of their federal Byrne grants. Hurdles to compliance include the high cost of implementation and objections to the juvenile registration requirement, which requires offenders as young as 14 who are adjudicated in juvenile court with a serious sex offense to be listed on law enforcement registers for 25 years. Critics of this SORNA requirement point to the growing body of empirical evidence that shows fewer than 10 percent of youth who commit sex offenses recidivate (National Juvenile Justice Network, 2012). In August of 2016, the Federal Court provided more flexibility to those states that have not yet complied with SORNA because of their objections to the requirement of placing all juveniles age 14 and older who have been convicted of a sex crime on this list (Department of Justice, 2016).

America's Promise Alliance

Another federal initiative is America's Promise Alliance. Established in 1997 with General Colin Powell as the founding chairman, America's Promise Alliance is the nation's largest partnership dedicated to improving the lives of youth, consisting of more than 360 corporations, nonprofits, communities, faith-based organizations, advocacy groups, educators, and policy makers. The Alliance's mission, as stated on its Web site, is to "inspire, engage, and unite individuals, institutions, and communities to create the conditions for success for every child in America" (America's Promise Alliance, 2016). The Alliance strives to keep Five Promises they believe should be made to each child: "We promise to young Americans that they will grow up with the help and guidance of caring adult relationships, healthy childhoods, safe surroundings, effective education and opportunities to serve others. When at least four of these promises are at work in young people's lives, they are more likely to succeed academically, socially and civically." By partnering with families, schools, and organizations in the community, the Alliance seeks to provide a foundation for success for all children. The America's Promise Alliance believes what research tells us, that if every child receives these five fundamental resources, he or she is 5 to 10 times more likely to stay in school, avoid drugs and alcohol, not get in trouble with the law, and grow up to be an engaged citizen in his or her community.

Project Safe Childhood

Project Safe Childhood was launched in 2006 by the Department of Justice to combat the proliferation of technology-facilitated crimes involving the sexual exploitation of children. Using a network of federal, state, and local law enforcement agencies and advocacy organizations, Project Safe Childhood aims to protect children by investigating and prosecuting offenders involved in child sexual exploitation. In May 2011, Project Safe Childhood was expanded to encompass all federal crimes involving the sexual exploitation of a minor, including sex trafficking of a minor and crimes against children committed in Indian country. Failure to register as a sex offender is now an offense that also falls within the reach of Project Safe Childhood (Project Safe Childhood, n.d.).

Safe Start National Resource Center

The Safe Start National Resource Center helps support those working with Children Exposed to Violence (CEV) by raising awareness, fostering effective community action, and moving from evidence to action to prevent and reduce the impact of direct and indirect violence on children and their families. Safe Start is designed to expand current partnerships among service providers in key areas such as early childhood education/development, health, mental health, child welfare, family support, substance abuse prevention/intervention, domestic violence/crisis intervention, law enforcement, the courts, and legal services. The project's goal is to create a comprehensive service delivery system that will meet the needs of children and their families at any point of entry into the system by expanding, enhancing, coordinating, and integrating services and support to families. This comprehensive system should improve the accessibility, delivery, and quality of services for young children who have been exposed to violence or are at high risk for exposure (Safe Start National Resource Center, n.d.).

The Safe Start Initiative funded 15 sites across the country from 2005 to 2010, all of which focused on implementing and measuring developmentally appropriate services for children exposed to violence within the context of the systems that serve them. Another 10 Safe Start sites were funded from 2010 to 2015 to provide evidence- or theory-based interventions to prevent and reduce the impact of children's exposure to violence in their homes and communities (Safe Start Center, 2013).

A PARTNERSHIP TO PREVENT JUVENILE DELINQUENCY

Horizons Youth and Family Services was founded on April 1, 1973 by the City Manager's office in Livermore, California. The program was transferred to the Livermore Police Department the next year, as a condition of funding, in an effort to more effectively reach those youth most at risk of delinquency. This purpose has remained for the past four decades. Although Horizons was original designed as a "youth outreach" program that involved the provision of recreational activities and informational counseling, it has evolved into a professionally staffed family counseling program (City of Livermore, n.d.). Horizons was selected to be the lead agency for the Comprehensive Youth Services in 1999, an alliance that brought together four local law enforcement agencies, four school districts, a community health center, and the local parks and recreation district to create a service plan for the entire area. This brought prevention and early intervention funds to Pleasanton and Livermore school districts, Valley Community Health Center, Horizons, and LARPD, providing to the entire valley under the Comprehensive Youth Services funding.

This alliance is based on interface and interdependence. Horizons Family Counseling and the Livermore Police Department literally work "shoulder to shoulder" because the counseling service is located inside the police department. Families of first-time youth offenders arrested for a minor offense have a unique opportunity in that the successful completion of three family sessions can change the arrest to a nonarrest. Police officers and counselors have different roles with these first-time offenders:

- Officers making the arrest interact with the family when emotions are running high.
- When families arrive for counseling after police have been at their home, they have had some time for reflection.
- Counselors have more permission to explore family members' lives.
- Counselors help weave emotional reconnections for a family.
- Families can then take responsibility for "inviting" a police intervention.

In moving from incident-driven policing to solution-focused policing, the department recognizes that outreach to young people and their families is important to community health and safety.

THE IMPORTANCE OF FAMILY AND PARENTAL INVOLVEMENT

The family is the foundation for the protection, care, and training of children. Because the family is usually the first teacher and model for behavior and misbehavior, the structure and interaction patterns of the home can sometimes influence whether children learn social or delinquent behavior. Children develop their sense of worth, capability, importance, and uniqueness from the attention and love given to them by their parents. They can also develop a sense of worthlessness, incapability, unimportance, and facelessness when attention and love are lacking, or when physical, sexual, or emotional abuse exists. Delinquency is highest when family interaction and controls are weak.

Findings released by the OJJDP suggest that violent acts of delinquency are less likely to be committed by youths who have adult supervision after school than by those who are unsupervised one or more days a week. Even more important than actual adult supervision is whether parents know where their children are after school.

Unfortunately, in many American families, the traditional bonds of discipline and respect between parent and child have loosened considerably, if not unraveled completely. If the integration process between parents and children is deficient, the children may fail to learn appropriate behaviors, and the stage may be set for delinquency.

> **LO3**
> The family is viewed by many as the cornerstone of the community.

THE IMPORTANCE OF SCHOOLS

Given the amount of time that youth and teens spend at school, it comes as no surprise that schools play an important role in the social development of children.

> **LO4**
> A school should be viewed as a community, not as an institution.

The Child Development Project (CDP) is a comprehensive, whole-school improvement program designed by the Developmental Studies Center in Oakland, California. This project fosters children's cognitive, ethical, and social growth by providing all students with engaging, challenging learning opportunities and creating a strong sense of community among students, teachers, and parents. CDP research suggests that increases in children's sense of community are linked to their later development of intrinsic academic motivation, concern for others, democratic values, skill and inclination to resolve conflicts equitably, intrinsic prosocial motivation, enjoyment of helping others learn, inclusive attitudes toward out-groups, and positive interpersonal behavior in class. In addition to building a sense of community within the school, schools should also partner with the community of which they are a part.

Students whose families are involved in their growth both inside and outside of school are more likely to experience school success and less likely to become involved in antisocial activities. School staff, students, and families should be involved in developing, discussing, and implementing fair rules. In addition, law enforcement can be brought into the school to get to know students and through select police–school programs can help students become mentors, peacekeepers, and problem solvers.

The President's Task Force on 21st Century Policing devoted much attention to the crucial role schools play and set forth numerous recommendations and action items pertaining to partnerships between police the schools, including (2015, pp. 47–50):

> **4.6.1 Action Item**: Education and criminal justice agencies at all levels of government should work together to reform policies and procedures that push children into the juvenile justice system.
>
> **4.6.2 Action Item:** In order to keep youth in school and to keep them from criminal and violent behavior, law enforcement agencies should work with

schools to encourage the creation of alternatives to student suspensions and expulsion through restorative justice, diversion, counseling, and family interventions.

A particularly salient action item, in the context of this discussion, is the following (2015, p. 48):

4.6.3 Action Item: Law enforcement agencies should work with schools to encourage the use of alternative strategies that involve youth in decision making, such as restorative justice, youth courts, and peer interventions.

Allowing youth an active role and voice in such strategies helps create legitimacy in the eyes of the youth involved, which can help build rapport with police and enhance youths' trust of the justice system as a whole. For example, youth courts, also called teen courts or peer courts, allow youth to determine the appropriate sanctions for first-time, nonviolent, misdemeanor juvenile offenders. In such courts, youth volunteers, supervised by adult volunteers, work as bailiffs, clerks, jury, and judges, questioning the offender, debating, and imposing sentences.

Youth courts generally have two main goals: (1) response to the behavior, with behavioral consequences such as restitution, community service, and personal restrictions, as well as the implied threat that failing to follow through will bring severe consequences and (2) building youth responsibility (Garrett, 2009). Studies show a low recidivism rate—less than 13 percent—among teen participants (Garrett, 2009).

School Teams

Some schools have developed teams to watch for signs of trouble and to step in to prevent problems. In California, Butte County's Safe Schools teams are one example. These teams are a partnership of the Chico (California) Police Department, which assigns a full-time youth services officer to each school in the program; the Butte County Probation Department, which redefined its caseloads to correspond to specific schools; and the Chico Unified School District, which provides office space and equipment and integrates its referral services with those of the police and probation department.

The officers monitor *all* students' behavior but focus on those on probation. They conduct safety checks, perform searches, and enforce curfew and attendance policies. The team also makes a point of supporting youths working hard to "stay on track" by attending sporting events, graduations, and other activities in which youths are taking part.

Another way the team is proactive is in forging relationships with gang members, their peers, and others "in the know." Students alert team members when they think something is "going down."

The School Resource Officer

School resource officers (SROs), also called education resource officers, are police officers assigned to schools on a full-time basis and function as an integral connection between the school and the community. The placement and use of SROs has grown considerably over the past two decades, with an estimated 17,000 sworn officers serving in our nation's schools (Raymond, 2010). SROs perform a variety of services and, while their duties may vary considerably from community to community, three primary roles have been generally recognized:

- safety expert and law enforcer
- problem solver and liaison to community resources
- educator

Local jurisdictions are finding encouragement and support through federal funding sources for SRO programs. However, as the use of SROs gains popularity, it has become important to understand when and how such assignments can be an appropriate strategy for schools and police agencies (Raymond, 2010). The practice was addressed by the President's Task Force on 21st Century Policing (2015, p. 48) in Action Item 4.6.8:

> Law enforcement agencies and schools should establish memoranda of agreement for the placement of School Resource Officers that limit police involvement in student discipline. Such agreements could include provisions for special training for School Resource Officers to help them better understand and deal with issues involving youth.

The following content is reprinted from the Office of Community Oriented Policing Service's Problem-Oriented Guide *Assigning Police Officers to Schools* (Raymond, 2010, pp. 3–5):

More than 17,000 school resource officers (SROs) exist in schools nationwide, serving as advisers to and positive role models for students and faculty. Partnerships with local law enforcement are an important element of safe and effective schools.

Syracuse Newspapers/J. Commentucci/The Image Works

Safety Expert and Law Enforcer

As sworn police officers, SROs play a unique role in preserving order and promoting safety on campus by, for example:

- Assuming primary responsibility for handling calls for service from the school and in coordinating the response of other police resources
- Addressing crime and disorder problems, gangs, and drug activities occurring in or around the school
- Making arrests and issuing citations on campus
- Providing leads and information to the appropriate investigative units
- Taking action against unauthorized persons on school property
- Serving as hall monitors, truancy enforcers, crossing guards, and operators of metal detectors and other security devices
- Responding to off-campus criminal mischief that involves students
- Serving as liaisons between the school and the police and providing information to students and school personnel about law enforcement matters.

Beyond serving in a crime prevention and response role, SROs are likely to serve as first responders in the event of critical incidents at schools, such as accidents, fires, explosions, and other life threatening events. In addition, SROs often support advance planning for managing crises, including assisting with:

- Developing incident response systems
- Developing and coordinating emergency response plans (in conjunction with other emergency responders)
- Incorporating law enforcement onto school crisis management teams
- Developing protocols for handling specific types of emergencies
- Rehearsing such protocols using tabletop exercises, drills, and mock evacuations and lockdowns.

Problem Solver and Liaison to Community Resources

In the school setting, problem solving involves coordinated efforts among administrators, teachers, students, parents, mental health professionals, and community-based stakeholders. SROs frequently assist in resolving problems that are not necessarily law violations, such as bullying or disorderly behavior, but which are nonetheless safety issues that can result in or contribute to criminal incidents. Helping resolve these problems frequently requires the officer to act as a resource liaison, referring students to professional services within both the school (guidance counselors, social workers) and the community (youth and family service organizations). In particular, SROs often build relationships with juvenile justice counselors, who are responsible for supervising delinquent youths, connecting them with needed services, and recommending diversionary activities.

Problem-solving activities commonly include:

- Developing and expanding crime prevention efforts for students
- Developing and expanding community justice initiatives for students
- Assisting in identifying environmental changes that can reduce crime in or around schools
- Assisting in developing school policies that address crime and recommending procedural changes to implement those policies.

Educator

A police officer can serve as a resource for classroom presentations that complement the educational curriculum by emphasizing the fundamental principles and skills needed for responsible citizenship, as well as by teaching topics related to policing. SROs can present courses for students, faculty, and parents. Although SROs teach a variety of classes, there is no research indicating which classes are most useful or how to ensure an officer's effectiveness in the teaching role. Topics commonly covered in an SRO curriculum include:

- Policing as a career
- Criminal investigation
- Alcohol and drug awareness
- Gang and stranger awareness and resistance
- General crime prevention
- Conflict resolution
- Restorative justice
- Babysitting safety
- Bicycling, pedestrian, and motor vehicle safety
- Special crimes in which students are especially likely to be offenders or victims, such as vandalism, shoplifting, and sexual assault by acquaintances.

The variety of program structures and activities can lead to confusion about what individual programs are meant to accomplish and how to assess and measure their effectiveness. In particular, school and police officials often conceptualize the role of the SRO differently. Although school officials tend to view SROs as first responders, SROs themselves often view their roles more broadly, giving greater weight to job functions that represent an expansion of the traditional security officer role. For instance, more police than principals report that SROs did more than maintain order. Police also report significantly more teaching activity than do principals.

Despite their rising popularity, little research has been conducted on the effectiveness of SRO programs (Raymond, 2010).

Crime and Violence in Our Schools

Unfortunately, the violence so prevalent within our society has found its way into our schools, as the school shootings in the past few years have dramatically shown. In addition, some youths turn to gangs for the support and feelings of self-worth they cannot find at home or school, as discussed in the next chapter. According to the most recently available *Indicators of School Crime and Safety* (Zhang, Musu-Gillette, & Oudekerk, 2016), crime in school is falling in most places. However, in 2014:

- Among students ages 12–18, there were about 850,100 nonfatal victimizations at school, which included 363,700 theft victimizations and 486,400 violent victimizations (simple assault and serious violent victimizations).

- Students ages 12–18 experienced 33 nonfatal victimizations per 1,000 students at school and 24 per 1,000 students away from school.

- Students residing in rural areas had higher rates of total victimization at school (53 victimizations per 1,000 students) than students residing in suburban areas (28 victimizations per 1,000 students).

Preliminary data also show that there were 53 school-associated violent deaths from July 1, 2012, through June 30, 2013 (Zhang et al., 2016). Other findings reported in the 2015 *Indicators of School Crime and Safety* include the following:

- During the 2013–14 school year, there were 1.3 million reported discipline incidents in the United States for reasons related to alcohol, drugs, violence, or weapons possession that resulted in a student being removed from the education setting for at least an entire school day.

- About 7 percent of students in grades 9–12 reported being threatened or injured with a weapon such as a gun, knife, or club on school property in 2013. The percentage of students who reported being threatened or injured with a weapon on school property has decreased over the last decade, from 9 percent in 2003 to 7 percent in 2013. In each survey year from 1993 to 2013, a higher percentage of males than of females in grades 9–12 reported being threatened or injured with a weapon on school property.

- During the 2011–12 school year, a higher percentage of public than private school teachers reported being threatened with injury (10 vs. 3%) or being physically attacked (6 vs. 3%) by a student from their school.

- Ten percent of elementary teachers and 9 percent of secondary teachers reported being threatened by a student from their school in 2011–12. The percentage of elementary teachers who reported being physically attacked by a student was higher than the percentage of secondary teachers (8 vs. 3%).

- The percentage of public schools that reported student bullying occurred at least once a week decreased from 29 percent in 1999–2000 to 16 percent in 2013–14. Similarly, the percentage of schools that reported the occurrence of student verbal abuse of teachers decreased from 13 percent in 1999–2000 to 5 percent in 2013–14.

- The percentage of public schools reporting student harassment of other students based on sexual orientation or gender identity was lower in 2013–14 (1%) than in 2009–10 (3%).

- During the 2013–14 school year, the percentage of public schools that reported student bullying occurred at least once a week was higher for middle schools (25%) than high schools/combined schools (17%), and the percentage for both of these school levels was higher than the percentage of primary schools (12%).

- The percentage of students ages 12–18 who reported that gangs were present at their school decreased from 18 percent in 2011 to 12 percent in 2013.

- A higher percentage of students from urban areas (18%) reported a gang presence than students from suburban (11%) and rural areas (7%) in 2013.

- A higher percentage of students attending public schools (13%) than of students attending private schools (2%) reported that gangs were present at their school in 2013.

- During the 2013–14 school year, the rate of illicit drug-related discipline incidents was 394 per 100,000 students in the United States.

- The percentage of students ages 12–18 who reported being the target of hate-related words decreased from 12 percent in 2001 (the first year of data collection for this item) to 7 percent in 2013.

- The percentage of students who reported carrying a weapon on school property in the previous 30 days declined from 12 percent in 1993 to 5 percent in 2013.

There is some concern that the government school crime reports do not tell the whole story. Unlike the FBI, which collects Uniform Crime Reports based upon actual reported crimes to law enforcement, federal education reports are based only on limited academic research surveys, not a comprehensive collection of actual reported crimes to law enforcement nationwide. Even if the *Indicators of School Crime* cited actual reported crimes, it would still underestimate the true level of offending and victimization because K–12 schools have no federal mandate requiring them to report crime; in contrast, colleges and universities are mandated to report such crimes (National School Safety and Security Services, n.d.). Although some states require reporting, there is no real auditing or enforcement to require compliance. Also, where inaccuracies have surfaced in local newspaper investigations, schools blame clerical orders or "a lack of understanding of the law and guidelines" for reporting. Consequently, the "persistently dangerous school" label that schools can be saddled with under the No Child Left Behind law creates pressure on local school administrators to underreport school crime. Many administrators worry about being seen as incompetent if crime and serious discipline problems become public or that talking about crime and security issues will alarm parents (National School Safety and Security Services, n.d.).

Because children are sometimes victimized on the way to or from school, programs that address this critical time period can be of great help. The University of Southern California (USC) has established a successful partnership with area schools and residents to keep students safe. The Kid Watch Program—a partnership between USC, the Los Angeles Unified School District, and the Los Angeles Police Department—recruits volunteers to watch over students on their way to and from school and to provide safe houses for kids who feel threatened or otherwise unsafe on the streets. Volunteers are vetted by the university and police department, free of charge, and safe houses are marked with a yellow sticker shaped like a house with stick figures of a boy and girl inside. In 2009, more than 1,000 neighbors watched over 9,000 children as they walked to and from school (Los Angeles Police Department, n.d.).

School Vandalism and Break-ins

The Center for Problem-Oriented Policing has studied the problem of school vandalism and break-ins, and their Problem-Oriented Guide for Police on the topic defines *school vandalism* as "willful or malicious damage to school grounds and buildings or furnishings and equipment," such as breaking windows, spraying graffiti, or generally destroying property (Dedel, 2005, p. 1). A *school break-in* is defined as "an unauthorized entry into a school building when the school is closed (e.g., after hours, on weekends, on school holidays)" (Dedel, 2005, p. 1). School break-ins typically fall into one of three categories (Dedel, 2005, p. 2):

- *Nuisance break-ins*, in which youth break into a school building, seemingly as an end in itself. They cause little serious damage and usually take nothing of value.

- *Professional break-ins*, in which offenders use a high level of skill to enter the school, break into storage rooms containing expensive equipment, and remove bulky items from the scene. They commit little incidental damage and may receive a lot of money for the stolen goods.

- *Malicious break-ins* entail significant damage to the school's interior and may include arson. Offenders sometimes destroy rather than steal items of value.

According to the Guide, although individual acts of school vandalism and break-ins are often trivial incidents, taken as a whole they pose a serious problem for schools and communities and for those charged with protecting them. For example, many school fires originate as arson or during an act of vandalism, having significant potential to harm students and staff. In the United Kingdom in 2000, about one-third of school arson fires occurred during school hours, when students were present.

Over the past 20 years, concerns about school violence, weapons, drugs, and gangs have eclipsed concern about school vandalism, its causes, and its possible responses. However, vandalism and break-ins continue to occur regularly and affect a significant number of U.S. schools. Although many education associations and national organizations routinely gather data on school-related violence, weapons, and gang activity, they do not gather data on school vandalism and break-ins. This may be because schools have different definitions of vandalism depending on what their insurance policies state or because school administrators may hesitate to report all cases of vandalism, break-ins, or arson, viewing some as trivial or fearing that such incidents will reflect poorly on their management skills. The failure to report vandalism and break-ins, however, may result in few perpetrators being apprehended and even fewer being prosecuted, thus allowing the problem to perpetuate (Dedel, 2005).

The lack of consistency in reporting school vandalism and break-ins also leads to imprecise cost estimates (Dedel, 2005). Such costs usually result from many small incidents rather than just a few more serious incidents. However, several estimates reveal that the costs of school vandalism are high and are increasing. In addition to the financial consequences of having to repair or replace damaged or stolen property and having to pay higher insurance premiums if property has not been self-insured, there may be difficulties in finding temporary accommodations in which to conduct classes and there may be negative effects on student, staff, and community morale.

The Guide (Dedel, 2005, pp. 32–34) highlights 28 effective responses, including the following community-focused responses:

- **Providing rewards for information concerning vandalism or break-ins:** Offender-focused responses require that vandals and intruders be identified and apprehended. Police investigations of vandalism incidents can be enhanced by high-quality information provided by students and community residents. As seen with traditional "Crime Stoppers" programs, setting up telephone or Internet-based tip lines, offering rewards for information, and guaranteeing anonymity encourage students and residents to come forward with specific information. The most effective programs actively involve students in collecting and synthesizing information for police, and in determining payout amounts in the event of apprehension.

- **Creating "School Watch" programs:** Similar to "Neighborhood Watch" efforts, community residents can conduct citizen patrols of school property during evenings and weekends. Membership and regular participation in voluntary patrols increase when some form of prestige is offered to volunteers. Effective practices include:
  - Patrolling regularly, but at unpredictable times.
  - Equipping volunteers with cell phones for prompt communication with police or other emergency services.
  - Engaging in passive surveillance only, and not interacting with potential vandals or intruders in any way.
  - Publicizing activities and outcomes among students and residents through school-based and local media outlets.

In response to a specific problem or rash of incidents, School Watch has produced short-term reductions in vandalism. However, community watch programs are difficult to sustain, have not been shown to reduce crime over the long term, and may actually increase the fear of crime.

- **Evaluating public use of school facilities after hours:** There is no consensus on how effective after-hours use of school facilities is in deterring vandalism and break-ins. On the one hand, making facilities and amenities available to residents increases the opportunities for natural surveillance to protect school buildings and property. Such access is also in keeping with the spirit of schools as hubs of community activity. However, residents who use the facilities after hours may not always have innocent intentions. If this response is adopted, rules and boundaries should be made very clear to participants, and only those areas required for the activities should be accessible, with other areas of the school secured by movable gates and locking partitions.

Responses with Limited Effectiveness

- **Controlling the sale of vandalism tools:** Some jurisdictions have attempted to control the various implements used for vandalism—for graffiti, in particular. Age-specific bans on the sale of spray paint or wide-tipped markers are designed to limit youth access to them. These bans are particularly difficult to implement and enforce because they require extensive cooperation from merchants.

- **Increasing penalties:** Responding to school vandalism and break-ins with excessively punitive criminal justice sanctions or harsh administrative punishments (e.g., expulsion) has been found to increase the incidence of vandalism.

Further, legal deterrents are generally ineffective when victim reporting and offender apprehension are not consistent, as is the case with school vandalism. Finally, most acts of vandalism are relatively minor, and thus are not serious enough to warrant severe consequences.

Bullying in Schools

Bullying—name calling, fistfights, purposeful ostracism, extortion, character assassination, repeated physical attacks, and sexual harassment—has been a common behavior in schools since they first opened their doors. Bullying is more accurately termed **peer child abuse**. Its occurrence is often taken lightly, with the belief that "kids will be kids."

The Virginia Youth Violence Project reports that bullying seems to have increased in recent years, although it is not clear if the increase reflects more bullying incidents or perhaps greater awareness of bullying as a problem (Virginia Youth Violence Project, n.d.). According to this project, student bullying is one of the most frequently reported discipline problems in schools, with 26 percent of elementary schools, 43 percent of middle schools, and 25 percent of high schools reporting problems with bullying.

Bullying is greatly underreported for many reasons, including the fact that most children and adults view reporting as tattling. Other reasons for underreporting include feelings of shame, fear of retaliation, and youngsters'

bullying

Name calling, fistfights, purposeful ostracism, extortion, character assassination, repeated physical attacks, and sexual harassment; also called *peer child abuse*.

peer child abuse

Another term for *bullying*—name calling, fistfights, purposeful ostracism, extortion, character assassination, repeated physical attacks, and sexual harassment.

belief that adults will not intervene even if they report the bullying. In that belief, they are often right.

Results of one study revealed that verbal bullying was the most prevalent form of bullying (53.6%), followed by relational (51.4%), physical (20.8%), and electronic (13.6%) (Wang, Iannotti, & Nansel, 2009). Gender differences in bullying involvement were also noted, with boys more involved in the physical and verbal forms of bullying and girls more involved in the relational form. With regard to cyberbullying, boys were more likely to be perpetrators and girls more like to be victims. A rather expected result of this study was the association between higher parental support and lower juvenile involvement across all forms and classifications of bullying. An interesting finding was the relationship between the number of friends a juvenile has and their involvement in bullying: "Having more friends was associated with more bullying and less victimization for the physical, verbal, and relational forms but was not associated with cyberbullying" (Wang et al., 2009, p. 368).

Several studies emphasizing the link between bullying and criminal behavior have led police and educators to reexamine their attitudes and responses to bullying: "Approximately 60 percent of boys identified as bullies were convicted of a crime by the age of 24, and an astonishing 40 percent of bullies had three or more convictions by age 24" (IACP, 2006). Research has found that men who reported bullying their childhood peers in school were at a significantly increased risk of committing intimate partner violence as adults (Falb, McCauley, Decker, Gupta, Raj, & Silverman, 2011). One implication of this finding is that programs seeking to reduce childhood bullying may also have potential to reduce later domestic violence.

Strategies to Mediate Bullying Strategies to mediate bullying include clear rules against such behavior applied consistently with appropriate sanctions for violation of the rules; a buddy system to pair younger students with older students; peer mediation; and close monitoring of cafeterias, playgrounds, and hot spots where bullying is likely to occur away from direct adult supervision.

tattling
Something done to get someone in trouble, in contrast to telling or reporting to keep someone safe.

A Johnson Institute program gives teachers step-by-step guidelines on how to teach students the difference between telling and tattling. Children, teenagers, and adults need to learn that **tattling** is something done to get someone in trouble, but telling or reporting is done to keep someone safe.

L05

The "tell or tattle" dilemma occurs when students hesitate to tell anyone that they are being bullied because it is seen as tattling—something they have been taught not to do.

Dr. Olweus of the University of Bergen, Norway, has been named "the world's leading authority" on bullying by *The Times* newspaper of London. His Olweus Bullying Prevention Program, used worldwide, is a multilevel, multicomponent school-based program designed to prevent or reduce bullying in elementary, middle, and junior high schools (students 6 to 15 years old).

A basic tenet is intervention by teachers when they see bullying behavior. Olweus recommends seven strategies: (1) adult supervision at recess, (2) strict enforcement of clear rules for student behavior, (3) consistent, nonphysical punishment of students who misbehave, (4) assistance to bullying victims that helps them to assert themselves, (5) parental encouragement that helps students develop and maintain friendships, (6) clear and positive communication between parents and school officials, and (7) clear and swift reaction to persistent physical or verbal bullying. Schools that implemented the program found a 40- to 50-percent reduction rate in bullying behavior within the first 2 years (*Substance Abuse and Mental Health Services Administration*, 2006). The Olweus Bullying Prevention Program has proven results:

- A 30-percent reduction in student reports of being bullied and bullying others; results are largely parallel with peer ratings and teacher ratings
- Significant reductions in student reports of general antisocial behavior—for example, vandalism, fighting, theft, and truancy
- Significant improvements in classroom order and discipline
- More positive attitude toward schoolwork and school

More recently, attention has turned to the role peer bystanders play in the perpetuation of bullying. Research has found that peers witness 85 percent of bullying episodes but intervene in only 10 percent of those observed (Jeffrey, 2004). Therefore, an important approach to preventing and mitigating bullying is to mobilize bystander reactions, particularly those of other students (Padgett & Notar, 2013).

A Partnership to Prevent Bullying   In December 2011, the Royal Canadian Mounted Police (RCMP) and researchers from the University of Victoria formed a partnership to address the issues of youth bullying and suicide. The effort draws on the evidence-based WITS Program to create communities that are responsive to the prevention of peer victimization and bullying. WITS stands for **W**alk away, **I**gnore, **T**alk it out, and **S**eek help—skills children can use to deal with bullying. Trained RCMP youth officers will partner with school staff, parents, and community leaders to take a unified approach to reducing bullying in their communities (Royal Canadian Mounted Patrol, 2011).

The Chula Vista Bullying Prevention Project   The Chula Vista (California) Police Department (CVPD) has implemented a successful bullying prevention program using the Olweus antibullying model. The program was funded by a School Community Policing Partnership grant for school districts, law enforcement, and community agencies to collaborate in reducing juvenile violence.

The project began by conducting annual surveys of students in three schools to determine the frequency, location, and types of bullying. Then, a CVPD public safety analyst created a training curriculum to educate SROs on the different types of bullying, bullying's long- and short-term effects, and the best practices in intervening with this behavior. Each school that participated in the program organized a Bullying Prevention Committee, consisting of teachers, administrators, parents, campus staff, SROs, and family resource coordinators. Each committee developed a consistent message about bullying and delivered it to parents, educators, and students, thereby preventing students from getting mixed messages.

The SROs were a driving force behind the expansion of the project. When they responded to a bullying call at a school, they advised the administration about proactive steps that could be taken to reduce bullying. The Chula Vista Bullying Prevention Project has been adopted by nine schools and recognized with a 2005 Helen Putnam Award from the League of California Cities. According to the continuing surveys, the following results have been achieved (IACP, 2006):

- Name calling has been reduced 17 percent, and racial name calling has decreased 2 percent
- Exclusion from groups decreased by 9 percent
- Hitting and kicking decreased by 18 percent
- False rumors dropped by 13 percent
- Threats decreased by 21 percent
- Bullying has been reduced
  - 23 percent in bathrooms
  - 27 percent in gym classes
  - 11 percent in lunchrooms
- More students (12%) were willing to intervene when witnessing bullying
- The vast majority of parents (82%) agreed that the school was treating bullying more seriously

Addressing bullying promises measurable returns in terms of crime prevention, violence reduction, and investment of scarce police resources. Unfortunately, bullying is not the only form of violence found in our schools.

School Shootings

Pearl, Mississippi; West Paducah, Kentucky; Jonesboro, Arkansas; Fayetteville, Tennessee; Springfield, Oregon; Richmond, Virginia; Littleton, Colorado; Conyers, Georgia; Santee, California; Red Lake, Minnesota; Chardon, Ohio; Newtown, Connecticut—these cities house schools that come to mind when school violence is mentioned. While such shootings are, statistically, relatively rare events, "Each attack has a terrible and lasting effect on the students, school, and surrounding community—and on the nation as a whole" (Schuster, 2009, p. 42). Consider the 1999 tragedy at Columbine High School in Littleton, Colorado, where two shooters killed a dozen students and a teacher and wounded 23 others before turning their guns on themselves. Further investigation revealed the shooters had been plotting for a year to kill at least 500 and blow up their school.

One resource that details school shootings and other violent deaths occurring within the nation's schools is the National School Safety Center's *School Associated Violent Deaths* (SAVD) report. According to this report, the vast majority (74.7%) of school-associated violent deaths that occurred between

1992 and 2010 were caused by shootings, 77.4 percent of fatally injured victims were male, and 66.5 percent of deaths occurred at high schools (National School Safety Center, 2010).

School Shooters "I hate being laughed at. But they won't laugh after they're scraping parts of their parents, sisters, brothers, and friends from the wall of my hate." These words were written in the journal of 15-year-old Kip Kinkel before he killed both parents and then moved into his Springfield, Oregon, high school and shot more than two dozen students, two fatally (Piazza, 2001).

In 40 cases of school violence in the past 20 years, the Secret Service's National Threat Assessment found that teenagers often told someone before they did the deed. Most of these kids were White and they preferred (and somehow acquired) semiautomatics. Almost half had shown some evidence of mental disturbance, including delusions and hallucinations.

School officials want to know if there are any clear signs to watch for and to tell parents about. They know they must be especially careful because any action they take has the potential of landing them in court. The problem is that few school psychologists have received training on this issue, so they are not sure what to do or what to look for. As with all dangerousness assessments, the most telling factor in what a child might do is what a child has already done. In other words, a history of violent actions or words is the best indicator of future violence potential.

Any pattern of behavior that persists over time tends to intensify. This does not necessarily mean that a bully will become a school killer, but it means that kids who develop an obsession with weapons or violent games and who tend to threaten violence are more likely to eventually act out than those who do not. Some of the behaviors to be especially concerned about include an increase in lying, blaming others, avoiding responsibility, avoiding effort to achieve goals, using deception or force or intimidation to control others, showing lack of empathy for others, exploiting others' weaknesses, or engaging in petty crimes like theft or damage to property.

Other behaviors are getting involved in gang behavior, having a pattern of overreacting, having a history of criminal acts without a motive, experiencing continual family discord, having a history of criminality in the family, having a history of running away from home, showing a pattern of anger, and being depressed or withdrawn. Other behaviors include showing inconsistencies, such as a sudden uncharacteristic interest in guns; developing an intense dislike of school; complaining about classmates treating him or her badly; having excessive television or video game habits (3 or more hours a day); carrying weapons such as a knife; complaining of feeling lonely; and showing intense resentment.

Preventing School Shootings and Other Targeted Attacks In the wake of several highly publicized school shootings during the 1990s, most notably the massacre at Columbine High School in Littleton, Colorado, on April 20, 1999, the U.S. Secret Service and the U.S. Department of Education formed the Safe School Initiative (SSI) to study incidents of violence occurring in the nation's schools. One particular focus of examination by the SSI was whether past school-based attacks were planned, or *targeted*, and how such attacker preparations could be detected in an effort to prevent future attacks.

One of the most salient findings from the SSI was that in most attacks, other people knew beforehand about the perpetrators' plans (Vossekuil, Fein, Reddy, Borum, & Modzeleski, 2002). In fact, in 81 percent of the incidents, at least one other person had some type of prior knowledge of the attacker's plan, and in 59 percent of the incidents, more than one person had such knowledge (Vossekuil et al., 2002). The overwhelming majority (93%) of those who knew of the plan in advance were the attacker's peers—friends, classmates, and siblings.

Many found it troubling that, despite advance knowledge about a planned attack at a school, the attacks still occurred. Thus, a follow-up study was conducted to explore how *bystanders*—those with some type of prior knowledge about planned school violence—decided what to do, if anything, after learning about the plan and to identify ways to encourage more students to share with an adult any information they learn about potential targeted school-based violence (Pollack, Modzeleski, & Rooney, 2008). One of the primary findings of the subsequent study was that the relationships between the bystanders and the attackers varied, as did the means by which bystanders came upon the information regarding the planned attacks (Pollack et al., 2008, p. 6):

- 34 percent of bystanders were friends with the attacker
- 29 percent of bystanders were acquaintances, co-workers, or schoolmates
- 6 percent of bystanders were family members
- In 31 percent of the cases, the relationship was of another type or unknown
- 82 percent of the bystanders received information directly from the attacker
- 13 percent of bystanders were told secondhand

In a majority of cases, bystanders received the information more than a day before the attack:

- 59 percent were told days or weeks in advance
- 22 percent were told months or years prior
- Only 19 percent were told a few hours or less before the attack

Other notable findings from the study were (Pollack et al., 2008):

- Bystanders shared information related to a threat along a continuum that ranged from bystanders who took no action to those who actively conveyed the information (p. 6).
- School climate affected whether bystanders came forward with information related to the threats (p. 7).
- Some bystanders disbelieved that the attacks would occur and thus did not report them (p. 7).
- Bystanders often misjudged the likelihood and immediacy of the planned attack (p. 7).
- In some situations, parents and parental figures influenced whether the bystander reported the information related to the potential attack to school staff or other adults in positions of authority (p. 7).

After-School Programs

For many students, the closing bell at the end of the school day does not necessarily mean it is time to go home. For some of these youths, the hours after school present the most dangerous time of day. Yet more than one in four of America's schoolchildren—more than 15 million youths—are alone and unsupervised in the hours right after school (Afterschool Alliance, 2014; The Children's Trust, 2014). After-school programs are often touted as one means to keep youths out of trouble and to help them succeed in school. Data have consistently shown that on school days, juvenile crime and delinquency peaks in the hours immediately after school, when youths are more likely to be unsupervised. Research also links after-school programs to increased school-day attendance and improved graduation rates (Lee, 2010). A metanalysis of 68 after-school studies found numerous benefits to students who participated in high-quality after-school programs, including better school attendance (lower truancy), better behavior, higher grades, and improved performance on tests compared to nonparticipants (After-school Alliance, 2014).

A Justice Based After-School (JBAS) Program has been piloted by the COPS Office, which asserts: "Without supervision between the hours of 2 and 10 P.M., children are more likely to be victimized and to engage in risk-taking behavior" (Office of Community Oriented Policing Services, 2002, p. 1). The JBAS program encourages law enforcement officers to work in partnership with community organizations, especially in high-crime neighborhoods, to develop a preventive approach to juvenile crime and victimization. In Minneapolis, Minnesota, for example, COPS funds have been used to expand an existing Police Athletic League (PAL) project in one school and to start programs in two other schools.

A poll of 1,200 youths between the ages of 13 and 18 found that 55.3 percent do not attend after-school programs other than sports because of lack of interest. Among the teens who do participate, 62.1 percent do so at school, 18.1 percent at a church, and 8.6 percent in a traditional after-school setting such as a YMCA. When asked what would increase their interest, 94.3 percent said they would like programs that offer opportunities for college scholarships; 92.1 percent said they would be interested if the programs offered an opportunity to earn college credit ("Teens Not Interested in After-School Programs," 2006).

Research on whether such programs are effective is mixed. In 2008, the Rand Corporation published results of a study of youth programs, including after-school programs (Beckett, 2008). The study concluded that some programs had positive effects whereas others did not. One after-school program was a low-cost program, open to all students. Participation in this program was found to have an overall negative effect on the participants themselves: "In the second year, participants were more likely to be suspended from school and to have been disciplined in school (e.g., missed recess or were sent out to the hall), and their teachers were more likely to have called parents about behavioral problems. Participation had no effects on academic outcomes, on social outcomes, on being supervised afterschool (by a parent, other adult, or

TECHNOLOGY IN COMMUNITY POLICING

PREVENTING LOITERING AND VANDALISM WITH THE MOSQUITO

When youth are unsupervised and lack structured activity, their idle minds and hands may turn to mischief. Sometimes that mischief manifests as nuisance behavior, such as loitering around businesses, and may escalate into delinquent or criminal behavior, including vandalism. While many businesses, such as gas station convenience stores, have successfully kept loitering youths at bay by playing classical or chill-out music over their outside speakers, new technology is providing a more subtle way to deter loitering and prevent vandalism.

The Mosquito is one such device capable of emitting a high-frequency sound audible only to people under a certain age. It has been marketed to cities, municipalities, school districts, and parks boards throughout North America as a loitering and vandalism prevention tool. The patented Mosquito uses a small speaker to produce a high-frequency sound similar to the buzzing of the insect it is named after. The latest version of the Mosquito—the MK4 Multi-Age—has two different settings: the 17 KHz setting can be heard only by young people approximately 13 to 25 years of age, whereas the 8 KHz setting is audible to persons of all ages.

Source: Moving Sound Technologies. (2012). *The Mosquito Device*. Vancouver, BC: Author. Retrieved October 12, 2016 from http://www.movingsoundtech.com

older sibling), or on homework completion" (Beckett, 2008, p. 18). After-school programs that targeted at-risk youth, however, tended to be more research-based and have a longer history of careful program assessment and evaluation. Thus, for either or both of these reasons, more-convincing evidence of positive behavioral impacts was found among targeted (specialized) programs (Beckett, 2008).

Another report by Miller (2003) found differently. After examining the results of research studies conducted over two decades regarding a broad range of after-school programs, Miller concludes that the evidence supports a link between after-school program participation and educational success. With school resources becoming more limited, the debate over whether to provide after-school programs is likely to continue.

Creating Safe Schools

Figure 12.1 illustrates the strategic process in designing a safe school.

New Jersey schools are using an iris recognition program to enhance security. The system, nicknamed T–PASS (Teacher–Parent Authorization Security System), links eye-scanning cameras with computers to identify people who have been preauthorized to enter the schools and, once their identity is confirmed, lets them in by unlocking the door. A review of the system noted: "Of the more than 9,400 times someone attempted to enter the schools using the iris scanner, there were no known false positives or other misidentifications" (Cohn, 2006, p. 14). The system appeared to make parents, teachers, and staff members feel safer in the school. A significant loophole in the system occurs, however, when someone who is authorized to enter, having passed the eye-scan check, holds the door open for

Figure 12.1	Strategic Process in Developing a Safe School

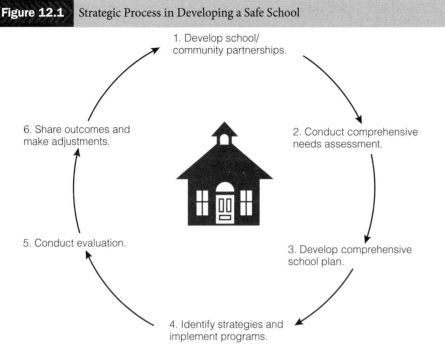

Source: Ira Pollack and Carlos Sundermann. "Creating Safe Schools: A Comprehensive Approach." *Juvenile Justice*, June 2001, p. 15.

others, who are then able to access the school without being scanned and authenticated.

Two highly successful programs to help build safe schools are Student Crime Stoppers and PeaceBuilders®. Student Crime Stoppers, like the adult program, offers youth tools to stand up against crime and violence without reprisal or peer pressure through an anonymous tip line to get the information to those who can stop the crime or violence. Those with information about solving crimes on school property or at school events can qualify for cash awards up to $100. The first Student Crime Stoppers program was started in a Boulder, Colorado, high school in 1983. Today, more than 2,000 programs exist in middle and high schools, community colleges, and colleges throughout the country.

PeaceBuilders® is a long-term, community-based, violence reduction or prevention program designed to help create an environment that reduces violence and establishes more peaceful ways of behaving, living, and working in families, schools, organizations, and communities. Schools may send up to four people to attend a 2 1/2-day training session to become site trainers. These site trainers then provide 4-hour PeaceBuilders® Staff Implementation Workshops at their schools or in their own districts. Up to 60 people may attend this workshop.

Safe schools depend not only on programs such as these but also on a comprehensive approach to safety.

LO6

A seven-pronged approach is needed for effective school security: (1) school/law enforcement/community partnerships, (2) education about nonviolence, (3) problem-solving training, (4) mediation and anger management training, (5) clear policies on accepted behavior with consequences for nonconformity, (6) security procedures and technology, and (7) crisis planning.

The COPS Office has a long-standing and proven commitment to school safety, having invested more than $913 million in America's schools through programs like Secure Our Schools (SOS), COPS in Schools, School-based Partnerships, and the Safe Schools Initiative. In fiscal year 2011, more than $13 million in SOS grant funding was awarded to law enforcement agencies to help schools respond to growing school safety and security concerns (Office of Community Oriented Policing Services, 2011).

The IACP has published a *Guide for Preventing and Responding to School Violence* (2nd edition, 2009), which includes as one topic developing partnerships with schools. One of the oldest and most commonly used partnerships is assigning police officers to schools—the school resource officer (SRO). The differences between traditional policing in the schools and community policing in the schools parallel those in the community, as summarized in Table 12.1.

Many school systems have successfully relied on counselors, nurses, and other specialists to supplement teachers' efforts to teach nonviolence, giving students a sense of a supportive network of adults available to help them resolve problems nonviolently.

When a dispute occurs on school grounds, the involved parties seek out a teacher or the program's adult coordinator. The coordinator assigns peer mediators to intervene and attempt to resolve the dispute peacefully through the parties' mutual agreement and commitment to a contract with set standards for conduct. Such mediation may substitute for detention or suspension of youths involved in fights, verbal threats, or intimidation of others on school grounds.

Table 12.1 Comparison between Traditional and Community Policing in Schools	
Traditional Policing in Schools	**Community Policing in Schools**
Reactive response to 911 calls	Law enforcement officer assigned to the school "community"
Incident driven	Problem oriented
Minimal school–law enforcement interaction, often characterized by an "us versus them" mentality	Ongoing school–law enforcement partnership to address problems of concern to educators, students, and parents
Police role limited to law enforcement	Police role extended beyond law enforcement to include prevention and early intervention activities
Police viewed as source of the solution	Educators, students, and parents are active partners in developing solutions
Educators and law enforcement officers reluctant to share information	Partners value information sharing as an important problem-solving tool
Criminal incidents subject to inadequate response; criminal consequences imposed only when incidents reported to police	Consistent responses to incidents are ensured—administrative and criminal, as appropriate
Law enforcement presence viewed as indicator of failure	Law enforcement presence viewed as taking a positive, proactive step to create orderly, safe, and secure schools
Police effectiveness measured by arrest rates, response times, calls for service, etc.	Policing effectiveness measured by the absence of crime and disorder

Source: From "Guide 5: Fostering School–Law Enforcement Partnerships." Reprinted by permission of Education Northwest (formerly Northwest Regional Educational Laboratory).

Potential obstacles to this strategy include lack of funds for staff to train students and faculty and coordinate mediator assignments. In addition, convincing students that violence can be prevented can be difficult.

Clear policies should be established for tardiness, absenteeism/class cutting, physical conflicts among students, student tobacco use, verbal abuse of teachers, drug use, vandalism of school property, alcohol use, robbery or theft, gangs, racial tensions, possession of weapons, physical abuse of teachers, and sale of drugs on school grounds. Many schools have adopted **zero tolerance** toward possession of guns, drugs, or alcohol in schools—that is, no matter what the underlying circumstances, a student bringing a weapon, drugs, or alcohol to school will be suspended or expelled.

zero tolerance
A policy of punishing all offenses severely, no matter how minor an offense may be.

HOPE FOR THE FUTURE

Despite the lack of progress in some areas, the outlook is not as bleak as some would paint it. Law enforcement agencies, particularly those embracing community policing, are part of the entire juvenile justice system, and that system appears to be changing. In introducing *The Future of American Children,* Steinberg (2008, p. 3) states: "American juvenile justice policy is in a period of transition.... State legislatures across the country have reconsidered punitive statutes they enacted with enthusiasm not so many years go. What we may be seeing now is a pendulum that has reached its apex and is slowly beginning to swing back toward more moderate policies, as politicians and the public come to regret the high economic costs and ineffectiveness of the punitive reforms and the harshness of the sanctions."

Combining this changing perspective with the focus of community policing on involving youths in partnerships and problem-solving efforts, the future for our youths can be more positive. In the words of James Baldwin: "For these are all our children. We will all profit by, or pay for, whatever they become."

L07
No data suggest that zero-tolerance policies reduce school violence. Such policies result in sometimes unreasonable suspensions and expulsions.

IDEAS IN PRACTICE URBAN HIGH SCHOOL DISORDER REDUCTION PROJECT: THE IACP 2011 COMMUNITY POLICING AWARD IN THE 100,001 TO 250,000 POPULATION CATEGORY

Over a 6-year period, Belmont High School in Dayton, Ohio, was the scene of a reported 145 violent crimes. Responding to calls for service in and around the school had led to a significant decline in patrol officer efficiency in the affected district, and a growing number of complaints from residents and businesses indicated that the problem had spread beyond the school grounds. In response, the Dayton Police Department (DPD) partnered with Dayton Public Schools, the Montgomery County Juvenile Court, and the Juvenile Division of the Montgomery County Prosecutor's Office to create the Urban High School Disorder Reduction Project, the goal of which was to implement community-policing strategies, such as crime prevention through

environmental design (CPTED) and the engagement of community stakeholders, to deny youths the opportunities for crime and disorder:

The project committee and stakeholders agreed on the following strategies:

1. Continuously communicating with all community partners
2. Identifying students requiring special intervention through arrest records
3. Reassigning classrooms to group students by grade level
4. Emphasizing a no-tolerance policy for violations and crimes

(Continues)

IDEAS IN PRACTICE   URBAN HIGH SCHOOL DISORDER REDUCTION
PROJECT: THE IACP 2011 COMMUNITY POLICING
AWARD IN THE 100,001 TO 250,000
POPULATION CATEGORY (*Continued*)

5. Assigning school staff members to monitor the lunch period, the school grounds, and nearby hot spots (alleyways, bus stops, bathrooms, hallways)

6. Assigning patrol officers to assist with monitoring hot spots and addressing violations

7. Establishing clear rules for student behavior

8. Reinforcing rules by making arrests, issuing citations, and subjecting students off school grounds to discipline

The project was successful on many levels. The number of crimes and calls for service were drastically reduced; there was a 76.6-percent drop in reported crime in the area, and a 92-percent decrease in the number of assaults (from 51 to 4). Educational goals were also enhanced, with the 9th grade graduation rate increasing 54 percent and the 10th grade rate increasing 38 percent. The number of 11th graders taking the ACT college entrance exam increased from just 8 percent during the 2008–2009 school year to www80 percent in the 2010–2011 school year. Finally, a safer environment was achieved for students and neighborhood residents. However, as the Dayton Police Department note, the work is far from over:

> Continued monitoring of the project is essential, as well as continued communication with Belmont High School's staff, students, and parents. DPD continues to improve those relationships by holding periodic in-school trainings like Prom DUI prevention. DPD also continues to monitor the school during monthly meetings with CAPERS (crime analysis police enforcement and response strategies), command staff, and other city agencies.

Source: "Urban High School Disorder Reduction Project." *IACP Community Policing Award: 2011 Winners and Finalists*. San Jose, CA: Cisco Systems, Inc., pp. 5–6. Retrieved October 12, 2016 from http://www.popcenter.org/library/awards/goldstein/2011/11-40(F).pdf

SUMMARY

Children and teenagers are an important segment of the community often overlooked when implementing the community policing philosophy. To counteract negative perceptions of police held by children and youths, many departments have programs aimed at fostering positive relations with them.

The developmental asset approach promotes (1) support, (2) empowerment, (3) boundaries and expectations, (4) constructive use of time, (5) commitment to learning, (6) positive values, (7) social competence, and (8) positive identity to help youngsters succeed in school and in life. Federal initiatives to protect our nation's youths include passage of the Adam Walsh Child Protection and Safety Act, America's Promise Alliance, Project Safe Childhood, and the Safe Start Initiative.

The family is viewed by many as the cornerstone of the community and should be included in community policing efforts focused on youths. Likewise, a school should be viewed as a community, not as an institution. Research suggests that students' academic motivation, commitment to democratic values, and resistance to problem behaviors depend on their experience of the school as a community. At a minimum, schools need to link with parents and with local law enforcement departments to teach students about the dangers of crime.

A precursor to school violence is bullying. Bullying is more accurately termed *peer child abuse*. Bullying has been seen as a rite of passage and has resulted in schools where violence is accepted. The "tell or tattle" dilemma occurs when students hesitate to tell anyone that they are being bullied because it is seen as tattling—something they have been taught not to do.

Two highly successful programs to build safe schools are Student Crime Stoppers and Peace-Builders®. In addition, a seven-pronged approach is needed for effective school security: (1) school/law enforcement/community partnerships, (2) education about violence, (3) problem-solving training, (4) mediation and anger management training, (5) clear policies on accepted behavior with consequences for nonconformity, (6) security procedures and technology, and (7) crisis planning. One of the oldest and most commonly used partnerships is assigning police officers to schools—the school resource officer (SRO).

One of the most popular strategies to promote safe schools is a zero-tolerance policy against violence, guns, and drugs in school. However, no data suggest that zero-tolerance policies reduce school violence. Such policies result in sometimes unreasonable suspensions and expulsions.

DISCUSSION QUESTIONS

1. Which of the programs for youths do you feel are the most effective?
2. Why do school administrators not consider drugs a security or crime problem?
3. What major differences in philosophy often exist between school administrators and police?
4. On which age group do you think police–school programs should focus? Why?
5. Was violence a problem in the high school you attended? If yes, what was the major problem?
6. What are the advantages and disadvantages of expelling disruptive students from school?
7. Is zero tolerance for violence, drugs, and weapons in school a workable policy? Why or why not?
8. How did you feel about the police when you were a child? Did that attitude change as you grew older? Why or why not? If so, how?
9. Do you think bullying is a serious problem? Did bullying occur in your school?
10. What risk factors for delinquent behavior do you think are most important?

The Challenge of Gangs: Controlling Their Destructive Force

Learning Objectives

LO1 Explain the prevalence of gangs in terms of membership and geographic prevalence.

LO2 Describe the three basic types of gang operating in the United States.

LO3 Identify the needs that are often served by gangs to their members.

LO4 Name the gang prevention efforts implicated by the Seattle study.

LO5 List the indicators of gang activity.

LO6 Know what strategies have been used to address the gang problem and which has been found to be the most effective.

Key Terms

community mobilization

gang

graffiti

moniker

organizational development

outlaw motorcycle gang (OMG)

prison gang

pulling levers

social intervention

social opportunities

street gang

suppression

turf

youth gang

The city of Chicago, Illinois, is as well known for its gang violence as it is for its nickname, the Windy City. In an attempt to control the violence spread by the city's two most prominent Hispanic gangs, the Latin Kings and the Two Six, local officials developed the Little Village Gang Violence Reduction Project.

The goal of this initiative was to decrease the hostility and aggression exhibited by 200 influential gang members and leaders between the two groups. The intervention team leading the initiative was comprised of members from local youth services, former gang members, case managers, police, and probation workers. In this project, officers on patrol would use standard Chicago Police Department (CPD) tactics to control the gang violence. When engaged with the gang members, officers would gather information from the individuals involved, which would then be shared at weekly meetings between youth workers and law enforcement in the hopes that the data would be passed to the gang intervention team. The intervention team would, in turn, offer the following services to the gang members: crisis intervention, family counseling and individual therapy, surveillance, and gang suppression activities.

Police officers found that the intervention efforts reduced individuals' interest in engaging with the gang and increased disinterest in overall gang attachment. Also, members who had engaged with the project became more involved in job seeking behavior and placement. Those hardcore individuals most targeted by the project spanned a variety of ages; however, the older gang youths tended to be more interested and successful in project graduation. This program, although not successful in reducing drug selling activities, accomplished a reduction in violent crime as well as a decrease in serious property offenses and various other wrongdoings.

Although the city of Chicago is still well known for their crime, gang violence among the two largest Hispanic gangs was greatly reduced due this program. By lessening the conflict among rival gang members, the initiative increased residents' feelings of safety in the surrounding neighborhoods and reduced the overall social disorganization of this once-hardened community.

INTRODUCTION

Gangs have spread through our country like a plague and now exist in rural, suburban, and inner cities—in every metropolitan area. Some analogize the gang problem to a societal cancer, where street gangs prey on the community like a malignant growth, eating away at its host until only a wasted shell remains. Gangs use harassment, intimidation, extortion, and fear to control their territory. Daily, countless news stories depict the tragedy of gang violence. The following examples document only the tip of the problem:

- A gang fight at a crowded park results in a 7-year-old girl being shot in the head while picnicking with her family.

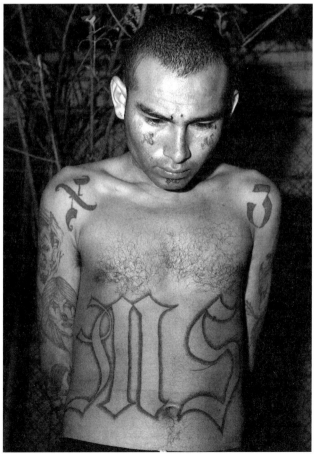

ES James/Shutterstock.com

A gang member displays his many tattoos that identify him as belonging to the Mara Salvatrucha-13 (MS-13) gang.

- Shotgun blasts from a passing car, intended for a rival gang member, strike a child.
- A shoot-out between rival gangs kills a high school athlete as he jogs around the school track.

To underscore the important role community policing plays in addressing the challenge of gangs, renowned gang researcher Malcolm Klein has asserted: "The gang is, first and foremost, a community problem. It is the community's kids who decide whether or not to form or join gangs, and it is the community's residents, institutions, and businesses that are most victimized by gang activity" (2007, pp. 84–85).

UNDERSTANDING GANGS AND GANG MEMBERS

The first step to devising a solution to a problem is to understand the true nature and scope of the problem. Numerous data collection tools are in place to measure the extent of gangs throughout our country, and although the numbers differ slightly from source to source, a singular reality exists that gangs do pose a serious threat to many communities in the United States. According to the National Gang Intelligence Center (NGIC), there are approximately 1.4 million active gang members comprising more than 33,000 gangs in the United States (NGIC, 2016). The 2014 National Youth Gang Survey (NYGS) estimates that 850,000 gang members, belonging to 30,700 gangs, were active across the country in 2012 (Egley, Howell, & Harris, 2014).

> **L01**
> An estimated 850,000 gang members are active in more than 30,700 gangs nationwide, with gang activity primarily concentrated in urban areas.

Roughly 3,100 jurisdictions throughout the United States, or slightly less than 30 percent of the responding agencies, reported an active gang presence in 2012, an estimate that shows a sPLlight downward trend in gang activity, a decrease that researchers attribute to a drop in gang presence in smaller cities. According to historic NYGS data, prevalence rates of gang activity across jurisdiction types followed a marked decline in the late 1990s, increased in the early 2000s, and, with the exception of smaller cities, have generally stabilized in recent years (Egley et al., 2014). Survey results show that gang activity remains concentrated primarily in urban areas, findings that do not support the popularly held notion that gang activity is spreading outward to less densely populated areas.

Figure 13.1 shows how the reported prevalence of gang activity has varied over the years by jurisdiction size.

Gangs Defined

Defining a gang is not always a simple, straightforward task. Some definitions emphasize criminal activity whereas others stress territoriality. The current federal law (18 USC § 521 (a)) defines a criminal street gang as "an ongoing group, club, organization, or association of five or more persons: (A) that has as one of its primary purposes the commission of one or more of the criminal offenses described in subsection (c); (B) the members of which engage, or have engaged within the past 5 years, in a continuing series of offenses described in subsection (c); and (C) the activities of which affect interstate or foreign

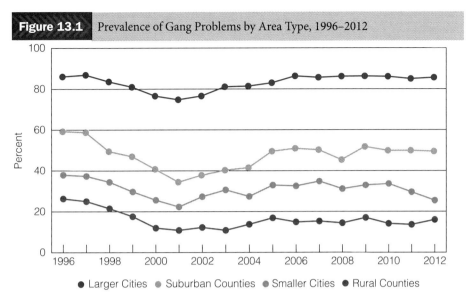

Figure 13.1 Prevalence of Gang Problems by Area Type, 1996–2012

● Larger Cities   ● Suburban Counties   ● Smaller Cities   ● Rural Counties

Source: National Gang Center. https://www.nationalgangcenter.gov/Survey-Analysis/Prevalence-of-Gang-Problems#preva lenceyouthgangstudy

commerce" (National Gang Center, 2015). The Organized Crime and Gang Section (OCGS) of the U.S. Department of Justice defines a gang as:

> (1) an association of three or more individuals; (2) whose members collectively identify themselves by adopting a group identity which they use to create an atmosphere of fear or intimidation frequently by employing one or more of the following: a common name, slogan, identifying sign, symbol, tattoo or other physical marking, style or color of clothing, hairstyle, hand sign or graffiti; (3) the association's purpose, in part, is to engage in criminal activity and the association uses violence or intimidation to further its criminal objectives; (4) its members engage in criminal activity, or acts of juvenile delinquency that if committed by an adult would be crimes; (5) with the intent to enhance or preserve the association's power, reputation, or economic resources; (6) the association may also possess some of the following characteristics: (a) the members employ rules for joining and operating within the association; (b) the members meet on a recurring basis; (c) the association provides physical protection of its members from other criminals and gangs; (d) the association seeks to exercise control over a particular location or region, or it may simply defend its perceived interests against rivals; or (e) the association has an identifiable structure. (7) this definition is not intended to include traditional organized crime groups such as La Cosa Nostra, groups that fall within the Department's definition of "international organized crime," drug trafficking organizations or terrorist organizations (U.S. Department of Justice, 2015).

The National Gang Center (NGC) notes that state and local jurisdictions often develop their own working definitions of gangs, and many agencies use terms such as *street gang* and *youth gang* interchangeably. A review of current state laws shows that 43 states and Washington, DC, have legislation that defines a "gang," and that every definition includes criminal/illegal activity or behavior (NGC, 2015):

- Thirty-four states define a gang as consisting of three or more persons.
- Thirty-six states refer to a gang as an "organization, association, or group."
- Twenty-seven states include a common name, identifying sign, or symbol as identifiers of gangs in their definitions.

In addition to defining what a gang is, 14 states have legislation that defines a "gang member," many of such laws involving a list of criteria that a person must meet to be considered a gang member. In addition, 31 states have legislation to define "gang crime/activity," 25 of which specify the exact crimes that are to be considered criminal gang activity (NGC, 2015). Law enforcement agencies that responded to the NYGS indicated that among the characteristics of greatest importance in defining a gang are engaging in criminal activity together; having a group name; and displaying signs, colors, and other symbols that outwardly represent the group to others (Egley et al., 2014). Other important definitional characteristics are hanging out together, claiming a turf or territory, and the designation of a leader or leaders.

For this discussion, a **gang** will be defined as a group of people who form an ongoing allegiance for a common purpose and engage in unlawful or criminal activity. Gangs are frequently identified by a name, **turf** (territory) concerns, symbols, signs, and colors. A gang is recognized by both its own members and by others.

gang
A group of people who form an ongoing allegiance for a common purpose and engage in unlawful or criminal activity. See also *street gang* and *youth gang*.

turf
Territory occupied by a gang, often marked by graffiti.

Types of Gangs

Gangs vary extensively in membership, structure, age, and ethnicity, but three basic types of gangs have been identified and defined by gang investigators: street gangs, prison gangs, and outlaw motorcycle gangs (OMGs). The National Gang Intelligence Center (NGIC) observes that, although these three types of gangs pursue the same objectives and commit the same crimes during those pursuits, they differ in how they operate because each gang is a product of its environment and, as such, has its own rules of conduct and methods of operation. Consequently, "street gangs differ from prison gangs, while prison and street gangs both differ from OMGs. Understanding the specific mentality of each gang type is integral to disruption and dismantlement" (NGIC, 2016, p. 8).

A **street gang** is a group of people whose allegiance is based on social needs, who have an identifiable leadership, who claim control over a specific territory in the community, and who engage in acts injurious to the public. Members of street gangs engage in an organized, continuous course of criminality, either individually or collectively, creating an atmosphere of fear and intimidation in a community. Most local law enforcement agencies prefer the term *street gang* because it includes juveniles and adults and designates the location of the gang and most of its criminal behavior. For criminal justice policy purposes, a **youth gang** is a subgroup of a street gang. It may refer to a juvenile clique within a gang.

street gang
A group of people whose allegiance is based on social needs, who have an identifiable leadership, who claim control over a specific territory in the community, and who engage in acts injurious to the public; the preferred term of most local law enforcement agencies.

youth gang
A subgroup of a street gang; may refer to a juvenile clique within a gang.

The NGIC define street gangs as "criminal organizations that formed on the street and operate in neighborhoods throughout the United States. Neighborhood-based gangs are confined to specific neighborhoods and jurisdictions, with no known leadership beyond their communities. National-level gangs have a presence in multiple jurisdictions" (NGIC, 2016, p. 11).

The NGIC (2016, p. 15) defines a **prison gang** as "a criminal organization that originates in the penal system and continues to operate within correctional facilities throughout the United States. Prison gangs are self-perpetuating criminal entities that also continue their operations outside of prison." An **outlaw motorcycle gang (OMG)** is defined as an ongoing organization, association, or group of three or more people "with a common interest or activity characterized by the commission of, or involvement in, a pattern of criminal conduct. Members must possess and be able to operate a motorcycle to achieve and maintain membership within the group" (NGIC, 2016, p. 22).

The NGIC assesses that the U.S. gang composition is approximately 88 percent street gang members, 9.5 percent prison gang members, and 2.5 percent OMG members (2016). Among the key findings of the *2015 National Gang Report* are (NGIC, 2016):

- Roughly half of all law enforcement agencies surveyed report that street gangs show few indicators of decreasing membership or criminal activity.

- As with previous years, neighborhood-based gangs remain the most significant threat, while national-level street gangs have a moderate-to-high impact in approximately half of reporting jurisdictions.

- More than two-thirds of jurisdictions responding indicate that prison gang membership has increased over the past 2 years and that the greatest threat of prison gangs lies in their nexus to street gangs and in their ability to corrupt prison officials.

- Larger OMGs have established new chapters and have attracted many new members, with the surging membership leading to clashes for geographic dominance and higher levels of violence. OMGs rely on support clubs for recruitment purposes, financial support, and to counter rival gangs.

Gang Member Demographics

The National Gang Center's *National Youth Gang Survey Analysis* (n.d.) provides demographic information about our country's gang population, including data about gang members' age, gender, and race and ethnicity. According to the most recently available data, more than three out of every five gang members nationwide are adults. In fact, since 1998, survey results have consistently shown that a greater percentage of gang members throughout the country are age 18 and older (NGC, n.d.). However, differences in gang member age do exist across different area type. For example, in larger cities and suburban counties, where gang problems tend to have existed for a longer time, law enforcement agencies report more adult gang members than juvenile ones. Conversely, in smaller cities and rural counties, where gang problems are often more recent, law enforcement is more likely to report equal proportions of juvenile and adult gang members (NGC, n.d.).

prison gang

a self-perpetuating criminal organization that originates in the penal system and continues to operate not only within correctional facilities throughout the United States but also outside of prison.

outlaw motorcycle gang (OMG)

an ongoing organization, association, or group of three or more people with a common interest or activity characterized by the commission of, or involvement in, a pattern of criminal conduct, and whose members must possess and be able to operate a motorcycle to achieve and maintain membership within the group.

LO2

Three basic types of gangs operating in the United States are street gangs, prison gangs, and outlaw motorcycle gangs (OMGs).

The overwhelming majority of gang members are male. However, nearly 25 percent of law enforcement agencies surveyed lacked data regarding the prevalence of female membership within their jurisdiction's gangs, a finding that suggests this issue is of secondary or lesser significance for law enforcement (NGC, n.d.). And despite a growing concern about females joining gangs, there has been no significant change observed in the past decade in terms of the percentage of female gang members—reported percentages have held fairly steady between 7 and 8 percent of total gang membership (NGC, n.d.).

A common misconception about gang demographics has been that they are comprised almost exclusively of racial or ethnic minorities (Howell, 2007). One explanation for the perpetuation of this fallacy is that most gang research has focused on high-risk neighborhoods in large cities—areas characterized by high rates of poverty, welfare dependency, single-parent households, and residential mobility. These highly socially disorganized communities, which tend to draw the attention of researchers, are also disproportionately inhabited by racial and ethnic minorities. Consequently, the assessment of the overall ethnic or racial composition of gangs becomes skewed (Howell, 2007). Nonetheless, law enforcement agencies do report a greater percentage of Hispanic/Latino and African American/Black gang members than other races or ethnicities, with the most recent data indicating an estimated 46 percent of gang members are Hispanic/Latino, 35 percent are African American/Black, 12 percent are White, and 7 percent are another race or ethnicity (NGC, n.d.). Table 13.1 shows the average race/ethnicity of gang members in jurisdictions of varying sizes in 2011.

Although many, if not most, gangs are organized around race or ethnicity and are highly homogeneous with respect to this variable, some street gangs are more racially or ethnically heterogeneous in their membership. Such mixed-race or mixed-ethnicity gangs are known as *hybrid gangs*, a term that originally referred to a gang's ethnic or racial composition. More recently, however, hybrid gangs have come to include a more diverse group of gangs, including those in which membership is comprised of both males and females.

The County and City of Los Angeles are considered to be the "gang capital" of the country, with more 45,000 active gang members in more than 450 gangs inflicting crime and violence on the city. Many of these gangs have existed for

Table 13.1	Average Race/Ethnicity of Gang Members by Area Type, 2011			
	Larger Cities	**Suburban Counties**	**Smaller Cities**	**Rural Counties**
Black or African American	39.0%	32.7%	20.3%	56.8%
Hispanic or Latino	45.5	51.0	53.8	24.8
White	9.7	9.1	14.6	14.9
Other	5.8	7.2	11.3	3.4

Source: National Gang Center (no date). *National Youth Gang Survey Analysis.* Washington, DC: Author. Retrieved October 24, 2016 from https://www.nationalgangcenter.gov/Survey-Analysis/Demographics

more than 50 years. Between 2009 and 2012, there were over 16,398 verified violent gang crimes in the City of Los Angeles, including 491 homicides, 98 rapes, more than 7,000 felony assaults, and approximately 5,500 robberies (Los Angeles Police Department, n.d.).

The Gang Subculture

A gang member's lifestyle is narrow and limited primarily to the gang and its activities. Members develop fierce loyalty to their respective gang and become locked into the gang's lifestyle, values, attitudes, and behavior, often making it difficult for a member to later break away from a gang.

A gang member may receive a new identity by taking on a nickname, or **moniker**, which others in the gang world would recognize. Monikers affirm a youth's commitment to gang life and may become their sole identity, the only way they see themselves and the only name they go by. They may no longer acknowledge their birth name, rejecting any previous identity or life outside the realm of the gang.

moniker
A nickname, often of a gang member.

Gang Activities

Gangs have different characteristics based on the activities in which they engage. Some gangs are violent; others focus on crime commission with violence as a by-product. The same is true with a gang's relationship to drugs. Some focus on the drug business; others engage in business to meet their own drug needs. The NGIC (2016) reports that the most common crimes committed by street gangs are street-level drug trafficking, large-scale drug trafficking, assault, threats and intimidation, and robbery. OMGs are well-known for their use of brute violence in carrying out a range of crimes, including assault, arson, extortion, weapons possession, and drug trafficking.

Egley et al. (2014) report that, with the exception of homicide, most law enforcement agencies do not routinely record offenses as "gang related." Respondents to the 2012 NYGS reported a total of 2,363 gang-related homicides in the United States. The Federal Bureau of Investigation's Uniform Crime Reports (UCR) also estimated that there were more than 14,800 homicides nationally in 2012: "Taken together, these findings suggest that gangs were involved in approximately 16 percent of all homicides in the United States in 2012 and underscore the considerable overlap between gang activity and violent crime" (Egley et al., 2014, p. 2).

Females are used by gangs in a variety of ways, often because they arouse less suspicion than male adults. Females may serve as lookouts for crimes in progress, conceal stolen property or tools used to commit crimes, carry weapons for males who do not want to be caught with them, carry information in and out of prison, and provide sexual favors (they are often drug dependent and physically abused).

Gangs use children to commit shoplifting, burglaries, armed robberies, and drug sales in schools. Their youthful appearance is an advantage because they often do not arouse suspicion. Furthermore, if they are caught, the juvenile justice system generally deals more leniently with them than with adults.

Youth and Gangs   Most youths who join gangs are already involved in delinquency and drug use, but once in a gang, they usually become more actively involved in delinquency, drug use, and violence—and are more likely to be victimized themselves. Gang involvement dramatically alters youths' life chances, particularly if they remain active in the gang. The street-life cycle of many gang members involves going from a community to detention, to juvenile corrections, to adult prisons, and back into a community. Howell (2006, p. 3) contends: "Gang members were more likely than nonmembers to be arrested, were rearrested more quickly following release from prison, were rearrested more frequently, and were more likely to be arrested for violent and drug offenses than were nongang members."

Research consistently demonstrates that youths are significantly more criminally active during periods of gang membership, particularly in serious and violent offenses. Furthermore, gang members commit more serious crimes. In general, gang members' violent offense rates are up to seven times higher than those of nongang members. Studies comparing the criminal behavior of gang members with nongang members show that gang members living in high-crime areas are responsible for far more than their share of all self-reported violent offenses committed by the entire sample (Howell, 2006).

In some large cities, youth gangs and drug gangs have taken over a number of public-housing developments: "Fear of crime and gangs was an 'immediate,' daily experience for people who lived in lower-income neighborhoods where gangs were more prevalent and dangerous. But for people in other areas, fear was generally an abstract concern about the future that became immediate only when they entered certain pockets of the county" (Howell, 2006, p. 3).

When they have a "substantial presence," youth gangs are linked with serious delinquency problems in elementary and secondary schools in the United States. A strong correlation exists between gangs in schools and both guns and availability of drugs in school. The presence of gangs at school more than doubles the likelihood of violent victimization at school. And while the economic impact of gang crimes cannot be estimated because most law enforcement agencies do not record such data, clearly there is a high social cost associated with gangs' presence in a community.

Gangs and Other Criminal Groups   Gangs have begun to form cooperative relationships with other criminal entities for mutual gain. For example, the NGIC (2016) notes that some gangs in the United States, particularly those active along the U.S.-Mexico border, have fostered partnerships with Mexican Transnational Criminal Organizations (MTCOs) to enhance their abilities to commit cross-border crimes, such as drug trafficking: "Cross-border crime remains a significant concern for law enforcement throughout the country, as these crimes directly impact border regions and indirectly impact jurisdictions throughout the country. Drug trafficking that emanates from the US southwest border affects all regions, as gangs fight to defend their drug distribution territory and distribute harmful drugs to communities throughout the United States" (NGIC, 2016, p. 28).

Gangs are also increasingly being connected to domestic extremist groups: "A mutually beneficial arrangement, extremists use gangs to spread their doctrine, while gangs turn to extremists to increase membership and facilitate collaboration with other criminal organizations. Gangs also refer to extremist ideology to respond to perceived injustices and to enact social change" (NGIC, 2016, p. 10). Groups such as the Black separatist extremists, White supremacist extremists, and sovereign citizen extremists have found gangs to be a fertile ground for recruitment.

Why Youths Join Gangs

Gangs have strong appeal for many children who live in communities where gangs thrive. Gangs can fulfill the need to belong or the need for attention. Children with low self-esteem can gain identity in the gang culture (Krohn, Schmidt, Lizotte, & Baldwin, 2011). Gang membership also can provide friendship and the emotional and psychological support lacking in a child's home (Miller, Barnes, & Hartley, 2011). Additional reasons youths may join gangs include the potential to make "easy money," to engage in exciting activities, and to express defiance by rebelling against parents and other authority figures. Additionally, to children living in crime-ridden neighborhoods with heavy gang activity, joining a gang may give them the only way they know to feel safe. They join to gain protection from violence and attack from rival gangs or because they are forced into membership by a gang's violent recruitment methods. And some children are simply following family tradition.

Gangs often fulfill survival functions for youths in low-income, socially isolated ghetto or barrio communities and in transitional areas with newly settled populations. In the text by Shelden and colleagues, an entire chapter is devoted to inequality in American society and concludes: "Unemployment, poverty, and general despair lead young people to seek out economic opportunities in the growing illegal marketplace, often done within the context of gangs" (Shelden, Tracy, & Brown, 2004, p. 191). It must be emphasized, however, that despite the numerous enticements, the vast majority of youths living in gang-ridden areas never join a gang.

> **LO3**
> Youths seeking protection, security, status, an identity, a sense of belonging, and economic security can fulfill all of these needs through gang membership.

PREVENTING GANG MEMBERSHIP

Common sense suggests that preventing a gang problem in the first place is preferable to finding strategies to deal with such a problem after it surfaces. Research has identified risk factors associated with gang membership, with implications for developing effective, targeted prevention and intervention methods.

Early Precursors of Gang Membership and Implications for Prevention

The Seattle Social Development Project (SSDP) is a long-term study that looked at the development of positive and problem behaviors among adolescents and young adults. The study began in 1981 to test strategies for reducing childhood risk factors for school failure, drug abuse, and delinquency. This project identified childhood risk factors that predict whether a youth is likely to join a gang and the duration of the membership. Findings from the SSDP support three implications for efforts to prevent youths from joining gangs (Hill, Lui, & Hawkins, 2001, p. 4).

Prevention Efforts Should Begin Early   Although research indicates that the peak age for joining a gang was 15, this does not mean that prevention efforts should be aimed only at 14-year-olds. Instead, prevention efforts should begin well before the peak age for joining a gang, around ages 10 to 12 (Hill et al., 2001).

Prevention Efforts Should Target Youths Exposed to Multiple Risk Factors   As with risk factors for generalized delinquency and youth victimization, risk factors for joining a gang fall into five broad categories: individual, family, peer groups, school, and neighborhood/community (Hill et al., 2001). The more risk factors present in a youth's environment, the higher his or her odds are of joining a gang. Compared with youths who experienced none or only 1 of the 21 risk factors, youths who experienced 7 or more were 13 times more likely to join a gang.

Prevention Efforts Should Address All Facets of Youths' Lives   Efforts to prevent youths from becoming gang members must address the different aspects of their lives. No single solution or "magic bullet" will prevent youths from joining gangs.

The G.R.E.A.T. Program

One program aimed at preventing gang membership is the Gang Resistance Education and Training (G.R.E.A.T.) program, a nationally used program with some proven success. G.R.E.A.T. is an evidence-based gang and violence prevention program built around school-based, law enforcement officer-instructed classroom curricula (G.R.E.A.T. Program, n.d.). The program is intended as an immunization against delinquency, youth violence, and gang membership for children in elementary and middle school—the years immediately before the prime ages for introduction into gangs and delinquent behavior. The G.R.E.A.T. program provides a continuum of components for children and their families, including a six-lesson elementary school curriculum, a summer component, a 13-lesson middle school curriculum, and a families component. More than 13,000 sworn officers from around the United States and various Central American countries have been trained and certified to teach the G.R.E.A.T. curricula, which have been delivered to more than 6 million children to date. G.R.E.A.T. allows law enforcement to foster strong relationships not only with participating students but also with their schools and communities.

A study supported by the National Institute of Justice (NIJ) documented the program benefits in a cross-sectional evaluation and showed that students who graduated from the G.R.E.A.T. course showed lower levels of delinquency, impulsive behavior, risk-taking behavior, and approval of violence. The study also found that students demonstrated higher levels of self-esteem, parental attachment, commitment to positive peers, antigang attitudes, perceived educational opportunities, and positive school environments.

An early study of the G.R.E.A.T. program, conducted from 1995 to 2000, returned promising but inconclusive results, which led to a rigorous retooling of the program and curriculum. A follow-up multicomponent evaluation conducted between 2006 and 2012 and commissioned by the National Institute of Justice found significant improvement to and effectiveness of the G.R.E.A.T. program. Specifically, the study compared students who had completed the G.R.E.A.T. curriculum with those who had not and found that 1 year after completing the program, students exposed to G.R.E.A.T. showed a 39 percent reduction in odds of joining a gang compared to those who did not and an average of 24 percent reduction in their odds of joining a gang 4 years after completing the program (Esbensen, Peterson, Taylor, & Osgood, 2012).

Gang Resistance Is Paramount

Another prevention program with some proven effectiveness is the Gang Resistance Is Paramount (GRIP) program developed by the city of Paramount, California, after it recognized in the early 1980s that it had a severe gang problem and that its efforts to dismantle established gangs had little success. Paramount decided the key to approaching their problem was prevention.

GRIP began in 1982 as an effort to reduce gang membership and prevent future gang involvement in the city. The program, which was originally called Alternatives to Gang Membership, aims to educate students about the dangers of gangs, discourage local youth from joining gangs, educate parents about the signs of gang involvement, and provide families with the resources needed for eliminating gang activities in their homes and neighborhoods (Solis, Schwartz, & Hinton, 2003).

GRIP has been evaluated six separate times, with positive results, and has been adopted by many other communities in California and elsewhere (Washington Violent Crime Prevention Partnership, 2010).

Connecting with Youths—*Cops and Kids*

Just as many departments are connecting with youths to combat the drug problem, many departments seek to connect with youths to prevent their involvement in gangs. One initiative aimed at improving the youth–police connection is Cops and Kids, a professional development training program created by the Pittsburgh-based Fred Rogers Company (producers of the well-known public television program Mr. Rogers' Neighborhood). The training is intended to increase officer's effectiveness in encounters and interactions with youth by (1) raising officers' awareness of the tremendous impact their presence has on children and (2) showing how basic knowledge of children's development can enhance an officer's impact, safety, and ability to achieve law enforcement goals (Meyers & Karpman, 2011). The program's success in the Pittsburgh area led to its receiving a COPS Office grant to conduct workshops in other cities throughout the country. The multiple goals of the training program are to equip officers with the tools they need to build trust among children and families in the communities they serve, increase officer's safety and effectiveness while on patrol, help officers promote greater cooperation and reporting of criminal activity from the public, strengthen partnerships with social service agencies that provide protective services to children, and ultimate enhance officers' overall ability to improve public safety. Efforts such as this can go far in equipping police with the skills they need to effectively connect with their community's teens and help steer them away from the destructive forces of gangs.

As law enforcement agencies across the country are recognizing the value a community- oriented policing philosophy has in repairing damaged relationships between the agency and the community, more departments are seeking to invest resources in innovative, cost-effective programs that build trust between citizens and officers. Wetzel (2015) outlines a five-point blueprint for how the *Cops and Kids* mentoring program can help bridge the trust gap between police officers and young people, especially those kids most at-risk and in need of direction:

1. Create Initial Strategic Development
2. Invite Kids to Roll Call and Ridealongs
3. Start Doing Monthly Lunches
4. Make Home Visits
5. Be Available

To this final point, Wetzel (2015) notes: "Being able to reach out to someone you can count on when feeling pressure or problems can be invaluable for a young person who is struggling with a situation."

The Role of Public Health in Preventing Gang Membership

Chapter 3 of *Changing Course: Preventing Gang Membership*, a publication co-authored by the Centers of Disease Control and Prevention (CDC) and the National Institute of Justice (NIJ), focuses on a relatively new approach that brings the public health sector into the mix of efforts aimed at steering at-risk youth away from gang involvement. Similar to the shift taking place with drug crimes and the addiction that often attaches to such behavior, gang membership is now being examined as not just a criminal justice issue but also as a public health problem. When viewed through the public health lens, gang membership prevention focuses on using applied science to understand the social determinants of health and mobilizing the best evidence from epidemiologic studies for prevention. This shift in thinking makes sense, considering that the CDC has focused on youth violence as a public health issue since the 1980s (Haegerich, Mercy, & Weiss, 2013).

Similar to the four-step SARA model for problem solving, the four-step public health approach to youth violence and gang membership prevention is:

1. Describe and monitor the problem.
2. Identify the factors that place youth at risk for, or protect youth from, engaging in gang membership and violence.

3. Develop and test prevention approaches.

4. Disseminate, implement, and adopt prevention approaches.

Researchers note: "A particularly difficult challenge is addressing the underlying social forces that play a key role in fueling gang membership and associated violence. Most gang-related violence, drug sales and turf wars occur between gang youth from similar marginal areas. The complex interplay between poverty, competition over scarce resources and crime creates environments that are conducive to the formation of gangs and their attractiveness to youth. Success in reducing gang membership and violence will require attention to these underlying social determinants, including, for example, the investigation of prevention strategies that focus on reducing the levels of economic stress (for example, through business development and improvements), reducing the concentration of poverty (for example, through urban planning approaches), and improving educational attainment and job skills to enhance success in the labor market and reduce the attraction of gangs" (Haegerich et al., 2013, p. 44). When taking these risk factors and social determinants into account, it becomes quite clear that the police, alone, cannot solve the problem of gang membership and youth violence.

RECOGNIZING THE PRESENCE OF GANGS AND IDENTIFYING GANG MEMBERS

When prevention efforts fail, it is important that communities recognize the presence of a gang or gangs in their neighborhoods and take steps to address the problem. "Gangs thrive on anonymity, denial, and lack of awareness by school personnel. The gang member whose notebook graffiti goes unaddressed today may be involved in initiations, assaults, and drug sales in school in the near future" (National School Safety and Security Services, n.d.).

When schools and communities turn a blind eye to gang activity or actively deny its existence, they only ripen the environment for further gang-related problems and allow the issue to become more entrenched. When the gang problem becomes so major or apparent that denial is no longer an option, the tendency for city officials or school administrators is to downplay the seriousness of the situation. However such "qualified admittance" does nothing more than put off dealing with the problem, allowing gang issues, and the community's and school's image, to continue to worsen.

Conversely, communities and schools must take care to not overstate a gang problem, which could cause unnecessary fear among residents, students, and parents and unintentionally raise the gang's image in the eyes of its rivals. Although a majority of students in school and residents in a community are not gang-involved, it takes only a few gang members to initiate a significant amount of violence in a short amount of time, if their presence and actions go unaddressed: "Both denial of gang problems and overreaction to them are detrimental to the development of effective community responses to gangs. Denial that gang problems exist precludes early intervention efforts. Overreaction in the form of excessive police force and publicizing of gangs may inadvertently serve to increase a gang's cohesion, facilitate its expansion, and lead to more crimes" (Howell, 2000, p. 53).

To prevent or reduce the risk of gangs becoming entrenched, community and school officials should train their staff on gang identification, behavior, prevention and intervention strategies, and related school security issues (National School Safety and Security Services, n.d.).

Once a community recognizes a gang problem, the next step is to identify the gang members. While gang identifiers vary from school to school and community to community, they may include (National School Safety and Security Services, n.d.):

> **L05**
>
> Indicators of gang activity include graffiti, drive-by shootings, intimidation assaults, murders, and the open sale of drugs.

- Graffiti
- Tattoos
- "Lit" (gang literature)
- Initiation activities
- Handsigns
- Wearing "colors"
- Behavior

While the presence of such identifiers can help others recognize a gang affiliation, it is important to recognize that a focus on behavior is especially important. Although many people often look for bandannas, graffiti, or other physical displays as the primary tipoffs of gang involvement, new information is showing that active gang members are often choosing to keep a lower profile in terms of outward appearance, particularly as law enforcement, school officials, parents, and others become more aware of these "typical" gang identifiers. For example, the Los Angeles Police Department (LAPD) Criminal Gang Homicide Division reports that gang members have toned down their dress and its obvious affiliation properties in recent years, realizing that such high-profile "announcements" can lead more easily to being shot by a rival gang member or arrested by the police (Campbell, 2015). Consequently, LAPD officers have noticed that gang colors are rarely overtly worn. However, many gang members still display a subtle sign of their gang, such as the bandana in a pocket.

According to Howell (2006, p. 27): "Determining a particular individual's gang involvement is as difficult as identifying true youth gangs. In many instances, a youth may associate occasionally with a gang, participate episodically in the activities of a gang, or desire gang membership without actually being a member. Likewise, many youths leave gangs by drifting out, gradually dissociating themselves. Because severe criminal sanctions can be applied to gang membership in certain jurisdictions, a valid determination is important." The following criteria (any one of which qualifies the individual) might be used to determine whether a youth is a gang member:

- The individual admits membership in a gang (i.e., self-reported)
- A law enforcement agency or reliable informant identifies an individual as a gang member

Joel Gordon

- An informant of previously untested reliability identifies an individual as a gang member, and this information is corroborated by an independent source
- The individual resides in or frequents a particular gang's area and adopts its style of dress, use of hand signs, symbols, or tattoos; maintains ongoing relationships with known gang members; and has been arrested several times in the company of identified gang members for offenses consistent with usual gang activity
- There is reasonable suspicion that the individual is involved in a gang-related criminal activity or enterprise

Because of the changing nature of gang identifiers, educators, police, parents, and other youth-service providers need training and periodic updates to stay current and equipped to recognize gangs and gang members in their communities and schools. The National School Safety and Security Services (n.d.) suggests that the best training on gang identifiers is often provided by local law enforcement and other gang specialists who are familiar with the latest local trends.

THE POLICE RESPONSE TO GANGS

Often, police chiefs in cities where gangs have recently arrived are slow to recognize the threat. If police chiefs deny a gang problem despite mounting evidence, the gang problem may become unmanageable. However, if police publicly acknowledge the existence of gangs, this places the police administrator in a catch-22 situation. Publicly acknowledging gangs validates them and provides notoriety.

An important task in most police departments is gathering information or intelligence on gangs and their members. Intelligence is knowing what gangs are out there, where they are, the names of the individual gang members and their gang affiliation, where they have been seen, and who they have been seen with. Howell (2006, p. 53) recommends: "Each city's gang program should be supported by a gang information system that provides sound and current crime incident data that can be linked to gang members and used to enhance police and other agency interventions. At a minimum, law enforcement agencies must ensure that gang crimes are coded separately from nongang crimes so that these events can be tracked, studied, and analyzed to support more efficient and effective antigang strategies."

A computerized Gang Intelligence System (GANGIS), including comprehensive gang profile data such as monikers and vehicle information, can be an effective crime-fighting tool. National networks of gang intelligence databases can greatly enhance a department's effort to understand and respond to gang activities in their jurisdiction. The Regional Information Sharing System (RISS) network links six regional intelligence databases, including a gang database, RISS-GANGS. Another computer technology used for tracking gangs is the General Reporting, Evaluation, and Tracking (GREAT) system—a combination hot sheet, mug book, and file cabinet. This system is not to be confused with the G.R.E.A.T. program used in schools to teach children about resisting gangs, discussed earlier in the chapter.

The proliferation of gang problems in jurisdictions of all sizes—urban, suburban, and rural—over the past two decades led to the development of a comprehensive, coordinated response to the nation's gang problem by the Office of Juvenile Justice and Delinquency Prevention (OJJDP), which has long supported a combination of activities, including research, evaluation, training and technical assistance, and demonstration programs, aimed at combating youth gangs. However, upon recognizing that street gang activities transcend the ages of gang members, the Office of Justice Programs merged its existing resources in October 2009 to create a new National Gang Center (NGC), to create a comprehensive approach to reduce gang involvement and levels of gang crime. The reinvigorated NGC is a single, more efficient entity, responsive to the needs of researchers, practitioners, and the public. The NGC Web site (www.nationalgangcenter.gov) features the latest research about gangs; descriptions of evidence-based, antigang programs; and links to tools, databases, and other resources to assist in developing and implementing effective community-based gang prevention, intervention, and suppression strategies. The site also posts data analysis of the findings from nearly 15 years of data collected by the annual National Youth Gang Survey (NYGS) of 2,500 U.S. law enforcement agencies.

Evolution of Strategies for Dealing with the Gang Problem

The OJJDP reports a distinct difference in the approach used in the 1950s and 1960s compared to that used in more recent years. In the 1950s and 1960s, law enforcement used a social services approach toward gangs. During more recent years, the focus has been on suppression. Neither approach is clearly superior. Some communities have adopted a comprehensive approach combining social services intervention and suppression strategies (National Gang Center, 2010).

Suppression includes tactics such as prevention, arrest, imprisonment, supervision, and surveillance. **Social intervention** includes crisis intervention, treatment for youths and their families, outreach, and referral to social services. **Social opportunities** include providing basic or remedial education, training, work incentives, and jobs for gang members. **Community mobilization** includes improved communication and joint policy and program development among justice, community-based, and grassroots organizations. **Organizational development** includes special police units and special youth agency crisis programs.

Gang Units

To combat the gang problem, a full-service gang unit uses the components of prevention, suppression, and intervention. Respondents to the National Youth Gang Survey provided information regarding operation of a gang unit in their agency, defined in the survey as "a specialized unit with at least two officers primarily assigned to handle matters related to youth gangs." The survey found (NGC, n.d.):

- Approximately 4 in 10 law enforcement agencies with a gang problem operated a gang unit in 2006, including 54 percent of larger cities.
- With the exception of smaller cities, the percentage of agencies operating a gang unit increased yearly and was highest in 2006.
- In 2006, 31 percent of law enforcement agencies with a gang problem that did not operate a gang unit reported that one or more officers were assigned to handle gang problems exclusively.

According to the most recent NYGS, by 2012, 64 percent of responding law enforcement agencies had a dedicated gang unit or gang officer to address jurisdictional gang issues (Egley et al., 2014).

These prevention and control strategies represent a major improvement over general deterrence tactics such as zero tolerance, sweeps, and crackdowns—broad tactics that are largely indiscriminate in target selection and independent of empirical information and that serve primarily to randomly and temporarily inconvenience gang members, expose police to claims of racial profiling, and create incentives for police corruption and excessive force.

L06

The OJJDP's Comprehensive Gang Model uses five strategies to address the gang problem: suppression, social intervention, social opportunities, community mobilization, and organizational development. Community mobilization has been found to be the most effective strategy to address the gang problem.

suppression
Strategy to address the gang problem that includes tactics such as prevention, arrest, imprisonment, supervision, and surveillance.

social intervention
Strategy to address the gang problem that includes crisis intervention, treatment for youths and their families, outreach, and referral to social services.

social opportunities
Strategy to address the gang problem that includes providing basic or remedial education, training, work incentives, and jobs for gang members.

community mobilization
Strategy to address the gang problem that includes improved communication and joint policy and program development among justice, community-based, and grassroots organizations.

organizational development
A law enforcement strategy to address the gang problem that includes special police units and special youth agency crisis programs.

FEDERAL EFFORTS TO ADDRESS THE GANG THREAT

Although there is no national strategy to address violent street gangs and the challenges they present to communities across the country—despite the fact many scholars and practitioners have been calling for such a plan—several approaches have been developed by various agencies and entities at the federal level.

The Federal Bureau of Investigation (FBI) Safe Streets Violent Crime Initiative

The Federal Bureau of Investigation's Safe Streets Violent Crime Initiative began in 1992 and was designed to allow each field office to address violent street gangs and drug-related violence through the establishment of FBI-sponsored, long-term, proactive task forces that focused on violent gangs, violent crime, and the apprehension of violent fugitives. The Violent Gang Safe Streets Task Force became the vehicle through which law enforcement agencies at all levels—local, state, and federal—could join together to address the gang-related violent crime plaguing their communities. The FBI's Safe Streets and Gang Unit administers 160 Violent Gang Safe Streets Task Forces nationwide.

The FBI also leads the National Gang Intelligence Center (NGIC), a multi-agency effort that integrates the gang intelligence assets of federal, state, and local law enforcement departments and serves as a centralized intelligence resource for gang information and analytical support. The mission of NGIC is to allow timely and accurate information sharing between law enforcement agencies and to facilitate strategic and tactical analysis of intelligence regarding the growth, migration, criminal activity, and association of gangs that pose a significant threat to communities throughout the United States. The NGIC is not connected with the National Gang Center, which is an OJJDP project. Other FBI antigang initiatives and partnerships include:

- Central American Intelligence Program
- Central American Law Enforcement Exchange
- MS-13 National Gang Task Force
- San Salvador Legal Attaché
- Transnational Anti-Gang Initiative

The National Crime Prevention Council (NCPC) Anti-Gang Initiative

In February of 2006, the Department of Justice announced a twofold strategy to combat gang violence. First, it recommended prioritizing prevention programs to provide America's youth and offenders returning to the community with opportunities that help them resist gang involvement. Second, it recommended ensuring robust enforcement policies when gang-related violence does occur. The cornerstones of this initiative were an expansion of the established Project Safe Neighborhoods (PSN) programs and included new and enhanced antigang efforts in six cities with significant gang problems (National Crime Prevention Council, 2006). This program addressed the full range of personal, family, and community factors that contribute to juvenile delinquency and gang activity, combining prevention, enforcement, and reentry efforts to address gang membership and gang violence.

The six target areas were Los Angeles; Tampa, Florida; Cleveland, Ohio; the "222 Corridor" that stretches from Easton to Lancaster, Pennsylvania (near Philadelphia); the Dallas/Fort Worth metroplex; and Milwaukee, Wisconsin. Supported by $2.5 million in grant funds per site, this new initiative incorporated prevention and enforcement efforts, as well as programs to assist released prisoners as they reenter society. By integrating prevention, enforcement, and prisoner reentry, this new initiative aims to address gang membership and gang violence at every stage.

The Office of Juvenile Justice and Delinquency Prevention Comprehensive Gang Model

The OJJDP's Gang Reduction Program, launched in 2003, was a multimillion-dollar initiative designed to reduce gang crime in targeted neighborhoods by incorporating research-based interventions to address individual, family, and community factors that contribute to juvenile delinquency and gang activity. The program leveraged local, state, and federal resources in support of community partnerships that implement progressive practices in prevention, intervention, suppression, and reentry (National Gang Center, 2010).

The foundation of the program is the Comprehensive Gang Model, developed by Dr. Irving Spergel and colleagues at the University of Chicago. This model, the product of decades of OJJDP-funded gang research, holds that two factors largely account for a community's youth gang problem: the lack of social opportunities available to gang members younger than 22 years old and the degree of social disorganization present in a community (National Gang Center, 2010). The model also suggests other contributing factors, including poverty, institutional racism, deficiencies in social policies, and a lack of or misdirected social controls. The model includes five strategies: mobilizing communities, providing youth opportunities, suppressing gang violence, providing social interventions and street outreach, and facilitating organizational change and development. According to Howell (2006, p. 7): "Based on research and community experience, the model is multifaceted and multilayered and involves individual youths, families, the gang structure, agencies, and the community."

The success of the model has led to its replication in sites nationwide. The Rural Gang Initiative funds adaptation of the Comprehensive Gang Model at four rural sites and funds evaluation, training, and technical assistance for these efforts.

The *Gang-Free Schools and Communities Initiative* (OJJDP, 2000), also a replication of the OJJDP's Comprehensive Gang Model, was launched in 2000 to address and reduce youth gang crime and violence in schools and communities throughout the nation. Four sites were selected (East Cleveland, Ohio; Houston, Texas; Miami/Dade County, Florida; and Pittsburgh, Pennsylvania).

In phase one, sites assembled steering committees and assessment teams, drawing on the wide range of stakeholders in each community. Sites then assessed gang problems extensively by using multiple sources of information, including school and law enforcement records, community leaders, students, parents, teachers, and youth gang members. Applying their assessment findings, sites developed strategic plans for implementing OJJDP's Comprehensive Gang Model. Implementation plans included designs for gang prevention, intervention, and suppression at the community level, with an emphasis on school involvement. In phase two, sites are now implementing their strategic plans and delivering services and antigang activities in schools and across the communities. Specific activities vary across sites, but all sites follow the five broad strategies outlined in the Comprehensive Gang Model.

The Gang Reduction Program is designed to reduce gang activity in targeted neighborhoods by incorporating a broad spectrum of research-based interventions to address the range of personal, family, and community factors that contribute to juvenile delinquency and gang activity. The program integrates local, state, and federal resources to incorporate state-of-the-art practices in prevention, intervention, and suppression in program activities and resources to enhance prosocial influences in the community. Pilot communities identify and coordinate current resources, programs, and services that address known risk factors in the community and use grant funding to fill gaps to address risk factors for delinquency across the broadest possible age spectrum. The program design includes a framework for coordinating a wide range of activities that have demonstrated effectiveness in reducing gang activity and delinquency.

The Gang Prevention through Targeted Outreach Program enables local boys' and girls' clubs to prevent youths from entering gangs, intervene with gang members early in their involvement, and divert youths from gang life into more constructive activities. In addition, the OJJDP provides publications, funding opportunities, training, and technical assistance.

LOCAL STRATEGIES TO ADDRESS A GANG PROBLEM AND GANG VIOLENCE

Several strategies have been implemented to address gang problems and gang violence on the local level, including establishing behavior codes, obtaining civil injunctions, establishing drug-free zones (DFZs) around schools, implementing conflict prevention strategies, applying community pressure, and instituting graffiti removal programs.

Behavior codes should be established and firmly, consistently enforced. These codes may include dress codes and bans on showing gang colors or using hand signals. On the positive side, schools should promote and reward friendliness and cooperation.

Another way to address the gang problem is through *civil injunctions*. This strategy was used by the Redondo Beach (California) Police Department in an award-winning experiment. The department obtained an injunction against the gang members who had essentially taken over a city park. The department sued them and won. The injunction resulted from a partnership between the community and the police department and exemplifies an innovative, proactive approach to ensuring public safety. The injunction restricted the following actions:

- Possessing, or remaining in the company of anyone with, dangerous weapons, including clubs, bats, knives, screwdrivers, BB guns, and so on
- Entering private property of another without prior written permission of the owner
- Intimidating, provoking, threatening, confronting, challenging, or carrying out any acts of retaliation
- Forbidding a gang member younger than 18 years of age to be in a public place after 8 P.M. unless going to a legitimate business, a meeting, or an entertainment activity
- Disallowing gang members to associate or congregate in groups of three or more in the park or within 10 yards of the outside fence surrounding the park

The constitutionality of such an approach needs to be considered by any community wishing to implement this innovative strategy.

Establishing *drug-free zones (DFZs) around schools* is another commonly used strategy. This may include rewiring any pay phones so that only outgoing calls can be made.

Conflict prevention strategies are also important to address the gang problem. Teachers should be trained to recognize and deal with gang members in nonconfrontational ways. Staff should identify all known gang members and try to build self-esteem and promote academic success for all students, including gang members.

pulling levers
Refers to a multiagency law enforcement team imposing all available sanctions on gang members who violate established standards for behavior.

 IDEAS IN PRACTICE   PULLING LEVERS IN BOSTON

Pulling levers refers to a multiagency law enforcement team imposing all available sanctions on gang members who violate established standards for behavior. This strategy was used in Boston, Massachusetts, with a small group of youths who had extensive involvement in the justice system and who accounted for a majority of youth homicides. Boston's pulling levers program, Operation Ceasefire, was initiated by a multiagency law enforcement team convening a series of meetings with the chronic gang offenders where law enforcement communicated new standards for behavior. Violence will no longer be tolerated.

The program sent a message to gang members that *all* members of the gang would suffer consequences if any *one* gang member committed a crime involving a gun. Consequences included saturation patrols in the gang's neighborhood, crackdowns on probation and parole violations and outstanding arrest warrants and even stringent enforcement of child support orders, public housing rules and other controls that might apply to gang members.

When the standards were violated, the multiagency law enforcement team responded by imposing all available sanctions. Since Boston implemented the strategy in 1996, youth homicides have decreased by two-thirds.

Source: Kennedy, D. M., Braga, A. A., & Piehl, A. M. (2001, September) "Developing and Implementing Operation Ceasefire." In *Reducing Gun Violence: The Boston Gun Project's Operation Ceasefire, pp. 1–53*. Washington, DC: National Institute of Justice, (NCJ 188741)

Community pressure is also needed to effectively reduce and prevent gang activity. Parents and the general public should be made aware of gangs operating in the community, as well as of popular heavy metal and punk bands that may be having a negative influence on youths. They should be encouraged to apply pressure to television and radio stations and to book and video stores to put an age limit on material that promotes use of alcohol, drugs, promiscuity, devil worship, or violence. This may raise constitutionality or censorship issues, but as long as it is private citizens who apply the pressure, it should not present a problem.

Graffiti removal programs should be put in place calling for the prompt removal of graffiti anywhere it appears. **Graffiti**, unauthorized writing or drawing on a public surface, is not only unattractive but is also the written language of the gang, allowing gang members to advertise their turf and authority. No longer limited to inner cities, graffiti has become universal. Beyond its unsightliness, graffiti damage is very expensive, now costing the American public more than $4 billion a year. In some instances, photographs of the graffiti may aid certain police investigations. School officials should give to the police remaining paint cans and paint brushes that might be used as evidence. As an alternative to graffiti, students might be encouraged to design and paint murals in locations where graffiti is most likely to occur.

The Beaverton (Oregon) Police Department's graffiti removal program targets taggers because tagger graffiti is the majority of what they experience (Beaverton Police Department, n.d.). A tagger takes on a nickname (or "tag") and then writes it on public and private property. Tagger graffiti is not territorial because the taggers are determined to place as many tags as possible throughout an area to seek recognition among their peers. Tagger vandals may operate as a crew. Most crew graffiti shows the tag name and the tag crew. A tag crew can be identified by the initials scrawled somewhere in the tag. Usually there are three initials, but sometimes two or four are used.

The Beaverton "Graffiti Removal Program" (n.d.) enlisted the cooperation of parents, teachers, community members, and businesses. The program alerts *parents* that taggers may proudly sport samples of their "art" on books or notebooks. Some even carry tagging scrapbooks, complete with samples of their writing. Taggers may also carry copies of magazines that support the tagging trade. Parents should check their children's fingers for paint and should also be aware that taggers often wear baggy pants and loose shirts so as to easily hide cans of spray paint. *Teachers* should take notice of graffiti on notebooks, desks, homework, and in lockers and should watch for students with paint on their fingers. Any tagging should be immediately reported to school security staff (Beaverton Police Department, n.d.).

The *community* has a responsibility to maintain their neighborhoods and keep them graffiti-free. When an area is hit repeatedly by graffiti, citizens may feel the area is unsafe and in a condition that may serve as a welcome to more serious crime. To defeat the vandals and keep neighborhoods safe, everyone must continually monitor the problem. Citizens should paint over graffiti on their property as soon as it appears. Not only is fresh graffiti easier to clean, but prompt removal discourages future tags, as taggers seek visibility. A quick cover-up of their work denies them this visibility, thus deterring future attacks.

graffiti
Painting or writing on buildings, walls, bridges, bus stops, and other available public surfaces; used by gangs to mark their turf.

Businesses also can participate by taking part in the police department's Responsible Retailer Program, keeping spray paint out of the hands of minors and immediately removing any graffiti that appears on their property.

A COMMUNITY APPROACH TO A GANG PROBLEM

Gangs are not only a law enforcement problem, they are the entire community's problem. To effectively tackle a gang problem, all affected parties—law enforcement, schools, parents, youths, businesses, religious groups, and social service organizations—must be engaged in finding a solution. Shelden et al. (2004, p. 223) explain: "The community approach, as the name suggests, reaches out to include a broad spectrum of individuals, groups, and organizations. The community itself makes it clear that certain unhealthy behaviors are unacceptable and will not be tolerated. This approach takes advantage of existing community resources in the broadest sense and pools them to develop a community-wide strategy. The mobilization process involves four specific steps: (1) involving key community leaders, (2) forming a community board or task force, (3) conducting a community risk and resource assessment, and (4) planning the program and deciding on evaluation methods."

Howell (2006, p. 53) stresses: "Community responses to gangs must begin with a thorough assessment of the specific characteristics of the gangs themselves, crimes they commit, other problems they present, and localities they affect. To conduct a thorough assessment, communities should look at community perceptions and available data. Data from law enforcement sources such as local gang and general crime data are critical. Other data should be collected from probation officers, schools, community-based youth agencies, prosecutors, and community residents."

IDEAS **IN PRACTICE**   RICHMOND, CALIFORNIA'S OPERATION PEACEMAKER

Four teens sit in the lobby of the Office of Neighborhood Safety (ONS) in Richmond, California, relaxing and chatting with their mentor about job opportunities and other needs and concerns the boys have:

"What can I do better?" the mentor, Kevin Yarbrough, asks.

"Help us get out of Richmond and stuff," one teen mumbles. "Get us far away."

The conversation sounds like one any mentor might have with a group of inner-city teens in America.

But this is no ordinary group. The mentor is an ex-con working for the city. The teens are suspected of the worst types of crimes but haven't faced prosecution, for lack of evidence. The mentor's job: Get them to put down their guns, stop their violent ways and transform their lives beyond the streets.

Richmond, California, which lies just north of Berkeley, was once considered to be one of the most violent cities in America. In 2007, with gang violence in Richmond having reached a record high and a shooting rate more than eight times the national average, DeVone Boggan knew something had to be done. He helped found the ONS, with a strategy of sending reformed ex-convicts into the most troubled neighborhoods to build rapport with community residents and

(Continues)

hopefully quell the violence. Although shooting deaths dropped the first year, they bounced back up in 2009. Analysis of the strategy showed that too much focus had been placed on "hot spots" and not enough on the "hot people" who made up the hot spots.

To place greater emphasis on these "hot individuals," the ONS program reached out to some of the most hardened youth in the city and invited them to be mentored by ex-cons, referred to as "neighborhood change agents." The effort became known as Operation Peacemaker and was loosely structured as an academic fellowship. The police were not involved in the program. As part of the arrangement, participating youth had to promise to put down their guns and adopt a more peaceful lifestyle. In turn, they received mentoring from reformed criminals now hired by the ONS. If the youths stayed on track for the first six months of the program, they were eligible to earn a stipend for continued good behavior

In its first 7 years, Operation Peacemaker has, by all accounts, been a success. Of the 68 youth who have completed the program, 64 are still alive and 54 have not been arrested for a new gun crime. Other cities have begun looking to the program as a model for addressing their own local gang and gun violence.

When asked about the lack of police involvement in the program, Boggan notes he wanted to give these at-risk youth another, more positive resource than the "scared straight" tactics they had been receiving from law enforcement. The Richmond police chief, for his part, commends the program and says the department appreciates any effort to reduce gang and gun violence in the community. "The police, the justice system can't do this whole thing," he said. "There has to be multiple interventions. We get it."

Source: Adapted from Drash, W., & Sambou, T. S. (2016, May 20). "Paying Kids Not to Kill." CNN online. Retrieved October 25, 2016 from http://www.cnn.com/2016/05/19/health/cash-for-criminals-richmond-california/

PROVIDING ALTERNATIVES TO GANGS

Many gang experts stress the need to provide alternatives for youths who may be drawn to a gang or who may already be in a gang but are becoming disenchanted. Following are several examples of successful programs offering alternatives to gangs, many involving parents and building a sense of family.

Homeboy Industries: Jobs for the Future

In 1992, responding to the civil unrest in Los Angeles, Father Gregory Boyle formed Homeboy Industries and its Jobs for a Future project to create businesses that provide counseling, training, work experience, and many other services (including free tattoo removal)—opportunities that allow at-risk youth to plan their futures, not their funerals. In providing employment services, Homeboy Industries targets and focuses on that segment of the community that finds it most difficult to secure employment on its own—former gang members, parolees, and at-risk youth. According to the Homeboy Web site, no organization in Los Angeles serves a greater number of gang-involved men and women, offering a much-needed intervention to those who deserve a second chance at life. Most importantly, Jobs for a Future provides the opportunity for rival gang members to work side by side. Although the program fell on hard times during the recession, the current picture looks bright. Roughly 250 people are currently enrolled in Homeboy's 18-month job training program and 500 to 600 people access the program's counseling services and other resources each week, adding to the tens of thousands who have sought and received help through Homeboy since its inception (Mejia, 2015).

The guiding principle of Homeboy Industries' Jobs for a Future project is both purposeful and pragmatic: "Nothing stops a bullet like a job." Located in the gang-afflicted East Los Angeles community of Boyle Heights, Homeboy Industries offers gang-involved and at-risk youth the opportunity to become productive members of society through a variety of employment-centered services.

Several economic development enterprises have been created since Homeboy Bakery, the first venture, was started: Homeboy Silkscreen, Homeboy/Homegirl Merchandise, Homeboy Graffiti Removal, Homeboy Diner, Homeboy Farmer's Market, and Homegirl Café and Catering. Homeboy Industries is supported by the OJJDP's Gang Reduction Program.

Pierce County, Washington: Safe Streets Campaign

Safe Streets is a community resource that helps individuals, families, communities, and organizations develop strategies to reduce gang violence and drug use. Programs for youths include the Interagency Gang Task Force, which unites the schools, the health department, local law enforcement, the prosecutor's office, and a children's commission to identify gang-involved youths and prevent the cycle of youth violence. The "Youth Leading Change" program engages area youth in leadership activities, working to promote healthier choices among their peers. Founded in 1996, the program has grown into and reaches out to high school-aged youth around Pierce County (Safe Streets Campaign, n.d.).

The Pierce County Prosecutor's Office is a proud supporter of the Safe Streets campaign, which is a nonprofit organization that brings people together, often for the first time, to take back their streets. By forming neighborhood block groups, the Safe Streets campaign helps plant the seed of grassroots, community leadership. That leadership helps hold communities together and links them with can-do people in agencies and organizations to make neighborhoods safe. Working together is the key to reversing crime trends in our neighborhoods. Safe Streets helps to create better, safer communities throughout Pierce County.

Los Angeles, California: Summer Night Lights

Summer Night Lights (SNL) is an antigang initiative that targets park facilities in Los Angeles's Gang Reduction and Youth Development (GRYD) zones—areas where rates of violent gang-related crime are significantly higher than in other parts of the city. SNL offers expanded programming, after-school activities, athletic leagues, art initiatives, family programs, and free food, with the hope that by keeping parks open after dark—during the peak hours for gang activity—at-risk youth will have a safe place to spend the summer (GRYD Foundation, 2016). Since 2008, the SNL program has grown from 8 parks to 32 parks across the city. According to the program's Web site, highlights of the 2014 season included 901,253 visits across all 32 SNL sites and 563,283 total meals served; a 15.4 percent reduction in gang-related crime over a 6-week summer period in the 32 SNL communities as compared to the same time frame in 2013; free HIV/STD testing for 228 participants; 10,611 youth participants in sports leagues; and the creation of 1,068 local jobs, including the hiring of 325 at-risk youth.

PROBLEM-SOLVING PARTNERSHIPS TO ADDRESS GANG CRIME AND GANG PROBLEMS

One national partnership aimed at reducing gang-related crime and attendant problems is Project Safe Neighborhoods (PSN), a networking initiative that connects existing local programs that target gun and gang crime and provides these programs with additional tools necessary to be successful (PSN was introduced in Chapter 7). Since its inception in 2001, billions of dollars have been committed to this initiative, with funds used to hire new federal and state prosecutors, support investigators, provide training, distribute gun-lock safety kits, deter juvenile gun crime, and develop and promote community outreach efforts as well as to support other gun and gang violence reduction strategies (Bureau of Justice Assistance, n.d.). In 2016, the Office of Justice Program's Bureau of Justice Assistance (BJA) awarded $5.7 million in grants to PSN (U.S. Department of Justice, 2016).

Local partnerships coordinated through the 94 U.S. Attorneys' Offices across the United States integrate five elements from successful gun crime reduction programs such as the Boston Operation Ceasefire Program and the Department of Justice's Strategic Approaches to Community Safety Initiative. The five elements are partnerships, strategic planning, training, outreach, and accountability.

SUMMARY

An estimated 850,000 gang members are active in more than 30,700 gangs nationwide, with gang activity primarily concentrated in urban areas. Three basic types of gangs operating in the United States are street gangs, prison gangs, and outlaw motorcycle gangs (OMGs). Many gangs are sophisticated and well organized; all use violence to control neighborhoods and boost their illegal money-making activities, which include robbery, drug and gun trafficking, prostitution and human trafficking, and fraud. Many gang members continue to commit crimes even after being sent to jail.

Youths seeking protection, security, status, an identity, a sense of belonging, and economic security can fulfill all of these needs through gang membership. Prevention efforts should (1) begin early, (2) target youths exposed to multiple risk factors, and (3) address all facets of youths' lives. The Gang Resistance Education and Training (G.R.E.A.T.) program is aimed at stopping gang membership. The Gang Resistance Is Paramount (GRIP) program seeks to prevent youths from joining gangs through education.

Indicators of gang activity include graffiti, drive-by shootings, intimidation assaults, murders, and the open sale of drugs. Indicators of gang membership include colors, tattoos, hand signs, and behavior.

The OJJDP's Comprehensive Gang Model uses five strategies to address the gang problem: suppression, social intervention, social opportunities, community mobilization, and organizational development. Community mobilization has been found to be the most effective strategy to address the gang problem.

Current strategies to address the gang problem include establishing behavior codes, obtaining civil injunctions, establishing drug-free zones (DFZs) around schools, implementing conflict prevention strategies, applying community pressure, and instituting graffiti removal programs.

DISCUSSION QUESTIONS

1. What do you think are the main reasons individuals join gangs?
2. How does a street gang member differ from other juvenile delinquents?
3. What are the advantages and disadvantages of expelling disruptive gang members from school?
4. Were gangs present in your high school? How did you know? If they were, did they present a threat?
5. Are there efforts in your community to combat the gang problem?
6. Why is a uniform definition of gangs important for the law enforcement profession and what has prevented it from being established?
7. Why do schools and policing agencies sometimes deny or downplay the presence of gangs?
8. Explain the consequences of denying the existence of gangs.
9. In your opinion, is it possible to prevent youngsters from joining gangs?

ADDITIONAL RESOURCES

Following are Web sites recommended for the study of gangs.

- Gangs and Security Threat Group Awareness, www.dc.state.fl.us/pub/gangs/index.html

  This Florida Department of Corrections Web site contains information on, photographs of, and descriptions of a wide variety of gang types, including Chicago- and Los Angeles-based gangs, prison gangs, nations, sets, and supremacy groups.

- Gangs OR Us, www.gangsorus.com

  This site offers a broad range of information, including a state-by-state listing of all available gang laws, gang identities, and behaviors applicable to all areas of the United States, and links to other sites that provide information for law enforcement, parents, and teachers.

- Southeastern Connecticut Gang Activities Group (SEGAG), www.segag.org

  This coalition of law enforcement and criminal justice agencies from southeastern Connecticut and New England provides information on warning signs that parents and teachers often observe first, along with a large number of resources and other working groups that are part of nationwide efforts to contain gang violence.

Understanding and Preventing Violence

Key Terms

bias crime
bias incident
cycle of violence
Ferguson effect
gun interdiction
hate crime
intimate partner violence (IPV)
process mapping
straw purchasers
violent crime

Social media infiltrates daily life. It is a tool used to help plan, organize, and detail the day-to-day interactions among people and has become the "new norm" of communication. Social media is more about sociology and psychology than about the application of technology. Considering that it invades the space of nearly every individual, recording private and public thought, police are now using social media as a crime prevention tool.

Officers with the Los Angeles Police Department (LAPD), with help from researchers at California-based RAND and Cardiff University in the United Kingdom, will be monitoring Twitter accounts for key words, phrases, and text patterns that might signal that a particular population or person is about to be a target of a hate crime based on race, religion, nationality, gender, sexual orientation, or disability. The theory is that evaluation of these derogatory key phrases or pattern, as determined by the researchers, can serve to identify hate speech as a key indicator in the hate crime. Funded with $600,000 from the U.S. Department of Justice, police and researchers will evaluate tweets to see how many hate crimes go unreported. Considering that the number of crimes motivated by ethnicity has risen from 22 percent in 2004 to 51 percent in 2012, and that crimes motivated by a religious bias grew from 10 percent in 2004 to 28 percent in 2012, researchers believe that this 3-year project will provide insight into the underreporting of hate crimes. It should be noted that there will be no monitoring of any active or current tweets by social media users.

Predictive policing is nothing new to the LAPD. By collecting such data, police and researchers hope to be better able to predict hate crimes based on their informatics. Such information can be used across their diverse jurisdiction, with particular attention being focused on immigrant communities where individuals may become victims of hate crime but are unlikely to report it because of their immigration status.

Although using technology is nothing new to law enforcement's monitoring of criminal activity, this project marks the first time social media is being used to form predictive policing models for the prevention of hate crimes. Since many people seem compelled to make their private life public through social media, police are recognizing the value in turning such posts into a tool to predict potentially criminal or hateful behavior.

INTRODUCTION

Our nation was born in the violence of the Revolutionary War. The Union remained intact after a bloody Civil War that pitted brother against brother. Since then America has been willing to fight for freedom. It also cherishes the peace and freedom at home, however, that others fought to secure. But violence continues to exist, as shown in Figure 14.1.

The Federal Bureau of Investigation (FBI) administers the Uniform Crime Reporting (UCR) Program and publishes UCR data in an annual report called *Crime in the United States*. In the UCR program, a **violent crime** is defined as an offense that involves force or threat of force. Violent crimes are categorized as one of the four offenses: murder and nonnegligent manslaughter, rape, robbery, and aggravated assault.

violent crime
an offense that involves force or threat of force; includes murder and non-negligent manslaughter, rape, robbery, and aggravated assault.

Figure 14.1	2014 Crime Clock

2014 Crime Clock STATISTICS

A Violent Crime occurred every	**26.3 seconds**
One murder every	36.9 minutes
One rape every	4.5 minutes
One robbery every	1.6 minutes
One aggravated assault every	42.5 seconds
A property crime occurred every	**3.8 seconds**
One burglary every	18.2 seconds
One larceny-theft every	5.4 seconds
One motor vehicle theft every	45.7 seconds

Source: Federal Bureau of Investigation. (2014a). *Crime in the United States 2014*. Washington, DC: Author. Retrieved October 27, 2016 from https://ucr.fbi.gov/crime-in-the-u.s/2014/crime-in-the-u.s.-2014/offenses-known-to-law -enforcement/browse-by/national-data

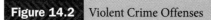

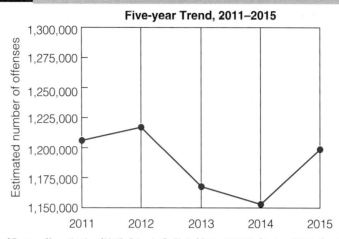

Figure 14.2 Violent Crime Offenses

Five-year Trend, 2011–2015

Source: Federal Bureau of Investigation. (2015). *Crime in the United States 2015*. Washington, DC: Author. Retrieved October 27, 2016 from https://ucr.fbi.gov/crime-in-the-u.s/2015/crime-in-the-u.s.-2015/offenses-known-to-law-enforcement/violent-crime/violentcrimemain_final

According to *Crime in the United States 2015* (FBI, 2015), an estimated 1,197,704 violent crimes occurred nationwide during 2015, an increase of 3.9 percent from the 2014 estimate. Although the nation seems to be experiencing an uptick in violent crime, it is worth considering 5- and 10-year trends, which show that the 2015 estimated violent crime total was 0.7 percent below the 2011 level and 16.5 percent below the 2006 level. Figure 14.2 illustrates the 5-year trend in violent crime offenses.

There were an estimated 372.6 violent crimes per 100,000 inhabitants in 2015, a rate that rose 3.1 percent when compared with the 2014 estimated violent crime rate. Other findings from the 2015 UCR report include:

- Aggravated assaults accounted for 63.8 percent of violent crimes reported to law enforcement in 2015. Robbery offenses accounted for 27.3 percent of violent crime offenses; rape (legacy definition) accounted for 7.5 percent; and murder accounted for 1.3 percent.

- Information collected regarding types of weapons used in violent crime in 2015 showed that firearms were used in 71.5 percent of the nation's murders, 40.8 percent of robberies, and 24.2 percent of aggravated assaults. (Weapons data are not collected for rape.)

It is important to note that the data presented in *Crime in the United States* reflect the Hierarchy Rule, which requires that only the most serious offense in a multiple-offense criminal incident be counted. The descending order of UCR violent crimes in terms of seriousness is murder and nonnegligent manslaughter, rape, robbery, and aggravated assault. Although arson is a property crime, the Hierarchy Rule does not apply to the offense of arson. Cases in which an arson occurs in conjunction with another violent or property crime, both the arson and the additional crime are reported.

Because the Hierarchy Rule presents a skewed image of the true extent of violent crime in the United States, many researchers and criminal justice practitioners advocate switching solely to the National Incident-Based Reporting System, or NIBRS, which records every offense committed during a single event. For example, if an armed assailant robbed a woman, raped her, and then shot her to death, all three offenses would be recorded: robbery, rape, and homicide. The UCR, however, would count only the homicide.

Crime rates are not evenly distributed, and the actual rate and risk of being victimized depends greatly on the region of the country, the city, and the neighborhood within the city. There also appears to be a strong correlation between crime rates and median household income. New England, the wealthiest region, has the lowest crime rates and the lowest homicide rates in the country. New York and New Jersey, though densely populated, have crime rates below the national average. The South historically has the highest crime rates in the country and the lowest median household income. The most current data on criminal victimization rates from the National Crime Victimization Survey (NCVS), the FBI, and other sources are available on the Bureau of Justice Statistics (BJS) Web site at bjs.ojp.usdoj.gov.

Violence occurs on our streets as road rage, in our schools and workplaces as shooting sprees, and behind closed doors as domestic abuse. It permeates and weakens our social fabric. After years of declining crime rates, law enforcement leaders grew alarmed when, in 2006, violent crime rates began to increase. Police chiefs from across the country suggested several plausible reasons: significant increases in gang activity; the movement of former gang members from New Orleans to other cities; release of offenders who were incarcerated at high rates during the 1990s; displacement of crime from cities where some crime-infested public housing units were dismantled; the changing nature of the drug market; and petty fights that escalated into major violent crimes.

Concern that these violent crime increases represented the front end of a tipping point of an epidemic of violence not seen for years, representatives from more than 50 cities—170 mayors, police chiefs, and public officials—met in August 2006 at the Police Executive Research Forum (PERF) National Violent Crime Summit to examine violent crime across the country and determine the nature and extent of the problem (Rosen, 2006). City after city reported that much of the violence was hitting the nation's minority communities hardest, both as victims and perpetrators of violent crime (Rosen, 2006, p. 8). Comments from participants included the following:

- "What is particularly frustrating about our homicides is that they occur for no apparent rhyme or reason. They come up over the smallest issue—someone feels disrespected." Chris Magnus, Richmond (Virginia) Police Chief (p. 4)

- "A big part of the problem is too many kids having kids and too many kids raising themselves." R. T. Rybak, Minneapolis (Minnesota) Mayor (p. 4)

- "A small segment of our youth has become a 'throwaway' generation. Nobody cares for them. They lack parental, educational, or social support." George Gascon, Mesa (Arizona) Police Chief (p. 8)

- "All the people we put in jail 10 years ago are now back. They come out of the system more hard core than when they went in." Richard Pennington, Atlanta (Georgia) Police Chief (p. 9)

Children and adults parade down a busy street during a peace march against violence in South Central Los Angeles. Nearly two dozen organizations took part in the event. Citizens are key stakeholders in violence prevention partnerships.

AP Images/Lee Celano

- "We are sacrificing hometown security for homeland security. Local police departments cannot be effective homeland security partners if they are overwhelmed by their core mission responsibilities." Douglas Palmer, Trenton (New Jersey) Mayor (p. 12)

The report on the summit concludes: "In 2006, American law enforcement finds itself once again facing a tipping point in violence on its streets, and it is spreading from city to city. While the nation has understandably focused on homeland security, it must recognize that there is a gathering storm of violent crime that threatens to erode the considerable crime reductions of the past" (Rosen, 2006, p. 14).

Despite the dire predictions, in the following year, violent crime resumed the downward trend of previous years and, despite a recent 1-year increase as mentioned earlier, crime rates in 2015 were still 16.5 percent below what they were in 2006. Criminologists are cautious as preliminary crime data for 2016 are being released, which indicates that violent crime may be once again tracking upward in dozens of major cities across the country (Sanburn, 2016). FBI Director James Comey has speculated that this phenomenon might be a reflection of the **Ferguson effect**, a theory that suggests policing practices have changed in the wake of the shooting of Michael Brown in Ferguson such

Ferguson effect

the theory that policing practices have changed in the wake of the shooting of Michael Brown in Ferguson, Missouri, where beat officers are backing off proactive policing and not getting out of their squad cars as often, which has emboldened criminals and fueled other social unrest, which has in turn led to a spike in violent crime.

that beat officers are backing off proactive policing and not getting out of their squad cars as often. This "hands off" policing approach has emboldened criminals and fueled other social unrest that has, in turn, led to a spike in violent crime (MacDonald, 2016). However, it should be kept in mind that when crime starts going up, it takes more than 2 or 3 years to determine a true trend.

CAUSES OF VIOLENCE

The causes of violence are as difficult to pinpoint as the causes of crime. Many suggest that the ready availability and lethal nature of guns, especially handguns, are major factors. In colonial America, however, every household had guns—survival depended on them—yet children did not shoot each other in their one-room schoolhouses. Nonetheless, the gun factor must be considered.

Another major cause of violence may be desensitization to violence. Violence permeates our television programs and movies, our video games and DVDs. Violence on our streets is graphically portrayed by the media.

Researchers Stretesky, Schuck, and Hogan (2004) examined 236 cities to determine if a relationship existed between poverty clustering and violent crime rates. They found that "disadvantage" has a much stronger relationship to homicide in cities with high levels of poverty clustering.

LO1
Causes of violence may include ready availability of guns, drugs, and alcohol; a desensitization to violence; disintegration of the family and community and the weakening of informal social control; social and economic deprivation; and increased numbers of children growing up in violent families.

PREVENTING VIOLENCE

Developing effective prevention tactics requires long-term collaborations between criminal justice and juvenile justice practitioners and other social service agencies. It also requires involvement of the entire community of which these agencies are a part. Prevention should include strategies directed toward children and their caregivers, especially those children at risk of becoming delinquent, as well as at areas with high levels of poverty and single-parent families. Efforts should also be directed at situations or locations where violent events cluster, such as illegal drug markets, certain places where alcohol and firearms are readily available, and physical locations conducive to crime.

LO2
A problem-solving approach to preventing violence must attempt to identify the underlying causes of specific violent situations that threaten a community before solutions can be devised.

Key partnerships in a *public dialogue and community mediation* strategy include schools, police, probation agencies, area courts, community organizations, and individual citizens, including youths. In addition, community newspapers and grassroots word-of-mouth networks help publicize the community dialogue and mediation services. A potential obstacle to the service is that it may be difficult to finance.

Another strategy is to *address violence as a public health problem.* A successful public health campaign against violence requires violence prevention curricula, community partnerships, public awareness involving the mass media, and clinical education and training. Community groups, the clergy, business leaders, schools, and parents can all contribute to a network of services. In addition, physicians, nurses, and other health care providers can be trained in violence prevention techniques, including counseling and teaching patients anger management.

The Boston City Department of Health and Hospitals initiated the Boston Violence Prevention Project in 1982 to prevent youth violence. It began in high

LO3
Strategies for general violence prevention include public dialogue and community mediation, and addressing violence as a public health problem.

school classrooms with lessons presenting violence statistics and addressing ways to avert violence and expanded into a comprehensive effort to reach the entire community.

This nationally known program also incorporates education and training for youth-serving agencies and has trained thousands of people and hundreds of agencies. The program also spurred development of the "Friends for Life, Friends Don't Let Friends Fight" media campaign and "Increase the Peace" weeks.

HATE CRIMES

No other nation is as culturally diverse as the United States, thrusting people of different customs, languages, lifestyles, and beliefs together and hoping they can coexist peacefully. Unfortunately, this does not always happen, and severe tension can result between cultural groups when their members are poorly informed and suspicious of cultures and lifestyles outside their own. Some people feel threatened by simply coming into contact with those who are culturally different. What people do not understand, they tend to fear, and what they fear, they often hate.

Hate can be classified into two categories: rational and irrational. Unjust or harmful acts, such as a rape, inspire rational hate. The victim and the victim's loved ones may rationally, with reason, hate the person who committed the rape. Conversely, hatred of someone based on his or her perceived race, religion, sexual orientation, ethnicity, or national origin constitutes irrational hate (Schafer & Navarro, 2003). A **hate** or **bias crime** is "a traditional offense like murder, arson, or vandalism with an added element of bias" (FBI, n.d.). For data collection purposes, Congress has defined a hate crime as a "criminal offense against a person or property motivated in whole or in part by an offender's bias against a race, religion, disability, ethnic origin, or sexual orientation. Hate itself is not a crime—and the FBI is mindful of protecting freedom of speech and other civil liberties" (FBI, n.d.).

Hate crimes include any act, or attempted act, to cause physical injury, emotional suffering, or property damage through intimidation, harassment, racial or ethnic slurs and bigoted epithets, vandalism, force, or the threat of force. The majority of hate crimes are against the person, including assault (the most common), harassment, menacing/reckless endangerment, and robbery. Crimes against property include vandalism/criminal mischief (most common), arson/cross burning, and burglary.

FBI investigations of hate crimes date as far back as the 1920s, but the protection of civil rights was considered to be a local rather than a federal concern. The murders of three African American civil rights workers in Mississippi, in June 1964, provided the impetus for a visible and sustained federal effort to protect and foster civil rights for all Americans and led to the passage of the Civil Rights Act in July 1964, which increased the role of the FBI in protecting civil rights. The Mississippi Burning (MIBURN) case became the largest federal investigation ever conducted in Mississippi. On October 20, 1967, seven men were convicted of conspiring to violate the constitutional rights of the slain

hate/bias crime
A criminal offense committed against a person, property, or society that is motivated, in whole or in part, by an offender's bias against an individual's or group's race, religion, ethnic/national origin, gender, age, disability, or sexual orientation. *Hate crime* and *bias crime* are considered synonymous.

civil rights workers and were sentenced to prison terms ranging from 3 to 10 years (FBI, n.d.).

As discussed, cultural tension commonly occurs in this country from an intolerance of racial and ethnic diversity. Although many would like to believe the intense racial hatred and slaughter of minorities is a relatively distant part of our nation's history and that we have come a long way from the "lynching era" of the late 1800s and early 1900s, events in the 1990s and early 2000s indicate otherwise.

- In 1998, James Byrd, Jr., a Black man, was hitchhiking home when a truck pulled up. Byrd was kidnapped, taken to a wooden area, beaten to unconsciousness, chained to the back of the truck, and then dragged for several miles. His head and right arm were torn from his body during the dragging. His assailants were three White men with links to racist groups.

- Also in 1998, openly gay college student Matthew Shepard was beaten with a pistol and then tied to a fence on the edge of town and left to die.

- In 2000, Jose Padilla was on a work break, sitting at a picnic table with two friends who worked at the adjoining business. The men were speaking Spanish. His friends' boss struck Padilla with a wooden two-by-four, telling him, "We don't speak Spanish here." Padilla suffered a fractured skull and permanent brain damage. The assailant went to prison.

Hate Crimes and Hate Groups by the Numbers

According to the most recent *Hate Crimes Statistics* (FBI, 2014b), law enforcement agencies across the country reported a total of 5,479 hate crime incidents involving 6,418 offenses to the UCR Program in 2014, crimes that left 6,727 individual victims in their wake and devastated. Data reported to the FBI show:

- In 2014, 15,494 law enforcement agencies participated in the Hate Crime Statistics Program. Of these agencies, 1,666 reported 5,479 hate crime incidents involving 6,418 offenses.

- There were 5,462 single-bias incidents that involved 6,385 offenses, 6,681 victims, and 5,176 known offenders.

- There were 17 multiple-bias incidents reported in 2014, involving 33 offenses, 46 victims, and 16 offenders.

As shown in Figure 14.3, of the 5,462 single-bias incidents reported in 2014:

- 47.0 percent were racially motivated.
- 18.6 percent resulted from sexual orientation bias.
- 18.6 percent were motivated by religious bias.
- 11.9 percent stemmed from ethnicity bias.
- 1.8 percent were motivated by gender identity bias.
- 1.5 percent were prompted by disability bias.
- 0.6 percent (33 incidents) resulted from gender bias.

Figure 14.3 Bias Breakdown

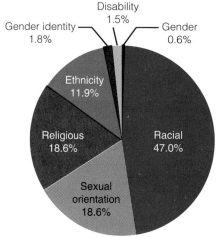

Analysis of the 5,462 single-bias incidents reported by law enforcement during 2014 revealed the following biases:

- Disability 1.5%
- Gender identity 1.8%
- Gender 0.6%
- Ethnicity 11.9%
- Religious 18.6%
- Racial 47.0%
- Sexual orientation 18.6%

Source: Federal Bureau of Investigation. (2014b). *Hate Crime Statistics 2014*. Washington, DC: Author. Retrieved October 27, 2016 from https://ucr.fbi.gov/hate-crime/2014

Of the 6,385 single-bias hate crime offenses reported in the above incidents:

- 48.3 percent stemmed from racial bias.
- 18.4 percent were motivated by sexual orientation bias.
- 17.1 percent resulted from religious bias.
- 12.4 percent were prompted by ethnicity bias.
- 1.7 percent stemmed from gender identity bias.
- 1.5 percent resulted from bias against disabilities.
- 0.6 percent (40 offenses) were prompted by gender bias.

Common crimes that might be motivated by hate include (Freilich & Chermak, 2013):

- Aggressive driving
- Assaults in and around bars
- Bullying in schools
- Cemetery vandalism
- Drive-by shootings
- Graffiti
- Homeless encampments
- School vandalism
- Stalking
- Street robbery

LO4
The majority of hate crimes are motivated by racial bias. Sexual orientation bias and religious bias are tied for the second most common type of motivator for hate crime.

However, victims do not always recognize that the crime they have just experienced was motivated, in part or in full, by hate or bias, and for this reason, the number of hate crimes remains significantly underreported. Studies have found that more than half (54%) of hate crime victims do not report the incident to police, with victims of disability hate being the least likely of all groups to report their victimization to law enforcement (Freilich & Chermak, 2013). Factors that affect whether a hate crime gets reported include whether the victim was aware that a crime occurred, whether the victim thought the offense was serious enough to report, whether the victim thought the police could do anything to solve the crime, and the victim's relationship to the perpetrator.

Researchers and law enforcement practitioners have observed that violent hate crimes tend to be more brutal than similar nonhate crimes and that hate crime offenders tend to use extreme violence going beyond that which is needed to subdue their victims. Consider that nearly 25 percent of hate crimes are serious violent crimes (i.e., rape/sexual assault, robbery, aggravated assault), compared to only 8 percent of nonhate crimes falling into those offense categories (Freilich & Chermak, 2013).

According to the Southern Poverty Law Center (SPLC), the number of active hate groups in the United States increased by 14 percent from 2014 to 2015, reaching a total of 892 such groups operating within the country at the end of 2015, nearly twice the number of hate groups observed in 1999 (SPLC, n.d.). All hate groups have beliefs or practices that attack or malign an entire class of people, typically for their immutable characteristics. The dramatic increase in such groups has been fueled by anger and fear over the nation's ailing economy, the influx of non-White immigrants, and the diminishing White majority. These factors have also fed a powerful resurgence of the antigovernment "Patriot" movement, including the formation of armed militias, which grew by 755 percent during the first 3 years of the Obama administration. Hate groups known to be active during 2015 included neo-Nazis, Klansmen, White nationalists, neo-Confederates, racist skinheads, Black separatists, Christian Identity, and border vigilantes (SPLC, n.d.).

Most states have passed mandatory reporting laws requiring police departments to keep statistics on the occurrence of bias and hate crimes. In 1990, the Federal Hate Crime Statistics Act was passed, mandating the justice department to secure data on crimes related to religion, race, sexual orientation, or ethnicity. Although the laws vary considerably, the most common elements are (1) enhanced penalties for common law crimes against persons or property motivated by bias based on race, ethnicity, religion, gender, or sexual orientation; (2) criminal penalties for vandalism of religious institutions; and (3) collection of data on bias crimes.

Effects of Hate Crime Victimization

After their victimization, the targets of hate crimes often experience psychological stress, including depression, anxiety, and feelings of heightened vulnerability; lack of concentration; and flashbacks. Comparisons between hate crime and nonhate crime victims indicate that victims of hate crime are significantly more likely to be fearful, expecting to be targeted again. Hate crime victims are also more likely to have employment problems and experience negative health issues. Furthermore, the families of hate crime victims, as well as the community at large, also often experience increased fear (Freilich & Chermak, 2013).

Because hate crimes impact the spatial mobility of people in the targeted communities, meaning residents restrict their everyday movements to only those environments where they feel unquestionably safe, hate crimes have the effect of undermining community cohesiveness and straining relationships between the community and the police. In addition, hate crimes sometimes lead to retaliation from the victim's family or community against members of the attackers' family or community, fueling a feud-like situation that further undermines community stability and public safety (Freilich & Chermak, 2013).

The police response also plays a role, whether positively or negatively, on how a hate crime affects the victim and community. If police minimize the crime or dismiss a victim's concerns, negative consequences often follow, leading victims to feel revictimized by the system that is supposed to protect them. Such a response can inflict long-term damage to police–community relations.

Addressing and Preventing Hate Crimes

The types of crimes committed against various minority groups differ. For example, antireligious hate crimes are more likely than other types to involve property damage and vandalism. Furthermore, different types of hate crimes vary across different locations in terms of their frequency and trends over time, and the way each group responds to their victimization varies (Freilich & Chermak, 2013).

Understanding the factors that contribute to a community's hate crime problem will help police frame local analysis questions, recognize key intervention points, and select appropriate responses. Scant evidence supports the idea that poor economic conditions lead to increases in hate crimes. However, factors that have been found to increase tension in the community that contribute to hate crimes include demographic change; social disorganization, or the "inability of a community...to realize the common values of its residents and maintain effective social controls"; and legal hate group activity (Freilich & Chermak, 2013). Legal hate-related activity includes hate group meetings, rallies, and leafleting, which are constitutionally protected behaviors. Using bigoted language does not violate hate crime laws and is frequently classified as a **bias incident**. However, hate crime laws apply when words threaten violence and when bias-motivated graffiti damages or destroys property.

To effectively address and prevent hate crimes, all stakeholders in the community must be brought to the table, including (Freilich & Chermak, 2013):

- criminal justice agencies
- mental health officials

bias incident
Use of bigoted and prejudiced language; does not in itself violate hate crime laws.

- victim services organizations
- watch groups (e.g., the Anti-Defamation League, the Southern Poverty Law Center, or the National Association for the Advancement of Colored People, or NAACP)
- community organizations representing hate crime victims
- community organizations from the offender's community
- media
- schools, colleges, and universities
- academic researchers

Police departments must also ask the right questions in forming an effective local response. Analysis of the current hate crime problem must include data pertaining to characteristics of the community (demographics, social organization), specific incidents (nature of offense, locations, time), victims, and offenders. An assessment of current police responses must also occur.

Many colleges and universities have responded to hate crimes on campus with broad-based public condemnation of bias, prejudice, and violence, including an open letter from the president or dean to the campus community and meetings open to the entire campus community. Several schools have implemented peer diversity education groups that promote understanding of diversity on campus. The Center for the Prevention of Hate Violence at the University of Southern Maine has initiated the Campus Civility Project to address bias, prejudice, and harassment.

Law enforcement can forge partnerships with local businesses and institutions to better understand and tackle hate crimes. In addition, the National Crime Prevention Council (NCPC) suggests various strategies for preventing the occurrence of bias crimes in a community, such as diversity and tolerance education in schools, ongoing police–cultural organization service partnerships, rapid response to reported incidents, media campaigns about community standards for tolerance, counseling for offenders involved in hate groups, and community-based dispute mediation services. Creating a strong and unified voice condemning the proliferation of hate is what is needed to stamp out bias and keep it from jeopardizing public safety.

Working with the families, friends, neighbors, and communities that surround a hate/bias incident becomes as important as working with the victim. Secondary victimization induces blame, outrage, or fear in a family, group of friends, or community. These groups may be motivated to act in response to a hate/bias crime and retaliate in their own ways unless they are educated and provided other options for response or healing. Training victims and communities to cooperate with law enforcement and other community programs takes the control out of the perpetrator's hands, instills confidence in the victim and community, and prevents future crimes.

The Center for Problem-Oriented Policing has set forth seven general considerations for an effective police strategy to address and prevent hate crimes in their community (Freilich & Chermak, 2013, pp. 31–33):

1. Prioritizing the response to hate crime within the police department
2. Establishing multi-agency task forces
3. Training police officers
4. Responding to hate crime victims' needs
5. Increasing police presence and attention in high-risk neighborhoods
6. Monitoring hate groups and tracking hate incidents
7. Reaching out to minority communities

Other actions a police department can take to-direct the community's energy into constructive actions include (Bune, 2004):

- Establishing a "zero tolerance" policy for any form of hate crime, regardless of its apparent seriousness
- Participate in or sponsor community events and activities promoting diversity, tolerance, bias reduction, and conflict resolution
- Collaborate with community organizations, schools, and other public agencies to develop coordinated approaches to hate crime prevention and response
- Engage the media as partners in restoring victimized communities and preventing bias-motivated incidents and crimes

GUN VIOLENCE

The issue of gun violence is a hot topic in our nation's dialogue on violence in general. Many in the United States mistakenly believe that the number of homicides caused by guns is rising dramatically. However, analysis of gun crime data by the Pew Research Center shows that the U.S. gun homicide rate has stabilized in recent years and that the overall gun death rate has dropped 31 percent since 1993 (Krogstad, 2015). Gun violence often manifests itself in specific types of violence that can be addressed through community policing strategies.

LO5

Gun violence may be considered as a three-phase continuum: (1) the illegal acquisition of firearms; (2) the illegal possession and carrying of firearms; and (3) the illegal, improper, or careless use of firearms.

Effective gun control strategies focus on one, two, or all three of these points of intervention. These strategies and programs focus on three points of intervention: (1) interrupting sources of illegal guns, (2) determining illegal possession and carrying of guns, and (3) responding to illegal gun use.

Strategies to Interrupt Sources of Illegal Guns

The strategies to interrupt sources of illegal guns include law enforcement initiatives that disrupt the illegal flow of firearms by using intelligence gathered through crime gun tracing and regulatory inspections or undercover operations involving suspected illegal gun dealers. Comprehensive crime gun tracing facilitates both the reconstruction of the sales history of firearms associated with crime and the identification of patterns of illegal gun trafficking. Similarly, focusing criminal and regulatory enforcement on suspect dealers allows law enforcement to efficiently focus limited resources. Suspect dealers include those at the greatest risk of selling firearms to **straw purchasers**—that is, purchasers fronting for people linked to illegal gun trafficking.

Illegal trafficking in firearms is a problem of supply and demand. Even though federal law prohibits the sale of firearms or ammunition to juveniles and people who have been convicted of felonies and some violent misdemeanors, and federally mandated background checks keep these "prohibited" people from buying firearms at licensed dealers, a black market exists to supply prohibited buyers with the weapons they demand. Those prohibited from legally purchasing a gun often turn to the largely unregulated secondary market—gun sales between private individuals—which is a major source of guns used in crimes.

The Boston Gun Project, Operation Ceasefire, was initiated in 1994 and included gun trafficking interdiction as one component in a broad strategy to stop gun violence (Operation Ceasefire was briefly introduced in Chapter 13). Partners in the project include the Bureau of Alcohol, Tobacco, Firearms, and Explosives (ATF); the Boston Police Department (BPD); the Suffolk County District Attorney's Office; and the U.S. Attorney's Office. A seasoned violent crime coordinator was assigned by ATF to pursue federal firearm arrests. Six ATF agents were also assigned to collaborate with ballistics and crime laboratories at BPD to trace recovered handguns and match them to other crimes. The National Institute of Justice (2013) explains how law enforcement can use trace data to detect illegal firearms markets:

> Records of firearms and ammunition sales can help law enforcement and researchers untangle these illegal firearms markets. If a gun is part of a criminal investigation, the Bureau of Alcohol, Tobacco, Firearms and Explosives (ATF) can trace it—that is, the ATF can provide information to law enforcement on a gun's movement through the supply chain to its first retail purchase. Some states, such as California, mandate the documentation of secondary-market firearms sales or require dealers to log ammunition sales. This information can help crime investigators develop leads about a gun-related crime.
>
> By analyzing patterns in these data, researchers and law enforcement can identify potential traffickers and begin to understand how firearms move into illegal use. For example, researchers in Los Angeles and those with Boston's Operation Ceasefire both found that there is very little interstate trafficking in firearms that are used in crimes. Instead, most crime guns, especially those that move very quickly from legal sale into criminal use, were originally purchased legally in the local area.
>
> Interventions to stop gun trafficking can use these data in different ways. The Operation Ceasefire Working Group, which first met in January 1995, decided to focus on traffickers of the types of guns used by Boston street

straw purchasers
Weapons buyers fronting for people linked to illegal gun trafficking.

gangs. The ATF worked closely with Boston police to flag guns that had recently been purchased illegally and used in a crime. In Los Angeles, a working group that was focused on reducing illegal trafficking created a warning letter campaign aimed at discouraging local citizens from selling their guns illegally.

The National Crime Prevention Council (NCPC) suggests that regulations and ordinances on gun licensing may interrupt sources of illegal guns, the first phase of gun violence. Municipal ordinances that interrupt the sale of illegal firearms may also simultaneously affect the second phase of gun violence—reducing the number of people possessing and carrying guns illegally.

Strategies to Deter Illegal Gun Possession and Carrying

Strategies to deter illegal gun possession and carrying include municipal gun ordinances; weapons hotlines; directed police patrols; focusing on hot spots where disproportionate amounts of crime and violence occur; and focusing on individuals most likely to possess and carry firearms illegally, including gang members and probationers.

A 1992 report by the Violence Policy Center showed that the United States had more licensed gun dealerships than it had gas stations—280,000. In response, the ATF implemented stiffer licensing requirements and raised the licensing fee from $30 to $200. Applicants were now to be fingerprinted and to undergo more extensive background checks aimed at weeding out unscrupulous dealers. The tougher laws and stricter enforcement cost nearly 200,000 U.S. gun dealers their licenses since the mid-1990s. Since 1994, the number of federally licensed firearms dealers has decreased 79 percent nationwide (Doyle, 2007).

This same strategy can be implemented locally if stakeholders work together to get legislation passed. For example, the East Bay Gun Violence Prevention Project was initiated by the East Bay Public Safety Corridor Partnership, a regional coordinating body formed to reduce crime and violence in response to an alarming level of gun violence among cities in the East Bay Corridor.

gun interdiction
Local police direct intensive patrols to specific geographic areas with high rates of gun-related incidents of violence.

Gun interdictions may be an effective deterrent to illegal gun possessing and carrying. A **gun interdiction** is a law enforcement-led strategy whereby local police direct intensive patrols to specific geographic areas with high rates of gun-related incidents of violence. Proactive patrols focus on traffic stops and other mechanisms to detect illegal or illegally concealed weapons and seize them. Community support for the interdiction strategy is vital because such searches and seizures can raise controversy. Community input should be sought in identifying the targeted areas to reduce the chance of charges of racial discrimination should the hot spot be inhabited by members of a minority group. Gun interdictions also affect the third phase of the gun violence continuum.

The COPS Guidelines for Responding to Drive-by Shootings

The Problem-Oriented Policing Center has published a problem-solving guide for police to help them prevent drive-by shootings (Dedel, 2007, pp. 2–6):

> A drive-by shooting refers to an incident when someone fires a gun from a vehicle at another vehicle, a person, a structure, or another stationary object. Many drive-by shootings involve multiple suspects and multiple victims....
>
> The specifics of a drive-by shooting—in which the shooter is aiming a gun out the window of a moving vehicle at a moving target, and is often inexperienced in handling a gun—mean that shots often go wild and injure people or damage property that was not the intended target. There are no national data on the volume of drive-by shootings. National statistical databases such as the Uniform Crime Reports record the outcome (e.g., homicide, aggravated assault, weapons law violations) rather than the method (i.e., drive-by shooting)....
>
> Although gang membership is certainly not a prerequisite to being involved in a drive-by shooting, studies have shown that larger proportions of gang members reported being involved in drive-by shootings than at-risk youth who were not gang-involved....
>
> *Motivations*: At the most basic level, the aggressors must have access to both a vehicle and a gun, but beyond that, these events appear to be rather unpredictable. Drive-by shootings that occur as an extreme form of road rage often occur in reaction to seemingly trivial events (e.g., another driver is driving "too slow," won't let another driver pass, is tailgating, fails to signal before turning).

Analyzing the local problem carefully is vital to designing an effective response strategy. The first step in such an analysis is to identify the stakeholders. In addition to criminal justice agencies, stakeholders might include local hospitals and emergency services, city public works agencies (e.g., parking, streets, transportation, utilities), federal law enforcement agencies (e.g., Drug Enforcement Administration [DEA]; ATF), probation and parole agencies, corrections departments, bar and nightclub owners and managers, social service providers, gang members, and members of other neighborhood "groups" and neighborhood associations (Dedel, 2007).

Effective Response Strategies   The following response strategies, drawn from a variety of research studies and police reports, provide a foundation of ideas that localities can tailor to address their unique drive-by shooting problems. In most cases, an effective approach involves implementing several different responses, including what police can do to involve the community in solving the problem.

A problem-focused approach would focus first on *proximate causes*, making drive-by shootings harder to carry out, for example, by decreasing offenders' mobility and/or the availability of weapons. In addition, Dedel (2007, pp. 16–23) suggests some combination of responses:

- *Targeting the activity, not the individual*—eliminating the perception that police are unfairly focusing on minorities and reinforcing their fair, unbiased approach to crime
- *Reducing weapon availability or prevalence* by conducting crackdowns, including saturating an area with patrols, using directed patrols, or setting up road blocks or checkpoints
- *Initiating "sweeps" targeting known offenders* in cooperation with parole and probation agencies; police can search offenders' residences, vehicles, and persons and confiscate any illegal weapons found
- *Obtaining consent to search for and seize weapons* from parents of at-risk youth who may be willing to consent, in exchange for a promise from police that neither the parents nor the youth will be charged or prosecuted if any weapons are found
- *Identifying situations with the potential for violence* by tracking current tensions and past altercations (many drive-by shootings are catalyzed by past altercations and ongoing tensions between individuals or among rival gang members); coordinating with hospitals

---

IDEAS **IN PRACTICE**　CEASEFIRE: WHO ARE THE VIOLENCE INTERRUPTERS? A UNIQUE APPROACH IN THE CRIMINAL JUSTICE FIELD

CeaseFire's use of violence interrupters made the program unique. Although many public health campaigns hire people who are adept at reaching target populations, hiring former gang members is not a common approach in the criminal justice field.

CeaseFire's violence interrupters were not always part of the program, however. As program officials realized that they needed better access to gang leaders, they made a strategic decision in 2004 to hire people who were uniquely suited to do this.

Violence interrupters must work in the netherworld of street gangs and pass muster with gang leaders. Interrupters cruise the streets of the toughest neighborhoods to identify and intervene in gang-related conflicts before they intensify. If a shooting has occurred, they seek out the victim's friends and relatives and try to prevent a retaliatory shooting.

People who fit this bill often lack traditional workplace experience, and finding and hiring them is not easy. Many have been in trouble with the law. However, the violence interrupters interviewed for the evaluation said they had turned their lives around and wanted to help others do the same.

CeaseFire set up many safeguards to ensure that the violence interrupters stayed clean. They are hired by a panel that includes police officers and local leaders. Background checks are run, with particular attention given to crimes against women and children. Some sites do not hire anyone with a felony conviction. Violence interrupters have to pass periodic drug tests.

Turnover can be high. The work is dangerous, and the pay—about $15 an hour at the time the researchers performed their evaluation—is modest. In many respects, violence interrupters are exposed to hazards from all sides. They are vulnerable to shootings, as well as stop-and-frisks by the police. Gangs are suspicious that violence interrupters are somehow associated with law enforcement, yet those who are ex-felons are at risk of legal repercussions from being "associated" with a gun.

Funding of Chicago CeaseFire has been unstable. Often, budget shortfalls forced short-term layoffs. Every time a site lost a violence interrupter, staff had to rebuild relationships with gang members and other high-risk youth who were the most likely to commit—or be the victims of—gun violence.

Source: Ritter, N. (2009). "CeaseFire: A Public Health Approach to Reduce Shootings and Killings." *NIJ Journal*, Issue No. 264, pp. 20–25. Retrieved October 27, 2016 from https://www.ncjrs.gov/pdffiles1/nij/228386.pdf

- *Prohibiting high-risk people from riding in cars with each other*, either as part of probation or parole conditions or as specified in a civil gang injunction

- *Making environmental changes* such as closing streets where drive-by shootings are concentrated, blocking entrances and exits, but coordinating these changes with first responders (e.g., firefighters, EMTs, ambulance drivers) to ensure their safe and efficient passage

- *Responding to incidents and increasing sanctions* by deploying response teams rapidly before physical evidence is destroyed or witnesses leave the scene or are influenced by discussions among witnesses and neighbors

- *Creating witness incentives* by minimizing the risks that witnesses who want to cooperate face, strengthening ties with the community, and offering support in the form of financial assistance and temporary relocation [to] encourage those with information to come forward

- *Implementing a "pulling levers" strategy* by targeting gang members with chronic involvement in serious crime, outlining the consequences for continued involvement in gun violence while offering prosocial alternatives (e.g., education and employment opportunities, drug treatment); in addition, if one member of the target group is involved in gun violence, all members of the group are subjected to intensified supervision and other forms of enhanced enforcement

Limited Effectiveness Responses Responses that appear to have limited effectiveness include targeting gun traffickers, teaching conflict resolution skills, implementing gun buyback programs, restricting entry to high-risk neighborhoods (which may anger residents and business owners and raise Fourth Amendment issues), and impounding cars that are not properly registered. The low yield of weapons and the inconvenience to residents suggest that impounding does not substantially decrease the number of drive-by shootings (Dedel, 2007, pp. 23–25).

Strategies to Respond to Illegal Gun Use

Strategies to respond to illegal gun use include identification, prosecution, and aggressive punishment of those who commit multiple violent crimes, are armed drug traffickers, or have used a firearm in a crime; intensive education; and strict monitoring of offenders. Local gun courts may also prove an effective strategy.

Local gun courts deal exclusively with gun law violations; they reinforce community standards against violence and ensure swift punishment of violators. The country's first adult gun court was established in the Providence (Rhode Island) Superior Court in 1994 by a statute creating a separate gun court calendar with concurrent jurisdiction with all other superior court calendars. Within 4 months of its implementation, the backlog of gun-related cases was reduced by two-thirds.

All cases are tried within 60 days, and most carry mandatory prison terms, including 10 years to life for a third offense. The mayor obtained support from the National Rifle Association (NRA) and from local advocates of gun control—a tricky combination.

LO6

Partners in gun violence reduction identified by the Office of Juvenile Justice and Delinquency Prevention (OJJDP) include the U.S. attorney, chief of police, sheriff, federal law enforcement agencies (FBI, ATF, DEA), district attorney, state attorney general, mayor/city manager, probation and parole officers, juvenile corrections officials, judges, public defenders, school superintendents, social services officials, leaders in the faith community, and business leaders.

Comprehensive Gun Violence Reduction Strategies

Comprehensive gun reduction involves partnerships through which the community, law enforcement, prosecutors, courts, and social services agencies undertake three objectives:

- Identify where gun violence occurs and who perpetrates it
- Develop a comprehensive plan
- Create strategies to carry out the plan

Reducing Access to Firearms   Child Access Prevention (CAP) laws, or "safe storage" laws, require adults to either store loaded guns in a place reasonably inaccessible to children or use a safety device to lock the gun if they choose to leave the weapon accessible. If a child obtains an improperly stored, loaded gun, the adult owner is criminally liable.

CAP laws also help reduce juvenile suicide by keeping guns out of the reach of children. For youths, particularly adolescents, rapid and intense fluctuations in mood are fairly common. A child going through a particularly difficult time emotionally may, with easy access to a firearm, turn a temporary situation into a permanent mistake.

Approximately one-third of U.S. households with children also have guns, and more than 40 percent of these residences do not keep their guns locked. Many children are unable to distinguish a real gun from a toy, and many toddlers are strong enough to pull the trigger on a real gun. Not surprisingly, children and teens commit more than half of all unintentional shootings in the United States (National Institutes of Health, 2016).

Teaching Gun-Safe Behavior   When adults fail to keep firearms securely locked away or to teach others in the house, especially children, proper gun safety techniques, they place their entire family and anyone who may be in or near their house at tremendous risk. One police officer, despite educating her two young sons about gun safety and how to handle firearms, lost her older boy to an accidental shooting. He had gone next door to play with a neighbor, who had found a gun in one of the bedrooms and, while playing with it, accidentally shot his friend in the face. His mother, like many parents, had never considered asking the parents of her children's playmates if they kept guns in their house.

Although the ultimate responsibility for teaching kids gun-safe behavior lies with parents, many adults themselves need coaching in this area. *Project ChildSafe*, the nation's largest firearm safety education program, aims to ensure safe and responsible firearm ownership. Since 2003, it has distributed more than 35 million safety kits that include a cable-style gun-locking device and safety education materials. It has partnered with governors, lieutenant governors, U.S. attorneys, mayors, and local law enforcement to promote Project ChildSafe's safety education measures. It also helps local law enforcement agencies to schedule firearm safety events in their communities. Project Child Safe was funded by the U.S. Department of Justice with a $50 million grant (*Bureau of Justice Assistance*, 2004).

Right-to-Carry Laws Right-to-carry (RTC) concealed handgun laws are a controversial issue. One fact is clear: Such laws do increase the number of concealed weapons on the streets. The argument in favor of such laws is that they will reduce crime and simultaneously give citizens a feeling of security.

Preventing gun violence may greatly affect the other types of violence discussed next: domestic violence and workplace violence.

SEXUAL VIOLENCE

Rape is one of the four violent crimes tracked by the FBI in its Uniform Crime Reports; however, the FBI documents only forcible rape of female victims, excluding all other illegal sex crimes. Rape or sexual assault is one of the most underreported crimes and, depending on the official source cited, the extent of the problem can be vastly underestimated. For example, in 2006, the FBI reported 90,427 forcible rapes. In contrast, that same year, the NCVS reported 272,350 rapes/sexual assaults. The NCVS counts all types of rape, regardless of gender or of whether the force was physical or psychological.

Like other violent crimes, the vast majority of sexual assaults are committed by someone the victim knows. Although women fear random attacks by strangers, the reality is that most victims are attacked by an acquaintance. Few sexual assaults (only about 10–20%) are ever reported to authorities. For the most part, the ones that are reported are those committed by strangers. Several factors account for the reluctance of victims of nonstranger rape to report assaults, including a fear that they will not be believed or that they will be blamed for their own victimization. Some victims are afraid to report because of threats by the assailant. Furthermore, many victims of sexual assault feel shame, blame themselves, and dread revealing what is normally very private information to police, courts, and possibly the public. They may be reluctant to report the rape if they had been drinking alcohol in excess or illegally or if they had used illegal substances at the time of the assault.

The most effective response to sexual assaults employs a collaborative team approach, which includes a police officer, victim advocate, and the physician or nurse who conducts the sexual assault examination and collects evidence from the victim's body. Ideally, each of these professionals should have specific training in sexual assault and each should understand the roles of the others. Advocates can make all the difference in these cases because their role is to support the victim throughout the process, helping her understand her choices at each stage and making her comfortable enough to be able to provide the necessary information for an investigation to go forward.

A little-understood phenomenon that affects people who have been in a recent traumatic situation is a type of amnesia that causes the victim to temporarily forget facts so important that it would seem, to others, that they would be impossible to forget. It is only after a night's sleep, or even a couple of nights' sleep, that the victim is able to remember these facts. Police officers often have difficulty believing people who "suddenly" remember an important fact, but officers suffer the very same phenomenon after a major incident involving gunfire or other violent action. For that reason, departments are often advised to let officers involved in a shooting incident "sleep on it" before being questioned in detail about the event. Rape victims commonly experience the same temporary memory loss.

Although there are some exemplary examples of departments that conduct professional, unbiased investigations, it is probably fair to say the majority of sexual assault victims are poorly served by the criminal justice system.

Problem-Solving Approach to Acquaintance Rape of College Students

Rape is the most common violent crime on college campuses today (Sampson, 2011). Women between the ages of 16 and 24 are four times more likely to become rape victims than all other women, and college women are at more risk for rape and other sexual assaults than noncollege women of the same age, yet fewer than 5 percent of women who are victims of rape or attempted rape report the assault to the police (Sampson, 2011).

Some police officers believe the number of false rape reports is unusually high. This may result from the fact that the sexual assault training most police officers receive is focused on stranger rape, giving officers the idea that only stranger rapes are valid cases. Another reason officers are skeptical of rape reports is that police are subjected to the same social stereotyping about rape and victims as the rest of society. Yet another reason is that the FBI does not separately track false rape reports; it tracks the total number of *unfounded* reports, which consist of both baseless cases in which the elements of the crime were never met and false reports. Officers need to know that unfounded reports are *not* the same as false reports.

Some officers believe incorrectly that a rape report is unfounded or false if any or all of the following conditions apply (Sampson, 2011, p. 10):

- The victim had a prior relationship with the offender, including being intimate
- The victim used alcohol or drugs at the time of the assault
- There is no visible evidence of injury
- The victim delays reporting and/or does not have a rape medical examination
- The victim fails to immediately label her assault as a rape and/or blames herself

Most college rape prevention activities consist of the campus police providing self-defense training, doing environmental assessments of outdoor areas where rapes could occur, providing safe escort for women on campus, and recommending the installation of cameras, lights, locks, and so on. These approaches, however, do not focus on preventing acquaintance rape and may actually be a disservice because they send a message that "real rape" is stranger rape and that stranger rape is what police are concerned with, whereas nonstranger rape can be dealt with by other campus departments or student organizations (Sampson, 2011). In fact, researchers have found that many young women heading off to college have been misled into thinking they can stay safe by being on guard against the stranger rapist who lurks in the deserted parking lots and campus shadows at night. What these women are not taught is that rape by an acquaintance or a romantic partner is a far more common scenario (Hoffman, 2015).

Sampson (2011, p. 15) stresses: "Colleges have a legal duty to warn students of known risks and to provide reasonable protection. If a crime is foreseeable, then a college can be held liable for not sufficiently protecting against it. As noted, acquaintance rape is the most common violent crime on college campuses. If acquaintance rape(s) occur at predictable times and places, the school must make reasonable efforts to prevent a recurrence; the school may be liable if it fails to deal effectively with repeat student offenders, including rapists, whose conduct eventually results in more damage."

Appropriate responses to sexual assault on campuses might include conducting acquaintance rape prevention programs for college men in general; conducting acquaintance rape risk-reduction programs for college women; developing risk-reduction plans to prevent repeat victimization; educating police about acquaintance rape of college students; conducting acquaintance rape prevention programs for college administrators, campus judicial officers, and other key campus personnel; and conducting acquaintance rape prevention programs geared toward campus athletes and fraternities (Sampson, 2011). Providing student escort and/or shuttle services and providing rape aggression defense training have limited effectiveness in preventing acquaintance rape on college campuses (Sampson, 2011).

The NotAlone.gov Web site was launched in connection with the White House Task Force to Protect Students from Sexual Assault, which was established on January 22, 2014. This site provides information for students, schools, and anyone interested in finding resources on how to respond to and prevent sexual assault. Since its inception, thousands of people have shared their experiences and ideas about how best to eliminate sexual assault in schools (U.S. Department of Justice, 2016).

Bystander Intervention

The Office of Health Promotion at Emory University in Atlanta, Georgia, has proposed an innovative approach to tackling sexual violence: bystander intervention. A bystander is someone who witnesses an event but is not a direct actor in that event. The direct actors in sexual violence are the victims and the perpetrators. Anyone else who is aware of the situation, either directly or indirectly, is a bystander. A bystander who ignores the situation is a passive bystander, one who engages in the situation is an active bystander, and one who makes the situation worse is a participant (Emory University, 2016).

The University has taken the stance that everyone has a role to play in preventing sexual violence and that bystander intervention, which simply means being an active bystander, is crucial to the safety and well-being of the student body and campus life as a whole. According to the University, "Research shows that bystander intervention is a promising practice to help prevent the national public health problem of sexual assault on college campuses" (Emory University, 2016). Training in bystander intervention aims to equip people with skills to be effective, supportive allies *before* a sexual assault ever occurs, teaching people when to intervene and why. The University stresses that "being an active bystander *does not mean* that you should risk your personal safety, or that you need to become a vigilante. There are a range of actions that are appropriate, depending on you and the risky situation at hand."

Mobilizing bystanders can be an effective strategy not only in preventing sexual assaults but also for preventing violence of all types. Community policing efforts that engage the community and other third parties, who traditionally consider themselves uninvolved or detached witnesses to an event, as bystanders who possess the skills needed to intervene and make a difference in the safety of their community and other individuals will help forge invaluable partnerships in the mission to achieve public safety.

DOMESTIC VIOLENCE

Domestic violence is an area where the system response has a real potential to save lives. In the words of the late Robert Trojanowicz, a community policing pioneer, "We must remember that until we are all safe, no one is truly safe." Building trust with the victims of domestic violence is crucial. Those who have been victimized by spousal abuse, stalking, child abuse, or elder abuse can be of great assistance in community efforts to prevent such victimization. This part of the chapter focuses on strategies to reduce or prevent domestic violence. In addition to collaboration among criminal justice agencies, all other stakeholders in the community need to be involved in identifying problems and working toward solutions.

Intimate Partner Violence

intimate partner violence (IPV)
Violence that occurs between two people in a close (intimate) relationship, whether the partners are of the same or opposite gender; can involve physical violence, sexual violence, threats, emotional abuse, and stalking.

Intimate partner violence (IPV) is defined by the Centers for Disease Control and Prevention (CDC) as that which occurs between two people in a close relationship (CDC, 2014). It can involve physical violence, sexual violence, threats, emotional abuse, and stalking. It can involve partners of the same or opposite gender. IPV is a serious problem in the United States, with an estimated 30 percent of women and 10 percent of men in this country having experienced rape, physical violence, and/or stalking by an intimate partner. In 2007, 2,340 deaths were attributed to IPV, and the majority (70%) of victims were females (CDC, 2014). Trend data indicate that, between 1980 and 2008, female homicide victims were more likely than male victims—in every age group—to have been killed by an intimate. And while the proportion of intimate homicides by a spouse has decreased since 1980, the proportion committed by a boyfriend or girlfriend has increased (Cooper & Smith, 2011).

Important Research Findings—Who Is at Risk?

Information on risk factors is helpful in developing prevention strategies and interventions. It is important to recognize that risk factors associated with a greater likelihood of IPV victimization or perpetration are merely contributing factors, not direct causes per se. Not everyone who is identified as "at risk" becomes involved in violence (Centers for Disease Control and Prevention, 2016):

> Some risk factors for IPV victimization and perpetration are the same, while others are associated with one another. For example, childhood physical or sexual victimization is a risk factor for future IPV perpetration and victimization.

> A combination of individual, relational, community, and societal factors contribute to the risk of becoming an IPV perpetrator or victim. Understanding these multilevel factors can help identify various opportunities for prevention.

Individual Risk Factors

- Low self-esteem
- Low income
- Low academic achievement
- Young age
- Aggressive or delinquent behavior as a youth
- Heavy alcohol and drug use
- Depression
- Anger and hostility
- Antisocial personality traits
- Borderline personality traits
- Prior history of being physically abusive
- Having few friends and being isolated from other people
- Unemployment
- Emotional dependence and insecurity
- Belief in strict gender roles (e.g., male dominance and aggression in relationships)
- Desire for power and control in relationships
- Perpetrating psychological aggression
- Being a victim of physical or psychological abuse (consistently one of the strongest predictors of perpetration)
- History of experiencing poor parenting as a child
- History of experiencing physical discipline as a child

Relationship Factors

- Marital conflict–fights, tension, and other struggles
- Marital instability–divorces or separations

- Dominance and control of the relationship by one partner over the other
- Economic stress
- Unhealthy family relationships and interactions

Community Factors

- Poverty and associated factors (e.g., overcrowding)
- Low social capital–lack of institutions, relationships, and norms that shape a community's social interactions
- Weak community sanctions against IPV (e.g., unwillingness of neighbors to intervene in situations where they witness violence)

Societal Factors

- Traditional gender norms (e.g., women should stay at home, not enter workforce, and be submissive; men support the family and make the decisions)

Women are more vulnerable to being assaulted or killed during separation and are particularly vulnerable when they are pregnant. A survey in Canada found that 21 percent of abused women were assaulted during pregnancy, and in 40 percent of these cases, this episode was the beginning of the abuse. The extreme vulnerability to violence by women in the sex trade often goes unnoticed. According to police reports submitted to Statistics Canada, between 1991 and 2004, 171 female prostitutes were killed. These cases are often never solved (Johnson, 2006).

Legislation to Prevent Stalking and Domestic Violence

Although several laws have been passed to prevent stalking and domestic violence, one law, the Violence against Women Act (VAWA), merits emphasis because it makes this serious problem a system-wide institutional priority. Passed in 1994 and reauthorized by the U.S. Congress in 2000, the Act was renewed in 2005 and again in 2013.

Animal Abuse and Domestic Violence

When looking at domestic violence cases, animal abuse serves as a predictor of other violent and abusive behavior. Animal abuse is often found in the background of homicide, vandalism, and arson perpetrators. In addition, many serial killers and even students involved in recent school shootings have histories of abusing animals first before moving on to human targets. Animal abuse has been identified as one component of the "MacDonald Triad," a conceptual model of violence risk that has been linked to multiple homicide, homicide, and sexual offending, the other two components being enuresis (bed wetting) and fire setting (Vaughn et al., 2010).

American Humane (2016) notes a correlation between animal abuse, family violence, and other forms of community violence and that abuse of both children and animals is connected in a self-perpetuating cycle of violence: "When animals in a home are abused or neglected, it is a warning sign that others in the household may not be safe. In addition, children who witness animal abuse are at a greater risk of becoming abusers themselves." The Humane Society of the United States (2016) presents findings from several studies that support the link between animal cruelty and domestic violence:

- A survey of domestic violence victims revealed that 71 percent reported that their abuser also targeted family pets.
- A study of families being investigated for suspected child abuse found that pet abuse co-occurred in 88 percent of these families.

American Humane (2016) also notes the findings of several studies that found evidence of the co-occurrence of animal abuse and domestic violence:

- Of women seeking shelter at one safe house who also had pets, 71 percent reported that their partner had threatened, hurt, or killed their pet. Among this same group of women, 32 percent of those who were mothers reported that their children had hurt or killed their pets.
- An assessment of violent offenders housed in a maximum-security prison found these inmates were significantly more likely than nonviolent offenders to have committed acts of cruelty toward pets during their youth.

A child who abuses an animal may be imitating parents who have abused them or other family members. The child may feel helpless and consequently hurt the only member of the family who is more vulnerable than he or she is—the family pet. Jeffrey Dahmer and Ted Bundy are "infamous examples" of this disturbing correlation.

Because many shelters do not allow animals, victims often choose to stay in their abusive homes for fear that leaving their pet behind would endanger the animals. In an effort to stop this cycle of violence, the Humane Society Legislative Fund supported the PAWS (Pets and Women's Safety) Act, introduced to Congress in 2015 as H.R. 1258 and S.B. 1559 (Humane Society Legislative Fund, 2015). This Act would give victims of domestic abuse their means to escape their abusers while keeping their companion animals safe.

In 2016, the FBI added animal cruelty as a category in the NIBRS program as part of an effort to obtain a clearer picture of animal abuse nationwide and guide strategies for intervention and enforcement. Data collection covers four categories: simple/gross neglect, intentional abuse and torture, organized abuse (such as dogfighting and cockfighting), and animal sexual abuse (FBI, 2016). The Humane Society of the United States has also formed the National Law Enforcement Council, comprised of current and former law enforcement officers and prosecutors, to help combat animal crimes nationwide. Members of the council have demonstrated leadership in protecting animals from neglect, violence, and other crimes.

The Law Enforcement Response to Domestic Violence

Domestic violence victims are less likely than other victims to call police because of privacy concerns, a fear of reprisal by their abuser, and their desire to protect offenders. This adds to the challenge of an effective police response to domestic violence.

One controversial law enforcement response is a mandatory arrest policy, and research results on the effectiveness of arresting domestic violence offenders are mixed. The *Spouse Assault Replication Program*, a field study cosponsored by the NIJ and the CDC and carried out between 1981 and 1991, analyzed more than 4,000 domestic violence incidents, from six jurisdictions, in which males had assaulted their female intimate partners. The first of the six studies within the SARP was the Minneapolis Domestic Violence Experiment (MDVE), conducted by Lawrence Sherman and Richard Berk, which found that arresting batterers reduced the rate of subsequent abuse involving the same victim by 50 percent within a 6-month follow-up period. The five replication studies added support to the MDVE results by finding that arresting batterers was consistently associated with less repeat offending. However, subsequent criticism of the studies' methodology led to the results being questioned and follow-up studies being conducted. Later research by Maxwell, Garner, and Fagan (2001, p. 2) led to several key findings:

- Arresting batterers was consistently related to reduced subsequent aggression against female intimate partners, although not all comparisons met the standard level of statistical significance.
- Regardless of the type of intervention (arrest vs. no arrest), most suspects had no subsequent criminal offense against their original victim within the follow-up period.
- The research found no association between arresting the offender and an increased risk of subsequent aggression against women.

The finding that most battering suspects discontinued their aggressive behaviors even without being arrested suggests that mandatory arrest policies for all batterers may unnecessarily misdirect a community's limited resources away from identifying and responding to the worst offenders and the victims at greatest risk (Maxwell et al., 2001).

A national survey found that approximately 11 percent of police departments in the United States have a specialized domestic violence unit, most of which work within investigative units. The majority of departments (56%) with 100 or more sworn officers have specialized domestic violence units (Klein, 2009). Studies have found that specialized domestic violence units, which put emphasis on repeat victim contact and evidence collection, significantly increase the likelihood of prosecution, conviction, and sentencing of abusers; are more likely to result in the victims leaving their abuser sooner (within 4 months, as opposed to the average 14 months for victims who do not receive a specialized police response); lead to higher victim reporting of reabuse; and increase the likelihood that victims will seek and secure a protective order against their abusers (Klein, 2009).

Corporate Partnership to Combat Domestic Violence

Most executives and managers in the corporate sector have given little or no thought to the impact of partner abuse on the health and safety of their employees. Potential barriers to understanding and helping employees who are victims of partner abuse include lack of awareness; denial; embarrassment; privacy and confidentiality concerns; victim blaming; expectations of self-identification by abused women; fear of advocating for change; and concern that outreach to abused women may alienate male employees, damage the company image, or be too expensive.

A survey of employee assistance professionals (EAPs) found that a large majority of EAP providers had been faced with cases of partner abuse, including restraining order violations and stalking in the workplace. General policies on workplace violence exist, but few specifically address domestic violence. Among larger corporations, EAP staff use a range of practices to assist employees affected by abuse, including use of leaves of absence, medical leaves, and short-term disability. The effect of domestic violence on the workplace is discussed shortly.

The Lakewood (Colorado) Police Department and Motorola joined forces to apply sophisticated law enforcement and business principles to develop new strategies for managing domestic violence cases. The partnership uses **process mapping**, a program Motorola developed as part of its quality management process. An alternative to traditional top-down methods of internal analysis, process mapping takes a horizontal view of a system and involves personnel at all levels. It uses a series of flowcharts or maps to visually depict how information, materials, and activities flow in an organization and how work is handed off from one unit or department to another. It also identifies how processes work currently and what changes should be made to attain a more ideal process flow. The Lakewood Police Department chose to apply process mapping to domestic violence because of the complexity of such cases and how the crime affects not only the victim but also branches out to affect the victim's children, other family members, neighbors, colleagues, and others. With process mapping, police can more effectively monitor the activities of various agencies involved in the response. Thus, the process mapping program not only identifies areas for improvement but also facilitates communication between the city, police department, and community.

process mapping
A method of internal analysis that takes a horizontal view of a system, in contrast to the traditional vertical view. It involves personnel at all levels and uses flowcharts to visually depict how information, materials, and activities flow in an organization; how work is handed off from one unit or department to another; and how processes work currently and what changes should be made to attain a more ideal process flow.

A Domestic Violence Reduction Unit

In 1992, the Portland (Oregon) Police Bureau identified a need to provide additional services to families. In keeping with the community policing philosophy, the agency turned to the community to help define the new programs. They consulted more than 100 community leaders and groups. To design the administrative framework for their Domestic Violence Reduction Unit, the bureau looked for models other agencies had designed. It also held discussions with the district attorney and judges as well as leaders in the battered women's movement. The participants agreed that officers would not only vigorously enforce the laws but that they would become advocates for victims, and that increased cooperation would be needed between the police and other public safety agencies to enhance reporting and enforcement.

The unit's activities are not confined to working with individual cases. Their work is also a source of training for other officers and for community education outside the Portland Police Bureau. In addition, the officers have provided training to more than 20 other police agencies in the country.

S*T*O*P Violence against Women

The Department of Justice's S*T*O*P Violence against Women grant program provides money directly to states and Native American tribes as a step in helping to restructure the criminal justice system's response to crimes of violence against women. The acronym stands for *services, training, officers,* and *prosecution,* the vital components in a comprehensive program for victims of domestic violence and its perpetrators. This program requires collaboration between victim advocates, prosecutors, and police. Funding from these grants can help build and maintain crisis centers and shelters for battered women, train and finance hundreds of new prosecutors for specialized domestic violence or sexual assault units, and help hundreds of volunteer coordinators run domestic violence hotlines.

Police–Community Partnership

A number of jurisdictions have attempted to bring together a wide range of criminal justice and social service agencies to provide a coordinated community response to domestic violence, an approach with the potential to positively impact both case processing and reabuse (Klein, 2009). An estimated 65 percent of police departments have established partnerships with community-based victim advocacy groups, according to a national survey of 14,000 police departments (Klein, 2009).

The Police Executive Research Forum (PERF), with funding from the Community Oriented Policing Services (COPS) Office, explored the nature, function, and impact of police–community partnerships to address domestic violence. *Police–Community Partnerships to Address Domestic Violence* (Reuland, Morabito, Preston, & Cheney, 2006) reports that about 62 percent of task force partnerships mentioned participation in coalitions or teams, and almost 60 percent of the partnerships listed victim services as an important component. On-scene responses were mentioned as an activity by only 42 percent. The majority of police respondents noted that the most important aspect of the partnership was how well the various parties communicate and work together to agree on the appropriate course of action and that they do it "almost automatically" despite their differences (Reuland et al., 2006, p. 29).

These partnerships are most successful in achieving those goals related to improving victim services and safety. Less success is noted for the goals of reducing the number of domestic violence incidents or repeated incidents. The predominant finding of this project is that partnerships between the police and a community-based organization have made tremendous

L07

When forming partnerships to prevent domestic violence, the issue of cultural diversity between male-dominated police organizations and female-dominated grassroots advocate groups must be addressed.

improvements in the way agencies communicate and channel their energies toward a shared goal of improving safety for the victims of domestic violence (Reuland et al., 2006).

Worst Mistakes   The most frequently noted mistake a police department can make is not partnering with the community to address domestic violence (Reuland et al., 2006). Almost all community partner sources said their worst mistake would be to overstep the bounds of the advocate's role by telling officers what to do, interfering in the criminal aspects of the situations, or confusing their role with that of the officers.

Recommendations   Based on research, communities that develop such partnerships with the police should:

- Involve as many stakeholders as possible when developing the partnership arrangements, including a wide range of community members (such as schools and animal shelters) and criminal justice agencies (such as prosecutors and judges).
- Develop strong personal relationships with partners, usually characterized by trust and shared goals; develop common ground by sharing frustration over the intractability of domestic violence and uncooperative victims.
- Demonstrate police leadership and commitment to addressing domestic violence by setting appropriate staff levels and developing mechanisms to enforce policy.
- Emphasize goals related to victim safety and services. Very few respondents focused on increased arrests *per se.* Instead, they hoped to increase victim safety, provide on-scene crisis intervention counseling, and ensure victim awareness of community resources to break the **cycle of violence** and get abuse victims out of their situation.
- Involve line-level staff (officers and counselors) in the process of developing and implementing partnership policies and procedures (Reuland et al., 2006, pp. 44–45).

cycle of violence
Violent or sexual victimization of children can often lead to these victims becoming perpetrators of domestic violence as adults.

When the Batterer Is a Police Officer

"Domestic violence in police families has always been one of the original 'don't ask, don't tell' issues—alternately ignored, hidden, or denied, firmly protected by the blue wall of silence" (Gallo, 2004, p. 60). Several studies have shown that at least 40 percent of police families experience officer-involved domestic violence (OIDV) each year, compared with about 10 percent of families in the general U.S. population (National Center for Women and Policing, 2005). Because of their training in using force, police officers can be the most dangerous of domestic abusers, but specialized training is only one factor that makes OIDV particularly perilous. The danger to victims of abuse by police officers is further heightened by the fact that the abuser has a gun; the weight of a close-knit, male-oriented police culture behind them; knowledge of the location of crisis centers and women's shelters; the ability and resources to track people down; and the know-how to manipulate the system to avoid penalty (Ammons, 2005).

Graves (2004) recommends a zero-tolerance posture against officer-involved domestic abuse, emphasizing the agency's commitment to maintaining community trust, discipline, and the like. He suggests that community members hold law enforcement officers to a higher standard of conduct both on and off duty: "No agency can afford the negative ramifications that come with a domestic abuse incident by one of their own" (Graves, 2004, p. 108).

The Lautenberg Amendment of 1996 is a federal law that prohibits anyone convicted of qualifying misdemeanor domestic violence crimes from possessing firearms. A qualifying misdemeanor domestic violence crime means that the crime has, as an element, the use or attempted use of physical force, or the threatened use of a deadly weapon, committed by a current or former spouse, parent, or guardian of the victim, by a person with whom the victim shares a child in common, by a person who is cohabiting with or has cohabited with the victim as a spouse, parent, or guardian, or by a person similarly situated to a spouse, parent, or guardian of the victim. The law does not exempt law enforcement officers and governmental employees (such as security guards or military personnel).

CHILD ABUSE

The link between child abuse and partner abuse and the risk factors involved in being abused as a child have been discussed. Figure 14.4 illustrates the overlap of child abuse and domestic violence, with data suggesting a 30-percent to 60-percent overlap between violence against children and violence against women in the same family.

Children in violent homes face three risks: (1) the risk of observing traumatic events, (2) the risk of being abused themselves, and (3) the risk of being neglected.

Children Exposed to Violence

Results of a 2009 study showed that more than 60 percent of the children surveyed had been exposed to violence within the past 12 months, either directly or indirectly, in their homes, schools, and communities. Childhood exposure to violence, regardless of whether it is as a victim or a witness, is often associated with long-term physical, psychological, and emotional harm, and

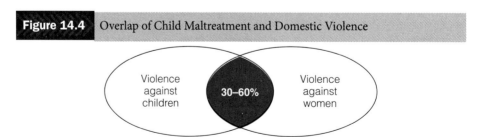

Figure 14.4   Overlap of Child Maltreatment and Domestic Violence

Source: Adapted from data from Bragg, H. L. (2003). *Child Protection in Families Experiencing Domestic Violence.* Washington, DC: U.S. Department of Health and Human Services, Office on Child Abuse and Neglect, p. 7. Retrieved October 28, 2016 from https://www.childwelfare.gov/pubPDFs/domesticviolence2003.pdf#page=12&view=CHAPTER 2 The Overlap Between Child Maltreatment and Domestic Violence

increases the risk of engaging in criminal behavior later in life, thus perpetuating the cycle of violence (Finkelhor, Turner, Ormrod, Hamby, & Kracke, 2009). Findings from this study include:

- Children are more likely to be exposed to violence and crime than adults.
- Children exposed to violence are more likely to abuse drugs and alcohol; suffer from depression, anxiety, and posttraumatic disorders; fail or have difficulty in school; and become delinquent and engage in criminal behavior.
- Almost 40 percent of children in the United States were direct victims of two or more violent acts, and 1 in 10 was victim of violence five or more times.
- Almost 1 in 10 American children saw one family member assault another family member, and more than 25 percent had been exposed to family violence during their life.
- A child's exposure to one type of violence increases the likelihood that the child will be exposed to other types of violence and exposed multiple times.

Training Professionals to Recognize Child Victims

Hospital personnel, lawyers, justice system officials, and psychiatrists need training to enable them to recognize child victims of violence and abuse, understand their special needs, and act as their advocates.

A potential obstacle is that professionals such as lawyers and physicians may be reluctant to admit their inability to recognize and assist child victims. The American Academy of Pediatrics and the Center to Prevent Handgun Violence sponsor educational and training materials for pediatric health care professionals through the Stop Firearm Injury program. The program provides doctors and others with brochures, posters, reading lists, and other information to help them recognize child victims of gun violence and refer them and their families to other service providers as needed. Thousands of physicians have received and used the materials.

The Child Development–Community Policing Model

The child development–community policing (CD–CP) model is a pilot initiative that emphasizes the importance of developing collaborative relationships between law enforcement and mental health communities to ensure that youths exposed to violence have access to a wide array of services offered in their communities.

LO8

The CD–CP model emphasizes cross-training of criminal justice and mental health professionals to develop collaborative problem-solving techniques that go beyond the reach of either "system" acting alone.

The distinction between law enforcement and child protection agencies is beginning to blur, with police spending more time in noninvestigative activities and child protection workers spending more time as investigators. Their spheres of influence have come to overlap in many areas, and both have shifted emphasis from reactive to proactive responses when possible.

The CD–CP program began in New Haven, Connecticut, in 1991 and has been facilitated by resources of and researchers at the Yale University Child

Study Center. Specifically, the CD–CP model's training and collaboration principles include:

- Child development fellowships for police supervisors, which provide supervisory officers with the necessary expertise to lead a team of community-based officers in activities and services related to children and families and create opportunities to interact with the child mental health professionals with whom they will collaborate in the future.
- Police fellowships for clinicians, which provide clinicians the opportunity to observe and learn directly from law enforcement officers about the responsibilities of community-based policing, while also building collaborative relationships with law enforcement officials.
- Seminars on child development, human functioning, and policing strategies for clinicians, community police officers, and related justice practitioners that incorporate case scenarios to apply principles of child development to the daily work of policing.
- Consultation services that give law enforcement the ability to make referrals and obtain immediate clinical guidance if necessary.
- Program conferencing, where CD–CP police officers and clinicians meet weekly to discuss difficult and perplexing cases (Office of Juvenile Justice and Delinquency Prevention, 1999).

The pioneering efforts of the CD–CP Program led the OJJDP to establish the National Center for Children Exposed to Violence (NCCEV) at the Yale Child Study Center in 1999, the mission of which is to increase public and professional awareness of the effects of violence on children. The NCCEV is a primary national resource center for anyone seeking information about the effects of violence on children and the initiatives designed to address this problem. It is also a provider of training, technical assistance, and consultation to a variety of collaborative community programs across the country.

Forming a Multidisciplinary Team to Investigate Child Abuse

Unfortunately, failure to respond to reports of child abuse in a timely and appropriate manner has happened many times—and is continuing to happen—in probably every state in the country and almost always for the same reason—a lack of and coordination among the agencies investigating reports of possible abuse. A key to avoiding tragedies is the formation of a multidisciplinary team representing the government agencies and private practitioners responsible for investigating crimes against children and protecting and treating children in the community.

Legislation to Increase Child Protections

The Adam Walsh Child Protection and Safety Act was passed in 2006. Among the numerous provisions of the Act are four that are especially significant:

1. The Act integrates the information in state sex offender registries and ensures that law enforcement agencies will have access to the same

information nationwide, "helping prevent sex offenders from evading detection by moving from state to state."

2. The Act imposes mandatory minimum prison terms for the most serious crimes against children and authorizes federal grants to the states to help them institutionalize, through civil commitment procedures, sex offenders found to be dangerous and about to be released from prison.

3. The Act aims to increase prosecutions of sexual predators who use the Internet to make contact with children, by authorizing funding for new regional Internet Crimes against Children Task Forces.

4. The Act establishes a new national child abuse registry and requires investigators to conduct background checks of prospective adoptive and foster parents before they are approved to take custody of a child. "By giving child protective service professionals in all 50 states access to this critical information, we will improve their ability to investigate child abuse cases and help ensure that vulnerable children are not put into situations of abuse or neglect."

Second-grade students in Austin, Texas look at a children's Internet safety program on library computers during a kickoff event for the "Cyber-Guardian for the Internet Age–Faux Paw the Techno Cat."

Bob Daemmrich/The Image Works

WORKPLACE VIOLENCE

Yet another type of violence that community policing efforts, partnerships, and problem solving can help address is workplace violence. The Occupational Safety and Health Administration (OSHA) defines workplace violence as "any act or threat of physical violence, harassment, intimidation, or other threatening disruptive behavior that occurs at the work site. It ranges from threats and verbal abuse to physical assaults and even homicide. It can affect and involve employees, clients, customers, and visitors" (OSHA, n.d.). Nearly 2 million Americans report being victims of workplace violence each year. According to the Bureau of Labor Statistics Census of Fatal Occupational Injuries (CFOI), of 4,821 fatal workplace injuries that occurred in the United States in 2014, 409 were workplace homicides. Of those homicides, 307 died of gun shots.

LO9

Common motivations behind violent behavior in the workplace include robbery, loss of a job, anger from feelings of mistreatment, substance abuse, and mental problems.

Most study results and experts identify the driving forces behind workplace violence as being (1) an economic system that fails to support full employment (downsizing), (2) a legal system that fails to protect citizens and releases criminals from prison early because of overcrowding, (3) a cultural system that glamorizes violence in the media, and (4) the universal availability of weapons.

Workplace violence shares many characteristics with school violence. School violence is, in fact, a form of workplace violence for school staff. Characteristics common to workplace violence and school violence include the profiles of the perpetrators, the targets, the warnings, the means, and the pathways to violence.

IDEAS IN PRACTICE WORKPLACE VIOLENCE INITIATIVE, BALTIMORE COUNTY, MARYLAND

After the Baltimore County Police Department responded to several workplace violence/stalking incidents in the suburban Cockeysville, Maryland, Precinct Seven area of the county, they realized they would be more effective if they could be proactive about these kinds of situations. The precinct had already handled two domestic workplace violence homicides in a 3-year period.

The officers did research on the issue of workplace violence, talking with leaders in the more than 750 businesses in the community. The information they gained, in combination with research results from the department's analysis unit, raised enough concern to lead to formation of a workplace violence prevention program.

With a focus on the *workplace avenger* and on domestic violence, which often spills over into the workplace, the department set up a workplace violence team as part of the behavioral assessment unit. The team set up a Web page with links and e-mail so that both police and businesses would have a confidential location to make requests and have their needs addressed. There is also an e-mail address for reporting potential problems anonymously to the police department.

The team also developed an internal tracking system for workplace violence cases. Previously, cases or calls were coded by offense because a workplace violence category did not exist; this system made it difficult to get a good idea of the scope of the problem. The new workplace violence tracking system has subcategories of assault, domestic violence, harassment, and stalking.

The team developed training seminars for managers, EAPs, and human resource professionals to address personnel problems and interventions. They offer help in case investigation, intervention, assessment, and management strategies for threats of violence and assistance with the prosecution of cases.

(Continues)

IDEAS **IN PRACTICE** WORKPLACE VIOLENCE INITIATIVE, BALTIMORE COUNTY, MARYLAND (*Continued*)

In the first 2 years, the team assessed 67 serious cases throughout Baltimore County. They have presented the training in workshops and at professional conferences throughout the country and appeared on television and radio to talk about workplace violence.

A workplace violence case protocol was created, and the team created a countywide workplace violence prevention committee. When they surveyed over 500 businesses in the targeted pilot area, 60 percent of them requested their assistance. The team assisted the Mid-Atlantic Region Community Policing Institute in designing manuals and handouts and worked with the Baltimore County state attorneys' office to have an assistant state attorney assigned to review and prosecute workplace violence cases.

The program expanded rapidly and was soon implemented throughout the county. It has received positive comments from other jurisdictions in the state of Maryland and across the country.

The new program was in step with the county's desire to attract and retain small and large businesses and with the police department's desire to assist the business community while improving the quality of life and safety for those who worked in the county.

Source: Center for Problem-Oriented Policing (2001). *Workplace Violence Initiative: Baltimore County.* Albany, NY: Author. Retrieved October 28, 2016 from http://www.popcenter.org/library/awards/goldstein/2001/01-04.pdf

HUMAN TRAFFICKING

The term *human trafficking* is used to describe many forms of exploitation of human beings. Human trafficking crimes are defined in Title 18, Chapter 77, of the U.S. Criminal Code and focus on "the act of compelling or coercing a person's labor, services, or commercial sex acts. The coercion can be subtle or overt, physical or psychological, but it must be used to coerce a victim into performing labor, services, or commercial sex acts. Because these statutes are rooted in the prohibition against slavery and involuntary servitude guaranteed by the Thirteenth Amendment to the United States Constitution, the Civil Rights Division [of the U.S. Department of Justice] plays a paramount role in enforcing these statutes," in partnership with the United States Attorneys' offices (USAOs) and law enforcement agencies (U.S. Department of Justice, 2015).

Human trafficking victims have been found in agricultural fields, sweatshops, suburban mansions, brothels, escort services, bars, and strip clubs. Many victims of human trafficking speak limited or no English and are fearful of strangers and the police: "While undocumented migrants can be particularly vulnerable to coercion because of their fear of authorities, traffickers have demonstrated their ability to exploit other vulnerable populations and have preyed just as aggressively on documented guest workers and U.S. citizen children. Indeed, because of the vulnerability of minors, where minors are offered for commercial sex the statutes do not require proof of force, fraud, or coercion" (U. S. Department of Justice, 2015).

The problem of human sex trafficking has become particularly acute, comprising the fastest-growing business among organized crime groups and the third largest criminal enterprise worldwide (Walker-Rodriguez & Hill, 2011). While data are limited regarding the exact number of children who are sex trafficked in the United States, an estimated 293,000 youths are currently at risk for such victimization in this country, the majority of whom are runaways or thrownaways and come from a background of abuse and neglect (Walker-Rodriguez & Hill, 2011).

In June 2012, the FBI initiated a 3-day law enforcement action called Operation Cross Country—the sixth iteration of its kind—which resulted in the recovery of 79 children and the arrest of 104 pimps on various prostitution-related charges. The operation partnered hundreds of FBI special agents with thousands of local police officers, deputy sheriffs, state troopers, and other law enforcement personnel throughout the United States to find and arrest those responsible for exploiting underage children through prostitution (FBI, 2012):

> Operation Cross Country is part of the Innocence Lost National Initiative that was created in 2003 by the FBI's Criminal Investigative Division, in partnership with the Department of Justice and National Center for Missing & Exploited Children (NCMEC), to address the growing problem of domestic child sex trafficking in the United States. ...

> To date, the 47 Innocence Lost Task Forces and Working Groups have recovered more than 2,200 children from the streets. The investigations and subsequent 1,017 convictions have resulted in lengthy sentences, including eight life terms and the seizure of more than $3.1 million in assets.

Because of enhanced criminal statutes, victim-protection provisions, and public awareness programs introduced by the Trafficking Victims Protection Act of 2000, the numbers of trafficking investigations and prosecutions have increased dramatically in recent years, as demonstrated by a 360-percent increase in convictions for the fiscal years 2001–2007 as compared to the previous 7-year period (U.S. Department of Justice, 2015). Unfortunately, however, research has found that most police departments still do not consider human trafficking a high priority, and that although some local law enforcement agencies are aware of the nature and seriousness of the crime, few have engaged in proactive endeavors to address the problem (Wilson, Walsh, & Kleuber, 2006). Police officers and citizens alike must be made more aware of suspicious activities to watch for, such as avoiding strangers, never leaving the place of employment, and showing fear of authorities.

A PROBLEM-SOLVING PARTNERSHIP IN ACTION

The 2002 Herman Goldstein Award was presented to the project entitled "Domestic Violence Intervention Project: Charlotte–Mecklenburg (North Carolina) Police Department" (Charlotte–Mecklenburg Police Department, 2002).

Scanning

The problem was an apparent increase in domestic assaults in the Charlotte–Mecklenburg Police Department's Baker One District.

Analysis

Analysis of domestic assault reports showed that the average victim had filed nine previous police reports, most involving the same suspect but sometimes filing reports in more than one police district. Many of the prior reports were for indicator crimes—offenses such as trespassing, threatening, and stalking. Within the Baker One District, most repeat call locations were domestic situations. Further analysis suggested the desirability of regarding the victim and suspect as "hot spots" instead of the traditional fixed geographic location.

Response

Baker One officers developed a tailored response plan for each repeat offense case, including zero tolerance of criminal behavior by the suspect and the use of other criminal justice and social service agencies. A Police Watch Program and a Domestic Violence Hotline voicemail system for victims were implemented. Officers developed detailed case files and created a database with victim/offender background data. The database tracks victims and offenders as moving "hot spots" from one address to another and across district boundaries.

The officers felt that building on existing partnerships with other components of the criminal justice system was critical to intervene effectively in these cases. They established a stronger partnership with the district attorney's office to achieve increased evidence-based prosecution. The department's research showed many of the offenders had prior criminal records and were frequently still on probation. The Baker One officers reached out to community corrections and probation and parole officers for Mecklenburg County to garner their support and understanding of the concept and to help them focus on the behavior of domestic violence suspects who were in violation of the terms of their probation and/or parole.

A variety of stakeholders developed these intervention tactics, including domestic violence investigators and counselors, prosecutors, probation officers, and practitioners in social programs that offer services to domestic violence victims and offenders. The social services agencies participating included New Options for Violent Actions (NOVA), Victim Assistance, Legal Services of the Southern Piedmont, and the Battered Women's Shelter. All agreed to work with Baker One officers in dealing with these complex cases. Guidelines were established to provide as uniform a response as possible to each case.

Assessment

Repeat calls for service were reduced by 98.9 percent at seven target locations. Domestic assaults decreased by 7 percent in the Baker One District but increased by 29 percent in other areas of the city. In 105 cases with indicator crimes, only three victims later reported a domestic assault. Only 14.8 percent of domestic violence victims in the project reported repeat victimization, as opposed to a benchmark figure of 35 percent. No internal affairs complaints were generated by officer contacts with suspects.

SUMMARY

Causes of violence may include ready availability of guns, drugs, and alcohol; a desensitization to violence; disintegration of the family and community; social and economic deprivation; and increased numbers of children growing up in violent families. A problem-solving approach to preventing violence must attempt to identify the underlying causes of specific violent situations that threaten a community before solutions can be devised.

Developing effective prevention tactics will require long-term collaborations between criminal justice and juvenile justice practitioners and other social service agencies. It also requires involvement of the entire community of which these agencies are a part. Strategies for general violence prevention include public dialogue and community mediation, and addressing violence as a public health problem.

Hate can be classified into two categories: rational and irrational. The majority of hate crimes are motivated by racial bias and involve violence.

Gun violence may be considered as a three-phase continuum: (1) the illegal acquisition of firearms; (2) the illegal possession and carrying of firearms; and (3) the illegal, improper, or careless use of firearms. The National Crime Prevention Council suggests that regulations and ordinances on gun licensing may interrupt sources of illegal guns. Gun interdictions may be an effective deterrent to illegal gun possessing and carrying.

Partners in gun violence reduction identified by the Office of Juvenile Justice and Delinquency Prevention (OJJDP) include the U.S. attorney, chief of police, sheriff, federal law enforcement agencies (FBI, ATF, DEA), district attorney, state attorney general, mayor/city manager, probation and parole officers, juvenile corrections officials, judges, public defenders, school superintendents, social services officials, leaders in the faith community, and business leaders.

Domestic violence is another type of problem in most communities. Animal abuse has a direct link to domestic violence. When forming partnerships to prevent domestic violence, the issue of cultural diversity between male-dominated police organizations and female-dominated grassroots advocate groups must be addressed.

Children in violent homes face three risks: (1) the risk of observing traumatic events, (2) the risk of being abused themselves, and (3) the risk of being neglected. The CD–CP model emphasizes cross-training of criminal justice and mental health professionals to develop collaborative problem-solving techniques that go beyond the reach of either "system" acting alone.

Yet another type of violence challenging communities is workplace violence. Common motivations behind violent behavior in the workplace include robbery, loss of a job, anger from feelings of mistreatment, substance abuse, and mental problems. Characteristics common to workplace violence and school violence include the profiles of the perpetrators, the targets, the warnings, the means, and the pathways to violence.

DISCUSSION QUESTIONS

1. Explain why some experts recommend a problem-solving approach to violence prevention.
2. What is the public health model of violence prevention?
3. Why do gun interdiction strategies frequently lead to charges that the police have targeted the minority community, and what can be done to allay such concerns?
4. Explain the difference researchers found between those who are violent to their partners and those who commit violent crimes against others.
5. What risks exist for children who live in homes where domestic violence occurs?
6. Corporations are suggested in this chapter as partners in violence prevention. Why would corporations have any interest in prevention or their ability to affect it?
7. Name some likely types of people who might pose a risk of violence in a workplace.
8. Discuss any instances of hate crimes in your community or your state. Does your state have mandatory reporting laws for hate crimes?
9. What type of person is the most likely victim of domestic violence?
10. What childhood experience increases the likelihood of being arrested later in life?

Understanding and Preventing Terrorism

Learning Objectives

LO1 List the common elements in definitions of terrorism.

LO2 Explain what motivates most terrorist attacks.

LO3 Know how terrorism is classified.

LO4 Identify the methods terrorists may use and which are the most common.

LO5 Name the two lead agencies in combating terrorism.

LO6 Summarize what the keys to combating terrorism are.

LO7 Understand what two concerns related to the war on terrorism are.

Key Terms

asymmetric warfare
contagion effect
deconfliction
fusion center
interoperability
Islamic State of Iraq and the Levant (ISIL)
jihad
terrorism

On July 8, 2016, in retribution for recent police-involved killings of Black men in Minnesota and Louisiana, a sniper in Dallas, Texas, set out to kill as many White police officers as possible. Michah Johnson, a 25-year-old U.S. Army Reserve veteran and supporter of the New Black Panther Party, opened fire on police as they were marshaling a peaceful community protest surrounding the police-involved shooting deaths of unarmed Black men across the country. What should have been a very peaceful ending to a nonviolent protest turned into bloodshed as the sniper trained his assault rifle on the police officers. In the end, the attack left five officers dead and seven others wounded.

Although the events garnered a lot of national attention, the Dallas Police Department (DPD) had already been very well respected prior to the shooting. The department, along with the chief and the officers, was revered for its changes in de-escalation tactics. As Dallas Mayor Mike Rawlings stated during one of the many press conferences following the 2016 shooting, "This police department trained in de-escalation far before cities across America did it. We're one of the premier community policing cities in the country and this year [2016] we have the fewest police officer-related shootings than any large city in America."

The impetus for the de-escalation tactics began in 2012, when an officer shot an unarmed man during a foot pursuit. Needless to say, the shooting garnered much media attention locally and led DPD Chief Brown to voluntarily review the police department's records on use-of-deadly-force incidents. Ultimately, the review generated reforms intended to reduce the unwarranted use of deadly force. Along with the change in deadly force policy execution came the following policies: new foot chase policy that aimed to limit precarious decision making while in pursuit, a contemporary method in reporting officer's use of force, a publically accessible Web site documenting all use of force by police officers, involvement of the F.B.I.'s Civil Rights Division in analyzing every officer-involved shooting, an increase in the amount of training with the department's deadly force policy, increased training on de-escalation tactics, and the purchasing of 1,000 body cameras for the department's officers.

Change, like anything, can be a difficult balance. DPD, though never claiming perfection, took multiple steps to properly and professionally change how officers patrolled their districts. Over the years though, the prospect of terrorism, including that perpetrated by homegrown offenders, has forced local law enforcement to morph into a more progressive and modern entity. Terrorism has no place in the United States, but continuously Americans find themselves prospective targets. No one could have predicted the tragedy, which would be inflicted upon the Dallas Police Department, but hopefully no other domestic agency will know of such loss.

INTRODUCTION

The September 11, 2001, attack on America galvanized the United States into action: "Tonight we are a country awakened to danger and called to defend freedom. Our grief has turned to anger, and anger to resolution," announced then-President George W. Bush. The horrific events of September 11 pulled together and unified the American people. Patriotism was immediately in vogue. Thousands of volunteers helped search for victims and donated blood and money. The American flag flew everywhere.

The events of that tragic day also added a new dimension to American policing. Experience now tells us that the first responders to any future terrorist incidents will most assuredly be local police, fire, and rescue personnel. As a result, law enforcement officials must now strategically rethink public security procedures and practices to maximize the full potential of their resources.

Boston Globe/Getty Images

Two backpack bombs explode near the finish line of the Boston Marathon on April 15, 2013, leaving 3 people dead and hundreds of others injured. The two suspects, brothers of Chechen descent, were self-radicalized Islamic extremists, the type of terrorists presenting unprecedented challenges to law enforcement in the United States.

TERRORISM: AN OVERVIEW

Terrorism has occurred throughout history for a variety of reasons: historical, cultural, political, social, psychological, economic, religious, or any combination of these. White (2012, p. 31) notes: "Terrorism is a method of fighting. It allows a very weak force to attack a stronger power, disrupting the social organization of established authority. Terrorism fluctuates over time, and it transforms with multiple political, social, and psychological circumstances. This means that terrorism is dynamic and ever changing." Terrorism can be perpetrated by an individual, a small group, or a large organization. National governments have at times aided terrorists to further their own foreign policy goals. State-sponsored terrorism is a form of covert warfare, a means to wage war secretly through the use of terrorist surrogates (stand-ins) as hired guns. The U.S. Department of State designates countries as state sponsors of terrorism if they actively assist or aid terrorists, if they harbor past terrorists, or if they refuse to renounce terrorism. Countries currently designed as state sponsors of terrorism are Iran, Sudan, and Syria (U.S. Department of State, 2016).

Definitions of Terrorism

terrorism
The unlawful use of force or violence against persons or property to intimidate or coerce a government, the civilian population, or any segment thereof, in furtherance of political or social objectives.

There is no single, universally accepted definition of terrorism. The Federal Bureau of Investigation (FBI) uses the guidelines set forth in the United States Code of Federal Regulations, which defines **terrorism** as "the unlawful use of force and violence against persons or property to intimidate or coerce a government, the civilian population, or any segment thereof, in furtherance of political or social objectives" (28 C.F.R. Section 0.85). Terrorists aim to create fear as a way to bring about political change. All terrorist acts involve violence or the threat of violence committed by nongovernmental groups or individuals.

L01

Common elements in definitions of terrorism include (1) systematic use of physical violence—actual or threatened, (2) against noncombatants, (3) but with an audience broader than the immediate victims in mind, (4) to create a general climate of fear in a target population, and (5) to cause political and/or social change.

Terrorism is by nature political because it involves acquiring and using power to force others to submit to terrorist demands. Terrorist attacks generate publicity and focus attention on the organization behind the attack, creating their power. Terrorists usually attempt to justify their violence by arguing that they have been excluded from the accepted process to bring about political or social change. They claim terrorism is their only option. Whether one agrees with this argument often depends on whether one sympathizes with the terrorists' cause or with the victims of the terrorist attack. The label *terrorism* can be highly subjective depending on one's sympathies. However, terrorist acts—including murder, kidnapping, bombing, and arson—have long been defined in both national and international law as crimes. Even in time of war, violence deliberately directed against innocent civilians is considered a crime.

Despite the lack of a single, universally accepted definition of terrorism, most definitions do have common elements.

Motivations for Terrorism

Terrorists act based on varying motivations. Religious motives are seen in Islamic extremism. Political motives include such elements as the Red Army Faction. Social motives are seen in single-issue groups such as antiabortion groups, animal rights groups, and environmentalists. Extremists begin believing that a specific situation is not right and that it is not fair. They focus blame on another group and then determine that group is evil. This process of ideological development is illustrated in Figure 15.1.

> **L02**
>
> Most terrorist acts result from dissatisfaction with a religious, political, or social system or policy and frustration resulting from an inability to change it through acceptable, nonviolent means.

Classification of Terrorist Acts

Although there are several ways to classify terrorist acts, the FBI generally distinguishes between two categories of terrorism.

International Terrorism   International terrorism is foreign based or directed by countries or groups outside the United States against the United States. According to the FBI (n.d.-a), *international terrorism* is an action that:

> **L03**
>
> The FBI categorizes terrorism as either international or domestic terrorism. Terrorism also includes acts by homegrown violent extremists (HVEs) and "lone wolf" attackers.

- Involves violent acts or acts dangerous to human life that violate federal or state law;

- Appears to be intended (i) to intimidate or coerce a civilian population; (ii) to influence the policy of a government by intimidation or coercion; or (iii) to affect the conduct of a government by mass destruction, assassination, or kidnapping; and

- Occurs primarily outside the territorial jurisdiction of the United States, or transcends national boundaries in terms of the means by which it is accomplished, the persons they appear intended to intimidate or coerce, or the locale in which their perpetrators operate or seek asylum.

Three categories of international terrorism are:

- foreign state sponsors of international terrorism using terrorism as a tool of foreign policy, for example, Iraq, Libya, and Afghanistan.

Figure 15.1	The Process of Ideological Development

It's not right   It's not fair   It's your fault   You're evil

Social and economic deprivation → Inequality and resentment → Blame/Attribution → Generalizing/Stereotyping

Blame/Attribution → Dehumanizing/Demonizing the enemy (cause)

Context   Comparison   Attribution   Reaction

Source: Randy Borum. "Understanding the Terrorist Mind-Set." *FBI Law Enforcement Bulletin*, July 2003, p. 9. Reprinted by permission.

Islamic State of Iraq and the Levant (ISIL)
A formalized international terrorist groups formerly known as al-Qa'ida in Iraq and Islamic State of Iraq (ISIS).

- formalized terrorist groups, such as Lebanese Hezbollah (alternately spelled Hizballah); Palestinian HAMAS; Palestinian Islamic Jihad (PIJ); core al-Qa'ida (alternately spelled al Qaeda) groups and their affiliates; and the **Islamic State of Iraq and the Levant (ISIL)**, formerly known as al-Qa'ida in Iraq and Islamic State of Iraq (ISIS).

- loosely affiliated international radical extremists who have a variety of identities and travel freely in the United States, unknown to law enforcement or the government.

The 1990s saw multiple terrorist attacks against U.S. military installations in Saudi Arabia and embassies in East Africa. On February 23, 1998, Osama bin Laden declared **jihad**, a holy war, on the United States, calling on "every Muslim who believes in God and wishes to be rewarded to comply with God's order to kill Americans and plunder their money wherever and whenever they find it" (Savelli, 2004, p. 3). Bin Laden was placed on the FBI's 10 Most Wanted List in connection with the August 7, 1998, bombings of U.S. embassies in dar Es Salaam, Tanzania and Nairobi, Kenya. Unfortunately, he was not apprehended and grew capable of even more horrific attacks, as Americans learned on that fateful September day in 2001. Since then, the U.S. government has been extremely aware of the threat of international terrorism and has shifted its focus from a war on drugs to a war on terrorism. Following a relentless 10-year search for this terrorist leader, U.S. special forces located and killed bin Laden on May 2, 2011, at his secret compound in Abbottabad, Pakistan.

jihad
Holy war.

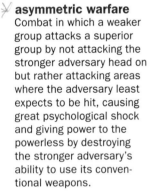

asymmetric warfare
Combat in which a weaker group attacks a superior group by not attacking the stronger adversary head on but rather attacking areas where the adversary least expects to be hit, causing great psychological shock and giving power to the powerless by destroying the stronger adversary's ability to use its conventional weapons.

International terrorist groups are likely to engage in what is often referred to as asymmetric warfare. **Asymmetric warfare** refers to combat in which a weaker group attacks a superior group by not attacking the stronger adversary head on but rather attacking areas where the adversary least expects to be hit, causing great psychological shock. Asymmetric warfare gives power to the powerless and destroys the stronger adversary's ability to use its conventional weapons. A prime example is al Qaeda terrorists using box cutters to convert airplanes into weapons of mass destruction, costing billions of dollars of losses to the U.S. economy and tremendous loss of life—all at an estimated cost to the terrorists of $500,000.

According to the Global Terrorism Index (GTI), terrorist activity increased worldwide in 2014 by 80 percent over the previous year, with Boko Haram overtaking ISIL as the deadliest terrorist group on the planet (Institute for Economics and Peace, 2015). The annual report notes the significant prevalence of lone wolf attacks in the West, with such attacks accounting for 70 percent of all terrorist deaths in the West since 2006. The Index also points out, however, that more than 437,000 people across the world are victims of homicide each year, a figure more than 13 times the number of people killed by terrorist acts.

Domestic Terrorism   The events of 9/11 shifted the FBI's focus to international terrorist groups operating inside the United States but not to the exclusion of domestic groups that threaten the safety of our citizens. The FBI defines *domestic terrorism* as an action that:

- Violates federal or state law;
- Appears to be intended to (1) intimidate or coerce a civilian population; (2) influence the policy of a government by intimidation or coercion; or

(3) affect the conduct of a government by mass destruction, assassination, or kidnapping; and

- Occurs primarily within the territorial jurisdiction of the United States" [18 U.S.C. § 2331 (5)].

The FBI expanded its definition of domestic terrorism when it stated, "The threat of domestic terror—Americans attacking Americans based on U.S.-based extremist ideologies—is alive and well. Today's domestic terror threats run the gamut from hate-filled White supremacists . . . to highly destructive ecoterrorists . . . to violence-prone anti-government extremists . . . to radical separatist groups" (FBI, 2009).

Domestic terrorist groups include White supremacists, Black supremacists, militia groups, other right-wing extremists, left-wing extremists, pro-life extremists, animal rights activists, and environmental extremists. Many of these groups are categorized as "hate groups," introduced briefly in Chapter 14, and the largest is the Ku Klux Klan (Southern Poverty Law Center, 2016). With regard to hate groups and other domestic terrorist groups, the FBI (2009) asserts:

> As with all forms of extremism, preventing homegrown attacks before they are hatched is our overriding goal. It's an especially tall order given the civil liberties we all enjoy as American citizens, including the right to free speech. Hate and anger are not crimes; neither are hard-line and poisonous ideologies. It's only when actions by groups or individuals cross the line into threats, the actual use of force or violence, or other law-breaking activities that we can investigate.

The bombing of the Alfred P. Murrah Federal Building in Oklahoma City; the pipe bomb explosions in Centennial Olympic Park in Atlanta, Georgia, during the 1996 Summer Olympic Games; the 2009 shooting of a guard at the Holocaust Museum in Washington, DC; the 2009 shooting at Fort Hood in Texas; and the 2010 flight of a small airplane into the IRS building in Austin, Texas—these incidents highlight the threat of domestic terrorists. These terrorists represent extreme right- or left-wing and special-interest beliefs. Many are antigovernment, antitaxation, and antiabortion; and some engage in survivalist training to perpetuate a White, Christian nation. The number of domestic terrorist attacks is almost double the number of international acts of terrorism.

Homegrown Violent Extremists   In the years immediately following 9/11, the United States naively believed that radical jihad was bred solely on foreign soil and looked almost exclusively to shoring up border security in an effort to keep out those with terrorist intentions. However, in recent years, it has become increasingly evident that terrorists can emerge from within our own citizenry and that it takes only a few homegrown jihadis to present a significant public safety threat (Straw, 2010).

There has been a rise in transnational Islamist terrorism, with growing domestic radicalization appearing in the United Kingdom, France, Germany, Australia, and other countries. Security forces in all of these countries routinely emphasize that the greatest threat they face is "homegrown terrorism"

(Chalk, 2010). This trend appears to be continuing in the United States, and concern is rising over the number of U.S. citizens who are traveling to Syria, Iraq, and other radicalized hotbeds, possibly to receive training and weapons to use against this country. An estimated 3,400 fighters from Western countries, including more than 150 people from the United States, are thought to have either traveled to Syria and surrounding conflict zones or have attempted to do so (Rasmussen, 2015).

Examples of alleged homegrown jihadists in the United States include Nidal Malik Hasan, the Virginia-born Army major who reportedly yelled "Allahu Akbar," an Islamic exclamation meaning "Allah is the Greatest," as he went on a murderous shooting rampage at Ft. Hood, Texas, in November 2009, killing 13 Americans and injuring another 31. Faisal Shahzad, a naturalized U.S. citizen of Pakistani descent, was convicted of the failed Times Square bombing attempt in May 2010 and is serving a life sentence without the possibility of parole. On April 15, 2013, two backpacks exploded near the finish line of the Boston Marathon, killing three people and injuring hundreds more, an attack was perpetrated by two self-radicalized brothers, 26-year-old Tamerlan and 23-year-old Dzhokhar Tsarnaev. Both of Chechen descent, Dzhokhar had become a naturalized U.S. citizen and Tamerlan was a permanent legal resident of the United States. Tamerlan was shot and killed by police shortly after the bombing; Dzhokhar is on death row. Syed Rizwan Farook, an American-born U.S. citizen of Pakistani descent, and his wife, Tashfeen Malik, a Pakistani-born lawful permanent resident of the United States, killed 14 people and wounded 22 others during a mass shooting and attempted bombing in San Bernardino, California, on December 2, 2015. The couple fled by car but were later found by police and killed during a shootout. The incident has spurred a federal terrorism investigation (FBI, 2015). Muhammad Youssef Abdulazeez, a 24-year-old Kuwait-born naturalized American citizen, went on a shooting rampage in Chattanooga, Tennessee, on July 16, 2015, in which he targeted military personnel. Four people were killed and two other wounded before police shot and killed Abdulazeez; another of his victims died several days later (Jaffe, Gibbons-Neff, & Goldman, 2015). An FBI investigation determined that Abdulazeez's attack was motivated by foreign terrorist organization propaganda, although a specific terrorist group was not identified (Sgueglia, 2015). And on June 12, 2016, 29-year-old American-born Omar Mateen, who had pledged his allegiance to ISIS, opened fire at a gay nightclub in Orlando, Florida, killing more than 50 people and wounding more than 50 others. Mateen was shot and killed by police after a 3-hour standoff (Grimson, Wyllie, & Fieldstadt, 2016). All of these attacks by HVEs can also be considered to be "lone wolf" attacks, as discussed shortly.

Radical Islamic jihadists are not the only HVEs of concern to police. In fact, a survey conducted in 2014 with the help of the Police Executive Research Forum (PERF) found that, as a whole, law enforcement agencies consider antigovernment violent extremists to be a greater threat than radicalized Muslims (Kurzman & Schanzer, 2015). Environmental extremism was also identified as a top threat.

Although "homegrown terrorists" often lack the training and resources to attack high-profile, well-protected facilities, they are perhaps the most difficult to detect because they often fly "under the radar" of typical law enforcement and intelligence agency detection methods (Chalk, 2010). A common thread running through many of the cases involving HVEs is the revelation that their radicalized views were acquired or nurtured via connections made online and through social media. John Carlin, the assistant attorney general for national security, has reported that the majority of people who have been charged in recent years by U.S. federal authorities with links to terrorism have had a social media connection to a terrorist organization. The Islamic State, says Carlin, is very adaptable and knows the audience it seeks through social media, as evidence by the fact that more than half of the cases involved suspects younger than 25 years of age (Baker & Schmitt, 2015).

In February 2015, the White House Summit on Countering Violent Extremists (CVE) was held, bringing in to focus the critical need for a collaborative government effort to prevent extremists from radicalizing and mobilizing recruits, especially those residing within our country (Department of Homeland Security [DHS], 2016). To that end, the DHS agreed to host the CVE Task Force, a permanent interagency group led by DHS and the DOJ, with additional members to include agents from the FBI and National Counterterrorism Center, as well as other supporting departments and agencies. The CVE Task Force will organize federal efforts into several areas, including research and analysis, engagements and technical assistance, communications, and interventions (DHS, 2016).

The "Lone Wolf" Offender   Similar to international terrorism, domestic terrorism is often committed by a "lone wolf" offender, an individual whose personal set of beliefs drives him or her to commit hateful attacks and who acts without the support or knowledge of a larger group (FBI, 2009). The Global Terrorism Index reports: "Lone wolf attackers are the main perpetrators of terrorist activity in the West. Seventy percent of all deaths from terrorism in the West since 2006 were by lone wolf terrorists with the rest being unknown or group attacks by more than three attackers" (Institute for Economics and Peace, 2015, p. 5). Calling lone wolf offenders a "particularly insidious concern that touches all forms of domestic extremisms," the FBI notes that in some cases, lone offenders have tried to join a group but were either kicked out for being too radical or chose to leave the group after a time because it was not extreme enough to match their level of radicalization (FBI, 2009).

The lengthy bombing spree of the Unabomber as well as the pipe bomb explosions in Centennial Olympic Park during the 1996 Summer Olympic Games highlight the threat of the lone bomber with a deep hatred of something or someone. More recent examples of lone wolf terrorists were ex-Los Angeles Police Department officer Christopher Dorner who, in early 2013, set out on a killing spree to exact revenge on the law enforcement community he felt had wronged him, and Dylann Roof, the Charleston church shooter, who wanted to start a race war.

Terrorists as Criminals

A documented nexus exists between traditional crime and terrorism, involving fraudulent identification, trafficking in illegal merchandise, and drug sales as means to terrorists' ends (Loyka, Faggiani, & Karchmer, 2005). Polisar (2004, p. 8) observes: "Suddenly agencies and officers who have been trained and equipped to deal with more traditional crimes are now focused on apprehending individuals operating with different motivations, who have different objectives, and who use much deadlier weapons than traditional criminals."

Linett (2005, p. 59) notes another striking difference between dealing with a terrorist and a street criminal: "The difference is not just one of semantics; it is a matter of life and death. When fighting terrorists, it's kill or be killed, not capture and convict." This blurring of the line between crime and war has drawn law enforcement directly into a new type of battle: "Local law enforcement will be expected to handle complex tactical situations such as chemical, biological, and nuclear events" (Page, 2004, p. 87).

The Rand Corporation studied how terrorist groups end and found, among other things, that police and intelligence efforts are more effective at eliminating terrorist groups than is the military: "The United States cannot conduct an effective long-term counterterrorism campaign against al Qaida or other terrorist groups without understanding how terrorist groups end," said the study's lead author and a political scientist at the Rand Corporation, a nonprofit organization. "In most cases, military force isn't the best instrument" (Rand Corporation, 2008). The most common way terrorist groups end (43%) is by a transition in the political process. The second most common way they end (40%) is through police and intelligence services: "Policing is especially effective in dealing with terrorists because police have a permanent presence in cities that enables them to efficiently gather information" (Rand Corporation, 2008). That is one of the same reasons community policing is so successful. Police must also be familiar with the arsenal of methods terrorists use.

Methods Used by Terrorists

Terrorists have used a variety of techniques in furtherance of their cause. Figure 15.2 illustrates the methods used in international terrorist attacks during 2014. Note that armed attacks and bombings accounted for the vast majority (more than three-fourths) of all terrorist attacks in 2014.

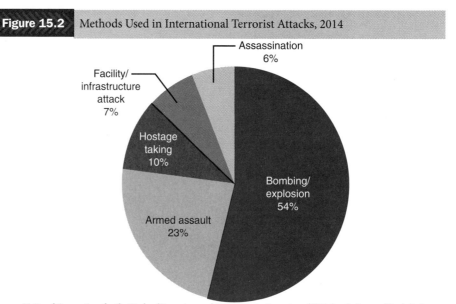

Figure 15.2 Methods Used in International Terrorist Attacks, 2014

Assassination 6%

Facility/infrastructure attack 7%

Hostage taking 10%

Bombing/explosion 54%

Armed assault 23%

Source: National Consortium for the Study of Terrorism and Responses to Terrorism. (2015, June). *Annex of Statistical Information: Country Reports on Terrorism 2014*. College Park, MD: University of Maryland. Retrieved October 30, 2016 from http://www.state.gov/documents/organization/239628.pdf

Some terrorism experts suggest that incendiary devices and explosives are most likely to be used because they are easy to make.

Explosives and Bombs   From 1978 to 1996, Theodore Kaczynski, the notorious Unabomber, terrorized the country, apparently in a protest against technology, with a string of 16 mail bombings that killed three people. Ramzi Ahmed Yousef, found guilty of masterminding the first World Trade Center bombing in 1993, declared that he was proud to be a terrorist and that terrorism was the only viable response to what he saw as a Jewish lobby in Washington. The car bomb used to shatter the Murrah Federal Building in 1995 was Timothy McVeigh's way of protesting the government and their raid on the Branch Davidians at Waco, Texas. In 2002, Lucas Helder terrorized the Midwest by placing 18 pipe bombs accompanied by antigovernment letters in mailboxes throughout five states. Six exploded, injuring four letter carriers and two residents. The most horrific act of terrorism against the United States occurred on September 11, 2001, when two airplanes were used as missiles to explode the World Trade Center and another plane was used to attack the Pentagon. A fourth plane crashed in a Pennsylvania field before it could reach its destination.

L04

Terrorists may use arson; explosives and bombs; weapons of mass destruction (biological, chemical, or nuclear agents); and technology. The majority of terrorism attacks are carried out by bombings and explosions. The second most common method is armed attacks.

Weapons of Mass Destruction   Weapons of mass destruction (WMD) include chemical agents, biological agents, and nuclear weapons and are defined under U.S. law (18 USC §2332) as:

- Any destructive device as defined in section 921 of this title (i.e., explosive device)
- Any weapon that is designed or intended to cause death or serious bodily injury through the release, dissemination, or impact of toxic or poisonous chemicals, or their precursors
- Any weapon involving a biological agent, toxin, or vector (as those terms are defined in section 178 of this title)
- Any weapon that is designed to release radiation or radioactivity at a level dangerous to human life (FBI, n.d.-b)

The Aum Shinrikyo attack in the Tokyo subway in 1995 initially focused the security industry's efforts on detecting and mitigating *chemical agent* threats. That incident confirmed that a nonstate entity could manufacture a viable chemical agent—sarin gas—and deliver it in a public location. Unfortunately, anyone with Internet access and a Web browser can obtain the chemical formula for sarin in less than 40 minutes and can produce it inexpensively. The four common types of chemical weapons are nerve agents, blood/choking agents, blistering agents, and radiological agents (White, 2012). One agent, ricin toxin, is both a biological and a chemical weapon.

Bioterrorism involves such biological WMD as anthrax, botulism, and smallpox, and the potential for bioterrorism in the United States has been identified as an increasingly unfortunate threat in the aftermath of the September 11 attacks and the anthrax scares (Hanson, 2005). Especially susceptible to bioterrorism are the nation's food and water supplies.

Although many people consider a nuclear weapon in the hands of a terrorist to be the most frightening scenario possible, it is a very difficult feat to accomplish: "It is much easier for terrorists to use conventional weapons than it is to build a nuclear weapon. Nuclear weapons are also difficult to obtain and detonate" (White, 2012, p. 143). Many scholars consider the probability of nuclear terrorism to be low based on the crime causation model where the victim, motivated offender, and opportunity to commit a crime intersect: "Al Qaeda—the only group that has made an effort to obtain a nuclear device—has the desire to make any one of their enemies victims, but it has consistently lacked the opportunity to strike. Further, there is no evidence to suggest that al Qaeda has the ability to obtain a nuclear weapon or to construct one" (White, 2012, p. 144). Local law enforcement agencies select and train officers to form a WMD team. The officers' time is not devoted solely to the unit, but they are ready if a need for their skills arises.

Technological Terrorism   Technological terrorism includes attacks *on* technology as well as *by* technology. The United States relies on energy to drive the nation's technology. An attack on the U.S. energy supply could be devastating. Likewise, an attack on the computer systems and networks critical to the functioning of businesses, health care facilities, educational institutions, the military, and all governmental agencies would be catastrophic. Cyberterrorism, a type of technological terrorism, has been defined as "the intimidation of civilian enterprise through the use of high technology to bring about political, religious, or ideological aims, actions that result in disabling or deleting critical infrastructure data or information" (Tafoya, 2011, p. 2). Damage to critical computer systems could put the nation's safety and security in jeopardy. Each of the preceding types of terrorism poses a threat to national security.

Funding Terrorism

Money is needed to carry out terrorism, not only for weapons but for general operating expenses. Many terrorist operations are financed by charitable groups and wealthy people sympathetic to the group's cause. Terrorist groups commonly collaborate with organized criminal groups to deal drugs, arms, and, in some instances, humans.

Fraud has become increasingly common among terrorists, not only as a way to generate revenue but also as a way to gain access to their targets. Fraudulently obtained drivers' licenses, passports, and other identification documents are often found among terrorists' belongings (Savelli, 2004). Common criminal methods of funding terrorist operations include kidnapping, extortion, robbery, fraud, larceny, smuggling, forgery, and counterfeiting: "Interpol estimates that counterfeiting and intellectual property theft is responsible for $200 billion in illegal profits in the United States alone" (White, 2012, p. 86).

THE FEDERAL RESPONSE TO TERRORISM: HOMELAND SECURITY

In 1996, the FBI established a Counterterrorism Center to combat terrorism. That same year, the Antiterrorism and Effective Death Penalty Act was passed, including several specific measures aimed at terrorism. This Act enhanced the federal government's power to deny visas to individuals belonging to terrorist groups and simplified the process for deporting aliens convicted of crimes.

In 1999, then-FBI Director Louis Freeh announced, "Our Number-One priority is the prevention of terrorism." To that end, the FBI added a new Counterterrorism Division with four subunits: the International Terrorism Section, the Domestic Terrorism Section, the National Infrastructure Protection Center, and the National Domestic Preparedness Office. These efforts, unfortunately, were not enough to avert the tragic events of September 11. It took a disaster of that magnitude to make the war on terrorism truly the first priority of the United States.

The National Counterterrorism Center (NCTC), created by Presidential Executive Order in 2004, is part of the Office of the Director of National Intelligence. NCTC serves as the primary organization in the U.S. government for integrating and analyzing all intelligence pertaining to terrorism possessed or acquired by the government (except purely domestic terrorism); serves as the central and shared knowledge bank on terrorism information; provides all-source intelligence support to government-wide counterterrorism activities; and establishes the information technology (IT) systems and architectures within the NCTC and between the NCTC and other agencies that enable access to, as well as integration, dissemination, and use of, terrorism information. NCTC's mission statement succinctly summarizes its key responsibilities and value-added contributions: "Lead our nation's effort to combat terrorism at home and abroad by analyzing the threat, sharing that information with our partners, and integrating all instruments of national power to ensure unity of effort" (NCTC, n.d.).

NCTC issues an annual *Report on Terrorism* to fulfill its mandate to collect statistics on the annual number of incidents of "terrorism," although its ability to track the specific groups responsible for each incident involving killings, kidnappings, and injuries is significantly limited by the availability of reliable open-source information, particularly for events involving small numbers of casualties or occurring in remote regions of the world. Moreover, specific details about victims, damage, perpetrators, and other incident elements are frequently not fully reported in open-source information. In deriving its figures for incidents of terrorism, the NCTC in 2005 adopted the definition of *terrorism* that appears in 22 USC §2656f(d)(2): "premeditated, politically motivated violence perpetrated against noncombatant targets by subnational groups or clandestine agents."

According to Gary LaFree, Director of the National Consortium for the Study of Terrorism and Responses to Terrorism (START), University of Maryland:

> Compared to most types of criminal violence, terrorism poses special conceptual and methodological challenges. To begin with, the term "terrorism" yields varying definitions, often loaded with political and emotional implications. As PLO Chairman Arafat famously noted in a 1974 speech before the United Nations, "One man's terrorist is another man's freedom fighter." Defining terrorism is no less complex for researchers. Researchers have identified dozens of different definitions of terrorism, and it is not unusual for academic conferences to dedicate hours of discussion to exploring and defending competing definitions (NCTC, 2009, p. 72).

The FBI's *Strategic Plan 2004–2009* declares: "The events of September 11th have forever changed our nation and the FBI. Since that terrible day, the FBI's overriding priority has been protecting America by preventing further attacks." In their list of priorities, that is number one. Priority nine is to support federal, state, local, and international partners: "To achieve its mission, the FBI must strengthen three inextricably linked core functions: intelligence, investigations, and partnerships. ... Partnerships are essential if the FBI is to effectively address evolving threats that are too complex or multijurisdictional for one agency to handle alone. To achieve its vital mission, the FBI is dependent upon the goodwill, cooperation, and expertise of our local, state, federal and international partners" (FBI, 2004, p. 19). No new strategic plan has been made available.

The Department of Homeland Security

The Department of Homeland Security (DHS) was established by Executive Order on October 8, 2001, in direct response to the September 11 attacks on the United States. Created through the integration of 22 different federal departments and agencies, either in whole or in part, the DHS is primarily responsible for protecting the country from terrorist attacks and responding to natural disasters. Agencies included under the umbrella of DHS are the U.S. Customs and Border Protection (CBP), U.S. Citizenship and Immigration Services (CIS), U.S. Immigration and Customs Enforcement (ICE), Domestic Nuclear Detection Office, Transportation Security Administration (TSA), Federal Law Enforcement Training Center (FLETC), Federal Emergency Management Agency (FEMA), U.S. Coast Guard (USCG), and U.S. Secret Service. With 240,000 employees, DHS is the third largest U.S. federal government department.

The mission of the DHS is stated in the department's Strategic Plan for 2008–2013 (DHS, 2008, p. 3): "We will lead the unified national effort to secure America. We will prevent and deter terrorist attacks and protect against and respond to threats and hazards to the nation. We will secure our national borders while welcoming lawful immigrants, visitors, and trade." All U.S. attorneys have been directed to establish antiterrorism task forces to serve as conduits for information about suspected terrorists between federal and local agencies.

The DHS serves in a broad capacity, facilitating collaboration between local and federal law enforcement to develop a national strategy to detect, prepare for, prevent, protect against, respond to, and recover from terrorist attacks within the United States. The DHS had previously established a five-level color-coded threat system which it used to communicate with public safety officials and the public at large. However, in April 2011, DHS Secretary Janet Napolitano announced that the five-tiered color-coded security advisory system would be replaced by a two-level National Terrorism Advisory System:

- Elevated Threat—warns of a credible terrorist threat against the United States

- Imminent Threat—warns of a credible, specific, and impending terrorist threat against the United States

L05

At the federal level, the FBI is the lead agency for responding to acts of domestic terrorism. The Federal Emergency Management Agency (FEMA) is the lead agency for consequence management (after an attack).

Fusion Centers

Another federal response to terrorism has been to support the development of a network of fusion centers across the country. A **fusion center** is "a collaborative effort of two or more agencies that provide resources, expertise, and information to the center with the goal of maximizing their ability to detect, prevent, investigate, and respond to criminal and terrorist activity" (*Fusion Center Guidelines*, 2006, p. 2).

The development of fusion centers throughout the country was spurred by the March 2002 summit held by the International Association of Chiefs of Police (IACP) and the COPS Office regarding criminal intelligence sharing in the United States. The FBI notes that fusion centers do not just *collect* information; they also *integrates* new data into existing information, *evaluates* it to determine its worth, *analyzes* it for links and trends, and *disseminates* its findings to the appropriate agency in the best position to do something about it.

Fusion centers pool the resources and personnel of multiple agencies into one central location to facilitate information sharing and intelligence development regarding criminal activities: "Combining data from multiple agencies enables policy makers and police managers to see trends and patterns not as apparent when using a single information source. Employing multiple sources helps present a more credible picture of crime and homeland security issues" (Lambert, 2010). Currently there are more than 75 fusion centers across the country, and they now take an "all threats/all hazards" approach to intelligence, expanding their focus from information on terrorism threats to include public safety matters and major criminal threats.

fusion center
A collaborative effort of two or more agencies that provide resources, expertise, and information to the center with the goal of maximizing their ability to detect, prevent, investigate, and respond to criminal and terrorist activity.

Joint Terrorism Task Forces

Often working in conjunction with fusion centers are joint terrorism task forces (JTTFs), multijurisdictional task forces created, coordinated, and managed by the FBI that combine the resources of federal and state, local, tribal, and territorial (SLTT) law enforcement to conduct terrorism-related investigations. The 104 JTTFs investigate terrorism cases across the FBI's 56 field offices and coordinate their efforts via the National Joint Terrorism Task Force, a fusion of local, state, and federal agencies acting as an integrated force to combat terrorism on a national and international scale.

As partners in the national homeland security initiative, fusion centers and JTTFs serve distinct yet complementary roles. Fusion centers analyze and share intelligence, and JTTFs conduct investigations. Fusion centers provide all threat-related tips and leads to JTTFs for investigation. For example, in the May 1, 2010 attempted bombing of Times Square by Faisal Shahzad, analysts at the Florida Fusion Center discovered Shahzad was associated with two subjects who had resided in their state and disseminated this information to JTTFs to further pursue leads, conduct investigations, and support corroboration. Shahzad was convicted on 10 charges and sentenced to life in prison.

Bombs are a key Part of this effort

The USA PATRIOT Act

On October 26, 2001, President George W. Bush signed into law the Uniting and Strengthening America by Providing Appropriate Tools Required to Intercept and Obstruct Terrorism (USA PATRIOT) Act, giving police unprecedented ability to search, seize, detain, or eavesdrop in their pursuit of possible terrorists. The law expands the FBI's wiretapping and electronic surveillance authority and allows nationwide jurisdiction for search warrants and electronic surveillance devices, including legal expansion of those devices to email and the Internet. The USA PATRIOT Act significantly improves the nation's counterterrorism efforts by:

- Allowing investigators to use the tools already available to investigate organized crime and drug trafficking.
- Facilitating information sharing and cooperation among government agencies so that they can better "connect the dots."
- Updating the law to reflect new technologies and new threats.
- Increasing the penalties for those who commit or support terrorist crimes.

Further, the USA PATRIOT Act makes it a federal crime to commit an act of terrorism against a mass transit system.

Increased Border Security

Enhancing security at our nation's borders is a fundamental step in keeping our citizenry safe. The DHS's United States Visitor and Immigrant Status Indicator Technology Program (US-VISIT) is an integrated, automated, biometric entry–exit system that records the arrival and departure of certain aliens (an *alien* is defined as any person not a citizen or national of the United States); conducts certain immigrations violation, criminal, and terrorist checks on aliens; and compares biometric identifiers (digital fingerprints and a photograph) to those collected on previous encounters to verify identity. The procedure applies to all non-U.S. citizens except Canadians applying for admission to the United States for business or pleasure (DHS, 2009). The program was implemented in January 2004 at 115 airports and 14 seaports and has been expanded to all land points of entry as well.

The National Incident Management System

The National Incident Management System (NIMS) was implemented in 2004 and revised in 2008. In 2016, as this text goes to print, NIMS was undergoing another revision. NIMS provides a systematic, proactive approach to guide departments and agencies at all levels of government, nongovernmental organizations, and the private sector to work seamlessly to prevent, protect against, respond to, recover from, and mitigate the effects of incidents, regardless of cause, size, location, or complexity, in order to reduce the loss of life and property and harm to the environment (FEMA, 2008).

Although the federal government has increased its efforts in the area of terrorism prevention and response, a large degree of responsibility for responding to threats of terrorism rests at the local level.

THE LOCAL POLICE RESPONSE TO TERRORISM: HOMETOWN SECURITY

The first line of defense against terrorism is the patrol officer in the field. State and local law enforcement agencies can and must play a vital role in the investigation and prevention of future terrorist attacks. Across the United States, there are nearly 17,985 state and local law enforcement agencies (U.S. Census Bureau, 2012). These agencies, and the 765,237 officers they employ, daily patrol our state highways and the streets of our cities and towns and, as a result, have an intimate knowledge of the communities they serve and have developed close relationships with the citizens they protect.

The IACP project *Taking Command* report, *From Hometown Security to Homeland Security* (IACP, 2005, p. 2), suggests that our nation's current homeland security strategy "is handicapped by a fundamental flaw. It does not sufficiently incorporate the advice, expertise, or consent of public safety organizations at state, tribal, or local levels." The IACP has identified five key principles that should form the basis for a national homeland security strategy (IACP, 2005, pp. 3–7):

1. All terrorism is local.
2. Prevention is paramount.
3. Hometown security is homeland security.
4. Homeland security strategies must be coordinated nationally, not federally.
5. Bottom-up engineering; the diversity of the state, tribal, and local public safety community; and noncompetitive collaboration are vital.

A study conducted by Rowan University found that one of the most significant changes in policing since September 11 may be how the nation's lowest-ranking officers approach their daily patrols. The study found that street officers, who see themselves as first responders, also recognize that they would be the ones most likely to be on the front lines of a terrorist attack. Therefore, they pay attention to things they did not used to pay attention to (Newswise, 2006).

Law enforcement officers must be aware of the possibility for contact with terrorists at any time during their normal course of duty. Following the 9/11 attacks, it was discovered that several of the hijackers had had contact with police officers in various parts of the country in the days and weeks leading up to the attack:

- September 9, 2001—Ziad Jarrah, hijacker of the plane that crashed in Shanksville, Pennsylvania, was stopped by police in Maryland for speeding. He was driving 90 mph in a 65-mph zone. He was issued a ticket and released.
- August 2001—Hani Hanjour, who hijacked and piloted the plane that crashed into the Pentagon, killing 289 persons, was stopped by police in Arlington, Virginia. He was issued a ticket for speeding and released. He paid the ticket, so he would not have to show up in court.

- April 2001—Mohammed Atta, who hijacked and piloted the plane that crashed into the north tower of the World Trade Center, was stopped in Tamarac, Florida, for driving without a valid license and issued a ticket. He did not pay the ticket, so an arrest warrant was issued. A few weeks later, he was stopped for speeding but let go because police did not know about the warrant.

This final incident underscores the critical importance not only of gathering information but also of sharing intelligence and data with the larger law enforcement community.

INFORMATION GATHERING AND INTELLIGENCE SHARING

It is not sufficient to simply gather data. Data must be analyzed and shared systematically with neighboring law enforcement agencies and also different levels of law enforcement (i.e., local, state, and federal) and other institutions, such as schools, hospitals, city departments, and motor vehicle divisions.

A distinction is made between *information* and *intelligence,* with intelligence broadening to become organized information: "Intelligence has come to mean information that has not only been selected and collected, but also analyzed, evaluated, and distributed to meet the unique policymaking needs of one particular enterprise" (Loyka et al., 2005, p. 7).

The application of such information in efforts to combat terrorism can be visualized as an intelligence cycle (Figure 15.3). In a threat-driven environment, *intelligence requirements*—identified information needs, or what

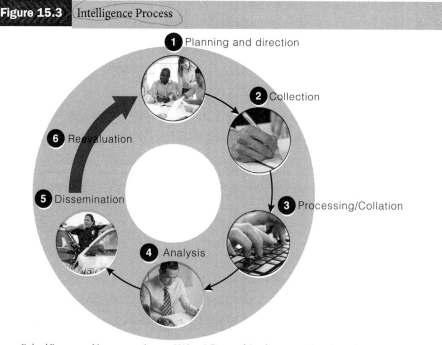

Figure 15.3 Intelligence Process

1. Planning and direction
2. Collection
3. Processing/Collation
4. Analysis
5. Dissemination
6. Reevaluation

Source: Federal Emergency Management Agency, 2010, p. 9. Retrieved October 31, 2016 from http://www.fema.gov/pdf/about/divisions/npd/cpg_502_eoc-fusion_final_7_20_2010.pdf

Pressmaster/Shutterstock.com; Iancu Cristian/Shutterstock.com; Zadorozhnyi Viktor/Shutterstock.com; Kaikoro/Shutterstock.com; Hill Street Studios/AGE Fotostock

This step is not in 15.3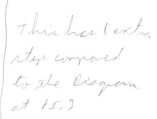

This has 1 extra step compared to the diagram at 15.3

must be known to safeguard the nation—are what drive investigations (Loyka et al., 2005, p. 35). Intelligence requirements are established by the Director of Central Intelligence under the guidance of the president and the National and Homeland Security Advisors. The attorney general and the director of the FBI also participate in the formulation of national intelligence requirements.

The second step in the intelligence cycle is *planning and direction,* a function of the FBI. Third is the *collection of raw information* from local, state, and federal investigations. Fourth is *processing and exploitation* of the raw information—that is, converting the collected information to a form usable for analysis. Fifth is *analysis and production,* converting the raw information into intelligence. The final step is *dissemination,* which leads back to refinement of intelligence requirements.

Loyka et al. (2005, p. 36) explain: "The Intelligence Cycle is just that, a continuing cycle, which overlaps and drives each of its functions and in turn, drives the investigative mission. This cycle or process is used across all programs—Counterterrorism, Counterintelligence, Cyber, and Criminal—to counter all threats."

Local and state law enforcement agencies are critical to the third step in the intelligence cycle and benefit from the sixth step as well. Many of the day-to-day duties of local law enforcement officers bring them into proximity with sources of information about terrorism. Patrol operations, especially traffic officers, properly trained in what to look for and what questions to ask when interacting with citizens, can be a tremendous source of intelligence, not only for local investigators but also for their state and federal homeland security counterparts.

TECHNOLOGY IN COMMUNITY POLICING

THE DOMAIN AWARENESS SYSTEM

The New York City Police Department (NYPD) has partnered with Microsoft Corporation to develop the Domain Awareness System (DAS), a sophisticated crime-prevention and counter-terrorism tool that aggregates and analyzes, in real time, information collected from the city's more than 3,000 closed-circuit surveillance cameras, license-plate readers, 911 calls, sensors, and other law enforcement databases. The system also archives information, allowing investigators and analysts to go back in time and track the movement of a suspect or vehicle before a particular event occurred. This technology provides law enforcement officers and investigators, public safety administrators, and intelligence analysts with a comprehensive view of criminal activity and potential threats. For example, DAS can notify analysts of suspicious packages or vehicles, and data collected can allow NYPD investigators to actively search for suspects by mapping their criminal history geospatially and chronologically, thus revealing patterns to their behavior. Police Commissioner Raymond Kelly notes: "The system is a transformative tool because it was created by police officers for police officers." And although the system is expected to cost the city $30–40 million, it also has the potential to generate revenue—because DAS was built by NYPD in partnership with Microsoft, sale of the technology to other jurisdictions will bring in revenue to help New York fund more crime prevention and counterterrorism efforts.

Source: Evans, B. (2012, August 12). *New York City Police Department and Microsoft Partner to Bring Real-Time Crime Prevention and Counterterrorism Technology Solution to Global Law Enforcement Agencies.* Redmond, WA: Microsoft News Center. Retrieved October 31, 2016 from http://www.microsoft.com/en-us/news/Press/2012/Aug12/08-08NYPDPR.aspx

The Regional Information Sharing Systems

The Regional Information Sharing Systems (RISS) program supports federal, state, and local law enforcement efforts to combat criminal activity, including terrorism. Six regional RISS intelligence centers provide investigative support services to law enforcement agencies across the nation. The RISS Program is the only multijurisdictional criminal intelligence system operated by and for state and local law enforcement agencies. The overall goal of the RISS Program is to enhance the ability of state and local criminal justice agencies to identify, target, and remove criminal conspiracies and activities spanning jurisdictional boundaries (RISS, 2015).

The National Criminal Intelligence Sharing Plan

Limitations on information sharing have caused tensions in the past because often information received by the FBI is classified. Rules of federal procedure and constraints associated with grand jury classified material also limit how much information can be shared.

A subtitle of the Homeland Security Act of 2002, called the Homeland Security Information Sharing Act, required the president to develop new procedures for sharing classified information, as well as unclassified but otherwise sensitive information, with state and local police. This charge was fulfilled in May 2002 when the IACP, the Department of Justice, the FBI, the DHS, and other representatives of the federal, state, tribal, and local law enforcement communities endorsed *The National Criminal Intelligence Sharing Plan* (NCISP). Originally published in 2003, this report was the first version of a plan intended to be a "living document" and periodically updated. The most recent update available was in 2013. Those charged with developing and implementing the plan will continue to solicit the involvement of the law enforcement and intelligence communities, national organizations and other government and public safety entities, in order to ensure that the plan is responsive to their needs for information and intelligence development and sharing.

Addressing Obstacles to Intelligence Sharing

Although progress has been made, obstacles persist to hamper the fluid exchange of intelligence. Two barriers to effective exchange of intelligence are lack of deconfliction protocols and interoperability issues. Polisar (2004, p. 8) asserts: "For far too long efforts to combat crime and terrorism have been handicapped by jurisdictional squabbles and archaic rules that prevented us from forging cooperative working relationships with our counterparts in local, regional, tribal, and federal law enforcement. This must end." The mass shooting at Fort Hood provided a more recent example of what can occur when information sharing is insufficient. On March 10, 2011, Senator Joseph Lieberman, who was chairing a Congressional Hearing of the Senate Homeland Security and Governmental Affairs Committee, stated: "This Committee's recent report on the Fort Hood attack shows that information sharing within and across agencies is nonetheless still not all it should be. And that allowed in that a case a ticking time bomb, namely Major Nidal

Hasan, now accused of killing 13 and wounding 32 others at Fort Hood, to radicalize right under the noses of the Department of Defense and the FBI. So we need to continue improving our information sharing strategies" (CQ Transcriptions, 2011).

A local networking module developed between local, state, and federal law enforcement agencies is the most effective way to discuss and share investigative and enforcement endeavors to combat terrorism. This networking module approach avoids compromising existing investigations or conducting conflicting cases and should have a built-in **deconfliction** protocol, which essentially means guidelines to avoid conflict. Deconfliction can be applied to declassified and confidential investigations (Savelli, 2004).

The 9/11 attacks, besides bringing attention to defective or ineffective routes of interagency communication, highlighted the importance of communications. **Interoperability** is the compatibility of communication systems such as emergency medical services (EMS), fire and rescue, and police, and across levels of government. The 9/11 Commission cited the inability to communicate as a critical failure on September 11 and stated that compatible and adequate communications among public safety organizations at the local, state, and federal levels remain a problem (9/11 Commission 2004, p. 397). The commission's recommendations were finally adopted in August 2007, almost 6 years after the attacks of September 11.

Hindsight reveals that many clues existed prior to the attack on September 11, but they were fragmented and never put together; thus, like a jigsaw puzzle with pieces scattered, the true scope of the picture went unrealized until it was too late. Seemingly insignificant information may be the one missing piece to put together an impending terrorist attack. Federal efforts rely on information from state and local officers. Local officers, in turn, will rely on citizen information and the networks formed through community policing.

deconfliction
Protocol or guidelines to avoid conflict.

interoperability
The compatibility of communication systems such as EMS, fire and rescue, and police, and across levels of government.

LO6
The keys to combating terrorism lie with the local police and the intelligence they can provide to federal authorities; how readily information is shared between agencies at different levels; and the interoperability of communications systems should an attack occur.

IDEAS **IN PRACTICE**   LAPD MODEL FOR CRIME REDUCTION AND COUNTERTERRORISM

CompStat, Operation Archangel, and the Critical Incident Management Bureau (CIMB)

In Los Angeles, Police Chief William Bratton, former New York City police commissioner and one of the driving forces behind the implementation of CompStat at the New York Police Department (NYPD), is in the process of installing CompStat at the Los Angeles Police Department (LAPD) to fully integrate criminal and terrorism-related intelligence collection and sharing. According to the LAPD Plan of Action released in October 2004: "Improved crime-fighting and counterterrorism tools are the LAPD's top priority for technology, along with data integration, and CompStat software is the vehicle to deliver such tools. For the first time in the nation, new CompStat technology will allow a multi-jurisdictional CompStat approach to integrate crime information and counterterrorism-related information collected, analyzed, and used by the LAPD to reduce crime in the region and to prevent terrorism incidents" (Bratton, 2006, p. 2).

The LAPD is not only using CompStat to accomplish its crime-reduction and counterterrorism mission—an all-hazards approach that maximizes the effectiveness of scarce resources—but will also include a "new automated community policing problem-solving

(Continues)

component as a strategic crime management tool." This will give officers in the field timely access to crime data and automate the inputting of crime locations, helping beat officers develop their own successful crime-reduction strategies.

To improve its ability to identify and protect critical infrastructure, the LAPD has also launched Operation Archangel, a partnership between the City and County of Los Angeles, the California Department of Homeland Security, and the U.S. Department of Homeland Security. Archangel is a proactive program used by the police to identify critical infrastructure locations in Los Angeles and develop a multiagency response. Archangel is geared toward facilitating the management of information and resources for the prevention, deterrence, response, and mitigation of major critical incidents. Again, at the heart of Archangel is a database-management tool that will "provide an automated system to assess threats and vulnerabilities to infrastructure, as well as the defenses available. The system will point out everything a responder would need to know before approaching a building, utility, or reservoir in an emergency."

The LAPD works closely in consultation with the owners and operators of critical infrastructure sites, who are asked to contribute detailed and up-to-date infrastructure information to Archangel, including floor plans, HVAC systems, entrances and exits, security centers, and fire-control stations. Archangel has been held up as a "proving ground for best practices as developed by the LAPD in conjunction with the Department of Homeland Security."

The LAPD has also taken the important step of institutionalizing its counterterrorism efforts through the creation of the Critical Incident Management Bureau (CIMB), which identifies critical infrastructure, coordinates security with private-sector partners,

and coordinates applications for homeland security grants to fund training, technology, and intelligence-gathering programs at the LAPD. The CIMB has established a forward, proactive counterterrorism posture for the LAPD and uses its officers to network throughout the public and private sectors in Los Angeles to collect intelligence and preemptively disrupt potential terrorist attacks.

Finally, the CIMB has not been hesitant to share its knowledge and expertise with private-sector partners. The CIMB has developed and disseminated al Qaeda countersurveillance training not only for selected LAPD personnel but private security officers at critical infrastructure sites. This training allows police and private security officers to identify terrorists as they conduct surveillance under the Safe Cities Project on prospective targets. This training has been carefully based on actual training that al Qaeda target teams received in the training camps in Afghanistan. This not only improves the effectiveness of private security officers but also improves their ability to pass credible intelligence to LAPD officers.

The LAPD, under the leadership of Chief Bratton, is dedicated to building a world-class counterterrorism capability by building on the proven crime-fighting success of problem-solving policing, CompStat information technology, and the relentless focus of the department on updating its knowledge of terrorist methods and planning. Problem-solving policing is the backbone that allows the LAPD and the CIMB to aggressively identify and prosecute potential terrorism precursor crimes and maximize the department's ability to disrupt and interdict terrorists without compromising its traditional crime-fighting mission.

Source: Reprinted by permission of the Manhattan Institute.

COMMUNITY POLICING AND THE WAR ON TERRORISM

The September 11 attacks undoubtedly shifted the priorities of policing. Law enforcement agencies must not, however, let the "war on terrorism" tempt them into abandoning or diminishing community policing efforts in favor of a return to the traditional model of policing with its paramilitary emphasis: "To do so would not only be counterproductive but would also arrest the progress policing has made over recent decades which has taken it to the high level of societal acceptance it now enjoys" (Murray, 2005, p. 347). In noting how the community policing philosophy can dovetail with homeland security efforts, Docobo (2005) asserts:

Both neighborhood crime and terrorism threaten the quality of life in a community and exploit the fear they create. Despite creative ways to stretch public safety budgets, local law enforcement cannot sustain two separate missions of traditional policing and terrorism prevention. Community policing and homeland security can share the same goals and strategies. Creating external partnerships, citizen involvement, problem solving, and transforming the organization to take on a new mission are all key elements of community policing and should be part of a comprehensive homeland security strategy. The lesson learned from fighting traditional crime is that prevention is the most effective approach in dealing with crime, fear, and social disorder. Fighting terrorism is no different.

A quote from former CIA director James Woolsey during his testimony before Congress in 2004 provides but one example of the invaluable role local police play in counterterrorism efforts: "Only an effective local police establishment that has the confidence of citizens is going to be likely to hear from, say, a local merchant in a part of town containing a number of new immigrants that a group of young men from abroad have recently moved into a nearby apartment and are acting suspiciously. Local police are best equipped to understand how to protect citizens' liberties and obtain such leads legally" (Newman & Clarke, 2008, p. 80).

The successful detection and prevention of terrorism depends on information, and a community–police relationship based on mutual trust is most likely to uncover matters helpful in identifying prospective terrorists. Chapman (2008) describes the importance of community partnerships in building trust and opening lines of communication in the effort to thwart terrorism: "Just as street-level knowledge is important to breaking up narcotics activities in a neighborhood, community partnerships and trusting relationships will inspire the confidence of citizens to pass along information that can help to uncover terrorist individuals or cells."

Risk Assessment and Identifying Potential Terrorist Targets

Potential terrorist targets might be a transit system hub, a chemical storage warehouse, or high-level government officials' residences. Although jurisdictions necessarily focus efforts on protecting logical, high-profile targets for terrorist attacks, soft targets should not be overlooked. Soft targets, those that are relatively unguarded or difficult to guard, include shopping malls, subways, trains, sporting stadiums, theaters, schools, hospitals, restaurants, entertainment parks, compressed gas and oil storage areas, chemical plants, pharmaceutical companies, and many others (Hanson, 2005).

Being Proactive

As with gangs, domestic violence, and other areas of concern to community policing, a proactive approach to terrorism is advocated: "Securing the homeland begins at the local level and 'first responders' must see themselves in a more proactive role as 'first preventers'" (Doherty & Hibbard, 2006, p. 78). Yet most of the dialogue has focused on efforts to share intelligence at the federal level, which has marginalized those assets consistently identified by research as being the most effective at detecting and interrupting terrorist plots: local police and private citizens (Ubinas, 2015). One study that looked at all publicly reported terrorist plots against U.S. targets found that, between 1999 and 2009, initial tips came from local police or the public more than 80 percent of the time, underscoring the reality that the first line of defense in detecting terrorist activity is law enforcement working in cooperation with the public. Emphasizing the pervasive of local law enforcement in communities throughout the country, Ubinas (2015) asserts: "The cop on the beat, the deputy on patrol or the trooper covering his usual assignment are in the neighborhoods and "outposts of society" where terrorists hide, plan and strike, and are more naturally sensitized to detect anomalies and act in real time to prevent an attack."

Success in terrorism prevention might be enhanced by cultivating numerous community information sources such as these (Doherty & Hibbard, 2006):

- Neighborhood Watch
- Hotels
- Real estate agents
- Storage facilities
- Religious groups
- Fraternal, social, and civic clubs
- Colleges and universities
- Printing shops
- Business managers
- Transportation centers and tourist attractions
- Major industrial enterprises
- Schools
- Health care providers
- Bar and liquor stores
- Inspectors and code enforcers
- Facility licenses
- Licenses and permits
- Delivery services
- Department of public works employees and refuse haulers
- Housing managers
- Meter readers
- Automobile and truck drivers
- Taxi and delivery drivers

The extent of the preceding list illustrates how broad in scope a community's information network can be for law enforcement officers faced with tackling terrorism, and it makes clear that the police are most certainly not "in this alone."

Chapter 15: Understanding and Preventing Terrorism **459**

CRUCIAL COLLABORATIONS AND PARTNERSHIPS TO PREVENT TERRORISM

The importance of partnerships between law enforcement agencies at all levels cannot be overstated as it applies to the war on terrorism. However, although these partnerships are obviously critical, broader partnerships are needed.

One of the key principles in the IACP's guide, *Using Community Policing to Counter Violent Extremism*, is that law enforcement should partner with public and private stakeholders—other criminal justice agencies, government services, nonprofits, faith- and community-based organizations, private companies, the media, and citizens themselves—to pool resources and accomplish what individual community members, organizations, or law enforcement agencies could not achieve alone.

Private security, a traditionally underutilized resource by law enforcement, can be an important partner in the war against terrorism. The 9/11 Commission confirmed just how dependent the nation is on private security, noting that the private sector owns and protects about 85 percent of the nation's infrastructure—buildings, power plants, utilities, transportation systems, and communications networks. The number of people employed in private security in the United States is estimated to be at least 2 million people—more than three times the number employed by public law enforcement (ASIS International, 2014). The Law Enforcement–Private Security Consortium (2009, p. 10) notes:

> Viewing private security as a force multiplier does not mean ignoring the differences between police and private security in legal authority, training, or accountability. Rather, it acknowledges the following:
>
>> Private security works in certain critical areas that law enforcement simply cannot cover because it lacks the human resources, mandate, or technology. Private security is a growth industry, whereas the number of sworn local and state law enforcement officers is not projected to grow significantly in the future.

A national summit held in January 2004 by the IACP was specifically designed to bring law enforcement and private security professionals together to build partnerships in a unified response to terrorism.

The American Society for Industrial Security (ASIS), which was founded in 1955 and officially changed its name to *ASIS* International in 2002, has also advocated for partnerships between public police and private security. Their latest initiative, Operation Partnership, is premised on the belief that public law enforcement and private security can do their jobs more effectively and efficiently through successful collaboration. Because both entities share the same mission—crime prevention through mitigation, detection, investigation, apprehension, and prosecution of those who would commit crimes—teaming up in the fight against terrorism is a natural extension of this shared mission. ASIS International highlights specific ways in which private security can be a force multiplier for law enforcement's efforts to detect terrorist activities in their communities (ASIS International, 2014, p. 11):

- Terrorist attacks do not occur in a vacuum. They require planning and preparation, such as the acquisition of certain materials or training in targeted activities. Terrorist operatives will try to obtain these in the private sector.

- Terrorists may portray themselves as legitimate customers in order to purchase or lease certain materials or equipment, to undergo certain formalized training to acquire important skills or licenses, may simply steal certain types of vehicles, equipment, or materials from the inventory of legitimate businesses.

- Through partnerships, business owners, operators and their employees may apply their particular business and industry knowledge and experience against each customer transaction or encounter to discern anything unusual or suspicious and to report such instances to authorities.

Tapping citizens' patriotism and inclination to voluntarily serve their community has, however, become more challenging as time has passed. In this regard, the very success of law enforcement in preventing further terrorist incidents on U.S. soil has, to some degree, worked against it. Many Americans have forgotten the shock, anger, and raw fear they felt on those days, weeks, and even months following September 11. Complacency has returned. In addition, some citizens have grown critical of a government they contend is too willing to infringe on individuals' civil rights in its overzealous attempt to keep Americans safe from terrorists. This is one of the basic concerns surrounding the war on terrorism. Nonetheless, citizens are an important force multiplier:

> They can help identify, prevent, and eliminate terrorist ideologies and behaviors before violence occurs. The importance of individual community members is embodied in the Nationwide Suspicious Activity Reporting (SAR) Initiative (NSI), which encourages individuals to take an active role in reporting any type of suspicious or criminal activity to authorities. During his 2011 State of the Union address, President Barack Obama called on American law enforcement and their communities to continue to work together to stop homegrown violent extremists before their plans become operational (International Association of Chiefs of Police, 2014, p. 2).

One way to reach citizens is through the media. Local media and their national affiliates are valuable stakeholders in the effort to combat violent extremism and can have an important impact on the public's perceptions of the police, which can, in turn, influence whether members of the community chose to actively engage with police as the "eyes and ears" of the neighborhoods. The media can increase public awareness of antiterrorism initiatives by covering police press conferences and events cosponsored by law enforcement and the community, which can help build familiarity and comfort among the jurisdiction's residents and increase the likelihood that they will attend future events and participate in community engagement efforts with the police (IACP, 2014).

One concern about the media involves the possible exploitation of this forum by terrorists looking to "get the word out." In this regard, the media can be a positive or negative influence on efforts to combat terrorism. Indeed, as the late Richard Clutterbuck, economics professor and expert on political violence, once observed, the media are like a loaded gun lying on the street—the first person to pick it up gets to decide how to use it. Governments try to use the media as their loaded gun by embedding reporters in active war zones, and terrorists use the media to justify their violent acts and spread their message: "One Algerian terrorist once said he would rather kill one victim in front of a news camera than one hundred in the desert where the world would not see them. His point should be noted: Modern terrorism is a media phenomenon" (White, 2012, p. 104). Certainly, without the 24-hour media coverage of the events of September 11 and the continuous stream of graphic visuals that poured into U.S. homes, the impact of that horrific attack would not have been so profound.

In exploring the dynamics of the relationship between Western media and terrorism, Rivera (2016) suggests that the intense coverage by the media of such events empowers terrorists, heightening their feelings of accomplishment and influence, which can be an especially effective tactic against Westerners, given the relative rarity of these acts in some locations of the world. A study by Sean Darling-Hammond, a sociologist and lawyer, examined the English media coverage of the more than 300 reported incidents of terrorism that occurred during 2015. Among his findings was that in the 2 months following terrorist attacks in the cities of Baghdad, Beirut, and Paris, there were 392 articles about the Baghdad attack; 1,292 articles about the Beirut attack; and more than 21,000 about the Paris attack: "The wars and turmoil in the Middle East, along with periodic massacres taking place in other of the world's hotspots, have caused a "horror fatigue" in our media when it comes to these regions. Terrorist acts in Western Europe and North America are still a relatively unusual occurrence, so broadcasters and publications deploy the bulk of their resources to cover these tragedies. The media also know that its viewers and readers are more likely to relate and identify with, to put it plainly, victims who look more like them" (Rivera, 2016).

White (2012, p. 120) raises the question of the **contagion effect**—that is, the coverage of terrorism inspires more terrorism. It is, in effect, contagious. This controversial issue leads to discussions about censorship in the war on terrorism, an idea to which the media are, not surprisingly, fundamentally opposed.

contagion effect
The media coverage of terrorism inspires more terrorism.

Law enforcement agencies attempting to engage the community in a collective effort to fight terrorism must, at some level, be aware of the negative undercurrent that exists among segments of society regarding the actions of the government, perpetuated in large part by the media.

CONCERNS RELATED TO THE WAR ON TERRORISM

After the bombings on the London transit system in 2005, the NYPD took the unprecedented step of making random checks of bags and backpacks at subway stations, buses, and commuter rail lines. The police department announced its intentions to the public a day in advance.

L07

Two concerns related to the "war on terrorism" are that civil liberties may be jeopardized and that people of Middle Eastern descent may be discriminated against or become victims of hate crimes.

Concern for Civil Rights

The first guiding principle of the DHS is to protect civil rights and civil liberties:

> We will defend America while protecting the freedoms that define America. Our strategies and actions will be consistent with the individual rights and liberties enshrined by our Constitution and the Rule of Law. While we seek to improve the way we collect and share information about terrorists, we will nevertheless be vigilant in respecting the confidentiality and protecting the privacy of our citizens. We are committed to securing our nation while protecting civil rights and civil liberties. (DHS, 2004, p. 6)

Civil libertarians are concerned, however, that valued American freedoms are being sacrificed in the interest of national safety. For example, the Justice Department has issued a new regulation giving itself the authority to monitor inmate–attorney communications if "reasonable suspicion" exists that inmates are using such communications to further or facilitate acts of terrorism. However, criminal defense lawyers and members of the American Civil Liberties Union (ACLU) have protested the regulation, saying it effectively eliminates the Sixth Amendment right to counsel because, under codes of professional responsibility, attorneys cannot communicate with clients if confidentiality is not assured. The ACLU has vowed to monitor police actions closely to see that freedoms protected under the Constitution are not jeopardized.

Retaliation or Discrimination against People of Middle Eastern Descent

Another concern is that some Americans may retaliate against innocent people of Middle Eastern descent, many of whom were either born in the United States or are naturalized citizens. In fact, such injustices have already occurred. Davies and Murphy (2004, p. 1), note: "Within hours of the Twin Towers' collapse and the attack on the Pentagon, U.S. residents and visitors, particularly Arabs, Muslims, and Sikhs, were harassed or attacked because they shared—or were perceived to share—the terrorists' national background or religion. ... Law enforcement's challenge since then has been to maintain an appropriate balance between the security interests of our country and the constitutional rights of every American." We must remember the Japanese internment camps during World War II and make sure we do not repeat that mistake.

A comprehensive public opinion poll conducted by the Pew Research Center in the summer of 2011, nearly 10 years after the 9/11 attacks, found no indication of an increased sense of alienation among Muslim Americans but did find that the vast majority of Muslim Americans are concerned about Islamic extremism, both within the United States and abroad; Muslims in the United States reject extremism by much larger margins than most other Muslim populations around the world; and an increasing number of Muslim Americans view U.S. efforts to combat efforts as being sincere (Pew Research Center, 2011).

A survey of policing in Arab American communities after September 11 found the following (Henderson, Ortiz, Sugie, & Miller, 2008, pp. 1–2):

> Surveys in 16 sites across the country where Arab Americans were geographically concentrated found that many Arab American respondents were troubled by increased government scrutiny of their communities following 9/11. Some reported they were more afraid of law enforcement agencies, particularly Federal agencies, than they were of being victims of hate crimes. They specifically mentioned fears about immigration enforcement, surveillance of their activities, and racial profiling.
>
> After September 11, law enforcement agencies on both the local and federal levels experienced great pressure to prevent further attacks. Some researchers and law enforcement officials suggested that local law enforcement agencies should play a greater role in intelligence-gathering and immigration enforcement. In addition, the FBI began to stress counterterrorism efforts, with Joint Terrorism Task Forces working in concert with local law enforcement agencies. Often, these efforts focused on Arab American communities.
>
> At the same time, local law enforcement agencies were called on to protect the Arab American community. After the attacks, some people of Arab descent said they experienced increased levels of harassment, ranging from workplace discrimination to verbal abuse and vandalism to severe hate crimes such as assault and homicide. To ensure the safety of Arab Americans, some local law enforcement agencies felt it necessary to step up their outreach efforts.
>
> Finally, some Arab Americans and law enforcement officers said that public suspicion of Arab Americans had led to an increase in false reporting. As one FBI special agent said, "The general public calls in some ridiculous stuff—it's really guilt by being Muslim." Because officers have to look into all reports, false reporting can be a significant strain on law enforcement agencies.
>
> Arab American communities have been deeply affected by the events of September 11 in other ways. Before the attacks, many Arab Americans were well assimilated into the American mainstream. But after September 11, some members of Arab American communities came to believe that many of their fellow citizens—not to mention some in the media and government—regarded them with suspicion. Although Arab Americans report a fair amount of goodwill towards local law enforcement agencies, some Arab Americans said these developments have strained relations between their communities and those agencies.

The study (2008, p. 2) identified four obstacles to improved relations between police and Arab American communities. One barrier is a persistent mutual mistrust; a second is police agencies' lack of knowledge about and sensitivity to the culture and religion of Arab Americans. The two other barriers are language differences and Arab American concerns about immigration status and deportation.

The study—which included surveys of local law enforcement officers and FBI agents in local field offices at each site—also produced some recommendations for ways to improve relations between Arab American communities and local law enforcement agencies and officers. Many of the recommendations reflect the priorities and practices of community policing. Recommendations include the creation of a police–community liaison position within local police departments, the recruitment of police officers from Arab American communities, and the training of officers in the cultural and religious values of Arab American communities. Such training should include guidance on how to deal with Arab Americans' mistrust of law enforcement officers (Henderson et al., 2008).

Local law enforcement can take these steps to prevent racial profiling and/ or discrimination against Arab Americans (Henderson, Ortiz, Sugie, & Miller, 2006):

- Increase communication and dialogue
- Develop person-to-person contact
- Provide cultural awareness training
- Identify community needs
- Create a community liaison position to work with the Arab American community
- Recruit more Arab Americans into law enforcement

Strategies for recruiting more Arab Americans into law enforcement include focusing on young people, translating recruitment materials into Arabic, providing incentives for Arabic-speaking officers, and expediting citizenship for recruits of Arab descent.

A FINAL CONSIDERATION

Research suggests that balancing traditional crime fighting and the new challenge of counterterrorism should not be a tremendous either/or proposition, as the philosophical principles governing each task complement each other and offer considerable overlap in policing's public safety mandate:

> As homeland security has gained contemporary recognition in an atmosphere of terrorism and fear, community policing has increasingly been relegated to far lesser importance by local, state, and federal organizations. However, through examining these two strategies, evidence suggests that they share a number of overlapping principles. Furthermore, community policing has been shown to satisfy the central concepts found within homeland security; namely, a) extensive information gathering, b) collaboration with local, federal, and state agencies, c) community involvement, and d) the formation of inter-agency cooperation. The value of community policing is revealed in the ability of law enforcement agencies, of varying styles and sizes, to adapt to community realities. Policy makers at each level of government will achieve better terrorism prevention and response when they wholly adhere to integrating the community policing philosophy into the homeland security strategy (Friedmann & Cannon, 2007, p. 18).

SUMMARY

The threat of terrorism has become a reality in America. Common elements in definitions of terrorism include (1) systematic use of physical violence—actual or threatened, (2) against noncombatants, (3) but with an audience broader than the immediate victims in mind, (4) to create a general climate of fear in a target population, and (5) to cause political and/or social change. Most terrorist acts result from dissatisfaction with a religious, political, or social system or policy and frustration resulting from an inability to change it through acceptable, nonviolent means.

The FBI categorizes terrorism as either international or domestic terrorism. Terrorism also includes acts by homegrown violent extremists (HVEs) and "lone wolf" attackers. Terrorists may use arson; explosives and bombs; weapons of mass destruction (biological, chemical, or nuclear agents); and technology. The majority of terrorism attacks are carried out by bombings and explosions. The second most common method is armed attacks.

As a result of September 11, the Department of Homeland Security was established, reorganizing the departments of the federal government. At the federal level, the FBI is the lead agency for responding to acts of domestic terrorism. The Federal Emergency Management Agency (FEMA) is the lead agency for consequence management (after an attack).

The first line of defense against terrorism is the patrol officer in the field. The keys to combating terrorism lie with the local police and the intelligence they can provide to federal authorities; how readily information is shared between agencies at different levels; and the interoperability of communications systems should an attack occur.

Two concerns related to the "war on terrorism" are that civil liberties may be jeopardized and that people of Middle Eastern descent may be discriminated against or become victims of hate crimes.

DISCUSSION QUESTIONS

1. Discuss the aphorism: "One man's terrorist is another man's freedom fighter." What kinds of examples can you think of that confirm this statement?

2. What can local law enforcement agencies do to prevent terrorism? What about communities? Will community partnerships have any effect on terrorism? How realistic do you think it is that any of these will affect terrorism?

3. Why does information sharing between government agencies seem like something they cannot or will not do, in spite of what's at stake?

4. Why was the Department of Homeland Security created? What is its purpose?

5. Police and private security rarely, if ever, collaborate. Why do you think this is so?

6. Discuss what is controversial about the USA PATRIOT Act. How did it change the government's ability to conduct investigations?

7. Is it *profiling* to focus security efforts on those who appear to be Middle Eastern or Arab?

8. Should the media report on terrorism events? How does media coverage affect terrorists?

9. The 9/11 Commission made recommendations to the government that would enhance safety for Americans. Why do you think that few of their recommendations have been adopted?

10. Do you think America's focus on fighting terrorism jeopardizes the progress of the community policing philosophy?

The Future of Community Policing

Following the incidents in Ferguson, Missouri, and Baltimore, Maryland, the social movement of Black Lives Matter, and the increased persistence of communities to create more transparency between police departments and citizens, the future of community policing faces considerable challenges. Many polls have found that confidence in police departments to meet the needs and desires of citizens as a top priority is at an all-time low. Other polls have found that distrust for police, especially in low-income areas, is at an all-time high.

However, an innovative approach by the Philadelphia Police Department (PPD) and the Philadelphia City Council has allowed for the rebirth of community policing within the city. In an attempt to earn back the trust of citizens, while at the same improving their quality of life, the city has moved to decriminalize public nuisance offenses. Officers are now able to use discretion when dealing with those who commit crimes such as disorderly conduct, public drunkenness, and vagrancy—offenses that once led to jail time—having the option to fine the offender instead of arresting him or her. Since the majority of the quality-of-life (nuisance) crimes have statistically been linked to low-income populations and, specially, people of color, the hope is that this "second chance" approach will have multiple positive results. For example, while an obvious objective of the program is an increased level of trust among police and citizens, a second objective is the reduction in the number of incarcerated individuals as a result of the program. If 5, 10, or 15 thousand fewer people are put in jail each year, the cost to the city and taxpayers is reduced, thus leaving more money for primary prevention programs, such as education and job training for the citizens. This further establishes the true essence of community policing. Substituting community programs for community imprisonment has the potential to deliver long-lasting benefits to all parties involved.

The Center on Media, Crime, and Justice spoke with the members of the PPD to gain their opinion on the changing definition of community policing. "We're telling officers that they can't arrest their way out of every problem," said Capt.

Francis Healy, legal adviser to Philadelphia Police Commissioner Richard Ross, who is overseeing the changes. "The future of community policing is happening here in Philadelphia." Philadelphia is no stranger to community policing strategies. Traditional strategies, such as bicycle and foot patrols to increase presence and community interaction, have been vigorously pursued over the past few decades with noticeable results. From 2007 to 2015, Philadelphia saw a decrease of more than 17,000 serious crimes, including a 28 percent reduction in the overall homicide rate. While these statistics are important for the safety of Philadelphians, the decline in crime rate has done little to increase overall trust between the citizens and the police. This new approach, aimed more at the well-being of the average citizen, especially those in high-crime, low-income areas, is an attempt to bridge the gap between the community and police, which has plagued the city for years. The future of community policing is still not clear, but innovative approaches aimed at assisting citizens before arresting citizens appears to be a step in the right direction.

INTRODUCTION

Policing in the United States has come a long way from its humble beginnings and, by all indications, the future will bring more changes more rapidly. Chuck Wexler, executive director of the Police Executive Research Forum, states (2014, p. ii): "Policing in the 21st century changes more in a year than it changed in a decade a generation ago. And these changes are not just about finding new ways to reduce crime; they go deeper, to evaluating the basic mission of the police, and what people want from the police."

Noting that police departments today are considerably more complex than they were a generation or two ago, the police mission has expanded beyond responding to calls for service and investigating crimes (PERF, 2014, p. 42): "Today's best police departments are always looking for ways to be proactive instead of reactive. And they have succeeded in this broader mission. Nationwide, violent crime rates are roughly half of what they were in the early 1990s. Police departments have achieved these goals in large part by deploying an endless array of new strategies and new technologies, such as:

- Community policing
- Problem-oriented policing
- CompStat
- Hot spots policing
- Crime mapping
- Predictive analytics
- Intelligence-led policing
- Closed-circuit video cameras, dash cams, and body cameras
- Automated license plate readers
- Gunshot detection systems
- Wireless transmission of nearly any type of data imaginable
- GPS devices to track suspects
- Sharing of information
- Regional task forces to address gun crime, drug crime, and other issues

- Partnerships with the community, the private sector, and corporations/businesses
- Social media"

Over the past several decades, police departments nationwide have begun to recognize the importance of community policing, public trust, accountability, and transparency in nearly everything they do. Buzz words in recent years have included "legitimacy" and "procedural justice" and reflect the growing expectation among the public that they be treated fairly and respectfully by the police: "Legitimacy and procedural justice sometimes are seen as a new, high-powered version of community policing. There is no turning back from these principles of public trust, community policing, and legitimacy in policing. Today's police executives understand that they must earn the trust of their community every day" (PERF, 2014, p. 45).

With the wealth of information related to community policing and strategies available in print and online, how can departments determine which ideas and programs are effective? Why is research important and what pitfalls might be encountered? What has been learned that will affect community policing efforts in the future?

Bratton (2006, p. 2) examines the relationship between practitioners and researchers and what can be done to improve and build on this critical, but often strained, relationship. In the evolving crime paradigm of the 21st century, intelligence-led policing will create new demands and challenges for law enforcement while simultaneously requiring law enforcement to combat the many facets of terrorism and cybercrime. Advocating a closer working relationships between researchers and police practitioners, Bratton calls for research partnerships focused on addressing these demands and maximizing the effectiveness and usefulness of the research conducted.

When the President's Task Force on 21st Century Policing began its mission of identifying best practices and formulating recommendations on how policing practices can promote effective crime reduction while building public trust, one of its tools was to hold listening sessions. At one such session on the Future of Community Policing, discussion led to a recommendation that emphasis must be placed on ways to research, improve, support, and implement policies and procedures for effective policing in the 21st century (President's Task Force on 21st Century Policing, 2015). Research is a key element to ensuring that policing remains effective, efficient, responsible, and trustworthy moving forward.

RELIABLE SOURCES OF LAW ENFORCEMENT RESEARCH

Several reliable sources of information are provided by criminal justice research organizations in the United States. Following are profiles of eight of the most prominent sources.

The *National Institute of Justice (NIJ)* is the research, development, and evaluation agency of the U.S. Department of Justice and is dedicated to researching crime control and justice issues. The NIJ provides objective, independent, evidence-based knowledge and tools to meet the challenges of crime and justice, especially at the state and local levels. Among its high-priority goals are to: (1) identify ways police and law enforcement agencies can improve their effectiveness, efficiency, and productivity; (2) enhance officer safety while minimizing unnecessary risks to suspects and others; (3) improve the police organizations' ability to collect, analyze, disseminate, and use information effectively and to communicate reliably and securely; (4) identify procedures, policies, technologies, and basic knowledge that will maximize appropriate and lawful police actions; and (5) enhance local investigative resources by identifying and disseminating investigative best practices and by developing technologies and techniques that help locate suspects and establish guilt.

The *Justice Research and Statistics Association (JRSA)* is a national nonprofit association of state Statistical Analysis Center (SAC) directors, researchers, and practitioners throughout government, academia, and criminal justice organizations. The JRSA is dedicated to the use of applied research and data analysis for sound development of criminal justice policy. The JRSA Web site is a gateway to online justice resources, providing links to statistical analysis centers and access to publications on key justice issues. It also provides access to the InfoBase of State Activities and Research (ISAR), a clearinghouse of current information on state criminal justice research, programs, and publications as well as reports on the latest research being conducted by federal and state agencies, including the annual *Directory of Justice Issues in the States* and *The JRSA Forum* newsletter.

The *Police Executive Research Forum (PERF)* is a national membership organization of police executives from city, county, and state law enforcement agencies dedicated to improving policing and advancing professionalism through research and involvement in public policy debate.

SEARCH, the *National Consortium for Justice Information and Statistics*, is a national membership organization created by and for the states, dedicated to improving the criminal justice system through effective application of information and identification technology. Since 1960, SEARCH's primary objective has been to identify and help solve the information management problems of state and local criminal justice agencies confronted with the need to exchange information with other local agencies, state agencies, agencies in other states, or the federal government.

The *Justice Research Association* is a private consulting firm and "think tank" focusing on issues of crime and justice. The Justice Research Association links agencies and practitioners in the justice field with specialized professional service providers. The service is free to those seeking professional services, with fees provided by the providers recommended.

The *Police Foundation* conducts national research on law enforcement and policing. Their first foundation study was the classic "Kansas City Preventive Patrol Experiment," which showed that increasing or decreasing the level of routine preventive patrol—the backbone of police work—had no appreciable effect on crime, fear of crime, or citizen satisfaction with police services. Many attribute the beginning of community policing with this study. Another study, "Policewomen on Patrol," conducted in cooperation with the Washington (DC) Police Department, concluded that women perform patrol work as well as men and that gender is not a valid reason to bar women from such work. Their follow-on study, "On the Move: The Status of Women in Policing," revealed that women have made major inroads into policing, but it also suggests that much more progress needs to be made in recruiting, promoting, and retaining women in policing.

Other classic research findings by the Police Foundation include the "Newark Foot Patrol Experiment," which found that foot patrol reduces citizen fear of crime and increases overall satisfaction with police services, a finding seminal to the evolution of community policing. An evaluation conducted with the San Diego (California) Police Department concluded that one officer is as effective and safe as two officers in a patrol car and markedly less expensive. As a partner in the Community Policing Consortium, the foundation plays a principal role in developing community policing research and technical assistance.

The *Vera Institute of Justice* is a private nonprofit organization that conducts research and offers consulting services in the area of criminal justice. The institute works closely with leaders in government and civil society to improve the services people rely on for safety and justice. The Vera Institute develops innovative, affordable programs that often grow into self-sustaining organizations, studies social problems and current responses, and provides practical advice and assistance to government officials in New York and internationally.

Each Vera Institute project begins with an empirical investigation of how some part of the justice system really works. That exploration may lead to designing a practical experiment. In other cases, officials are brought together with their peers and constituents to plot a rational course for reform. The aim is to help government partners achieve measurable improvements in the quality of justice they deliver and share what they have learned with others around the globe. For more than 40 years, the institute has been a pioneer in developing practical, affordable solutions to some of the toughest problems in the administration of justice.

The *International Association of Chiefs of Police (IACP) Research Center's* mission is to identify issues in law enforcement and conduct timely policy research, evaluation, follow-up training, and technical assistance and direction to law enforcement leaders, the justice system, and the community. The IACP calls for practical, relevant research in policing. The IACP's Research Advisory Committee (RAC) has published a nationwide, survey-based, focused research agenda to guide both police leaders and researchers as they undertake research initiatives. This *National Law Enforcement Research Agenda (NLERA)* is a list of priority research topics for law enforcement aimed at (1) promoting research on these topics, (2) encouraging police/researcher partnerships to conduct that research, and (3) ensuring that research topic selection results in relevant policy to assist the law enforcement community (IACP Research Advisory Committee, 2008). Using the information gained from all prior work, particularly the survey of IACP members, RAC members agreed on a final set of eight research areas that function as the core elements of the NLERA:

- Leadership
- Management and administration
- Training and education

- Systems approaches
- Technology
- Response to crime and victimization
- Emergency preparedness
- Emerging issues

The *NLERA* includes examples of specific research questions for each of the eight areas. For example, a few of the research questions included in the management and administration category are (IACP Research Advisory Committee, 2008, p. 11):

- What are the best practices in communicating policies and procedures to employees?
- What are the best practices in developing and implementing goals and objectives?
- How do agencies define community policing and measure its implementation and effectiveness?
- What is the impact of accreditation on an agency? How can the accreditation process be more effective?
- Is CompStat effective? What variations of the concept are most effective and for which types of agencies? Can CompStat accommodate community policing?
- What recruitment issues are agencies facing, and what strategies have agencies successfully employed to overcome them?
- What programs and selection procedures are effective to recruit officers in agencies with various missions?
- What issues arise with combat veterans returning from active duty to policing? What methods are effective in facilitating that transition?

IDEAS **IN PRACTICE** THE COMMISSION ON ACCREDITATION FOR LAW ENFORCEMENT AGENCIES

The Commission on Accreditation for Law Enforcement Agencies, Inc. (CALEA) was created in 1979 through the joint efforts of the International Association of Chiefs of Police (IACP), the National Organization of Black Law Enforcement Executives (NOBLE), the National Sheriff's Association (NSA), and the Police Executive Research Forum (PERF). The purpose in forming CALEA was to enhance law enforcement as a profession and to improve law enforcement by providing credentialing for law enforcement agencies that meet certain standards of professionalism (CALEA, 2010).

The benefits for agencies that become accredited are many. Once accredited, they will have greater accountability within the agency; they will experience a reduced risk and liability exposure often reflected in reduced insurance costs; and they will have a stronger defense against civil lawsuits, staunch support from government officials, and increased community support.

The accreditation process is lengthy and requires agencies to examine their management practices and, in most cases, adjust those practices. Accreditation is also not free. CALEA charges agencies based on their size for the guidance, assessment, and other services they provide during the process. Once accredited, agencies must pay an annual fee to CALEA.

Hundreds of agencies across the United States and Canada have become accredited, and more are going through the process every year.

Source: The Commission on Accreditation for Law Enforcement. (2010). *The Commission.* Fairfax, VA: Author. Retrieved November 3, 2016, from http://www.calea.org/content/commission

THE IMPORTANCE OF PRACTICAL, RELEVANT RESEARCH

"Contrary to conventional wisdom, law enforcement agencies are actually quite open to the research process" (Cosner & Loftus, 2005, p. 64). However, much of the research done is conducted by criminal justice scholars who are more interested in getting their studies published than in providing useful information and findings for departments to implement. This emphasis on publishing over practicality naturally fosters distrust by the police regarding research. What is needed is a research model that includes those affected by the results and that is practical and relevant.

Research as a Partnership

Many partnerships between law enforcement leaders and academic researchers have been successful over the last 30 years (Sanders & Fields, 2009). Policing has been influenced by research projects leading to substantive, sound policy recommendations. Despite these successes, however, much remains to be done. Existing research partnerships often suffer from many unresolved problems.

Police agencies and researchers need to identify and locate each other, determine mutually interesting projects, and set ground rules for how the project will proceed. Partnerships between police agencies and academic researchers can benefit both groups.

Undoubtedly, for most researchers, the main benefit is access to data. Sanders and Fields (2009) suggest these benefits for police agencies:

- Employing data to make hiring decisions
- Applying job analysis data to make promotions more objective
- Collecting data for writing grant applications
- Surveying citizens about crime priorities or quality of life
- Gathering data to justify requests for money or equipment
- Using data to improve services in general (identifying priorities, understanding citizen fears)

In addition, through partnerships, agencies can provide internship opportunities for professors' students as well as potential future job opportunities for graduates. Police officers can also provide professors with teaching aids such as case studies and guest speakers, providing access to real-life examples of motivation, leadership, organizational structure, personnel issues, and organizational communication. A further mutual benefit is that networks at local colleges might provide future opportunities for adjunct teaching for police administrators with advanced degrees.

"Research is a partnership, and its best application and realization of meaningful results begins when the user is directly involved in the process" (Cosner & Loftus, 2005, p. 65). Experts in police research recommend that to improve police–researcher coordination, law enforcement agencies should:

- Partner with skilled researchers to carefully design research.
- Train their leaders in evaluating potential research to ensure their ability to identify suitable research partners and to recognize relevant research topics.
- Establish regular forums through which their own research interests and priorities are communicated.
- Be willing to initiate research partnerships on regional, national, and local levels.
- Use the action research model for conducting research in law enforcement.

Action Research

One of the best models for police–researcher alliance is an action research approach, first used by Lewin in the 1940s. **Action research** emphasizes full participation in the research by everyone directly affected by the process and results. When police officers participate in designing and conducting the research, they are more likely to use the results.

Kinds of Research

Research can be very formal and rigorous or more informal and less rigorous. It is important to recognize what type of research is being reported.

Experimental Design   Among the most formal research is that based on an experimental design.

In **random assignment**, the individuals participating in the study are selected with no definite design (randomly) and placed into an experimental (treatment) or control (no treatment) group purely by chance.

Although support for experiments is strong, experiments in criminal justice are not without critics.

The ethical issue centers around denying those in the control group "treatment." However, the American Society of Criminology (ASC) conducted an email poll, which resulted in "virtually unanimous" support for random assignment.

Support for experimental research is attested to by the formation of the Academy of Experimental Criminology in 2000, with Lawrence Sherman as its first president. Assistance in experiments in criminal justice is available through the NIJ's Locally Initiated Research Partnerships in Policing. In this NIJ initiative, partners share responsibility throughout the entire project, jointly selecting an area of interest to the department (locally initiated) and collaborating on the research design, implementation, and interpretation of findings. Started in 1995, the NIJ partnership program currently has 41 projects. Usually the partnerships involve a local police department or

action research
Emphasizes full participation in the research by everyone directly affected by the process and results.

LO1

At the heart of **experimental design** is the random assignment of individuals to experimental and control conditions.

experimental design
Research method involving the random assignment of individuals to experimental (treatment) and control (no treatment) conditions.

random assignment
Dependence on a random number table or machine-generated random number that indicates the particular group to which an individual or entity will be assigned. Whether a person is a member of the treatment group or the control (no treatment) group is determined purely by chance.

LO2

Experiments in criminal justice raise ethical issues as well as privacy issues.

other law enforcement agency and a local university. Often graduate students are used and can receive credit for research projects.

At the heart of the partnerships is the Action Research Model, illustrated in Figure 16.1. The cyclical, multistep process starts with nomination of a research topic, continues with development and implementation of the research design, and ends with communicating and applying the findings.

Surveys

One commonly used method to evaluate the effectiveness of a strategy is the survey—either in person, mailed, or phoned. Sometimes a **two-wave survey** is used, the first wave consisting of a pretest before a strategy is implemented and the second wave a posttest after the strategy has been implemented for a given amount of time.

PERF has established a center for survey research to help agencies design, conduct, and analyze surveys. Surveys also play an important part in the *agency-level* Performance Measurement System that PERF developed for the law enforcement community: "The PERF measurement system is unique because it focuses law enforcement agencies' attention on a broader spectrum of activities—ones that have not been measured consistently, but are imperative to understanding what law enforcement agencies produce for their communities" (Milligan & Fridell, 2006, p. 5). Figure 16.2 illustrates how law enforcement outcomes contribute to overall community health.

Several surveys included in the Performance Measurement System will help agencies measure their performance and provide the accountability the public rightfully expects. Community surveys available in the Performance Measurement System include surveys that measure victimization of community members and businesses and self-reported delinquency surveys for juveniles. Self-reporting is an important way to measure crime in a community, as not all victims report crimes to the police. Also included in this list are measures that relate to perceptions of safety and security, confidence, trust, and satisfaction

two-wave survey
Study method where the first wave consists of a pretest before a strategy is implemented, and the second wave consists of a posttest after the strategy has been implemented for a given amount of time.

LO3
To validate an evaluation conducted by survey, 60 percent of distributed surveys must be returned.

| Figure 16.1 | The Action Research Model |

Source: Tom McEwen. "NIJ's Locally Initiated Research Partnerships in Policing Factors that Add Up to Success." *National Institute of Justice Journal*, Issue 238, January 1999, p. 7.

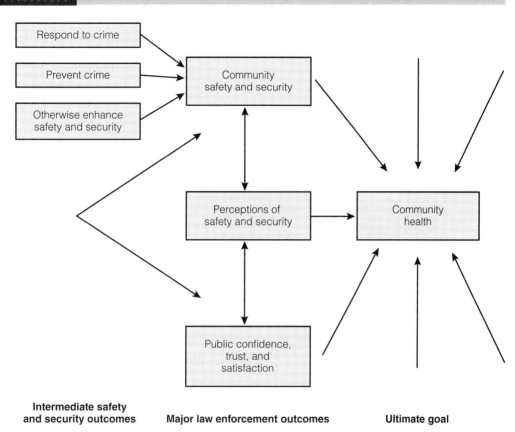

Figure 16.2 Law Enforcement Outcomes Contributing to Overall Community

Intermediate safety and security outcomes   **Major law enforcement outcomes**   **Ultimate goal**

Note: The "orphaned" arrows pointing toward Community Health from the top and bottom of the model indicate that there are many other contributors to a community's health besides law enforcement. Certainly, a healthy community is partially defined by a low crime rate, residents' feelings of security, and residents' trust and confidence in local law enforcement agency, but it is also dependent on the actions of many other agencies, organizations, and individuals.

Source: Milligan, S. O., & Fridell, L. (2006, April). *Implementing an Agency-Level Performance Measurement System: A Guide for Law Enforcement Executives.* Washington, DC: Police Executive Research Forum.

and traffic safety, since they clearly affect community safety. Departments wishing to use surveys might benefit from the Bureau of Justice Assistance's free report, *A Police Guide to Surveying Citizens and Their Environment* (Bureau of Justice Assistance, 1993).

Evidence-Based Policing

In 1998, criminologist Larry Sherman proposed a new model of law enforcement he called evidence-based policing (EBP): "Of all the ideas in policing, one stands out as the most powerful force for change: police practices should be based on scientific evidence about what works best." He notes that often, even after research has shown that something does not work, law enforcement continues to do it as a result of political pressure, inertia, or ignorance (Jensen, 2006, p. 98).

In reality, EBP is more a philosophy than a model to use when confronted with an issue or problem. As a starter, specific outcomes or goals should be established and used to drive every other aspect of a project. The next step is to determine best practices as identified in recent, relevant literature. A wealth of cutting-edge research is already available through most major city police departments and state police organizations and on the Internet. Sherman stresses that all research is not created equal. Some studies involve an adequate number of subjects and use random assignment and control groups; others do not. It is critical to understand how well a study was conducted.

After best practices are determined, the agency must adapt them to their local laws, agency policies, and community realities to formulate guidelines. What works in one jurisdiction may not work, or be acceptable, in another jurisdiction. Once guidelines are in place, they can be used to develop outputs or means to accomplish a task. Finally, and perhaps most important, is a means of measuring whether the plan actually works—that is, if it accomplishes what it was designed to do.

Predictive Policing

predictive policing
A data-driven model that uses an algorithm to convert crime data into crime forecasting.

Predictive policing, also known as PredPol, is a data-driven model considered by many to be the next emerging era of policing. PredPol, which uses an algorithm to convert crime data into crime forecasting in the same way modeling technology is used by meteorologists to predict weather events, was developed by two university professors in California and first used by the Los Angeles Police Department as a tool to forecast where burglaries and auto thefts were most likely to occur (Beck & McCue, 2009).

A fundamental premise of predictive policing is that crime is not randomly distributed across people, places, or times; therefore, with enough "big data," analysts can forecast when and where crimes may be more likely to occur (location-based prediction) and which individuals are more likely to be involved, either as victims or perpetrators (person-based prediction) (Brayne, Rosenblat, & Boyd, 2015).

Predictive policing does not replace traditional policing but, rather, enhances existing approaches such as POP, community policing, intelligence-led policing (ILP), and hot spot policing (NIJ, 2014). Building on the principles of ILP, the PredPol model casts a wide net to collect data on factors that can affect crime rates in an area—demographic trends; economic conditions; parolee populations; seasonality factors; historical crime data; neighborhood risk factors such as vacant lots, ATMs, and parks; and numerous other factors. These data are then fed into the predictive algorithms to produce a picture of statistical probabilities where crime is more likely to occur within a jurisdiction. These models, which are supported by prior crime and environmental data, have been shown to be more accurate predictive tools than human analysis and can help agencies make better informed intervention decisions and deploy their resources more efficiently and effectively (NIJ, 2014).

LO4

The predictive policing process involves a four-stage cycle: data collection, data analysis, police intervention, and target response, which leads back to data collection and the cycle continues.

In the fourth stage, responses to the intervention create new data that are fed back into the cycle, showing how the predictive process becomes increasingly complex over time (Brayne et al., 2015). Because this process involves collecting copious amounts of different types of data, predictive policing has generated considerable rhetoric and controversy:

> Civil rights advocates suggest predictive policing will be used to profile and harass people who have not committed any crime, and that it can do so under the patina of objectivity. . . . Mirroring debates occurring over discriminatory lending, some of the variables included in predictive models may simply be a proxy for race or other protected categories. Individuals in law enforcement argue predictive models should not substitute experience, "street smarts," and officer intuition. . . .
>
> Some (but not all) concerns are driven by misconceptions. The major pervasive misconception is the Minority Report myth. Minority Report, a book and subsequent film that depicts a dystopian world in which individuals are arrested for crimes "precogs" foresee them committing in the future, is relentlessly invoked in discourse around predictive policing. . . . Predictive policing is not akin to a crystal ball. It does not foretell the future. Rather, when used correctly, it can give police officers probabilistic information about where to go and who to police. Much of the time, predictive models serve to confirm police intuitions. (Brayne et al., 2015, p. 5)

In an effort to quell concerns, particularly those of officers who are unsure about how PredPol will impact their day-to-day duties, University of California–Los Angeles (UCLA) Professor Jeffrey Brantingham explains that although predictive analysis can help highlight where and when crime is likely to take place, it will never replace officer skills or the need for officers to choose a course of action in how to disrupt the criminal opportunity. LAPD Captain Sean Captain Malinowski tells his officers that predictive policing gives them a way to "play the probabilities" in fighting crime: "Using this data will allow them to deny criminals the opportunity to commit a crime, . . . but when they spend time in the high-probability areas, they need to be doing problem solving. There is something there that is attracting criminals; we tell officers to look for the magnets. What are they, and how can they be mitigated? The goal isn't more arrests, the goal is crime prevention" (Police Executive Research Forum, 2014, p. 6).

RESEARCH FINDINGS ON COMMUNITY POLICING DEPARTMENTS

The Chicago Internet Project conducted online surveys of target communities and provided feedback to those communities. The project was based on the premise that, while much has been done under the community policing and problem-oriented policing models, progress in reforming police organizations and communities has been restricted by failure to explore new measures of success and new methods of accountability that are grounded in the community (Rosenbaum, Schuck, Graziano, & Stephens, 2007).

If police–community relations are a priority, accountability systems should examine the day-to-day interactions between police and citizens. The project sought to learn the police response to residents as victims, witnesses, suspects, complainants, callers, and concerned citizens, as well as to gain insight about how residents respond to the police.

The project developed, field-tested, and validated three primary types of community assessment: general assessments of police officers, experience-based assessments of police officers, and assessments of the police organization as a whole.

Rosenbaum et al. (2007, p. ix) suggest: "From management and research perspectives, the Internet allows for hundreds of performance comparisons within and across jurisdictions. This tool can be used, for example, to assess the impact of localized interventions (e.g., the impact of installing cameras in crime hot spots on residents' awareness, fear, and risk of detection compared to control locations), to compare performance across beats or districts (e.g., police visibility and response times across different Latino beats), or to compare performance across jurisdictions (e.g., perceived police demeanor during traffic stops in African American neighborhoods in Chicago, London, and Los Angeles)."

Institutionalized organizations may experience **isomorphism** or structural conformity becoming more like each other through three mechanisms: mimetic, coercive, and normative (Willis, Mastrofski, & Weisburd, 2007). **Mimetic isomorphism** occurs when an organization copies or imitates another organization. **Coercive isomorphism** occurs when organizations adopt something as a result of pressure either from the state or other organizations, with perhaps the greatest source of coercive isomorphism being the U.S. Justice Department, which controls billions of dollars in funding. **Normative isomorphism** results from professionalism, with influences coming from organizations such as PERF and IACP.

isomorphism

Similar in structural characteristics. Isomorphism results in a one-size-fits-all approach to community policing; in contrast to refraction.

mimetic isomorphism

Occurs when an organization copies or imitates another.

coercive isomorphism

Occurs when organizations adopt something due to pressure either from the state or other organizations.

normative isomorphism

Results from professionalism, with influences coming from other organizations involved in the same profession.

COMMUNITY POLICING AND EVALUATION

The effectiveness of community policing is often measured using crime rates for a given jurisdiction. Decreasing crime rates would indicate success. As discussed in Chapter 10, the national decline in violent crime rates from the late 1990s through 2004 was attributed by many to the implementation of community policing throughout the country. Some, however, suggest that community policing is just one factor, others being a robust economy, a graying population, and fewer teenagers. The COPS Office has added thousands of officers, but whether these officers are implementing community policing strategies is not as clear.

When using crime reduction as a measure of community policing's effectiveness, the question often arises as to whether crime is, instead, simply displaced—moved to another community. Another question, in the case of crime actually being prevented, concerns how to measure incidents or events that do not happen.

If departments want more effective approaches to evaluating community policing efforts, they must incorporate communitywide information in the process. It is especially important to use data collected and maintained by public and private agencies other than law enforcement agencies. Therefore, to evaluate the effectiveness of specific community policing strategies, police

LO5
Crime statistics are seldom sufficient to understand the extent and character of a particular strategy's impact. Most research on community policing strategies shows only modest and statistically insignificant effects on crime rates, drug abuse and trafficking, and fear of crime.

departments should consider data from the health care system (especially emergency rooms), schools, housing and licensing departments, and community surveys.

When evaluating the effectiveness of family violence prevention programs, the number of abused women referred by medical personnel to shelters may be a more reliable indicator of program success or lack thereof than the number of domestic violence arrests. Similarly, strategies aimed at youths might use data on truancy, suspensions, and expulsions as one means of measuring effectiveness.

Several researchers have suggested that law enforcement not concentrate on crime statistics but rather focus on whether community policing efforts are able to build stronger communities—a major goal of the philosophy. One such measure might be the number and nature of citizen complaints. However, in some studies, community policing and traditional policing officers generated a similar proportion of complaints, similar types of complaints, and a similar number of complaints.

THE IMPACT OF THE ECONOMIC DOWNTURN ON POLICING IN THE UNITED STATES

According to the COPS Office: "Police agencies are some of the hardest hit by the current economic climate. Curtailing revenues nationwide have forced local governments to make cuts in spending across the board, which includes public safety operating budgets. While budget cuts threaten the jobs of law enforcement officers, the duties and responsibilities to ensure public safety remain" (Office of Community Oriented Policing Services, 2011, p. 3).

Faced with the need to cut budgets and continue to "do more with less," law enforcement administrators must not only identify different ways to deliver police services more cost-effectively but also articulate what the revised public safety models will look like to their communities. Highlighting the importance of community policing during tough financial times, the COPS Office notes that many of the cost-saving techniques being implemented by agencies throughout the country are directly related to community policing efforts (Office of Community Oriented Policing Services, 2011, pp. 33–34):

> The three tenets of community policing—community partnerships, organizational transformation, and problem solving—are of increased importance when facing budget cuts that reduce the number of officers on the streets.

> Collaborative partnerships to develop solutions to problems and increase trust in police can be seen in many of the solutions police agencies are using in light of the economic downturn. Specifically, the use of volunteers, partnerships between the police and private agencies, and the use of social media as a means to communicate effectively with the community in order to meet their needs, are all examples of how collaborative partnerships act as a cost-saving tool.

> Organizational transformation exists through the alignment of organizational management, structure, personnel, and information systems to support community partnerships and proactive problem solving. From its inception,

community policing's goal is one of forging strong relationships between law enforcement and the communities they serve. It aims to redesign the practice of public safety into a collective, collaborative effort....

Unfortunately, when agencies are forced to make widespread budget cuts, some have done so by reducing or eliminating some of their community policing programs. In fact, according to the [Major Cities Chiefs Association] MCCA survey, 39 percent of respondents who have reduced budgets stated that those budgets cuts were made to their community policing efforts.

Herein lies one of the major fallacies as it relates to community policing. Community policing should not be viewed as a particular program within a department, but rather as a department-wide philosophy. Programs are typically initiated as a response to a specific problem, in which only a small portion of the organization is involved and once the problem has been addressed the program is dissolved. Instead, community policing must be understood as a philosophy that promotes the systematic use of partnerships and problem-solving techniques to proactively address the conditions within a community that are cause for public concerns over crime and social disorder issues....

Some have made the argument that these economic challenges may compel us to abandon community policing because we simply cannot afford it. However, experience has shown that community policing is a more cost-effective way of utilizing available resources than simple traditional policing practices, for a number of reasons. Primarily, community participation in crime-prevention amplifies the amount of available resources, while community partnerships used to address problem solving provides a more efficient distribution of combined police and community resources than simply reactive policing program models.

RETHINKING THE "GET TOUGH" ON CRIME APPROACH

Armed with an increasing body of empirical data regarding "get tough" measures and criminal recidivism, many jurisdictions are now revisiting their mandatory minimum laws, three-strikes laws, and other nondiscretionary sentencing schemes, particularly for low-level drug offenders. Many of our nation's correctional institutions have become severely overcrowded by the long-term warehousing of these repeat, albeit generally nonviolent, offenders. As the economic recession has worsened, many policy makers have been forced to examine whether we can afford to continue the "get tough" approach of incarcerating the mass number of offenders who "strike out." Data provided by the National Conference of State Legislatures (NCSL) indicate that, of the 24 states that passed three-strikes laws during the 1990s, at least 16 have since modified their legislation to allow judges more discretion in sentencing or to narrow the types of crimes that count as a "strike" (Michels, 2012). In addition, at least 14 states have either eliminated mandatory minimum sentencing for low-level drug offenders or have granted greater judicial discretion concerning correctional alternatives to incarceration (Michels, 2012).

HOW INNOVATIONS IN TECHNOLOGY ARE TRANSFORMING POLICING

Technology was the topic of a recent Police Executive Research Forum (PERF) Executive Session as part of their Critical Issues in Policing Series. At this conference, police chiefs unanimously expressed how impactful technology has been in helping bring crime rates down and helping their officers be more efficient and effective (PERF, 2012). They also all agreed that a new Age of Technology will sweep through American policing in the next two decades, as the technologies that have recently emerged begin to take hold and technologies no one is yet aware of are developed and become available:

> Policing today bears very little resemblance to the policing of the 1970s. For those of us who have been watching this happen day by day, the differences are simply stunning. Back then, police officers thought they were doing a fine job if they responded quickly to calls for service and investigated crimes thoroughly. Today's police departments have given themselves a much larger and more important mission: working with their communities to solve crime problems, and in so doing, [using technology to] actually [prevent] crimes from being committed and [reduce] crime rates. (Wexler, 2012, p. iii)

Technologies discussed at the session included gunshot detection systems, license plate readers, use of communication technology/social media, cameras in squads, body cameras, cameras in hot spots, wireless video streaming, online crime reporting and case tracking for crime victims, and the use of GPS (global positioning systems) to track criminals and officer locations. Readers are encouraged to give a closer look to the PERF report generated from that Executive Session: *How Are Innovations in Technology Transforming Policing?* (also available online at policeforum.org).

Other technologies not mentioned at the PERF Executive Session that have been implemented by various law enforcement agencies throughout the country include:

- Camera-equipped aerial drones—These can be controversial in that while such technology enables officers to obtain a bird's-eye view of a crime scene in an emergency, such surveillance capabilities also raise privacy concerns.
- Tablet computers—Portable, lightweight devices, such as the Apple iPad, can be used to take notes and record victim and witness statements in the field. Various police-specific applications are available, such as crime scene diagramming tools.
- GPS vehicle pursuit darts—Squads involved in potentially dangerous high-speed pursuits can fire an adhesive GPS-equipped "dart" at a fleeing vehicle and then track the vehicle's movements from a safe distance.
- Throwable robotic cameras—A robotic camera is a small remote-controlled device that can withstand being thrown over a wall and then right itself, climb stairs, and maneuver into small, poorly lit spaces to allow officers to view potential threats from a safe distance.

Another technology with the potential to significantly alter police practices are autonomous (driverless) cars (Washington, 2016). This technology

Technology is making policing safer, more efficient, and more transparent. Body-worn cameras, such as the one shown here, record everything that transpires during a police-citizen contact, giving greater protection to both officers and citizens.

Al Seib/Los Angeles Times/Getty Images

could put an end to traffic stops and high-speed pursuits, as it would be futile for police to attempt to ticket occupants of self-driving cars, and many such cars will likely be owned not by the rider but by a corporation with a fleet of autonomous vehicles. As can often be the case with technology, driverless car technology can present a double-edged sword, being exploitable by terrorists, who will be able to place a vehicle-borne improvised explosive device (VBIED) inside such a vehicle and maneuver it to a target-rich environment.

Bernard Levin, a retired professor of psychology and co-author of *The Future of Policing*, notes that while technology can increase police efficiency and effectiveness, it will never replace the need for live officers (Washington, 2016): "Most of policing isn't about technology, it's about people, and the technology is an add-on. There still will be tremendous need for a street cop, a patrol cop, to go to where the problem is and help people solve the problem. Sometimes you help people by arresting them. Most of the time, you just talk people out and help them wind up better than they were."

TRENDS IN POLICE RECRUITING AND TRAINING

Pillar 5 of the Final Report of the President's Task Force on 21st Century Policing is entitled: "Training and Education," underscoring the crucial importance of hiring and training the right people to serve as our country's next generation of police officers (President's Task Force on 21st Century Policing, 2015, p. 51):

> As our nation becomes more pluralistic and the scope of law enforcement's responsibilities expands, the need for more and better training has become critical. Today's line officers and leaders must meet a wide variety of challenges including international terrorism, evolving technologies, rising immigration, changing laws, new cultural mores, and a growing mental health crisis. All states and territories and the District of Columbia should establish standards for hiring, training, and education.

> The skills and knowledge required to effectively deal with these issues requires a higher level of education as well as extensive and ongoing training

in specific disciplines. The task force discussed these needs in depth, making recommendations for basic recruit and in-service training, as well as leadership development in a wide variety of areas:

- Community policing and problem-solving principles
- Interpersonal and communication skills
- Bias awareness
- Scenario-based, situational decision making
- Crisis intervention
- Procedural justice and impartial policing
- Trauma and victim services
- Mental health issues
- Analytical research and technology
- Languages and cultural responsiveness

Police executives are now discussing how changes in the younger generations, the cohort from which new recruits are drawn, are affecting police department organization and management: "Some of the wisest police chiefs today are saying they can't expect the younger generation to accept the hierarchical, paramilitary structures of most police departments. Rather, they say, police departments must do the adapting, or they will miss out on hiring and retaining many of the brightest young people" (PERF, 2014, p. 44). Yet many departments across the country are understaffed and finding it difficult to recruit and retain police officers, including the Chicago Police Department, the New York Police Department, and many other departments in Michigan, Texas, and California. In 2006, the Seattle Police Department received 3,000 applications for 10 openings. Ten years later, they are getting 1,000 applicants for 70 openings, a decline of more than 90 percent (Libaw, 2016). Departments in smaller cities are having a particularly difficult time finding recruits to fill vacancies. Reasons for such hiring difficulties include low pay and the stigma that many think surrounds the profession as the result of high-profile police shootings.

The crossroads at which policing finds itself, in which not enough "qualified bodies" are applying to fill existing openings, has led some to predict a growing involvement of state training and certification agencies, commonly called Peace Officers Standards and Training, or POST, in assisting local agencies (Church, 2007). It is also anticipated that more nonprofit organizations will get involved in mentoring candidates and even fund them through the academy.

Where does community policing fit into the context of basic police academy training? Shults (2007) examined this question and found clear support from police training experts for community policing training to become an integral part of basic police training academies. In both 2002 and 2006, more than 90 percent of academies provided basic training on community policing topics. Additionally, 90 percent of academies provided basic training on terrorism-related topics in 2006, up from 80 percent in 2002 (Reaves, 2009).

A LOOK TOWARD THE FUTURE

The FBI forecasts that subnational and nongovernmental entities will play an increasing role in world affairs for years to come, presenting new "asymmetric" threats to the United States. Although the United States will continue to occupy a position of economic and political leadership, and although other governments will also continue to be important actors on the world stage, terrorist groups, criminal enterprises, and other nonstate actors will assume an increasing role in international affairs. Nation-states and their governments will exercise decreasing control over the flow of information, resources, technology, services, and people.

Globalization and the trend of an increasingly networked world economy will become more pronounced within the coming years. The global economy will stabilize some regions, but widening economic divides are likely to make areas, groups, and nations that are left behind breeding grounds for unrest, violence, and terrorism. As corporate, financial, and nationality definitions and structures become more complex and global, the distinction between foreign and domestic entities will increasingly blur. This will lead to further globalization and networking of criminal elements, directly threatening the security of the United States.

Most experts believe that technological innovation will have the most profound impact on the collective ability of the federal, state, and local governments to protect the United States. Advances in information technology, as well as other scientific and technical areas, have created the most significant global transformation since the Industrial Revolution. These advances allow terrorists, disaffected states, weapons proliferators, criminal enterprises, drug traffickers, and other threat enterprises easier and cheaper access to weapons technology. Technological advances will also provide terrorists and others with the potential to stay ahead of law enforcement countermeasures. For example, it will be easier and cheaper for small groups or individuals to acquire designer chemical or biological warfare agents and correspondingly more difficult for forensic experts to trace an agent to a specific country, company, or group (Federal Bureau of Investigation, 2004).

As this chapter has discussed, and as is aptly stated by John Schaar, American writer and scholar: *The future is not some place we are going to, but one we are creating. The paths are not to be found, but made, and the activity of making them changes both the maker and the destination.*

SUMMARY

At the heart of experimental design is the random assignment of individuals to experimental and control conditions. Experiments in criminal justice raise ethical issues as well as privacy issues. Assistance in experiments in criminal justice is available through the NIJ's Locally Initiated Research Partnerships in Policing. Surveys are commonly used by police departments.

To validate an evaluation conducted by survey, 60 percent of distributed surveys must be returned.

Crime statistics are seldom sufficient to understand the extent and character of a particular strategy's impact. Most research on community policing strategies shows only modest and statistically insignificant effects on crime rates, drug abuse and trafficking, and fear of crime.

DISCUSSION QUESTIONS

1. Why has the relationship between law enforcement practitioners and researchers often been difficult?
2. How can partnerships make research more effective?
3. What percentage of returned surveys is required for validation, and why?
4. Why do crime and arrest statistics fall short of explaining the success or failure of a particular strategy? What other kinds of data should also be looked at?
5. Discuss the importance of research in criminal justice.
6. Some police agencies conduct citizen surveys to gauge public attitudes toward the police. Discuss the impact different methods of conducting surveys can have on the results.
7. Do the 10 trends affecting policing listed by Proteus USA appear valid in your community?
8. How does the availability of funding affect patterns of community policing within police departments?
9. What is a two-wave survey, and when might it be appropriate to use?
10. What do you think will be law enforcement's biggest future challenge and why?

A HELPFUL RESOURCE

The Criminal Justice Distance Learning Consortium. (1999). *The Definitive Guide to Criminal Justice and Criminology on the World Wide Web.* Upper Saddle River, NJ: Prentice Hall.

GLOSSARY

Number in parentheses indicates the chapter in which the term is introduced.

A

acculturation—Occurs when a society takes in or assimilates other cultures. Also called *assimilation*. (6)

action research—Emphasizes full participation in the research by everyone directly affected by the process and results. (16)

Alzheimer's disease (AD)—A progressive, irreversible, and incurable brain disease with no known cause that affects 4 million elderly Americans; the classic symptom is memory loss. (6)

Americans with Disabilities Act (ADA)—Legislation signed in 1990 that guarantees that persons with disabilities will have equal access to any public facilities available to persons without disabilities. (6)

analysis (in SARA)—Examines the identified problem's causes, scope, and effects; includes determining how often the problem occurs and how long it has been occurring, as well as conditions that appear to create the problem. (4)

assessment (in SARA)—Refers to evaluating how effective the intervention was; was the problem solved? (4)

assimilation—Occurs when a society takes in or assimilates various other cultures to become a "melting pot." Also called *acculturation*. (6)

asymmetric warfare—Combat in which a weaker group attacks a superior group by not attacking the stronger adversary head on but rather attacking areas where the adversary least expects to be hit, causing great psychological shock and giving power to the powerless by destroying the stronger adversary's ability to use its conventional weapons. (15)

attention-deficit hyperactivity disorder (ADHD)—A common disruptive behavior disorder characterized by heightened motor activity (fidgeting and squirming), short attention span, distractibility, impulsiveness, and lack of self-control. (6)

B

bias—A prejudice that inhibits objectivity; can evolve into hate. (6)

bias crime—A criminal offense committed against a person, property, or society that is motivated, in whole or in part, by an offender's bias against an individual's or group's race, religion, ethnic/national origin, gender, age, disability, or sexual orientation. *Hate crime* and *bias crime* are considered synonymous. (14)

bias incident—Use of bigoted and prejudiced language; does not in itself violate hate crime laws. (14)

bifurcated society—The widening of the gap between those with wealth (the "haves") and those living in poverty (the "have-nots"), with a shrinking middle class. (3)

binge drinking—Five or more drinks in a row during the previous 2 weeks. (11)

broken windows phenomenon—Suggests that if it appears no one cares about the community, as indicated by broken windows not being repaired, then disorder and crime will thrive. (3)

bullying—Name calling, fistfights, purposeful ostracism, extortion, character assassination, repeated physical attacks, and sexual harassment; also called *peer child abuse*. (12)

C

call management—Calls are prioritized based on the department's judgment about the emergency nature of the call (e.g., imminent harm to a person or a crime in progress), response time, need for backup, and other local factors. (7)

call stacking—A process performed by a computer-aided dispatch system in which nonemergency, lower-priority calls are ranked and held or "stacked" so that the higher priorities are continually dispatched first. (7)

change management—The development of an overall strategy to examine the present state of an organization, envision the future state of the organization, and devise a means of moving from one to the other. (5)

charge bargaining—Legal negotiations between the prosecutor and the defense lawyer or the defendant to reach an agreement or compromise on the charge(s) the defendant will plead guilty to, thus avoiding a court trial, conserving time, and reducing expense. (3)

closed drug market—Dealers sell only to people they know or who are vouched for by other buyers. (11)

cocoon neighborhood watch—Focusing on only those living around at-risk places rather than an entire neighborhood. (10)

coercive isomorphism—Occurs when organizations adopt something due to pressure either from the state or other organizations. (16)

collaboration—Occurs when a number of agencies and individuals make a commitment to work together and contribute resources to obtain a common, long-term goal. (7)

communication process—Involves a sender, a message, a channel, a receiver, and, sometimes, feedback. (6)

community—The specific geographic area served by a police department or law enforcement agency and the individuals, organizations, and agencies within that area; also refers to a feeling of belonging—a sense of integration, a sense of shared values, and a sense of "we-ness." (3)

community justice—An ethic that transforms the aim of the justice system into enhancing community life or sustaining communities; partnerships between the formal criminal justice system, the private sector, and community groups to promote public safety and enhance

quality of life in the community. (3, 7)

community mobilization—Strategy to address the gang problem that includes improved communication and joint policy and program development among justice, community-based, and grassroots organizations. (13)

community policing—A philosophy that promotes organizational strategies that support the systematic use of partnerships and problem-solving techniques to proactively address the immediate conditions that give rise to public safety issues, such as crime, social disorder, and fear of crime. (1)

community relations—Efforts to interact and communicate with the community—team policing, community resource officers, and school liaison officers. See also *public relations.* (1)

conservative crime control—Comes down hard on crime; wages "war" on crime and drugs. (11)

contagion—Suggests that when offenders notice one criminal opportunity they often detect similar opportunities they have previously overlooked; crime then spreads; the broken windows theory is an example. (10)

contagion effect—The media coverage of terrorism inspires more terrorism. (15)

CPTED—Crime Prevention through Environmental Design—altering the physical environment to enhance safety, reduce the incidence and fear of crime, and improve the quality of life. (9)

crack children—Children who were exposed to cocaine while in the womb. (6)

criminogenic needs—Those characteristics or variables that can be changed, such as drug addiction, antisocial attitudes and values, the tendency to hang

out with criminal peers, family dysfunction, and unemployment; also called *dynamic risk factors.* (7)

crisis behavior—Results when a person has a temporary breakdown in coping skills; not the same as mental illness. (6)

critical mass—The smallest number of citizens and organizations needed to support and sustain the community policing initiative. (5)

CSI effect—A phenomenon created when the viewing public believes that every police force has access to the same high-tech crime-solving gadgets they see on popular police television shows. (8)

cycle of violence—Violent or sexual victimization of children can often lead to these victims becoming perpetrators of domestic violence as adults. (14)

D

dark side of crime—The large amount of crime that goes unreported. (9)

deadly force—Any force that can reasonably be expected to cause or is intended to cause death or serious physical injury. (2)

decentralization—An operating principle that encourages flattening of the organization and places decision-making authority and autonomy at the level where information is plentiful, usually at the level of the patrol officer. (5)

deconfliction—Protocol or guidelines to avoid conflict. (15)

demographics—The characteristics of a human population or community. (3)

developmental assets—Forty ideals, experiences, and qualities established by the Search Institute to "help young people make wise decisions, choose positive paths, and grow up competent, caring, and responsible." (12)

diffusion—Occurs when criminals believe that the opportunity blocking of one type of criminal activity is also aimed at other types of criminal activity. (10)

discretion—Freedom to make choices among possible courses of action or inaction, for example, to arrest or not arrest. (2)

displacement—The theory that successful implementation of a crime-reduction initiative does not really prevent crime; instead, it just moves the crime to another area. (3)

Diversion—The practice of removing juvenile status offenders and delinquents from the jurisdiction of the courts, when possible, in an effort to avoid stigmatization and further criminalization. (3)

DOC model—Dilemmas–Options–Consequences challenges officers to carefully consider their decisions and the short- and long-term consequences of those decisions, with the goal of fusing problem solving and morality. (4)

doctor shopping—Occurs when a person obtains controlled substances from multiple health care practitioners without the prescribers' knowledge of the other prescriptions already acquired. (11)

drug diversion—The rerouting of drugs from legally and medically necessary and authorized uses to uses that are illegal and typically neither medically authorized nor necessary. (11)

dynamic risk factors—Those characteristics or variables that can be changed, such as drug addiction, antisocial attitudes and values, the tendency to hang out with criminal peers, family dysfunction, and unemployment; also called *criminogenic needs*. (7)

E

EBD—Emotionally/behaviorally disturbed. (6)

effectiveness—Producing the desired result or goal; doing the right things. (4)

efficiency—Minimizing waste, expense, or unnecessary effort; results in a high ratio of output to input; doing things right. (4)

empirical study—Research based on observation or practical experience. (9)

empowered—Granting authority and decision making to lower-level officers. (5)

entrapment—An act of government agents to induce a person to commit a crime that is not normally considered by the person for the purpose of prosecuting them. (4)

ethnocentrism—The preference for one's own way of life over all others. (6)

excessive force—Force greater than that reasonably necessary to accomplish a legitimate law enforcement purpose. (2)

experimental design—Research method involving the random assignment of individuals to experimental (treatment) and control (no treatment) conditions. (16)

F

Ferguson effect—The theory that policing practices have changed in the wake of the shooting of Michael Brown in Ferguson, Missouri, where beat officers are backing off proactive policing and not getting out of their squad cars as often, which has emboldened criminals and fueled other social unrest, which has in turn led to a spike in violent crime. (14)

fetal alcohol syndrome (FAS)—The leading known cause of mental retardation in the Western world; effects include impulsivity, inability to predict consequences or to use appropriate judgment in daily life, poor communication skills, high levels of activity, distractibility in small children, and frustration and depression in adolescents. (6)

flat organization—Unlike a typical pyramid organization chart, the top is pushed down and the sides are expanded at the base. In a police department, this means fewer lieutenants and captains, fewer staff departments, and fewer staff assistants but more sergeants and more patrol officers. (5)

force—That amount of effort required by police to compel compliance from an unwilling subject. (2)

formal power structure—Includes divisions of society with wealth and political influence such as federal, state, and local agencies and governments, commissions, and regulatory agencies. (3)

frankpledge system—The Norman system requiring all free men to swear loyalty to the king's law and to take responsibility for maintaining the local peace. (1)

fusion center—A collaborative effort of two or more agencies that provide resources, expertise, and information to the center with the goal of maximizing their ability to detect, prevent, investigate, and respond to criminal and terrorist activity. (15)

G

gang—A group of people who form an ongoing allegiance for a common purpose and engage in unlawful or criminal activity. See also *street gang* and *youth gang*. (13)

gateway theory—Teaches that milder illicit drugs—such as marijuana—lead directly to experimentation with and an addiction to hard drugs such as crack cocaine and heroin. (11)

geographic information system (GIS)—Creating, updating, and analyzing computerized maps. (4)

geographic profiling—A crime-mapping technique that takes the locations of past crimes and, using a complex mathematical algorithm, calculates probabilities of a suspect's residence. (4)

graffiti—Painting or writing on buildings, walls, bridges, bus stops, and other available public surfaces; used by gangs to mark their turf. (13)

Guardian Angels—Private citizen patrols who seek to deter crime and to provide a positive role model for young children. (9)

gun interdiction—Local police direct intensive patrols to specific geographic areas with high rates of gun-related incidents of violence. (14)

H

hate crime—A criminal offense committed against a person, property, or society that is motivated, in whole or in part, by an offender's bias against an individual's or group's race, religion, ethnic/national origin, gender, age, disability, or sexual orientation. *Hate crime* and *bias crime* are considered synonymous. (14)

heterogeneous—Involving things (including people) that are unlike, dissimilar, different; the opposite of *homogeneous.* (3)

homogeneous—Involving things (including people) that are basically similar, alike; the opposite of *heterogeneous.* (3)

hot spots—Areas where incidents of crime and disorder tend to cluster in close proximity to one another. (4)

hue and cry—The summoning of all citizens within earshot to join in pursuing and capturing a wrongdoer. (1)

human relations—Efforts to relate to and understand other individuals or groups. (1)

I

impact evaluation—Determines if the problem declined. (4)

implicit bias—The unintentional, subconscious associations every individual makes among groups of people and stereotypes about those groups. (6)

incident—An isolated event that requires a police response; the primary work unit in the professional model. (4)

incivilities—Occur when social control mechanisms have eroded and include unmowed lawns, piles of accumulated trash, graffiti, public drunkenness, fighting, prostitution, abandoned buildings, and broken windows. (3)

informal power structure—Includes religious groups, wealthy subgroups, ethnic groups, political groups, and public interest groups. (3)

interoperability—The compatibility of communication systems such as EMS, fire and rescue, and police, and across levels of government. (15)

intimate partner violence (IPV)—Violence that occurs between two people in a close (intimate) relationship, whether the partners are of the same or opposite gender; can involve physical violence, sexual violence, threats, emotional abuse, and stalking. (14)

Islamic State of Iraq and the Levant (ISIL)—A formalized international terrorist group formerly known as al-Qa'ida in Iraq and Islamic State of Iraq and Syria (ISIS). (15)

isomorphism—Similar in structural characteristics. Isomorphism results in a one-size-fits-all approach to community policing; in contrast to refraction. (16)

J

jargon—The technical language of a profession. (6)

jihad—Holy war. (15)

K

kinesics—The study of body movement or body language. (6)

L

least-effort principle—Concept proposing that criminals tend to commit acts of crimes within a comfort zone located near but not too close to their residence. (4)

less-lethal force—Force that has less potential for causing death or serious injury than do traditional tactics. (2)

liberal crime control—Emphasizes correctional policies and broader social reforms intended to expand opportunities for those "locked out" of the American Dream; wages "war" on poverty and inequality of opportunity. (11)

Lucifer effect—The transformation of good people into evil. (2)

M

magnet phenomenon—Occurs when a phone number or address is associated with a crime simply because it was a convenient number or address to use. (4)

mediation—The intervention of a third party into an interpersonal dispute, where the third party helps disputants reach a resolution; often termed alternative dispute resolution (ADR). (4)

mimetic isomorphism—Occurs when an organization copies or imitates another. (16)

mission statement—A written declaration of purpose. (2)

moniker—A nickname, often of a gang member. (13)

N

negative contacts—Unpleasant interactions between the police and the public; may or may not relate to criminal activity. (2)

news media echo effect—The theory that the media have the power, through their coverage of isolated, high-profile cases, to influence the operations of the criminal justice system and even the disposition of individual cases. (8)

NIMBY syndrome—"Not in my backyard"; the idea that it is fine to have a halfway house—across town, not in my backyard. (3)

911 policing—Incident-driven, reactive policing. (2)

nonverbal communication—Includes everything other than the actual words spoken in a message, such as tone, pitch, and pacing. (6)

normative isomorphism—Results from professionalism, with influences coming from other organizations involved in the same profession. (16)

O

open drug market—Dealers sell to all potential customers, eliminating only those suspected of being police or some other threat. (11)

opportunity blocking—Changes to make crime more difficult, risky, less rewarding, or less excusable; one of the oldest forms of crime prevention. (10)

organizational development—A law enforcement strategy to address the gang problem that includes special police units and special youth agency crisis programs. (13)

outlaw motorcycle gang (OMG)—An ongoing organization, association, or group of three or more people with a common interest or activity characterized by the commission of, or involvement in, a pattern of criminal conduct, and whose members must possess and be able to operate a motorcycle to achieve and maintain membership within the group. (13)

P

paradigm—A model or a way of viewing a specific aspect of life such as politics, medicine, education, and the criminal justice system. (1)

paradigm shift—A new way of thinking about a specific subject. (1)

participatory leadership—A management style in which each individual has a voice in decisions, but top management still has the ultimate decision-making authority. (5)

patronage system—Politicians rewarded those who voted for them with jobs or special privileges; prevalent during the political era. Also called the *spoils system*. (1)

peer child abuse—Another term for *bullying*—name calling, fistfights, purposeful ostracism, extortion, character assassination, repeated physical attacks, and sexual harassment. (12)

perp walks—The police practice of parading suspects before the media, often simply for the publicity provided by news media coverage. (8)

place—A very small area reserved for a narrow range of functions, often controlled by a single owner and separated from the surrounding area. (10)

plea bargaining—Legal negotiations between the prosecutor and the defense lawyer or the defendant to reach an agreement on how a defendant will plead to a specific charge, thus eliminating the time and expense of a trial. (3)

police culture—The informal values, beliefs, and expectations passed on to newcomers in the department; may be at odds with the formal rules, regulations, procedures, and role authority of managers. (2)

political era—Extended into the first quarter of the 20th century and witnessed the formation of police departments. (1)

polyvictimization—Experiencing multiple forms of victimization (emotional, physical). (12)

posttraumatic stress disorder (PTSD)—A persistent reexperiencing of a traumatic event through intrusive memories, dreams, and a variety of anxiety-related symptoms. (6)

poverty syndrome—Includes inadequate housing, education, and jobs and a resentment of those who control the social system. (6)

predictive policing—A data-driven model that uses an algorithm to convert crime data into crime forecasting. (16)

prison gang—A self-perpetuating criminal organization that originates in the penal system and continues to operate not only within correctional facilities throughout the United States but also outside of prison. (13)

privatization—Using private security officers or agencies to provide services typically considered to be law enforcement functions. (3)

proactive—Anticipating problems and seeking solutions to those problems, as in community policing. The opposite of *reactive*. (1)

problem-oriented policing (POP)—A department-wide strategy aimed at solving persistent community problems by grouping incidents to identify problems and to determine possible underlying causes. (4)

problem-solving approach—Involves proactively identifying problems and making decisions about how best to deal with them. (4)

procedural justice—The idea of being treated fairly during a process or procedure. (2)

process evaluation—Determines if the response was implemented as planned. (4)

process mapping—A method of internal analysis that takes a horizontal view of a system, in contrast to the traditional vertical view. It involves personnel at all levels and uses flowcharts to visually depict how information, materials, and activities flow in an organization; how work is handed off from one unit or department to another; and how processes work currently and what changes should be made to attain a more ideal process flow. (14)

professional model—Emphasized crime control by preventive automobile patrol coupled with rapid response to calls. The predominant policing model used during the reform era (1970s and 1980s). (1)

progressive era—Emphasized preventive automobile patrol and rapid response to calls for service. Also called the *reform era*. (1)

protective factor—A condition, characteristic, or variable that increases the likelihood that a child will avoid delinquency; often the opposite of a *risk factor*. (12)

public information officer (PIO)—An officer trained in public relations and assigned to disseminate information to the media, thereby providing accurate, consistent information while controlling leaks of confidential or inaccurate information and managing controversial or negative situations to the department's benefit. (8)

public relations—Efforts to enhance the police image. See also *community relations*. (1)

pulling levers—Refers to a multiagency law enforcement team imposing all available sanctions on gang members who violate established standards for behavior. (13)

Q

qualitative data—Examines the excellence (quality) of the response, that is, how satisfied were the officers and the citizens; most frequently determined by surveys, focus groups, or tracking complaints and compliments. (4)

qualitative evaluations—Assessments that are more descriptive and less statistical than empirical studies; the opposite of quantitative evaluation. (9)

quantitative data—Examines the amount of change (quantity) as a result of the response; most frequently measured by before-and-after data. (4)

R

racial profiling—A form of discrimination that singles out people of racial or ethnic groups because of a belief that these groups are more likely than others to commit certain types of crimes. Race-based enforcement is illegal. (6)

random assignment—Dependence on a random number table or machine-generated random number that indicates the particular group to which an individual or entity will be assigned. Whether a person is a member of the treatment group or the control (no treatment) group is determined purely by chance. (16)

reactive—Responding after the fact; responding to calls for service. The opposite of *proactive*. (1)

reasonable force—Force no greater than that needed to achieve the desired end. (2)

reform era—Emphasized preventive automobile patrol and rapid response to calls for service. Also called the *progressive era*. (1)

response (in SARA)—Acting to alleviate the problem, that is, selecting the alternative solution or solutions. (4)

restorative justice—Seeks not retribution (punishment) but, rather, restitution to repair the damage of crime as much as possible and to restore the victim, the community, and the offender. (7)

risk factor—A condition, characteristic, or variable that increases the likelihood that a child will become delinquent; often the opposite of a *protective factor*. (12)

risk factor prevention paradigm—Seeks to identify key risk factors for offending and then implement prevention methods designed to counteract them. (10)

routine activity theory—Principle of environmental criminology that states crime occurs at the intersection of a motivated offender, a suitable target, and an absent or ineffective guardian. (4)

S

scanning (in SARA)—Refers to identifying recurring problems and prioritizing them to select one problem to address. (4)

selective enforcement—The use of police discretion, deciding to concentrate on specific crimes such as drug dealing and to downplay other crimes such as white-collar crime. (2)

social capital—Refers to the strength of a community's social fabric and includes the elements of trustworthiness and obligations. Two levels of social capital are local and public. (3)

social contract—A legal theory that suggests that for everyone to receive justice, each person must relinquish some individual freedom. (3)

social intervention—Strategy to address the gang problem that includes crisis intervention, treatment for youths and their families, outreach, and referral to social services. (13)

social opportunities—Strategy to address the gang problem that includes providing basic or remedial education, training, work incentives, and jobs for gang members. (13)

soundbites—Good, solid information stated briefly, that is, within 7 to 12 seconds. (8)

spoils system—Politicians rewarded those who voted for them with jobs or special privileges; prevalent during the political era. Also called the *patronage system*. (1)

stakeholders—Those people who have an interest in what happens in a particular situation. (7)

static risk factors—Those characteristics or variables that cannot be changed, such as an offender's prior criminal record. (7)

stereotyping—Assuming all people within a specific group are the same, lacking individuality. (6)

strategic planning—Long-term, large-scale, futuristic planning. (5)

straw purchasers—Weapons buyers fronting for people linked to illegal gun trafficking. (14)

street gang—A group of people whose allegiance is based on social needs, who have an identifiable leadership, who claim control over a specific territory in the community, and who engage in acts injurious to the public; the preferred term of most local law enforcement agencies. (13)

suppression—Strategy to address the gang problem that includes tactics such as prevention, arrest, imprisonment, supervision, and surveillance. (13)

symbiotic—Describes a relationship of mutual dependence upon each other. (8)

syndrome of crime—A group of signs, causes, and symptoms that occur together to foster specific crimes. (3)

synergism—Occurs when individuals channel their energies toward a common purpose and accomplish what they could not accomplish alone. (10)

T

target hardening—Refers to making potential objectives of criminals more difficult to obtain through the use of improved locks, alarm systems, and security cameras. (10)

tattling—Something done to get someone in trouble, in contrast to telling or reporting to keep someone safe. (12)

terrorism—The unlawful use of force or violence against persons or property to intimidate or coerce a government, the civilian population, or any segment thereof, in furtherance of political or social objectives. (15)

thin blue line—The distancing of the police from the public they serve. (1)

tipping point—That point at which an ordinary, stable phenomenon can turn into a crisis. (3)

tithing—A group of 10 families. (1)

tithing system—The Anglo-Saxon principle establishing the principle of collective responsibility for maintaining local law and order. (1)

traffic calming—Describes a wide range of road and environmental design changes that either make it more difficult for a vehicle to speed or make drivers believe they should slow down for safety. (10)

TRIAD—A three-way partnership among the American Association of Retired Persons (AARP), the

International Association of Chiefs of Police (IACP), and the National Sheriffs' Association (NSA) to address criminal victimization of older people. (7)

turf—Territory occupied by a gang, often marked by graffiti. (13)

two-wave survey—Study method where the first wave consists of a pretest before a strategy is implemented, and the second wave consists of a posttest after the strategy has been implemented for a given amount of time. (16)

V

violent crime—An offense that involves force or threat of force; includes murder and nonnegligent manslaughter, rape, robbery, and aggravated assault. (14)

vision—Intelligent foresight; starts with a mental image that gradually evolves from abstract musings to a concrete series of mission statements, goals, and objectives. (5)

W

White flight—The departure of White families from neighborhoods experiencing racial integration or from cities experiencing school desegregation. (3)

working in "silos"—Occurs when agencies with common interests work independently with no collaboration. (7)

Y

youth gang—A subgroup of a street gang; may refer to a juvenile clique within a gang. (13)

Z

zero tolerance—A policy of punishing all offenses severely, no matter how minor an offense may be. (12)

1

Bayley, D. H. (1994). *Police for the Future.* New York, NY: Oxford.

Bratton, W. J. (1996, Spring). "New Strategies for Combating Crime in New York City." *Fordham Urban Law Journal*, 23, pp. 781–795.

Bureau of Justice Assistance. (1994, August). *Understanding Community Policing: A Framework for Action.* Washington, DC: Author. Retrieved June 3, 2016, from https://www.ncjrs.gov/pdffiles/commp.pdf

Burger, W. E. (1991, May/June). "Introduction." *The Bench and Bar of Minnesota*, p. 26.

Cordner, G. W. (1999). "The Elements of Community Policing." In *Policing Perspectives: An Anthology*, edited by Larry K. Gaines and Gary W. Cordner, pp. 137–149. Los Angeles: Roxbury.

Dulaney, W. M. (1996). *Black Police in America.* Bloomington, IN: Indiana University Press.

Foner, P. S. (1975). *History of Black Americans: From Africa to the Emergence of the Cotton Kingdom.* Westport, CT: Greenwood.

Ford, J. K. (2007). "Building Capability Throughout a Change Effort: Leading the Transformation of a Police Agency to Community Policing." *American Journal of Community Psychology*, 39(3–4), pp. 321–334.

Garmire, B. L., ed. (1989, August). *Local Government Police Management.* Washington, DC: International City Management Association.

Kelling, G. L. (1994, April). "Defining Community Policing." *Subject to Debate*, p. 3.

Kelling, G. L. (1988, June). "Police and Communities: The Quiet Revolution." *Perspectives on Policing.* Washington, DC: U.S. Department of Justice, National Institute of Justice.

Kelling, G. L., & Moore, M. H. (1991). "From Political to Reform to Community: The Evolving Strategy of Police." In *Community Policing: Rhetoric or Reality?*, edited by Jack R. Greene and Stephen D. Mastrofski, pp. 3–25. New York: Praeger.

Klockars, C. B. (1983). *Thinking about Police: Contemporary Readings.* New York, NY: McGraw-Hill.

Lincoln, A. (1863, November 19). *The Gettysburg Address.* Dedication of the Soldiers' National Cemetery. Gettysburg, PA.

Lord, V. B., & Friday, P. C. (2008, June). "What Really Influences Officer Attitudes toward COP? The Importance of Context." *Police Quarterly*, 11(2), pp. 220–238.

Maguire, E. R., & Katz, C. M. (1997, November). "Community Policing and Loose Coupling in American Police Agencies." Paper presented at the annual meeting of the American Society of Criminology, San Diego, CA.

Maguire, E. R., & Mastrofski, S. D. (2000, March). "Patterns of Community Policing in the United States." *Police Quarterly*, 3(1), pp. 4–45.

Melekian, B. K. (2011, March). "The Office of Community Oriented Policing Services." *The Police Chief*, p. 14.

Mentel, Z. (2008, May). "Policing in a Democratic Society." *Community Policing Dispatch.* Retrieved July 12, 2016, from http://cops.usdoj.gov/html/dispatch/may_2008/policing_DS.htm

Morabito, M. S. (2010, October). "Understanding Community Policing as an Innovation: Patterns of Adoption." *Crime & Delinquency*, 56(4), pp. 564–587.

National Commission on Law Observance and Enforcement. (1931). *Report on Lawlessness in Law Enforcement.* Washington, DC: Government Printing Office.

Office of Community Oriented Policing Services. (2014). *Community Policing Defined.* Washington, DC: Author. Retrieved July 12, 2016, from http://www.cops.usdoj.gov/pdf/vets-to-cops/e030917193-CP-Defined.pdf

Peak, K., & Barthe, E. P. (2009, December). "Community Policing and CompStat: Merged, or Mutually Exclusive?" *The Police Chief*, pp. 72, 73 ,74 ,76–78, 80–82, 84. Retrieved June 6, 2016, from http://www.policechiefmagazine.org/magazine/index.cfm?fuseaction=display_arch&article_id=1968&issue_id=122009

Peed, C. R. (2008, November). "The Community Policing Umbrella." *FBI Law Enforcement Bulletin*, 77(11), pp. 22–25.

Potter, G. (2013, June 25). *The History of Policing in the United States, Part I.* Richmond, KY: Eastern Kentucky University. Retrieved June 3, 2016, from http://plsonline.eku.edu/insidelook/history-policing-united-states-part-1

President's Task Force on 21st Century Policing. (2015, May). *Final Report of the President's Task Force on 21st Century Policing.* Washington, DC: Office of Community Oriented Policing Services. Retrieved July 12, 2016, from http://www.cops.usdoj.gov/pdf/taskforce/TaskForce_Final Report.pdf

Reichel, P. L. (1999). "Southern Slave Patrols as a Transitional Police Type." In *Policing Perspectives: An Anthology*, edited by Larry K. Gaines and Gary W. Cordner, pp. 79–92. Los Angeles, CA: Roxbury.

Richardson, J. F. (1970). *The New York Police.* New York, NY: Oxford University Press.

Rohe, W. M., Adams, R. E., Arcury, T. A., Memory, J., & Klopovic, J. (1996). *Community Oriented Policing: The North Carolina Experience*. Chapel Hill, NC: The Center for Urban and Regional Studies.

Rosenberg, H., Sigler, R. T., & Lewis, S. (2008, September). "Police Officer Attitudes toward Community Policing: A Case Study of the Racine, Wisconsin, Police Department." *Police Practice and Research*, 9(4), pp. 291–305.

Roth, J. A., & Johnson, C. C. (1997, November). "COPS Context and Community Policing." Paper presented at the annual meeting of the American Society of Criminology, San Diego, CA.

Simmons, R. C. (1976). *The American Colonies*. New York, NY: McKay.

Skogan, W. G. (2004). "Community Policing: Common Impediments to Success." In *Community Policing: The Past, Present, and Future*, edited by Lorie Fridell and Mary Ann Wycoff, pp. 159–168. Washington, DC: The Annie E. Casey Foundation and Police Executive Research Forum.

Skolnick, J. H., & Bayley, D. H. (1988). "Theme and Variation in Community Policing." In *Crime and Justice: A Review of Research*, edited by M. Tonry and N. Morris, pp. 1–37. Chicago, IL: University of Chicago Press.

Sparrow, M. K. (1998, November). *Implementing Community Policing*. Washington, DC: U.S. Department of Justice, National Institute of Justice.

Trojanowicz, R., & Bucqueroux, B. (1990). *Community Policing: A Contemporary Perspective*. Cincinnati, OH: Anderson.

Upper Midwest Community Policing Institute. (n.d.). *Community Policing Defined*. New Brighton, MN: Author.

Vollmer, A. (1936). *The Police and Modern Society*. Berkeley, CA: University of California Press.

Walker, S. (1997). *Popular Justice: A History of American Criminal Justice*, 2nd ed. New York, NY: Oxford University Press.

Walker, S. L., & Macdonald, M. (2009). "An Alternative Remedy for Police Misconduct: A Model State 'Pattern or Practice' Statute." *Civil Rights Law Journal*, 19(3), pp. 479–552.

Williams, H., & Murphy, P. V. (1990, January). *The Evolving Strategy of Police: A Minority View*. Washington, DC: National Institute of Justice, Perspectives on Policing, No. 13. (NCJ 121019)

Wilson, O. W. (1950). *Police Administration*. New York, NY: McGraw-Hill.

Wilson, O. W. (1952). *Police Planning*. Springfield, IL: Thomas.

2

Basich, M. (2008, April). "A Love-Hate Relationship." *Police*, pp. 54–57.

Bittner, E. (1974). "Florence Nightingale in Pursuit of Willie Sutton: A Theory of Police." In *The Potential for Reform of Criminal Justice*, edited by H. Jacob, pp. 17–44. Beverly Hills, CA: Sage.

Blanchard, K., & Peale, N. V. (1988). *The Power of Ethical Management*. New York: Fawcett Crest.

Borrello, A. (2005, January). "Defining the Building Blocks of Ethics." *Law and Order*, pp. 65–68.

Commission on Accreditation of Law Enforcement Agencies. (2012). *Standards for Law Enforcement Agencies*. 5th ed. Fairfax, VA: Author.

"Considering Police Body Cameras." (2015, April 10). *Harvard Law Review*, 128(6), pp. 1794–1817. Retrieved July 15, 2016, from http://harvardlawreview.org/2015/04/considering-police-body-cameras/

DeLone, G. J. (2007, June). "Law Enforcement Mission Statements Post-September 11." *Police Quarterly*, 10(2), pp. 218–235.

Ederheimer, J., & Johnson, W. (2007, April). "Introduction." In *Strategies for Resolving and Minimizing Use of Force*, edited by Joshua A. Ederheimer, pp. 1–11. Washington, DC: Police Executive Research Forum, Critical Issues in Policing Series.

Everett, B. (2006, Spring). "Officer Discretion and Serving the Community." *Minnesota Police Chief*, pp. 10–11.

Famega, C. N., Frank, J., & Mazerolle, L. (2005). "Managing Police Patrol Time: The Role of Supervisor Directives." *Justice Quarterly*, 22(4), pp. 540–559.

Federal Bureau of Investigation. (2010, March 30). *A Different Kind of Training: What New Agents Learn from the Holocaust*. Washington, DC: Author. Retrieved June 20, 2016, from https://www.fbi.gov/news/stories/2010/march/leas_033010/a-different-kind-of-training-what-new-agents-learn-from-the-holocaust

Futterman, C., Mather, M., & Miles, M. (2007, November 15). "Report Says 'Culture of Denial' Allows Police Abuse in Chicago." *Criminal Justice Newsletter*, pp. 3–4.

Gilmartin, K. M., & Harris, J. J. (1998). "The Continuum of Compromise." *The Police Chief*, 65(1), pp. 25–28.

Goldstein, H. (1990). *Problem-Oriented Policing*. New York: McGraw-Hill.

Goldstein, J. (2004). "Police Discretion Not to Invoke the Criminal Process: Low-Visibility Decisions in the Administration of Justice." In *The Criminal Justice System: Politics and Policies*, 9th ed., edited by George F. Cole, Marc G. Gertz, and Amy Bunger, pp. 77–95. Belmont, CA: Thomson Wadsworth.

Horowitz, J. (2007). "Making Every Encounter Count: Building Trust and Confidence in the Police." *NIJ Journal*, (256), pp. 8–11.

Hyland, S., Langton, L., & Davis, E. (2015, November). *Police Use of Nonfatal Force, 2002-11*. Washington, DC: Bureau of Justice Statistics. (NCJ 249216). Retrieved July 14, 2016, from http://www.bjs.gov/content/pub/pdf/punf0211.pdf

Independent Police Complaints Commission, (n.d.). *Complaints and Appeals*. Sale, United Kingdom: Author. Retrieved July 15, 2016, from http://www.ipcc.gov.uk/complaints

International Association of Chiefs of Police. (n.d.). *Ethics Training in Law Enforcement*. Report by the Ethics Training Subcommittee of the IACP Ad Hoc Committee on Police Image and Ethics, Ethics Toolkit. Retrieved July 15, 2016, from http://www.iacp.org/-Ethics-Training-in-Law-Enforcement

International Association of Chiefs of Police. (2008, May). *Police Chiefs Desk Reference: A Guide for Newly Appointed Police Leaders*, 2nd ed. Boston, MA: McGraw Hill Learning Solutions. Retrieved July 14, 2016, from http://www.theiacp.org/Portals/0/documents/pdfs/PCDR2updated.pdf

Johnson, R. R. (2015, July). *Citizen Satisfaction with the Police: The Impact of a Negative Police Contact*. Plainfield, IN: Legal & Liability Risk Management Institute. Retrieved July 16, 2016, from http://www.llrmi.com/articles/legal_update/2015_johnson_citizensatisfaction2.shtml

Kindy, K., Fisher, M., Tate, J., & Jenkins, J. (2015, December 26). "A Year of Reckoning: Police Fatally Shoot Nearly 1,000." *The Washington Post.* Retrieved July 14, 2016, from http://www.washingtonpost.com/sf/investigative/wp/2015/12/26/2015/12/26/a-year-of-reckoning-police-fatally-shoot-nearly-1000/

Klockars, C. B. (1985). *The Idea of Police.* Newbury Park, CA: Sage.

Klockars, C. B. (1991). "The Rhetoric of Community Policing." In *Community Policing: Rhetoric or Reality,* edited by Jack R. Greene and Stephen D. Mastrofski, pp. 239–258. New York: Praeger.

Lohner, W. (2011, August). "What Does It Take to Excel?" *FBI Law Enforcement Bulletin,* pp. 20–23.

Marcou, D. (2009, February 18). "'Community Oriented' SWAT." *Police One.* Retrieved July 15, 2016, from https://www.policeone.com/community-policing/articles/1787649-Community-Oriented-SWAT/

Martin, R. (2011, May). "Police Corruption: An Analytical Look into Police Ethics." *FBI Law Enforcement Bulletin,* pp. 11–17.

Martinelli, T. J. (2011, March). "Noble Cause Corruption and Police Discretion." *The Police Chief,* pp. 60–62.

Miller, L., & Toliver, J. (2014, September). *Implementing a Body-Worn Camera Program: Recommendations and Lessons Learned.* Washington, DC: Police Executive Research Forum.

National Institute of Justice. (2005, December). *Enhancing Police Integrity.* Washington, DC: Author.

Oldham, S. (2006, May). "Proud of the Police Culture." *Law and Order,* pp. 18–21.

Paoline, E. A., III. (2004, June). "Shedding Light on Police Culture: An Examination of Officers' Occupational Attitudes." *Police Quarterly,* 7(2), pp. 205–236.

Police Executive Research Forum. (2015). *Re-engineering Training on Police Use of Force.* Critical Issues in Policing Series. Washington, DC: Author.

President's Task Force on 21st Century Policing. (2015, May). *Final Report of the President's Task Force on 21st Century Policing.* Washington, DC: Office of Community Oriented Policing Services. Retrieved July 12, 2016, from http://www.cops.usdoj.gov/pdf/taskforce/TaskForce_FinalReport.pdf

Quinn, M. W. (2005). *Walking with the Devil: The Police Code of Silence.* Minneapolis, MN: Quinn and Associates.

Ramsey, D. X. (2015, August 7). "Tracking Police Violence a Year after Ferguson." *FiveThirtyEight.* Retrieved July 14, 2016, from http://fivethirtyeight.com/features/ferguson-michael-brown-measuring-police-killings/

Reaves, B. A. (2015, May). *Local Police Departments, 2013: Personnel, Policies, and Practices.* Washington, DC: Bureau of Justice Statistics (NCJ 248677). Retrieved June 22, 2016, from http://www.bjs.gov/content/pub/pdf/lpd13ppp.pdf

Rosenbaum, D. P., Schuck, A. M., Costello, S. K., Hawkins, D. F., & Ring, M. K. (2005, September). "Attitudes toward the Police: The Effects of Direct and Vicarious Experience." *Police Quarterly,* 8(3), pp. 343–365.

Saad, L. (2015, December 21). *Americans' Faith in Honesty, Ethics of Police Rebounds.* Washington, DC: Gallup. Retrieved July 13, 2016, from http://www.gallup.com/poll/187874/americans-faith-honesty-ethics-police-rebounds.aspx

San Jose Police Department. (2016). *San Jose Police Department Vision, Mission, and Values Statements.* San Jose, CA: Author. Retrieved June 22, 2016, from http://www.sjpd.org/COP/MissionStatement.html

Scrivner, E. (2006). *Innovations in Police Recruitment and Hiring: Hiring in the Spirit of Service.* Washington, DC: U.S. Department of Justice, Office of Community Oriented Policing Services. Retrieved July 13, 2016, from http://www.cops.usdoj.gov/pdf/vets-to-cops/innovationpolicerecruitmenthiring.pdf

Skogan, W. G. (2005, September). "Citizen Satisfaction with Police Encounters." *Police Quarterly,* 8(3), pp. 295–321.

Skolnick, J. H. (1966). "A Sketch of the Policeman's 'Working Personality.'" In *Justice without Trial: Law Enforcement in a Democratic Society,* pp. 42–62. New York: John Wiley & Sons. Reprinted in *The Criminal Justice System: Politics and Policies,* 9th ed., edited by George F. Cole, Marc G. Gertz, and Amy Bunger, pp. 109–126. Belmont, CA: Thomson Wadsworth, 2004.

Smith, D. (2011, August). "DVR Dreams." *Police,* p. 84.

Son, I. S., & Rome, D. M. (2004, June). "The Prevalence and Visibility of Police Misconduct: A Survey of Citizens and Police Officers." *Police Quarterly,* 7(2), pp. 179–204.

Sourcebook of Criminal Justice Statistics Online. (n.d.) Washington, DC: Bureau of Justice Statistics. Retrieved July 13, 2016, from http://www.albany.edu/sourcebook/pdf/t2202012.pdf

Sutton, R. (2005, March). "Ethical Survival." *Law Officer Magazine,* pp. 64–65.

Trautman, N. (2000). *Police Code of Silence Facts Revealed.* 2000 Conference Materials, Legal Officers Section, International Association of Chiefs of Police.

United States Department of Justice. (2015, March 4). *Investigation of the Ferguson Police Department.* Washington, DC: Author. Retrieved July 14, 2016, from https://www.justice.gov/sites/default/files/opa/press-releases/attachments/2015/03/04/ferguson_police_department_report.pdf

Walls, K. G. (2003, July). "Not a Token Effort." *FBI Law Enforcement Bulletin,* pp. 16–17.

Wargo, E. (2006, August). "Bad Apples or Bad Barrels? Zimbardo on 'The Lucifer Effect.'" *The Association for Psychological Science Observer,* 19(8). Retrieved July 15, 2016, from http://www.psychologicalscience.org/index.php/publications/observer/2006/august-06/bad-apples-or-bad-barrels-zimbardo-on-the-lucifer-effect.html

Wexler, C. (2015, August). "Summary: What You Will Find in This Report." In *Re-Engineering Training on Police Use of Force,* pp. 3–10. Washington, DC: Police Executive Research Forum.

Wilson, J. Q., & Kelling, G. L. (1989, February). "Making Neighborhoods Safe." *Atlantic Monthly,* pp. 46–52.

3

Agnew, R. (2005). *Why Do Criminals Offend? A General Theory of Crime and Delinquency.* Los Angeles, CA: Roxbury Publishing Company.

Ankerfelt, J., Davis, M., & Futterer, L. (2011). "The Brooklyn Park, Minnesota, Police's Joint Community-Police Partnership." *The Police Chief,* 77(3), pp. 22–31.

Beaver, K. M., DeLisi, M., Mears, D. P., & Stewart, E. (2009, December). "Low Self-Control and Contact with the Criminal Justice System in a Nationally Representative Sample of Males." *Justice Quarterly*, 26(4), pp. 696–715.

Blake, A. (2016, March 3). "NYPD To Stop Arresting People for Public Urination, Alcohol Consumption in Manhattan." *The Washington Times*. Retrieved July 17, 2016, from http://www.washingtontimes.com/news/2016/mar/3/nypd-stop-arresting-people-public-urination-alcoho/

Braga, A. A., Welsh, B. C., & Schnell, C. (2015). "Can Policing Disorder Reduce Crime? A Systematic Review and Meta-Analysis." *Journal of Research in Crime and Delinquency*, 52(4), pp. 567–588.

Brewster, J., Stoloff, M. L., & Sanders, N. (2005, Fall). "Effectiveness of Citizen Police Academies in Changing the Attitudes, Beliefs, and Behavior of Citizen Participants." *American Journal of Criminal Justice*, pp. 21–34.

Bureau of Labor Statistics. (2016, March 30). *May 2015 National Occupational Employment and Wage Estimates, United States.* Washington, DC: Author. Retrieved July 18, 2016, from http://www.bls.gov/oes/current/oes_nat.htm#43-0000

Center for Evidence-Based Crime Policy. (2013). *Broken Windows Policing.* Fairfax, VA: Author. Retrieved July 17, 2016, from http://cebcp.org/evidence-based-policing/what-works-in-policing/research-evidence-review/broken-windows-policing/

Colby, S. L., & Ortman, J. M. (2015, March). *Projections of the Size and Composition of the U.S. Population: 2014 to 2060.* Current Population Reports, P25-1143. Washington, DC: U.S. Census Bureau. Retrieved July 18, 2016, from http://www.census.gov/content/dam/Census/library/publications/2015/demo/p25-1143.pdf

Coleman, J. (1990). *Foundations of Social Theory.* Cambridge: Harvard University Press.

Correia, M. E. (2000). *Citizen Involvement: How Community Factors Affect Progressive Policing.* Washington, DC: Police Executive Research Forum.

Devers, L. (2011, January 24). *Plea and Charge Bargaining.* Washington, DC: Bureau of Justice Assistance. Retrieved July 18, 2016, from https://www.bja.gov/Publications/PleaBargainingResearchSummary.pdf

Gonzalez-Barrera, A. (2015, November 19). *More Mexicans Leaving Than Coming to the U.S.* Washington, DC: Pew Research Center. Retrieved July 18, 2016, from http://www.pewhispanic.org/2015/11/19/more-mexicans-leaving-than-coming-to-the-u-s/

Gottfredson, M. R., & Hirschi, T. (1990). *A General Theory of Crime.* Stanford, CA: Stanford University Press.

Harcourt, B. E., & Ludwig, J. (2006). "Broken Windows: New Evidence from New York City and a Five-City Social Experiment." *The University of Chicago Law Review*, 73, pp. 271–320.

International Association of Chiefs of Police. (2011). *Volunteers in Police Service Add Value While Budgets Decrease.* Alexandria, VA: Author. Retrieved July 18, 2016, from http://www.iacp.org/Portals/0/documents/pdfs/VIPS_police_service_add_value_while_budgets_decrease.pdf

Jargowsky, P. A. (2009, January). "Cause or Consequence? Suburbanization and Crime in U.S. Metropolitan Areas." *Crime & Delinquency*, 55(1), pp. 28–50.

Kaste, M. (2015, February 21). "Police Are Learning to Accept Civilian Oversight, But Distrust Lingers." Retrieved July 18, 2016, from http://www.npr.org/2015/02/21/387770044/police-are-learning-to-accept-civilian-oversight-but-distrust-lingers

Kaufman, J. M. (2009, September). "Gendered Responses to Serious Strain: The Argument for a General Strain Theory of Deviance." *Justice Quarterly*, 26(3), pp. 410–444.

Kingman, K. (2005, Winter). "Volunteers: Three Ingredients for Success." *Community Links*, pp. 4–5.

Kolb, N. (2005, June). "Law Enforcement Volunteerism: Leveraging Resources to Enhance Public Safety." *The Police Chief*, pp. 22–30.

Mangino, M. T. (2014, January 7). "How Plea Bargains Are Making Jury Trials Obsolete." *The Crime Report.* Retrieved July 18, 2016, from http://www.thecrimereport.org/viewpoints/2014-01-how-plea-bargains-are-making-jury-trials-obsolete

Messner, S. F., & Rosenfeld, R. (2007). *Crime and the American Dream*, 4th ed. Belmont, CA: Wadsworth.

National Crime Prevention Council. (2016). *About Teens, Crime, and the Community.* Gambrills, MD: Author. Retrieved July 18, 2016, from http://www.ncpc.org/programs/teens-crime-and-the-community/about-tcc

Office of Community Oriented Policing Services. (n.d.). *Private Security and Public Law Enforcement.* Washington, DC: Author. Retrieved July 18, 2016, from http://www.cops.usdoj.gov/Default.asp?Item=2034

President's Task Force on 21st Century Policing. (2015, May). *Final Report of the President's Task Force on 21st Century Policing.* Washington, DC: Office of Community Oriented Policing Services. Retrieved July 12, 2016, from http://www.cops.usdoj.gov/pdf/taskforce/TaskForce_FinalReport.pdf

Rosenblum, M. R., & Soto, A. G. R. (2015, August). *An Analysis of Unauthorized Immigrants in the United States by Country and Region of Birth.* Washington, DC: Migration Policy Institute. Retrieved July 18, 2016, from http://www.migrationpolicy.org/research/analysis-unauthorized-immigrants-united-states-country-and-region-birth

Skogan, W. G. (2004). "Community Policing: Common Impediments to Success." In *Community Policing: The Past, Present, and Future*, edited by Lorie Fridell and Mary Ann Wycoff, pp. 159–168. Washington, DC: The Annie E. Casey Foundation and Police Executive Research Forum.

Tribune News Service. (2012, August 9). "As Police Budgets Dwindle, More U.S. Residents, Cities Hiring Private Security." *Governing.* Retrieved July 18, 2016, from http://www.governing.com/news/local/mct-more-residents-cities-hiring-private-security.html

United States Census Bureau. (2016). *U.S. and World Population Clock.* Washington, DC: Author. Retrieved July 18, 2016, from http://www.census.gov/popclock/?eml=gd&intcmp=home_pop&utm_medium=email&utm_source=govdelivery

Wilson, J. Q., & George L. K. (1982). "The Police and Neighborhood Safety: Broken Windows." *Atlantic Monthly* (March), pp. 29–38.

4

Bichler, G., & Gaines, L. (2005, January). "An Examination of Police Officers' Insights into Problem Identification and Problem Solving." *Crime and Delinquency,* 51(1), pp. 53–74.

Brito, C. S., & Allan, T., eds. (1999). *Problem-Oriented Policing.* 2nd vol. Washington, DC: Police Executive Research Forum.

Bruinius, H. (2014, August 24). "N.Y.C. Crime Is Low: But At What Cost?" *The Christian Science Monitor.* Retrieved July 20, 2016, from http://www.csmonitor.com/USA/2014/0824/N.Y.C.-crime-is-low-But-at-what-cost

Burke, T., & Hermacinski, E. (2011). *Armadillos: Starting a Trend.* Peoria, IL: Peoria Police Department. Retrieved July 20, 2016, from http://www.popcenter.org/library/awards/goldstein/2011/11-07.pdf

Center for Problem-Oriented Policing. (2012a). *The Herman Goldstein Award Projects.* Washington, DC: Author. Retrieved July 20, 2016, from http://www.popcenter.org/library/awards/goldstein

Center for Problem-Oriented Policing. (2012b). *Tilley Award Projects.* Washington, DC: Author. Retrieved July 20, 2016, from http://www.popcenter.org/library/awards/tilley

Clarke, R. V., & Eck, J. E. (2005, August). *Crime Analysis for Problem Solvers in 60 Small Steps.* Washington, DC: Office of Community Oriented Policing Services. Retrieved July 20, 2016, from http://www.cops.usdoj.gov/pdf/CrimeAnalysis-60Steps.pdf

Crisp, H. D., & Hines, R. J. (2007, February). "The CompStat Process in Columbia." *The Police Chief,* pp. 46–48.

Eck, J. E. (2002). *Assessing Responses to Problems: An Introductory Guide for Police Problem-Solvers.* Washington, DC: Office of Community Oriented Policing Services.

Eck, J. E. (2005, August). "Crime Hot Spots: What They Are, Why We Have Them, and How to Map Them." In *Mapping Crime: Understanding Hot Spots,* edited by John E. Eck, et al., pp. 1–15. Washington, DC: National Institute of Justice. (NIJ 209393)

Eck, J. E., & Spelman, W. (1987). *Problem-Solving: Problem-Oriented Policing in Newport News.* Washington, DC: The Police Executive Research Forum.

Goldstein, H. (1990). *Problem-Oriented Policing.* New York: McGraw-Hill.

Goldstein, H. (2001). *What Is POP?* Albany, NY: Center for Problem-Oriented Policing. Retrieved July 19, 2016, from http://www.popcenter.org/about/?p=whatiscpop

Goldstein, H., & Susmilch, C. E. (1981, March). *The Problem-Oriented Approach to Improving Police Service: A Description of the Project and an Elaboration of the Concept.* Madison, WI: Madison, Wisconsin Police Department and the Project on Development of a Problem-Oriented Approach to Improving Police Service at the Law School, University of Wisconsin—Madison.

Harries, K. (1999, December). *Mapping Crime: Principle and Practice.* Washington, DC: Institute of Justice.

Hoelzer, G., & Gorman, J. (2011, November). "Incorporating Hot-Spots Policing into Your Daily Patrol Plan." *FBI Law Enforcement Bulletin,* pp. 10–15.

Jang, H., Hoover, L. T., & Joo, H. (2010, December). "An Evaluation of CompStat's Effect on Crime: The Fort Worth Experience." *Police Quarterly,* 13(4), pp. 387–412.

Kates, G. (2012, May). "Cracking the 'Blue Wall of Silence.'" *The Crime Report.* New York: John Jay College of Criminal Justice. Retrieved July 20, 2016, from http://www.thecrimereport.org/news/inside-criminal-justice/2012-05-cracking-the-blue-wall-of-silence

Markovic, J., & Scalisi, N. (2011). "Full Spectrum Use of GIS by Law Enforcement: It's Not Just about Mapping Crime." *Geography and Public Safety,* 3(1), pp. 2–4.

McCue, C. (2011). "Proactive Policing: Using Geographic Analysis to Fight Crime." *Geography and Public Safety,* 2(4), pp. 3–5.

National Association for Community Mediation. (n.d.). *Purpose.* Louisville, KY: Author. Retrieved July 19, 2016, from http://www.nafcm.org/?page=Purpose

National Institute of Justice. (2009). *Geographic Profiling.* Washington, DC: National Institute of Justice. Retrieved July 20, 2016, from https://www.ncjrs.gov/html/nij/mapping/ch6_1.html

Newman, G. R., & Socia, K. (2007). *Sting Operations.* Washington, DC: Center for Problem-Oriented Policing, Response Guide No. 6.

Office of Community Oriented Policing Services. (2011, July). *Problem-Solving Tips: A Guide to Reducing Crime and Disorder through Problem-Solving Partnerships,* 2nd ed. Washington, DC: Author. (e050600069)

Peed, C., Wilson, R. E., & Scalisi, N. J. (2008, September). "Making Smarter Decisions: Connecting Crime Analysis with City Officials." *The Police Chief,* pp. 20–28.

Police Executive Research Forum. (2008, May). *Violent Crime in America: What We Know about Hot Spots Enforcement.* Washington, DC: Author.

Rossmo, D. K. (2005, July 1). *What Is Crime Mapping? Briefing Book.* Washington, DC: National Institute of Justice. Retrieved July 20, 2016, from http://www.cops.usdoj.gov/html/cd_rom/tech_docs/pubs/WhatIsCrimeMapping-BriefingBook.pdf

Schmerler, K., Perkins, M., Philips, S., Rinehart, T., & Townsend, M. (2011, July). *Problem-Solving Tips: A Guide to Reducing Crime and Disorder through Problem-Solving Partnerships.* 2nd ed. Washington, DC: Office of Community Oriented Policing Services. Retrieved July 20, 2016, from http://www.popcenter.org/library/reading/pdfs/ProbSolvTips_2ed.pdf

Scott, M. S. (2000). *Problem-Oriented Policing: Reflections on the First 20 Years.* Washington, DC: U.S. Department of Justice, Office of Community Oriented Policing Services.

Scott, M., & Goldstein, H. (1988). *The Key Elements of Problem-Oriented Policing.* Washington, DC: Center for Problem-Oriented Policing. Retrieved July 19, 2016, from http://www.popcenter.org/about/?p=elements

Serpas, R. W., & Morley, M. (2008, May). "The Next Step in Accountability-Driven Leadership: 'CompStating' the CompStat Data." *The Police Chief,* pp. 60–70.

White, M. B. (2008, February). *Enhancing the Problem-Solving Capacity of Crime Analysis Units.* Washington, DC: Center for Problem-Oriented Policing, Problem-Solving Tools Series, Guide No. 9. Retrieved July 20, 2016, from http://www.popcenter.org/tools/PDFs/enhancing_capacity.pdf

Wilson, J. Q., & Kelling, G. L. (1989, February). "Making Neighborhoods Safe." *Atlantic Monthly,* pp. 46–52.

Wintersteen, J. D. (2007, February). "CompStat and Crime Prevention in Paradise Valley." *The Police Chief,* pp. 52–58.

5

Braga, A. A., & Weisburd, D. L. (2007, May). "Police Innovation and Crime Prevention: Lessons Learned from Police Research over the Past 20 Years." Unpublished paper presented at the National Institute of Justice (NIJ) Policing Research Workshop: Planning for the Future, Washington, DC. (Document No. 218585) Retrieved August 2, 2016, from https://www.ncjrs.gov/pdffiles1/nij/grants/218585.pdf

Broken Arrow Police Department Leadership Team. (2006). "How to Implement Shared Leadership." *The Police Chief,* 73(4), pp. 34–37.

Community Policing Consortium. (n.d.). *Recruitment and Selection for Community Policing.* (Monograph). Washington, DC: Author.

Community Policing Consortium. (2000). *The Police Organization in Transition: Organization and Framework.* Washington, DC: Author.

Connors, E., & Webster, B. (2001, January). *Transforming the Law Enforcement Organization to Community Policing.* (Final Monograph). Unpublished report prepared for the National Institute of Justice, Washington, DC. Retrieved August 2, 2016, from https://www.ncjrs.gov/pdffiles1/nij/grants/200610.pdf

Correia, M. E. (2000). *Citizen Involvement: How Community Factors Affect Progressive Policing.* Washington, DC: Police Executive Research Forum.

Davis, M. (1998, March). *Community Policing and Law Enforcement.* Washington, DC: U.S. Department of Agriculture, Office of Community Development, OCD Technote 14.

Florida Regional Community Policing Institute. (2004, September). *Changing Roles: Supervising Today's Community Police Officer* (Course Manual). St. Petersburg, FL: Author. Retrieved July 26, 2016, from http://cop.spcollege.edu/training/supervising/chaningroles.pdf

Goldstein, H. (1990). *Problem-Oriented Policing.* Philadelphia: McGraw-Hill.

Haberfeld, M. R. (2006). *Police Leadership,* Upper Saddle River, NJ: Pearson/Prentice Hall.

Harr, J. S., & Hess, K. M. (2010). *Seeking Employment in Criminal Justice and Related Fields.* 6th ed. Belmont, CA: Wadsworth.

Hess, K. M., Orthmann, C. H., & LaDue, S. (2016). *Management and Supervision in Law Enforcement,* 7th ed. Boston, MA: Cengage Learning.

Kennedy, D. M. (2006). "Chapter 8: Old Wine in New Bottles: Policing and the Lessons of Pulling Levers." In *Police Innovation: Contrasting Perspectives,* edited by David L. Weisburd and Anthony A. Braga, pp. 155–170. New York: Cambridge University Press.

Kohlhepp, K., & Phillips, T. (2009). "DiscoverPolicing.org: A Nationwide Online Recruiting Resource for the Law Enforcement Profession." *The Police Chief,* 76(1).

Kurz, D. L. (2006, Summer). "Strategic Planning: Building Police–Community Partnerships in Small Towns." *Big Ideas for Small Police Departments,* pp. 1–9.

Los Angeles Police Department. (2006, May 12). "Los Angeles Police Department News Release: LAPD Unveils Blog." *Los Angeles Times.* Retrieved November 1, 2016, from http://lapdonline.org/may_2006/news_view/29954

Matrix Group. (2009, February 25). *International Association of Chiefs of Police Wins the 2008 Interactive Media Awards Best in Class for the Discover Policing Web Site.* Alexandria, VA: Author. Retrieved August 2, 2016, from http://www.matrixgroup.net/news-events/news/2009/02/25/international-association-of-chiefs-of-police-wins-the-2008-interactive-media-awards-best-in-class-for-the-discover-policing-web-site

McEwen, T., Spence, D., Wolff, R., Wartell, J., & Webster, B. (2003, July). *Call Management and Community Policing: A Guidebook for Law Enforcement.* Washington, DC: Office of Community Oriented Policing Services.

National Research Council. (2004). *Fairness and Effectiveness in Policing: The Evidence.* Committee to Review Research on Police Policy and Practices. Wesley Skogan and Kathleen Frydl, editors. Committee on Law and Justice, Division of Behavioral and Social Sciences and Education. Washington, DC: The National Academies Press.

Nelson, T. (2004, July 1). *PTO: An Overview and Introduction.* Washington, DC: Police Executive Research Forum and the COPS Office. Retrieved July 28, 2016, from http://ric-zai-inc.com/Publications/cops-w0150-pub.pdf

Newburn, T. (2008). *Handbook of Policing.* Devon, UK: Willan.

Office of Community Oriented Policing Services. (2006, January 9). *Regional Community Policing Institutes.* Fact sheet. Washington, DC: Author. Retrieved July 28, 2016, from http://www.cops.usdoj.gov/txt/fact_sheets/e01063526.txt

Peak, C. (2014, December 17). "Minorities Should Want to Be Police Officers." *NationSwell.* Retrieved July 28, 2016, from http://nationswell.com/strategies-to-increase-number-of-minority-police-officers/#ixzz4EmN3m0G3

President's Task Force on 21st Century Policing. (2015, May). *Final Report of the President's Task Force on 21st Century Policing.* Washington, DC: Office of Community Oriented Policing Services. Retrieved July 12, 2016, from http://www.cops.usdoj.gov/pdf/taskforce/TaskForce_FinalReport.pdf

Reaves, B. A. (2015, May). *Local Police Departments, 2013: Personnel, Policies, and Practices.* Washington, DC: Bureau of Justice Statistics. (NCJ 248677) Retrieved July 28, 2016, from http://www.bjs.gov/content/pub/pdf/lpd13ppp.pdf

Scheider, M. (2008). "Community Policing Nugget: Community Policing Specialists vs. Generalists." *Community Policing Dispatch,* 1(4). Retrieved November 1, 2016, from https://cops.usdoj.gov/html/dispatch/april_2008/nugget.htm

Scott, M. S. (2000, October). *Problem-Oriented Policing: Reflections on the First 20 Years.* Washington, DC: Community Oriented Policing Services.

Scrivner, E. (2006). *Innovations in Police Recruitment and Hiring: Hiring in the Spirit of Diversity*. Washington, DC: Office of Community Oriented Policing Services.

Skogan, W. G. (2004a). "Community Policing: Common Impediments to Success." In *Community Policing: The Past, Present, and Future*, edited by Lorie Fridell and Mary Ann Wycoff, pp. 159–167. Washington, DC: The Annie E. Casey Foundation and the Police Executive Research Forum.

Skogan, W. G. (2004b). "Representing the Community in Community Policing." In *Community Policing (Can It Work?)*, edited by Wesley G. Skogan, pp. 57–75. Belmont, CA: Wadsworth.

Walker, S. (1993). "Does Anyone Remember Team Policing? Lessons of the Team Policing Experience for Community Policing." *American Journal of Police*, 12(1), pp. 33–56.

Wuestewald, T., & Steinheider, B. (2006a). "Can Empowerment Work in Police Organizations?" *The Police Chief,* 73(1), pp. 48–55.

Wuestewald, T., & Steinheider, B. (2006b). "The Changing Face of Police Leadership." *The Police Chief,* 73(4), pp. 26–33.

6

Alzheimer's Association. (2016). *2016, Alzheimer's Disease Facts & Figures.* Chicago, IL: Author. Retrieved August 8, 2016, from http://www.alz.org/documents_custom/2016-facts-and-figures.pdf

America's Youngest Outcasts: A Report Card on Child Homelessness. (2014). Needham, MA: The National Center on Family Homelessness at American Institutes for Research. Retrieved August 8, 2016, from http://www.air.org/sites/default/files/downloads/report/Americas-Youngest-Outcasts-Child-Homelessness-Nov2014.pdf

Association for Children with Learning Disabilities. (2016). *About Specific Learning Disabilities.* Pittsburgh, PA: Author. Retrieved August 8, 2016, from http://www.acldtillotsonschool.org/Definition.aspx

Colby, S. L., & Ortman, J. M. (2015, March). *Projections of the Size and Composition of the U.S. Population: 2014 to 2060.* Current Population Reports, P25-1143. Washington, DC: U.S. Census Bureau. Retrieved August 5, 2016, from http://www.census.gov/content/dam/Census/library/publications/2015/demo/p25-1143.pdf

Comey, J. N. (2015, February 12). *Hard Truths: Law Enforcement and Race.* Washington, DC: Federal Bureau of Investigation. Retrieved August 7, 2016, from https://www.fbi.gov/news/speeches/hard-truths-law-enforcement-and-race

Cordner, G. (2006, May). *People with Mental Illness.* Problem-Oriented Guides for Police, Problem-Specific Guides Series, No. 40. Washington, DC: Office of Community Oriented Policing Services.

Curtin, S. C., Warner, M., & Hedegaard, H. (2016, April). *Increase in Suicide in the United States, 1999-2014* (NCHS Data Brief, No.241). Washington, DC: U.S. Department of Health and Human Services, National Center for Health Statistics. Retrieved August 8, 2016, from http://www.cdc.gov/nchs/data/databriefs/db241.pdf

Dasgupta, N. (2013). "Implicit Attitudes and Beliefs Adapt to Situations: A Decade of Research on the Malleability of Implicit Prejudice, Stereotypes, and the Self-Concept." *Advances in Experimental Social Psychology*, 47, pp. 233–279.

A Dream Denied: The Criminalization of Homelessness in U.S. Cities. (2006, January). A Report by the National Coalition for the Homeless and the National Law Center on Homelessness and Poverty. Retrieved August 8, 2016, from http://www.nationalhomeless.org/publications/crimreport/report.pdf

Ekins, E. (2014, October 14). *Poll: 70% of Americans Oppose Racial Profiling by the Police.* Washington, DC: Reason Foundation. Retrieved August 8, 2016, from http://reason.com/poll/2014/10/14/poll-70-of-americans-oppose-racial-profi

Epilepsy Foundation. (n.d.). *Law Enforcement/EMS Response to Seizures.* Landover, MD: Author. Retrieved August 8, 2016, from http://www.epilepsy.com/get-help/services-and-support/training-programs/first-responder-training/law-enforcementems-response

Fridell, L. (2011). *Fair and Impartial Policing.* PowerPoint. Retrieved November 1, 2016, from http://www.cops.usdoj.gov/pdf/conference/2011/FairandImpartialPolicing-Fridell.pdf

Fridell, L. (2015). *Fair and Impartial Policing.* Tampa, FL: Fair and Impartial Policing. Retrieved August 7, 2016, from http://static1.squarespace.com/static/54722818e4b0b3ef26cdc085/t/5623ec8ce4b0099ac-9caaada/1445194892676/Extended_About+FIP_2015.pdf

Glenn, R. W., Panitch, B. R., Barnes-Proby, D., Williams, E., Christian, J., Lewis, M. W., Gerwehr, S., & Brannan, D. W. (2003). *Training the 21st Century Police Officer: Redefining Police Professionalism for the Los Angeles Police Department.* Santa Monica, CA: Rand Public Safety and Justice.

Giles, H., Fortman, J., Dailey, R., Barker, V., & Hajek, C. (2005). *Hate, Violence, and Death on Main Street USA: A Report on Hate Crimes and Violence against People Experiencing Homelessness, 2005.* Washington, DC: National Coalition for the Homeless.

Gonzalez-Barrera, A. (2015, November 19). *More Mexicans Leaving Than Coming to the U.S.* Washington, DC: Pew Research Center. Retrieved August 5, 2016, from http://www.pewhispanic.org/2015/11/19/more-mexicans-leaving-than-coming-to-the-u-s/

Haddad, R. (2011). "Building Trust, Driving Relationships with the Dearborn, Michigan, Arab American Community." *The Police Chief,* 78(3), pp. 42–47.

Henderson, N. J., Ortiz, C. W., Sugie, N. F., & Miller, J. (2006). *Law Enforcement and Arab American Community Relations after September 11, 2001: Engagement in a Time of Uncertainty.* New York, NY: Vera Institute of Justice.

Hill, R., Guill, G., & Ellis, K. (2004). "The Montgomery County CIT Model: Interacting with People with Mental Illness." *FBI Law Enforcement Bulletin,* 73(7), pp. 18–25.

Hoefer, M., Rytina, N., & Baker, B. C. (2011, February). *Estimates of Unauthorized Immigrant Population Residing in the United States: January 2010.* Washington, DC: Department of Homeland Security, Office of Immigration Statistics.

Homes Not Handcuffs: The Criminalization of Homelessness in U.S. Cities. (2009, July). Washington, DC: National Law Center on Homelessness & Poverty and the National Coalition for the Homeless. Retrieved August 8, 2016, from http://www.nationalhomeless.org/publications/crimreport/crimreport_2009.pdf

"Justice Department Offers Local Police Guidance for Complying with ADA." (2006, May 15). *Criminal Justice Newsletter,* pp. 1–3.

Khashu, A., Busch, R., & Latif, Z. (2005, August). *Building Strong Police–Immigrant Community Relations: Lessons from a New York City Project.* New York, NY: Vera Institute of Justice. Retrieved August 5, 2016, from http://archive.vera.org/sites/default/files/resources/downloads/300_564.pdf

Lysakowski, M., Pearsall, A. A., III, & Pope, J. (2009, June). *Policing in New Immigrant Communities.* Washington, DC: Office of Community Oriented Policing Services. (e060924209)

Mohandie, K., Meloy, J. R., & Collins, P. I. (2009). "Suicide by Cop among Officer-Involved Shooting Cases." *Journal of Forensic Sciences,* 54(2), pp. 456–462.

Moore, C. (2006). "Policing the Mentally Ill." *Law Enforcement Technology,* 33(8), p. 134.

National Coalition for the Homeless. (2010, January). *Hate Crimes against the Homeless: Violence Hidden in Plain View.* Washington, DC: Author.

National Initiative for Building Community Trust and Justice. (2015). *Implicit Bias.* Community-Oriented Trust and Justice Briefs. Washington, DC: Office of Community Oriented Policing Services. Retrieved August 7, 2016, from http://ric-zai-inc.com/Publications/cops-w0793-pub.pdf

National Institute of Mental Health. (2015). *Suicide in America: Frequently Asked Questions (2015).* Washington, DC: Author. Retrieved August 8, 2016, from http://www.nimh.nih.gov/health/publications/suicide-faq/index.shtml

National Law Center on Homelessness and Poverty. (2011, June). *"Simply Unacceptable": Homelessness and the Human Right to Housing in the United States 2011.* Washington, DC: Author.

Passel, J., Cohn, D., & Gonzalez-Barrera, A. (2012, May 3). *Net Migration from Mexico Falls to Zero—and Perhaps Less.* Washington, DC: Pew Research Center. Retrieved August 8, 2016, from http://www.pewhispanic.org/2012/04/23/net-migration-from-mexico-falls-to-zero-and-perhaps-less/

Pew Research Center. (2011, December 6). *Illegal Immigration: Gaps between and within Parties.* Washington, DC: Author. Retrieved August 5, 2016, from http://www.people-press.org/files/legacy-pdf/12-6-11%20Immigration%20Release.pdf

President's Task Force on 21st Century Policing. (2015, May). *Final Report of the President's Task Force on 21st Century Policing.* Washington, DC: Office of Community Oriented Policing Services. Retrieved July 12, 2016, from http://www.cops.usdoj.gov/pdf/taskforce/TaskForce_FinalReport.pdf

Ryan, C. (2013, August). *Language Use in the United States: 2011* (American Community Survey Reports, ACS-22). Washington, DC: Bureau of the Census. Retrieved August 2, 2016, from https://www.census.gov/content/dam/Census/library/publications/2013/acs/acs-22.pdf

Schafer, R., & McNiff, J. (2011). "Awareness of Alzheimer's Disease." *FBI Law Enforcement Bulletin,* 80(10), pp.12–16.

Scoville, D. (2010, April). "Suicide by Cop." *Police,* pp. 32–41.

Shah, S., & Estrada, R. (2009, February). *Bridging the Language Divide: Promising Practices for Law Enforcement.* New York, NY: Vera Institute of Justice, Center on Immigration and Justice.

Skogan, W., & Frydl, K., eds. (2004). *Fairness and Effectiveness in Policing: The Evidence.* Washington, DC: National Academies Press.

Tactical Response Staff. (2006). "Crisis Intervention Team." *Tactical Response,* 4(9), pp. 54–59.

Telhami, S. (2015, December 9). "What Americans Really Think about Muslims and Islam." Washington, DC: Brookings Institution. Retrieved August 8, 2016, from https://www.brookings.edu/2015/12/09/what-americans-really-think-about-muslims-and-islam/

Thompson, G. (2006, March 31). "Community Policing: The 'Gap' Theory." *PoliceOne.com.* Retrieved August 8, 2016, from http://www.correctionsone.com/corrections/articles/1841228-Community-Policing-The-gap-theory

Thompson, G. (2009, March 27). "Tactical Civility: The Path of Power and Safety." *PoliceOne.com.* Retrieved August 8, 2016, from http://www.correctionsone.com/corrections-training/articles/1882989-Tactical-Civility-The-path-of-power-and-safety

Treatment Advocacy Center. (2006). *Law Enforcement and People with Severe Mental Illness.* Arlington, VA: Author.

United States Census. (2015). *QuickFacts.* Washington, DC: Author. Retrieved August 8, 2016, from https://www.census.gov/quickfacts/table/PST045215/00

United States Interagency Council on Homelessness. (2013). *Opening Doors: Federal Strategic Plan to Prevent and End Homelessness. Update 2013.* Washington, DC: Author. Retrieved August 8, 2016, from https://www.usich.gov/resources/uploads/asset_library/USICH_Annual_Update_2013.pdf

University at Albany, Hindelang Criminal Justice Research Center. (n.d.). *Sourcebook of Criminal Justice Statistics.* Table 2.26. Retrieved August 8, 2016, from http://www.albany.edu/sourcebook/pdf/t226.pdf

Venkatraman, B. A. (2006). "Lost in Translation: Limited English Proficient Populations and the Police." *The Police Chief,* 73(4), pp. 40–50.

Walker, S., Spohn, C., & DeLone, M. (2012). *The Color of Justice: Race, Ethnicity, and Crime in America.* 5th ed. Belmont, CA: Wadsworth.

Worden, R. E., McLean, S. J., & Wheeler, A. P. (2012). "Testing for Racial Profiling with the Veil-ofDarkness Method." *Police Quarterly,* 15(1), pp. 92–111.

7

Baum, K., Catalano, S., Rand, M., & Rose, K. (2009, January). *Stalking Victimization in the United States.* Washington, DC: Bureau of Justice Statistics Special Report. (NCJ 224527)

Berman, G., & Anderson, D. (2010). *Engaging the Community: A Guide for Community Justice Planners.* New York, NY: Center for Court Innovation. Retrieved August 11, 2016, from http://www.courtinnovation.org/sites/default/files/EngagingtheCommunity.pdf

Berman, G., & Feinblatt, J. (2001). "Problem-Solving Courts: A Brief Primer." *Law and Policy,* 23(2), pp. 125–140.

Bureau of Justice Assistance. (1994, August). *Understanding Community Policing: A Framework for Action*. Monograph. Washington, DC: Author. (NCJ 148457) Retrieved August 9, 2016, from https://www.ncjrs.gov/pdffiles/commp.pdf

Campbell, N., & Wolf, R. V. (2004). *Beyond Big Cities: The Problem-Solving Innovations of Community Prosecutors in Smaller Jurisdictions*. New York, NY: Center for Court Innovation.

Center for Court Innovation. (n.d.). *Red Hook Community Justice Center: Documented Results*. New York, NY: Author. Retrieved August 12, 2016, from http://www.courtinnovation.org/sites/default/files/RH_Fact_sheet.pdf

Centre for Justice and Reconciliation. (2016). *Restorative Justice*. Washington, DC: Author. Retrieved August 11, 2016, from http://restorativejustice.org/restorative-justice/

Chapman, R., & Scheider, M. (2006). *Community Policing for Mayors: A Municipal Service Model for Policing and Beyond*. Washington, DC: Office of Community Oriented Policing Services.

Council of State Governments Justice Center. (2013, April). *Lessons from the States: Reducing Recidivism and Curbing Corrections Costs through Justice Reinvestment*. New York: Author.

Cunningham, W. S., Renauer, B. C., & Khalifa, C. (2006). "Sharing the Keys to the Courthouse: Adoption of Community Prosecution by State Court Prosecutors." *Journal of Contemporary Criminal Justice, 22*(3), pp. 202–219.

Dodge, M. (2006, July/August). "The State of Research on Policing and Crime Prevention: Expanding Roles and Responses." *Criminal Justice Research Reports*, pp. 84–85.

Doniger, K. (2009, February). "Inspiring the Judiciary: Community Courts Adapt Community Policing Principles." *Community Policing Dispatch, 2*(1). Retrieved November 1, 2016, from https://cops.usdoj.gov/html/dispatch/February_2009/courts_adapt.htm

Fanflik, P. L., Budzilowicz, L. M., & Nugent-Borakove, M. E. (2007, October). *Managing Innovation: A Closer Look at Community Prosecution Management Issues*. Alexandria, VA: National District Attorneys Association, American Prosecutors Research Institute.

Jansen, S., & Dague, E. (2006). "Working with a Neighborhood Community Prosecutor." *The Police Chief, 73*(7), pp. 40–44.

Kaeble, D., Maruschak, L. M., & Bonczar, T. P. (2015, November). *Probation and Parole in the United States, 2014*. Washington, DC: Bureau of Justice Statistics. (NCJ 249057) Retrieved August 12, 2016, from http://www.bjs.gov/content/pub/pdf/ppus14.pdf

Karp, D. R., & Clear, T. R. (2000). "Community Justice: A Conceptual Framework." In *Boundary Changes in Criminal Justice Organizations*, edited by Charles M. Friel, vol. 2, pp. 323–368. Washington, DC: National Institute of Justice. Retrieved August 11, 2016, from https://www.ncjrs.gov/criminal_justice2000/vol_2/02i2.pdf

Lang, J. (2011). *What Is a Community Court? How the Model Is Being Adapted across the United States*. New York, NY: Center for Court Innovation.

Lee, E., & Martinez, J. (1998). *How It Works: Summary of Case Flow and Interventions at the Midtown Community Court*. New York, NY: Center for Court Innovation.

Malvestuto, R. J., & Snyder, F. M. (2005). "Office of the Chief Probation Officers." In *2005 Annual Report*. Philadelphia, PA: Philadelphia Adult Probation and Parole Department. Retrieved August 12, 2016, from http://www.courts.phila.gov/pdf/report/2005appd.pdf

Matz, A. K., DeMichele, M. T., & Lowe, N. C. (2012, October). "Police-Probation/Parole Partnerships: Responding to Local Street Gang Problems." *The Police Chief, 78*, pp. 24–38. Retrieved August 12, 2016, from http://www.policechiefmagazine.org/magazine/index.cfm?fuseaction=display&article_id=2777&issue_id=102012

Mazerolle, L., Rogan, D., Frank, J., Famega, C., & Eck, J. E. (2005, February). *Managing Calls to the Police with 911/311 Systems*. Washington, DC: National Institute of Justice. (NCJ 206256)

McEwen, T., Spence, D., Wolff, R., Wartell, J., & Webster, B. (2003, February). *Call Management and Community Policing: A Guidebook for Law Enforcement*. Washington, DC: Office of Community Oriented Policing Services.

New York City Police Department. (2016). *Crime Prevention: Citywide Vandals Task Force*. New York, NY: Author. Retrieved August 12, 2016, from http://www.nyc.gov/html/nypd/html/crime_prevention/citywide_vandals_taskforce.shtml

Office of Community Oriented Policing Services. (2004, June 18). *COPS and Homeland Security*. COPS Fact Sheet. Washington, DC: Office of Community Oriented Policing Services. Retrieved June 17, 2012, from http://www.cops.usdoj.gov/Publications/e06042393.pdf

Office of Community Oriented Policing Services. (2007, November 8). *311 for Non-Emergencies: Helping Communities One Call at a Time*. Fact Sheet. Washington, DC: Author. (e01060007)

Office of Community Oriented Policing Services. (2009, April 3). *Community Policing Defined*. Washington, DC: Author. (e030917193) Retrieved August 9, 2016, from http://cops.usdoj.gov/Publications/e030917193-CP-Defined.pdf

Perry, S. W. (2006, July). *Prosecutors in State Courts, 2005*. Washington, DC: Bureau of Justice Statistics. (NCJ 213799)

President's Task Force on 21st Century Policing. (2015, May). *Final Report of the President's Task Force on 21st Century Policing*. Washington, DC: Office of Community Oriented Policing Services. Retrieved August 10, 2016, from http://www.cops.usdoj.gov/pdf/taskforce/TaskForce_FinalReport.pdf

Rinehart, T. A., Laszlo, A. T., & Briscoe, G. O. (2001). *Collaboration Toolkit: How to Build, Fix, and Sustain Productive Partnerships*. Washington, DC: Office of Community Oriented Policing Services.

Schweig, S. (2014, April). *Beyond a Single Neighborhood: Community Justice in Washington, D.C., Newark, N.J., and Milliken, Colo*. Washington, DC: Canter for Court Innovation. Retrieved August 11, 2016, from http://www.courtinnovation.org/sites/default/files/documents/Neighborhood.pdf

Sickmund, M., Sladky, A., & Kang, W. (2015). *Easy Access to Juvenile Court Statistics: 1985-2013*. Washington, DC: Office of Juvenile Justice and Delinquency Prevention. Retrieved August 12, 2016, from http://www.ojjdp.gov/ojstatbb/ezajcs/

Velazquez, S. E., Garcia, M., & Joyce, E. (2009). "Mobilizing a Community Response to Stalking: The Philadelphia Story." *The Police Chief*, 76(1), pp. 30–37.

Wolf, R. V. (2006). *How Do We Pay for That? Sustaining Community Prosecution on a Tight Budget*. New York, NY: Center for Court Innovation.

Wolf, R. V. (2007). *Principles of Problem-Solving Justice*. New York, NY: Center for Court Innovation.

Wolf, R. V., & Worrall, J. J. (2004, November). *Lessons from the Field: Ten Community Prosecution Leadership Profiles*. Alexandria, VA: American Prosecutors Research Institute.

8

Brown, B. (2015, March 11). "Is the Media Altering Our Perceptions of Crime?" *International Policy Digest*. Retrieved August 15, 2016, from http://intpolicydigest.org/2015/03/11/is-the-media-altering-our-perceptions-of-crime/

Buice, E. (2003, October). "The PIO Triangle." *Law and Order*, p. 32.

Chermak, S., & Weiss, A. (2006). "Community Policing in the News Media." *Police Quarterly*, 9(20), pp. 135–160.

Cochran, A. (2013, May 7). "'America's Most Wanted' Host John Walsh on Cancellation: Show Needs to Be on TV." *CBSNews*. Retrieved August 18, 2016, from www.cbsnews.com/news/americas-most-wanted-host-john-walsh-on-cancellation-show-needs-to-be-on-tv/

Cotterman, C. (2015, September 8). "Focus on Media Relations: A Recipe for Success with News Outlets." *FBI Law Enforcement Bulletin*. Retrieved August 18, 2016, from https://leb.fbi.gov/2015/september/focus-on-media-relations-a-recipe-for-success-with-news-outlets

Davis, P. (2010, July). "The PIO and Today's Digital News Environment." *FBI Law Enforcement Bulletin*, pp. 1–8.

Donlon-Cotton, C. (2006, July). "TV Interview Tips." *Law and Order*, pp. 20–22.

Edmond, R. G. (n.d.). "The PIO Triangle."

Fairfax County (Virginia) Police Department. (n.d.). *Media Advisory Cards*. Fairfax, VA: Author, Victim Services Section.

France, L. R. (2009, March 13). "Police Departments Keeping Public Informed on Twitter." *CNN.com*. Retrieved August 18, 2016, from http://www.cnn.com/2009/TECH/03/13/police.social.networking/index.html

Goldman, R. (2012, September 19). "'CSI' Inspires NYPD to Video Tape Interrogations, Commissioner Says." *ABCNews*. Retrieved August 16, 2016, from http://abcnews.go.com/US/csi-inspires-nypd-video-tape-interrogations-commissioner/story?id=17272394

Knoxville Police Department. (n.d.). *Knoxville Police Department (KPD) Public Information Officer*. Knoxville, TN: Author. Retrieved August 18, 2016, from http://www.knoxvilletn.gov/government/city_departments_offices/police_department/chief_of_police_office/public_information_officer/

Krajicek, D. (2003). "Chapter One: The Crime Beat." In *Covering Crime and Justice: A Guide for Journalists*. Berkeley, CA: Institute for Justice and Journalism.

Morley, E. M., & Jacobson, M. J. (2007). "Building a Successful Public Information Program." *The Police Chief*, 74(12), pp. 66–68.

National Crime Prevention Council. (2016). *About McGruff: History*. Gambrills, MD: Author. Retrieved August 18, 2016, from http://www.ncpc.org/about/about-mcgruff/history

Parrish, P. (2012). Parrish Institute of Law Enforcement and Media and retired media relations instructor, FBI Academy. Personal conversation with the author.

Tricchinelli, R. (2013, Spring). "Pretrial Publicity's Limited Effect on the Right to a Fair Trial." *The News Media and the Law*, 37(2). Retrieved August 16, 2016, from https://www.rcfp.org/browse-media-law-resources/news-media-law/news-media-and-law-spring-2013/pretrial-publicitys-limited

Tucker, E., Freking, K., & Sullivan, E. (2016, June 27). "Comey's Refusal to Name Gunman Marks Change in Terror Talk." *Associated Press*. Retrieved August 18, 2016, from http://www.foxnews.com/us/2016/06/27/comey-refusal-to-name-gunman-marks-change-in-terror-talk.html

Tufekci, W. (2012, December 19). "The Media Needs to Stop Inspiring Copycat Murders. Here's How." *The Atlantic*. Retrieved August 16, 2016, from http://www.theatlantic.com/national/archive/2012/12/the-media-needs-to-stop-inspiring-copycat-murders-heres-how/266439/

Whitehead, C. (2004). "Seasonal Press Releases." *Law and Order*, 52(6), p. 21.

Wisconsin Department of Justice. (n.d.). "Rights and Services for Crime Victims and Witnesses." Madison, WI: Author, Office of Crime Victim Services. Retrieved August 18, 2016, from https://www.doj.state.wi.us/sites/default/files/ocvs/navigating/rights-services-brochure-english.pdf

9

Angel, S. (1968). *Discouraging Crime through City Planning*. Berkeley, CA: University of California Press.

Barthe, E. (2006, June). *Crime Prevention Publicity Campaigns*. Washington, DC: U.S. Department of Justice, Office of Community Oriented Policing Services, Problem-Oriented Guides for Police, Response Guides Series, Guide No. 5.

Blincoe, L. J., Miller, T. R., Zaloshnja, E., & Lawrence, B. A. (2015, May). *The Economic and Societal Impact of Motor Vehicle Crashes, 2010* (Revised) (Report No. DOT HS 812 013). Washington, DC: National Highway Traffic Safety Administration.

Craven, K. (2009). "Foot Patrols: Crime Analysis and Community Engagement to Further the Commitment to Community Policing." *Community Policing Dispatch*, 2(2).

Fleissner, D., Fedan, N., & Klinger, D. (1992, August). "Community Policing in Seattle: A Model Partnership between Citizens and Police." *NIJ Journal*, (225), pp. 9–18.

Fowler, F. J., Jr., & Mangione, T. W. (1986). "A Three-Pronged Effort to Reduce Crime and Fear of Crime: The Hartford Experiment." In *Community Crime Prevention: Does It Work?*, edited by Dennis P. Rosenbaum, pp. 87–108. Beverly Hills, CA: Sage Publications.

Greene, J. R., & Taylor, R. B. (1991). "Community-Based Policing and Foot Patrol: Issues of Theory and Evaluation." In *Community Policing: Rhetoric or Reality*, edited by Jack R. Greene and Stephen D. Mastrofski, pp. 195–223. New York, NY: Praeger Publishers.

Guyot, D. (1992, May). "Problem-Oriented Policing Shines in the Stats." In *Source Book: Community-Oriented Policing: An Alternative Strategy*, edited by Bernard L. Garmire, pp. 317–321. Washington, DC: International City/County Management Association (ICMA).

Heinzelmann, F. (1986). "Foreword." In *Community Crime Prevention: Does It Work?*, edited by Dennis P. Rosenbaum, pp. 7–8. Newbury Park, CA: Sage Publications.

Holloway, K., Bennett, T., & Farrington, D. P. (2008, April). *Crime Prevention Research Review No. 3: Does Neighborhood Watch Reduce Crime?* Washington, DC: Office of Community Oriented Policing Services.

Jacobs, J. (1961). *The Death and Life of Great American Cities.* New York, NY: Vintage.

Lindsay, B., & McGillis, D. (1986). "Citywide Community Crime Prevention: An Assessment of the Seattle Program." In *Community Crime Prevention: Does It Work?*, edited by Dennis P. Rosenbaum, pp. 46–67. Beverly Hills, CA: Sage Publications.

Mastrofski, S. D. (1992, August). "What Does Community Policing Mean for Daily Police Work?" *NIJ Journal*, (225), pp. 23–27.

Mentel, Z. (2009, July). "Shutting the Door on Foreclosure and Drug-Related Problem Properties: Two Communities Respond to Neighborhood Disorder." *Community Policing Dispatch*, *The e-Newsletter of the COPS Office*, 2(7)

Mothers against Drunk Driving. (2016). *Drunk Driving.* Irving, TX: Author. Retrieved September 2, 2016, from http://www.madd.org/drunk-driving/

National Association of Town Watch. (2015). "National Night Out 2015: An Impressive Display of Police-Community Partnerships." *New Spirit.* Wynnewood, PA: Author. Retrieved September 1, 2016, from https://d3j566vp3nvche.cloudfront.net/wp-content/uploads/2016/01/Newsletter2015.pdf

Newman, O. (1972). *Defensible Space: Crime Prevention through Urban Design.* New York, NY: Macmillan.

Pate, A. M. (1986). "Experimenting with Foot Patrol: The Newark Experience." In *Community Crime Prevention: Does It Work?*, edited by Dennis P. Rosenbaum, pp. 137–156. Beverly Hills, CA: Sage Publications.

Ratcliffe, J. (2006). *Video Surveillance of Public Places.* Washington, DC: Center for Problem-Oriented Policing.

Ratcliffe, J. H., Taniguchi, T., Groff, E. R., & Wood, J. D. (2011). "The Philadelphia Foot Patrol Experiment: A Randomized Controlled Trial of Police Patrol Effectiveness in Violent Crime Hotspots." *Criminology*, 49(3), pp. 795–831.

Repetto, T. A. (1974). *Residential Crime.* Cambridge, UK: Ballinger.

Rosenfeld, B. (2008, April 8). "Letter to the Mayor of the City and County of San Francisco, the Members of the Board of Supervisors, and the Members of the San Francisco Police Commission." City and County of San Francisco, CA: Office of the Controller. Retrieved September 2, 2016, from http://sfcontroller.org/ftp/uploadedfiles/controller/reports/Foot%20Patrol%20Final%20Report%20Transmittal%20Letter%20(Final)%204-8-07.pdf

Sadd, S., & Grinc, R. M. (1996, February). *Implementation Challenges in Community Policing.* Washington, DC: National Institute of Justice Research in Brief.

Schneider, A. L. (1986). "Neighborhood-Based Antiburglary Strategies: An Analysis of Public and Private Benefits from the Portland Program." In *Community Crime Prevention: Does It Work?*, edited by Dennis P. Rosenbaum, pp. 68–86. Beverly Hills, CA: Sage Publications.

Skogan, W. G. (2004). "Community Policing: Common Impediments to Success." In *Community Policing: The Past, Present, and Future*, edited by Lorie Fridell and Mary Ann Wycoff, pp. 159–168. Washington, DC: The Annie E. Casey Foundation and Police Executive Research Forum.

Skogan, W. G., & Wycoff, M. A. (1986). "Storefront Police Offices: The Houston Field Test." In *Community Crime Prevention: Does It Work?*, edited by Dennis P. Rosenbaum, pp. 179–199. Beverly Hills, CA: Sage Publications.

Skolnick, J. H., & Bayley, D. H. (1986). *The New Blue Line: Innovation in Six American Cities.* New York, NY: The Free Press.

Stoughton, S. (2015, April 10). "Law Enforcement's 'Warrior' Problem." *Harvard Law Review*, 128(6), pp. 225–234. Retrieved September 2, 2016, from http://harvardlawreview.org/2015/04/law-enforcements-warrior-problem/

Sulton, A. T. (1990). *Inner-City Crime Control: Can Community Institutions Contribute?* Washington, DC: The Police Foundation.

Taft, P. B., Jr. (1986). *Fighting Fear: The Baltimore County C.O.P.E. Project.* Washington, DC: Police Executive Research Forum.

Trojanowicz, R. C. (1986). "Evaluating a Neighborhood Foot Patrol Program: The Flint, Michigan, Project." In *Community Crime Prevention: Does It Work?*, edited by Dennis P. Rosenbaum, pp. 157–178. Beverly Hills, CA: Sage Publications.

Wycoff, M. A. (1991). "The Benefits of Community Policing: Evidence and Conjecture." In *Community Policing: Rhetoric or Reality,* edited by Jack R. Greene and Stephen D. Mastrofski, pp. 103–120. New York, NY: Praeger Publishers.

Zahm, D. (2007). *Using Crime Prevention through Environmental Design in Problem Solving.* Washington, DC: Center for Problem-Oriented Policing.

10

Bishop, D. G. (2007). "Identity Theft and Fraud Prevention Program." *The Police Chief,* 74(5), pp. 36–38, 41.

Boba, R., & Santos, R. (2006, August). *Burglary at Single-Family House Construction Sites.* Washington, DC: Office of Community Oriented Policing Services, Problem-Oriented Guides for Police, Problem-Specific Guides Series, Guide No. 43.

Harrell, E. (2015, September). *Victims of Identity Theft, 2014.* Washington, DC: Bureau of Justice Statistics. (NCJ 248991) Retrieved September 16, 2016, from http://www.bjs.gov/content/pub/pdf/vit14.pdf

Casstevens, S. (2008, August). "Traffic Enforcement Is Real Police Work." *Law and Order*, 57(8), pp. 44–46.

CBS News. (2016, May 16). "Cops' Latest Tool in High-Speed Chases: GPS Projectiles." *CBS News.* Retrieved September 13, 2016, from http://www.cbsnews.com/news/police-test-gps-tracking-bullets-high-speed-chase-starchase/

Centers for Disease Control and Prevention. (2016, August 2). *Youth Violence: Using Environmental Design to Prevent School Violence.* Atlanta, GA: Author. Retrieved September 15, 2016, from http://www.cdc.gov/violenceprevention/youthviolence/cpted.html

Chamard, S. (2006, April). *Partnering with Businesses to Address Public Safety Problems.* Washington, DC: Office of Community Oriented Policing Services, Problem-Oriented Guides for Police, Problem-Specific Guides Series, Guide No. 5.

Compton, R. P., & Berning, A. (2015, February). *Drug and Alcohol Crash Risk* (Traffic Safety Facts Research Note. DOT HS 812 117). Washington, DC: National Highway Traffic Safety Administration. Retrieved September 13, 2016, from http://www.nhtsa.gov/Driving+Safety/Research+&+Evaluation/Alcohol+and+Drug+Use+By+Drivers

Crowe, T. D. (2000). *Crime Prevention through Environmental Design: Applications of Architectural Design and Space Management Concepts.* Boston: Butterworth-Heinemann.

Dedel, K. (2006, July). *Witness Intimidation.* Washington, DC: Office of Community Oriented Policing Services, Problem-Oriented Guides for Police, Problem-Specific Guides Series, Guide No. 42.

Dewey-Kollen, J. (2006, September). "Ten Ways to Improve DUI Enforcement." *Law and Order,* 54(9), pp. 10–17.

Eck, J. E. (1997). "Preventing Crime at Places." In *Preventing Crime: What Works, What Doesn't, What's Promising,* edited by the University of Maryland, Department of Criminology and Criminal Justice. Washington, DC: Office of Justice Programs, U.S. Department of Justice.

Farrington, D. P. (2000). "Explaining and Preventing Crime: The Globalization of Knowledge—The American Society of Criminology 1999 Presidential Address." *Criminology,* 38(1), pp. 1–24.

Federal Bureau of Investigation. (2016). *Preliminary Semiannual Uniform Crime Report, January-June 2015.* Washington, DC: Author. Retrieved September 12, 2016, from https://ucr.fbi.gov/crime-in-the-u.s/2015/preliminary-semiannual-uniform-crime-report-januaryjune-2015

Federal Trade Commission. (n.d.). "The Importance of the Police Report." Memorandum to Law Enforcement. Washington, DC: Author. Retrieved September 19, 2016, from https://www.consumer.ftc.gov/sites/default/files/articles/pdf/pdf-0088-ftc-memo-law-enforcement.pdf

Frank, T. (2015a, September 29). "Feds Fail to Track Deadly Police Pursuits." *USA Today.* Retrieved September 13, 2016, from http://www.usatoday.com/story/news/2015/09/29/nhtsa-police-high-speed-pursuit/72617864/

Frank, T. (2015b, July 30). "High-Speed Police Chases Have Killed Thousands of Innocent Bystanders." *USA Today.* Retrieved September 13, 2016, from http://www.usatoday.com/story/news/2015/07/30/police-pursuits-fatal-injuries/30187827/

Governors Highway Safety Association. (2012, March 1). *Speeding and Aggressive Driving.* Washington, DC: Author. Retrieved September 13, 2016, from http://www.ghsa.org/html/files/pubs/survey/2012_speed.pdf

Ingraham, C. (2015, July 25). "Police Chases Kill More People Each Year than Floods, Tornadoes, Hurricanes, and Lightning—Combined." *The Washington Post.* Retrieved September 13, 2016, from https://www.washingtonpost.com/news/wonk/wp/2015/07/25/why-police-shouldnt-chase-criminals/

Insurance Institute for Highway Safety. (2011, February 1). "City Uses Cameras as Safety Tool, not Moneymaker." *Status Report* (Publication by the Insurance Institute for Highway Safety), 46(1), pp. 1–2, 6–7.

Insurance Institute for Highway Safety. (2016, July 29). *Turning Off Red Light Cameras Costs Lives, New Research Shows.* Ruckersville, VA: Author. Retrieved September 13, 2016, from http://www.iihs.org/iihs/news/desktopnews/turning-off-red-light-cameras-costs-lives-new-research-shows

iSqFt. (2016, February 24). *Five High-Tech Ways to Control Construction Site Theft.* Cincinnati, OH: Author. Retrieved September 15, 2016, from http://www.isqft.com/start/blog-five-high-tech-ways-to-control-construction-site-theft/

Kauffman, G. (2015, June 8). "Could This New Technology Put a Stop to Drunk Driving?" *The Christian Science Monitor.* Retrieved September 13, 2016, from http://www.csmonitor.com/USA/USA-Update/2015/0608/Could-this-new-technology-put-a-stop-to-drunk-driving-video

Kloberdanz, K. (2016, January 20). "Taxi Drivers: Years of Living Dangerously." Retrieved September 19, 2016, from https://consumer.healthday.com/encyclopedia/work-and-health-41/occupational-health-news-507/taxi-drivers-years-of-living-dangerously-646377.html

Lent, C. (2006, October 26). "Police ID Theft Work Earns International Recognition." *Beaverton Valley Times.*

Maggard, D. L., & Jung, D. (2009). "Irvine's Area Traffic Officer Program." *The Police Chief,* 77(3), pp. 46–50.

Marshall, M. A. (2011). "'The Greatest Threat' to Public Safety." *The Police Chief,* 78(7), p. 6.

Martinez, C. (2016, April 17). "LAPD Task Force Aims to Put the Brakes on Street Racing." *CBS News.* Retrieved September 13, 2016, from http://www.cbsnews.com/news/lapd-task-force-aims-to-put-the-brakes-on-street-racing/

Mrazek, P. J., & Haggerty, R. J., eds. (1994). *Reducing Risks for Mental Disorders: Frontiers for Preventative Intervention Research.* Washington, DC: National Academy Press.

National Crime Prevention Council. (1995). *350 Tested Strategies to Prevent Crime: A Resource for Municipal Agencies and Community Groups.* Washington, DC: Author.

National Highway Traffic Safety Administration. (n.d.). *Community Traffic Safety Resource Center: Building Coalitions.* Washington, DC: Author. Retrieved September 14, 2016, from http://www.nhtsa.gov/Driving+Safety/Community+Traffic+Safety/Community+Traffic+Safety+Building+Coalitions

National Highway Traffic Safety Administration. (2012a, June). *Overview* (Traffic Safety Facts: 2010 Data). Washington, DC: Author. (DOT HS 811 630) Retrieved September 12, 2016, from https://crashstats.nhtsa.dot.gov/Api/Public/ViewPublication/811630

National Highway Traffic Safety Administration. (2012b, May). *Speeding* (Traffic Safety Facts: 2009 Data). Washington, DC: Author. (DOT HS 811 397) Retrieved September 12, 2016, from https://crashstats.nhtsa.dot.gov/Api/Public/ViewPublication/811397

National Highway Traffic Safety Administration. (2015, June 4). *Alcohol-Impaired Driving Crashes Kill Nearly 10,000 People*

Annually; This Alcohol-Detection Vehicle Technology Could Potentially Save Thousands of Lives Each Year. Washington, DC: Author. Retrieved September 13, 2016, from http://www.nhtsa.gov/About-NHTSA/Press-Releases/nhtsa_dadss_event_06042015

National Highway Traffic Safety Administration. (2016a, July 1). *NHTSA Data Shows Traffic Deaths Up 7.7 Percent in 2015.* Washington, DC: Author. Retrieved September 12, 2016, from http://www.nhtsa.gov/About+NHTSA/Press+Releases/nhtsa-2015-traffic-deaths-up-07012016

National Highway Traffic Safety Administration. (2016b, August). *2015 Motor Vehicle Crashes: Overview* (Traffic Safety Facts Research Note. Report No. DOT HS 812 318). Washington, DC: Author. Retrieved September 13, 2016, from https://crash-stats.nhtsa.dot.gov/Api/Public/ViewPublication/812318

National Institute of Justice. (2010, May 25). *How to Identify Hot Spots.* Washington, DC: Author. Retrieved September 14, 2016, from http://www.nij.gov/topics/law-enforcement/strategies/hot-spot-policing/identifying.htm

National Science and Technology Council. (2011, September). *The National Biometrics Challenge.* Washington, DC: Author, Subcommittee on Biometrics and Identity Management. Retrieved September 19, 2016, from http://www.biometrics.gov/Documents/BiometricsChallenge2011_protected.pdf

Newman, G. R. (2004, June). *Identity Theft.* Washington, DC: Office of Community Oriented Policing Services, Problem-Oriented Guides for Police, Problem-Specific Guides Series, Guide No. 25.

Office of Community Oriented Policing Services. (2015, February 2). *FY 2016, Performance Budget.* Washington, DC: Author. Retrieved September 15, 2016, from https://www.justice.gov/sites/default/files/jmd/pages/attachments/2015/02/02/29._community_oriented_policing_services_cops.pdf

Pickrell, T. M., & Li, R. (2016, February). *Seat Belt Use in 2015—Overall Results* (Traffic Safety Facts Research Note. Report No. DOT HS 812 243). Washington, DC: National Highway Traffic Safety Administration. Retrieved September 13, 2016, from https://crashstats.nhtsa.dot.gov/Api/Public/ViewPublication/812243

Police Executive Research Forum. (2012, January). *How Are Innovations in Technology Transforming Policing?* Washington, DC: Author, Critical Issues in Policing. Retrieved September 15, 2016, from http://www.policeforum.org/assets/docs/Critical_Issues_Series/how%20are%20innovations%20in%20technology%20transforming%20policing%202012.pdf

Ratcliffe, J. (2011, August). *Video Surveillance of Public Places.* Washington, DC: Office of Community Oriented Policing Services, Problem-Oriented Guides for Police, Problem-Specific Guides Series, Guide No. 4.

Rosen, M. S. (2006, October). *Chief Concerns: A Gathering Storm—Violent Crime in America.* Washington, DC: Police Executive Research Forum.

Sampson, R. (2007, January). *Domestic Violence.* Washington, DC: Office of Community Oriented Policing Services, Problem-Oriented Guides for Police, Problem-Specific Guides Series, Guide No. 45.

Scott, M. S. (2001a, September 14). *Robbery at Automated Teller Machines.* Washington, DC: Office of Community Oriented Policing Services, Problem-Oriented Guides for Police, Problem-Specific Guides Series, Guide No. 8.

Scott, M. S. (2001b, August 14). *Speeding in Residential Areas.* Washington, DC: Office of Community Oriented Policing Services, Problem-Oriented Guides for Police, Problem-Specific Guides Series, Guide No. 3.

Scott, M. S., & Dedel, K. (2006a, August). *Assaults in and around Bars.* 2nd ed. Washington, DC: Office of Community Oriented Policing Services, Problem-Oriented Guides for Police, Problem-Specific Guides Series, Guide No. 1.

Scott, M. S., & Dedel, K. (2006b, August 6). *Street Prostitution.* 2nd ed. Washington, DC: Office of Community Oriented Policing Services, Problem-Oriented Guide for Police, Problem-Specific Guides Series, Guide No. 2.

Shader, M. (2002). *Risk Factors for Delinquency: An Overview.* Washington, DC: Office of Juvenile and Delinquency Prevention.

Smith, M. J. (2005, March). *Robbery of Taxi Drivers.* Washington, DC: Office of Community Oriented Policing Services, Problem-Oriented Guides for Police, Problem-Specific Guides Series, Guide No. 34.

Sourcebook of Criminal Justice Statistics Online. (2011). Retrieved September 19, 2016, from http://www.albany.edu/sourcebook/pdf/t2392011.pdf

Strawn, J. (2014, December). "Protecting Yourself from Theft." *Water Well Journal,* pp. 19–22. Retrieved September 15, 2016, from http://ner.net/events/protecting-yourself-from-theft.pdf

Thornton, P. (2015, May 6). "How an App Destroyed Their Streets: Readers Count the Waze." *Los Angeles Times.* Retrieved September 13, 2016, from http://www.latimes.com/opinion/opinion-la/la-ol-waze-traffic-app-neighborhoods-readers-20150506-story.html

Tucker, A. S., Van Hasselt, V. B., Vecchi, G. M., & Browning, S. L. (2011, October). "Responding to Persons with Mental Illness." *FBI Law Enforcement Bulletin,* 80(10), pp. 1–6.

Wieder. (2013, March 19). *You Can Never Be Too Cautious.* Encinitas, CA: ATMDepot. Com. Retrieved September 15, 2016, from http://www.atmdepot.com/atm-robberies/

11

Botvin LifeSkills Training. (n.d.). *Program Overview.* White Plains, NY: Author. Retrieved October 5, 2016, from http://lifeskillstraining.com/overview.php

Caulkins, J. P., Reuter, P., Iguchi, M. Y., & Chiesa, J. (2005). *How Goes the "War on Drugs?" An Assessment of U.S. Drug Problems and Policy.* Occasional paper. Santa Monica, CA: The Rand Corporation.

CBS News (2012, June 6). *98 Arrested in NY Prescription Drug Sweep.* New York, NY: Author. Retrieved October 6, 2016, from http://www.cbsnews.com/news/98-arrested-in-ny-prescription-drug-sweep/

Center for Behavioral Health Statistics and Quality. (2015, September). *Behavioral Health Trends in the United States: Results from the 2014 National Survey on Drug Use and Health* (HHS Publication No. SMA 15-4927, NSDUH Series H-50).

Rockville, MD: Author. Retrieved September 26, 2016, from http://www.samhsa.gov/data/sites/default/files/NSDUH-FRR1-2014/NSDUH-FRR1-2014.pdf

Centers for Disease Control and Prevention. (2015, November 12). *Fact Sheets—Underage Drinking.* Atlanta, GA: Author. Retrieved October 6, 2016, from http://www.cdc.gov/alcohol/fact-sheets/underage-drinking.htm

Combating Underage Drinking through a Collaborative Community Response Program. (2009). City of New Britain, CT: Central Connecticut State University (CCSU) Police Department and New Britain Police Department, Herman Goldstein Award Submission. Retrieved October 6, 2016, from http://www.popcenter.org/library/awards/goldstein/2009/09-32.pdf

Degenhardt, L., Dierker, L., Chiu, W. T., Medina-Mora, M. E., Neumark, Y., Sampson, N., Alonso, J., Angermeyer, M., Anthony, J. C., Bruffaerts, R., de Girolamo, G., de Graaf, R., Gureje, O., Karam, A. N., Kostyuchenko, S., Lee, S., Lépine, J. P., Levinson, D., Nakamura, Y., Posada-Villa, J., Stein, D., Wells, J. E., & Kessler, R. C. (2010). "Evaluating the Drug Use 'Gateway' Theory Using Cross-National Data: Consistency and Associations of the Order of Initiation of Drug Use among Participants in the WHO World Mental Health Surveys." *Drug and Alcohol Dependence,* 108(1–2), pp. 84–97.

DeJong, W., & Blanchette, J. (March 2014). "Case Closed: Research Evidence on the Positive Public Health Impact of the Age 21 Minimum Legal Drinking Age in the United States." *Journal of Studies on Alcohol and Drugs,* Supplement No. 17, pp. 108–115.

Des Moines (Iowa) Police Department. (1990). *Drugs: A "Municipal Approach."* Des Moines, IA: Des Moines Police Department.

Drug Enforcement Administration. (2015a, April). *National Heroin Threat Assessment Summary.* Washington, DC: Author. (DEA-DCT-DIR-039-15) Retrieved September 29, 2016, from http://www.dea.gov/divisions/hq/2015/hq052215_National_Heroin_Threat_Assessment_Summary.pdf

Drug Enforcement Administration. (2015b, October). *2015 National Drug Threat Assessment.* Washington, DC: Author. (DEA-DCT-DIR-008-16) Retrieved September 28, 2016, from https://www.scribd.com/doc/290654459/2015-NDTA-Report-National-Drug-Threat-Assessment-Summary

Governing. (2016, May 25). *State Marijuana Laws Map.* Washington, DC: Author. Retrieved September 30, 2016, from http://www.governing.com/gov-data/state-marijuana-laws-map-medical-recreational.html

Grossi, D. (2009, April). "Going Under." *Law Officer Magazine,* pp. 24–28.

Guerino, P., Harrison, P. M., & Sabol, W. J. (2012, January 9). *Prisoners in 2010.* Washington, DC: Bureau of Justice Statistics. (NCJ 236096)

Hughes, A., Lipari, R. N., & Williams, M. R. (2016, July 26). *Marijuana Use and Perceived Risk of Harm from Marijuana Use Varies Within and Across States* (The CBHSQ Report). Rockville, MD: Center for Behavioral Health Statistics and Quality, Substance Abuse and Mental Health Services Administration. Retrieved September 29, 2016, from http://www.samhsa.gov/data/sites/default/files/report_2404/ShortReport-2404.pdf

Jabeen, A. (2012). "Using Technology to Combat Pharmacy Robberies." *Community Policing Dispatch,* 5(4). Retrieved October 6, 2016, from http://cops.usdoj.gov/html/dispatch/04-2012/technology-and-pharmacy-robberies.asp

Johnston, L. D., O'Malley, P. M., Miech, R. A., Bachman, J. G., & Schulenberg, J. E. (2016, February). *Monitoring the Future National Survey Results on Drug Use, 1975-2015: Overview, Key Findings on Adolescent Drug Use.* Ann Arbor: Institute for Social Research, The University of Michigan. Retrieved September 26, 2016, from http://monitoringthefuture.org/pubs/monographs/mtf-overview2015.pdf

Katel, P. (2006). "War on Drugs." *CQ Researcher Online,* 16(21), pp. 481–504.

Leonhart, M. (2008, October). "Target America: Opening Eyes to the Damage Drugs Cause." Paper presented at the California Science Center, Los Angeles, CA.

Macher, R., Burke, T. W., & Owen, S. S. (2012, May). "Synthetic Marijuana." *FBI Law Enforcement Bulletin,* pp. 17–22.

Marlowe, D. B. (2010, December). *Research Update on Adult Drug Courts.* Alexandria, VA: National Association of Drug Court Professionals. Retrieved October 5, 2016, from http://www.nadcp.org/sites/default/files/nadcp/Research%20Update%20on%20Adult%20Drug%20Courts%20-%20NADCP_1.pdf

Marlowe, D. B., & Carey, S. M. (2012, May). *Research Update on Family Drug Courts.* Alexandria, VA: National Association of Drug Court Professionals. Retrieved October 5, 2016, from http://www.nadcp.org/sites/default/files/nadcp/Reseach%20Update%20on%20Family%20Drug%20Courts%20-%20NADCP.pdf

Mazerolle, L., Soole, C. W., & Rombouts, S. (2007, July 22). *Crime Prevention Research Reviews No. 1: Disrupting Street-Level Drug Markets.* Washington, DC: Office of Community Oriented Policing Services.

Messner, S. F., & Rosenfeld, R. (2007). *Crime and the American Dream.* 4th ed. Belmont, CA: Wadsworth Thomson Learning.

National Association of Drug Court Professionals. (2016). *What Are Drug Courts?* Alexandria, VA: Author. Retrieved May 30, 2016, from http://www.nadcp.org/learn/drug-courts-work/what-are-drug-courts

National Center on Addiction and Drug Abuse. (2009, May). *Shoveling Up II: The Impact of Substance Abuse on Federal, State, and Local Budgets.* New York, NY: Author. Retrieved September 24, 2016, from http://www.centeronaddiction.org/addiction-research/reports/shoveling-ii-impact-substance-abuse-federal-state-and-local-budgets

National Drug Intelligence Center. (2009, April). *National Prescription Drug Threat Assessment, 2009.* Washington, DC: Author. Retrieved October 6, 2016, from https://www.justice.gov/archive/ndic/pubs33/33775/33775p.pdf

National Institute on Alcohol Abuse and Alcoholism. (2014). "Measuring the Burden of Alcohol." *Alcohol Alert,* 87. Rockville, MD: Author. Retrieved October 6, 2016, from http://pubs.niaaa.nih.gov/publications/aa87/AA87.pdf

National Institute on Drug Abuse. (2015a, November). *Drug-Facts: Synthetic Cannabinoids*. Bethesda, MD: Author. Retrieved September 30, 2016, from https://www.drugabuse.gov/publications/drugfacts/synthetic-cannabinoids

National Institute on Drug Abuse (2015b, August). *Trends and Statistics*. Bethesda, MD: Author. Retrieved October 5, 2016, from https://www.drugabuse.gov/related-topics/trends-statistics

National Institute on Drug Abuse. (2016a, June). *DrugFacts: Drugged Driving*. Bethesda, MD: Author. Retrieved October 5, 2016, from https://www.drugabuse.gov/publications/drugfacts/drugged-driving

National Institute of Drug Abuse. (2016b, February). *Understanding Drug Abuse and Addiction: What Science Says*. Bethesda, MD: Author. Retrieved October 5, 2016, from https://www.drugabuse.gov/understanding-drug-abuse-addiction-what-science-says

National Institute of Justice. (n.d.). *Program Profile: Mandatory-Random Student Drug Testing*. Washington, DC: Author. Retrieved October 5, 2016, from https://www.crimesolutions.gov/ProgramDetails.aspx?ID=223

News Medical. (2005, April 19). *Best School Drug Prevention Programs Teach Life Skills, Studies Find*. London, UK: Author. Retrieved October 5, 2016, from http://www.news-medical.net/news/2005/04/19/9334.aspx

Office of National Drug Control Policy. (2011, May). *Drug Courts: A Smart Approach to Criminal Justice*. Washington, DC: Author. Retrieved November 22, 2016, from https://www.whitehouse.gov/sites/default/files/ondcp/Fact_Sheets/drug_courts_fact_sheet_5-31-11.pdf

Office of National Drug Control Policy. (2015). *National Drug Control Strategy 2015*. Washington, DC: Author. Retrieved October 5, 2016, from https://www.whitehouse.gov//sites/default/files/ondcp/policy-and-research/2015_national_drug_control_strategy_0.pdf

Office of National Drug Control Policy. (2016, February). *FY 2017 Funding Highlights*. Washington, DC: Author. Retrieved October 5, 2016, from https://www.whitehouse.gov/sites/default/files/ondcp/press-releases/fy_2017_budget_highlights.pdf

Paulozzi, L. J., Mack, K. A., & Hockenberry, J. M. (2014, July 4). "Vital Signs: Variation among States in Prescribing of Opioid Pain Relievers and Benzodiazepines—United States, 2012." *Morbidity and Mortality Weekly Report*, 63(26), pp. 563–568. Retrieved October 6, 2016, from http://www.cdc.gov/mmwr/pdf/wk/mm6326.pdf

Police Executive Research Forum. (2012, January). "PERF Survey Shows Widespread Use of Many Technologies in Policing." In *How Are Innovations in Technology Transforming Policing?*, pp. 1–3. (Critical Issues in Policing Series) Washington, DC: Author.

President's Task Force on 21st Century Policing. (2015, May). *Final Report of the President's Task Force on 21st Century Policing*. Washington, DC: Office of Community Oriented Policing Services. Retrieved October 6, 2016, from http://www.cops.usdoj.gov/pdf/taskforce/TaskForce_FinalReport.pdf

Rand Corporation. (2009, February 4). *Methamphetamine Use Estimated to Cost the U.S. about $23 Billion in 2005*. Press release. Santa Monica, CA: Author. Retrieved October 5, 2016, from http://www.rand.org/news/press/2009/02/04/meth.html

Rudd, R. A., Aleshire, N., Zibbell, J. E., & Gladden, R. M. (2016, January 1). "Increases in Drug and Opioid Overdose Deaths—United States, 2000-2014." *Morbidity and Mortality Weekly Report*, 64(50), pp. 1378–1382. Retrieved October 6, 2016, from http://www.cdc.gov/mmwr/preview/mmwrhtml/mm6450a3.htm

Sacks, J. J., Gonzales, K. R., Bouchery, E. E., Tomedi, L. E., & Brewer, R. D. (2015). "2010 National and State Costs of Excessive Alcohol Consumption." *American Journal of Preventive Medicine*, 49(5), pp. 73–79.

Scott, M. S., & Dedel, K. (2006). *Clandestine Methamphetamine Labs*. 2nd ed. Washington, DC: Office of Community Oriented Policing Services, Problem-Oriented Guides for Police, Problem-Specific Guides Series, Guide No. 16.

Sinnema, C. (2003, May). "Residents Learn Ways to Best Serve Sheriff's Office in Fight against Meth." *Community Links*, pp. 10–12.

Substance Abuse and Mental Health Services Administration (2016, March 2). *Stimulants*. Rockville, MD: Author. Retrieved September 29, 2016, from http://www.samhsa.gov/atod/stimulants

Taylor, C. M. (2011, February 1). *Rocky Pomerance Excellence in Policing Award*. Ocala, FL: Ocala Florida Police Department. Retrieved October 6, 2016, from http://www.nnscommunities.org/Rocky_Pomerance_Excellence_in_Policing_Award.pdf

Townsend, R. (2012, June 13). *Neighbors Stunned by Drug Raid at Olathe Home*. Kansas City, MO: *Fox 4 News Kansas City*. Retrieved October 6, 2016, from http://fox4kc.com/2012/06/13/neighbors-stunned-by-drug-raid-at-olathe-home

Wilson, F. A., Stimpson J. P., & Pagán, J. A. (2014). "Fatal Crashes from Drivers Testing Positive for Drugs in the U.S., 1993-2010." *Public Health Reports*, 129(4), pp. 342–350.

12

Afterschool Alliance. (2014). *Afterschool Programs Keep Kids Safe, Engage Kids in Learning and Help Working Families*. Washington, DC: Author. Retrieved October 11, 2016, from http://afterschoolalliance.org//documents/National_fact_sheet_10.07.14.pdf

America's Promise Alliance. (2016). *Mission and Purpose*. Washington, DC: Author. Retrieved October 11, 2016, from http://www.americaspromise.org/mission-purpose

Beckett, M. K. (2008). *Current-Generation Youth Programs: What Works, What Doesn't, and at What Cost?* Santa Monica, CA: The Rand Corporation.

The Children's Trust. (2014, August 4). *After-School Programs Keep Kids Safe, Inspire Learning and Help Working Families*. Miami, FL: Author. Retrieved October 11, 2016, from https://www.thechildrenstrust.org/providers/news/102-news/news-releases/1093-after-school-programs-keep-kids-safe-inspire-learning-and-help-working-families

City of Livermore. (n.d.). *Horizons*. Livermore, CA: Author. Retrieved October 11, 2016, from http://www.cityoflivermore.net/citygov/horizons/services/history.htm

Cohn, J. P. (2006). "Keeping an Eye on School Security: The Iris Recognition Project in New Jersey." *NIJ Journal,* 254, pp. 12–15.

Dedel, K. (2005, August). *School Vandalism and Break-ins.* Washington, DC: Office of Community Oriented Policing Services Problem-Oriented Guides for Police, Problem-Specific Guides Series, Guide No. 35. Retrieved October 12, 2016, from http://www.popcenter.org/problems/pdfs/schoolVandalism.pdf

Department of Justice. (2016, August 1). "Supplemental Guidelines for Juvenile Registration under the Sex Offender Registration and Notification Act." *Federal Register,* 81(147). Retrieved October 11, 2016, from https://www.federalregister.gov/documents/2016/08/01/2016-18106/office-of-the-attorney-general-supplemental-guidelines-for-juvenile-registration-under-the-sex#h-7

Falb, K. L., McCauley, H. L., Decker, M. R., Gupta, J., Raj, A., & Silverman, J. G. (2011). "School Bullying Perpetration and Other Childhood Risk Factors as Predictors of Adult Intimate Partner Violence Perpetration." *Archives of Pediatric and Adolescent Medicine,* 165(10), pp. 890–894.

Federal Interagency Forum on Child and Family Statistics. (2016). *America's Children: Key National Indicators of Well-Being, 2016.* Washington, DC: U.S. Government Printing Office. Retrieved October 12, 2016, from http://www.childstats.gov/pdf/ac2016/ac_16.pdf

Forman, J., Jr. (2004). "Community Policing and Youth as Assets." *Journal of Criminal Law and Criminology,* 95(1), pp. 1–48.

Garrett, R. (2009, July). "A Jury of Their Peers." *Law Enforcement Technology,* pp. 44–50.

International Association of Chiefs of Police. (2006, May). *Developing an Anti-Bullying Program: Increasing Safety, Reducing Violence.* Alexandria, VA: Author. Retrieved October 11, 2016, from http://www.theiacp.org/portals/0/pdfs/bullyingbrief.pdf

International Association of Chiefs of Police. (2009). *Guide for Preventing and Responding to School Violence,* 2nd ed. Alexandria, VA: Author. Retrieved October 12, 2016, from https://www.bja.gov/Publications/IACP_School_Violence.pdf

Jeffrey, R. (2004). "Bullying Bystanders." *Prevention Researcher,* 1(3), pp. 7–8.

Los Angeles Police Department. (n.d.). *Kid Watch.* Los Angeles, CA: Author. Retrieved October 11, 2016, from http://lapdonline.org/juvenile_division/content_basic_view/6285

Lee, B. (2010). *California's After-School Commitment: Keeping Kids on Track and out of Trouble.* San Francisco, CA: Fight Crime: Invest in Kids California.

Mannes, M., Roehlkepartain, E. C., & Benson, P. L. (2005). *Unleashing the Power of Community to Strengthen the Well-Being of Children, Youths, and Families: An Asset-Building Approach.* Washington, DC: Child Welfare League of America.

Marcus, C. R., & Stepansky, J. (2015, August 14). "NYPD Commissioner Bill Bratton Congratulates 1,800 Youth Police Academy Graduates." *New York Daily News.* Retrieved October 11, 2016, from http://www.nydailynews.com/new-york/bratton-congratulates-1-800-nypd-youth-academy-graduates-article-1.2325532

McPherson, L. (2007). "Practitioner's Guide to the Adam Walsh Act." *Update* (published by the American Prosecutors Research Institute's National Center for Prosecution of Child Abuse), 20, pp. 9–10.

Metropolitan Police Department. (n.d.). *Youth Advisory Council.* Washington, DC: Author. Retrieved October 10, 2016, from http://mpdc.dc.gov/page/youth-advisory-council-yac

Miller, B. M. (2003, May). *Critical Hours: After-School Programs and Educational Success.* Quincy, MA: Nellie Mae Education Foundation. Retrieved from http://www.nmefoundation.org/getmedia/08b6e87b-69ff-4865-b44e-ad42f2596381/Critical-Hours?ext=.pdf

Moving Sound Technologies. (2012). *The Mosquito Device.* Vancouver, BC: Author. Retrieved October 2, 2016, from http://www.movingsoundtech.com

National Juvenile Justice Network. (2012, January 17). *The Adam Walsh Act: The Cost of Compliance and the Danger to Juveniles in the Justice System.* Washington, DC: Author. Retrieved from http://www.njjn.org/article/the-adam-walsh-act--the-cost-of-compliance-and-the-danger-to-juveniles-in-the-justice-system

National School Safety Center. (2010). *School Associated Violent Deaths.* Westlake Village, CA: Author. Retrieved October 11, 2016, from http://www.schoolsafety.us/media-resources/school-associated-violent-deaths

National School Safety and Security Services. (n.d.). *School Crime Reporting and School Crime Underreporting.* Cleveland, OH: Author. Retrieved October 11, 2016, from http://www.schoolsecurity.org/trends/bak/school_crime_reporting.html

New York Police Department. (2016). *Community Programs: Summer Youth Police Academy.* New York, NY: Author. Retrieved October 10, 2016, from http://www.nyc.gov/html/nypd/html/community_affairs/youth_programs_summer_academy.shtml

Office for Victims of Crime. (2015). *Engaging Communities, Empowering Victims: 2015 NCVRW Resource Guide.* Washington, DC: Author. Retrieved October 11, 2016, from http://ovc.ncjrs.gov/ncvrw2015/pdf/FullGuide.pdf

Office of Community Oriented Policing Services. (2002, October). *Justice Based After-School Program.* Fact sheet. Washington, DC: Author. Retrieved October 12, 2016, from https://ric-zai-inc.com/Publications/cops-w0122-pub.pdf

Office of Community Oriented Policing Services. (2011, September). *Secure Our Schools.* Fact sheet. Washington, DC: Author. Retrieved October 11, 2016, from http://www.cops.usdoj.gov/pdf/2011AwardDocs/CSPP-SOS-CHP/2011-SOS-Post-FactSheet.pdf

Padgett, S., & Notar, C. E. (2013). "Bystanders Are the Key to Stopping Bullying." *Universal Journal of Education Research,* 1(2), pp. 33–41. Retrieved October 11, 2016, from http://www.hrpub.org/download/201308/ujer.2013.010201.pdf

Piazza, P. (2001, November 1). "Scourge of the Schoolyard: Technology Alone Isn't Enough." *Security Management,* pp. 68–73.

Pollack, I., & Sundermann, C. (2001). "Creating Safe Schools: A Comprehensive Approach," *Juvenile Justice,* 8(1), pp. 13–20.

Pollack, W. S., Modzeleski, W., & Rooney, G. (2008, May). *Prior Knowledge of Potential School-Based Violence: Information Students Learn May Prevent a Targeted Attack.* Washington, DC: U.S. Secret Service and U.S. Department of Education.

President's Task Force on 21st Century Policing. (2015, May). *Final Report of the President's Task Force on 21st Century Policing.* Washington, DC: Office of Community Oriented Policing Services. Retrieved October 6, 2016, from http://www.cops.usdoj.gov/pdf/taskforce/TaskForce_FinalReport.pdf

Project Safe Childhood. (n.d.). *Fact Sheet: Project Safe Childhood.* Washington, DC: Department of Justice. Retrieved from https://www.justice.gov/psc/file/842426/download

Rand Corporation. (2005). *Stopping Violence before It Starts: Identifying Early Predictors of Adolescent Violence.* Santa Monica, CA: Author.

Raymond, B. (2010, April). *Assigning Police Officers to Schools.* Problem-Oriented Guides for Police, Response Guide No. 10. Washington, DC: Office of Community Oriented Policing Services. Retrieved October 11, 2016, from http://www.popcenter.org/Responses/pdfs/school_police.pdf

Royal Canadian Mounted Patrol. (2011, December 8). *RCMP to Pilot WITS Bullying Prevention Program.* Ottawa, ON: Author. Retrieved October 11, 2016, from http://nationaltalk.ca/story/rcmp-to-pilot-wits-bullying-prevention-program

Regional Youth Voice Forums. (n.d.). Washington, DC: Office of Youth Development.

Safe Start Center. (2013, March). *Safe Start Promising Approaches Communities: Improving Outcomes for Children Exposed to Violence.* North Bethesda, MD: Author. Retrieved October 11, 2016, from http://www.ojjdp.gov/programs/safestart/ImprovingOutcomesforChildrenExposedtoViolence.pdf

Safe Start National Resource Center. (n.d.). *About Safe Start.* Retrieved October 11, 2016, from https://safestartcenter.wordpress.com/

Schuster, B. (2009). "Preventing, Preparing for Critical Incidents in Schools." *NIJ Journal,* 262, pp. 42–46. (NCJ 225765)

Shader, M. (2002). *Risk Factors for Delinquency: An Overview.* Washington, DC: Office of Juvenile Justice and Delinquency Prevention. Retrieved October 12, 2016, from https://www.ncjrs.gov/pdffiles1/ojjdp/frd030127.pdf

Sheppard, D. (1999, February). *Promising Strategies to Reduce Gun Violence.* Washington, DC: Office of Juvenile Justice and Delinquency Prevention. (NCJ 173950)

Steinberg, L. (2008). "Introducing the Issue." *Juvenile Justice: The Future of Children,* 18(2), pp. 3–14.

Substance Abuse and Mental Health Services Administration. (2006). *The Olweus Bullying Prevention Program.* Washington, DC: Author.

TAPS Academy. (2015). *About TAPS Academy.* Houston, TX: Author. Retrieved October 10, 2016, from http://www.tapsacademy.org/about

"Teens Not Interested in After-School Programs." (2006). *American School Board Journal,* 193(9), pp. 74–75.

"Urban High School Disorder Reduction Project." (2011). In *IACP Community Policing Award: 2011 Winners and Finalists*, pp. 5–6. San Jose, CA: Cisco Systems. Retrieved October 12, 2016, from http://www.popcenter.org/library/awards/goldstein/2011/11-40(F).pdf

Virginia Youth Violence Project. (n.d.). *Bullying.* Charlottesville, VA: University of Virginia. Retrieved October 11, 2016, from http://curry.virginia.edu/research/projects/bullying

Vossekuil, B., Fein, R., Reddy, M., Borum, R., & Modzeleski, W. (2002). *The Final Report and Findings of the Safe School Initiative: Implications for the Prevention of School Attacks in the United States.* Washington, DC: U.S. Department of Education, Office of Elementary and Secondary Education, Safe and Drug-Free Schools Program, and U.S. Secret Service, National Threat Assessment Center.

Wang, J., Iannotti, R. J., & Nansel, T. R. (2009). "School Bullying among U.S. Adolescents: Physical, Verbal, Relational, and Cyber." *Journal of Adolescent Health,* 45(4), pp. 368–375.

Zahn, M. A., Agnew, R., Fishbein, D., Miller, S., Winn, D., Dakoff, G., Kruttschnitt, C., Giordano, P., Gottfredson, D., Payne, A. A., Feld, B. C., & Chesney-Lind, M. (2010, April). *Causes and Correlates of Girls' Delinquency.* Washington, DC: Office of Juvenile Justice and Delinquency Prevention. (NCJ 226358)

Zhang, A., Musu-Gillette, L., & Oudekerk, B. A. (2016, May). *Indicators of School Crime and Safety: 2015* (NCES 2016-079/NCJ 249758). Washington, DC: National Center for Education Statistics, U.S. Department of Education, and Bureau of Justice Statistics, Office of Justice Programs, U.S. Department of Justice. Retrieved October 11, 2016, from http://nces.ed.gov/pubs2016/2016079.pdf

13

Beaverton Police Department. (n.d.). *Graffiti Removal Program.* Beaverton, OR: Author. Retrieved October 25, 2016, from http://beavertonpolice.org/200/Graffiti-Removal-Program

Bureau of Justice Assistance. (n.d.). *Project Safe Neighborhoods (PSN).* Washington, DC: Author. Retrieved October 25, 2016, from https://www.bja.gov/programdetails.aspx?program_id=74

Campbell, J. (2015, June 6). "Prevalence of Gang Colors Fades, But They Can Still Be Deadly." *Los Angeles Times.* Retrieved October 24, 2016, from http://homicide.latimes.com/post/gang-colors/

Drash, W., & Sambou, T. S. (2016, May 20). "Paying Kids Not to Kill." *CNN online.* Retrieved October 25, 2016, from http://www.cnn.com/2016/05/19/health/cash-for-criminals-richmond-california/

Egley, A., Jr., Howell, J. C., & Harris, M. (2014, December). *Highlights of the 2012 National Youth Gang Survey.* Fact sheet. Washington, DC: Office of Juvenile Justice and Delinquency Prevention.

Esbensen, F., Peterson, D., Taylor, T. J., & Osgood, D. W. (2012). *Is G.R.E.A.T. Effective? Does the Program Prevent Gang Joining? Results from the National Evaluation of G.R.E.A.T.* St. Louis, MO: University of Missouri-St. Louis.

G.R.E.A.T. Program. (n.d.). *What Is G.R.E.A.T.?* Tallahassee, FL: Author. Retrieved October 24, 2016, from https://www.great-online.org/Home/About/What-Is-GREAT

GRYD Foundation. (2016). *Summer Night Lights.* Los Angeles, CA: Author. Retrieved October 25, 2016, from http://grydfoundation.org/programs/summer-night-lights/

Haegerich, T. M., Mercy, J., & Weiss, B. (2013). "What Is the Role of Public Health in Gang-Membership Prevention?" Chapter 3 in *Changing Course: Preventing Gang Membership*, edited by T. R. Simon, N. M. Ritter, and R. R. Mahendra, pp. 31–49. Washington, DC: National Institute of Justice. Retrieved October 25, 2016, from https://www.ncjrs.gov/pdffiles1/nij/239234.pdf

Hill, K. G., Lui, C., & Hawkins, J. D. (2001, December). *Early Precursors of Gang Membership: A Study of Seattle Youth.* Washington, DC: Office of Juvenile Justice and Delinquency Prevention. (NCJ 190106)

Howell, J. A. (2000, August). *Youth Gang Programs and Strategies.* Washington, DC: Office of Juvenile Justice and Delinquency Prevention. Retrieved October 24, 2016, from https://www.ncjrs.gov/pdffiles1/ojjdp/171154.pdf

Howell, J. C. (2006, August). *The Impact of Gangs on Communities.* Washington, DC: Office of Juvenile Justice Delinquency Prevention, National Youth Gang Center. Retrieved October 24, 2016, from https://www.nationalgangcenter.gov/Content/Documents/Impact-of-Gangs-on-Communities.pdf

Howell, J. C. (2007). "Menacing or Mimicking? Realities of Youth Gangs." *Juvenile and Family Court Journal,* 58(2), pp. 39–50.

Kennedy, D. M., Braga, A. A., & Piehl, A. M. (2001, September). "Developing and Implementing Operation Ceasefire." In *Reducing Gun Violence: The Boston Gun Project's Operation Ceasefire*, pp. 1–53. Washington, DC: National Institute of Justice. (NCJ 188741)

Klein, M. W. (2007). *Chasing after Street Gangs: A Forty-Year Journey.* Upper Saddle River, NJ: Pearson Prentice-Hall.

Krohn, M. D., Schmidt, N. M., Lizotte, A. J., & Baldwin, J. M. (2011). "The Impact of Multiple Marginality on Gang Membership and Delinquent Behavior for Hispanic, African American, and White Male Adolescents." *Journal of Contemporary Criminal Justice,* 27(1), pp. 18–42.

Los Angeles Police Department. (n.d.). *Gangs.* Los Angeles, CA: Author. Retrieved October 24, 2016, from http://www.lapdonline.org/la_gangs/content_basic_view/1396

Mejia, B. (2015, March 7). "Homeboy Industries Hopes More Space Will Better Serve Gang Community." *Los Angeles Times.* Retrieved October 25, 2016, from http://www.latimes.com/local/california/la-me-adv-homeboy-expansion-20150308-story.html

Meyers, M., & Karpman, M. (2011, June 13). *National Rollout of Training Program Aims to Improve Police Interactions with Children.* Washington, DC: National League of Cities. Retrieved October 24, 2016, from http://www.nlc.org/find-city-solutions/institute-for-youth-education-and-families/violence-prevention/national-rollout-of-training-program-aims-to-improve-police-interactions-with-children

Miller, H. V., Barnes, J. C., & Hartley, R. D. (2011). "Reconsidering Hispanic Gang Membership and Acculturation in a Multivariate Context." *Crime and Delinquency,* 57(3), pp. 331–355.

National Crime Prevention Council. (2006, May). "Anti-Gang Initiative Announced." *Catalyst Newsletter.* Retrieved October 24, 2016, from http://www.ncpc.org/programs/catalyst-newsletter/catalyst-newsletter/archives/may-2006-catalyst/anti-gang-initiative-announced

National Gang Center (n.d.). *National Youth Gang Survey Analysis.* Tallahassee, FL: Author. Retrieved October 24, 2016, from https://www.nationalgangcenter.gov/Survey-Analysis/Demographics

National Gang Center. (2010, October). *Best Practices to Address Community Gang Problems: OJJDP's Comprehensive Gang Model.* 2nd ed. Washington, DC: Office of Juvenile Justice and Delinquency Prevention. (NCJ 231200)

National Gang Center. (2015, December). *Brief Review of Federal and State Definitions of the Terms "Gang," "Gang Crime," and "Gang Member."* Tallahassee, FL: Author. Retrieved October 24, 2016, from https://www.nationalgangcenter.gov/Content/Documents/Definitions.pdf

National Gang Intelligence Center. (2016). *2015 National Gang Report.* Washington, DC: Federal Bureau of Investigation, U.S. Department of Justice. Retrieved October 24, 2016, from https://www.fbi.gov/file-repository/stats-services-publications-national-gang-report-2015.pdf/view

National School Safety and Security Services. (n.d.). *Gangs and School Safety.* Cleveland, OH: Author. Retrieved October 25, 2016, from http://www.schoolsecurity.org/trends/gangs/

Office of Juvenile Justice and Delinquency Prevention. (2000). *Gang-Free Schools and Communities Initiative.* Washington, DC: Author. (NCJ 189464) Retrieved October 25, 2016, from https://www.ncjrs.gov/pdffiles1/Digitization/189464NCJRS.pdf

Safe Streets Campaign. (n.d.). *Who We Are.* Tacoma, WA: Author. Retrieved October 25, 2016, from http://safest.org/who-we-are/

Shelden, R. G., Tracy, S. K., & Brown, W. B. (2004). *Youth Gangs in American Society.* 3rd ed. Belmont, CA: Wadsworth.

Solis, A., Schwartz, W., & Hinton, T. (2003, October 1). *Gang Resistance Is Paramount (GRIP) Program Evaluation: Final Report.* Los Angeles, CA: University of Southern California. Retrieved October 25, 2016, from https://ced.usc.edu/files/2014/07/GRIP_Evaluation.pdf

U.S. Department of Justice. (2015, May 28). *About Violent Gangs.* Washington, DC: Author. Retrieved October 24, 2016, from https://www.justice.gov/criminal-ocgs/about-violent-gangs

U.S. Department of Justice. (2016, September 14). *Justice Department's Office of Justice Programs Awards Nearly $6 Million to Project Safe Neighborhoods Program.* Washington, DC: Author. Retrieved October 25, 2016, from https://www.justice.gov/opa/pr/justice-department-s-office-justice-programs-awards-nearly-6-million-project-safe

Washington Violent Crime Prevention Partnership. (2010, September 14). *Strategies to Address Gang Activity: Suppression, Intervention and Prevention.* Olympia, WA: Office of Superintendent of Public Instruction. Retrieved October 24, 2016, from http://www.k12.wa.us/SafetyCenter/Gangs/pubdocs/StrategiesAddressGangActivitySupressionInterventionPrevention.pdf

Wetzel, T. (2015, March 12). "Cops and Kids: 5 Steps to Create a Mentoring Program." *Police One.com.* Retrieved October 24,

2016, from https://www.policeone.com/police-jobs-and-careers/articles/8423462-Cops-and-kids-5-steps-to-create-a-mentoring-program/

14

American Humane. (2016, August 25). *Understanding the Link between Animal Abuse and Family Violence*. Washington, DC: Author. Retrieved October 28, 2016, from http://www.americanhumane.org/fact-sheet/understanding-the-link-between-animal-abuse-and-family-violence/

Ammons, J. (2005). *Batterers with Badges: Officer-Involved Domestic Violence*. San Diego, CA: California Western School of Law. Retrieved October 28, 2016, from http://www.americanbar.org/content/dam/aba/migrated/domviol/priorwinners/Ammons1.authcheckdam.pdf

Bune, K. L. (2004). "Law Enforcement Must Take Lead on Hate Crimes." *The Police Chief*, 71(4), pp. 41–55.

Bureau of Justice Assistance. (2004). *Project ChildSafe*. Washington, DC: Author. (NCJ 204959)

Centers for Disease Control and Prevention. (2014). *Understanding Intimate Partner Violence*. Fact sheet. Atlanta, GA: Author. Retrieved October 28, 2016, from http://www.cdc.gov/ViolencePrevention/pdf/IPV-FactSheet.pdf

Centers for Disease Control and Prevention. (2016, July 20). *Intimate Partner Violence: Risk and Protective Factors*. Atlanta, GA: Author. Retrieved October 27, 2016, from http://www.cdc.gov/violenceprevention/intimatepartnerviolence/risk-protectivefactors.html

Center for Problem-Oriented Policing (2001). *Workplace Violence Initiative: Baltimore County*. Albany, NY: Author. Retrieved October 28, 2016, from http://www.popcenter.org/library/awards/goldstein/2001/01-04.pdf

Charlotte–Mecklenburg Police Department. (2002). "Domestic Violence Intervention Project: Charlotte–Mecklenburg (North Carolina) Police Department." In *Excellence in Problem-Oriented Policing: The 2002 Herman Goldstein Award Winners*, pp. 19–25. Washington, DC: Police Executive Research Forum.

Cooper, A., & Smith, E. L. (2011, November). *Homicide Trends in the United States, 1980–2008 (Annual Rates for 2009 and 2010)*. Washington, DC: Bureau of Justice Statistics. (NCJ 236018)

Dedel, K. (2007, March). *Drive-by Shootings*. Washington, DC: Office of Community Oriented Policing Services, Problem Specific Guides Series, Guide No. 47.

Doyle, M. (2007, August 16). "Licensed Gun Dealers Down 79%." *The Seattle Times*. Retrieved October 28, 2016, from http://seattletimes.com/html/nationworld/2003838480_gundealers16.html

Emory University. (2016). *Bystander Intervention*. Atlanta, GA: Author. Retrieved October 27, 2016, from http://studenthealth.emory.edu/hp/respect_program/learn_more/bystander_intervention.html

Federal Bureau of Investigation. (n.d.). *Hate Crime—Overview*. Washington, DC: Author. Retrieved October 27 from http://www.fbi.gov/about-us/investigate/civilrights/hate_crimes/overview

Federal Bureau of Investigation. (2012, June 25). *Nearly 80 Juveniles Recovered in Nationwide Operation Targeting underage Prostitution*. Washington, DC: Author. Retrieved October 28, 2016, from https://archives.fbi.gov/archives/news/pressrel/press-releases/nearly-80-juveniles-recovered-in-nationwide-operation-targeting-underage-prostitution

Federal Bureau of Investigation. (2014a). *Crime in the United States 2014*. Washington, DC: Author. Retrieved October 27, 2016, from https://ucr.fbi.gov/crime-in-the-u.s/2014/crime-in-the-u.s.-2014/offenses-known-to-law-enforcement/browse-by/national-data

Federal Bureau of Investigation. (2014b). *Hate Crime Statistics 2014*. Washington, DC: Author. Retrieved October 27, 2016, from https://ucr.fbi.gov/hate-crime/2014

Federal Bureau of Investigation. (2015). *Crime in the United States 2015*. Washington, DC: Author. Retrieved October 27, 2016, from https://ucr.fbi.gov/crime-in-the-u.s/2015/crime-in-the-u.s.-2015/offenses-known-to-law-enforcement/violent-crime/violentcrimemain_final

Federal Bureau of Investigation. (2016, February 1). *Tracking Animal Cruelty*. Washington, DC: Author. Retrieved October 28, 2016, from https://www.fbi.gov/news/stories/-tracking-animal-cruelty

Finkelhor, D., Turner, H., Ormrod, R., Hamby, S., & Kracke, K. (2009). *Children's Exposure to Violence: A Comprehensive National Survey*. Bulletin. Washington, DC: U.S. Department of Justice, Office of Justice Programs, Office of Juvenile Justice and Delinquency Prevention. Retrieved October 28, 2016, from https://www.ncjrs.gov/pdffiles1/ojjdp/227744.pdf

Freilich, J. D., & Chermak, S. M. (2013, June). *Hate Crimes*. Washington, DC: Center for Problem-Oriented Policing. Retrieved October 27, 2016, from http://www.popcenter.org/problems/pdfs/hate_crimes.pdf

Gallo, G. (2004, July). "The National Police Family Violence Prevention Project Helps Departments Address Domestic Abuse in Police Families." *Law Enforcement Technology*, 32(7), pp. 60–64.

Graves, A. (2004). "Law Enforcement Involved Domestic Abuse." *Law and Order*, 52(11), pp. 108–111.

Hoffman, J. (2015, June 10). "College Rape Prevention Program Proves a Rare Success." *New York Times*. Retrieved October 27, 2016, from http://www.nytimes.com/2015/06/12/health/college-rape-prevention-program-proves-a-rare-success.html?_r=0

Humane Society of the United States. (2016). *Animal Cruelty Facts and Stats*. Washington, DC: Author. Retrieved October 28, 2016, from http://www.humanesociety.org/issues/abuse_neglect/facts/animal_cruelty_facts_statistics.html?referrer=https://www.google.com/#domestic

Johnson, H. (2006). *Measuring Violence against Women: Statistical Trends 2006*. Ottawa, Ontario: Minister of Industry, Statistics Canada. Retrieved October 28, 2016, from http://ywcacanada.ca/data/research_docs/00000043.pdf

Klein, A. R. (2009, June 5). *Practical Implications of Current Domestic Violence Research: For Law Enforcement, Prosecutors, and Judges*. Washington, DC: National Institute of Justice. (NCJ 225722)

Krogstad, J. M. (2015, October 21). *Gun Homicides Steady after Decline in '90s; Suicide Rate Edges Up*. Washington, DC: Pew

Research Center. Retrieved October 27, 2016, from http://www.pewresearch.org/fact-tank/2015/10/21/gun-homicides-steady-after-decline-in-90s-suicide-rate-edges-up/

MacDonald, H. (2016, January 13). "The Ferguson Effect in Los Angeles—More Crime." *Los Angeles Times* online. Retrieved October 27, 2016, from http://www.latimes.com/opinion/op-ed/la-oe-mac-donald-ferguson-effect-in-los-angeles-20160113-story.html

Maxwell, C. D., Garner, J. H., & Fagan, J. A. (2001, July). "The Effects of Arrest on Intimate Partner Violence: New Evidence from the Spouse Assault Replication Program." *Research in Brief.* Washington, DC: National Institute of Justice. (NCJ 188199)

National Center for Women and Policing. (2005). *Police Family Violence Fact Sheet.* Fact sheet. Beverly Hills, CA: Author. Retrieved October 28, 2016, from http://www.womenandpolicing.org/violenceFS.asp

National Institute of Justice. (2013, April 10). *Illegal Firearms Trafficking.* Washington, DC: Author. Retrieved October 27, 2016, from http://www.nij.gov/topics/crime/gun-violence/trafficking/Pages/welcome.aspx

National Institutes of Health (2016, March 18). *Gun Safety.* Bethesda, MD: U.S. National Library of Medicine. Retrieved October 27, 2016, from https://medlineplus.gov/gunsafety.html

Occupational Safety and Health Administration. (n.d.). *Workplace Violence.* Washington, DC: U.S. Department of Labor. Retrieved October 28, 2016, from http://www.osha.gov/SLTC/workplaceviolence/index.html

Office of Juvenile Justice and Delinquency Prevention. (1999, February). *Promising Strategies to Reduce Gun Violence.* 1999 (February). Report. Washington, DC: Author. Retrieved October 28, 2016, from http://www.ojjdp.gov/pubs/gun_violence/173950.pdf

Reuland, M., Morabito, M. S., Preston, C., & Cheney, J. (2006, March 20). *Police–Community Partnerships to Address Domestic Violence.* Washington, DC: Police Executive Research Forum and the Office of Community Oriented Policing Services. Retrieved October 28, 2016, from https://ric-zai-inc.com/Publications/cops-p091-pub.pdf

Ritter, N. (2009). "CeaseFire: A Public Health Approach to Reduce Shootings and Killings." *NIJ Journal,* (264), pp. 20–25. Retrieved October 27, 2016, from https://www.ncjrs.gov/pdffiles1/nij/228386.pdf

Rosen, M. S. (2006). *Chief Concerns: A Gathering Storm—Violent Crime in America.* Washington, DC: Police Executive Research Forum.

Sampson, R. (2011, August). *Acquaintance Rape of College Students.* Washington, DC: Office of Community Oriented Policing Services, Problem-Specific Guide Series, Guide No. 17.

Sanburn, J. (2016, May 13). "Murders Are Up in Many U.S. Cities Again This Year." *Time.* Retrieved October 27, 2016, from http://time.com/4329688/murder-rate-u-s-cities-increase-2016/

Schafer, J. R., & Navarro, J. (2003, March). "The Seven-Stage Hate Model: The Psycho-pathology of Hate Groups." *FBI Law Enforcement Bulletin.* Retrieved October 27, 2016, from http://www.au.af.mil/au/awc/awcgate/fbi/7stage_hate_model.htm

Southern Poverty Law Center. (n.d.). *Hate Groups.* Montgomery, AL: Author. Retrieved October 27, 2016, from https://www.splcenter.org/hate-map

Stretesky, P. R., Schuck, A. M., & Hogan, M. J. (2004). "Space Matters: An Analysis of Poverty, Poverty Clustering, and Violent Crime." *Justice Quarterly,* 21(4), pp. 817–841.

U.S. Department of Justice. (2015, November 20). *Human Trafficking Prosecution Unit (HTPU).* Washington, DC: Author. Retrieved October 28, 2016, from https://www.justice.gov/crt/human-trafficking-prosecution-unit-htpu

U.S. Department of Justice. (2016, October 27). *Protecting Students from Sexual Assault.* Washington, DC: Author. Retrieved October 27, 2016, from https://www.justice.gov/ovw/protecting-students-sexual-assault

Vaughn, M. G., Fu, Q., DeLisi, M., Wright, J. P., Beaver, K. M., Perron, B. E., & Howard, M. O. (2010). "Prevalence and Correlates of Fire-Setting in the United States: Results from the National Epidemiologic Survey on Alcohol and Related Conditions." *Comprehensive Psychiatry,* 51(3), pp. 217–223.

Walker-Rodriguez, A., & Hill, R. (2011, March). "Human Sex Trafficking." *FBI Law Enforcement Bulletin,* pp. 1–9.

Wilson, D. G., Walsh, W. F., & Kleuber, S. (2006, May). "Trafficking in Human Beings: Training and Services among U.S. Law Enforcement Agencies." *Police Practice and Research,* 7(2), pp. 149–160.

15

ASIS International. (2014). *Operation Partnership: Primer on Getting Started.* Alexandria, VA: Author. Retrieved October 31, 2016, from https://foundation.asisonline.org/Scholarships-and-Awards/Awards/Matthew-Simeone-Award/Documents/Operation%20Partnership%20Primer.pdf

Baker, P., & Schmitt, E. (2015, December 5). "California Attack has U.S. Rethinking Strategy on Homegrown Terror." *New York Times.* Retrieved October 31, 2016, from http://www.nytimes.com/2015/12/06/us/politics/california-attack-has-us-rethinking-strategy-on-homegrown-terror.html?_r=1

Borum, R. (2003). "Understanding the Terrorist Mind-Set." *FBI Law Enforcement Bulletin,* 72(7), pp. 7–10.

Bratton, W. J. (2006). "The Need for Balance." *Subject to Debate,* 20(4), pp. 2–3.

Chalk, P. (2010, March 18). "Below the Radar." RAND Newsroom Commentary. Retrieved October 30, 2016, from http://www.rand.org/multimedia/audio/2010/04/12/below_the_radar.html

Chapman, R. (2008). "Community Partnerships: A Key Ingredient in an Effective Homeland Security Approach." *Community Policing Dispatch,* 1(2).

CQ Transcriptions. (2011, March 10). *Senate Homeland Security and Governmental Affairs Committee Holds Hearing on Information Sharing in the Era of WikiLeaks.* Washington, DC: CQ Congressional Transcriptions. Retrieved October 31, 2016, from https://www.ise.gov/sites/default/files/Senate_HSGAC_Hearing_InfoSharing_Mar2011.pdf

Davies, H. J., & Murphy, G. R. (2004). *Protecting Your Community from Terrorism: Strategies for Local Law Enforcement Series: Volume 2: Working with Diverse Communities.* Washington,

DC: The Office of Community Oriented Policing Services and the Police Executive Research Forum.

Department of Homeland Security. (2004). *Securing Our Homeland: U.S. Department of Homeland Security Strategic Plan.* Washington, DC: Author.

Department of Homeland Security. (2008, May 20). *One Team, One Mission, Securing Our Homeland: U.S. Department of Homeland Security Strategic Plan Fiscal Years 2008–2013.* Washington, DC: Author. Retrieved October 31, 2016, from http://www.hsdl.org/?view&did=235371

Department of Homeland Security. (2009, March). *Fact Sheet: Upgrade to 10-Fingerprint Expansion.* Washington, DC: Author. Retrieved October 31, 2016, from https://www.dhs.gov/xlibrary/assets/usvisit/usvisit_edu_10-fingerprint_collection_fact_sheet.pdf

Department of Homeland Security. (2016, January 8). *Countering Violent Extremism Task Force.* Washington, DC: Author. Retrieved October 31, 2016, from https://www.dhs.gov/news/2016/01/08/countering-violent-extremism-task-force

Docobo, J. (2005, June). "Community Policing as the Primary Prevention Strategy for Homeland Security at the Local Law Enforcement Level." *Homeland Security Affairs,* 1(1). Retrieved October 31, 2016, from http://www.hsaj.org/?fullarticle=1.1.4

Doherty, S., & Hibbard, B. G. (2006). "Special Focus: Community Policing and Homeland Security." *The Police Chief,* 73(2), pp. 78–86.

Evans, B. (2012, August 8). *New York City Police Department and Microsoft Partner to Bring Real-Time Crime Prevention and Counterterrorism Technology Solution to Global Law Enforcement Agencies.* Redmond, WA: Microsoft News Center. Retrieved October 31, 2016, from http://www.microsoft.com/en-us/news/Press/2012/Aug12/08-08NYPDPR.aspx

Federal Bureau of Investigation. (n.d.-a). *Terrorism.* Washington, DC: Author. Retrieved October 29, 2016 from, https://www.fbi.gov/investigate/terrorism

Federal Bureau of Investigation. (n.d.-b). *Weapons of Mass Destruction: Frequently Asked Questions.* Washington, DC: Author. Retrieved October 30, 2016, from http://www.fbi.gov/about-us/investigate/terrorism/wmd/wmd_faqs

Federal Bureau of Investigation. (2004). *Federal Bureau of Investigation Strategic Plan 2004–2009.* Washington, DC: Author.

Federal Bureau of Investigation. (2009, September 7). *Domestic Terrorism in the Post-9/11 Era.* Washington, DC: Author. Retrieved October 29, 2016, from https://www.fbi.gov/news/stories/2009/september/domterror_090709

Federal Bureau of Investigation. (2015, December 4). *FBI Will Investigate San Bernadino Shootings as Terrorist Act.* Washington, DC: Author. Retrieved October 30, 2016, from https://www.fbi.gov/news/news_blog/fbi-will-investigate-san-bernardino-shootings-as-terrorist-act

Federal Emergency Management Agency. (2008, December). *National Incident Management System (NIMS): What's New.* Washington, DC: Author. Retrieved October 31, 2016, from http://www.fema.gov/pdf/emergency/nims/NIM-SWhatsNew.pdf

Friedmann, R. R., & Cannon, W. J. (2007). "Homeland Security and Community Policing: Competing or Complementing Public Safety Policies." *Journal of Homeland Security and Emergency Management,* 4(4): Article 2. Retrieved November 1, 2016, from http://scholarworks.gsu.edu/cgi/viewcontent.cgi?article=1000&context=cj_facpub

Fusion Center Guidelines—Developing and Sharing Information in a New Era. (2006, August). Washington, DC: U.S Department of Justice and U.S. Department of Homeland Security.

Grimson, M., Wyllie, D., & Fieldstadt, E. (2016, June 13). "Orlando Nightclub Shooting: Mass Casualties after Gunman Opens Fire in Gay Club." *NBC News.* Retrieved October 31, 2016, from http://www.nbcnews.com/storyline/orlando-nightclub-massacre/orlando-nightclub-shooting-emergency-services-respond-reports-gunman-n590446

Hanson, D. (2005, August). "What's Next—Soft Target Attacks." *Law Enforcement Technology,* 33(8), pp. 18–27.

Henderson, N. J., Ortiz, C. W., Sugie, N. F., & Miller, J. (2006, June). *Law Enforcement and Arab American Community Relations after September 11, 2001: Engagement in a Time of Uncertainty.* New York: Vera Institute of Justice.

Henderson, N. J., Ortiz, C. W., Sugie, N. F., & Miller, J. (2008, July). *Policing in Arab American Communities after September 11.* Washington, DC: National Institute of Justice. (NCJ 221706) Retrieved November 1, 2016, from http://archive.vera.org/sites/default/files/resources/downloads/Arab_American_community_relations.pdf

Institute for Economics and Peace. (2015, November). *Global Terrorism Index 2015.* Sydney, Australia: Author. Retrieved October 29, 2016, from http://economicsandpeace.org/wp-content/uploads/2015/11/Global-Terrorism-Index-2015.pdf

International Association of Chiefs of Police. (2005, May 17). *From Hometown Security to Homeland Security: IACP's Principles for a Locally Designed and Nationally Coordinated Homeland Security Strategy.* Alexandria, VA: Author. Retrieved October 31, 2016, from http://www.theiacp.org/portals/0/pdfs/HomelandSecurityWP.pdf

International Association of Chiefs of Police. (2014). *Using Community Policing to Counter Violent Extremism: Five Key Principles for Law Enforcement.* Washington, DC: Office of Community Oriented Policing Services. Retrieved October 31, 2016, from http://www.theiacp.org/Portals/0/documents/pdfs/Final%20Key%20Principles%20Guide.pdf

Law Enforcement–Private Security Consortium. (2009, July). *Operation Partnership: Trends and Practices in Law Enforcement and Private Security Collaborations.* Washington, DC: Office of Community Oriented Policing Services. (e08094224)

Jaffe, G., Gibbons-Neff, T., & Goldman, A. (2015, July 17). "Chattanooga Shooter's Real, Online Lives Seem to Take Divergent Paths." *The Washington Post.* Retrieved October 30, 2016, from https://www.washingtonpost.com/world/national-security/as-investigators-probe-motive-in-chattanooga-rampage-a-portrait-of-the-shooter-emerges/2015/07/17/4b2ff26a-2c97-11e5-bd33-395c05608059_story.html

Kurzman, C., & Schanzer, D. (2015, June 25). *Law Enforcement Assessment of the Violent Extremist Threat.* Durham, NC: Triangle Center on Terrorism and Homeland Security, Duke University. Retrieved October 31, 2016, from https:

//sites.duke.edu/tcths/files/2013/06/Kurzman_Schanzer_Law_Enforcement_Assessment_of_the_Violent_Extremist_Threat_final.pdf

Lambert, D. (2010, December). "Intelligence-Led Policing in a Fusion Center." *FBI Law Enforcement Bulletin*, 79(12), p. 16.

Linett, H. (2005, August). "Counter-Terrorism 101." *Police*, pp. 58–64.

Loyka, S. A., Faggiani, D. A., & Karchmer, C. (2005, February). *Protecting Your Community from Terrorism: Strategies for Local Law Enforcement. Volume 4: The Production and Sharing of Intelligence.* Washington, DC: Community Oriented Policing Services and the Police Executive Research Forum.

Murray, J. (2005). "Policing Terrorism: A Threat to Community Policing or Just a Shift in Priorities?" *Police Practice and Research,* 6(4), pp. 347–361.

National Consortium for the Study of Terrorism and Responses to Terrorism. (2015, June). *Annex of Statistical Information: Country Reports on Terrorism 2014.* College Park, MD: University of Maryland. Retrieved October 30, 2016, from http://www.state.gov/documents/organization/239628.pdf

National Counterterrorism Center. (n.d.). *About Us.* Washington, DC: Author. Retrieved October 31, 2016, from https://www.nctc.gov/overview.html

National Counterterrorism Center. (2009, April 30). *2008 Report on Terrorism.* Washington, DC: Author. Retrieved October 31, 2016, from https://www.fbi.gov/file-repository/stats-services-publications-terror_08.pdf/view

Newman, G. R., & Clarke, R. V. (2008, July). *Policing Terrorism: An Executive's Guide.* Washington, DC: Office of Community Oriented Policing Services.

Newswise. (2006, August 2). *9/11 Changed Culture, Attitude of Street Cops.* Charlottesville, VA: Author. Retrieved October 31, 2016, from http://www.newswise.com/articles/911-changed-culture-attitude-of-street-cops

9/11 Commission. (2004). *Final Report of the National Commission on Terrorist Attacks upon the United States.* Edited by T. Kean. New Haven, CT: Avalon Project, Yale University Law School. Retrieved October 31, 2016, from http://avalon.law.yale.edu/sept11/911Report.pdf

Page, D. (2004, March). "Law Enforcement Renaissance: The Sequel." *Law Enforcement Technology,* 32(3), pp. 86–90.

Pew Research Center. (2011, August 30). *Muslim Americans: No Signs of Growth in Alienation or Support for Extremism.* Poll. Washington, DC: The Pew Forum on Religion and Public Life. Retrieved November 1, 2016, from http://www.pewforum.org/2011/08/30/muslim-americans-no-signs-of-growth-in-alienation-or-support-for-extremism/

Polisar, J. M. (2004). "The National Criminal Intelligence Sharing Plan." President's message. *The Police Chief,* 71(6), p. 8.

Rand Corporation. (2008, August 6). *U.S. Should Rethink 'War on Terrorism' Strategy to Deal with Resurgent Al Qaida.* Santa Monica, CA: Author.

Rasmussen, N. J. (2015, February 11). *Countering Violent Islamist extremism: The Urgent Threat of Foreign Fighters and Homegrown Terror.* Washington, DC: National Counterterrorism Center. Retrieved October 30, 2016, from http://www.nctc.gov/docs/Countering_Violent_Islamist_Extremism.pdf

Regional Information Sharing Systems. (2015, July). *Frequently Asked Questions.* Washington, DC: Bureau of Justice Assistance. Retrieved October 31, 2016, from https://www.riss.net/pdf/RISS.FAQ.pdf

Rivera, J. D. (2016, May 24). *The Symbiotic Relationship between Western Media and Terrorism.* New York, NY: Carnegie Council for Ethics in International Affairs. Retrieved November 1, 2016, from http://www.carnegiecouncil.org/publications/ethics_online/0117

Savelli, L. (2004). *A Proactive Law Enforcement Guide for the War on Terrorism.* Flushing, NY: LooseLeaf Law Publications, Inc.

Scheider, M. C., Chapman, R. E., & Seelman, M. F. (2004). "Connecting the Dots for a Proactive Approach." *Border and Transportation Security,* pp. 158–162. Retrieved October 31, 2016, from http://ric-zai-inc.com/Publications/cops-w0245-pub.pdf

Sgueglia, K. (2015, December 16). "Chattanooga Shootings 'Inspired' by Terrorists, FBI Chief Says." *CNN.* Retrieved October 30, 2016, from http://www.cnn.com/2015/12/16/us/chattanooga-shooting-terrorist-inspiration/

Southern Poverty Law Center. (2016, February 17). *Active Hate Groups in the United States in 2015.* Montgomery, AL: Author. Retrieved October 29, 2016, from https://www.splcenter.org/fighting-hate/intelligence-report/2016/active-hate-groups-united-states-2015

Straw, J. (2010, April). "The Evolving Terrorist Threat." *Security Management,* pp. 47–55.

Tafoya, W. L. (2011, November). "Cyber Terror." *FBI Law Enforcement Bulletin,* 80(11), pp. 1–7.

Ubinas, R. (2015, December 6). "Police Lieutenant: Local Force Is Best Line of Defense against Terror." *Tampa Bay Times.* Retrieved November 22, 2016, from http://www.tbo.com/list/news-opinion-commentary/rick-ubinas-drawing-a-thin-blue-line-between-the-dragon-and-its-wrath-why-local-police-must-lead-way-for-homeland-security-20151206/

U.S. Census Bureau. (2012). *Statistical Abstract of the United States: 2012.* Washington, DC: Author, p. 216. Retrieved October 31, 2016, from http://www2.census.gov/library/publications/2011/compendia/statab/131ed/tables/law.pdf

U.S. Department of State. (2016, June). *Country Reports on Terrorism 2015.* Washington, DC: Author. Retrieved October 29, 2016, from http://www.state.gov/documents/organization/258249.pdf

White, J. R. (2012). *Terrorism and Homeland Security.* 7th ed. Belmont, CA: Wadsworth.

16

Beck, C., & McCue, C. (2009, November). "Predictive Policing: What Can We Learn from Wal-Mart and Amazon about Fighting Crime in a Recession?" *The Police Chief,* 76(11), pp. 18–24.

Bratton, W. J. (2006). "Working Together to Meet the Challenges of 21st-Century Policing." *Subject to Debate* 20(9), p. 2.

Brayne, S., Rosenblat, A., & Boyd, D. (2015, October 27). *Predictive Policing.* Data & Civil Rights: A New Era of Policing and Justice, conference presentation. Washington, DC. Retrieved November 3, 2016, from http://www.datacivilrights.org/pubs/2015-1027/Predictive_Policing.pdf

Bureau of Justice Assistance. (1993, October). *A Police Guide to Surveying Citizens and Their Environment.* Monograph. Washington, DC: Author. (NCJ 143711) Retrieved November 4, 2016, from https://www.ncjrs.gov/pdffiles/polc.pdf

Church, J. (2007, February). "Future Trends in Law Enforcement Recruiting." *Officer.com.* Retrieved November 4, 2016, from http://www.officer.com/article/10250151/future-trends-in-law-enforcement-recruiting

The Commission on Accreditation for Law Enforcement. (2010). *The Commission.* Fairfax, VA: Author. Retrieved November 3, 2016, from http://www.calea.org/content/commission

Cosner, T. L., & Loftus, G. M. (2005). "Law Enforcement-Driven Action Research." *The Police Chief,* 72(10), pp. 62–68.

Federal Bureau of Investigation. (2004). *Federal Bureau of Investigation Strategic Plan 2004–2009.* Washington, DC: Author.

International Association of Chiefs of Police. (2008, September). *Improving 21st-Century Policing through Priority Research: The IACP's National Law Enforcement Research Agenda.* Arlington, VA: IACP Research Advisory Committee.

Jensen, C. J. (2006). "Consuming and Applying Research: Evidence-Based Policing." *The Police Chief,* 73(2), pp. 98–101.

Libaw, O. Y. (2016, July 10). "Police Face Severe Shortage of Recruits." *ABC News.* Retrieved November 4, 2016, from http://abcnews.go.com/US/story?id=96570&page=1

McEwen, T. (1999, January). "NIJ's Locally Initiated Research Partnerships in Policing Factors that Add Up to Success." *NIJ Journal,* (238), pp. 2–10.

Michels, S. (2012, June 28). "Rethinking 'Tough on Crime.'" *The Crime Report.* Retrieved November 4, 2016, from http://thecrimereport.org/2012/06/28/2012-06-rethinking-tough-on-crime/

Milligan, S. O., & Fridell, L. (2006, April). *Implementing an Agency-Level Performance Measurement System: A Guide for Law Enforcement Executives.* Washington, DC: Police Executive Research Forum.

National Institute of Justice. (2014, June 9). *Predictive Policing.* Washington, DC: Author. Retrieved November 3, 2016, from http://www.nij.gov/topics/law-

Office of Community Oriented Policing Services. (2011, October). *The Impact of the Economic Downturn on American Police Agencies.* Washington, DC: Author. Retrieved November 4, 2016, from http://www.ncdsv.org/images/COPS_ImpactOfThe EconomicDownturnOnAmericanPoliceAgencies_10-2011.pdf

Police Executive Research Forum. (2012, January). *How Are Innovations in Technology Transforming Policing?* Washington, DC: Author, Critical Issues in Policing Series. Retrieved November 4, 2016, from http://www.policeforum.org/assets/docs/Critical_Issues_Series/how%20are%20innovations%20in%20technology%20transforming%20policing%202012.pdf

Police Executive Research Forum. (2014). *Future Trends in Policing.* Washington, DC: Office of Community Oriented Policing Services. Retrieved November 3, 2016, from http://www.policeforum.org/assets/docs/Free_Online_Documents/Leadership/future%20trends%20in%20policing%202014.pdf

President's Task Force on 21st Century Policing. (2015, May). *Final Report of the President's Task Force on 21st Century Policing.* Washington, DC: Office of Community Oriented Policing Services. Retrieved November 3, 2016, from http://www.cops.usdoj.gov/pdf/taskforce/TaskForce_FinalReport.pdf

Reaves, B. A. (2009, February 26). *State and Local Law Enforcement Training Academies, 2006.* Special report. Washington, DC: Bureau of Justice Statistics. (NCJ 222987)

Rosenbaum, D. P., Schuck, A. M., Graziano, L. M., & Stephens, C. D. (2007, November 25). *Measuring Police and Community Performance Using Web-Based Surveys: Findings from the Chicago Internet Project Final Report.* Chicago, IL: Center for Research in Law and Justice, Department of Criminal Justice, University of Illinois at Chicago.

Sanders, B. A., & Fields, M. L. (2009). "Partnerships with University-Based Researchers." *The Police Chief,* 76(6), pp. 58–61.

Shults, J. F. (2007, August). *The Future of Community Policing in the Context of Basic Police Academy Training.* D.Ed. dissertation. Columbia, MO: Graduate School of the University of Missouri–Columbia.

Washington, R. (2016, September 29). *Driverless Cars Are Coming. What Does That Mean for Policing?* New York, NY: The Marshall Project. Retrieved November 4, 2016, from https://www.themarshallproject.org/2016/09/29/driverless-cars-are-coming-what-does-that-mean-for-policing#.bZrWalP8L

Wexler, C. (2012, January). "Introduction." In *How Are Innovations in Technology Transforming Policing?,* pp. iii–iv. Washington, DC: Police Executive Research Forum, Critical Issues in Policing Series. Retrieved November 4, 2016, from http://www.policeforum.org/assets/docs/Critical_Issues_Series/how%20are%20innovations%20in%20technology%20transforming%20policing%202012.pdf

Willis, J. J., Mastrofski, S. D., & Weisburd, D. (2007). "Making Sense of COMPSTAT: A Theory-Based Analysis of Organizational Change in Three Police Departments." *Law and Society Review,* 41(1), pp. 147–188.

CASES CITED

Adams v. City of Fremont, 80 Cal. Rptr. 2d 196 (1998)

Escobedo v. Illinois, 378 U.S. 478 (1964)

Gideon v. Wainwright, 372 U.S. 335 (1963)

Graham v. Connor, 490 U.S. 386 (1989)

Johnson v. Board of Police Commissioners, 351 F. Supp. 2d 929 (E.D. Mo. 2004)

Mapp v. Ohio, 367 U.S. 643 (1961)

Miranda v. Arizona, 384 U.S. 436 (1966)

Pottinger v. City of Miami, 76 F.3d 1154 (11th Cir. 1996)

Sorrells v. United States, 287 U.S. 435 (1932)

Tennessee v. Garner, 471 U.S. 1 (1985)

Terry v. Ohio, 392 U.S. 1 (1968)

Torrey Dale Grady v. North Carolina, 575 U. S. ___ (2015)

United States v. Jones, 565 U.S. ___ (2012)

United States v. Jones, 565 U.S. _____ 132 S.Ct. 945 (2012)

United States v. Knights, 534 U.S. 112 (2001)

United States v. Russell, 411 U.S. 423 (1973)

Weeks v. United States, 232 U.S. 383 (1914)

AUTHOR INDEX

Rosenfeld, R., 74, 329
Rossmo, D. K., 112
Roth, J. A., 22
Rudd, R. A., 317
Ryan, C., 155
Rytina, N., 160

S

Saad, L., 39
Sabol, W. J., 300
Sacks, J. J., 318
Sadd, S., 259
Sambou, T. S., 392
Sampson, N., 305
Sampson, R., 416, 417
Sanburn, J., 400
Sanders, B. A., 472
Sanders, N., 89
Santos, R., 286
Savelli, L., 440, 446, 455
Scalisi, N. J., 20, 115
Schafer, J. R., 402
Schafer, R., 177, 402
Schanzer, D., 442
Scheider, M. C., 143, 207
Schmerler, K., 120
Schmidt, N. M., 377
Schmitt, E., 443
Schneider, A. L., 255
Schnell, C., 70
Schuck, A. M., 43, 401, 477, 478
Schulenberg, J. E., 301
Schuster, B., 358
Schwartz, W., 379
Schweig, S., 200
Scott, M. S., 54, 55, 98, 99, 140, 269, 288, 290,
    291, 292, 315
Scoville, D., 175
Scrivner, E., 33, 136
Sgueglia, K., 442
Shader, M., 283, 337
Shah, S., 151, 155, 161
Shelden, R. G., 377, 391
Sheppard, D., 341
Shults, J. F., 483
Sickmund, M., 205
Sigler, R. T., 20
Silverman, J. G., 356
Simmons, R. C., 9
Sinnema, C., 322
Skogan, W. G., 5, 43, 71, 131, 137, 154, 251, 258, 261
Skolnick, J. H., 21, 35, 249, 251, 259, 262
Sladky, A., 205
Smith, D., 40

Smith, E. L., 418
Smith, M. J., 40, 293
Snyder, F. M., 207
Socia, K., 109
Solis, A., 379
Son, I. S., 60
Soole, C. W., 195
Soto, A. G. R., 78
Sparrow, M. K., 17
Spelman, W., 95, 99, 101, 114, 117
Spence, D., 127, 194
Spohn, C., 161, 166
Stein, D., 305
Steinberg, L., 365
Steinheider, B., 128
Stepansky, J., 340
Stephens, C. D., 477, 478
Stewart, E., 74
Stimpson J. P., 306
Stoloff, M. L., 89
Stoughton, S., 259
Straw, J., 441
Strawn, J., 286
Stretesky, P. R., 401
Sugie, N. F., 162, 167, 463, 464
Sullivan, E., 222
Sulton, A. T., 258
Sundermann, C., 363
Susmilch, C. E., 104
Sutton, R., 58, 59

T

Tafoya, W. L., 446
Taft, P. B., Jr., 252
Taniguchi, T., 257
Tate, J., 53
Taylor, C. M., 329
Taylor, R. B., 249, 252
Taylor, T. J., 379
Telhami, S., 167
Thompson, G., 153
Thornton, P., 269
Toliver, J., 55
Tomedi, L. E., 318
Townsend, M., 120
Townsend, R., 311
Tracy, S. K., 377, 391
Trautman, N., 36
Tricchinelli, R., 218
Trojanowicz, R.C., 5, 249, 251, 418
Tucker, A. S., 293
Tucker, E., 222
Tufekci, W., 220
Turner, H., 427

SUBJECT INDEX

Key: figure (*f*), table (*t*)